DATE DUE

~~MY 21~~ '93			

Fodor's 92
Scandinavia

Fodor's Travel Publications, Inc.
New York and London

 Published in the United States by Fodor's Travel Publications, Inc., a subsidiary of Random House, Inc., New York, and simultaneously in Canada by Random House of Canada Limited, Toronto. Distributed by Random House, Inc., New York.

ISBN 0-679-02089-6

Fodor's Scandinavia

Editor: Nancy van Itallie
Assistant Editor: Amanda B. Jacobs
Contributors: Susan M. Bain, Robert Blake, Andrew Collins, Melody Favish, Holly Hughes, Margaret Hunter, Hilary Jacobs, Chris Mosey, Anita Peltonen, Karina Porcelli, Paul Psychas, Linda K. Schmidt, Jon Asgeir Sigurdsson
Creative Director: Fabrizio La Rocca
Cartographer: David Lindroth
Illustrator: Karl Tanner
Cover Photograph: A. Woolfitt/Westlight

Design: Vignelli Associates

Special Sales

MANUFACTURED IN THE UNITED STATES OF AMERICA
10 9 8 7 6 5 4 3 2 1

Contents

Maps

Foreword

We would like to express our gratitude to Lillian Hess of the Danish Tourist Board, Ritva Muller of the Finnish Tourist Board, Harald Hansen of the Norwegian Tourist Board, Inga Maria Magnusdottir of the Icelandic Tourist Board, and Annika Goldfarb, Jenny Lundstrøm, and Maria Winkler of the Swedish Tourist Board in New York City for their valuable assistance during the preparation of this new edition of Fodor's *Scandinavia*.

While every care has been taken to ensure the accuracy of the information in this guide, the passage of time will always bring change, and consequently the publisher cannot accept responsibility for errors that may occur.

All prices and opening times quoted here are based on information supplied to us at press time. Hours and admission fees may change, however, and the prudent traveler will avoid inconvenience by calling ahead.

Fodor's wants to hear about your travel experiences, both pleasant and unpleasant. When a hotel or restaurant fails to live up to its billing, let us know and we will investigate the complaint and revise our entries where the facts warrant it. Send your letters to the editors of Fodor's Travel Publications, 201 E. 50th Street, New York, NY 10022.

Highlights '92 and Fodor's Choice

Highlights '92

For travelers to Scandinavia, the dramatic **changes in Eastern Europe** and the former Soviet Union mean shifts in prices, new opportunities to combine visits to the two regions, and a greater need to reserve ahead, as Eastern Europeans start to visit Scandinavia. The car parked next to yours in Norway, for example, now may well be a Trabant; the other visitors in your tour of Christianborg Palace in Copenhagen may include Poles, Czechs, or Hungarians.

European Community harmonization has lowered the prices of beer and other goods in Denmark (a member of the EC since 1972) as cheaper imports from Germany introduced competition. Airline connections between Scandinavia and the rest of Europe have improved, with frequent-flyer programs and weekend bargain flights. Sweden and Finland have applied for Common Market membership since the easing of Cold War tensions made their historic neutrality relatively meaningless. In Norway, an ancient emphasis on self-sufficiency has long divided public opinion on EC membership, but Sweden's decision may change that. Iceland remains untempted.

The warm and snowless winters of the late '80s, particularly disappointing in the Swiss and Italian Alps, have paid off for Scandinavia: a variety of resorts in northern Norway and Sweden now offer **snow guarantees:** if a specified number of ski lifts don't operate during your visit, your hotel stay is free.

In **Lillehammer, Norway,** where the **1994 Winter Olympics** will take place, Norwegian and Swedish firms are building new hotels, apartment complexes, and downhill courses and setting up a transportation system of buses and limousines to ferry Olympic fans to the slopes. This year Oslo celebrates the 100th anniversaries of the Holmenkollen Ski Jump (January) and the Polar ship *Fram* (from April 1).

Copenhagen, Denmark, in 1992 hosts the ballet event of the year: a **Bournonville Festival** in honor of the 150th anniversary of the first performance of the 19th-century composer/choreographer August Bournonville's ballet *Napoli*. Eight ballets, two major museum exhibits, video presentations, and lectures are scheduled. The city of **Aalborg,** founded by the Vikings 1,300 years ago, celebrates **Two Times 650** this year: it received its charter 650 years ago. Yearlong festivities include music, art, and folk-life performances and exhibitions.

In addition to being the 75th anniversary of **Finland's** independence, 1992 has been declared the official **homecoming year** for all emigrants and people of Finnish descent. Parades, music and dance festivals, and sporting events designed to bring Finnish descendants and friends from around the world home to explore their roots and rediscover Finland will take place throughout the country all year long. Contact the Finnish Tourist Board for information on special discount travel packages available for the festivities.

During the summer **Iceland's Biennial Arts Festival** will fill Reykjavík's concert halls, theaters, and galleries with music, drama, and art from around the world.

The defeat of **Sweden**'s Social Democrats in the fall 1991 elections was the latest sign of the changes that are taking place in Swedish society, with high taxes and a stagnant economy generating discontent among voters. The new minority government faces a volatile parliament and an uncertain future. Competition among the parties for popularity and admission to the EC will bring alterations in Sweden's welfare system. **Stockholm**'s authorities have recently trained the city's 400 *Lapp-Lisas* (parking meter maids) in the art of helping tourists: They now distribute city maps and answer questions.

Fodor's Choice

No two people will agree on what makes a perfect vacation, but it can be fun and helpful to know what others think. We hope you'll have a chance to experience some of Fodor's Choices yourself while visiting Scandinavia. For detailed information on individual entries, see the relevant sections of this guidebook.

Dining

Denmark Skt. Gertrudes Kloster, Copenhagen (*Very Expensive*)

Havfruen, Copenhagen (*Moderate*)

Ida Davidsen, Copenhagen (*Moderate*)

Finland Ravintola Valhalla, Helsinki (*Very Expensive*)

Bellevue, Helsinki (*Expensive*)

Garlic Restaurant Kynsilaukka, Helsinki (*Moderate*)

Iceland Fiðarinn, Akureyri (*Expensive*)

Við Tjørnina, Reykjavík (*Expensive*)

Norway Refnes Gods, Moss (*Expensive*)

Spisestuen (Alexandra Molde Hotel), Molde (*Expensive*)

Bryggestuen & Bryggeloftet, Bergen (*Moderate*)

Stefan, Oslo (*Moderate*)

Sweden Operakällaren, Stockholm (*Very Expensive*)

Anno 1990, Malmö (*Expensive*)

Wasahof, Stockholm (*Moderate*)

Jukkasjärvis Wärdshus och Hembyggdsgård, Jukkasjärvi (*Inexpensive*)

Lodging

Denmark D'Angleterre, Copenhagen (*Very Expensive*)

Falsled Kro, Faborg, Fyn (*Very Expensive*)

Vandrehjem (Family and Youth Hostels), anywhere in Denmark (*Inexpensive*)

Finland Lord, Helsinki (*Expensive*)

Anna, Helsinki (*Moderate*)

Iceland Valhøll, Þingvellir (*Expensive*)

Norway Ambassadeur, Oslo (*Expensive*)

Hotel Park, Bergen (*Moderate*)

Kvikne's Hotel, Balestrand (*Moderate*)

Sweden Grand Hotel, Stockholm (*Very Expensive*)

Clas på Hörnet, Stockholm (*Expensive*)

Grand Hotel, Helsingborg (*Expensive*)

Castles and Churches

Denmark Valdemars Slot, Troense, Fyn

Frederikborg, Hillerod, Sjælland

Kronborg, Helsingør, Sjælland

Finland Temppeliaukion Kirkko, Helsinki

Turun Linna (Turku Castle), Turku

Norway Heddal Stave Church, Heddal

Akershus Slott, Oslo

Sweden Drottningholm Palace, Drottningholm

Läckö Slott, Läckö

Riddarholmskyrkan, Stockholm

Royal Palace, Stockholm

Towns and Villages

Denmark Ribe, Jylland

Finland Eckero

Rauma

Iceland Bakkagerði

Norway Lyngør

Røros

Lom

Sweden Rättvik

Sigtuna

Strömstad

Visby

Parks and Gardens

Denmark Frederiksberg Haven, Copenhagen

Kong Have, Copenhagen

Dyrehaven, Copenhagen

Finland Urho Kekkonen National Park, Saariselkä

Kulturanta's rose gardens, Luonnonmaasaari

Iceland Grasagruðurinn, Reykjavík

Skaftafell National Park

Norway Frogner Park, Oslo

Hardangervidda, Geilo

Jostedalsbreen (glacier), Loen

Sweden Djurgården, Stockholm

Muddus National Park, Norrland

Trädgårdsföreningen, Göteborg

Museums

Denmark Louisiana Modern Art Museum, Copenhagen

Carlsberg Glyptoteket, Copenhagen

Finland Suomen Kansallismuseo, Helsinki

Iceland Arni Magnusson Institute, repository of the Saga manuscripts, Reykjavík

Norway Norwegian Folk Museum, Bygdøy, Oslo

Vikingskiphuset, Bygdøy, Oslo

Sami Collections, Karasjok

Sweden Millesgården, Stockholm

Modern Museum, Stockholm

Zorn Museum, Mora

Lakes, Fjords, and Islands

Denmark Aerø, off Fyn

Bornholm

Strømfjord, Greenland

Finland Suomenlinna Fortress Island, Helsinki

Iceland Flatey, Breiðafjöður

Lake Mývatn

Norway Lofoten Islands

Svalbard

Geirangerfjord

Sweden Siljan and Sollerön

Mälaren and Björkö

Special Moments

Denmark Eating an old-fashioned ice-cream cone on a Bornholm beach

Watching a bonfire on Skt. Hansaften (the longest day of the year)

Walking through Tivoli at dusk

Finland Blueberry-picking in August

Watching the moon rise over Lake Inari (spring and fall)

Watching the sailboat regatta in Hanko

Iceland Watching the northern lights in December from Þingvellir

Bobbing among glacial ice chunks in Jökulsárlón lagoon

Spying golden rainbows shimmering in the mists of Gullfoss

Norway Eating shrimp from the boats at the pier in Oslo

Midsummer at the North Cape

Riding the train from Flåm to Myrdal

Sweden Eating a Fat Tuesday bun during Lent

Sailing in the Stockholm archipelago

Scandinavia

NORGE
(NORWAY)
DANMARK
(DENMARK)
RUSSIA
ESTONIA
LATVIA
LITHUANIA
BYELORUSSIA
POLAND
GERMANY
North
Sea
Baltic
Sea
Gulf of Finland
Skagerrak
Kattegat
Oslofjord
Sognefjord
Hardangerfjord
Jostedalsbreen
Jotunheimen
Østerdalen
Lake Mjøsa
Vänern
Vättern
Mälaren
Klarälven
Ljusnan
Saimaa
Haukivesi
Åland
Gotland
Öland
Bornholm
Hiiumaa
Saaremaa
TO FAROE ISLANDS
Faroe Islands (Denmark)
KEY
Ferry
0
500 miles
0
750 km
N
Florø
Ålesund
Molde
Geiranger
Åndalsnes
Dombås
Oppdal
Støren
Røros
Tynset
Koppang
Rena
Lillehammer
Hamar
Eidsvoll
Oslo
Hønefoss
Drammen
Kongsberg
Porsgrunn
Larvik
Arendal
Kristiansand
Grimstad
Evje
Mandal
Stavanger
Sandnes
Haugesund
Bergen
Voss
Geilo
Fredrikstad
Halden
Strömstad
Uddevalla
Göteborg
(Gothenburg)
Trollhättan
Mellerud
Karlstad
Borlänge
Mora
Idre
Tännäs
Östersund
Sundsvall
Bollnäs
Falun
Fagersta
Avesta
Västerås
Örebro
Uppsala
Stockholm
Nynäshamn
Norrköping
Linköping
Jönköping
Nässjö
Borås
Värnamo
Falkenberg
Halmstad
Helsingborg
Kristianstad
Karlskrona
Växjö
Kalmar
Oskarshamn
Malmö
Ystad
Rønne
Visby
Slite
Gävle
Söderhamn
Hudiksvall
Mariehamn
(Maarianhamina)
Vaasa
Pori
Rauma
Turku
Salo
Hämeenlinna
Tampere
Parkano
Jyväskylä
Äänekoski
Varkaus
Savonlinna
Punkaharju
Imatra
Lappeenranta
Mikkeli
Heinola
Lahti
Kouvola
Kotka
Porvoo
Helsinki
Ekenäs
Hanko
St. Petersburg
Tallinn
Pskov
Riga
Daugavpils
Liepaja
Klaipeda
Skagen
Aalborg
Thisted
Århus
Silkeborg
Ringkøbing
Esbjerg
Ribe
Fredericia
Middelfart
Flensburg
København
(Copenhagen)
Nakskov

World Time Zones

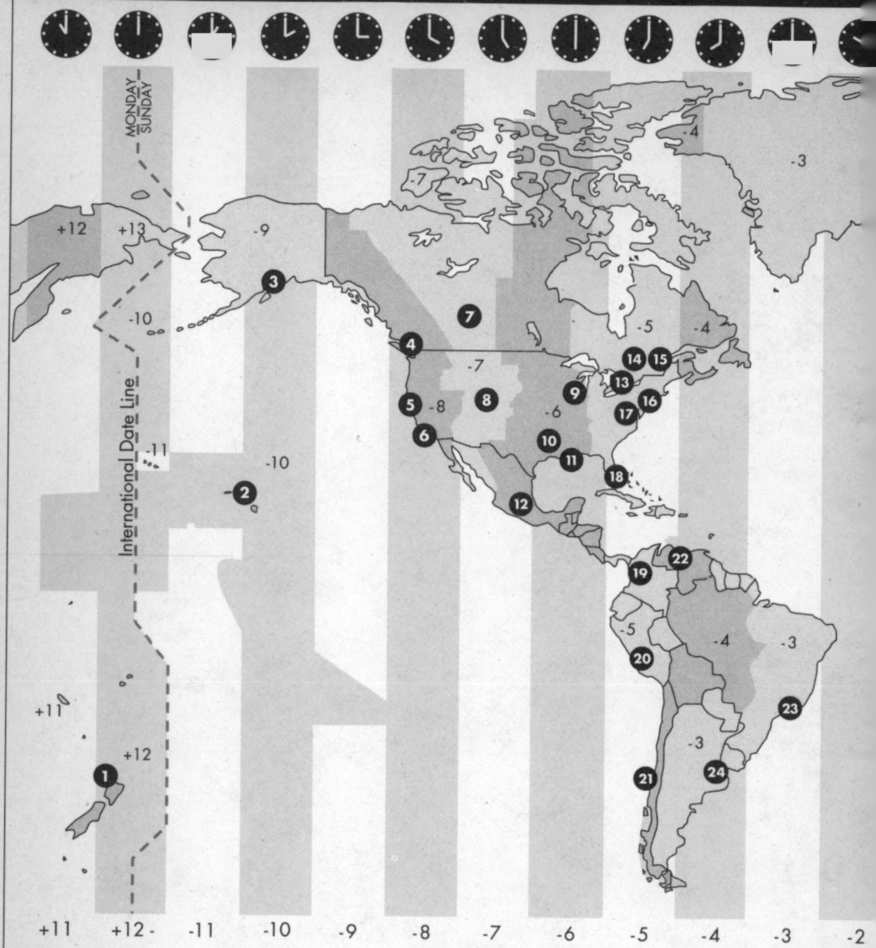

Numbers below vertical bands relate each zone to Greenwich Mean Time (0 hrs.).
Local times frequently differ from these general indications,
as indicated by light-face numbers on map.

Algiers, **29**
Anchorage, **3**
Athens, **41**
Auckland, **1**
Baghdad, **46**
Bangkok, **50**
Beijing, **54**
Berlin, **34**
Bogotá, **19**
Budapest, **37**
Buenos Aires, **24**
Caracas, **22**
Chicago, **9**
Copenhagen, **33**
Dallas, **10**
Delhi, **48**
Denver, **8**
Djakarta, **53**
Dublin, **26**
Edmonton, **7**
Hong Kong, **56**
Honolulu, **2**
Istanbul, **40**
Jerusalem, **42**
Johannesburg, **44**
Lima, **20**
Lisbon, **28**
London (Greenwich), **27**
Los Angeles, **6**
Madrid, **38**
Manila, **57**

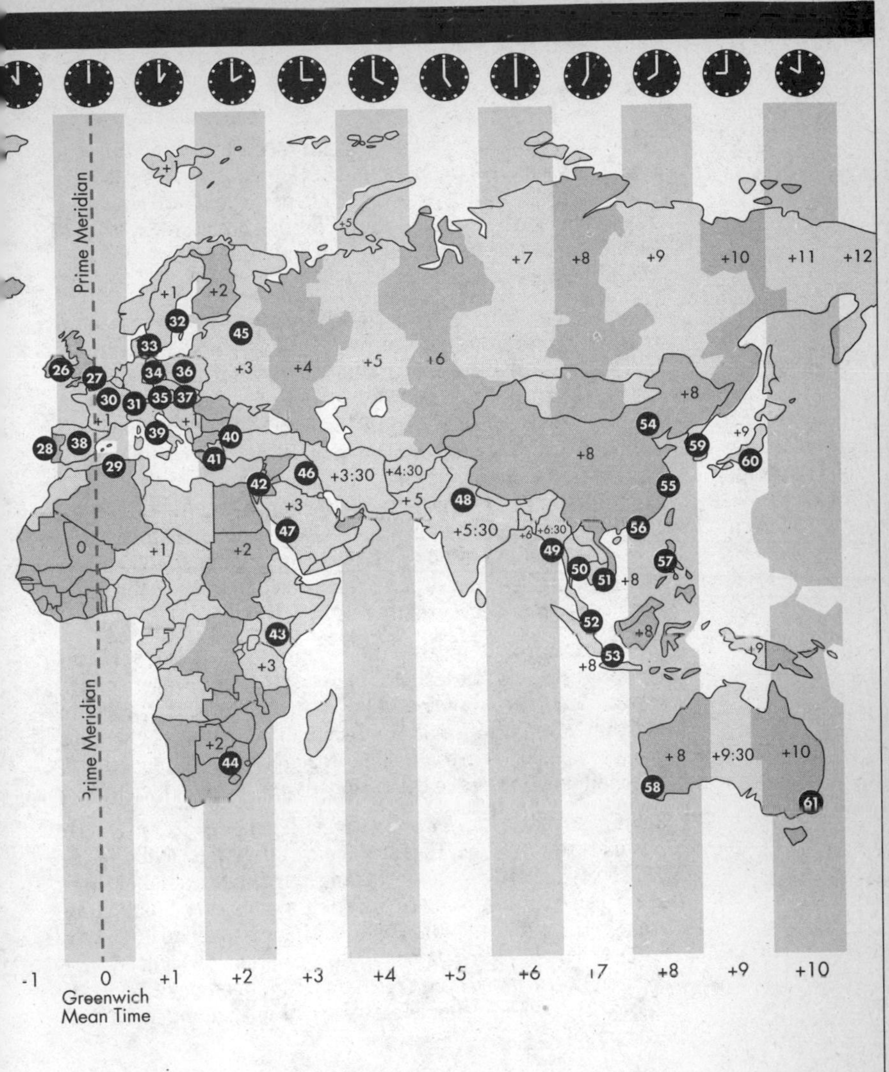

Mecca, **47**
Mexico City, **12**
Miami, **18**
Montreal, **15**
Moscow, **45**
Nairobi, **43**
New Orleans, **11**
New York City, **16**

Ottawa, **14**
Paris, **30**
Perth, **58**
Reykjavík, **25**
Rio de Janeiro, **23**
Rome, **39**
Saigon, **51**

San Francisco, **5**
Santiago, **21**
Seoul, **59**
Shanghai, **55**
Singapore, **52**
Stockholm, **32**
Sydney, **61**
Tokyo, **60**

Toronto, **13**
Vancouver, **4**
Vienna, **35**
Warsaw, **36**
Washington, DC, **17**
Yangon, **49**
Zürich, **31**

Introduction

by Eric Sjogren

Eric Sjogren, a Swedish travel writer based in Brussels, is a frequent contributor to The New York Times *and other publications. He has also served as area editor for* Fodor's Belgium and Luxembourg.

The islands of Stockholm mirrored in the water, the ships and Little Mermaid of Copenhagen, Oslo and its majestic fjord, the bay and peninsulas of Helsinki, Reykjavík with its busy deep-blue harbor: the capitals of Scandinavia are unthinkable without the water that surrounds and sustains them.

What is true for the capitals is equally true for the countries. Denmark consists of one peninsula and 400 islands, half of them inhabited. Finland and Sweden used to dispute which country was really "the land of a thousand lakes." Finland settled it, after counting almost 190,000. An island summer in the archipelago is part of every Stockholmer's childhood memory. The mail packets of Norway's Hurtigruten sail north from Bergen along the fjord-indented coast and turn around at Kirkenes on the Russian border, 1,250 miles later. Iceland is so dependent on the surrounding sea that it has been known to take on the British navy to protect its fishing limits.

Water has never separated the Scandinavian nations. In the early days it was far easier to cross a stretch of water than it was to penetrate dense and trackless forests. It was their mastery of shipbuilding that enabled the Vikings to rule the waves 1,000 years ago. Their ocean-going ships could be beached, and this gave them the advantage of surprise.

Viking exploration and conquests ranged from North America to the Black Sea and from Greenland to Mallorca. These voyagers developed the angular Runic alphabet, ideal for carving in stone. In Sweden alone, over 2,000 rune stones still stand, in memory of Vikings who fell in far-away battles. The Vikings also devised a complex mythology and created literature of such realism and immediacy that even today the Icelandic sagas can be read with admiration and enjoyment.

You might think that, with so much in common, the Scandinavians would keep peace among themselves, but this was not to be. By the 11th century the passion that had inflamed the Vikings was spent, and Christianity defeated the old beliefs. The Swedes departed on a dubious crusade to conquer the Finns and annex their land. The Norwegians, having colonized Iceland, squabbled among themselves and disappeared as a nation for 500 years. By the 16th century, Scandinavia was divided between Denmark and Sweden, bound together by mutual antagonism. The two countries were at war with one another for a total of 134 years, and the conflict was perpetuated by history books written from nationalistic points of view.

What happened in the distant past acquires the status of myth and influences in many ways the image that a people has of itself. What has happened more recently sometimes leaves more obvious marks. Allegiances and dependencies were reshuffled early in the 19th century, as a consequence of the Napoleonic Wars, which transformed the European landscape. Sweden lost Finland, which spent the next 100 years as a czarist province. Norway declared its independence from Denmark but was thrust into a union with Sweden.

Finland learned more about her cultural identity while a Russian province than she did during centuries of Swedish rule. Akseli Gallen Kallela painted the scenes of a mythological past that Jean Sibelius fashioned into tone poems. Norway, too, was to experience a cultural renaissance, led by artists such as Edvard Grieg, Henrik Ibsen, and Edvard Munch. From Denmark came philosopher Soren Kierkegaard, writer Hans Christian Andersen, and the composer Carl Nielsen. Sweden produced the painters Anders Zorn and Carl Larsson and dramatist August Strindberg.

Large-scale emigration to the United States (including a million Swedes) peaked during the latter half of the century, only decades before new industries transformed the old farming economy.

In the early years of this century the Norwegians finally became masters in their own house. This could not have happened without strong nationalist sentiment, and it is to the credit of both Norway and Sweden that the divorce was amicable. The Russian revolution brought civil war to Finland, followed by independence, for the first time in that nation's history. Finland was attacked again in 1939, by Stalin's forces, and was eventually defeated but never occupied. Denmark and Norway, attacked by Germany in 1940, were not spared that fate. After the war had ended, Iceland declared its independence from Denmark.

Denmark, Norway, and Iceland are members of NATO. Denmark is also a paid-up member of the European Community; and Sweden is on the brink of applying for membership, with Norway and Finland bringing up the rear.

Scandinavians, like the British, often talk of Europe as though they were not part of it. They see themselves as different. They dream of the *joie de vivre* that they believe all southerners enjoy but believe that the moral fiber and know-how of the Scandinavians are superior to anything you find south of the border.

Nevertheless, it is sometimes said that sick-leave levels are now so high in Sweden that there are more sick people in a factory than in a hospital. As people often do with the good things in life, Scandinavians in all five countries have become used to high levels of social services. The political coloration of the government seems to matter less, as long as the services are delivered. This requirement is not easily squared with the vociferous demand for lower taxes.

More than the rest of Europe, Scandinavia has been influenced by the American lifestyle and its ethos of professionalism. This coexists, sometimes precariously, with the "socialism with a human face" that has influenced these societies for the past 50 years or more. Among the measures introduced recently is Sweden's 12-month maternity/paternity leave. Husband and wife can split it between them as they see fit: An idea that was decried as madness has done wonders for marriage and fatherhood.

Scandinavian women know how to assume power with ease and grace. Denmark's Queen Margarethe was pushed into her position as reigning monarch but has acquitted herself so well that royalism in Denmark is at an all-time high. President Vigdis of Iceland first achieved narrow victory on a platform that emphasized cultural values; she has subsequently seen her majority grow by leaps and bounds. When Gro Harlem Bruntland became prime minister of Norway, she appointed a cabinet consisting of 40% women. Her popularity may have influenced the main opposition party to elect another woman as their leader. Sweden's Antonia Axelsson Johnson runs one of the country's largest business empires. And, with more than 250 policemen reporting to her, Margareta Linderoth is district police commissioner of one of Stockholm's most difficult precincts. "I have had nothing but support from my male colleagues," she says. Officially 101 languages are spoken in her district. This can be read as an indication of the richness of new ethnic contributions to Scandinavian culture, although it is not necessarily seen that way by the host country.

There is still much truth in the myth of the taciturn Scandinavian. A story tells of the two Danes, two Norwegians, and two Swedes who were marooned on a desert island. When a rescue party arrived six months later, they found that the two Danes had started a cooperative, and the two Norwegians had founded a local chapter of the patriotic society Sons of Norway. The two Swedes were waiting to be introduced.

Stereotypes about national characteristics abound among Scandinavians. Danes believe the saving grace of humor will take the sting out of most of life's vicissitudes. The Finns attribute their survival to their *sisu*, or true grit. Icelanders are known as a nation of hard workers, singers, and drinkers, who think there is always a way for things to get fixed. The Norwegians find virtue in being, like Ibsen's Peer Gynt, *sig selv nok*, which means self-reliant in all things. The Swedes, the most introspective of the lot, take pride in their reliability and admit to "Royal Swedish envy" as their principal vice.

There's no denying that there is a definite strain of melancholy in the Scandinavian character, more pronounced the farther you penetrate into the lonely north. In Finland, the most popular dance—one in which dance halls specialize to the exclusion of all others—is the tango, precisely because it is so sad. But there's no need to look only to Argentine imports: Virtually all Scandinavian folk music, even when rhythms are rapid and gay, is in a minor key.

The Scandinavians are not bound by a native language. Iceland was colonized from Norway, but present-day Icelandic is incomprehensible to other Scandinavians. Finnish, like Hungarian, is one of the enigmatic Finno-Ugrian languages. Danish, a language rich in glottal stops, is not understood by many Swedes, and Danish TV programs have to be subtitled. Norwegian, in pronunciation and vocabulary halfway between the two, sometimes serves as an intra-Scandinavian mode of communication. But get a group of Scandinavians together, and what are they most likely to speak? English.

Those who think a sauna is nothing but a steam bath are greatly mistaken. To the Finns, who invented it, a sauna has a spiritual dimension, with the cleansing of the body accompanied by the enjoyment of nature, because a beautiful location is a vital part of a true Finnish sauna. Most of the major decisions made in the country are reached during a sauna.

Denmark is in many ways a garden of delight. The Denmark of beech woods, dappled paths, half-timber farmhouses, and rolling fields still exists. Only Skåne, the southernmost Swedish province, which was part of Denmark until the 17th century, resembles agricultural Denmark.

Farther north the woods close in, pine and spruce mingling with white-trunked birches, with here and there a clearing or a field. As you continue north, the hegemony of the forest becomes complete, challenged only by the lakes. On a clear night, from an aircraft, the moonlight is reflected in so many lakes that it seems to cut a shining path to the horizon.

The forest is not as silent and lonely as you might think. Walk along a Scandinavian country road on an evening in early summer, and you will hear roe deer barking at your approach, and the forlorn hooting of loons from the lakes. You will see stately moose coming out of the woods to graze in the fields. Juniper bushes cast long, eerie shadows, and on a hilltop skeletal pines are silhouetted against a still clear sky. No wonder that in ages past popular imagination peopled these forests with sprites and trolls and giants.

Having a summer home is not a great luxury in Scandinavia. On Friday afternoon there are traffic jams in Oslo, as the Norwegians escape to their cabins in the mountainous interior. In Stockholm the waterways are clogged with motorboats heading for summer cottages in the archipelago. The Finns and Icelanders, less urbanized than their neighbors, almost always have a village or isolated farmstead they consider their real home.

Modern Scandinavia is largely a secular society, but woods and lakes hold a special mystique. A midnight boat ride on an island-studded lake, with the moon suspended just above the treetops, is very close to a religious experience for the people of the North, as their souls fill with a tremendous wistfulness and a sense of simultaneous sadness and joy.

1 Essential Information

Before You Go

Government Tourist Offices

In the United States **Danish Tourist Board,** 655 3rd Ave., New York, NY 10017, tel. 212/949–2333, fax 212/983–5260. **Finnish Tourist Board,** 655 3rd Ave., New York, NY 10017, tel. 212/949–2333, fax 212/983–5260; 1900 Ave. of the Stars, Los Angeles, CA 90067, tel. 213/277–5226. **Iceland Tourist Board,** 655 3rd Ave., New York, NY 10017, tel. 212/949–2333, fax 212/983–5260. **Norwegian Tourist Board,** 655 3rd Ave., New York, NY 10017, tel. 212/949–2333, fax 212/983–5260; 8929 Wilshire Blvd., Beverly Hills, CA 90211, tel. 213/657–4808, fax 213/657–4686. **Scandinavian Tourist Board,** 150 N. Michigan Ave., Suite 2145, Chicago, IL 60601, tel. 312/726–1120, fax 312/726–3774; 8929 Wilshire Blvd., Beverly Hills, CA 90211, tel. 213/657–4808, fax 213/657–4686. **Swedish Tourist Board,** 655 3rd Ave., New York, NY 10017, tel. 212/949–2333, fax 212/983–5260.

In Canada **Danish Tourist Board,** Box 115, Station N, Toronto, Ontario M8V 3S4, tel. 416/823–9620, fax 416/823–8860. **Finnish Tourist Board,** 1200 Bay St., Suite 604, Ontario M5R 2A5, tel. 416/964–9159.

In the United Kingdom **Danish Tourist Board,** Sceptre House, 169–173 Regent St., London W1R 8PY, 071/734–2637, fax 071/494–2170. **Finnish Tourist Board,** Greener House, 66–68 Haymarket, London SW1 4RF, tel. 071/839–4048, fax 071/321–0696. The Icelandic Tourist Board does not have an address in London, but **Icelandair** (172 Tottenham Court Rd., London WP1 9LG, tel. 081/388–5599) can supply tourist information. **Norwegian Tourist Board,** Charles House, 5–11 Lower Regent St., London SW1Y 4LR, tel. 071/839–6255, fax 071/839–6014. **Swedish National Tourist Office,** 29–31 Oxford St., London W1R 1RE, tel. 071/437–5817, fax 071/287–0164.

ASK
1) Inn
checks

Tour Groups

If you're traveling to the Land of the Midnight Sun for the first time, you might want to consider a group tour. Escorted bus tours provide comprehensive sightseeing coverage of Scandinavia's modern capitals, ancient villages, and historic sites. All you have to do is enjoy the view. As an added bonus, these tours also tend to save you money on air fare and hotels. If group travel is not your style, or if you're returning to Scandinavia for a second time, consider an independent package. Many tour operators offer deals that let you design your own itinerary and choose from a variety of travel options, stringing together hotel packages, following a pre-arranged itinerary independently, or creating your own fly-drive trip. And if you don't feel like driving, you can always hop on a cruise ship. When evaluating any tour, find out exactly what expenses are included (particularly tips, taxes and service charges, side trips, additional meals, and entertainment); ratings of all hotels and the facilities they offer; cancellation policies for both you and the tour operator; and, if you are traveling alone, the cost of a single supplement.

Listed below is a sampling of operators and packages to give you an idea of what is available. For additional resources, contact your travel agent or the countries' tourist offices. Most tour operators request that bookings be made through a travel agent at no additional charge.

General-interest *U.S. Tour Operators*

Bennett Tours (270 Madison Ave., New York, NY 10016, tel. 212/532–5060 or 800/221–2420) is a veritable supermarket, offering more than a dozen Scandinavian tours and cruises. **Caravan Tours** (401 N. Michigan Ave., Chicago, IL 60611, tel. 312/321–9800) and **TWA Getaway Vacations** (tel. 800/GETAWAY) offer 14-day Scandinavian tours that wind through Denmark, Sweden, and Norway at a leisurely pace. Other Caravan itineraries include Finland and the Soviet Union. **Maupintour** (Box 807, Lawrence, KA 66044, tel. 913/843–1211 or 800/255–4266) offers an in-depth overview of the area on its three tours, which range from 15 to 20 days. **American Express Vacations** (Box 5014, Atlanta, GA 30302, tel. 800/241–1700; in Georgia, 800/282–0800) has a choice of seven tours, several of which combine Scandinavia and the Soviet Union. On its 15-day tour, **Olson-Travelworld** (100 N. Sepulveda Blvd., Suite 1010, El Segundo, CA 90245, tel. 213/546–8400 or 800/421–2255; in California, 800/421–5785) takes you to Norway's North Cape to watch the sun shine at midnight. Three other Scandinavian tours are available. All are limited to 28 participants. The 17-day "Fjord Adventure" from **Trafalgar Tours** (21 E. 26th St., New York, NY 10010, tel. 212/689–8977 or 800/854–0103) features a cruise on two of Norway's most scenic fjords. Other Scandinavian tours range from 18 to 23 days in length. For the budget-minded, Trafalgar offers 14- and 16-day CostSaver tours that use tourist-class hotels. At the upper end of the price spectrum, **Abercrombie & Kent** (1420 Kensington Rd., Oak Brook, IL 60521–2106, tel. 708/954–2944 or 800/323–7308) offers a nine-day luxury rail-and-road tour through Scandinavia. **UniTravel Holidays** (1177 N. Warson Rd., Box 12485, St. Louis, MO 63132, tel. 800/325–2222), **Gadabout Tours** (700 E. Tahquitz Way, Palm Springs, CA 92262, tel. 619/325–5556), **American Airlines Fly AAway Vacations** (tel. 817/355–1234 or 800/433–7300), **Delta Dream Vacations** (tel. 305/522–1440 or 800/872–7786), **TWA Getaway Vacations** (tel. 800/GETAWAY), and **Continental's Grand Destinations** (tel. 800/634–5555) offer tours of Denmark, Sweden, and Norway, ranging from nine to 15 days.

British Tour Operators

Arctic Experience Ltd (29 Nork Way, Banstead, Surrey SM7 1PB, tel. 0737/362321) specializes in holidays to unusual and remote destinations. It offers some 30 tours to Iceland, including Land Rover safaris, ski treks, and bird-watching; dogsled tours in Swedish Lapland; and a grand tour of Scandinavia by bus. **Finlandia Travel** (223 Regent St., London W1R 7DB, tel. 071/409–7334) offers city packages to Helsinki and 15 other cities throughout Finland, including excursions to Stockholm and the Soviet Union, and Christmas programs in Lapland. **Finnchalet Holidays Ltd** (Dunira, Comrie, Perthshire PH6 2JZ, tel. 0764/70020) will arrange sea crossings and flexible itineraries for motorists, with accommodations in hotels, chalets, inns, and farmhouses in Denmark, Sweden, Norway, and Finland. **Frames Rickards** (11 Herbrand St., London WC1N 1EX, tel. 071/637–4171) includes Norway, Denmark, and Sweden, as well as other countries en route from London, on its 17-day "Discover Scandinavia" bus tour. **Hamilton Travel Ltd.** (3 Heddon St., London W1R 7LE, tel. 071/437–4627) features a nine-day dogsledding program in the Arctic Circle area of Sweden. Packages to Bergen, Oslo, Stavanger, Copenhagen, Helsinki, Stockholm, and Gothenburg are also available. **Holiday Scandinavia Ltd.** (28 Hillcrest Rd., Orpington, Kent BR6 9AW, tel. 0689/824958) arranges winter and summer holidays in chalets and apartments in Norway, Sweden, Denmark, and Finland and offers touring options such as a Norwegian coastal voyage and self-drive itineraries. **Icelandair** (172 Tottenham Court Rd., London W1P 9LG, tel. 071/388–5599) offers packages to Reykjavík from two to seven nights, with optional excursions to other places of interest. **NSR (Norwegian State Railways) Travel** (21–24 Cockspur St., London SW1Y 5DA, tel. 071/930–6666) offers summer and winter tours to all five Scandinavian countries, including two-, three-, and seven-night Scandinavian Fare Deals to major city centers. **Page & Moy Ltd.** (136–140 London Rd., Leicester LE2 1EN, tel. 0533/552521) offers an eight-day tour of Norway, including a fjord cruise and sightseeing tours of Bergen and Oslo. **DFDS/Scandinavian Seaways** (Scandinavia House, Parkeston Quay, Harwich, Essex CO12 4QG, tel. 0255/241234) offers a number of holiday packages to Denmark and Sweden in conjunction with its sailings from Harwich, including touring by car; self-catering apartments or cabins; city breaks in Copenhagen, Stockholm, and Gothenburg; and bus tours for festive breaks at Christmas, New Year's, and Easter. **Scanscape Holidays** (Hillgate House, 13 Hillgate St., London W8 7SP, tel. 071/221–3244) offers a range of options, including fjord cruises, bus tours, motoring holidays, farmhouse or summerhouse holidays, multicity tours, and wilderness-adventure tours. **Scantours Ltd.** (8 Spring Gardens, Trafalgar Square, London SW1A 2BG, tel. 071/839–2927) will arrange inclusive tours of Scandinavia, along with special holidays such as Christmas in Lapland, a husky expedition, a snowmobile safari, Baltic cruises, and a white reindeer ski trek. **Taber Holidays** (Norway House, 126 Sunbridge Rd., Bradford, West Yorkshire BD1 2SX, tel. 0274/393480) has a large selection of inclusive holidays to Norway, including single- and multicenter holidays for the pedestrian and motorist, self-catering holidays, escorted tours, coastal voyages, and a bus tour departing from the United Kingdom. **Top Deck Travel** (Top Deck House, 131–135 Earls Court Rd., London SW5 9RH, tel. 071/370–4555) offers a 30-day bus tour of Scandinavia and Lapland during the summer months, and bus tours combining Scandinavia and Russia. **Trafalgar Tours** (15 Grosvenor Pl., London SW1X 7HH, tel. 071/235–7090) features fjord cruises, 18- to 23-day Best of Scandinavia tours, and, for the cost-conscious, 14- and 16-day Cost Saver tours that use tourist-class hotels. **Winge Travel Ltd.** (3 Whitcomb St., London WC2H 7HA, tel. 071/839–5341) offers City Breaks in six cities in Denmark, Norway, and Sweden.

Special-interest

An amazing variety of specialty tours is sponsored each year by trade organizations, alumni groups, hobby associations, and others. Topics range from archaeology to architecture, food and wine to chicken farms, and gardening to textile design. The firms below may be able to help you find a group organizing a tour that matches your interest. None of these firms are retailers, and none will sell you a ticket, but all make it their business to organize special-interest tours for other organizations that act as travel retailers. Such tour organizers include: **Academic Travel Abroad Inc.** (3210 Grace St. NW, Washington, DC 20007, tel. 202/333–3355), **Arrangement Abroad** (50 Broadway,

New York, NY 10004, tel. 212/514–8921), **Associated Travel Coordinators Inc.** (1207 33rd St. NW, Washington, DC 20007, tel. 202/333–1800), **Bryan International Travel Inc.** (421 Powell St, Suite 210, San Francisco, CA 94102–1594, tel. 415/986–0967), **International Ambassador Program** (Dwight D. Eisenhower Building, Spokane, WA 99202, tel. 509/534–0430), **Ritzau Special Tours** (Østbanegade 39, DK–2100 Copenhagen Ø, tel. 45/31–26–48–88, fax 45/31–26–34–45), and **Travel Dynamics Inc.** (132 E. 70 St., New York, NY 10021, tel. 212/517–7555).

Package Deals for Independent Travelers

TWA Getaway Vacations (*see* General-interest, *above*) offers three-day "city break" packages to Copenhagen and Stockholm. Additional nights are available. **Bennett Tours** (*see* General-interest, *above*) has three-day packages to Helsinki, Oslo, Bergen, Copenhagen, and Stockholm. **Travel Bound** (599 Broadway, New York, NY 10012, tel. 212/334–1350 or 800/456–8656) has three-night packages to Stockholm and Oslo that include one-way airfare from London. Preferred rates at hotels in Bergen, Copenhagen, Helsinki, Oslo, and Stockholm are also available when you book a total of three nights. **American Express Vacations** (*see* General-interest, *above*) gives you three-night packages in Copenhagen and Stockholm with the option to book additional nights. **KLM Royal Dutch Airlines** (tel. 800/777–1668) has a "Europe By Design" program that gives you one night in Amsterdam and three nights in Copenhagen, including all air transportation. Six optional excursions are available in each city. **Jet Vacations** (888 7th Ave., New York, NY 10106, tel. 212/247–0999 or 800/JET–0999) and **Central Holiday Tours** (206 Central Ave., Jersey City, NJ 07307, tel. 201/798–5777 or 800/526–6045) offer special nightly rates at hotels in Stockholm, Oslo, and Copenhagen. Central Holiday also has fly/drive packages in Denmark, Norway, and Sweden. **American Airlines Fly AAway Vacations** (*see* General-interest, *above*) gives you two days in Stockholm and a cruise to Helsinki. The eight-day package is air-and-land inclusive. Four-day packages to Stockholm, Copenhagen, Oslo, Göteborg, and Bergen are also offered. Ports of call on the 15-day luxury cruise offered by **Gadabout Tours** (*see* General-interest, *above*) include Helsinki, Stockholm, Copenhagen, Oslo, Leningrad, and Gdansk. **Continental's Grand Destinations** (*see* General-interest, *above*) lets you design a self-drive itinerary in Denmark, Norway, Finland, and Sweden. Round-trip air transportation to Stockholm, Oslo, or Copenhagen is included. The airline also offers a six-night Norwegian ski package to Oslo and Lillehammer.

When to Go

Tourist season is in June, July, and August, when daytime temperatures are often in the 70s (21°C to 26°C) and sometimes rise into the 80s (27°C to 32°C). Detailed temperature charts are included in individual country chapters. In general, the weather is not overly warm, and a brisk breeze and brief rainstorms are possible anytime.

Truly delightful are the incredibly long days, particularly in June, when the sun rises in Copenhagen at 4 AM and sets at 11 PM, making long evenings of sightseeing possible. Days are even longer farther north. Many attractions extend their hours during the summer, and some shut down altogether in winter. Fall, spring, and even winter are pleasant, despite the area's reputation for gloom. The days become shorter quickly, but the sun casts a golden light one does not see farther south.

The Gulf Stream warms Denmark, the western coast of Norway, and Iceland, making winters in these areas similar to those in New York or London. Even the harbor of Narvik, far to the north in Norway, remains ice-free year-round. Away from the protection of the Gulf Stream, however, northern Norway, Sweden, and Finland experience bitter cold that attracts skiers.

Climate Current weather information for more than 750 cities around the world may be obtained by calling **WeatherTrak** information service at 900/370–8728 (cost: 95¢ per minute). A taped message will tell you to dial the three-digit access code for the destination in which you're interested. The code is either the area code (in the United States) or the first three letters of the foreign city. For a list of all access codes, send a stamped, self-addressed envelope to Cities, 9B Terrace Way, Greensboro, NC 27403. For more information, call 800/247–3282.

A similar service operated by **American Express** can be accessed by dialing 900/WEATHER. As well as supplying a three-day weather forecast for 600 cities worldwide, this service provides international travel information and time and day. Cost is 75¢ per minute.

What to Pack

Pack light, then take half of what you thought you needed and leave it at home as well. A light suitcase is a real joy, as porters are usually difficult to find and baggage restrictions are tight on international flights. Be sure to check your airline's policy before you pack. Make sure, too, to leave room for the bulky sweaters, furs, and crystal that you may bring home from Scandinavian shops.

Clothing Don't forget to bring a bathing suit to Iceland, even in winter, as volcanic springs are particularly delightful then. Also bring a warm sweater, socks, and slacks during summer, wherever you travel in Scandinavia. Fresh summer days become cool evenings, and the wind is often brisk, particularly on the water, if you plan to travel by boat.

Don't bother with an umbrella, as gusty winds quickly destroy even the sturdiest. A lightweight raincoat is a much better choice and can double as a windbreaker. You will probably find yourself taking it with you every day, everywhere you go, as it is common for the sky to be clear at 9 AM, rainy at 11 AM, and clear again in time for lunch. Don't forget that your feet get wet, as well: an extra pair of walking shoes that dry quickly will come in handy.

Perhaps because of the climate, Scandinavians tend to be practical and resilient, and fashion follows suit. It is safe to generalize that, with the possible exception of the Swedes, most Scandinavians—from bicyclists in Copenhagen, to businesspeople in Oslo, to shopkeepers in Reykjavík and Helsinki—dress more casually than their Continental brethren in Germany and Italy. Slacks and comfortable shoes are almost always acceptable attire. That said, don't forget to bring one nice outfit for your visit to a fancy Stockholm restaurant.

Miscellaneous If you can't sleep when it is light and you are traveling during summer, bring a comfortable eye-mask, so you won't wake up automatically at the 4 AM sunrise.

Bug repellent is a good idea if you plan to venture away from the capital cities. Large mosquitoes can be a real nuisance on the southern Danish pig farms that produce all those hams for export, as well as in the far northern reaches of Norway and Sweden.

Because of the far northern latitude, the sun slants at angles unseen elsewhere on the globe, and a pair of dark sunglasses can prevent eyestrain if, for example, you're unlucky enough to drive westward at sundown. Sunscreen is less a requirement here than in most places but can nonetheless be a good idea during summer and for winter skiing.

Carry-on Luggage Airlines generally allow each passenger one piece of carry-on luggage on international flights from the United States. The bag cannot exceed 45″ (length + width + height) and must fit under the seat or in the overhead luggage compartment.

Checked Luggage Passengers are generally allowed to check two pieces of luggage, neither of which can exceed 62″ (length + width + height) or weigh more than 70 pounds. Baggage allowances vary slightly among airlines, so check with the carrier or your travel agent before departure.

Taking Money Abroad

Traveler's checks and major U.S. credit cards—particularly American Express—are accepted in larger cities and resorts. In smaller towns and rural areas you may need cash. Businesses in Jutland in Denmark, for example, are known for refusing to accept credit cards. You'll get a better exchange rate abroad than home, but even so it's wise to change a small amount of money before you go; lines at airport currency-exchange booths can be long. If your local bank can't change your currency, you can exchange money through **Thomas Cook Currency Service.** To find the office nearest you, contact the service at 29 Broadway, New York, NY 10006, tel. 212/635–0515.

For safety and convenience, it's always best to take traveler's checks. The most widely recognized traveler's checks are American Express, Barclay's, Thomas Cook, and those issued through major commercial banks such as Citibank and Bank of America. Some banks will issue the checks free to established customers, but most charge a 1% commission fee. Buy some of the traveler's checks in small denominations, to cash toward the end of your trip. This will save you having to cash a large check and ending up with more foreign money than you need. (Hold on to your receipts after exchanging your traveler's checks; it's easier to convert foreign currency back into dollars if you have the receipts.) Remember to take the addresses of offices where you can get refunds for lost or stolen traveler's checks. The *American Express Traveler's Companion,* a directory of offices to contact worldwide in case of loss or theft of American Express traveler's checks, is available at most travel-service locations.

Getting Money from Home

There are at least three ways to get money from home: (1) Have it sent through a large commercial bank with a branch in the town where you're staying. The only drawback is that you must have an account with the bank; if not, you'll have to go through your own bank, and the process will be slower and more expensive. (2) Have it sent through American Express. If you are a cardholder, you can cash a personal check or a counter check at an American Express office for up to $1,000 ($2,500 for gold-card holders) in cash or traveler's checks. There is a 1% commission on traveler's checks. American Express also provides another service, which you don't have to be a cardholder to use: the American Express MoneyGram. You will have to call home and have someone go to an American Express office or MoneyGram agent and fill out the necessary form. The amount sent must be in increments of $50 and must be paid for with cash, MasterCard, Visa, or the Optima card. The American Express MoneyGram agent authorizes the transfer of funds to an American Express office in the town where you're staying. You'll need to show identification when picking up the money. If possible, it helps to know the transaction reference number, but it can be traced by your last name. In most cases, the money will be available in 15 minutes. Fees vary according to the money sent. For sending $300, the fee is $35; for $1,000, $70; for $5,000, $170. For the American Express MoneyGram location nearest your home and the locations of offices throughout Scandinavia, call 800/543–4080. (3) Have it sent through Western Union (tel. 800/325–6000). If you have a MasterCard or Visa, you can have money sent for any amount up to your credit limit. If not, have someone at home take cash or a certified cashier's check to a Western Union office. The money will be delivered in two business days to a UniBank of Denmark (Aarhus, Copenhagen, Esbjerg, and Odense). Fees vary with the amount of money being sent. For $1,000 the standard fee is $47, plus an additional $10 for a phone transaction and another $25 for sending it to Europe ($82 total).

Cash Machines Express Cash allows American Express cardholders to withdraw up to $1,000 ($500 cash and $500 in American Express traveler's checks) in a seven-day period (21 days overseas) from their personal checking accounts at ATMs worldwide. Gold-card members can receive up to $2,500 ($500 cash and $2,000 in traveler's checks) in a seven-day period (21 days overseas). Express Cash is not a cash-advance service; only money already in the linked checking account can be withdrawn. Every transaction carries a 2% fee with a minimum charge of $2 and a maximum of $6. Apply for a PIN (Personal Identification Number) to link your accounts at least two to three weeks before departure. Call 800/CASH–NOW to receive an application or to locate the nearest Express Cash machine. In Scandinavia, Express Cash machines are located in Helsinki, Finland, and in Stavanger, Norway, only.

Scandinavian Currency

Currency fluctuations, unfortunately, have not favored American citizens recently. As of early 1991 the dollar was near a decade-long record low relative to the Scandinavian currencies. The pound has maintained a more stable relationship with the various kroner/or. Currencies are abbreviated DKr (Danish kroner), FM (Finnish mark), IKr (Icelandic kroner), NKr (Norwegian kroner), and SKr (Swedish kronor) in this book. In individual countries you may see prices indicated with Kr only, and you may see exchange rates in banks quoted for DEK, FIM, ISK, NOK, and SEK respectively. The currency-exchange rates quoted in the following chapters fluctuate daily, so check them at the time of your departure.

What It Will Cost

Costs are high in Denmark and Norway, higher still in Sweden and Finland, and highest in Iceland, where so many things must be imported. Throughout the region, be aware that sales taxes can be very high, but foreigners can avoid some sales tax by finding stores hooked into the country's tax-free shopping system. *See* Shopping, *below*, for details.

There are, of course, ways to cope with costs. Breakfast is usually included in the hotel bill. Eating lunch out and sticking to a simple dinner from materials bought at a grocery store is one method of holding down costs. Avoiding beer and liquor in restaurants is another; a bottle of beer costs four times as much in a restaurant as the same brand in a grocery store.

Passports and Visas

U.S. Citizens A traveler is required to have a valid passport to enter any Scandinavian country for a stay of up to three months. However, note that these countries begin calculating that three-month period from the time you enter any country in Scandinavia.

To obtain a new passport, apply in person; renewals can be obtained in person or by mail. First-time applicants should apply to one of the 13 U.S. Passport Agency offices at least five weeks in advance of their departure date. In addition, local county courthouses, many state and probate courts, and some post offices accept passport applications. Necessary documents include (1) a completed passport application (Form DSP–11); (2) proof of citizenship (birth certificate with raised seal or naturalization papers); (3) proof of identity (unexpired driver's license, employee ID card, military ID, student ID, or any other document with your photograph and signature); (4) two recent, identical, two-inch-square photographs (black-and-white or color); and (5) a $42 application fee for a 10-year passport (those under 18 pay $27 for a five-year passport). Passports are mailed to you in about 10–15 working days. If you are paying in cash, you must have exact change; no change is given.

To renew your passport by mail, you'll need to send a completed Form DSP–82; two recent, identical passport photographs; your current passport (less than 12 years old); and a check or money order for $35.

If your passport is lost or stolen abroad, report it immediately to the nearest U.S. embassy or consulate and to local police authorities. If you can provide the consular officer with the information contained in the passport, he or she will most likely be able to issue you a new passport. For this reason, it is a good idea to keep a copy of the data page of your passport in a separate place or to leave the passport number, date, and place of issuance with a relative or friend in the United States.

British Citizens You need a valid passport to enter any of the Scandinavian countries (cost £15 for a standard 32-page passport, £30 for a 94-page passport). Application forms are available from most travel agents and major post offices and from the Passport Office (Clive House, 70 Petty France, London SW1H 9HD, tel. 071/279–3434 for recorded information, or 071/279–4000). You do not need a visa. A British Visitor's Passport is valid for a stay in Scandinavia, provided you will be there less than three months. It is valid for one year, costs £7.50, and is nonrenewable. You'll need two passport photographs and identification. Apply at your local post office.

Canadian Citizens A traveler is required to have a valid passport to enter any Scandinavian country for a stay of up to three months. However, note that these countries begin calculating that three-month period from the time you enter any country in Scandinavia.

To obtain a passport, send a completed application (available at any post office or passport office) to the Bureau of Passports, Suite 215, West Tower, Guy Favreau Complex, 200 boulevard René Lévèsque Ouest, Montréal, Québec H2Z 1X4. Include $25, two photographs, a guarantor, and proof of Canadian citizenship. Applications can be made in person at regional passport offices in many locations, including Edmonton, Halifax, Montréal, Toronto, Vancouver, and Winnipeg. Passports are valid for five years and are nonrenewable.

Customs and Duties

On Arrival Limits on what you can bring in duty-free vary from country to country. See individual chapters for limits on alcohol, cigarettes, and other items. Also be careful to check before bringing food of any kind into Iceland.

On Departure If you are bringing any foreign-made equipment, such as a camera, with you from home, it's wise to carry the original receipt or to register it with customs before you leave (U.S. Customs Form 4457). Otherwise, you may end up paying duty on the item on your return.

U.S. Citizens You may bring home duty-free up to $400 worth of foreign goods, as long as you have been out of the country for at least 48 hours and you haven't claimed that exemption in the past 30 days. Each member of the family is entitled to the same exemption, regardless of age, and exemptions may be pooled. For the next $1,000 worth of goods, a flat 10% rate is assessed; above $1,400, duties vary with the merchandise. Included in the allowances for travelers 21 or older are one liter of alcohol, 100 cigars (non-Cuban), and 200 cigarettes. Only one bottle of perfume trademarked in the United States may be imported. There is no duty on antiques or works of art over 100 years old. Anything exceeding these limits will be taxed at the port of entry and may be taxed additionally in the traveler's home state. Gifts valued at under $50 may be mailed duty-free to friends or relatives at home, but you may not send more than one package per day to a single addressee, and packages may not include tobacco, liquor, or perfumes costing more than $5.

British Citizens Returning to the United Kingdom, a traveler 17 or over can take home (1) 200 cigarettes or 100 cigarillos or 50 cigars or 250 grams of tobacco; (2) one liter of alcohol over 22% volume or two liters of alcohol under 22% volume or two liters of fortified or sparkling wine; (3) two liters of still table wine; (4) 60 ml of perfume and 250 ml of toilet water; (5) other goods to a value of £32 but no more than 50 liters of beer or 25 mechanical lighters.

Canadian Citizens Exemptions for returning Canadians range from $20 to $300, depending on length of stay out of the country. For the $300 exemption, you must have been out of the country for one week. In any given year, you are only allowed one $300 exemption. You may bring in duty-free up to 50 cigars, 200 cigarettes, 2.2 pounds of tobacco, and 40 ounces of liquor, provided these are declared in writing to customs on arrival and accompany you in hand or in checked baggage. Personal gifts should be mailed labeled "Unsolicited Gift—Value under $40." Obtain a copy of the Canadian Customs brochure *I Declare* for further details.

Traveling with Film

If your camera is new, shoot and develop a few rolls of film before leaving home. Pack some lens tissue and an extra battery for your built-in light meter. Invest about $10 in a skylight filter: It will protect the lens and reduce haze.

Film doesn't like hot weather, so if you're driving in summer, don't store film in the glove compartment or on the shelf under the rear window. Put it behind the front seat on the floor, on the side opposite the exhaust pipe.

On a plane trip, never pack unprocessed film in checked luggage: if your bags are X-rayed, you can say good-bye to your pictures. Always carry undeveloped film with you through security and ask to have it inspected by hand. (It helps to keep your film in a plastic bag, ready for quick inspection.) Inspectors at American airports are required by law to honor requests for hand inspection.

The newer airport scanning machines used in all U.S. airports are safe for anything from five to 500 scans, depending on the speed of your film. The effects are cumulative; you can put the same roll of film through several scans without worry. After five scans, though, you're asking for trouble.

If your film becomes fogged and you want an explanation, send it to the **National Association of Photographic Manufacturers** (550 Mamaroneck Ave., Harrison, NY 10528). It will try to determine what went wrong. The service is free.

Language

Despite the fact that four of the five Scandinavian tongues are in the Germanic family of languages, it is a myth that someone who speaks German can understand Danish, Swedish, and Norwegian. Fortunately, English is widely spoken in Scandinavia. German is the most common third language. Outside major cities, English becomes rarer, and it's a good idea to take along a dictionary or phrase book. Even here, however, anyone under the age of 50 is likely to have studied English in school.

Danish, Norwegian, and Swedish are similar, and fluent speakers can generally understand each other. A foreigner will most often be struck by the lilting rhythm of spoken Swedish, which takes a bit of getting used to for Danes and Norwegians, who often choose to speak English with Swedes.

Characters special to these three languages are the Danish "ø" and the Swedish "ö," pronounced somewhat like the "oo" in "goop," but with a bit more r-sound to it; "æ"or "ä," which sounds like the "a" in "ape" but with a glottal stop; and the "å," which sounds like the "o" in "ghost." The important thing about these characters isn't that you pronounce them correctly—foreigners usually can't—but that you know to find them in the phone book at the very end. Mr. Søren Åstrup, for example, will be found after "Z." Æ or Ä and Ø or Ö follow.

Icelandic, because of its island isolation, is the language closest to what the Vikings spoke 1,000 years ago. Although Norwegian, Danish, and Swedish have clearly evolved away from the roots common to all four languages, Icelandic retains a surprising amount of its ancient heritage, and Icelanders want to keep it that way: a governmental committee in Iceland has the express task of coming up with Icelandic versions of new words such as "computer." Two characters are unique to Icelandic and Faroese: the "Þ" or "þ," which is pronounced like the "th" in "thing"; and "Ð" or "ð," which is pronounced like the "th" in "the."

Finnish is a non-Germanic language more closely related to Livonian and Hungarian than to any of the other Scandinavian languages. A visitor isn't likely to recognize anything on the average newspaper's front page. A linguistic cousin to Finnish is still spoken by the Sami (Lapps), who wander in the northernmost parts of Norway, Sweden, Finland, and Russia.

Staying Healthy

If you have a health problem that may require purchase of prescription drugs, have your doctor write a prescription using the drug's generic name, as brand names vary from country to country. If possible, take enough from home to last the trip, and remember to hand-carry prescriptions and medicines, so they aren't lost if your luggage is.

If necessary, many clinics in Scandinavia will write a prescription for you free of charge, which you can pick up at a nearby *apotek* (drug store), often at subsidized prices.

The **International Association for Medical Assistance to Travelers (IAMAT)** (417 Center St., Lewiston, NY 14092, tel. 716/754–4883; in Canada, 40 Regal Rd., Guelph, Ontario N1K 1B5; in Europe, 57 Voirets, 1212 Grand-Lancy, Geneva, Switzerland) is a worldwide association that offers a list of approved physicians and clinics whose training meets British and American standards. For a list of Scandinavian physicians and clinics that are part of this network, contact IAMAT. Membership is free.

Inoculations are not required for entry into any of the Scandinavian countries.

Insurance

Travelers may seek insurance coverage in four areas: health and accident, lost luggage, trip cancellation, and flight. Your first step is to review your existing health and home-owner policies; some health-insurance plans cover health expenses incurred while traveling, some major medical plans cover emergency transportation, and some home owner policies cover the theft of luggage.

Health and Accident

Several companies offer coverage designed to supplement existing health insurance for travelers:

Carefree Travel Insurance (Box 310, 120 Mineola Blvd., Mineola, NY 11501, tel. 516/294–0220 or 800/323–3149) provides coverage for emergency medical evacuation and accidental death and dismemberment. It offers 24-hour medical phone advice.

International SOS Assistance (Box 11568, Philadelphia, PA 19116, tel. 215/244–1500 or 800/523–8930) provides emergency evacuation services, worldwide medical referrals, and optional medical insurance.

Travel Assistance International (1133 15th St. NW, Suite 400, Washington, DC 20005, tel. 202/331–1609 or 800/821–2828) provides emergency evacuation services and 24-hour medical referrals.

Travel Guard International, underwritten by Transamerica Occidental Life Companies (1145 Clark St., Stevens Point, WI 54481, tel. 715/345–0505 or 800/782–5151), offers emergency evacuation services and reimbursement for medical expenses with no deductibles or daily limits.

Wallach and Company, Inc. (243 Church St. NW, Suite 100D, Vienna, VA 22180, tel. 703/281–9500 or 800/237–6615) offers comprehensive medical coverage, including emergency evacuation services worldwide.

WorldCare Travel Assistance Association (1150 S. Olive St., Suite T–233, Los Angeles, CA 90015, tel. 213/749–0909 or 800/666–4993) provides unlimited emergency evacuation, 24-hour medical referral, and an emergency message center.

Lost Luggage and Trip Cancellation

On international flights, airlines are responsible for lost or damaged property up to $9.07 per pound (or $20 per kilo) for checked baggage and up to $400 per passenger for unchecked baggage. If you're carrying valuables, either take them with you on the plane or purchase additional insurance for lost luggage. Some airlines will issue extra luggage insurance when you check in, but many do not. Insurance for lost, damaged, or stolen luggage is available through travel agents or directly through various insurance companies. Luggage-loss coverage is usually part of a comprehensive travel-insurance package that includes personal accident, trip cancellation, and sometimes default and bankruptcy. Two companies that issue luggage insurance are **Tele-Trip** (Box 31685, 3201 Farnam St., Omaha, NE 68131, tel. 800/228–9792), a subsidiary of Mutual of Omaha, and **The Travelers Corporation** (Ticket and Travel Dept., 1 Tower Sq., Hartford, CT 06183, tel. 203/277–0111 or 800/243–3174). Tele-Trip operates sales booths at airports and also issues insurance through travel agents. Rates vary according to the length of the trip. The Travelers Corporation will insure checked or hand luggage at $500–$2,000 valuation per person, for a maximum of 180 days. Rates for 1–5 days for $500 valuation are $10; for 180 days, $85. Other companies with comprehensive policies include **Access America Inc.,** a subsidiary of Blue Cross–Blue Shield (Box 11188, Richmond, VA 23230, tel. 800/334–7525 or 800/284–8300), **Near Services** (450 Prairie Ave., Suite 101, Calumet City, IL 60409, tel. 708/868–6700 or

800/654–6700), **Travel Guard International,** and **Carefree Travel Insurance** (*see* Health and Accident Insurance, *above*).

Before you go, itemize the contents of each bag in case you need to file an insurance claim. Be certain to put your home or business address on each piece of luggage, including carry-on bags. If your luggage is lost or stolen and later recovered, the airline will deliver the luggage to your home free of charge.

Flight Flight insurance is often included in the price of a ticket when paid for with American Express, Visa, or other major credit cards. It is usually included in combination travel-insurance packages available from most tour operators, travel agents, and insurance agents.

Car Rentals

Driving through Scandinavia is delightful; you'll notice that drivers keep their headlights on even during the day—it is required by law in most of Scandinavia. Take a good pair of sunglasses—the slanting sunlight creates a lot of glare. Drivers' licenses from Britain, Canada, and the United States are valid in Scandinavia. Several countries require drivers to be over 20 years old, but some car-rental companies require drivers be at least 25, so it is wise to ask.

Major companies include **Avis, Hertz, Europcar, Bonus, Budget,** and **InterRent,** which have offices throughout Scandinavia. Frequently it is cheaper and more certain to reserve a car before leaving home than to do so from a Scandinavian airport. Reduced rates are sometimes available if you travel on domestic air services and for train travelers at major stations. Special car-rental rates are often available on weekends and sometimes to those with foreign passports. Always ask if the price includes tax, which can add 20% or more.

In most Scandinavian countries green-card liability insurance is not generally necessary while driving a car rented in Scandinavia. Green-card insurance is, however, required to drive a Scandinavian rental car elsewhere in continental Europe, and in Iceland. Such insurance is usually free, but you must remember to ask the rental agency to do the necessary paperwork.

Personal accident insurance covers medical injuries. One expense not generally covered by rental-car personal accident insurance policies is emergency transportation home (*see* Insurance, *above*).

For British citizens, a personal accident insurance policy on a rented car does not make sense in Denmark, because EC-wide agreements cover all medical expenses and transportation home. For British citizens traveling in the rest of Scandinavia, which is not a part of the EC, however, major medical bills must be paid by insurance from home.

Rail Passes

The **EurailPass,** valid for unlimited first-class train travel through 17 countries, including Norway, Sweden, Denmark, and Finland, is an excellent value if you plan to travel around the Continent.

The ticket is available for periods of 15 days ($390), 21 days ($498), one month ($616), two months ($840), and three months ($1,042). For two or more people traveling together, a 15-day rail pass costs $298 each. Between April 1 and September 30, you need a minimum of three in your group to get this discount. For those younger than 26, there is the **Eurail Youthpass**, for one or two months of unlimited second-class train travel at $425 and $560.

If you like to spread out your train journey, you can use the **Eurail Flexipass.** With the 15-day Flexipass ($230), you will get five days of unlimited first-class train travel spread out over 15 days; a 21-day pass gives you nine days of travel ($398), and a one-month pass gives you 14 days ($498).

The **EurailPass** is available only if you live outside Europe and North Africa. You can apply through an authorized travel agent or through **Rail Europe** (610 5th Ave., New York, NY 10020, tel. 800/345–1990).

The **Scandinavian Rail Pass** is valid throughout Scandinavia and can be purchased from Rail Europe (*see above*). A second-class pass costs $139 for 15 days, $229 for 21 days, and $319 for one month. The first-class rates are $179, $299, and $459 respectively.

The **Nordturist Card** gives unlimited travel on the state railway systems of Denmark, Sweden, Norway, and Finland. The 21-day card costs DKr 1,650, for example (about $275 or £140), but tickets can be bought at any train station in the four countries. Reservations are not necessary. Young people ages 12 to 25 pay DKr 1,250, and children 4 to 11, DKr 825. The ticket is also valid on several ferries: Helsingør/Helsingborg, Frederikshavn/Göteborg, Hirtshals/Kristiansand, and Stockholm/Åbo. Further rebates of up to 50% are granted on some ferries and coaches and by some hotels.

Student and Youth Travel

The **International Student Identity Card (ISIC)** entitles students to special fares on local transportation, rail passes, and intra-European student charter flights and to discounts at museums, theaters, sports events, and many other attractions. If the ISIC card is purchased in the United States, the $14 cost also includes $3,000 in emergency medical coverage plus hospital coverage of $100 a day for up to 60 days. Apply to the **Council on International Educational Exchange (CIEE)** (205 E. 42nd St., New York, NY 10017, tel. 212/661–1414). In Canada, the ISIC is available for $12 (Canadian) from **Travel Cuts** (187 College St., Toronto, Ontario M5T 1P7, tel. 416/979–2406). In the United Kingdom, students enrolled in university programs can purchase the ISIC at any students union or student-travel company upon presentation of a valid university ID.

Travelers (students and nonstudents) under age 26 can apply for a **Youth International Educational Exchange Card (YIEE)** issued by the **Federation of International Youth Travel Organizations** (FIYTO, 81 Islands Brugge, DK–2300 Copenhagen S, Denmark). It provides services and benefits similar to those of the ISIC card and is available in the United States from CIEE (*see above*) or from **International Student Exchange** (ISE, Europa House, 802 W. Oregon St., Urbana, IL 61801, tel. 217/

344–5863). In Canada contact the **Canadian Hostelling Association (CHA)** (1600 James Naismith Dr., Suite 608, Gloucester, Ontario K1B 5N4, tel. 613/748–5638).

get "Lets go" book.

An **International Youth Hostel Federation (IYHF)** membership card is the key to inexpensive dormitory-style accommodations at more than 5,000 hostel locations in 68 countries around the world. Hostels provide separate sleeping quarters for men and women at rates ranging from $7 to $20 a night per person, and many have family accommodations. Youth-hostel memberships, which are valid for 12 months from the time of purchase, are available in the United States through **American Youth Hostels (AYH)** (Box 37613, Washington, DC 20013, tel. 202/783–6161), in Canada through the **Canadian Hostelling Association** (*see above*), and in the United Kingdom through the **Youth Hostel Association of England and Wales** (Trevelyan House, 8 St. Stephen's Hill, St. Albans, Herts AL1 2DY, tel. 0727/55215). By joining one of these national youth-hostel associations, members automatically become part of the International Youth Hostel Federation and are entitled to special reductions on rail and bus travel around the world. Handbooks listing these special concessions are available from the associations. The cost of a first-year membership is $25 for adults 18–54. Renewal is $15 per year thereafter. For young people 17 and under the rate is $10, and for senior citizens (55 and older) the rate is $15. Family membership is available for $35.

Economical bicycle tours for small groups of adventurous, energetic students are a popular AYH student-travel service. For information on these and other AYH activities and publications, contact AYH at the address above.

Council Travel, a CIEE subsidiary, is the foremost U.S. student travel agency, specializing in low-cost charters and serving as the exclusive U.S. agent for many student airfare bargains and tours. CIEE's 80-page *Student Travel Catalog* and Council Charter brochures are available free from any Council Travel office in the United States (enclose $1 postage if ordering by mail; *see* address *above*). In addition to CIEE headquarters at 205 East 42nd Street (tel. 212/661–1450) in New York City, there are Council Travel offices in California (Berkeley, La Jolla, Long Beach, Los Angeles, San Diego, San Francisco, and Sherman Oaks); Colorado (Boulder); Connecticut (New Haven); Washington, DC; Georgia (Atlanta); Illinois (Chicago and Evanston); Louisiana (New Orleans); Massachusetts (Amherst, Boston, and Cambridge); Minnesota (Minneapolis); North Carolina (Durham); Oregon (Portland); Rhode Island (Providence); Texas (Austin and Dallas); Washington (Seattle); and Wisconsin (Milwaukee).

The **Educational Travel Center** (438 N. Frances St., Madison, WI 53703, tel. 608/256–5551) is another student-travel specialist worth contacting for information on student tours, bargain fares, and bookings.

Students who would like to work abroad should contact CIEE's **Work Abroad Department** (206 E. 42nd St., New York, NY 10017, tel. 212/661–1414, ext. 1130). The council arranges paid and voluntary work experiences overseas for up to six months. CIEE also sponsors study programs in Europe, Latin America, Asia, and Australia and produces several books of interest to the student traveler. These include *Work, Study, Travel*

Abroad: The Whole World Handbook ($10.95 plus $1 book-rate postage or $2.50 first-class postage); *Volunteer! The Comprehensive Guide to Voluntary Service in the U.S. and Abroad* ($6.95 plus $1 book-rate postage or $2.50 first-class postage); and *The Teenager's Guide to Travel, Study, and Adventure Abroad* ($9.95 plus $1 book-rate postage or $2.50 first-class postage.) The **Information Center at the Institute of International Education (IEE)** (809 U. N. Plaza, New York, NY 10017, tel. 212/984–5413) has reference books, foreign-university catalogs, study-abroad brochures, and other materials that may be consulted free of charge. The center is open weekdays 10–4 and is closed holidays.

Most major cities in Scandinavia (including Helsinki, Oslo, Stockholm, Reykjavík, and Copenhagen) offer special **City Cards,** which entitle the holder to unlimited, reduced-rate travel on public transportation as well as free or discounted admission to museums, theaters, and other attractions. The cards can be purchased at tourist offices and major rail stations. (For more information, *see* individual destination chapters.) Additional information is available from the **Scandinavian Tourist Board.** For information on the Eurail Youthpass, *see* Rail Passes, *above.*

Traveling with Children

Publications "Family Travel Times" is a newsletter published 10 times a year by **Travel With Your Children (TWYCH),** (80 8th Ave., New York, NY 10011, tel. 212/206–0688). A one-year subscription costs $35 and includes access to back issues. The organization also offers a free phone-in service that gives advice and information on specific destinations.

Great Vacations with Your Kids, by Dorothy Jordan and Marjorie Cohen, offers complete advice on planning your trip with children, from toddlers to teens. It is available for $12.95 (paperback) from E. P. Dutton (2 Park Ave., New York, NY 10016, tel. 212/725–1818).

"Kids and Teens in Flight," a useful brochure about children flying alone, is available from the U. S. Department of Transportation. To order a free copy, call 202/366–2220.

Innocents Abroad: Traveling with Kids in Europe, by Valerie Wolf Deutsch and Laura Sutherland, is a new guide to child- and teen-friendly activities, food, and transportation on the Continent, with individual sections on each country. It is available for $14.95 (paperback) from the New American Library (Penguin USA, 375 Hudson St., New York, NY 10014, tel. 212/366–2000).

Getting There All children, including infants, must have a valid passport for foreign travel. On international flights, children under two not occupying a seat pay 10% of the adult fare. Various discounts apply to children from ages two to 12, so check with your airline when making reservations. Regulations about infant travel on airplanes are changing, and, until a standard is set, you must bring your own infant car seat and buy a separate ticket if you want to be sure your infant is secure. Check with the airline in advance to be sure your seat meets the required standard. If possible, reserve a seat behind one of the plane's bulkheads, where there's usually more legroom and enough space to fit a bassinet (which is available from the airlines). The booklet "Child/Infant Safety Seats Acceptable for Use in Aircraft" is available from the **Federal Aviation Administration** (APA–200, 800 Independence Ave. SW, Washington, DC 20591, tel. 202/267–3479). If you opt to hold your baby on your lap, do so with the infant outside the seat belt rather than inside it so he or she doesn't get crushed in case of a sudden stop. When reserving tickets, also ask about special children's meals or snacks. The February 1992 issue of "Family Travel Times" includes TWYCH's "Airline Guide," which contains a rundown of the children's services offered by 46 different airlines.

Getting Around Children are entitled to discount tickets (often as much as 50% off) on buses, trains, and ferries throughout Scandinavia, as well as reductions on special City Cards. During summer months children under 12 pay $20 to $40 and children under two fly free on SAS and Linjeflyg round-trips. The only restriction on this discount is that the family travel together and return to the originating city in Scandinavia at least two days later. Under the Scanrail plan—good for rail journeys throughout Scandinavia—children under four travel free and children four to 11 pay half-fare.

Hotels In most Scandinavian hotels children stay free or at reduced rates when sharing their parents' rooms; there is a nominal charge for an extra bed.

Home Exchange Exchanging homes is a surprisingly inexpensive way to enjoy a vacation abroad, especially if you plan a lengthy visit. The largest home-exchange company, **International Home Exchange Service** (Box 190070, San Francisco, CA 94119, tel. 415/435-3497), publishes three directories each year. The $45 membership entitles you to one listing and all three directories (there is an additional charge for postage). Photos of your property cost an additional $10, and listing a second home costs $10.

Loan-a-Home (2 Park La., Apt. 6E, Mount Vernon, NY 10552, tel. 914/664–7640), which publishes two directories (in December and June) and two supplements (in March and September) each year, is popular with academics on sabbatical, businesspeople on temporary assignment, and retirees on extended vacations. There is no annual membership fee or charge for listing your home, but one directory and a supplement cost $35. All four books cost $45.

Hostels In Scandinavia many youth hostels offer special facilities (including multiple-bed rooms and separate kitchens) for families with children. Family hostels also provide an excellent opportunity for children to meet youngsters from other countries. Contact the **AYH** (*see* Student and Youth Travel, *above*) for information.

Baby-sitting Services For information on local baby-sitting agencies, contact the tourist office in the city or region you are visiting.

Hints for Disabled Travelers

In Scandinavia Facilities for the disabled in Scandinavia are generally good, and most of the major tourist offices offer special booklets and brochures on travel and accommodations for disabled visitors.

Hotels Some hotels are suitable for unaccompanied travelers, but, in many others, individuals will require the assistance of an able-bodied companion. Contact the organizations listed below for further information.

The **Best Western** chain (tel. 800/528–1234) offers properties with wheelchair-accessible rooms in Helsinki, Oslo, and Stockholm and just outside Copenhagen. If wheelchair rooms are not available, ground-floor rooms are provided.

In the United States The **Information Center for Individuals with Disabilities** (Fort Point Pl., 1st floor, 27–43 Wormwood St., Boston, MA 02210, tel. 617/727–5540; TDD 617/727–5236) offers useful problem-solving assistance, including lists of travel agents who specialize in tours for the disabled.

Moss Rehabilitation Hospital Travel Information Service (1200 W. Tabor Rd., Philadelphia, PA 19141–3009, tel. 215/456–9600, TDD 215/456–9602) for a small fee provides information on tourist sights, transportation, and accommodations in destinations around the world. They also provide toll-free airline reservation telephone numbers with special lines for the hard of hearing.

Travel Industry and Disabled Exchange (TIDE) (5435 Donna Ave., Tarzana, CA 91356, tel. 818/368–5648) publishes a quarterly newsletter and a directory of travel agencies and tours catering to the disabled. The annual membership fee is $15.

Mobility International USA (Box 3551, Eugene, OR 97403, tel. 503/343–1284, voice and TDD) is an internationally affiliated organization with 500 members. For a $20 annual fee, it coordinates exchange programs for disabled people around the world and offers information on accommodations and organized study programs.

The **Society for the Advancement of Travel for the Handicapped** (26 Court St., Penthouse Suite, Brooklyn, NY 11242, tel. 718/858–5483) provides access information and lists of tour operators specializing in travel for the disabled. Annual membership costs $45, or $25 for students and senior citizens. Send $1 and a stamped, self-addressed envelope for information on a specific destination.

In the United Kingdom The main British sources of advice on travel for the handicapped are the **Royal Association for Disability and Rehabilitation (RADAR)** (25 Mortimer St., London W1N 8AB, tel. 071/637–5400), the **Holiday Care Service** (2 Old Bank Chambers, Station Rd., Horley, Surrey), and **Mobility International** (228 Borough Hight St., London SE1 1JX, tel. 081/403–5688).

Publications **The Itinerary** (Box 2012, Bayonne, NJ 07002, tel. 201/858–3400) is a bimonthly travel magazine for the disabled. Call for a subscription ($10 for one year, $20 for two); the magazine is not available in bookstores.

Access to the World: A Travel Guide for the Handicapped, by Louise Weiss, offers tips on travel and accessibility around the world. It is available from Henry Holt & Co. for $12.95 (tel. 800/247–3912; the order number is 0805 001417).

Twin Peaks Press (Box 129, Vancouver, WA 98666, tel. 206/694–2462 or 800/637–2256 for orders only) specializes in books for the disabled. *Travel for the Disabled* offers helpful hints as well as a comprehensive list of guidebooks and facilities geared to the disabled. The *Directory of Travel Agencies for the Disabled* lists more than 350 agencies throughout the world. Twin Peaks also offers a "Traveling Nurse's Network," which provides registered nurses to accompany and assist disabled travelers.

Hints for Older Travelers

In Scandinavia When booking tickets of any kind or reserving hotel rooms or train seats, always ask if a discount is available for older travelers. Rental cars are also available at a discount. For additional information on senior discounts and seasonal savings plans, contact the Scandinavian Tourist Board (*see* Government Tourist Offices, *above*).

In the United States The **American Association of Retired Persons (AARP)** (1909 K St. NW, Washington, DC 20049, tel. 202/662–4850) arranges group tours, cruises, and apartment living in Europe through **American Express Vacations** (Box 5014, Atlanta, GA 30302, tel. 800/241–1700 or, in GA, 800/637–6200). AARP members must be 50 years or older; annual dues are $5 per person or couple.

Elderhostel (75 Federal St., 3rd floor, Boston, MA 02110–1941, tel. 617/426–7788) is an innovative educational program for people 60 and older. Participants live in dorms on some 1,200 campuses around the world. Mornings are devoted to lectures and seminars; afternoons to sightseeing and field trips. Fees for two- to three-week trips—including room, board, tuition, and round-trip transportation—range from $1,800 to $4,500.

Saga International Holidays (120 Boylston St., Boston, MA 02116, tel. 800/343–0273) specializes in group travel for people over 60. A selection of variously priced tours allows you to choose the package that meets your needs.

Publications The ***International Health Guide for Senior Citizen Travelers,*** by W. Robert Lange, M.D., is available for $4.95 plus $1 for shipping, from Pilot Books (103 Cooper St., Babylon, NY 11702, tel. 516/422–2225).

The ***Discount Guide for Travelers Over 55,*** by Caroline and Walter Weintz, lists helpful addresses, package tours, and reduced-rate car rentals in the United States and abroad. To order, send $7.95 plus $1.50 shipping and handling to NAL/Cash Sales (Bergenfield Order Dept., 120 Woodbine St., Bergenfield, NJ 07621, tel. 800/526–0275).

Contacts with Scandinavians

A nonprofit organization known as **Friends Overseas** (68–04 Dartmouth St., Forest Hills, NY 11375) provides contacts with welcoming locals for travelers in Denmark, Finland, Norway, and Sweden. Send a note listing your name, address, age, occupation, and those with whom you are traveling, along with a business-size, self-addressed, stamped (or include a $1 international postal coupon) envelope in order to receive an application form and more information. The membership fee is $25.

Further Reading

A History of the Vikings (Oxford University Press, 1984) recounts the story of the aggressive warriors and explorers who, by the time of their defeat at Hastings, in 1066, had influenced a large portion of the world, extending from Constantinople to

America. Gwyn Jones's lively account makes learning the history enjoyable.

Arriving and Departing

From North America by Plane

Be sure to distinguish between the three types of flights: nonstop—no changes, no stops; direct—no changes, but one or more stops; and connecting—two or more planes, one or more stops.

Airlines The following is a list of the major airlines that fly nonstop from the United States or Canada to Scandinavia. Additional airlines offer connecting flights to Scandinavia.

Scandinavian Airlines (SAS) (tel. 800/221–2350) is the airline offering the largest number of nonstop flights to Scandinavia, with flights linking Copenhagen to New York, Chicago, Seattle, Los Angeles, Anchorage, London, Reykjavík, and Toronto. SAS also offers direct flights from New York to Oslo.

Delta Airlines (tel. 800/221–1212) now flies to Copenhagen from Atlanta. **Finnair** (tel. 800/950–5000) offers nonstop flights between Helsinki and Copenhagen, Göteborg, London, Los Angeles, Malmö, New York, Oslo, Stockholm, and Toronto.

Icelandair (in the U.S., tel. 800/223–5500; in Oslo, 02/42–39–75; in Copenhagen, 33–12–33–88) offers nonstop flights linking Reykjavík to New York, Copenhagen, London, Orlando, Oslo, Stockholm, Amsterdam, Baltimore, and Glasgow. All flights between North America and Denmark stop in Reykjavík. Overnight stopovers are available; during winter months, stopovers are free and include hotel.

From the United Kingdom by Plane

Many of the airlines listed above make stops in London en route to Scandinavia. The list below includes other major carriers from Great Britain.

SAS (in London, tel. 071/734–6777; fax 071/465–0125) offers nonstop flights connecting London to Århus, Bergen, Copenhagen, Göteborg, Malmö, Oslo, Stavanger, and Stockholm.

British Airways (tel. 081/897–4000) offers nonstop flights from Heathrow to Bergen, Copenhagen, Gothenburg, Helsinki, Oslo, Stavanger, and Stockholm. **Maersk Air** (tel. 071/638–7920) flies between London and Copenhagen. **Air Europe** (tel. 0345/444737), **Aer Lingus** (tel. 0345/01–01–01; in Ireland, 0001/377–777), **Cimber Air** (tel. 0652/688491), **Business Air** (tel. 0382/66345), **Midtfly** (tel. 0224/723357), and **Icelandair** (tel. 071/388–5599; or 081/745–7051 at Heathrow Airport) all have flights between Great Britain or Ireland and major Scandinavian cities.

Flying Time The following are typical in-air times between major airports in North America, London, and Scandinavia. Add extra time for stopovers and connections.

From New York: to Reykjavík, 5 hours 30 minutes; to Copenhagen, 7 hours 40 minutes; to Stockholm, 8 hours; to Oslo, 7 hours 30 minutes; to Helsinki, 8 hours.

From Los Angeles: to Copenhagen, 9 hours 50 minutes; to Helsinki, 11 hours 15 minutes.

From London (Gatwick): to Copenhagen, 2 hours; to Stockholm, 2 hours 25 minutes; to Reykjavík, 3 hours 10 minutes; to Helsinki, 3 hours.

From Reykjavík: to Copenhagen, 3 hours 15 minutes.

From Helsinki: to Stockholm, 55 minutes; to Copenhagen, 1 hour 45 minutes; to Oslo, 1 hour 45 minutes.

From Copenhagen: to Oslo, 1 hour; to Stockholm, 1 hour 10 minutes; to Reykjavík, 2 hours 20 minutes; to Helsinki, 2 hours 35 minutes.

Enjoying the Flight

If you're lucky enough to be able to sleep on a plane, it makes sense to fly at night. Many experienced travelers, however, prefer to take a morning flight to Scandinavia and arrive in the evening, just in time for a good night's sleep. Because the air on a plane is dry, it helps, while flying, to drink a lot of nonalcoholic beverages; drinking alcohol contributes to jet lag, as does eating heavy meals on board. Feet swell at high altitudes, so it's a good idea to remove your shoes at the beginning of your flight. Sleepers usually prefer window seats to curl up against; those who like to move about the cabin should ask for aisle seats. Bulkhead seats (located in the front row of each cabin) have more legroom, but seat trays are attached rather awkwardly to the arms of the seat rather than to the back of the seat ahead. Generally, bulkhead seats are reserved for the disabled, the elderly, or parents traveling with babies.

Discount Flights

The major airlines offer a range of tickets that can increase the price of any given seat by more than 300%, depending on the day of purchase. As a rule, the farther in advance you buy the ticket, the less expensive it is and the greater the penalty (up to 100%) for canceling. Check with airlines for details.

APEX (advance-purchase) tickets carry certain restrictions: They must be bought in advance (usually 21 days); they restrict your travel, usually with a minimum stay of seven days and a maximum of 90; and they also penalize you for changes—voluntary or not—in your travel plans. But if you can work around these drawbacks (and most travelers can), they are among the best-value fares available.

Travelers willing to put up with some restrictions and inconveniences in exchange for a substantially reduced airfare may be interested in flying as an **air courier.** A courier accompanies shipments between designated points. There are two sources of information on courier deals: (1) For a telephone directory listing courier companies by the cities to which they fly, send $5 and a self-addressed, stamped, business-size envelope to Pacific Data Sales Publishing, 2554 Lincoln Blvd., Suite 275–F, Marina Del Rey, CA 92091. (2) For "A Simple Guide to Courier Travel," send $14.95 (includes postage and handling) to Box 2394, Lake Oswego, OR 97035. For more information, call 800/344–9375.

Charter flights offer the lowest fares but often depart only on certain days, and seldom on time. Though you may be able to arrive at one city and return from another, you may lose all or most of your money if you cancel your trip. Don't sign up for a charter flight unless you've checked with a travel agency about the reputation of the packager. It's particularly important to know the packager's policy concerning refunds, should a flight be canceled; some travel agents recommend that travelers purchase trip-cancellation insurance if they plan to book charter flights. One of the most popular charter operators to Europe is **Council Charter** (205 E. 42nd St., New York, NY 10017, tel. 212/661–0311 or 800/223–7402), a division of the Council on International Educational Exchange (CIEE). Other companies advertise in the travel sections of Sunday newspapers.

Somewhat more expensive—but up to 50% below the cost of APEX fares—are tickets purchased through **consolidators,** companies that buy blocks of tickets on scheduled airlines and sell them at wholesale prices. Tickets are subject to availability, so passengers must generally have flexible travel schedules. Here again, you may lose all or most of your money if you change plans, but at least you will be on a regularly scheduled flight with less risk of cancellation than on a charter. As an added precaution, you may want to purchase trip-cancellation insurance. Once you've made your reservation, call the airline to confirm it. Among the best-known consolidators are **UniTravel** (Box 12485, St. Louis, MO 63132, tel. 314/569–2501 or 800/325–2222) and **Access International** (101 W. 31st St., Suite 1104, New York, NY 10001, tel. 212/465–0707 or 800/825–3633). Others advertise in the travel sections of Sunday newspapers.

Another option is to join a **travel club** that offers special discounts to its members. Several such organizations are **Discount Travel International** (114 Forrest Ave., Narberth, PA 19072, tel. 215/668–7184), **Moment's Notice** (425 Madison Ave., New York, NY 10017, tel. 212/486–0503), **Travelers Advantage** (CUC Travel Service, 49 Music Sq. W, Nashville, TN 37203, tel. 800/548–1116), and **Worldwide Discount Travel Club** (1674 Meridian Ave., Miami Beach, FL 33139, tel. 305/534–2082). These cut-rate tickets should be compared with APEX tickets on the major airlines.

Smoking If cigarette smoke bothers you, ask for a seat far from the smoking section. It is best to request a nonsmoking seat at the time you book your ticket. If a U.S. airline representative tells you there are no seats available in the nonsmoking section, insist on one: Department of Transportation regulations require U.S. flag carriers to find seats for all nonsmokers on the day of the flight, provided they meet check-in time restrictions.

From North America by Ship

Only one firm now offers trans-Atlantic crossings: **Cunard** (tel. 800/221–4770; in the United Kingdom, through British Airways, *see* From North America by Plane, *above*), sailing the famed *Queen Elizabeth 2* between New York and Southampton. The trip takes five days, and passengers fly home. Those arriving at Southampton wishing to sail on to Scandinavia should be aware that the Scandinavian ferries leave from Harwich, on the other side of London from Southampton.

Staying in Scandinavia

Getting Around

Particularly between Sweden, Norway, and Denmark, travel is practical by car, bus, train, boat, and plane. The choice depends on personal preference.

The Norwegian Tourist Office publishes an unglamorous brochure called "Tourist Timetables" that is particularly useful. It includes information about ships, trains, planes, buses, and ferries traveling to and around Norway, but much of the information is pertinent to all of Scandinavia.

By Plane Scandinavia is larger than it looks on a map, and many native travelers choose to fly between the capital cities, using trains and buses for domestic travel.

If you are traveling from south to north in Norway, Sweden, or Finland, flying is a necessity: Stavanger in southern Norway is as close to Rome, Italy, as it is to the northern tip of Norway.

For international travelers, one or two stopovers can often be purchased more cheaply along with an international ticket. With SAS, however, the least expensive tickets can be bought only within Scandinavia and only in summer, between July 1 and August 15. These Northern Price tickets require a seven-day advance purchase. Slightly more expensive are SAS Impulse Tickets, which require no advance purchase and are available year-round. SAS also gives couples traveling together a 50% discount off one of their two tickets, or 25% off the total ticket price.

By Car Driving is a marvelous way to explore Scandinavia. The roads are generally excellent and well marked but it is expensive: The price of gasoline runs roughly $1.25 per liter of lead-free gas, or roughly four times the typical American price. Ferry costs are steep, and reservations are vital. Tolls on some major roads add to the expense.

Also be aware of the relatively low legal blood-alcohol limits in Scandinavia and of the tough penalties for driving while intoxicated. Penalties include suspension of the driver's license and fines or imprisonment and are enforced by random police roadblocks in urban areas on weekends. In addition, an accident involving a driver with an illegally high blood-alcohol level usually voids all insurance agreements, so the driver becomes responsible for his own medical bills and damage to the cars.

In a few remote areas, especially in Iceland and northern Norway, Sweden, and Finland, road conditions can be unpredictable, and careful planning is required for safety's sake. It is wise to use a four-wheel-drive vehicle and to travel with at least one other car in these areas.

By Train Trains are clean, comfortable, on schedule, and deliver passengers directly downtown. They also offer special smoking and quiet sections, plus bunk beds for overnight trips. The prices are reasonable, and the network is wide, allowing passengers to go wherever they wish, either by train or by links to local bus networks, which are coordinated with train schedules. Trains aren't necessarily cheaper than flying, and they do take longer; one advantage, though, is that an overnight train is cheaper than many Scandinavian hotels, with reasonably comfortable bunk-style accommodations.

If you are over 65 or traveling with children, ask about discounts whenever you buy single-trip train tickets, as special prices are available in many places on many routes. Reservations are almost never necessary.

For details on the EurailPass and Scandinavian Rail Pass *see* Rail Passes in Before You Go, *above*.

By Bus Buses are ideal for local trips, as public transportation tends to be good. Detailed information on bus routes is available through local tourist offices (*see* Essential Information in destination chapters).

By Ship Taking a ferry isn't just fun, it's often necessary in Scandinavia. Many of the operators below arrange package trips, some offering a rental car and hotel as part of the deal.

Cruises often last overnight. The trip between Copenhagen and Oslo, for example, lasts approximately 16 hours, most lines leaving at about 5 PM and arriving about 9 the next morning. The cruise between Stockholm and Helsinki takes 12 hours, usually leaving at about 3 PM and arriving the next morning at 9. The shortest ferry route, however, runs between Helsingør, Denmark, and Helsingborg, Sweden, and takes only 20 minutes.

The main shipping operators running within Scandinavian waters are: **Larvik Line** (Box 30, 9900 Frederikshavn, Denmark, tel. 45/98–42–14–00), **Fred Olsen Lines** (Box 1159 Sentrum, N–0107 Oslo 1, Norway, tel. 472/67–80 00, fax 472/68–66–33), and **Scandinavian Ferry Lines** (Kronborgvej 9, Postboks 1, DK–3000 Helsingør, Denmark, tel. 45/42–23–95–22, fax 45/42–23–96–04).

The chief operator between England and many points within Scandinavia is **DFDS/Scandinavian Seaways** (Axelborg, Vesterbrogade 4A, 1620 Copenhagen V, Denmark, tel. 45/33–11–22–55) with ships connecting Harwich and Newcastle to Esbjerg, Göteborg, and ports farther up the Norwegian coastline. Another cruise connects Travemünde, Stockholm, Helsinki, and Leningrad.

Connections from Holland and Germany to Norway are available through DFDS and the **Stena Line** (Trafikhavnen, DK–9900 Frederikshavn, Denmark, tel. 45/98–42–00–13).

Connections to the Faroe Islands from Norway are available through the **Smyril Line** (Engelgården, Nye Bryggen, Box 4135, N–5015 Dreggen, Norway, tel. 475/32–09–70).

Connections to Finland are available through **Vaasanlaivat Oy** (Box 213, SF–65101 Vaasa, Finland, tel. 358/961–116–181).

Travel by car often necessitates travel by ferry. There are some well-known ferries running between Dragør, Denmark, just south of Copenhagen, and Limhamn, Sweden, just south of Malmö; between Helsingør, Denmark, and Helsingborg, Sweden; and between Copenhagen and Göteborg, Sweden.

An easy trip runs between Copenhagen and Göteborg on **Stena Line** (in Sweden, tel. 031/75–00–00). The Helsingør/Helsingborg ferry takes only 20 minutes and is available on **Scandinavian Ferry Lines** (in Denmark, tel. 49/21–25–58). Taking a car along one way costs DKr 250 ($41 or £22). The Dragør/Limhamn ferry is also a Scandinavian Ferry line. Taking a car one way costs DKr 516 ($83 or £44).

Shopping

Prices in Scandinavia are never low, but quality is high, and specialties are sometimes less expensive here than elsewhere. Swedish crystal, Icelandic sweaters, Danish Lego blocks and furniture, Norwegian furs, and Finnish fabrics—these are just a few of the items to look for.

One way to beat the prices is to take advantage of tax-free shopping. In all of Scandinavia, you can make major purchases free of tax if you have a foreign passport. Ask about tax-free shopping when you make a purchase for roughly $50 (£25) or more. When your purchases exceed a specified limit (which varies from country to country), you receive a special export receipt. Keep the parcels intact and take them out of the country within 30 days of purchase. When you leave, you can obtain a refund of the tax in cash from a special office at the airport, or, upon arriving home, you can send your receipts to an office in the country of purchase to receive your refund by mail. Be aware that limits for EC tourists are higher than for those coming from outside the EC. In Sweden, for non-EC tourists, the refund is about 14%; in Finland, 11% to 15% for purchases over FM200; in Norway, 16.67% of purchases over NKr300; in Denmark, 18% of purchases over DKr600; in Iceland, 15% of purchases over IKr5,000.

Sports

Skiing—downhill, cross-country, and trekking—is excellent here, as snow in northern Sweden and Norway lasts often as late as May, and in some areas is present year-round. Disadvantages in winter include short days and bitter cold, as low as −35°C (any temperature below −10°C makes the danger of frostbite great enough to prohibit skiing, advises one experienced Scandinavian skier). It is a good idea to ski here in fall or spring, when the days are longer and warmer—November and March are preferable. Other popular sports in Scandinavia include **hiking, bicycling, fishing, boating,** and **mountain climbing.** *See* the individual country chapters for details.

Beaches

Although Scandinavia is better known for its craggy coastlines, the region does have some lovely beaches. After the last great Ice Age, the retreating glaciers left the southern parts of Norway, Sweden, and all of Denmark with a flattened landscape and rich soil, which is why these regions are today known for their farmland—and for their beaches. This fact is not lost on landlocked Germans, who drive northward in such numbers every summer that many shopkeepers advertise their wares in three languages. All national tourist offices (*see* Government Tourist Offices in Before You Go, *above*) have information on beaches in their areas, with additional resources listed below.

Truly hot summer days are rare in Scandinavia, and frequently a cool sea breeze can chill wet skin. So take plenty of towels, a light jacket or sweater, and perhaps a beach umbrella as a wind break. Look for sand dunes when you arrive: Sleeping behind a warm sand dune in the Scandinavian sun is a cozy, but not sweaty, experience.

Dining

Eating is fun in Scandinavia, and consists of a lot more than the well-known *smörgåsbord,* which can be found throughout the region. Because it's inevitable you'll encounter one of these lavish buffets, here's how the locals tackle them: Begin with strong-tasting herring, served in a myriad of cream- and vinegar-based marinades, eaten with whole-grain brown bread or a hot boiled potato with a spoonful of fermented cream and chives. Follow with marinated or smoked salmon with dill sauce. Then the main course: cold meats; salads; fish; "Swedish" meatballs (actually eaten throughout Scandinavia); and occasionally reindeer meat or the Swedish Jansson's temptation, made with potatoes, onions, and anchovies. Desserts include well-ripened cheeses, cakes, and terrific amounts of chocolate and whipped cream.

Local liquor laws arouse almost obsessional interest among Scandinavians. In most of Scandinavia, liquor and strong beer (over 3% alcohol) can be purchased only in state-owned shops, at very high prices, during weekday business hours, usually 9:30 to 6. A 750 centiliter bottle of whiskey in Sweden, for example, can easily cost SKr230 to SKr260, or about $40. Denmark takes a less restrictive approach, with liquor and beer available in the smallest of grocery stores, open weekdays and on Saturday morning. Danish prices, too, are high, though. (When you visit relatives in Scandinavia, a bottle of whiskey bought duty-free on the trip over is often a much-appreciated gift.)

Lodging

In the larger cities, lodging ranges from first-class business hotels run by SAS, Sheraton, and Scandic, to good-quality tourist-class hotels, such as SARA, RESO, Best Western, and Scandic Budget, to a wide variety of single-entrepreneur hotels. In the countryside, look for independently run inns and motels. In Denmark they're called *kro;* in Norway, *fjellstue* or *pensjonat;* in Finland, *kienvari;* and elsewhere, guest houses.

Two things about hotels usually surprise North Americans: the size of Scandinavian beds and the size of Scandinavian breakfasts. Scandinavian double-size beds are often around 60″ wide or slightly less, closer in size to the U.S. queen size. King-size beds (72″ wide) are difficult to find and, if available, require special reservations.

Older hotels may have some rooms described as "double," which in fact have one double bed plus one fold-out sofa big enough for two people. This arrangement is occasionally called a "combi-room" because it was designed to suit businessmen during the weekdays and tourists with families on weekends. They are being phased out, however.

Many hotels, particularly the country inns and independently run smaller hotels in the cities, do not have private bathrooms. Ask ahead if this is important to you.

Scandinavian breakfasts resemble what many people would call lunch, usually including breads, cheeses, marmalade, hams, lunch meats, eggs, juice, cereal, milk, and coffee. In contrast, the typical Continental breakfast served in other parts of Europe is just a roll and coffee. A general rule is that the farther north you go, the larger the breakfasts become. Breakfast is usually included in the price of the hotel, except in Finland and in deluxe establishments elsewhere.

All five Scandinavian countries offer **Inn Checks,** or prepaid hotel vouchers, for accommodations ranging from first-class hotels to country cottages. These vouchers, which must be purchased from travel agents or from the Scandinavian Tourist Board (*see* Government Tourist Offices, *above*) before departure, are sold individually and in packets for as many nights as needed and offer savings of up to 50%. Most countries also offer summer bargains for foreign tourists. For further information about Scandinavian hotel vouchers, contact the Scandinavian Tourist Board.

Reservations The need for reservations depends on where you want to stay and when. It is virtually impossible to get a room on a weekday in Stockholm in the late spring, for example, because large conventions soak up all available space. Countryside inns usually have space, but not always: Norwegians and Danes call vacationing Germans *vandhunde* (water-dogs) because waterside areas attract them in large numbers. With eastern Germans suddenly more mobile, some coast-side inns have recently been filling their summer vacancies by January.

Be aware that different countries define their tourist seasons differently: Sweden's official season is much shorter than Norway's, for example. Some hotels lower prices during tourist season; others, perversely, raise prices during the same period. It's best to ask when making reservations.

In general, reservations are a good idea, and doing the planning at least two months ahead assures an organized trip.

Ratings No region-wide rating system exists in Scandinavia. Instead, each of the national tourist offices distributes lists of hotels with information about opening times, pricing, handicapped accommodations, and discounts for children.

Credit Cards

The following credit card abbreviations have been used: AE, American Express; D, Discover; DC, Diners Club; MC, MasterCard; V, Visa. It's a good idea to call ahead to check current credit card policies.

Great Itineraries

The itineraries that follow suggest ways in which Scandinavian destinations can be combined and give an idea of reasonable (minimum) amounts of time needed in various destinations. Elements from different itineraries can be combined to create an itinerary that suits your interests. Note that Denmark, Norway, and Sweden are six hours ahead of New York, one hour ahead of London and Iceland, and one hour behind Finland.

Sand, Surf, and Ships, Scandinavia-style

Scandinavia is defined by water. Glaciers, rivers, and sea tides shape the geography; oceans define the history and culture. Tiny Denmark, for example, would probably not exist today, except that it sticks up like a cork in the bottleneck entrance to the Baltic Sea, making it strategically important for great shipping and trading countries such as England, which has both attacked and defended the country over trading issues during the last 400 years. What better way, then, to see the land of the Vikings, than by water?

Length of Trip Two weeks

The Main Route **Two nights: Iceland.** After an overnight flight from New York, set aside one day to recover. Flying from London is easier, but it's still pleasant to spend one day relaxing at the volcanic pools outside Reykjavík and the next day exploring the city itself.

Three nights: Denmark. Fly to Copenhagen. Explore the beaches north of Copenhagen on Sjælland, and spend a day sailing the Øresund. If the winds are not too strong, go all the way around Sjælland; otherwise, drive or take a train to the lake by Fredensborg palace (one hour by car, two by train). Explore the palace and go sailing. Spend one day in Copenhagen, taking a cruise around the harbor area, where the *Little Mermaid* perches on her rock. A walking tour will take you to the Royal Danish Library, which sits on what was a pier 400 years ago (the large iron rings used to moor boats can still be seen in the garden walls), and to the Royal Naval Museum, which was recently relocated in Copenhagen's old naval hospital, in the charming Christianshavn quarter.

Five nights: Norway. Fly to Bergen. Take a cruise up the magnificent Norwegian coastline to Trondheim. Fly to Oslo, visit the Viking Ship Museum. Take the ferry to Göteborg, Sweden.

Four nights: Sweden. Use Göteborg as a center from which to explore beaches to the south toward Halmstad and north to the Norwegian border. Both areas are warmed by the Gulf Stream. Go sea fishing one day; try windsurfing the next. In Göteborg, see the island of Elfsborg; its 17th-century fortress was built to guard the harbor entrance and is now used for marine archaeology. Ride the ferry from Göteborg to Copenhagen, and fly home.

Information *See* Chapters 2, 4, 5, and 6.

Scandinavian Mountains

For those who like snow-clad mountains, Scandinavia has plenty to offer: glacier climbing, reindeer sledding, cross-country skiing, and just plain old hiking in gorgeous surroundings.

Length of Trip Two weeks

The Main Route **Five nights: Norway.** Fly to Oslo then on to Bodø or another destination in northern Norway. Some of the country's most striking ranges are the Lofoton and Vesterålen mountains, near Bodø, along with the Lyngen peninsula in Troms. Begin with a four-day hiking tour or a glacier walk guided by **Den Norske Turistforening (DNT, Norwegian Mountain Touring Association)** (Postboks 1963 Vika, N–0125 Oslo 1, tel. 02/832550 or 02/

838040). From Bodø, fly to Narvik then take the train to Kiruna, Sweden, the largest town in Swedish Lapland.

Five nights: Sweden. Welcome to the Arctic Circle, where the sun is above the horizon 24 hours during summer solstice. In Kiruna, join a three-day white-water-canoeing trip. Take a rest, rent a car, and visit the beaver colonies at Ramsele and the fine collection of Lapp art in Jokkmokk. Drive to Gällivare, where the Lapps celebrate their annual church festivals, and go monster-spotting on Storsjön (Great Lake) near Østersund. Drive or take the train to Rovaniemi, Finland, about 323 kilometers (200 miles) from Kiruna, a five- or six-hour drive. Watch out for deer and other animals on the road.

Four nights: Finland. Rovaniemi is the beginning point for The Road of the Four Winds, or, simply, the Arctic Road, which runs 1,000 kilometers (620 miles) north to the Arctic Circle. In summer, look for the salmon-fishing competition, reindeer herding, gold panning, logging, and the Russian Orthodox Skolt Lappish festivals that are held throughout the region. Fly from Rovaniemi to Helsinki and then home.

Information *See* Chapters 3, 5, and 6.

Tracing the Vikings

Traces can still be found of the seafaring warriors who, from the eighth through 11th centuries, traded with, settled in, or raided what today is the Soviet Union, western Europe, Iceland, Greenland, Labrador, and Newfoundland. The Vikings' 1,000-year-old remains are scattered throughout Scandinavia and provide a fascinating record of their culture.

Length of Trip 10 days

The Main Route **Three nights: Denmark.** Begin in Copenhagen with a visit to the Danish National Museum, which has many Viking exhibits in English, one of which attempts to explain how the Vikings navigated their ships across vast oceans at a time when most people believed the world was flat. Take the train to the Viking Ship Hall in Roskilde (an easy day trip less than an hour west of Copenhagen), where five ships, found in the Roskilde Fjord and dating from around AD 1000, have been restored. On the way back, visit Trelleborg in western Sjælland, where you'll find the remains of a staging area for troops led by Knud, who in 1016 became king of England, Denmark, Norway, and part of Sweden.

Rent a car or take a train and stay overnight in Vejle, on the large peninsula of Jylland, then head for Jelling, where two Viking kings—Gorm the Old and his son, Harald Bluetooth, Knud's great-grandfather—reigned. They left two large burial mounds and two runic stones, dating from around AD 950. In June, attend a performance of the Viking play *The Stoneship* on Fårup Sø.

If you have time, you can visit many other Viking sites in Denmark: Ribe, Denmark's oldest town; Hedeby; Høje, where graves are marked by four-foot-tall stones placed in the pattern of a ship; Moesgård, with an excellent museum; Fyrkat, with a 10th-century ring fortress; Lindholm; Høbro; Mammen; Århus; Aggersborg; and Viborg. Return to Copenhagen and fly to Oslo, Norway.

Three nights: Norway. Go straight to the Oslo Viking Ship Hall, where you'll see the finest single collection of excavated and preserved Viking ships, once used as burial sepulchers for nobles. The next day, in Oslo's Historical Museum, you'll find beautiful jewelry from the 9th century: gold necklaces, silver ornaments, and "gripping beasts," whimsical monsters fashioned from amber and other materials. Fly to Stockholm.

Four nights: Sweden. In the State Historical Museum, you'll find swords and amulets in the shape of a hammer, the symbol of Thor, the thunder god. At Gamla Uppsala (old Uppsala), an easy drive north of Stockholm, there are burial grounds for three sixth-century Viking monarchs. In summer take the ferry to the island of Gotland in time for the Folk Sports Olympiad to see games played the way they were in the distant past. One contest, known as *varpa*, is won by tossing a stone nearest a stake. Another, *stångstörtning*, involves the tossing of 16-foot poles. In the Gotland Historical Museum, you'll find valuables that were buried with the Vikings, including Arabic, Byzantine, German, Bohemian, Hungarian, and Anglo-Saxon coins that reflect the warriors' wanderings. Return to Stockholm and then home.

Architecture and Handicrafts

Scandinavian furniture, architecture, and handicrafts are world renowned.

Length of Trip 11 days

The Main Route **Three nights: Denmark.** If you visit Copenhagen in April, you're in for a treat: The Scandinavian Furniture Fair is a fast introduction to leading names in Scandinavian furniture design. In August a smaller show is held in Herning, on the other side of Denmark, in Jylland. Many of the remaining family-run furniture producers are located in Jylland, and, if you're willing to rent a car, you can visit several factories within a few days.

Copenhagen showrooms are open year-round. Don't miss Paustian, located in Frihavn in a building designed by the architect who designed the Sydney, Australia, opera house. Illums Bolighus on the Strøget has memorable examples of Danish interior furnishing. Other showrooms include Tre Falke Møbler in the Falkoner Center; and Lysberg, Hansen & Therp on Bredgade, just off Kongens Nytorv. There's also the Georg Jensen Museum and the Kunstindustrimuseet, with its Rococo buildings and fine exhibits of European and Oriental handicrafts. Historical walking tours of the city are held each day and are the best introduction to the city's architecture. They are often led by Helge Jacobsen, a local historian. Take the overnight sleeper-train to Stockholm.

Two nights: Sweden. Visit the Vasa Ship, and stroll the city. Spend a day at the Design Center, then enjoy lunch at its café before spending the afternoon at the Museum of Architecture, with its archives and book store. Drive to Insjöen to visit Säterglänten, a center for courses in traditional handicrafts. Return to Stockholm and take the overnight ferry to Helsinki.

Five nights: Finland. Begin by spending a day at the Museum of Finnish Architecture and the Museum of Applied Arts, which will give you an overview of the development of Finnish design.

Next day, call the University of Industrial Arts in Helsinki, the largest of its kind in Scandinavia, to check on its current exhibits, often held in collaboration with Design Forum Finland. Visit the Artek factory, which features furniture by Alvar Aalto; the Marimekko and Vuokko textile factories; and the Temppeliaukio church, excavated out of rock, with only the shallow cupola visible from the outside. Rent a car to visit the Finnish Glass Museum, located just north of Helsinki in Riihimäki, with permanent exhibits on glass technology and rotating exhibitions of contemporary designers. Stop by the Hvitträsk, a turn-of-the-century studio designed by and for three Finnish architects as a laboratory for their aesthetic principles. One of the three, Eliel Saarinen, later immigrated to the United States, after he, who had never seen a skyscraper, won a competition to design one.

If there is still time, visit the Suomenlinna Island Fortification, an important fortress partly built by Russians, where you will also find the Nordic Art Center. A ferry leaves from the Kauppatori market square every half-hour. Also stop in the garden city of Käpylä, a residential area built in the 1920s in a unique neoclassical style reminiscent of traditional Finnish wood architecture. For a more solemn shade of neoclassical, visit the Finnish Parliament House, built in the same period.

Information *See* Chapters 2, 3, and 6.

Scandinavia at a Glance: A Chronology

c 12,000 BC The first migrations into Sweden.

c 10,000 BC Stone Age culture develops in Denmark.

c 8,000 BC The earliest human settlers reach the coast of Norway.

c 7,000 BC First nomadic settlers come to Finland.

2,000 BC Tribes from Southern Europe migrate toward Denmark. The majority of early settlers in Scandinavia were of Germanic origin.

c 500 BC Migration of Celts across central Europe impinges on Denmark's trade routes with the Mediterranean world. Trade becomes less economically crucial because of the growing use of abundant iron.

---

c AD 100 Ancestors of present-day Finns move to Finland.

c 770 The Viking Age begins. For the next 250 years, Scandinavians set sail on frequent expeditions stretching from the Baltic to the Irish seas and even to the Mediterranean as far as Sicily, employing superior ships and weapons and efficient military organization.

c 800–c 1000 Swedes control river trade routes between the Baltic and Black seas; establish Novgorod, Kiev, and other cities.

830 Frankish monk Ansgar makes one of the first attempts to Christianize Sweden and builds the first church in Slesvig, Denmark. Sweden is not successfully Christianized until the end of the 11th century, when the temple at Uppsala, a center for pagan resistance, is destroyed.

c 870 The first permanent settlers arrive in Iceland from western Norway.

911 Scandinavian, Rollo, rules Normandy by treaty with French king.

930 Iceland's parliament, the Althing, is founded.

995 King Olaf I Tryggvasson introduces Christianity into Norway.

1000 Leif Eriksson visits America. Olaf I sends a mission to Christianize Iceland.

1016–1035 Canute (Knud) the Great is king of England, Denmark (1018), and Norway (1028).

1070 Adam of Bremen composes *History of the Archbishops of Hamburg-Bremen*, the first important contemporary source for Danish history.

1169 King Valdemar, who was acknowledged as the single king of Denmark in 1157 and who undertook repeated crusades against the Germans, captures Rugen and places it under Danish rule, signifying the beginning of the Danish medieval empire. It culminates in 1219 when Valdemar marches to Estonia and builds a fortress at Ravel. In 1225, Valdemar, after being kidnapped by a German vassal, is forced to give up all his conquests, except for Rugen and Estonia, in exchange for freedom.

1217 Haakon IV becomes king of Norway, beginning its "Golden Age." His many reforms modernize the Norwegian administration; under him, the Norwegian empire reaches its greatest extent when Greenland and Iceland form unions with Norway in 1261.

1248 In Sweden, Erik Eriksson appoints Birger as Jarl, in charge of military affairs and expeditions abroad. Birger improves women's rights, makes laws establishing peace in the home and church, and begins building Stockholm.

1250 Stockholm, Sweden, is officially founded.

1282 At a meeting of the Hof, or Danish parliament, Danish king Erik Glipping signs a coronation charter that becomes the first written constitution of Denmark.

1319 Sweden and Norway form a union that lasts until 1335.

1349 The Black Death strikes Norway and kills two-thirds of the population.

1370 The Treaty of Stralsund gives the north German trading centers of the Hanseatic League free passage through Danish waters and full control of Danish herring fisheries for 15 years. German power increases throughout Scandinavia.

1397 The Kalmar union is formed as a result of the dynastic ties between Sweden, Denmark, and Norway, the geographical position of the Scandinavian states, and the growing influence of Germans in the Baltic. Erik of Pomerania is crowned king of the Kalmar Union.

1477 University of Uppsala, Sweden's oldest university, is founded.

1479 University of Copenhagen is founded.

1520 Christian II, ruler of the Kalmar Union, executes 82 people who oppose the Scandinavian union, an event known as the "Stockholm blood bath." Sweden secedes from the Union three years later. Norway remains tied to Denmark and becomes a Danish province in 1536.

1523 Gustav Ericsson founds Swedish Vasa dynasty as King Gustav I Vasa.

1534 Count Christoffer of Oldenburg and his army demand the restoration of Christian II as king of Denmark, initiating civil war between supporters of Christian II and supporters of Prince Christian (later King Christian III).

1611–1613 The Kalmar War: Denmark wages war against Sweden in hope of restoring the Kalmar Union.

1611–1660 Gustav II Adolphus reigns in Sweden. Under his rule, Sweden defeats Denmark in the Thirty Years War and becomes the greatest power in Scandinavia as well as Northern and Central Europe.

1660 Peace of Copenhagen establishes modern boundaries of Denmark, Sweden, and Norway.

1668 Bank of Sweden, the world's oldest central bank, is founded.

1700–1721 Sweden, led by Karl XII, first broadens then loses its position to Russia as Northern Europe's greatest power in the Great Northern War.

1754 Royal Danish Academy of Fine Arts is established.

1762 Duke of Gottorp becomes tsar of Russia and declares war on Denmark. Catherine, the tsar's wife, overrules her husband's war declaration and makes a peaceful settlement.

1763 The first Norwegian newspaper is founded.

c 1780 A volcanic eruption causes a famine in Iceland that kills one-fifth of the population.

1801–1814 The Napoleonic wars are catastrophic for Denmark economically and politically: The policy of armed neutrality fails, the English destroy the Danish fleet in 1801, Copenhagen is devastated at the bombardment of 1807, and Sweden, after Napoleon's defeat at the Battle of Leipzig, attacks Denmark and forces the Danish surrender of Norway. The Treaty of Kiel, in 1814, calls for a union between Norway and Sweden despite Norway's desire for independence. The Danish monarchy is left with three parts: the Kingdom of Denmark and the duchies of Schleswig and Holstein.

1807 During the Napoleonic wars, Swedish king Gustav III joins the coalition against France and reluctantly accepts war with France and Russia.

1809 Sweden surrenders the Åland Islands and Finland to Russia, Finland becomes a Grand Duchy of the Russian Empire, and the Instrument of Government, Sweden's constitution, is adopted.

1811 University of Oslo is established.

1813 Sweden takes a Frenchman as king: Karl XIV Johann establishes the Bernadotte dynasty.

1818 National Library of Iceland is founded.

1849 Denmark's absolute monarchy is abolished and replaced by the liberal June constitution, which establishes freedom of the press, freedom of religion, the right to hold meetings and form associations, and rule by parliament with two elected chambers as well as the king and his ministers.

c 1850 The building of railroads begins in Scandinavia.

1863 National Museum of Iceland is established.

1864 Denmark goes to war against Prussia and Austria; the hostilities end with the Treaty of Vienna, which forces Denmark to surrender the duchies of Schleswig and Holstein to Prussia and Austria.

1874 Iceland adopts a constitution.

1884 A parliamentary system is established in Norway.

1885 The Art Gallery of Iceland is founded.

1887 The Norwegian Labor Party is founded.

1889 The Swedish Social Democratic Party is founded.

1901 Alfred Nobel, the Swedish millionaire chemist and industrialist, initiates the Nobel prizes.

1904 Iceland is granted home rule. The first Icelandic minister takes office. Rule by parliamentary majority is introduced.

1905 Norway's union with Sweden is dissolved.

1914 At the outbreak of World War I, Germany forces Denmark to lay mines in an area of international waters known as the Great Belt. Because the British fleet makes no serious attempts to break through, Denmark is able to maintain neutrality. Norway and Sweden also declare neutrality but are effectively blockaded.

1916 Iceland establishes a national organization of trade unions.

1917 Finland declares independence from Russia. Danish writer Henrik Pontoppidan is awarded the Nobel prize for Literature.

1918 Iceland becomes a separate state under the Danish crown; only foreign affairs remains under Danish control. Sweden, Denmark, and Norway grant women the right to vote.

1919 A republican constitution is adopted by Finland. Kaarlo Juho Stahlberg is elected president.

1920 Scandinavian countries join the League of Nations.

1929–1937 The first social democratic governments take office in Denmark, Sweden, and Finland. During this period, Norway is ruled by a labor government.

c 1930 The Great Depression causes unemployment, affecting 40% of the organized industrial workers in Denmark.

1939 Denmark and the other Nordic countries declare neutrality in World War II. Finnish novelist Frans Eemil Sillanpaa wins the Nobel prize for literature.

1939–1940 Russia defeats Finland in the Winter War. Russia invades Finland primarily for its larger strategic interests in the area and not because Finland poses a threat.

1940 Germany occupies Norway and Denmark. British forces occupy Iceland until 1941 when U.S. forces replace them.

1941–1944 The Continuation War begins when Finland joins Nazi Germany in attacking the Soviet Union. After Russia defeats Finland, an agreement is signed calling for Finnish troops to withdraw to the 1940 boundary lines of Finland and for German troops on Finnish soil to disarm.

1944 The Icelandic Republic, with British and U.S. support, is founded on June 17. Sveinn Bjørnsson is Iceland's first president.

1945 Norway joins the United Nations.

1948 Treaty of Friendship, Cooperation, and Mutual Assistance between Finland and the Soviet Union obligates Finland to defend the U.S.S.R. in the event of an attack through Finnish territory.

1949 Denmark, Norway, and Iceland become members of NATO. Sweden and Finland decline membership.

1952 The Nordic Council, which promotes cooperation among the Nordic parliaments, is founded.

1955 Finland joins the United Nations and the Nordic Council. Halldor Laxness of Iceland receives the Nobel prize for literature.

1970 Finland hosts the Strategic Arms Limitation Talks (SALT).

1972 Sweden, on the basis of its neutral foreign policy, and Norway decline membership in the EC; Denmark becomes a member in 1973.

1975 Sweden's Instrument of Government of 1809 is revised and replaced with a new Instrument of Government. This constitution reduces the voting age to eighteen and removes many of the king's powers and responsibilities.

1976 The "cod wars," between Britain and Iceland over the extent of Iceland's fishing waters, end.

1980 Fifty-eight percent of Sweden's voters advocate minimizing the use of nuclear reactors at Sweden's four power plants. Iceland elects as president Vigdis Finnbogadottir, the world's first popularly elected female head of state.

1981 Gro Harlem Brundtland, a member of the Labor party, becomes Norway's first female prime minister.

1982 Poul Schluter becomes Denmark's first Conservative prime minister since 1894.

1983 In Finland, the Greens gain parliamentary representation, making them the first elected environmentalists in the Nordic region.

1985 The Alþing, Iceland's parliament, unanimously approves a resolution banning the entry of nuclear weapons into the country.

1986 U.S. president Ronald Reagan and Soviet premier Mikhail Gorbachev discuss nuclear disarmament at a summit meeting in Reykjavík, Iceland. Sweden's prime minister, Olof Palme, is assassinated for unknown reasons. Ingvar Carlsson succeeds him.

1988 Due to U.S. pressure, Iceland consents to reducing its quota of whales caught for "scientific purposes." The United States argues that Iceland is acting against a moratorium imposed by the International Whaling Commission.

1989 Tycho Brahe Planetarium opens in Copenhagen; and Denmark becomes the first NATO country to allow women to join front-line military units.

1990 Finland becomes the fourth major route for Jewish emigration from the Soviet Union. Helsinki, Finland, hosts the summit meeting between George Bush and Mikhail Gorbachev.

1991 The Karen Blixen Museum, in Rungstedlund, Denmark, is founded.

2 Denmark

Introduction

by Karina Porcelli

Karina Porcelli is a freelance travel writer who divides her time between Copenhagen, Denmark, and Washington, D.C. She contributes to a number of American and Danish magazines and newspapers, often in collaboration with her husband, photographer Jesper Westley Jorgensen.

The kingdom of Denmark dapples the Baltic Sea in an archipelago of some 450 islands and the arc of one peninsula. Measuring 43,069 square kilometers (17,028 square miles), with a population of 5 million, it is the geographical link between Scandinavia and Europe. Half-timbered villages and well-groomed agriculture cozy up to provincial towns and a handful of cities, where footsteps, not traffic, mark the tempo. Mothers safely park baby carriages outside bakeries, while outdoor cafés fill with cappuccino-sippers, and lanky Danes pedal to work in lanes thick with bicycle traffic. Clearly this is a land where the process of life is the greatest reward.

Many visitors pinch themselves in disbelief and make long lists of resolutions to emulate the Danes. The lifestyle is certainly enviable. Many of the qualities that have pressure-cooked life in other Western countries have barely touched this land. Long one of the world's most liberal countries, Denmark has a highly developed social-welfare system. The hefty taxes are the subject of grumbles and jokes, but Danes remain proud of their state-funded medical and educational systems and their high standard of living. They enjoy life with month-long vacations, 7.6-hour workdays, and overall security.

Educated, patriotic, and keenly aware of their tiny international stance, most Danes travel extensively and have a balanced perspective of their nation's benefits and shortfalls. As in many provincial states, egalitarianism is often a constraint for the ambitious. In Denmark, this "Don't think you're anything special" notion is the *Jante* law, an insidious cultural barrier to talent and aspiration. On the other hand, free education and state support allow refugees, immigrants, and the underprivileged an opportunity to begin new, often prosperous lives.

The history of the tiny country stretches back 250,000 years, when Jylland (Jutland) was inhabited by nomadic hunters, but it wasn't until AD 500 that a tribe from Sweden, called the Danes, migrated south and christened the land Denmark.

The Viking expansion that followed, based on the country's strategic position in the north, saw struggles for control of the North Sea with England and Western Europe, for the Skagerrak (the strait between Denmark and Norway) with Norway and Sweden, and for the Baltic with Germany, Poland, and Russia. With high-speed ships and fine-tuned warriors, intrepid navies navigated to Europe and Canada, invading and often pillaging, until, under King Knud (Canute) the Great (995–1035), they captured England.

After the British conquest, Viking supremacy declined as feudal Europe learned to defend itself. Internally, the pagan way of life was threatened by the expansion of Christianity, which became reality under Harold Bluetooth, who in AD 980 "baptized" the country, essentially to avoid war with Germany. For the next several hundred years, the country tried to maintain its Baltic power under the influence of the German Hanseatic League. Under the leadership of Valdemar IV (1340–1375), Sweden, Norway, Iceland, Greenland, and the Faroe Islands became a part of Denmark. Sweden broke away by the mid-15th century and battled Denmark for much of the next several hundred years, while Norway remained under Danish rule un-

Denmark

North Sea
Skagerrak
TO GREENLAND
TO FAROE ISLANDS
SWEDEN
Skagen
Hirtshals
Hjørring
Frederikshavn
Sæby
Brønderslev
Læsø
Hanstholm
Limfjord
Aalborg
Thisted
Limfjord
Ålborg Bugt
Kattegat
Nykøbing
Hadsund
Lemvig
Skive
Anholt
Struer
Viborg
Randers
Holstebro
Jylland
Grenå
Silkeborg
Ringkøbing
Herning
Århus
Ebeltoft
Skanderborg
Tisvildeleje
Hornbaek
Horsens
Samsø
Helsingør
Nykøbing
Grindsted
Frederikssund
Hillerød
Skjern
Billund
Vejle
Samsøbælt
Kalundborg
Holbæk
Copenhagen
Fredericia
Esbjerg
Holsted
Storebælt
Jyderup
Roskilde
Middelfart
Fanø
Kolding
Amager
Kerteminde
Sjælland
Odense
Slagelse
Køge Bugt
Ribe
Vojens
Assens
Ringsted
Køge
Rømø
Fyn
Haderslev
Lillebælt
Nyborg
Korsør
Skærbæk
Næstved
St. Heddinge
Åbenrå
Fåborg
Tønder
Langeland
Karrebæksminde
Svendborg
Als
Tranekær
Troense
Vordingborg
Sønderborg
Rudkøbing
Stege
Ærøskøbing
Nakskov
Møn
Ærø
Marstal
Nykøbing
Maribo
Falster
Rødby
TO BORNHOLM
Lolland
Nysted
Ostsee
SWEDEN
Baltic Sea
Bornholm
Rønne
GERMANY
N
0
50 miles
0
75 km

til 1814, and Iceland until 1943. Greenland and the Faroe Islands are still self-governing Danish provinces.

Denmark prospered again in the 16th century, thanks to the Sound Dues, a levy charged to ships crossing the Øresund, the slender waterway between Denmark and Sweden. Under King Christian IV, a construction boom crowned the land with what remain architectural gems, but his fantasy spires and castles, compounded with the Thirty Years' War in the 17th century, led to state bankruptcy.

By the 18th century, absolute monarchy gave way to representative democracy, and culture flourished. Then, in a fatal mistake, Denmark sided with France and refused to surrender its navy to the English during the Napoleonic Wars. In a less than valiant episode of British history, Lord Nelson turned his famous blind eye to the destruction, and bombed Copenhagen to bits. The defeated King Frederik VI handed Norway to Sweden. Denmark's days of glory were unequivocally over.

Though Denmark was unaligned during World War II, the Nazis invaded in 1940. Against them, the Danes used the only weapons they had: a cold shoulder and massive underground resistance. After the war, Denmark focused inward, refining its welfare system and concentrating on its main industries of agriculture, shipping, and financial and technical services. In spring 1991 it was still the sole Scandinavian member of the European Community.

Though expensive, Denmark is in many ways less pricey than the rest of Scandinavia. At the height of summer, when businesses shut down (usually for all of July), conference hotels often lower prices and offer weekend specials. Denmark is also the only Nordic country with relaxed drinking laws and moderate beer and wine prices, an attraction that induces other Scandinavians to hop over for splurge weekends.

Copenhagen fidgets with its modern identity, trying to integrate its role as a Scandinavian-European link and cozy capital. The center of Danish politics, culture, and finance, it copes through balance and an absurd sense of humor. Stroll the streets and you'll pass classical architecture painted in candy colors, businessmen clad in jeans and T-shirts, and on sunny days, ebullient Danes stripping down on beaches and in parks.

Copenhagen is the attention-getter, but it would be a shame to miss the surrounding countryside of Sjælland (Zealand). Less than an hour away, the land is checkered with fields and half-timbered cottages. Roskilde, to the east, has an impressive 12th-century cathedral, while in the north, Helsingør is crowned with the Kronborg castle, of *Hamlet* fame. Beaches, some chic, some deserted, are powdered by fine white sand that drives Danes to bliss.

Fyn (Funen) has rightly earned its storybook reputation by making cute a local passion. The city of Odense, Hans Christian Andersen's birthplace, is cobbled with crooked old streets and lilliputian cottages. Jylland's (Jutland's) landscape is the most severe, with Ice Age–chiseled fjords and hills (which the Danes sheepishly call mountains). Nonetheless, its provincial towns have timbered neighborhoods, while the cities of Århus and Aalborg offer museums and nightlife rivaling Copenhagen's.

The best way to discover Denmark is to strike up a conversation with a Dane. Affable and hospitable, they'll probably approach you before you get the chance to ask the time. They have a wonderful word, *hyggelig*, which defies definition but comes close to meaning a cozy and charming hospitality. A summertime beach picnic can be as hyggelig as tea on a cold winter's night. The only requirement is the company of a Dane.

Before You Go

Government Tourist Offices

In the United States **Danish Tourist Board,** 655 3rd Ave., New York, NY, 10017, tel. 212/949-2333

In Canada **Danish Tourist Board,** Box 115 Station N, Toronto, Ontario, M8V 3S4, tel. 416/823-9620

In the United Kingdom **Danish Tourist Board,** Sceptre House, 169–173 Regent St., JB London W1R 8PY, tel. 071/734-2637

When to Go

Most travelers visit Denmark in the warmest months, July and August, but there are advantages to coming in May, June, or September when sights are less crowded and many establishments offer off-season discounts. However, few places in Denmark are ever unpleasantly crowded, and when the Danes make their annual exodus to the beaches, the cities have more breathing space. In winter months the days are short and dark, and when important attractions such as Tivoli are closed.

Climate The climate is greatly tempered by the Gulf Stream, which makes for warm summers and soggy, gray winters, with little snow. The following are average daily maximum and minimum temperatures for Copenhagen.

Jan.	36F	2C	**May**	61F	16C	**Sept.**	64F	18C
	28	-2		46	8		52	11
Feb.	36F	2C	**June**	66F	19C	**Oct.**	54F	12C
	27	-3		52	11		45	7
Mar.	41F	5C	**July**	72F	22C	**Nov.**	45F	7C
	30	-1		57	14		37	3
Apr.	52F	11C	**Aug.**	70F	21C	**Dec.**	39F	4C
	37	3		57	14		34	1

Festivals and Seasonal Events

April: Aalborg's 1,300th anniversary begins a year-long series of events, including indoor and outdoor concerts and theater.
April 16: The Queen's Birthday is celebrated with the royal guard in full ceremonial dress, as the royal family appears before the public on the balcony of Amalienborg Castle.
May: The Copenhagen Carnival includes boat parades in Nyhavn and costumed revelers in the streets.
May–August: The Tivoli Gardens in Copenhagen open with amusement rides, concerts, and entertainment.
May–September: Legoland, a park constructed of 35 million Lego blocks, opens in Billund, Jylland.

June: The Around Fyn Regatta starts in Kerteminde.
June: The Round Zealand Regatta, one of the largest yachting events in the world, starts and ends in Helsingør.
Mid-June: The Aalborg Jazz Festival fills the city with four days of indoor and outdoor concerts, many free.
June: The Viking Festival in Frederikssund includes open-air performances of a Viking play.
June: On Midsummer's Night, Danes celebrate the longest day of the year with bonfires and picnics.
June–July: The Roskilde Festival, the largest rock concert in northern Europe, attracts dozens of bands and 75,000 fans.
July 4: The Fourth of July celebration in Rebild Park, near Aalborg, sets off the only American Independence Day festivities outside the United States.
July: The Copenhagen Jazz Festival gathers international and Scandinavian jazz greats for a week of concerts, many free.
Mid-July: The Århus Jazz Festival gathers European and world-renowned names, with indoor and outdoor concerts.
July–August: The Hans Christian Andersen Festival brings the author's fairy tales to life in street theater and free events for children and adults.
September: The Århus Festival, Denmark's most comprehensive fete, fills the city with concerts, sports, and theater.

Danish Currency

The monetary unit in Denmark is the krone (DKr), which is divided into 100 øre. At press time (fall 1991), the krone stood at 6.00 to the dollar, 10.97 to the pound sterling, and 5.29 to the Canadian dollar. Most major credit cards are accepted in Denmark, American Express less frequently than others, and Carte Blanche rarely. Traveler's checks can be exchanged in banks and in many hotels, restaurants, and shops.

What It Will Cost

Denmark's economy is stable, and inflation remains reasonably low. While considerably cheaper than Norway and Sweden, the Danish cost of living is nonetheless high, especially for such luxuries as cigarettes and alcohol. Prices are highest in Copenhagen, lower elsewhere in the country.

Taxes All hotel, restaurant, and departure taxes and VAT (what the Danes call MOMS) are automatically included in prices. VAT is 22%, of which non-EC citizens can obtain an 18% refund. The more than 1,500 shops that participate in the tax-free scheme have a white sticker that says "Tax Free" on the window. Purchases must be at least DKr600 per store and must be sealed and unused in Denmark. At the shop, you'll be asked to fill out a form and show your passport. The form can then be turned in at any airport or ferry customs desk, where you can choose a check or charge-card credit. Keep all your receipts and tags; occasionally, the customs authorities ask to see purchases, so pack them where they are accessible.

Sample Costs Cup of coffee, DKr12–16; bottle of beer, DKr15–25; soda DKr12–15; ham sandwich DKr35; 1-mile taxi ride, DKr25.

Passports and Visas

U.S., Canadian, and British citizens must have a valid passport to enter Denmark for a stay of up to three months. Visas and health certificates are not required. If you lose your passport, go to the police immediately and report it. Bring the report, with positive ID and a photocopy of the photo page (do this before you leave home, and keep it separate from your passport) to the embassy in Copenhagen, (*see* Copenhagen, *below*, for embassy addresses).

U.S. Citizens For more information, contact the **Royal Danish Embassy** (3200 Whitehaven St. NW, Washington, DC 20008, tel. 202/234-4300).

British Citizens **Royal Danish Embassy,** 55 Sloane St., London SW1, tel. 071/235-1255

Canadian Citizens **Royal Danish Embassy,** 85 Range Rd., Apt. 702, Ottawa, Ontario, KEN 816, tel. 613/234-0704

Customs and Duties

On Arrival U.S., Canadian, and U.K. residents entering Denmark from an EC country may bring in 1.5 liters of alcohol or 3 liters of strong wine (not more than 22% alcohol); 5 liters of table wine; 300 cigarettes, 75 cigars or 400 grams of tobacco; 75 grams of perfume. Other articles include DKr3,100 worth of goods, with a single item costing no more than DKr2,725. Taxes must be paid in the country of purchase.

From a non-EC country, duty-free allowances include: 1 liter liquor or 2 liters strong wine; 2 liters wine; 200 cigarettes, 75 cigars or 250 grams tobacco and 50 grams of perfume. Other articles include DKr350. worth of goods.

On Departure *See* Customs and Duties in Chapter 1.

Language

Students of Danish are taught that if they can't pronounce a word, they should say it faster and swallow most of it. It's a difficult language for foreigners, except Norwegians and Swedes, to learn to understand, let alone speak. Most Danes, except those in rural areas, speak English well, but it's a good idea to ask before launching into a conversation. Bring a phrase book if you plan on visiting the countryside or the smaller islands.

Car Rentals

Major international car rentals are available throughout Denmark. Smaller companies include: **InterRent** (Kastrup Airport, tel. 32/50-30-900) and **Pitzner Auto** (Kastrup Airport, tel. 32/50-90-65). In Copenhagen, most car-rental agencies are located on Vester Farimagsgade, near the Vesterport Station.

Rail Passes

The **Copenhagen Card** provides unlimited transportation on trains and buses in the metropolitan area as well as admission to a number of attractions in Copenhagen and surroundings, and discount passage to Sweden. The card costs DKr115 (one day), DKr155 (two days), or DKr200 (three days) and is available at tourist offices and hotels and through travel agents.

The **Danish State Railways (DSB)** also offers discount tickets for senior citizens, children, and groups of three or more traveling together. Inquire at any train station for **Gruppe Rabat (group rebate), Gruppe Billetter (group tickets),** or off-peak fare, which offers considerable reductions on certain days of the week.

Student and Youth Travel

Copenhagen's main railway station features a useful **Inter Rail Center** where young travelers can meet, exchange notes, and even partake of a free shower. Students can obtain information on inexpensive accommodations in Copenhagen at the **Youth Information Center** (Raadhusstraede 13, DK–1466 Copenhagen K; tel. 33/15–65–18). It is open June 15 to September 14, daily 9 AM to 7 PM; and September 15 to June 14, Monday to Friday 10 AM to 3 PM.

Hints for Disabled Travelers

In Denmark, wheelchair users will find rail travel difficult, because **Danish State Railways (DSB)** has few special carriages or toilets for disabled passengers. Travelers are advised to bring a companion to help them on and off trains. On the Copenhagen–Esbjerg and Copenhagen–Aalborg route, however, two trains offer special facilities for the disabled, including hydraulic wheelchair lifts and accessible toilets. Advance reservations are required. A number of major stations provide wheelchairs for customer use. A brochure with information about train facilities is available from the state railroad, in train stations, and from the state railroad's travel agency, **DSB Rejsebureau** (Terminus Vesterbrogade 5, DK–1620 Copenhagen V, Denmark).

In Denmark, most buses and coaches are not equipped to carry wheelchair users, though all long-distance routes now have a minimum of one daily departure each way, using buses with lifts and extra space for wheelchairs. Advance reservations are required. Some Danish taxi firms also have large, London-size cabs for passengers in wheelchairs. For information on travel and accommodation in Denmark, ask the Danish Tourist Board for its 100-page booklet "Access in Denmark—A Travel Guide for the Disabled," or contact the **Dansk Handicap Forbund** (The Danish Handicapped Association, Kollektivhuset, Hans Knudsens Plads, 1A, 1, DK–2100, Copenhagen Ø, tel. 31/29–35–55).

Many hotels, particularly among the larger chains, have facilities for the disabled. You also can contact the **Committee for Housing, Transportation and Technical Aids: Bolig-, Motor- or Hjælpemiddeludvalget** (Hans Knudsens Plads 1A, DK–2100 Copenhagen Ø, tel. 31/18–26–66). Ask the tourism board for the excellent booklet *Access in Denmark: A Travel Guide for the Disabled*, which covers transportation, accommodation, and sightseeing.

Hints for Older Travelers

One of the only travel agencies that offers tailor-made senior-citizen tours is **Robinson Scandinavia** (Carit Etlarsvej 3, 1814 Frederiksberg, Copenhagen, tel. 31/31–71–77). Packages and special arrangements inside Scandinavia include bus tours, accommodations, and sightseeing tours at rates substantially cheaper than those for independent travel.

Further Reading

Excellent reading on Denmark includes: those works of Karen Blixen (Isak Dinesen) set in Denmark; *Pelle the Conqueror* (volumes I and II) by Martin Andersen Nexø (a novel about a young Swedish boy and his father who work on a stone farm in Bornholm under hateful Danish landowners); *Laterna Magica* by William Heinesen (a novel of the Faroe Islands by perhaps Denmark's greatest writer since Karen Blixen); and the satirical trilogy by Hans Scherfig—*Stolen Spring, The Missing Bureaucrat*, and *Idealists*. Wallace Stegner's novel *The Spectator Bird* follows a man's exploration of his Danish heritage. Finally, **Fjord Press** (Box 16501, Seattle, WA 98116, tel. 206/625–9363, fax 206/938–1991) has one of the most comprehensive selections of Danish titles of any bookseller in the United States.

Arriving and Departing

From North America by Plane

Airports and Airlines Copenhagen's **Kastrup Airport**, the hub of Scandinavian air travel, is 10 kilometers (6 miles) from the capital's center. **Scandinavian Airlines System (SAS)** (tel. 800/251–2350), the main carrier, makes nonstop flights from Anchorage, Chicago, Los Angeles, Newark, and Seattle. **British Airways** (tel. 800/AIR–WAYS) makes connecting flights via London from Atlanta, Boston, Chicago, Dallas, Detroit, Los Angeles, Miami, New York, Orlando, Philadelphia, Pittsburgh, San Francisco, Seattle, and Washington, D.C. **Icelandair** (tel. 800/223–5500) makes connecting flights via Reykjavík from Baltimore and New York. **Tower Air** (tel. 800/221–2500), a charter carrier, makes weekly direct flights from New York. **Delta** (tel. 800/221–1212) is planning to start direct service from Pittsburgh.

Flying Time From New York, flights to Copenhagen take 7 hours, 40 minutes. From Chicago they take 8 hours, 15 minutes. From Los Angeles the flight time is 10 hours, 55 minutes.

Discount Flights Airfare to Denmark is expensive, but it is possible to save money on regular coach tickets. Start with a flexible schedule and make your reservations as early as possible. Discounted, advance-purchase tickets sell out quickly. Generally, the airfare is much more economical if you travel with a tour operator.

From the United Kingdom by Plane, Car, Ferry, Train, and Bus

By Plane
Airlines The major airlines flying to Copenhagen from the United Kingdom include **British Airways** (156 Regent St., London W1, tel. 081/897–4000), which flies nonstop from Heathrow, Gatwick, and Manchester; **SAS Scandinavian Airlines** (SAS House, 52–53

Condute St., W1R 0AU, London, tel. 071/734–4020), which flies nonstop from Heathrow, Birmingham, Manchester, Aberdeen, and Glasgow; **Air Europe** (Europe House, Manor Royal, Crawley, West Sussex, RH10 2QD, tel. 293/562–626), which flies nonstop from Gatwick; **Birmingham European Airways** (Birmingham International Airport, Coventry Road, Birmingham, B26 3QB, tel. 021/782–0711), which flies nonstop from Birmingham; and **Aer Lingus** (67 Deans Gate, Manchester, tel. 061/832–5771) which flies direct from Manchester. SAS also flies round-trip from London to Århus, while **Maersk Air** (Liverpool Station, London EC2, tel. 071/623–3813) flies nonstop from Gatwick to Billund and Copenhagen.

Flying Time From London to Copenhagen the flight takes 1 hour, 55 minutes.

Discount Flights Though intra-European flights into Scandinavia are often as expensive as flying directly from the United States, it's worth scanning the newspapers and London's local *Time Out* magazine for fares. The major airlines also offer APEX tickets that must be bought at least two weeks in advance, require a Saturday night stay, and have other restrictions, including severe penalties if you cancel your flight.

By Car and Ferry **Scandinavian Seaways Ferries (DFDS)** (Scandinavian Seaways, DFDS Ltd., Scandinavia House, Parkeston Quay, Harwich, Essex, CO12 4QG, England, tel. 0255/24–02–40; in Denmark, tel. 33/11–22–55) sail from Harwich to Esbjerg (20 hours) on Jutland's west coast daily in the summer, three times weekly in the winter, and from Newcastle to Esbjerg (21 hours), mid-June–mid-August twice a week. There are many discounts, including 50% for senior citizens, the disabled, and children between the ages of four and 16.

The only part of Denmark connected to the European continent is Jylland on the E–45 highway from Germany. The E–20 highway then leads to Middelfart on Fyn and east to Knudshoved. From there a ferry crosses to Korsør on Sjælland and E–20 east leads to Copenhagen. Another option is to take the three-hour car ferry from Århus directly to Kalundborg in western Sjælland. From there, Route 23 leads to Copenhagen. Make reservations for the ferry in advance through the **Danish State Railway (DSB)** (tel. 33/14–88–80). (*Note:* During the busy summer months, passengers without reservations for their vehicles can wait hours.) The completion of the Storebælt bridge, connecting Fyn and Sjælland, should speed up rail connections by 1993 and auto traffic by 1996.

By Train Trains within Europe are well connected to Denmark, with Copenhagen serving as the main hub; however, it's often little cheaper than flying. **Eurorail-** and **Eurail Saverpass** passes, which can only be purchased in the United States, are accepted by the **Danish State Railway** and on some ferries operated by DSB. From London, the crossing (25 hours including ferry) can be arranged through the **British Rail European Travel Center** (Victoria Station, London, tel. 071/834–2345), **Eurotrain** (52 Grosvenor Gardens, London SW1 (tel. 071/730–3402) and **Wasteels** (121 Wilton Rd., London SW1, tel. 071/834–7066).

By Bus Not particularly comfortable or fast, bus travel is inexpensive. The **JCP Sally Express** (23 Bourne End Rd., Northwood, Middlesex, tel. 0923/835–696) departs from the Great Eastern Hotel (Liverpool St., London) at 2:15 Saturday and makes stops in

Copenhagen (26 hours), as well as Århus (24 hours), Odense (24 hours), and Frederikshavn (22 hours). **Eurolines** (52 Grosvenor Gardens, London, SW1, tel. 071/730–0202) travels from London's Victoria Station Saturday at 7 PM and arrives in Copenhagen 26 hours later.

Staying in Denmark

Getting Around

By Plane Copenhagen's **Kastrup Airport** is the hub of all domestic routes. Most other airports are located in areas that serve several cities. Flight times in country are all less than one hour. Probably the best bet for tourists for intra-Scandinavian travel, which is usually expensive, is the SAS 5-coupon ticket (about $250) for unlimited air travel in Scandinavia; it is sold only in the United States. Coupons can be be used for flights in July and August and are sold from April on in conjunction with transatlantic flights.

The major carriers in Denmark are **SAS** (tel. 33/13–62–66), **Danair** (tel. 31/51–50–55), **Maersk Air** (tel. 32/45–35–35), and **Cimber Air** (tel. 74/42–22–77).

By Train and Bus Traveling by bus or train is easy because DSB and a few private companies cover the country with a dense network of services, supplemented by buses in remote areas. Hourly intercity trains connect the main towns in Jylland and Fyn with Copenhagen and Sjælland, using high-speed diesels, called Lyntog (lightning trains), on the most important stretches. All these trains make one-hour ferry crossings of the Great Belt, the waterway separating Fyn and Sjælland. You can reserve seats on intercity trains and Lyntog, and you *must* have a reservation if you plan to cross the Great Belt. Buy tickets at stations for trains, buses, and connecting ferry crossings. Bus tickets are usually sold on the bus itself. Children under five travel free and those between five and 12 travel at half-price. Ask about discounts for senior citizens and groups of three or more. The **Scanrail Pass,** for travel anywhere within Scandinavia, **Interail** and **Eurail** are also valid on all DSB trains, as well as some ferry passages.

By Car Roads here are good and largely traffic-free (except the manageable traffic around Copenhagen); you can reach the many islands by toll-free bridges.

Rules of the Road Drivers need a valid driver's license, and, if you're using your own car, it must have a certificate of registration and national plates. A triangular hazard-warning sign is compulsory in every car and is provided with a rental car. No matter where you sit in a car, you must wear a seat belt, and cars must have low beams on at all times. Motorcyclists must wear helmets and use low-beam lights as well.

Drive on the right and give way to traffic—*especially to cyclists*—on the right. A red-and-white YIELD sign or a line of white triangles across the road means you must yield to traffic on the road you are entering. Do not turn right on red unless there is a green arrow indicating it is allowed. Speed limits are 50 kilometers per hour (30 miles per hour) in built-up areas; 100 kph (60 mph) on highways; and 80 kph (50 mph) on other roads. If you are towing a trailer, you must not exceed 70 kph (40 mph). Speeding and, especially, drinking and driving, are treated severely, even if no damage is caused. Americans and foreign tourists must pay fines on the spot.

Parking You can usually park on the right-hand side of the road, though not on main roads and highways.

PARKERING/STANDSNING FORBUNDT means no parking or stopping, though you are allowed a three-minute grace period for loading and unloading. In town, parking discs are used where there are no automatic ticket-vending machines. Get discs from gas stations, post offices, police stations, or tourist offices, and set them to show your time of arrival. For most downtown-parking, you must buy a ticket from an automatic vending machine and display it on the dash. Parking costs about DKr9 per hour in town, DKr7 elsewhere.

Gasoline Gasoline costs about DKr6.85 per liter.

Breakdowns Before leaving home, consult your insurance company. Members of organizations affiliated with **Alliance International de Tourisme (AIT)** can get technical and legal advice from the **Danish Motoring Organization (FDM)** (Firskovvej 32, 2800 Lyngby, tel. 45/93–08–00, open 10–4 weekdays). All highways have emergency phones, and you can call the rental company for help. If you cannot drive your car to a garage for repairs, the rescue corps, **Falck** (tel. 33/14–22–22) can help anywhere, anytime.

Telephones

Telephone exchanges throughout Denmark, especially those in Sjælland and Bornholm, are in the process of being changed (through 1993). If you hear a recorded message or three loud beeps, chances are the number you are trying to reach has been changed. KTAS information (tel. 0033) can always find current numbers.

Local Calls Phones accept 1-, 5-, 10-, and 20-kroner coins. Pick up the receiver, dial the number, always including the area code, and wait until the party answers, then deposit the coins. You have roughly four minutes per krone, so you can make another call on the same payment if your time has not run out. When it does, you will hear a beep and your call will be disconnected unless you deposit another coin. Dial the eight-digit number for calls anywhere within the country. For calls to the Faroe Islands (298) and Greenland (299), dial 009, then the three-digit code, then the five-digit number.

International Calls Dial 009, then the country code (1 for the United States and Canada, 44 for Great Britain), the area code, and the number. It's very expensive to telephone or fax from hotels, and Danish Telephone offers no discount times, so it's best to make calls from either main rail stations or post offices, many of which have telephone offices.

Operators and Information Most operators speak English. For national directory assistance, dial 0033; for an international operator, dial 0039; for a directory-assisted international call, dial 0015. To reach an AT&T direct operator in the United States, for collect, person-to-person, or credit card calls, dial 80–01–0010.

Mail

Postal Rates Airmail letters to the United States cost DKr4.75 for 20 grams and postcards. Letters and postcards to the United Kingdom and EC countries cost DKr3.50. You can buy stamps at post offices or from shops selling postcards.

Receiving Mail You can arrange to have your mail sent general delivery (called *Poste Restante* in Denmark) to any post office, hotel, or inn. If you do not have an address, **American Express** (Dagmarhus, Amagertorv 18, 1461 KBH K, tel. 33/12–23–01) will also receive and hold cardholders' mail at no charge.

Tipping

The egalitarian Danes do not expect to be tipped. Service is included in bills for hotels, bars, and restaurants. Taxi drivers round up the fare to the next krone but expect no tip. The exception is hotel porters, who receive around DKr5 per bag.

Opening and Closing Times

Banks Most banks are open weekdays 9:30 to 4, Thursday until 6, but check in smaller towns, where times vary.

Museums As a rule, museums are open 10 to 3 or 11 to 4 and are closed on Monday. In winter, opening hours are shorter, and some museums close for the season. Check the local papers or ask at tourism offices for current times.

Shops Shops are generally open weekdays 9 to 5:30; most stay open Friday until 7 or 8, and close Saturday at 1 or 2. Everything, except bakeries and kiosks, is closed on Sunday, and most bakeries take Monday off. The first Saturday of the month is a Long Saturday, where shops, especially in the larger cities, stay open until 4 or 5.

Shopping

Danish design has earned an international reputation for form and function, and any visitor will have a hard time resisting the boutiques and crafts shops. The summer season is as good as any to shop, though the most drastic sales are after Christmas until February. Skip clothing and stick to the best buys, which are to be found in glassware, stainless steel, pottery, ceramics, and fur, though antiques and silver also are much cheaper than in the United States. The best selection of shops and department stores is in Copenhagen, though crafts shops are also located in the pedestrian streets of most smaller towns.

Sports and Outdoor Activities

Bicycling Without a doubt, Denmark is one of the world's best places for cycling. Three-quarters of the population have bicycles, and over half make use of them, on roads that effectively coordinate public transportation and cycle traffic. Many towns, particularly Odense and Copenhagen, have good cycling lanes alongside auto traffic, but the cyclist should be aware of cars at all times and pedal with caution, especially at intersections. The countrysides are also lined with paths, especially Jylland and the island of Bornholm. Bicycles can be sent as baggage between most train stations and can also be carried onto most trains and ferries. Contact **DSB** (tel. 33/14–17–01) for more information. All cabs must be able to take bikes and are equipped with racks. Most towns have rentals, but check with local tourism offices for referrals. For more information, contact the **Danish Cyclist Federation** (Rømersgade 7, DK–1362 KBH K, tel. 33/32–31–21). The Danish Tourist Board also publishes bicycle maps and brochures.

Boating and Sailing Well-marked channels and nearby anchorages make sailing and boating easy and popular throughout the 7,300-kilometer (4,500-mile) coastline. Waters range from the open seas of the Kattegat and the Baltic to Smålandshavet (between Sjælland and Lolland Falster) and the calm Limsfjord in Jylland. Boat rentals are available in most areas. Canoe and kayak rentals are also available to explore the country's calm streams. For details, contact the Danish Tourist Board.

Camping *See* Camping, in Lodging, *below*.

Golf Because of its low greens fees and the over 60 well-maintained courses, golfers throughout Europe and Japan are heading to Denmark. Visitors are welcome to all courses, but you do need a valid membership card from your own club. For package tours, contact **Dan Golf** (Esbønderupvej 71, DK–3230 Græsted, tel. 42/29–20–50). For more general information about golfing in Denmark, contact the **Danske Golf Union** (Golfsvinget 12, DK–2625 Vallensbæk, tel. 42/64–06–66).

Hiking Because Denmark is basically flat, the most interesting hikes are day walks between towns. Local tourism offices have maps of paths and can help plan specific routes.

Horseback Riding Riding schools throughout the country rent horses for day or package holidays. You can also rent a covered wagon for an inexpensive and unusual accommodation and transport (*see* Off the Beaten Track in Fyn, *below*). For details, contact the Danish Tourist Board.

Tennis Tennis, as well as badminton, handball, and other court-and-ball games, is extremely popular in Denmark, which boasts some of the world's best players and teams. Courts are at a premium, but most cities and towns have public gyms where you might get a court. Ask at your hotel or the local tourist board.

Water Sports Surfing and scuba diving take second place to windsurfing, which is quite popular, especially in southern and northern Sjælland and off the shores north of Copenhagen and southern Fyn. A wet suit is advisable year-round. The Danish Tourist Board has more information.

Beaches

Denmark's best beaches are located on the northwest coast of Jylland and just north of Copenhagen on the northeast coast of the island of Sjælland. Topless sunbathers are common on Danish beaches and in public parks. In addition to information from the national tourist office, an up-to-date map of Danish beaches can be purchased for DKr48 from the **Dansk Miljø Styrelsen (Danish Environmental Department)** (Strandgade 29, 1401 Copenhagen K, Denmark, tel. 31/57–83–10).

Dining

Danes take their food seriously, and Danish food, however simple, is excellent, with an emphasis on fresh ingredients and careful presentation. Fish and meat are both of top quality in this farming and fishing country, and both are staple ingredients of the famous *smørrebrød* (open-face sandwich). Some smørrebrød are huge meals in themselves: Innocent snackers find themselves faced with dauntingly large (but delicious) mounds of meat or fish, slathered with pickle relish, all atop *rugbrød* (black bread) and *franskbrød* (white bread). Among the other specialties are *frikadeller* (butter-fried pork meatballs), *flæskesteg* (pork roast baked with crisp rind), *æggekage* (fluffy bacon, tomato, and cucumber omelettes), *biksemad* (cubed potatoes, bacon, and beef pan fried and served with an egg), and the original Danish pastries, called *wienerbrød*, which shame all imitations.

All Scandinavian countries have versions of the cold table, but the Danes claim that theirs, *det store kolde bord*, is the original and the best. It's a celebration meal: The setting of the long table is a work of art—often with paper sculpture and silver platters—and the food itself is a minor miracle of design and decoration.

In hotels and restaurants, the cold table is served at lunch only, though you'll find more limited versions at hotel breakfasts—a good bet for budget travelers because you can eat as much as you like. The price conscious should also be on the lookout for establishments with fixed-price menus (look for *tilbud*, which means "special") and cafés, where an overstuffed sandwich and steaming cup of cappuccino rarely cost more than DKr45. Even less expensive are the *pølservogn* (sausage wagons), where you can pick up a lip-smacking Danish sausage or hot dog and a separate roll for less than DKr18. Vegetarians sometimes feel slighted in this meat-and-potatoes land, but there are vegetarian restaurants in the larger cities, and fresh fruit and vegetable stands are almost everywhere. Fresh fish, including plaice, cod, eel, and the ubiquitous herring, are also excellent.

Liquid refreshment is top-notch. Denmark boasts more than 50 beers; the best known are Carlsberg and Tuborg. Those who like harder stuff should try the *snaps*, the famous akvavit traditionally drunk with cold food.

Ratings Meal prices vary little between town and country. While approximate ratings are given below, remember that careful ordering can get you a Moderate meal at a Very Expensive restaurant. Prices are per person and include a first course, entrée and dessert, plus taxes and tip, but not wine. Best bets are indicated by a star. At press time (spring 1991), there were DKr5.88 to the dollar.

Category	Copenhagen	Other Areas*
Very Expensive	over DKr400	over DKr350
Expensive	DKr250–DKr400	DKr350–DKr200
Moderate	DKr150–DKr250	DKr100–DKr200
Inexpensive	under DKr150	under DKr100

Lodging

Accommodations in Denmark range from spare to resplendent. Even inexpensive hotels offer simple designs in good materials, and good, firm beds. Many Danes prefer a shower to a bath, so if you particularly want a bath, ask for it, but be prepared to pay more. Farmhouses and *kro* (inn) accommodations offer a terrific alternative to more traditional hotels. Except in the case of rentals, breakfast and taxes are usually included in prices, but check when making a reservation.

Hotels Luxury hotels in the city or countryside offer rooms of a high standard, and in a manor–house hotel, you may find yourself sleeping in a four-poster bed. Less expensive accommodations, however, are uniformly clean and comfortable. Make your reservations well in advance, especially in resort areas near the coasts, to avoid having to overnight in costly, last-minute hotels. Many places offer summer reductions to compensate for the slowdown in business travelers and conferences.

Inns A cheaper and charming alternative to hotels are the kro (old stagecoach inns) scattered throughout Denmark. You can save money by investing in **Inn Checks,** valid at 65 inns. Each check costs DKr325 for a single room in Fyn and Jylland, DKr425 in Sjælland; double room anywhere in Denmark, DKr495. Prices include one overnight stay in a room with bath, breakfast included. Contact **Dansk Kroferie** (Søndergade 31, DK–8700 Horsens, tel. 75/62–35–44).

Farm Vacations These are perhaps the best way to see how the Danes live and work. You stay on a farm and share meals with the family and can even get out and help with the chores. There's a minimum stay of three nights; half-board runs around DKr220, while lunch and dinner can often be purchased directly from the family for DKr25 to 35. Contact the **Horsens Tourist Information Office** (Søndergade 26, DK–8700 Horsens, Jylland, tel. 75/62–38–22).

Youth and Family Hostels The country's 100 youth hostels are excellent, with kitchen and family rooms available to all, regardless of age. If you have an International Youth Hostels Association card (obtainable before you leave home), the average cost is DKr60 per person. Without the card, there's a surcharge of DKr22. The hostels fill up quickly in the summer, so make your reservations early. Most hostels are particularly sympathetic toward students and will usually find them at least a place on the floor. Bring your own linens or sheet sleeping bags, though these can usually be rented at the hostel. Sleeping bags are not allowed. Contact **Landsforeningen Danmarks Vandrehjem** (Vesterbrogade 39, DK–1620, Copenhagen V, tel. 31/31–36–12).

Rentals Many Danes rent out their summer homes, and a stay in one is another good way to see the countryside on your own. A simple house with room for four will cost from DKr2,500 per week upward. Contact **DanCenter** (Falkoner Allé 7, DK–2000 Frederiksberg, tel. 31/19–09–00).

Camping Denmark has over 500 approved campsites, with a rating system of one, two, or three stars. You need an International Camping Carnet or Danish Camping Pass (available at any campsite and valid for one year). For more details on camping and discounts for groups and families, contact **Campingrådet**

(Olof Palmes Gade 10, DK-2100 Copenhagen, tel. 31/42-32-22).

Ratings Prices are for two people in a double room and include service and taxes, and usually breakfast. Best bets are indicated by a star. At press time (spring 1991), there were DKr5.88 to the dollar.

Category	Copenhagen	Other Areas*
Very Expensive	over DKr1,300	over DKr850
Expensive	DKr1,000–DKr1,300	DKr650–DKr850
Moderate	DKr800–DKr1,000	DKr450–DKr650
Inexpensive	under DKr800	under DKr450

Copenhagen

Introduction

Copenhagen (København in Danish) has no glittering skylines, few killer views, and only a handful of meager skyscrapers. Traffic is manageable, events are organized, and the pace is utterly human. Even at the height of the busy summer, there is always a quiet café or a lakeside bench available to ponder this European capital with a provincial soul.

In the streets, bicycles spin alongside smooth auto traffic. In the early morning in the pedestrian streets of the city's core, Strøget, the air is redolent of freshly baked bread and soap-scrubbed store fronts. If there's such a thing as a cozy city, this is it.

Extremely livable and relatively calm, Copenhagen is not a microcosm of Denmark; indeed, it speeds past the rest of the mostly rural country. The headquarters of Denmark's political, cultural, and financial operations, it is inhabited by 1.5 million Danes, a fifth of the population, as well as a growing immigrant community. Filled with museums, restaurants, cafés, and lively nightlife, it has its greatest resource in its spirited inhabitants. Imaginative and unconventional, the affable Copenhageners exude a Do-What-You-Wanna-Do philosophy that embraces and respects nearly all lifestyles and leanings.

The town was a fishing colony until 1157, when Valdemar the Great gave it to Bishop Absalon, who built a castle on what is now Christianborg. It grew as a center on the Baltic trade route and became known as *købmændenes havn* (merchants' harbor), and eventually København. In the 15th century, it became the royal residence, and the capital of Norway and Sweden. A hundred years later, Christian IV, a Renaissance king obsessed with fine architecture, began a building boom that crowned the city with towers and castles, many of which still exist. They are almost all that remain of the city's 800-year history; much of the city was destroyed during two major fires in the 18th century and Lord Nelson's bombings during the Napoleonic Wars.

Despite a tumultuous history, Copenhagen survives as the liveliest Scandinavian capital. With the backdrop of copper towers and crooked rooftops, the venerable city is humored by playful street musicians and performers, spangled by the thousand lights and gardens of Tivoli, and moved by one of the hottest jazz scenes in the world.

Important Addresses and Numbers

Tourist Information The main tourist information office is **Danmarks Turistråd** (Danish Tourist Board, H.C. Andersens Blvd. 22, tel. 33/11-13-25). It is open May through September, weekdays 9–6, Saturday 9–2, Sunday 9–1; and October through April, weekdays 9–5 and Saturday 9–noon. Packed with brochures and maps covering Copenhagen and the rest of the country, it's run by a pleasant and knowledgeable staff. Youth information in Copenhagen is available at **Use-It** (Huset, Rådhusstræde 13, tel. 33/15–65–18), which also has a café, a video gallery, and three music clubs.

Embassies **U.S. Embassy,** Dag Hammarskjölds Allé 24, tel. 31/42–31–44. **Canadian Embassy,** Kristen Bernikows Gade 1, tel. 33/12–22–99. **U.K. Embassy,** Kastesvej 36–40, tel. 35/26–46–00.

Emergencies For **police, fire,** and **ambulance,** dial 000. If you cannot drive your car to a garage for repairs, the rescue corps, **Falck** (tel. 31/14–22–22) can help.

Hospital Emergency Rooms **Rigshospitalet** (Blegdamsvej 9, tel. 31/38–66–33 or 31/39–66–33) is located north of the city, next to the large Fælled park. **Frederiksberg Hospital** (Nordre Fasanvej 57, tel. 38/34–77–11) is two blocks north of the zoo.

Doctors After normal business hours, **emergency doctors** make house calls in the central city. In Osterbro and Norrebro, call 33/12–00–41; in Frederiksberg, 31/10–00–41; and in Vesterbro, Valby, and Sydhaven, 31/22–00–41. Fees are payable in cash only; night fees are approximately DKr300–400.

Dentists **Emergency dentists** (14 Oslo Plads, no tel.) near Østerport station, are available daily 8 PM–9:30 PM and Saturday, Sunday, and holidays 10 AM–noon. Only cash is accepted as payment.

Where to Change Money Almost all banks (including Den Danske Bank at the airport) exchange money. Most hotels cash traveler's checks and major foreign currency, but they charge a substantial fee and give a lower rate. After normal banking hours, an exchange is open at the **main railway station,** October to mid-April, daily 7 AM–9 PM, and mid-April to September 6:45 AM–10 PM. **American Express** (Amagertorv 18, tel. 33/12–23–01) is open weekdays 9–5 and Saturday 9–noon. **Tivoli** (Vesterbrogade 3, tel. 33/15–10–01) also exchanges money; it is open May to September, daily noon–11 PM.

English-language Bookstores **Steve's Books and Records** (Ved Stranden 10, tel. 33/11–94–60) has new and used English books. **Boghallen** (Rådhuspladsen 37, tel. 33/11–85–11, ext. 764) and **Arnold Busck** (Kobmagergade 49, tel. 33/12–24–53) are Danish bookstores with excellent English-language sections.

Late-night Pharmacies **Steno Apotek** (Vesterbrogade 6C, tel. 33/14–82–66) and **Sønderbro Apotek** (Amangerbrogade 158, tel. 31/58–01–40) are open 24 hours a day.

Travel Agencies **American Express** (Amagertorv 18, tel. 33/12–23–01), **Thomas Cook, c/o Wagons Lit** (Vesterbrogade 2B, tel. 33/14–27–47), and **Budget Rejser** (Vesterbrogade 26, tel. 31/31–11–12) are among the leading agencies. For student and budget travel, try **DIS Rejser** (Skindergade 28, tel. 33/11–00–44). **Spies** (Nyropsgade 41, tel. 33/11–84–84) handles charter packages.

Arriving and Departing by Plane

Airport and Airlines Copenhagen's recently renovated and expanded **Kastrup Airport,** 10 kilometers (6 miles) southeast of downtown, is the gateway to Scandinavia. In addition to international flights, domestic flights are served by **SAS** (tel. 33/13–72–77). Among the many airlines that serve Kastrup are **British Airways** (tel. 33/14–60–00), **Icelandair** (tel. 33/12–33–88), and **TWA** (tel. 33/32–80–88).

Between the Airport and Downtown Traffic in Copenhagen, even during the rush hour, is manageable; you will find that travel between the airport and downtown is both quick and easy.

By Bus **SAS coach buses** leave the international arrival terminal every 15 minutes, from 5:42 AM to 9:45 PM, cost DKr28, and take 25 minutes to reach Copenhagen's main train station on Vesterbrogade. Another SAS coach from Christianborg, on Slotsholmsgade, to the airport, runs every 15 minutes between 8:30 AM and noon, and every half-hour from noon to 6 PM. The **HT** city buses depart from the international arrival terminal every 15 minutes, from 4:30 AM (Sunday 5:30) to 11:52 PM, but take a longer, more circuitous route. Take bus Nos. 32, 32H for the Town Hall Square (Rådhuspladsen), No. 9 for Kongens Nytorv and Østerport, and No. 38E for Valby Station. Tickets cost DKr13.50.

By Taxi The 20-minute ride downtown costs DKr75 to 120. Lines form at the international arrival terminal. In the unlikely event a taxi is not available, call 31/35–35–35.

Arriving and Departing by Car, Train, and Ship

By Car The E–20 highway, via bridges and ferry routes, connects Fredericia (on Jylland) to Middelfart (on Fyn) to Copenhagen. Farther north, from Århus (in Jylland), there is a direct ferry service to Kalundborg (on Sjælland). From there, Route 23 leads to Copenhagen. Make reservations for the ferry in advance through **DSB** (tel. 33/14–88–80).

Once in Copenhagen, leave your car in the garage and walk. The charm of the pedestrian malls comes at the cost of a complicated system of one-way streets and difficult (and expensive) parking. Attractions are relatively close together, and public transportation to them is excellent.

By Train Copenhagen's **Hovedbanegården** (central station) is the hub of the DSB network. Intercity trains leave every hour, usually on the hour, from 6 AM to 10 PM for principal towns in Fyn and Jylland. Find out more from **DSB Information** (tel. 33/14–17–01). You can make reservations at the central station, at most other stations, and through travel agents. In Copenhagen, if you have an Inter-Rail card, there is an Inter-Rail Center at the main station, which also offers rest and a bath. The center is open July to mid-September, daily 7 AM–midnight.

By Ship If you are coming from Sweden, there are frequent ferry connections, including several daily ships from Malmö, Limhamn, Landskrona, and Helsingborg that arrive in Copenhagen. There is also a high-speed craft from Malmö.

Getting Around

Copenhagen is small, with most sights within its square-mile center. Wear comfortable shoes and explore it on foot. Or follow the example of the Danes and rent a bike. An efficient transit system is available, for the footsore.

By Train and Bus The **Copenhagen Card** affords unlimited travel on buses and suburban trains, admission to over 40 museums and sights around Sjælland, and a reduction on the ferry crossing to Sweden. You can buy the card, which costs DKr115 (one day), DKr155 (two days), or DKr200 (three days), at tourist offices and hotels and from travel agents.

Trains and buses operate from 5 AM (Sunday 6 AM) to midnight. After that, night buses run every half-hour from 1 AM to 4:30 AM, from the main bus station at the Town Hall Square to most areas of the city and surroundings. Trains and buses operate on the same ticket system and divide Copenhagen and surrounding areas into three zones. Tickets are validated on a time basis: On the basic ticket, which costs DKr9 per hour, you can travel anywhere in the zone you started in. A discount *klip kort,* good for 10 rides, costs DKr80 and must be stamped in the automatic ticket machines on buses or at stations. Get zone details from the 24-hour information service (tel. 36/45–45–45 for buses, 33/14–17–01 for S trains).

By Taxi The shiny computer-metered Mercedes and Volvo cabs are not cheap. The base charge is DKr12, plus DKr8 to 10 per kilometer. A cab is available when it displays the sign FRI (Free); it can be hailed or picked up in front of the main train station or at taxi stands, or tel. 31/35–35–35.

By Bicycle Bikes are delightfully well suited to Copenhagen's flat terrain and are popular among Danes, as well as among visitors. Bike rental costs DKr25 to 60 a day, with a deposit of DKr100–200. Contact **Københavns Cyclebørs** (Track 12, Copenhagen main train station, tel. 33/14–07–17), **Danwheel-Rent-a-Bike** (Colbjørnsensgade 3, tel. 31/21–22–27), or **Urania Cykler** (Gammel Kongevej 1, tel. 31/21–80–88). You can also *borrow* a bike for free by inserting a 20-kroner coin in one of hundreds of special bike racks around the city. Return it to any rack and your deposit will be refunded. Contact **Bycyklen Aps** (Nyhavn 6E, tel. 33/13–28–37) for information.

Opening and Closing Times

Banks and businesses follow the same hours as the rest of the country, but grocery stores stay open later, until 7 most nights. Shops stay open until 5:30 Monday through Thursday, and until 6 or 7 Friday. On the first Saturday of the month some shops stay open until 4 or 5.

Guided Tours

The Copenhagen Tourist Board monitors all tours and has brochures and information. Most tours run through the summer until September. Only the Grand Tour of Copenhagen is year-round.

Orientation All tours begin at Lurblæserne (Lur Blower Column) at the Town Hall Square, and reservations are not necessary. **The Royal Tour of Copenhagen** (2¾ hours) covers the exhibitions at Christiansborg and Rosenborg, and visits Amalienborg Square. **The Grand Tour of Copenhagen** (2½ hours) includes Tivoli, the Carlsberg Glyptotek, Christiansborg Palace, Børsen, the Royal Theater, Nyhavn, Amalienborg Palace, the Gefion Fountain, the Grundtvig Church, and Rosenborg Castle. The **City Tour** (1½ hours) is more general, passing the Carlsberg Glyptotek, Christiansborg Palace, Thorvaldsen's Museum, the National Museum, Børsen, the Royal Theater, Rosenborg, the National Art Gallery, the Botanical Gardens, Amalienborg, the Gefion Fountain, and stopping at the Little Mermaid. For more information on all tours, call **Copenhagen Excursions** (tel. 31/54–06–06).

Special-interest Tours of the **Carlsberg Brewery** meet at the Elephant Gate (Ny Carlsbergvej 140, tel. 31/21–12–21, ext. 1312), weekdays at 9 and 2. **Tuborg Breweries** also provides tours (Strandvejen 54, Hellerup, tel. 31/29–33–11, ext. 2212). **The Royal Porcelain Factory** (Smallegade 45, tel. 31/86–48–48) has tours, which end at its shop, on weekdays at 9, 10, and 11 from September until March and weekdays 9, 10, 11, 1, and 2 from April through August.

Boat Tours The **Harbor and Canal Tour** (1 hour) leaves from Gammel Strand and the east side of Kongens Nytorv from May to mid-September. Contact Canal Tours via the Tourist Board. The **City and Harbor Tour** (2½ hours) includes a short bus trip through town and sails from the Fish Market on Holmens Canal through several more waterways, ending near Strøget. Call Copenhagen Excursions (*see above*).

Walking Tours **Guided strolls** (2 hours) with English-speaking guides start at 4:30 Sunday and 5:30 Wednesday, May through September, at the town hall, and include the double square of Gammel and Nytorv, Vor Frue Kirke, the university, and the Round Tower. Other walks are also planned. Call 31/51–25–90 or 39/69–65–05, or look for the latest schedule in the tourist magazine *Copenhagen This Week*.

Highlights for First-time Visitors

Amalienborg Castle (*see* Tour 2)
Christiansborg Palace (*see* Tour 1)
Langelinie and **the Little Mermaid** (*see* Tour 2)
Ny Carlsberg Glyptotek (*see* Tour 3)
Nyhavn (*see* Tour 2)
Rosenborg Castle (*see* Tour 3)
Rundetårn and **Trinitas Church** (*see* Tour 3)
Strøget (*see* Tour 3)
Tivoli (*see* Tour 3)
Vor Frelsers Kirke (*see* Tour 1)

Exploring Copenhagen

Numbers in the margin correspond with points of interest on the Copenhagen map.

The city core consists of the five consecutive pedestrian strands known as Strøget and the surrounding tangle of roads and courtyards. Less than a mile square, it is best explored on foot. North of Kongens Nytorv, the city becomes a fidgety grid of wider boulevards and parks that point toward the upscale Østerbro area. To the south are the working-class and immigrant neighborhoods of Vesterbro, where you'll find a good selection of inexpensive ethnic restaurants and shops. Across the main harbor is the smaller, historic haven of Christianshavn.

The city is surrounded by water, be it sea or canal; it is built on two islands—Sjælland and Amager—and connected by bridges and drawbridges. The maritime atmosphere is indelible, especially around Nyhavn and Christianshavn. Leave enough time in your tours to linger, to enjoy the views of life from the sidewalk cafés in the shady squares.

Tour 1: Town Hall Square to the Citadel

The best place to begin a stroll is **Rådhus Pladsen** (City Hall Square), the hub of Copenhagen's commercial district. The
1 mock-Renaissance building dominating it is **Københavns Rådhus** (Copenhagen's City Hall), completed in 1905. A statue of Copenhagen's 12th-century founder, Bishop Absalon, sits atop the main entrance. Inside, you can see the first World Clock, multidialed, super-accurate astronomical timepiece that took inventor Jens Olsen 27 years to complete before it was put into action in 1955. It contains a 570,000-year calendar. If you're feeling energetic, take a guided tour up the 106-meter (350-foot) bell tower for the panoramic, but not particularly inspiring, view. *Rådhus Pladsen, tel. 33/15–38–00. Admission: DKr10. Open weekdays 10–3. Tower tours, Oct.–May, Mon.–Sat. noon; June–Sept., weekdays 10, noon, and 2 and Sat. noon.*

Diagonally across the square, atop a corner office building, you can check the local weather forecast. Look above the neon thermometer to the gilded barometer: On sunny days, a golden sculpture of a girl on a bicycle appears, on rainy days, a girl with an umbrella. The bronze sculpture was created by the Danish artist E. Utzon Frank in 1936.

2 On the right of Rådhus Pladsen is **Lurblæserne** (the Lur Blower's Column), topped by two Vikings blowing an ancient trumpet called a *lur.* The 1914 sculptor took a great deal of artistic license—the lur dates to the Bronze Age, 1500 BC, while the Vikings lived a mere 1,000 years ago.

If you continue to the square's northeast corner and turn right, you are in **Frederiksberggade,** the first of the five pedestrian
3 streets that make up **Strøget,** Copenhagen's shopping district. Walk past the cafés and trendy boutiques to the double square of **Gammeltorv** (Old Square) and **Nytorv** (New Square), where on April 16, golden apples (gilded metal balls) dance on water jets to celebrate the queen's birthday. In 1728 and again in 1795, this area was heavily damaged by fire, with the later blaze destroying the original 15th-century town hall. In the renovation process, the city fathers straightened and widened the streets. Between the swanky boutiques and newer architecture, you can still see buildings from this reconstruction period, as well as a few that survived the fires.

Amalienborg, **15**
Amalienhavn, **16**
Børsen, **10**
Botanisk Have, **29**
Christiansborg Slot, **5**
Frihedsmuseet, **20**
Gefion Springvandet, **23**
Helligånds Kirken, **12**
Den Hirschsprungske Samling, **31**
Kastellet, **21**
Københavns Bymuseum, **35**
Københavns Rådhus, **1**
Københavns Synagoge, **26**
Københavns Universitet, **25**
Det Kongelige Bibliotek, **7**
Kongelige Teater, **14**
Kunstindustrimuseet, **19**
Den Lille Havfrue, **22**
Lurblæserne, **2**
Marmorkirken, **17**
Nationalmuseet, **4**
Nikolaj Kirke, **13**
Ny Carlsberg Glyptotek, **33**
Rosenborg Slot, **28**
Rundetårn, **27**
Russiske Ortodoks Kirke, **18**
Statens Museum for Kunst, **30**
Strøget, **3**
Teaterhistorisk Museet, **8**
Thorvaldsens Museum, **6**
Tivoli, **32**
Tøjhusmuseet, **9**
Tycho Brahe Planetarium, **34**
Vor Frelsers Kirke, **11**
Vor Frue Kirke, **24**

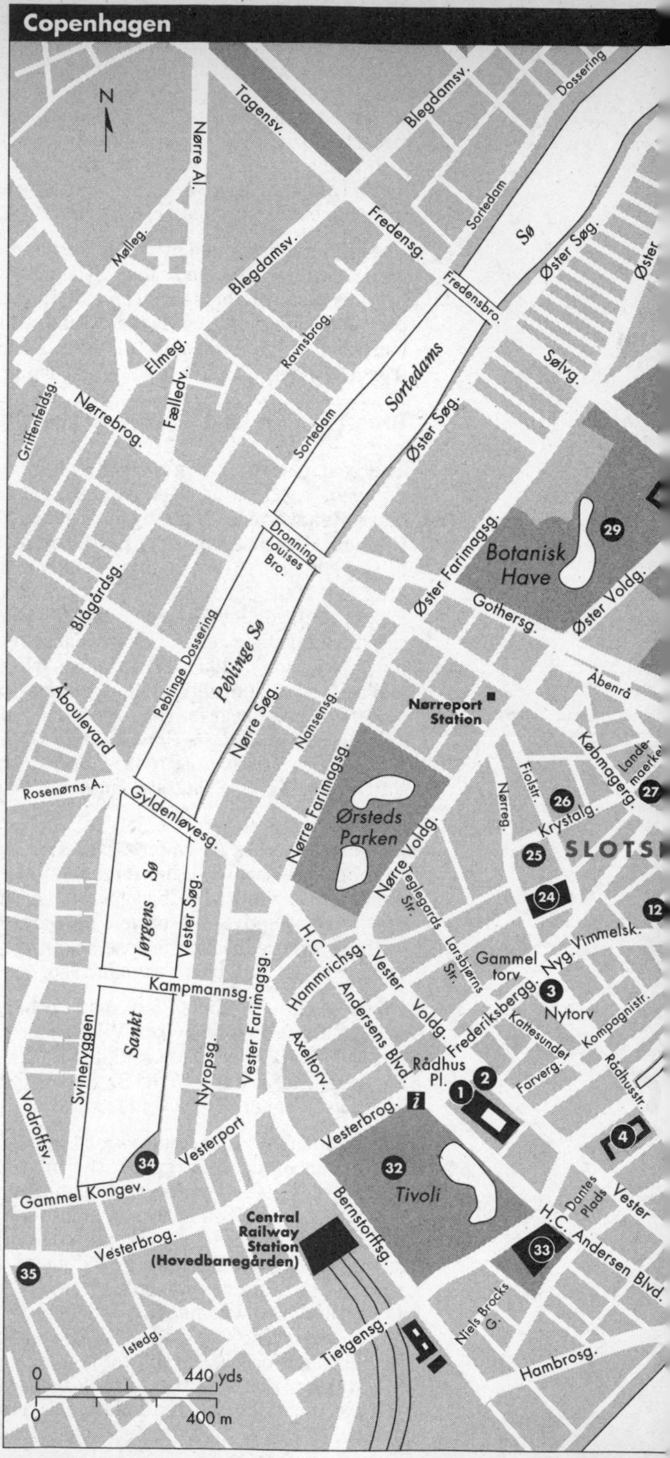

Langeliniebrd.
Hammerskjölds Al.
Kristianiag.
Østbaneg.
Folke Bernadottes Al.
Østerport Station
Oslo Plads
Stockholmsg.
Øster Anlæg
Churchill-parken
Forbindelsesv.
Langelinie
Yderhavn
Grønningen
St. Kongensg.
Esplanaden
Rigensg.
Sølvg.
Fredericiag.
Bredg.
Amalieg.
Toldbog.
Kongens Have
Kronprincesseg.
Store Kongensg.
Dronningens Tværg.
Adelg.
Borgerg.
Sankt Annæ Plads
Vognmagerg.
Gammelmønt
Pilestræde
Gothersg.
Ny Østerg.
Kongens Nytorv
Nyhavn
Nyhavn Canal
Inderhavn
OLMEN
Kr. Bernikg.
Østerg.
Heibergsg.
Amagertorv
Højbro
Læderstr.
Gammel Strand
Bremerholm
Holmens
Holbergsg.
Havnegade
Vindelbrog
Christiansborg Slotsplads
Chr. IV's Bro
Børsg.
Knippelsbro
Tøjhusgade
Frederiksholms Kanal
Christians Brygge
Voldg.
Sankt Annæg.
CHRISTIANSHAVN
Torveg.
Dronningensg.
Princessg.
Christianshavns Voldg.
Langerbrog.
Langebro
Amager Blvd.
Stadsgraven
Amagerbrog.
Vermlandsg.
5
6
7
8
9
10
11
13
14
15
16
17
18
19
20
21
22
23
28
30
31

Turn down Rådhusstræde toward Frederiksholms Kanal. Here
4 you'll find the **National Museet** (National Museum), with extensive collections that chronicle Danish cultural history to modern times, including one of the largest collections of Stone-Age tools in the world, as well as Egyptian, Greek, and Roman antiquities. If you are a Viking enthusiast, check out the Runic stones in the Danish cultural history section. *Frederiksholms Kanal 12, tel. 33/13-44-11. Admission free. Open June 16–Sept. 15, Tues.–Sun. 10–4; Sept. 16–June 15, Tues.–Fri. 11–3, weekends noon–4.*

Cross Frederiksholms Kanal to Christiansborg Slotsplads, a small atoll divided by the canal and dominated by the massive
5 granite **Christiansborg Slot** (Christiansborg Castle), where the queen officially receives guests. The complex, which contains the **Folketinget** (Parliament House), **De Kongelige Repræsantationlokaler** (the Royal Reception Chambers; where you'll be asked to don slippers to protect the floors), and **Højesteret** (the Supreme Court), is located on the site of the city's first fortress, built by Bishop Absalon in 1167. While the castle was being built at the turn of the century, the National Museum excavated the **ruins** lying beneath the site. From 1441 until the fire of 1795 Christiansborg was used as the royal residence. *Christiansborg, tel. 33/92-64-92. Ruins: admission DKr11 adults, DKr5 children; open daily 10–4; closed Sat., Sept. 11–May. Reception chambers: admission DKr18 adults, DKr7 children; open to guided tours only: June–Aug., Tues.–Sun., English tour at 12, 2, and 4; Sept.–May, Tues.–Fri. and Sun., English tour at 2. Folketinget: tel. 33/37-55-00; admission free, tours Sun. hourly 10–4.*

6 Also on the island, north of the castle, is **Thorvaldsens Museum.** The 19th-century artist Bertel Thorvaldsen (1770–1844), perhaps Denmark's greatest sculptor, is buried at the center of the museum. Greatly influenced by the statues and reliefs of classical antiquity, he is recognized as one of the world's greatest neoclassical artists and completed many commissions all over Europe. In addition to his own interpretations of classical and mythological figures, there is an extensive collection of paintings and drawings by other artists that he assembled while living in Italy. *Prins Jørgens Gård, tel. 33/32-15-32. Admission free. Open May–Sept., daily 10–4; Oct.–Apr., Wed.–Mon. 10–3.*

7 Nearby **Det Kongelige Bibliotek** (the Royal Library) houses the country's largest collection of books, newspapers, and manuscripts. Look for records of the Viking journeys to America and Greenland, as well as original manuscripts by Hans Christian Andersen and Karen Blixen (Isak Dinesen). Afterward, leave time to ramble around the statue of philosopher Søren Kierkegaard (1813–1855), the formal gardens, and tree-lined avenues that surround the scholarly building. *Christians Brygge 8, tel. 33/93-01-11. Admission free. Open weekdays 9–7, Sat. 9–6.*

8 Close to the library is **Teaterhistorisk Museet** (the Theater History Museum), in the Royal Court Theater of 1766, which was founded by Ludvig Holberg, a satirist often compared to Molière. You can see extensive exhibits in theater and ballet history and then wander around the boxes, the stage, and the dressing rooms. *Christiansborg Ridebane 18, tel. 33/11-51-76. Admission: DKr20 adults, DKr10 senior citizens and stu-*

dents, DKr5 children. Open June Sept., Wed. 2-4, Sun. noon–4.

Also at this address are **De Kongelige Stald** (the Royal Stables), which display vehicles used by the Danish monarchy from 1776 to the present day. *Admission: DKr5 adults, DKr2 children. Open Nov.–Apr., daily 2–4; May–Oct., Fri.–Sun. 2–4.*

9 Across the street that bears its name is **Tøjhusmuseet** (the Royal Arsenal Museum) with impressive displays of uniforms, weapons, and armor in an arched hall 200 yards long. *Tøjhusgade 3, tel. 33/11–60–37. Admission free. Open May–Sept., Tues.–Sat. 1–4, Sun. 10–4; Oct.–Apr., Tues.–Sat. 1–3, Sun. 11–4.*

10 A few steps from Tøjhuset is **Børsen,** believed to be the oldest stock exchange still in use, though now only on special occasions. It was built between 1619 and 1640 by Christian IV, a scholar and warrior, and architect of much of the city. The king is said to have helped to twist the tails of the four dragons that form the structure's whimsical green copper spire. With its steep roofs, tiny windows, and gables, the building is one of Copenhagen's treasures. *Not open to the public.*

To the left (near Højbro Plads) is a delightful row of houses bordering the northern edge of Slotsholmen. The quays in front of them were long used for Copenhagen's fish market, though today a couple of early-morning fisherwomen hawking fresh fish, marinated herring, and slithering eel are the only people who carry on the tradition.

Across from Børsen is **Holmens Kirke** (the Islet's Church), where two of the country's most revered naval heroes—Niels Juel, who crushed the Swedish fleet at Køge in 1677, and Peder Tordenskjold, who defeated Charles XII of Sweden during the Great Northern War in the early 18th century—are buried. *Holmens Kanal, tel. 33/13–61–78. Admission free. Open May 15–Sept. 15, Mon.–Fri. 9–2, Sat. 9–noon; Sept. 16–May 14, Mon.–Sat. 9–noon.*

From Børsen, look east across the drawbridge (Knippelsbro) that connects Slotsholmen with **Christianshavn,** one of the oldest parts of Copenhagen. Three hundred years ago, it was designed for trade, commerce, housing for the shipbuilding workers, and as a defense area against sea attacks. Now gentrified, its old tangles of cobbled avenues, antique street lamps, and Left Bank atmosphere have been preserved, as has the old system of earthworks—the best preserved of Copenhagen's original fortification walls. Restaurants, cafés, and boutiques have moved in, and the ramparts are now edged with green areas and walking paths—a popular neighborhood for afternoon and evening promenades.

11 Dominating the scene is the green-and-gold spire of **Vor Frelsers Kirke** (Our Savior's Church). The Gothic structure was built in 1696. Local legend has it that the staircase encircling it was built curling the wrong way around, so that when its architect reached the top and realized what he'd done, he jumped. The less impulsive should climb the 400 steps to the top—being careful of strong winds and slippery surfaces—for the wonderful view of Copenhagen. *Skt. Annægade, tel. 31/57–27–98. Admission: DKr10 adults, DKr4 children. Open Mar. 15–May, Mon.–Sat. 9–4:30, Sun. noon–3:30; June–Aug., Mon.–Sat.*

9–4:30, Sun. noon–4:30; Sept.–Oct., Mon.–Sat. 9–3:30, Sun. noon–3:30; Nov.–Mar. 14, Mon.–Sat. 10–1:30, Sun. noon–1:30. Tower closed Dec.–Mar. 14.

Cross the Knippels Torvegade Bridge and walk straight down the street about a mile (or take bus No. 8 to the canal and walk about two blocks north) to the Amagertorv section of Strøget. 12 On your left is the 18th-century **Helligånds Kirken** (Church of the Holy Ghost), one of the city's oldest. The choir contains a font by the sculptor Thorvaldsen. *Niels Hemmingsengade 5, tel. 33/12–95–55. Admission free. Open Mon.–Fri. noon–4.*

In Østergade, the easternmost of the streets that make up 13 Strøget, you'll see the green spire of **Nikolaj Kirke** (Nicholas Church). The current building was finished in 1914; the previous structure, which dated from the 13th century, was destroyed by the 1728 fire. Today, the church is an art gallery and an exhibition center. *Nikolaiplads, tel. 33/93–16–26. Admission free. Open daily noon–5.*

Time Out **Café Nikolaj,** inside Nikolaj Kirke, is a reliable, inexpensive café for a Danish pastry or a light meal.

Although Strøget is a famous shopping area, and elegant stores and trendy boutiques abound, it's also where Copenhagen comes to stroll. Outside the posh displays of the fur and porcelain shops, the bustling cafés and restaurants, the sidewalks have the festive air of a street fair.

Tour 2: Around the Royal Palace

Kongens Nytorv (the King's New Square) marks the end of Strøget. In its center is a mounted statue of Christian V. Every year, at the end of June, graduating high-school students wearing white caps arrive in horse-drawn carriages and dance 14 around the austere statue. The stoic, pillared **Kongelige Teater** (Danish Royal Theater), flanked by statues of Danish authors Adam Oehlenschläger and Ludvig Holberg, sits on the south side. Its two stages and sumptuous red-velvet interiors are the home of Danish opera and ballet, as well as theater. The Danish Royal Ballet remains one of the world's great companies, with a repertoire ranging from classical to modern works (*see* The Arts and Nightlife, *below*). *Tordenskjoldsgade 3, tel. 33/14–10–02. Not open for tours.*

Located just behind the theater is **Charlottenborg,** which 300 years ago was planned as a residential palace with a large garden. Since 1754, however, the main section of the palace (which was built in 1670) has housed the faculty and students of the Danish Academy of Fine Art. On the western side of the square, you'll see the stately white New Georgian facade of the 200-year-old **D'Angleterre** (*see* Lodging, *below*), the grande dame of Copenhagen hotels.

The street leading southeast from Kongens Nytorv is **Nyhavn** (New Harbor). The harbor is actually a canal that was dug 300 years ago to draw traffic and commerce to the center of the city. The plan worked, attracting merchants and warehouses to the area, many of which have been well preserved and give Nyhavn its authentic 18th-century maritime atmosphere. Until 1970, this area was the favorite haunt of sailors. Now gentrified, the restaurants, boutiques, and antiques stores outnumber the tattoo parlors, but the area still retains a genuine charm, with a fleet of old-time sailing ships that you can view from the quay. Hans Christian Andersen lived at numbers 18, 20, and 67.

Time Out Dozens of restaurants and cafés line Nyhavn. Among the best, try **Cap Horn** or **Nyhavn 21** (tel. 33/12–85–04) for both moderately priced hearty and light Danish specialties served in a ship's galley atmosphere, or **La Glace** (Kongens Nytorv 2, tel. 33/14–46–46) where elegantly dressed Danes flock on the weekend for some of the best—albeit pricey—pastries and coffee in town.

Beside the main harbor are old shipping warehouses, including two—Nyhavn 71 and the Admiral—that have been converted into comfortable hotels (*see* Lodging, *below*). The end of Nyhavn is the departure point for the high-speed craft to Malmö, while on the other side, on Kvævthusbroen (at the end of Skt. Annæ Plads) are boats to Oslo and Bornholm.

Turn left at the end of Nyhavn to see the harbor front and then take an immediate left onto Skt. Annæ Plads and the second right onto Amaliegade. Walk through the imposing wood colon-
15 nade and you'll be in the cobbled square of **Amalienborg,** the four identical Rococo buildings that have been the royal residence since 1784. Every day at noon, the Royal Guard and band march from Rosenborg Slot through the city for the changing of the guard. The palace interior is closed to the public. In the center of the square is a magnificent statue of King Frederik V by the French sculptor Jacques Francois Joseph Saly. One of the finest equestrian statues in the world, it reputedly cost as much as all the buildings.

On the palace's harbor side are the trees, gardens, and foun-
16 tains of **Amalienhaven** (Amalia's Gardens). Across the square, it's a step to Bredgade and the ponderous Frederikskirke, com-
17 monly called **Marmorkirken** (the Marble Church), a Baroque church begun in 1749 in high-priced Norwegian marble that lay unfinished (because of budget restraints) from 1770 to 1874 before it was finally completed and consecrated in 1894. Perched around the exterior are 16 statues of various religious leaders from Moses to Luther, and below them stand sculptures of outstanding Danish ministers and bishops. *Bredgade, tel. 33/15–37–63. Admission free. Open daily 11–2. Dome: Admission free. Open Sat.*

Bredgade is also home to the exotic gilded onion domes of the
18 **Russiske Ortodoks Kirke** (Russian Orthodox Church).

19 Farther on is the fine Rococo building of the **Kunstindustrimuseet** (Museum of Decorative Art), which was formerly a royal hospital. Inside, there's a large selection of European and Oriental handicrafts, as well as ceramics, silverware, and tapestry. Leave yourself enough time for coffee in the lovely café. *Bredgade 68, tel. 33/14–94–52. Admission July, Aug., Sun., and holidays: DKr20; other times free. Open Tues.–Sun. 1–4.*

Parallel to Bredgade, you can walk down Store Kongensgade to the neat mustard-colored enclave of **Nyboder,** a perfectly laid-out compound of flat, long, former sailors' homes built by Christian IV. Like Nyhavn, this salty sailors' area was seedy and boisterous at the beginning of the 1970s, but today, it's among Copenhagen's more fashionable neighborhoods.

Back on Store Kongensgade, turn right onto Esplanaden, and
20 you'll arrive at **Frihedsmuseet** (the Liberty Museum), situated in Churchill Park. Flanked by a homemade tank the Danes used to spread the news of the Nazi surrender after World War II, the museum gives an evocative picture of the heroic Danish resistance movement, which managed to save 7,000 Jews from the Nazis by hiding them, then smuggling them to Sweden. When the Germans demanded that all Jews in Denmark wear a gold star, King Christian X, the present Queen Margrethe II's grandfather, became a legend among his people when he told the Germans that if the Jews were forced to wear a star, he would, too. *Churchillparken, tel. 33/13–77–14. Admission free. Open Sept. 16–Apr., Tues.–Sat. 11–3, Sun. 11–4; May–Sept. 15, Tues.–Sat. 10–4, Sun. 10–5.*

At the park's entrance stands the English church, St. Albans,
21 and, in the center, **Kastellet** (the Citadel), with two rings of moats. This was the city's main fortress in the 18th century, but in a grim reversal during World War II, the Germans used it as the focal point of their occupation. *Admission free. Open 6 AM–sunset.*

Continue to Langelinie, which on Sundays is thronged with
22 promenading Danes, and at last to **Den Lille Havefrue** (the Little Mermaid), the somewhat overrated 1913 statue commemorating Hans Christian Andersen's lovelorn creation, and the subject of hundreds of travel posters. Unfortunately, the innocent waif has also been the subject of some cruel practical jokes, including decapitation and the loss of an arm. Back to-
23 ward Esplanaden, the **Gefion Springvandet** (Gefion Fountain) illustrates another dramatic myth, that of the goddess Gefion, who was promised as much of Sweden as she could carve in a night. The story goes that she changed her sons to oxen and carved out the island of Sjælland.

Time Out A less than 10-minute walk back down Esplanaden is the **Charlotte II Café** (Esplanaden 8, tel. 33/12–33–80), which serves cappuccino, sandwiches, and other light meals off ceramics by Copenhagen artist Jesper Packness; all the works are for sale.

Tour 3: Around Strøget and down Vesterbrogade

From Langelinie, take the train from Østerport station to
24 Nørreport station and walk down Fiolstræde to **Vor Frue Kirke** (Church of Our Lady), Copenhagen's cathedral since 1924. The site itself has been a place of worship since the 13th century, when Bishop Absalon built a chapel here, but was reconstructed in neoclassical style after destruction during the Napoleonic Wars. Inside, you can see Thorvaldsen's marble sculptures of Christ and the Apostles, and Moses and David in bronze. *Nørregade, Frue Plads, tel. 33/15–10–78. Open Mon.–Sat. 9–5, Sun. 12–5. Closed during mass.*

25 Head north again on Fiolstræde to the main building of **Københavns Universitet** (the Copenhagen University), constructed in the 19th century on the site of the medieval bishops' palace. Past the university, turn right on Krystalgade. On the left is
26 the arklike **Københavns Synagoge** (Copenhagen Synagogue), designed by the noted contemporary architect Gustav Friederich Hetsch.

27 Just across Købmagergade is the **Rundetårn** (round tower), built as an observatory in 1642 by Christian IV and still maintained as the oldest in Europe. It is said that Peter the Great of Russia drove a horse and carriage up the 600 feet of its smooth, spiraling ramp. You'll have to walk, but the view of the twisted streets and crooked roofs of old Copenhagen is worth it. *Købmagergade, tel. 33/93–66–60. Admission: DKr10 adults, DKr4 children. Open Dec.–Mar., daily 10–4; Apr.–May and Sept.–Oct., daily 10–5; June–Aug., daily 10–8.*

Straight down from Rundetårn on Landemærket is Gothersgade and **Kongens Have** (the King's Garden), with expansive lawns, park benches, and shady walking paths. Carefully
28 tended gardens surround **Rosenborg Slot,** the Dutch Renaissance castle built by Christian IV. Intending it first as a summer residence, the king loved the castle so much that he ended up living, and dying, there. It remained the royal residence until the early 19th century, when it became a museum. It still contains the crown jewels, as well as a collection of costumes and royal memorabilia—Christian IV's pearl-studded saddle and bejeweled tables are showstoppers. In 1849, when the absolute monarchy was abolished, the royal castles became state property, except for Rosenborg, which is still inherited from monarch to monarch. *Øster Voldgade 4A, tel. 33/15–32–86. Admission: DKr30 adults, DKr5 children. Open Apr.–May, daily 11–3; June–Aug., daily 10–4; Sept.–Oct., daily 11–3; Nov.–Mar., Tues. and Fri. 11–2, Sun. 10–3.*

29 Across Øster Voldgade from the palace is **Botanisk Have,** (the Botanical Garden), 25 acres of trees, flowers, ponds, sculptures, and a rather spectacular *Palmehuset* (Palm House) containing tropical and subtropical plants. There's also an observatory and a geological museum. *Gothersgade 128, tel. 33/12–74–60. Admission free. Gardens open May–Aug., daily 8:30–6; Sept.–Apr., daily 8:30–4. Palm house open daily 10–3.*

30 Leave the gardens through the north exit to get to the **Statens Museum for Kunst** (National Art Gallery), where the official doorman greets you wearing a uniform with buckled shoes and a cocked hat. The collections range from Danish art to works by Rubens, Dürer, the Impressionists, and Matisse. *Sølvgade 48–50, tel. 33/91–21–26. Admission free. Open Tues.–Sun. 10–4:30.*

31 An adjacent building houses **Den Hirschsprungske Samling** (the Hirschsprung Collection) of 19th-century Danish art. The modest museum features works from the country's Golden Age, in particular a group of late-19th-century painters called the Skagen School, whose illuminated images capture the play of light and water that is so characteristic of the Danish countryside. *Stockholmsgade 20, tel. 31/42–03–36. Admission free. Open Wed.–Sun. 1–4; Oct.–Apr. also Wed. 7–10 PM.*

Walk back to the Nørreport station and take a train to the Main Copenhagen Station. When you exit on Vesterbrogade, make a right and you'll see Copenhagen's best-known attraction,
32 **Tivoli.** In the 1840s, Danish architect George Carstensen persuaded a worried King Christian VIII to let him build an amusement park on the edge of the city's fortifications, rationalizing that "when people amuse themselves, they forget politics." In the comparatively short season, from May to September, more than 4 million people come through the gates.

Tivoli is more sophisticated than a mere funfair: It boasts a pantomime theater, an open-air stage, elegant restaurants (24 in all), and frequent classical, jazz, and rock concerts. There are also fantastic flower displays both in the lush gardens and floating on the swan-filled ponds. On weekends elaborate fireworks displays are presented, as well as maneuvers by the Tivoli Guard, a youth version of the Queen's Royal Guard. See Tivoli at least once by night, when 100,000 colored lanterns illuminate the Chinese Pagoda and the main fountain. *Vesterbrogade 3, tel. 33/15–10–01 Admission, not including rides: DKr30 adults, DKr15 children. Open Apr. 24–Sept. 15, daily 10 AM–midnight.*

At the southern end of the gardens, on Hans Christian Ander-
33 sen Boulevard, is the neoclassical **Ny Carlsberg Glyptotek** (New Carlsberg Museum), one of Copenhagen's most imposing museums. Its nucleus is a lush indoor garden—a green sanctuary where you can write a few postcards and relax. From there, start to explore the nooks and chambers that house a vast collection of works by Gauguin and Degas and other Impressionists, as well as an extensive assemblage of Egyptian, Greek, Roman, and French sculpture—and what is considered the largest collection of Etruscan art outside Italy. The museum was a gift to the city from Carl Jacobsen, founder of the Carlsberg Breweries, and is maintained by the Carlsberg Foundation, one of the largest cultural and scientific benefactors in Denmark. *Dantes Plads 7, tel. 33/91–10–65. Admission: DKr15 adults (free Wed. and Sun.), children free. Open Sept.–Apr., Tues.–Sat. noon–3, Sun. 10–4; May–Aug., Tues.–Sun. 10–4.*

Tucked between St. Jørgens Lake and the main arteries of
34 Vesterbrogade and Gammel Kongevej is the **Tycho Brahe Planetarium,** opened in 1989. The modern, cylindrical building (which appears sliced at an angle) is filled with astronomy exhibits and an Omnimax Theater that takes visitors on a visual journey up through space and down under the seas. *Gammel Kongevej 10, tel. 33/12–12–24. Admission: DKr40 for exhibition and theater, noon–5; DKr50 for exhibition and theater, 6–10 PM; exhibition only DKr10. Reservations advised for theater. (Planetarium officials advise that movie is not suitable for children under 7.) Open daily 10:30–9.*

Continue down Vesterbrogade into Copenhagen's equivalent of New York's Lower East Side. Populated with many of the city's immigrants, students, and union workers, it's full of ethnic groceries, discount shops, and inexpensive international restaurants. Parallel to it is **Istedgade,** Copenhagen's half-hearted red-light district, where Mom 'n' Pop kiosks stand side by side with seedy porn shops. Though relatively safe, with several fine hotels, avoid it for a late-night stroll.

35 Farther down Vesterbrogade is **Københavns Bymuseum** (Copenhagen City Museum), a 17th-century building flanked by a meticulously maintained model of medieval Copenhagen. Inside, there are exhibits chronicling the city's history and a memorial room for philosopher Søren Kierkegaard, the father of existentialism. *Vesterbrogade 59, tel. 31/31–07–72. Admission free. Open May–Sept., Tues.–Sun. 10–4; Oct.–Apr., Tues.–Sun. 1–4.*

Short Excursions from Copenhagen

Eksperimentarium

Eight kilometers (6 miles) north of Copenhagen is the beachside town of Hellerup, where the newest attraction is the user-friendly **Eksperimentarium** (Experimentarium). More than 200 exhibitions are clustered in 15 Discovery Islands, each exploring a different facet of science, technology, and natural phenomena with a dozen hands- and body-on exhibits. Visitors can take skeleton-revealing bike rides, measure their lung capacity, stir up magnetic goop, play ball on a jet stream, and gyrate to gyroscopes. Take bus No. 6 from Rådhus Plads or the S-train to Hellerup. *Tuborg Havnevej, tel. 39/27–33–33. Admission: DKr40 adults Mon., Tues., and Fri. before 1; DKr45 adults Tues. and Fri. after 1; DKr50 adults weekends and holidays; DKr30 children Mon.–Fri. and DKr35 children weekends and holidays. Discounts for combined adult/child admission. Open Mon., Wed., and Fri. 9–6; Tues. and Thurs. 9–9; weekends 11–6.*

Louisiana

A world-class collection of modern art is housed in the **Louisiana,** a museum on the "Danish Riviera," the north Sjælland coast. Even those who can't tell a Rauschenberg from a Rembrandt should make the 35-kilometer (22-mile) trip to see this elegant rambling structure surrounded by a large park. In the permanent collection, Warhols vie for space with Giacomettis and Picassos. There are contemporary exhibits, as well as concerts and films. In the summer, Danes bring their children and picnic in the sculpture garden. The museum is a half-hour train ride from Copenhagen and a 10-minute walk from the station. It's also accessible by the E4 highway and the more scenic coastal road, Strandvejen. *Gammel Strandvej 13, Humlebæk, tel. 42/19–07–19. Admission: DKr40 adults, children free. Open Mon., Tues., and Thurs.–Sun. 10–5; Wed. 10–10.*

Dragør

On the island of Amager, less than an hour from Copenhagen, is the quaint fishing town of **Dragør** (pronounced Drah-wer). The town's history is separated from the rest of Copenhagen's because it was settled by Dutch farmers in the 16th century. The community was ordered by King Christian II to provide fresh produce and flowers for the royal court. Still meticulously maintained, it has neat rows of white, terra-cotta tiled houses trimmed with wandering ivy, roses, and the occasional waddling goose. The oldest house in town contains a museum of furniture, costumes, drawings, and model ships. Its chimney is twisted (so the devil won't find his way down). The small **museum** in Store Magleby, an old half-timbered farmhouse, displays Amager furniture, dresses, and needlework. Take bus No. 30 or 33 from Råhuspladsen. *Strandlinien 4, tel. 31/53–41–06. Admission: DKr10. Open May–Sept., weekdays 2–5, weekends noon–6.*

Frilandsmuseet

Just north of Copenhagen is Lyngby, and the **Frilandsmuseet,** an open-air building museum. About 100 farmhouses representing different periods of Danish history have been painstakingly deconstructed, moved, reconstructed, and filled with period furniture and tools. In addition to its historical appeal, the museum is located in a verdant setting of trees and gardens. Bring a lunch and plan to spend the day. Take the S-train to either the Lyngby or Jægersborg Station and then the local Jægersborg–Nærum train. *Frilandsmuseet. 100 Kongevejen, Lyngby, tel. 42/85–02–92. Admission: DKr15 adults, DKr5* *children. Open Mar. 15–Sept., Tues.–Sun. 10–5; Oct.–Nov. 14, Tues.–Sun. 10–3.*

Copenhagen for Free

Many museums in Copenhagen skip admission fees or offer free entrance on certain evenings or days. These museums include the Hirschsprungske Collection (admission free), the Royal Library (admission free), Frihedsmuseet (admission free), the Ny Carlsberg Glyptotek (admission free Wed. and Sun.), Kunstindustrimuseet (admission free weekdays), and the Bymuseum (admission free). The **Davids Samling** (Kronprinsessegade 30, tel. 33/13–55–64), which has an unusual exhibition of Islamic art, European handicrafts, and porcelain; the **Royal Copenhagen Museum** (Amagertorv on Strøget 6, tel. 33/13–71–81); and the **Zoological Museum** (Universitetsparken 15, tel. 31/35–41–11), with models and exhibits of animal life, are also free. Of course, the green parks and gardens, which include the Botanical and Kings Gardens are free, too, and on a sunny day, priceless.

What to See and Do with Children

Few cities are as accommodating to children and families. Most museums have free or half-price admission for kids, in addition to providing strollers and changing facilities for the smallest travelers. **Tivoli** shouldn't be missed, but as it costs between DKr10 and 20 per ride, the most zealous thrill-seekers should buy a **Tur-Pas,** which affords admission and tickets for all rides for about DKr100. Nearby is the **Benneweis Circus** (Jernbanegade 8, tel. 31/14–44–43), an old-fashioned family-run circus with acrobats, seals, horses, and an army of clowns. Also in town is the **Sømods Bolcher** (Nørregade 36, tel. 33/12–60–46, open Mon.–Fri. 10–5:30 and Sat. 10–1), where hard candy is made the traditional way by pulling and cutting it by hand. Up north, near the Klampenborg train station, Copenhagen's other amusement park, **Bakken** (tel. 31/63–73–00; admission free; open Apr.–Sept., daily noon–midnight) has more old-time fun. Once you arrive at the train station, walk through the lush Dyrehaven (Deer Park) or take a horse-drawn carriage. The park-bound **Zoological Gardens** (Roskildevej 32; tel. 36/30–25–55; admission DKr40 adults, DKr20 children 3–11; open daily 9–6) boasts more than 2,000 animals and a small petting zoo. There's also the fantasy world of the **Toy Museum** (Valkendorfsgade 13; tel. 33/14–10–09; admission DKr20 adults, DKr10 children; open weekdays 9–4, weekends 10–4) and **Danmarks Akvarium** (Charlottenlund; tel. 31/62–32–83; admission DKr30 adults, DKr15 children; open Apr.–Sept., daily 10–6 and Oct.–Mar., daily 10–4).

Off the Beaten Track

Those nostalgic for the '60s counterculture can head to **Christiania** (at the corner of Prinsessegade and Badsmandsstræde, on Christianshavn), an anarchists' commune founded in 1971 when students occupied army barracks. Giant wall cartoons preach drugs and peace, but the inhabitants are less fond of cameras and picture-taking—which they forbid within the compound.

The **Arbejdermuseet** (Workers Museum; Rømersgade 22, tel. 33/13–01–52; admission DKr20 adults, DKr5 children; open Tues.–Fri. 10–3, Wed. 10–8, weekends 11–4), chronicles the history of the working class from 1850 to the present, with life-size "day-in-the-life-of" exhibits.

W.Ø. Larsens Tobaksmuseet (the W.Ø. Larsen's Tobacco Museum; Amagertorv 9, tel. 33/12–20–50; admission free; open weekdays 9:30–5) exhibits pipes made in every conceivable shape from every conceivable material (including a tiny one not bigger than an embroidery needle), paintings, drawings, and an amazing collection of smoking accoutrements.

The former Danish Surgical Academy is now home of the **Medicinsk Historisk Museum** (Medical History Museum; Bredgade 62, tel. 33/15–25–01; admission free; open Tues., Thur., and Sat. at 2 for tour in English) and has a small collection of human body parts, primitive surgical apparatus, and other exhibits.

Shopping

Copenhagen seems designed with shoppers in mind. Small, easy to explore on foot, and conveniently crammed with boutiques and specialty stores, the city's core is a showcase for world-famous Danish design and craftsmanship. The best buys are luxury items like crystal, porcelain, silver, and furs. Look for sales (*tilbud* or *udsalg* in Danish) and check antique and second-hand shops for classics at cut-rate prices.

Although prices are inflated by a hefty 22% Value Added Tax (Danes call it MOMS), non-EC citizens can receive an 18% refund (*see* Shopping in Staying in Denmark, *above*). For more details and a list of all tax-free shops, ask at the tourist board for a copy of the *Tax-Free Shopping Guide*, or call 36/72–00–66.

Shopping Districts/ Streets/Malls

The pedestrian-only **Strøget** and adjacent **Købmagergade** are *the* shopping streets, but wander down the smaller streets for lower priced, offbeat stores. You'll find the most exclusive shops on **Ny Adelgade, Grønnegade,** and **Pistolstræde,** but remember taxes and transportation costs push designer prices up in Denmark. **Scala,** the city's glittering café- and boutique-studded mall is across the street from Tivoli and boasts a trendy selection of clothing stores. Farther down, on **Vesterbrogade,** you'll find discount stores—especially leather and clothing shops.

Department Stores

Illums (Østergade 52, tel. 31/14–40–02), not to be confused with Illums Bolighus (*see* Design, *below*), is a well-stocked department store with a lovely rooftop café. **Magasin** (Kongens Nytorv 13, tel. 31/11–44–33), the largest department store in Scandinavia, occupies nearly an entire block and includes an excellent gourmet grocery.

Street Markets

Check with the tourist board or the tourist magazine *Copenhagen This Week* for flea markets. Bargaining is expected. For a good overview of antiques and junk, visit the flea market at **Israels Plads** (near Nørreport Station; open May–Oct., Sat. 8–2). It is run by more than 100 professional dealers, and prices are steep, but there are loads of classic Danish porcelain, silver, jewelry, and crystal, plus books, prints, postcards, and more. Slightly smaller, with lower prices and more junk, are the markets behind **Frederiksberg Rådhus** (Saturday morning) and at

Lyngby Storcenter near the Lyngby station (every Sunday morning), both in summer.

Specialty Stores

Antiques For silver, porcelain, and crystal, the well-stocked shops on **Bredgade** are upscale and expensive. Visit **Royal Copenhagen Antiques** (Bredgade 11, tel. 33/14–02–29), **Kaabers Antikvariat** (Skindergade 34, tel. 33/15–41–77) for old and rare books and prints, **Branner's Old Book Shop** (Bredgade 10, tel. 33/15–91–87), **Antik 14** (Læderstræde 14, tel. 33/14–41–58) for Oriental antiques, **H. Danielsens** (Læderstræde 11, tel. 33/13–02–74) for silver, Christmas plates, and porcelain, and **Danborg Gold and Silver** (Holbergsgade 17, tel. 33/32–93–94) for estate jewelry and silver flatwear. For furniture, **Ravnsborggade** has dozens of stores that carry traditional pine, oak, and mahogany furniture, in addition to smaller items like lamps and tableware. (Most sell tax free and can arrange shipping.) Call the **Association of Antique Dealers in Ravnsborggade** (tel. 35/37–27–17) for information.

Audio Equipment For high-tech design and acoustics, **Bang & Olufsen** (Østergade 3, tel. 33/15–04–22) is so renowned, its products are in the permanent design collection of New York's Museum of Modern Art. **Fredgaard** (Østergade 26, tel. 33/13–60–80) shows off B&O audio and video products, too, but in *HG*-style showrooms.

Clothing Retail clothing tends to be expensive and trendy, so stick to the best stores—where you can be sure of the quality. These include: **Brødrene Andersen** (Østergade 7–9, tel. 33/15–15–77), for Hugo Boss, Hermes, and Pringle sweaters for men; **Jens Sørensen** (Østergade 61, tel. 33/12–26–02) for fine men's and women's clothing and outerwear, and a Burberry's collection; **Petitgas Chapeaux** (Købmagergade 5, tel. 33/13–62–70) for old-fashioned men's hats, and the **Company Store** (Frederigsgade 24, tel. 33/11–35–55) for trendy, youthful styles. If you are interested in the newest Danish designs, keep your eyes open for cooperatives and designer-owned stores. For inventive, handmade women's clothing by two of the city's best young designers, visit **Met Mari** (Vestergade 11, tel. 33/15–87–25) and **McVerdi** (St. Regnegade 22, tel. 33/15–10–14). Thick traditional patterned and solid Scandinavian sweaters are available at the **Sweater Market** (Frederiksberggade 15, tel. 33/15–27–73), while there's a smaller selection of more modern styles (and loads of gift ideas) at **Artium** (Vesterbrogade 1, tel. 33/12–34–88).

Crystal and Porcelain Minus the VAT, Danish classics like Holmegaard crystal and Royal Copenhagen porcelain are less expensive than back home. Signed art glass is always more expensive, but be on the lookout for seconds, secondhand, and unsigned pieces. Among the specialists: **Bing & Grøndahl** (a part of Royal Copenhagen) (Amagertorv 6, tel. 33/12–26–86), **Chicago** (Vimmelskaftet 47 on Strøget, tel. 33/12–30–31), **Skandinavisk Glas** (Ny Østergade 4, tel. 33/13–80–95), and **Holmegaards Glass** (Østergade 15, tel. 33/12–44–77). Both the main Royal Copenhagen shop (Amagertorv 6, tel. 33/13–71–81) and the **Royal Porcelain Factory** (Smallegade 45, tel. 31/86–48–48) have firsts and seconds.

Design Part gallery, part department store, **Illums Bolighus** (Amagertorv 10, tel. 31/14–19–41) shows off cutting-edge Danish and international design—art glass, porcelain, silverware, carpets, and loads of grown-up toys. **Lysberg, Hansen and Therp** (Bredgade 3, tel. 33/14–47–87), one of the most prestigious interior-design firms in Denmark, has sumptuous showrooms done up in traditional and modern styles. There's also an exquisite gift shop with silk, silver, and leather accessories. **Interieur** (Gothersgade 91, tel. 33/13–15–56) displays fresh Danish style as well as a chic kitchenware shop. Master florist **Tage Andersen** (Ny Adelgade 12, tel. 33/93–09–13) has a fantasy-infused shop and studio full of one-of-a-kind gifts and arrangements.

Fur Because of a glut in the international market, fur prices—especially for mink—have dropped dramatically. A SAGA label means that the animals (often mink or fox) are ranched—never trapped in the wild. Furs are graded on a system of Xs, with a 4X the best. **A.C. Bang** (Østergade 27, tel. 33/15–17–26) is Copenhagen's venerable furrier—and that of the Royal Court since 1817. **Birger Christensen** (Østergade 38, tel. 33/11–55–55) is just slightly less expensive. **Otto D. Madsen** (Vesterbrogade 1, tel. 33/13–41–10), not as chichi, has some of the best prices in town.

Silver Check the silver standard of a piece by its stamp. Three towers and "925S" (which means 925 parts out of 1,000) mark sterling. Two towers are used for silver plate. The "826S" stamp was used until the 1920s. For the best, visit **Georg Jensen** (Østergade 40, tel. 33/11–40–80), an elegant, austere shop aglitter with velvet-cushioned sterling. (The same pieces are available at Royal Copenhagen, down the street, which owns Georg Jensen.) **Peter Krog** (4 Bredgade, tel. 33/12–45–55), **Ketti Hartogsohn** (Palægade 8, tel. 33/15–53–98), and the **English Silver House** (Pilestræde 4, tel. 33/14–83–81) are excellent for used silver at prices 20% to 40% lower. Also visit the city's largest (and brightest) silver store, **Sølvkælderen** (Kompagnistræde 1, tel. 33/13–36–34). The **Tin Centret** (Pewter Center; Ny Østergade 2, tel. 33/14–82–00) has a huge selection of mostly new Scandinavian and European pewter, and a small selection of secondhand pieces.

Sports and Fitness

Bicycling Copenhagen is a cyclist's city. Bike rentals (DKr100–200 deposit and DKr30–50 per day) and free city bikes are available throughout the city (*see* Getting Around, *above*), and most roads have bike lanes. Follow all traffic signs and signals; bicycle lights must be used at night. For more information, contact the **Dansk Cyclist Forbund** (Danish Cyclist Federation, Rømersgade 7, tel. 33/32–31–21).

Golf Denmark's best course (where international tournaments are played) is the 18-hole **Rungsted Golf Klub** (Vestre Stationsvej 16, tel. 42/86–34–44) with a 24 handicap for men, 29 for women. The 18-hole **Københavns Golf Klub** (Dyrehaven 2, tel. 31/63–04–83) is said to be Scandinavia's oldest. Admission (green fees, DKr150–200) must be reserved at least two days in advance—longer in the summer.

Health and Fitness Clubs A day-pass for weights and aerobics at the **Fitness Club** is DKr80 (Vesterbrogade at Scala, tel. 33/32–10–02). **Form og Figur** (Form and Figure) offers one-hour aerobic classes for DKr50 at the SAS Globetrotter Hotel in Amager (Engvej 171, tel. 31/55–00–70), and weights, treadmill, and stationary bikes for DKr75 at the SAS Scandinavia Hotel (Amager Boulevard 70, tel. 31/54–28–88) and Øbro-Hallen (Ved Idrætsparken 1, tel. 35/26–79–39).

Horseback Riding You can ride at the **Dyrehavebakken** (Deer Forest Hills) in Lyngby, at the **Fortunens Ponyudlejning** (Pony Rental) (Ved-Fortunen 33, tel. 45/87–60–58). A 50-minute session, where both experienced and inexperienced riders go out with a guide, costs DKr70.

Jogging The 6-kilometer (4-mile) loop around the three swan-filled lakes just west of the center of the city—**St. Jorgens, Peblinge,** and **Sortedams**—is a runner's heaven. There are also paths at the **Rosenborg Have, Frederiksberg Garden** (near the Frederiksberg station, at the corner of Frederiksberg Allé and Pile Allé), and the **Dyrehaven** north of the city near Klampenborg.

Swimming Swimming is very popular and pools are crowded but well maintained. Separate bath tickets can also be purchased. Local pools (admission: DKr20–40) include **Frederiksberg Svømmehal** (Helgesvej 29, tel. 38/88–00–71), **Øbro Hallen** (Ved Idrætsparken 3, tel. 31/42–13–65), **Vesterbro Svømmehal** (Angelgade 4, tel. 31/22–05–00), and **Lyngby Svømmehal** (Lundoftevej 53, tel. 42/87–44–56).

Tennis Courts for guests (DKr100 per hour; open to guests before 1 PM only) are available at **Københavns Boldklub** (Pile Allé14, tel. 31/30–23–00), **Hellerup Idræts Klub** (Hartmannsvej 37, tel. 31/62–14–28), the **Skovshoved Idræts Forening** (Krersvej 5A, tel. 31/64–23–83), and the **Gentofte Tennis Club** (Skolevej 23, tel. 31/68–26–63).

Spectator Sports

Soccer Danish soccer fans call themselves *Rolegans* (which loosely translates to well-behaved fans), as opposed to hooligans, and idolize the national team's soccer players as super-stars. When the rivalry is most intense (especially against Sweden and Norway), fans don face-paint, wear head-to-toe red-and-white, incessantly wave the *Dannebrog* (Danish flag), and have a good time whether or not they win. The biggest stadium in town for national and international games is **Idrætsparken** (P.H. Lengs Allé, tel. 31/42–14–30). Tickets (DKr100 for standing room, DKr200 for seats) can be bought at the gates or at Ved Vesterport 7 (tel. 33/15–13–11).

Beaches

North of Copenhagen along the old beach road, **Strandvejen,** there's a string of lovely old seaside towns and beaches. The **Bellevue beach** (across the street from the Klampenborg station) is packed with locals and also has cafés, kiosks, and surfboard rentals, while **Charlottelund** (bus No. 6 from Rådhusplads) is a bit more private. **Vedbæk,** farther north, is less crowded. The summer water temperature along this coast is 65°–68°F.

Dining

Food is one of the great pleasures of a stay in Copenhagen, a city with over 2,000 restaurants. Traditional Danish fare spans all price categories: You can order a light lunch of traditional *smørrebrød* (sandwiches), munch alfresco from a street-side *pølser* (sausage) cart, or dine out on Limfjord oysters and local plaice. Even the most upscale restaurants have moderate-price fixed menus, but the cost of wine increases totals enormously. Happily, the local Tuborg and Carlsberg beers complement the traditional fare better than wine.

The Danes are Francophiles when it comes to fine dining, and many restaurants are fond of combining fresh, local ingredients with French preparation. The city's more affordable ethnic restaurants are concentrated in Vesterbro, Nørrebro, and the side streets off Strøget.

Highly recommended restaurants are indicated by a star ★.

Very Expensive

Fiskekælderen. Copenhagen's finest seafood restaurant has dark wooden benches and an air of minimalist chic, but in its lime-and-white setting, the menu remains classic—with such offerings as turbot in puff pastry, grilled fjord salmon with a hunk of lobster butter, and a sumptuous bouillabaisse. *Ved Stranden 18, tel. 33/12–20–11. Reservations required. Dress: casual but neat. AE, DC, MC, V. No weekend lunch. Closed Dec. 24–26 and 30, Jan. 1, Easter.*

Kong Hans. Five centuries ago, this was a Nordic vineyard, but now it's one of Scandinavia's finest restaurants. Chef Daniel Letz's French-inspired cuisine uses the freshest local and French ingredients, while the setting is subterranean and mysterious, with whitewashed walls and arched ceilings. Try the airy duck-liver mousse, surrounded by fresh tomato purée, or the oysters Charentaise. *Vingårdsstræde 6, tel. 33/11–68–68. Reservations advised. Jacket advised. AE, DC, MC, V. No lunch. Closed mid-July–mid-Aug. and Sun.*

★ **Skt. Gertrudes Kloster.** The history of this medieval monastery goes back 600 years, when even then, its vaulted stone interiors welcomed tradesmen and wayfarers. The dining room is bedecked with hundreds of icons, the only light provided by 1,500 candles. The French menu is extensive, with such specials as fresh fillet of halibut steamed in oyster sauce and l'Alsace duck breast in sherry vinaigrette. *32 Hauser Plads, tel. 33/14–66–30. Reservations required. Jacket and tie advised. AE, DC, MC, V. No lunch. Closed Dec. 24–Jan. 1 and Easter.*

Expensive

Els. When it opened in 1853, the intimate Els was the place to be seen before the theater, and the painted muses on the walls still watch diners rush to make an eight o'clock curtain. The antique wooden columns and furniture complement owner and chef Ole Mathiesen's nouvelle Danish/French menu. It changes daily and incorporates game, fish, and market produce. *Stora Strandestræde 3, tel. 33/14–13–41. Reservations advised. Jacket advised. AE, DC, MC, V.*

Kommandanten. Fancifully decorated by master florist Tage Andersen, with brushed iron and copper furniture, down pillows and foliage-flanked lights, this is among the city's most chic dinner spots, attracting well-heeled business people and local celebrities. The adventuresome international fare includes rabbit with bouillon-cooked lentils, herbs, and bacon and marinated salmon with oysters and parsley. *Ny Adelgade 7, tel. 33/12–09–90. Reservations advised. Jacket advised. AE, DC, MC, V. Closed July, Sat. lunch, and Sun.*

La Brasserie. This is the place where Copenhagen's see-and-be-seen set goes to eat, drink, and mingle. Diners enjoy French-

Dining

L'Alsace, **14**
La Brasserie, **15**
Cafe Asbæk, **10**
Café Restaurant Philippe, **7**
Els, **11**
Fiskekælderen, **23**
Flyvefisker, **21**
Greens, **8**
Havfruen, **16**
Ida Davidsen, **6**
Kasmir, **2**
Kommandanten, **9**
Kong Hans, **24**
Pakhuskælderen, **25**
Peder Oxe, **13**
Quatro Fontane, **1**
Riz Raz, **22**
Skt. Gertrudes Kloster, **5**

Lodging

Altea Hotel Scala, **29**
Ascot, **19**
Copenhagen Admiral, **17**
D'Angleterre, **15**
Kong Frederik, **20**
Missionhotellet Nebo, **28**
Neptun, **12**
Nyhavn71, **25**
Plaza, **27**
SAS Scandinavia, **30**
Sheraton, **18**
Skovshoved, **3**
Triton, **26**
Viking, **4**

Copenhagen Dining and Lodging

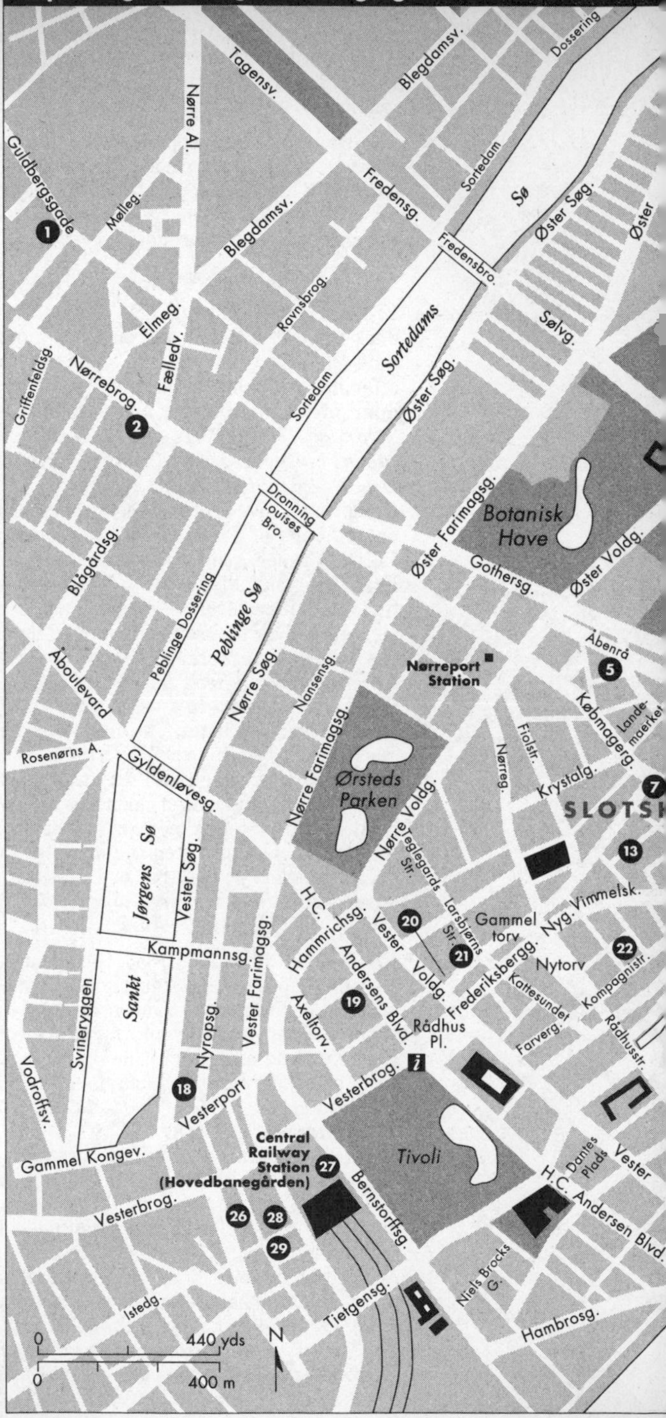

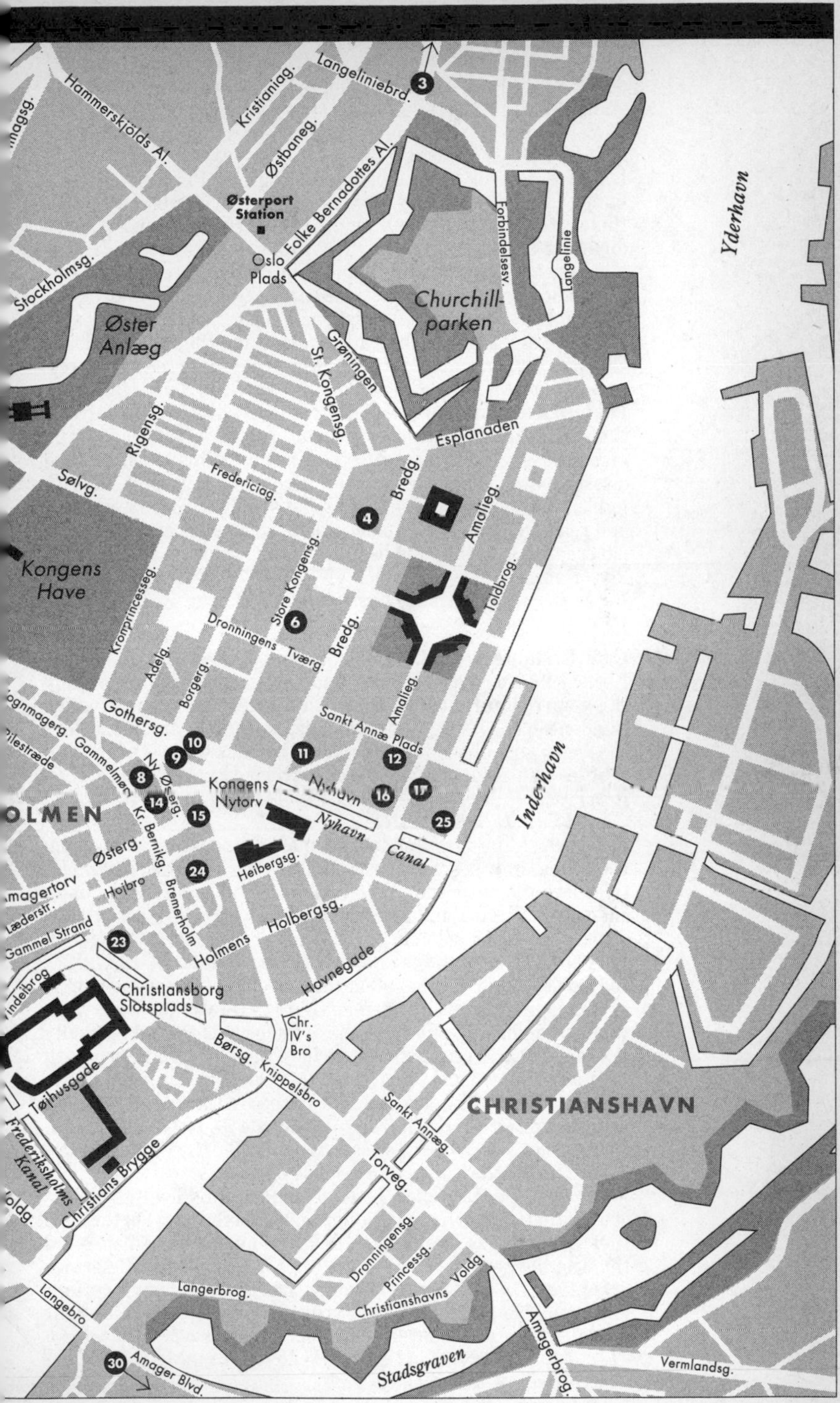
Langeliniebrd.
3
Hammerskjölds Al.
Kristianiag.
Østbaneg.
Folke Bernadottes Al.
Østerport Station
Oslo Plads
Stockholmsg.
Øster Anlæg
Churchill-parken
Forbindelsesv.
Langelinie
Yderhavn
Grøningen
St. Kongensg.
Rigensg.
Esplanaden
Sølvg.
Fredericiag.
Bredg.
Amalieg.
4
Kongens Have
Kronprincesseg.
Store Kongensg.
Toldbrog.
6
Dronningens Tværg.
Adelg.
Borgerg.
Gothersg.
Sankt Annæ Plads
10
9
11
12
8
Ny Østerg.
Kongens Nytorv
Nyhavn
16
17
14
15
25
OLMEN
Inderhavn
Nyhavn Canal
Østerg.
Kr. Bernikg.
24
Heibergsg.
Amagertorv
Højbro
Bremerholm
Læderstr.
Gammel Strand
Holbergsg.
23
Holmens
Havnegade
Christiansborg Slotsplads
Chr. IV's Bro
Børsg.
Knippelsbro
Tøjhusgade
CHRISTIANSHAVN
Sankt Annæg.
Frederiksholms Kanal
Christians Brygge
Torveg.
Dronningensg.
Princessg.
Langerbrog.
Christianshavns Voldg.
Langebro
Amagerbrog.
30
Amager Blvd.
Stadsgraven
Vermlandsg.

inspired food in charming bistro surroundings under a giant illuminated clock. During lunch, there's a smørrebrød menu, while at night, the vivacious crowds relish à la carte items like antipasto, salads, escargot, sautéed duck liver, and more substantial entrées. *Hotel D'Angleterre, Kongens Nytorv 34, tel. 33/32-01-22. Reservations advised. Dress: casual but neat. AE, DC, MC, V. Closed Sun.*

★ **L'Alsace.** Set in the cobbled courtyard of Pistolstræde and hung with paintings by Danish surrealist Wilhelm Freddie, this restaurant is peaceful and quiet, attracting such diverse diners as Queen Margrethe, Elton John, and Pope Paul II. The hand-drawn menu lists oysters from Brittany, terrine de foie gras, and choucrôute à la Strasbourgeois (a hearty mélange of cold cabbage, homemade sausage, and pork, among other specialties). Ask to sit in the patio overlooking the courtyard. *Ny Østergade 9, tel. 33/14-57-43. Reservations advised. Dress: casual but neat. AE, DC, MC, V. Closed Sun. and holidays.*

Pakhuskælderen. Surrounded by thick white walls and raw timbers, Nyhavn 71 Hotel's intimate restaurant attracts a mix of business and holiday guests. Known for his fresh seafood classics, Chef Finn Lytje often accompanies fresh fish with light cream sauces. Baked red mullet soufflé with lobster meat, and roast venison with homemade herb noodles and horseradish cream are among his best creations. There's also an excellent Danish buffet at lunch. *Nyhavn 71, tel. 33/11-85-85. Reservations required. Dress: casual but neat. AE, DC, MC, V.*

Moderate

★ **Cafe Restaurant Philippe.** Checkered tablecloths and corny French music, Francophiles and love-struck couples supply this cozy restaurant with Gallic ambience. The Franco-Danish kitchen serves hearty warm salads, fresh fish, and meat. Try the warm goat cheese salad followed by duck thigh stuffed with truffles in a cognac sauce. *Gråbrødretorv 2, tel. 33/32-92-92. Reservations advised. Dress: casual but neat. AE, DC, MC, V. Closed Sun. lunch and Dec. 23-Jan. 1.*

Havfruen. A life-size wooden mermaid swings decorously from the ceiling in this small, rustic fish restaurant in Nyhavn. Natives love the cozy, maritime-bistro air and come for the daily changing French-and-Danish menu, which utilizes cream sauces and fresh salmon, turbot, and cod. *Nyhavn 39, tel. 33/11-11-38. Reservations advised. Dress: casual. DC, MC, V.*

Ida Davidsen. Five generations old, this world-renowned lunch spot is synonymous with smørrebrød. Dimly lit, with worn wooden tables and photographs of famous visitors, it's usually packed. Creative sandwiches include the H.C. Andersen with liver pâté, bacon, and tomatoes and the airplane clipper—steak tartare shaped like a plane and topped with caviar, smoked salmon, and egg yolk. *Store Kongensgade 70, tel. 33/91-36-55. Reservations required. Dress: casual. DC, MC, V. No dinner. Closed weekends, July, and Dec. 24-Jan. 1.*

Peder Oxe. Located on a historic square, this lively bistro is countrified, with rustic antiques and 15th-century Portuguese tiles. All entrées, which include grilled steaks and fish—and the best burgers in town—come with an excellent self-service salad bar. Damask-covered tables are set with heavy cutlery and opened bottles of hearty Pyrenées wine. A clever call-light for the waitress is above each table. *Gråbrødretorv 11, tel. 33/11-00-77. Reservations advised. Dress: casual. D, MC, V. Closed Dec. 24-26 and Jan. 1.*

Inexpensive

Café Asbæk. The ground level of a four-story modern art gallery, this bright little establishment makes creative use of fresh ingredients. The menu changes every month—though typical offerings include inventive salads, soups, sandwiches, and omelets—while the art on the walls changes with every exhibition. The artist showing in the downstairs gallery designs the tablecloths as well! *Ny Adelgade 8, tel. 33/12–24–16. Reservations not required. Dress: casual. AE, DC, MC, V. No dinner.*

Flyvefisker. Silvery stenciled fish swim along blue and yellow walls in this funky vegetarian eatery. More experimental than Greens (*see below*), the constantly changing daily menu makes use of salads, nuts, legumes, and fish. Popular specialties include an apple and beet salad, vegetable burgers, and salmon with shiitake mushrooms. *Lars Bjørnstræde 18, tel. 33/14–95–15. No reservations. Dress: casual. No credit cards. Closed Sat. evening, Sun., and holidays.*

Greens. Located off Strøget on a small courtyard, Greens is fashionably rustic and a mecca for the health-conscious. Well-dressed bohemians duck in here for the classical music and the vegetarian choices like hummus and warm pita bread, organic pizza, stuffed eggplants, and other healthful options from a buffet that relies heavily on grains, natural sweeteners, fresh fruits, and vegetables. *Grønegade 12–14, tel. 33/15–16–90. No reservations. Dress: casual. MC, V. Closed Sun.*

Kasmir. This quiet, carpet-shrouded Indian restaurant is a favorite with locals, who come for the unusual vegetarian and fish menu. Specialties include tandoori-fried salmon, a hearty lentil soup, and the basic side dishes—like *bhajis* (fried vegetables in a tomato sauce), *raita* (yogurt and cucumbers), and *nan* (thick round bread). *Nørrebrogade 35, tel. 35/37–54–71. Reservations advised on weekend. Dress: casual but neat. AE, MC, V. Closed Dec. 24–25.*

Quatro Fontane. On a corner west of the lakes, one of Copenhagen's best Italian restaurants is a busy, noisy, two-story affair, packed tight with marble-topped tables and a steady flow of young Danes. Served by chatty Italian waiters, the homemade food includes cheese or beef ravioli or cannelloni, linguine with clam sauce, and thick pizza. Leave room for the totally immoral ice cream or take some with you from the carry-out in Frederiksberg (Falkonér Allé, tel. 38/39–49–82). *Guldbergsgade 3, tel. 31/39–39–31. Reservations advised. Dress: casual. No credit cards.*

★ **Riz Raz.** Located on a corner off Strøget, this Middle Eastern restaurant hops with young locals, who pack it to bursting on weekends. The all-you-can-eat buffet is heaped with lentils, tomatoes and potatoes, olives, hummus, warm pita bread, *kufte* (Middle Eastern meatballs), yogurt and cucumbers, pickled vegetables, bean salads, and occasionally pizza. *Kompagnistræde 20, tel. 33/15–05–75. Reservations advised (required on weekend). Dress: casual. DC, MC, V. Closed Dec. 24–25 and Jan. 1.*

Lodging

Copenhagen is well served by a wide range of hotels, but overall, they are among Europe's most expensive. The hotels around the seedy red-light district of Istedgade (which looks more dangerous than it is) are the least expensive. During summer, reservations are recommended, but should you arrive without one, try the booking service at the **Væelseavivsning** kiosk (Room Service booth) in the central station. This service will also locate rooms in private homes, with rates starting at DKr140 for a single. Young travelers should head for **Huset** (Rådhusstræde 13, tel. 33/15–65–18); after hours, check the bulletin board outside for suggestions on accommodations. Breakfast is included in the room rate at the following hotels unless indicated otherwise.

Highly recommended establishments are indicated by a star ★.

Very Expensive

★ **D'Angleterre.** Just off Kongens Nytorv, the city's finest hotel welcomes royalty and rock stars in palatial surroundings. Behind its imposing New Georgian facade is an English-style sitting room, while standard guest rooms are furnished in pastels, with overstuffed chairs and modern and antique furniture. The spit-and-polish staff accommodates every wish. *Kongens Nytorv 34, 1050 KBH K, tel. 33/12–00–95, fax 33/12–11–18. 130 rooms with bath, 28 suites. Facilities: 2 restaurants, bar, 24-hour room service, concierge, meeting rooms, shops, parking. Breakfast not included. AE, DC, MC, V.*

Nyhavn 71. Located in a 200-year-old warehouse, this quiet hotel is a good choice for privacy-seekers. It overlooks the old ships of Nyhavn and the maritime interiors have been preserved with the original thick plaster walls and exposed brick. The rooms are tiny but cozy, with warm woolen spreads, dark woods, soft leather furniture, and criss-crossing timbers. Outside, the Fyrskib 71 Nyhavn, an old light ship, transforms into a summer café. *Nyhavn 71, 1051 KBH K, tel. 33/11–85–85, fax 33/93–15–85. 82 rooms with bath, 6 suites. Facilities: restaurant, bar, room service, concierge, small meeting rooms, parking. Breakfast not included. AE, DC, MC, V.*

SAS Scandinavia. Near the airport, this is Northern Europe's largest hotel, and Copenhagen's token skyscraper. An immense lobby, with cool, recessed lighting and streamlined furniture, gives access to the city's first (and only) casino. The guest rooms are large and somewhat institutional, but offer every modern convenience: It is a good choice if you prefer convenience to character. *Amager Blvd. 70, 2300 KBH S, tel. 33/11–24–23, fax 31/57–01–93. 542 rooms with bath, 41 suites. Facilities: 4 restaurants, 2 bars, casino, health club, pool, sauna, solarium, room service, concierge, meeting rooms, shops, parking. Breakfast not included. AE, DC, MC, V.*

Expensive

Altea Hotel Scala. One of the city's newest, this hotel looks as trendy as Danish hotels can get. A few steps from the main train station, its frescoed and neon exterior stands out in the dingy neighborhood. Inside, the reception area and the nearby bar are art-directed with streamlined teak tables, leather chairs, and granite pillars. Cool purple spreads and furniture are in the slick rooms. Downstairs, there's a sunny breakfast restaurant. *Colbjørnsensgade 13, 1652 KBH V, tel. 31/22–11–00, fax 31/22–21–99. 134 rooms with bath, 3 suites. Facilities: bar, meeting rooms. AE, DC, MC, V. Closed Dec. 24–Jan. 2.*

Kong Frederik. West of Rådhus Pladsen, and a two-minute walk from Strøget, this intimate hotel has the same British style as its sister hotels, the D'Angleterre and Plaza. The difference is the sun-drenched Queen's Garden restaurant, where a hearty hot and cold morning buffet is served in addition to lunch and dinner. The rooms are elegant, with Oriental vases, mauve carpets, and plain blue spreads. Ask for a top room, with a view of the city's towers. *Vester Voldgade 25, 1552 KBH V, tel. 33/12-59-02, fax 33/93-59-01. 110 rooms with bath, 13 suites. Facilities: restaurant, bar, room service, meeting rooms, parking. Breakfast not included. AE, DC, MC, V. Closed Dec. 23–Jan. 2.*

★ **Neptun.** Recently expanded, this elegant, centrally situated hotel was bought years ago with the intention of making it the bohemian gathering place of Copenhagen, but proprietress Bente Noyens has also made it practical. The lobby and lounge are light, with slender furnishings and peach schemes, and next door, there's a fine restaurant. The rooms are posh, with thoughtful details—like pivotal desk and bed lights and bathroom-floor heating. *Skt. Annæ Plads 18–20, 1250 KBH K, tel. 33/13-89-00, fax 33/14-12-50. (In the United States, call Best Western, at 800/528-1234.) 129 rooms with bath, 10 suites. Facilities: restaurant, sauna, solarium, 24-hour room service, meeting rooms, parking, AE, DC, MC, V. Closed Dec. 22–Jan. 2.*

Plaza. The smallest of Copenhagen's three Royal Classic Hotels, the Plaza is more modest than the D'Angleterre or Kong Frederik, but attracts the likes of Tina Turner, Keith Richards, and Willy Brandt. Close to Tivoli and the main station, the Flatiron-style building opens with a stately lobby. The older rooms are scattered with antiques, while newer ones are furnished in a more modern style. *Bernstorffsgade 4, 1557 KBH V, tel. 33/14-92-62, fax 33/93-93-62. 93 rooms with bath, 6 suites. Facilities: restaurant, bar, room service, concierge, small meeting rooms, parking. Breakfast not included. AE, DC, MC, V. Closed Dec. 23–Jan. 2.*

Sheraton. Near the Tycho Brahe Planetarium and Lake District, this 18-story hotel offers impeccable service and standard Sheraton style. The lobby is modern and vast, with dim lighting, plants, and leather sofas, while the rooms are generous and bright, done up in mint and peach and furnished with modern, gray wood furniture. *Vester Søgade 6, 1601 KBH V, tel. 33/14-35-35, fax 33/32-12-23. 471 rooms with bath, 35 suites. Facilities: 2 restaurants, piano bar, massage and beauty services, sauna, solarium, 24-hour room service, nonsmoking floor, concierge, meeting rooms, shops, parking. AE, DC, MC, V.*

Moderate

Ascot. Recently renovated, this charming downtown building features a wrought-iron staircase and an excellent breakfast buffet. The lobby has been classically remodeled in marble and columns, while the recently refurbished guest rooms remain cozy, with modern furniture and bright colors; a few have kitchenettes. *Studiestræde 57, 1554 KBH V, tel. 33/12-60-00, fax 33/14-60-40. 125 rooms with bath, 5 suites, 10 apartments. Facilities: restaurant, bar, meeting rooms, parking. AE, DC, MC, V.*

Copenhagen Admiral. A five-minute stroll from Nyhavn, overlooking old Copenhagen and Amalienborg, the monolithic Admiral was once a grain warehouse, but now affords travelers no-nonsense accommodation. With massive stone walls, broken by rows of tiny windows, it's one of the less expensive top hotels, cutting frills and prices. The guest rooms are spare, with jutting beams and modern prints. *Toldbodgade 24–28, 1253 KBH K, tel. 33/11-82-82, fax 33/32-55-42. 365 rooms with bath, 52 suites. Facilities: restaurant, bar, nightclub, sauna,* *solarium, meeting rooms, shop, parking. Breakfast not included. AE, MC, V.*

Triton. Despite its seedy surroundings, this streamlined hotel attracts a cosmopolitan clientele thanks to a central location in Vesterbro. The large rooms, in blond wood and warm tones, have all been updated with new bathrooms and state-of-the-art fixtures. The buffet breakfast is exceptionally generous, the staff friendly. There are also family rooms, with separate bedroom and foldout couch. *Helgolansgade 7–11, 1653 KBH V, tel. 31/31–32–66. 123 rooms with bath, 2 suites, 4 family rooms. Facilities: bar, meeting room. AE, DC, MC, V.*

Inexpensive

★ **Missionhotellet Nebo.** This budget hotel is located between the main train station and Istedgade's seediest porn shops. The dubious location has no effect on the prim hotel, which is comfortable and well maintained by a friendly staff. The dormlike guest rooms are furnished with industrial carpeting, polished pine furniture, and gray-striped duvet-covers. There are baths, showers, and toilets at the center of each hallway, and downstairs, there's a breakfast restaurant with a tiny courtyard. *Istedgade 6, 1653 KBH V, tel. 31/21–12–17, fax, 31/23–47–74. 96 rooms with bath.*

Skovshoved. A delightful inn 8 kilometers (5 miles) north of town, the Skovshoved is neighbors with a few old fishing cottages beside the yacht harbor. Licensed since 1660, it has retained its provincial charm, though it is fully modernized. Rooms differ—some overlook the sea, while small ones rim the courtyard. The Saison restaurant serves gourmet dishes, but is expensive. *Strandvejen 267, 7920 Charlottelund, tel. 31/64–00–28, fax 31/64–06–72. 20 rooms with bath. Facilities: restaurant, bar, meeting room. AE, DC, MC, V.*

Viking. A comfortable, century-old former mansion near Amalienborg, Nyhavn, and Langelinie, this hotel is close to most sights and Strøget—making it a favorite for inner-city guests. While the halls are decorated with antiques, the rooms are filled with '60s and '70s furniture. Despite the dated decor, they are clean, comfortable, and spacious. *Bredgade 65, 1260 KBH K, tel. 33/12–45–50, fax, 33/12–46–18. 60 rooms, 30 with shower. Facilities: restaurant, 24-hour bar, small meeting room, parking. AE, DC, MC. Closed Dec. 22–Jan. 2.*

The Arts and Nightlife

The Arts

The most complete English calendar of events is included in the tourist magazine ***Copenhagen This Week*** and includes musical and theatrical events, as well as films and exhibitions. Concert and festival information is available from the **Dansk Musik Information Center** (Vimmelskaftet 48, tel. 33/11–20–86). The free newspaper *Neon Guilden* is available in most record shops, cafés, and the tourist office, and lists rock, pop, and jazz concerts, as well as restaurants and events. Copenhagen's main theater and concert season runs from September through May, and tickets can be obtained either directly from theaters and concert halls or from ticket agencies. Box offices include **Arte** (64 Hvidkilevej, no tel.), **Scala** (2 Axeltorv, no tel.), **Fiolstræde/Nørregade Kiosk** for half-price tickets the day of the performance (opposite Norreport Station, no tel.), **Jazzhus Montmartre** (Nørregade 41, 1165 KBH K, tel. 33/13–69–66), **Saga Billetcenter** (Vesterbrogade 25, tel. 31/23–88–00), and **Tivoli Billetcenter** (Vesterbrogade 3, tel. 33/15–10–12).

Opera, Ballet, and Theater Tickets at the **Kongelige Teater** (Royal Theater, tel. 33/14–10–02) are reasonably priced at DKr140 to DKr230. All performances are in Danish. For information and reservations, call the theater. For English-language theater, attend a performance at the **Mermaid Theater** (27 Skt. Peder Stræde, tel. 33/11–43–03).

Film Films open in Copenhagen a few months to a year after their U.S. premier. Nonetheless the Danes are avid viewers, willing to pay DKr60 per ticket, wait in lines for premiers, and read subtitles. Monday nights are traditionally half-price, but tickets go fast and often reservations are not accepted. Any other night, call the theater for a reservation and pick up tickets (which include a seat number) an hour before the movie. Most theaters have a café, so it's not hard to sit back and people-watch before the show. Among the city's alternative venues are **Vester Vov Vov** (Absalonsgade 5, tel. 31/24–42–00), **Klaptræet** (Kultorvet 11–13, tel. 33/13–00–09), and the **Grand** (Mikkel Bryggersgade 8, 33/15–16–11), all of which tend to include arty and foreign films—which are naturally subtitled in Danish.

Nightlife Most nightlife is concentrated in the area in and around **Strøget**, though there are student and "left" cafés and bars in **Nørrebro,** and more upscale and alternative spots in **Østerbro.** Many restaurants, cafés, bars, and clubs stay open after midnight, a few until 5 AM. Copenhagen is famous for jazz, but you'll find night spots catering to almost all musical tastes, from bop to ballroom music—and for the younger crowd, house and rap clubs soundtracked by local DJs. The **Minefield,** the district around Nikolaj Kirke, boasts the highest concentration of trendy discos and dance spots, with cover prices averaging DKr40.

Bars and Lounges Business travelers flock to **Fellini** (SAS Royal Hotel, 1 Hammerichsgade, 33/14–14–12) to dance, mingle, drink outrageously expensive booze, and ogle the not-so-risqué dancers. **Peder Oxe's** basement (Gråbrødretorv 11, tel. 33/11–00–77) is much more casual and young, though nearly impossible to squeeze into on late weekends. The **Library,** located in the Plaza Hotel (4 Bernstorffsgade, tel. 33/14–92–62), is an elegant and romantic spot for a quiet drink, whereas **Hviids Vinstue** (Kongens Nytorv 19, 33/15–10–64) attracts all kinds, young and old, single and coupled, for a quiet glass of wine or cognac. **Vin & Ølgod** (Skindergade 45, tel. 33/13–26–25) is where the same crowd goes to sing, drink vast quantities of beer, and link arms for old-fashioned dancing to corny swing bands.

Cafés Café life appeared in Copenhagen in the '70s and quickly became a compulsory part of its urban existence. The cheapest sit-down eateries in town, with a cappuccino and sandwich often costing less than DKr40, they are lively and relaxed at night. **Café Sommersko** (Kronprinsensgade 6, tel. 33/14–81–89) is the granddaddy, attracting an eclectic crowd during the day and night and hosting classical concerts on Sunday morning. **Krasnapolsky** (Vestergade 10, tel. 33/32–88–00) packs a young, hip, and excruciatingly well-dressed audience at night, a more mixed group for its quiet afternoons. **Café Dan Turrell** (Skt. Regnegade 3, tel. 33/14–10–47), another old café, is as mixed as Sommersko and a favorite with students and intellectuals. **Victors Café** (Ny Østergade 8, tel. 33/13–36–13) is all brass and dark wood, lovely for a light lunch. Among the newer cafés is the very chic **Europe** (Amagertorv 1, tel. 33/14–28–89), where the people-watching and coffee far surpass the fare.

Casinos Casinos are new to Denmark, having just opened in 1991. The **Casino Copenhagen** is at the SAS Scandinavia (Amager Boulevarden 70, tel. 33/11–51–15), with American and French roulette, blackjack, baccarat, and slot machines. Admission is DKr40, and the casino is open 4 PM to 2 AM.

Discos and Dancing Most discos open at 11 PM, have a cover charge (about DKr40), and pile on steep drink prices. Among the popular clubs: **Annabel's** (Lille Kongensgade 16, tel. 33/11–20–20) is young and upscale, while **U-Matic** (Vestergade 10, tel. 33/32–88–00) is young, funky, and full of far-out costumes. The newest club in town is **Axel's** (in Scala on Vesterbrogade, tel. 33/13–03–78), which has three bars and a large dance floor. Chic attendees run tabs on cards that work like temporary credit cards, then pay up when they exit. **Privé** (Ny Østergade 14, tel. 33/13–75–20) attracts a hip, young, well-dressed (tie included) crowd who come for the rock and disco. At **Woodstock** (Vestergade 12, tel. 33/11–20–71) a mixed audience grooves to music of the '60s. **Søpavillionen** (Gyldenløvesgade 24, tel. 33/15–12–24) between St. Jørgen's and Peblinge lakes glows white on the outside, with pop and disco for an older crowd inside. There's also the **Røde Pimpernel** (Hans Christian Andersen Blvd. 7, tel. 33/12–20–32) where an adult audience gathers for dancing to live orchestras, trios, and old-time music.

Jazz Clubs What Copenhagen lacks in cabarets and comedy clubs, it makes up for in jazz clubs. The largest and best-known is **Jazz House Montmartre** (Nørregade 41, tel. 33/12–78–36), which attracts international and Scandinavian greats, often at ticket prices of upwards of DKr145. **De Tre Musketerer** (Nikolaj Plads 25, tel. 33/12–50–67) is dark, brooding, and smoky, with Dixieland to fusion musicians. **La Fontaine** (Kompagnistræde 11, tel. 33/11–60–98) also hosts Scandinavian and, occasionally, international artists. **Tivoli's Jazzhus Slukefter** (Bernstorffsgade 1, tel. 33/11–11–13) attracts some of the biggest names in the world, but it's only open in the summer.

Rock Clubs Copenhagen has a good selection of rock clubs, most of which cost less than DKr40. Almost all are filled with young, fashionable ripped-jean crowds. **Cafeen Funk** (Blegdamsvej 2, tel. 31/35–17–41) plays hard-core funk, while **Pumpehuset** (Studiestræde 52, tel. 33/93–19–60) plays rap and rock. **Huset** (Rådhusstræde 13, tel. 33/32–00–66) has three venues, all under the same roof: **Musikcafeen** hosts international rock, soul, reggae, and funk groups; **Foyérscenen Jazz** hosts local and European jazz names, and occasionally classical groups; **Bar Bue** is the place for punk and experimental Danish and European rock. **Hånd i Hanke** (Griffenfeldstgade 20, tel. 35/37–20–70) sticks to heavier blues and rock.

Gay Bars For more information, call or visit the **Lesbiske og Bøser Landsforening** (Lesbian and Gay Association; Knabostræde 3, Box 1023, 1007 KBH K, tel. 33/13–19–48), which also has a café, bookshop, and 46 years of experience. Check the local free paper *Pan* for listings of nightlife events and clubs, or call the **Gay and Lesbian Information Hotline** (tel. 33/13–01–12).

The **Amigo Bar** (Schønbergsgade 4, tel. 31/21–49–15) serves light meals and is popular with men of all ages, but shouldn't be confused with the mammoth **Club Amigo** (Studiostræde 31A, tel. 33/15–33–32), which includes a sauna, solarium, and cinema. The **Pan Club** (Knabrostræde 3, tel. 33/32–49–08) is the biggest gay disco in town, with two dance floors. The **Stable Bar** (Teglgårdsstræde 3, tel. 33/12–73–03) and the **Cosy Bar** (Studiestræde 24, tel. 33/12–74–27) are the motorcycle and leather clubs. **Babushka** (Turesensgade 6, tel. 33/15–05–36) is a cozy lesbian café that welcomes men, while the **Club Rosenborg** (Sølvgade 18, tel. 33/93–48–28) café pub is lesbians-only Friday from midnight to 5 AM.

Sjælland and Its Islands

Introduction

The Goddess Gefion is said to have carved Sjælland (Zealand) from Sweden. If she did, she must have wrestled with the north, slicing it deep with a fjord, while she chopped the south to pieces and left the sides bowing west. Though the coasts are dramatically serrated, Gefion's myth is more dramatic than the flat, fertile land of rich meadows and beech stands.

Slightly larger than the state of Delaware, Sjælland is the largest of the Danish islands. From Copenhagen, almost any point on it can be reached in an hour and a half, making it the most traveled portion of country. To the north of the capital, the ritzy beach towns line up between Hellerup and Humlebæk. Helsingør's Kronborg, which Shakespeare immortalized in *Hamlet,* and Hillerød's stronghold of Frederiksborg, considered one of the most magnificent Renaissance castles in Europe, are also north. To the west of Copenhagen is Roskilde, medieval Denmark's most important town, which boasts an eclectic cathedral that was northern Europe's spiritual center 1,000 years ago.

West and south, rural towns and farms edge up to beach communities and fine white beaches, often surrounded by forests. Even more unspoiled are the lilliputian islands around southern Sjælland, virtually unchanged over the past century.

Important Addresses and Numbers

Tourist Information Tourist offices in the chief towns covered in this chapter are at: **Helsingør** (Havnepladsen 3, tel. 49/21–13–33), **Hillerød** (Rosenhaven, Slotsgade 52, tel. 42/26–28–52), **Køge** (Vestergade 1, tel. 53/65–58–00), **Lolland** (at Nykøbing Falster) (Østergade 2B, tel. 54/85–13–03), **Roskilde** (Fondens Bro 3, tel. 42/35–27–00), **Sakskøbing** (in summer, Torvegade 4, tel. 53/89–56–30; in winter, tel. 53/89–45–72); and **Stege** and **Møn** (Storegade 5, Stege, tel. 55/81–44–11).

Emergencies For **police, fire,** or **ambulance,** dial 000.

Hospital Emergency Rooms Emergency care is available at **Helsingør** (Esrumvej 145, tel. 49/21–61–00) and **Roskilde** (Roskilde Amtssygehus, Køgvej, tel. 42/37–02–37).

Late-night Pharmacies **Helsingør** (Axeltorvs, Groskenstæde 2A, tel. 49/21–12–23; Stengades, Stengade 46, tel. 49/21–86–00) and **Roskilde** (Dom Apoteket, Algade 8, tel. 42/35–40–16, and Svane Apoteket, Skomagergade 12, tel. 42/35–83–00) have pharmacies that are open late. In each town, pharmacies rotate 24-hour service, so call first to see which is open.

Arriving and Departing by Plane

Copenhagen's **Kastrup Airport** is Sjælland's only airport (*see* Arriving and Departing by Plane in Copenhagen, *above*).

Arriving and Departing by Car and Train

By Car There are several **DSB** car ferries from Germany. They connect Kiel to Bagenkop, on the island of Langeland (from there, drive north to Spodsbjerg and take another ferry to Lolland, which is connected to Falster and Sjælland by bridges); Puttgarden to Rødbyhavn on Lolland; Travemünde and Wanemünde to Gedser on Falster. Sjælland is connected to Fyn, which is connected to Jylland, by bridges and frequent ferries. If you are driving from Sweden, take a car ferry from either Helsingborg to Helsingør or Limhamn to Dragør. Or sail directly to Copenhagen (*see* Arriving and Departing by Car, in Copenhagen, *above*). In Denmark, call **DSB** (tel. 33/14–88–80); in Sweden, call **Scandlines** (tel. 42/18–61–00).

By Train Most train routes to Sjælland, whether international or domestic, are directed to Copenhagen. Routes to north and south Sjælland usually require a transfer at Copenhagen's main station. For timetables, call **DSB** (tel. 33/14–17–01).

Getting Around

By Car Highways and country roads throughout Sjælland are excellent, and traffic—even around Copenhagen—is manageable most of the time.

By Train and Bus The **Copenhagen Card,** which affords free train and bus transport, as well as admission to museums and sights, is valid within the HT-bus and rail system, which extends north to Helsingør, west to Roskilde, and south to Køge (*see* Getting Around in Copenhagen, *above*). Every town in Sjælland has a central train station, usually within walking distance of hotels and sights. (For long distances, buses are not convenient.) The only part of the island not connected to the DSB network is the sliver of northwestern peninsula known as **Sjællands Odde** (Zealand's Tongue). Trains leave from Holbæk to Højby, where you can bus to the tip of the point. For information, call the private bus company, **Odsherrede** (tel. 53/41–00–03). Two vintage trains (dating from the 1880s) run from Helsingør (tel. 42/30–89–35) and Hillerød (tel. 48/30–00–30 or 42/12–00–98) to Gilleleje.

Guided Tours

Check with the local tourism boards for general sightseeing tours in the larger towns or for self-guided walking tours. The following tours begin in Copenhagen: The Roskilde **Vikingland Tour** (6 hours) includes the market and cathedral, Christian IV's Chapel, and the Viking Ship Museum. The **Afternoon Hamlet Tour** (4½ hours), includes Frederiksborg Castle and Fredenborg Palace, while the **Castle Tour of North Zealand** (7 hours) also stops at Kronborg Castle. Less historical is the lovely **Afternoon of History and Romance** (4 hours), which includes the old half-timbered district of Bondebyen, a cruise on Furesø, a stop at the Lyngby open-air museum, and a return through the Royal Deer Park. For information, call **Vikingbus** (tel. 31/57–26–00) or **Copenhagen Excursion** (tel. 31/54–06–06).

Boat Tours The turn-of-the-century ***Sagafjord*** (the Viking Ship Museum, Vikingeskibshallen, tel. 42/35–35–75) plies the waters of the Roskildefjord from April through September, and meals are served. Schedules vary.

Exploring Sjælland and Its Islands

Numbers in the margin correspond with points of interest on the Sjælland and Its Islands map.

Most of Sjælland can be explored in day trips from Copenhagen. The exceptions are the northwestern beaches around the Sejerø Bugt (Sejerø Bay) and those south of Møn, all of which require at least a night's stay and a day's loll.

Tour 1: North Sjælland

North of Copenhagen on Route 152, the Strandvejen (Beach Road), Sjælland's east coast is lined with upscale seaside neigh-
1 borhoods. In **Rungsted,** between Copenhagen and Helsingør, is **Rungstedlund,** the former manor of Baroness Karen Blixen. The author of *Out of Africa* and several accounts of aristocratic Danish life, Blixen wrote under the pen-name Isak Dinesen. The manor, where she lived as a child and returned in 1931, recently opened as a museum and includes manuscripts, photographs, and memorabilia documenting her years in Africa and Denmark. *Rungstedlund, tel. 42/57–10–57. Admission: DKr30 adults, children free. Open May–Sept., daily 10–5; Oct.–Apr., weekdays and Sun. 1–4.*

2 Another 10 kilometers (6 miles) northward is **Humlebæk** and the must-see **Louisiana** museum. Housed in a pearly 19th-century villa, surrounded by dramatic views of the Øresund waters, the permanent collection includes modern American paintings and Danish painting from the COBRA and Deconstructivism movements. Be sure to see the haunting collection of Giacomettis backdropped by picture windows overlooking the sound. *Gamle Strandvej 13, tel. 42/19–07–19. Admission: DKr40, children free. Open daily 10–5.*

3 At the northeastern tip of the island is **Helsingør,** the departure point for ferries to Helsingborg, Sweden, and the site of **Kronborg Slot.** William Shakespeare based *Hamlet* on Danish mythology's Amleth, and—never having seen the castle—used it as the setting nonetheless. Built in the late 16th century, it's 600 years younger than the Elsinore we imagine from the tragedy and was built as a Renaissance tollbooth. From its cannon-mounted bastions, forces collected Erik of Pomerania's much-hated Sound Dues, a tariff charged to all ships crossing the sliver of water between Denmark and Sweden. Well worth seeing are the 200-foot-long dining hall and the dungeons, where a brooding statue of Holger Danske sits. According to legend, the Viking chief sleeps, but will awaken to defend Denmark when it is in danger. *Helsingør, tel. 49/21–30–78. Admission: DKr14 adults, DKr7 children. Open May–*

Sjælland and Its Islands

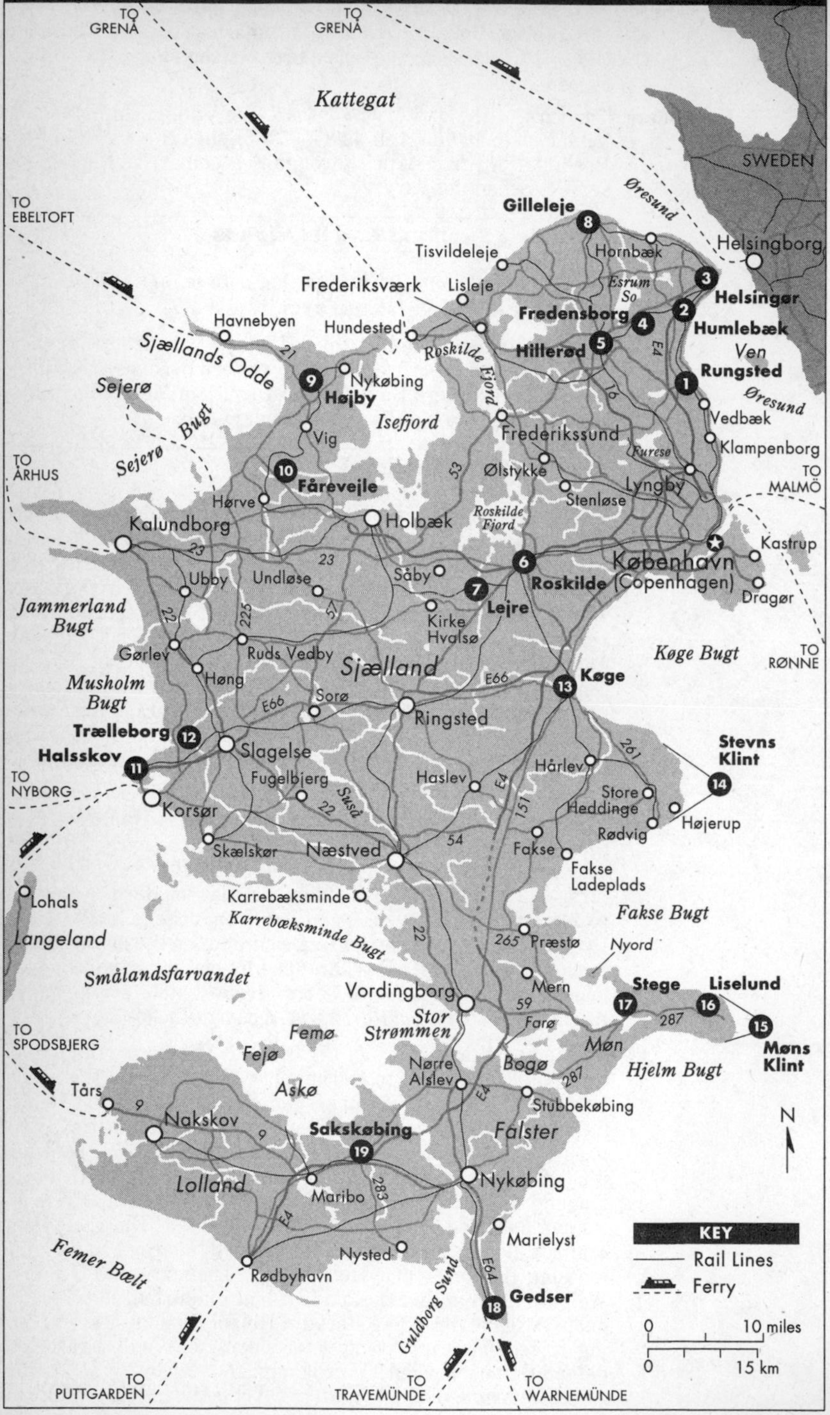

Sept., daily 10–5; Oct. and Apr., daily 11–4; Nov.–Mar., daily 11–3.

Thanks to the hefty tolls, the town prospered. Stroll past the carefully restored medieval merchants' and ferrymen's houses in the middle of town, and on the corner of Stengade and Skt. Annæ Gade near the harbor, you'll come to **Skt. Olai's Kirke** (St. Olai's Church), the country's largest town-church, which is worth poking into for its elaborately carved wooden altar. Next door is the 15th-century **Carmelite Kloster** (Carmelite Convent), one of the most well-preserved examples of medieval architecture in Scandinavia. After the Reformation, it was used as a hospital, and by 1630, a poor house. *Admission: DKr10 adults, DKr5 children. Guided tours year-round, daily 2 PM.*

Next door is the **By Museum** (Town Museum), with exhibits of 19th-century handicrafts, dolls, and a model of the town. *Skt. Annæ Gade 36, tel. 49/21–00–98. Admission: DKr10 adults, DKr5 children. Open daily 12–4.*

If you are interested in castles, visit the Louis XVI-style **Marienlyst Slot,** about 1 kilometer (½ mile) north of Helsingør. Built in 1587 at the queen's behest, it provided her a delicate change of scenery from the militant Kronborg. Today, the gardens have been replanted, and the interiors contain paintings by North Sjælland artists. *Marienlyst Allé, tel. 49/21–16–27. Admission: DKr20 adults, children free. Open daily 12–5.*

4 Southwest 15 kilometers (9 miles) is the town of **Fredensborg and the Fredensborg Slot** (Castle of Peace), built by Frederik IV to commemorate the 1720 peace treaty with Sweden. The Castle of Peace was originally inspired by French and Italian castles, with a towering domed hall in the center; however, 18th-century reconstructions conceal the original design and instead serve as a review of domestic architecture. The castle became a favorite of Frederik V, who lined the marble gardens with sculptures of ordinary people. It is now the summer residence of the royal family; interiors are closed except during July. The neatly trimmed park around the palace, connecting with Lake Esrum, is a lovely spot for a stroll. *Tel. 42/28–00–25. Palace open July, daily 1–4. Park open year-round.*

5 **Hillerød** and the **Frederiksborg Slot** (castle) lie another 10 kilometers (6 miles) south. Acquired and rebuilt by Frederik II, the fortress was demolished by his son, king–cum–architect Christian IV, and rebuilt as one of Scandinavia's most magnificent castles. With three wings and a low entrance portal, the moated Dutch-Renaissance structure covers three islets. It is peaked with dozens of gables, spires, and turrets. The interiors include a two-storied marble gallery known as the Great Hall. Audaciously festooned with drapery, paintings, and reliefs, it's atop the vaulted Chapel where 17th- to 19th-century monarchs were crowned. Devastated by a fire in 1859, the castle was reconstructed with the support of the Carlsberg Foundation, and it now includes a museum of Danish history. *Tel. 42/26–04–39. Admission: DKr25 adults, DKr5 children. Open Apr. and Oct., daily 10–4; May–Sept., daily 10–5; Nov.–Mar., daily 11–3.*

Forty kilometers (24 miles) south of Hillerød (on Rte. 6) and 32 kilometers (20 miles) west of Copenhagen (on Rte. 156) is
6 **Roskilde,** Sjælland's second largest town, and one of its oldest. Over a weekend at the end of June, it's filled with the rock mu-

sic of the **Roskilde Festival,** said to be the largest outdoor concert in northern Europe, attracting 75,000 people.

Roskilde was the royal residence in the 10th century and became the spiritual capital of Denmark and northern Europe in 1170 when Bishop Absalon built the **Roskilde Domkirke** (Roskilde Cathedral) on the site of a church erected 200 years earlier by Harald Bluetooth. Overwhelming the center of town, the current structure took more than 300 years to complete and thus provides a one-stop crash-course in Danish architecture. Inside, there's an ornate Dutch altarpiece, as well as the sarcophagi, ranging from opulent to modest, of 38 Danish monarchs. Predictably, Christian IV is interred in a magnificent chapel with a massive painting of himself in combat, as well as a bronze sculpture by Thorvaldsen. In modest contrast is the newest addition, the simple brick chapel outside the church, of King Frederik IX, who died in 1972. On the interior south wall above the entrance is a 16th-century clock that depicts St. George charging a dragon, which hisses and howls, echoing throughout the church and causing Peter Døver, "The Deafener," to sound the hour. A squeamish Kirsten Kiemer, "The Chimer," shakes her head in fright but manages to strike the quarters. *Domkirkestræde 10, tel. 42/35–16–24. Admission: DKr3 adults, DKr1 children. Open Apr.–Sept., weekdays 9–5:45, Sat. 11:30–5:45; Oct.–Mar., weekdays 10–3:45; May–Aug. also open Sun. 12:30–5:45; Sept.–Apr. also open Sun. 12:30–3:45.*

Less than a kilometer (½ mile) north of the cathedral, on the fjord, is the **Vikingeskibshallen** (Viking Ship Museum), a modern museum that contains five Viking ships sunk in the fjord 1,000 years ago to block enemy ships. They were discovered in 1957. The painstaking recovery involved building a watertight dam and then draining the water from that section of the fjord. The splinters of wreckage were then preserved and reassembled in an ongoing process. A deep-sea trader, a warship, a ferry, a merchant ship, and a fierce 92½-foot man of war, which is still being reconstructed, attest to the Vikings' sophisticated and aesthetic boat-making skills. *Strandengen, tel. 42/35–65–55. Admission: DKr25 adults, DKr16 children. Open Apr.–Oct., daily 9–5; Nov.–Mar., daily 10–4.*

7 Another 10 kilometers (6 miles) west of Roskilde in **Lejre** is the **Lejre Forsøgscenter** (Lejre Archaeological Research Center). Within the 50-acre compound, a village dating from the Iron Age and two 19th-century farmhouses have been reconstructed and during the summer are inhabited by a handful of hardy Danish families. Under the observation of researchers, the inhabitants go about their daily routine—grinding grain, herding goats, wearing skins—and give a clearer picture of ancient ways of life. In Bodalen (the Fire Valley), visitors (especially children) can grind corn, file an ax, and sail in a dugout canoe. *Slangæleen, tel. 46/48–02–45. Admission: DKr35 adults, DKr15 children. Open May–Sept., daily 10–5.*

Time Out There are picnic tables but no cafeteria at the archaeological center, so bring your lunch, or head back to **Druedahl's Konditori** (Skomagergade 40, tel. 42/35–01–13) in Roskilde, which has freshly baked pastries and bread. There's also a cafeteria at the Viking Ship Museum, overlooking the fjord.

Tour 2: West and South Sjælland

Sjælland's northwest coast is characterized by level land and summerhouse communities. Within this pastoral setting is
8 **Gilleleje,** at the very top of the island. Once a small fishing community, it experiences a population explosion every summer, when northern Europeans take to its woods and fine, sandy beaches. It was a favorite getaway of philosopher Søren Kierkegaard, who wrote, "I often stood there and reflected over my past life. The force of the sea and the struggle of the elements made me realize how unimportant I was." The less existential will go for a swim and visit the philosopher's monument on a nearby hill. The old part of town, with its thatched-roofed and colorfully painted houses, is also good for a walk.

Farther west is the hammer-shaped **Odsherred,** which is curved by the Sejerø Bugt (bay) and dotted with hundreds of burial mounds. If you are a devotee of ecclesiastical art, make a pilgrimage to explore the frescoes of several 12th- to 15th-century
9 churches, among them the Roman/Gothic/Renaissance **Højby kirke** (in the town of **Højby,** near Nykøbing Sjælland) and the
10 Gothic **Fårevejle kirke** (in the town of **Fårevejle**), with the earl of Bothwell's chapel. Alternatively, you can simply bask on the powdery beaches.

While the England–France Chunnel is creating a stir on the Continent, Europe's second biggest tunnel-bridge (18-kilometers/11¼-miles) is in the process of linking **Halsskov,** on west
11 Sjælland, to Nyborg, on east Fyn. The **Storebælt Udstillings Center** (Great Belt Exhibition Center), detailing the roadwork, which will be completed in 1993 for rail passage and 1996 for auto traffic, includes videos and models and makes for an informative stop while you're waiting for a ferry. *Halsskov, tel. 58/35-01-00. Admission: DKr25 adults, DKr15 children. Open daily 10–8.*

If you are a Viking enthusiast, head instead 14 kilometers (8½
12 miles) northeast, just outside Slagelse, to **Trælleborg,** an excavated Viking encampment, with a reconstructed army shelter. No longer content to rely on farmer warriors, the Viking hierarchy designed the geometrically exact camp within a circular, moated rampart, thought to be of Oriental inspiration. The 16 barracks, of which there is one model, could accommodate 1,300 men. *Trælleborg Allé, tel. 53/54-95-06. Admission: DKr8 adults, DKr4 children. Open Apr.–Sept., daily 10–6.*

On the east coast, 40 kilometers (24 miles) south of Copenha-
13 gen, is the well-preserved medieval town of **Køge,** which used to be a witch-hunting town. In the **Køge Museum,** a 17th-century merchant's house, you will see souvenirs from Hans Christian Andersen, costumes, local artifacts, an executioner's sword, and a 13th-century stone font. A story is told that the font had to be removed from the town church after a crippled woman committed an unsavory act into it, hoping her bizarre behavior would cure her. Also on exhibit are 16th-century silver coins from a buried treasure of more than 2,000 coins found in the courtyard of Langkildes Gård. *Nørregade 4, tel. 54/65-02-62. Admission: DKr10 adults, DKr5 children. Open Oct.–May, weekdays 2–5, Sat.–Sun. 1–5; June–Sept., daily 10–5.*

On a calmer scale, the old part of Køge is filled with 300 half-timbered houses, all protected by the National Trust; it's a lovely area for a stroll. At the end of Kirkestræde, the 15th-century **Skt. Nikolai Kirke** (St. Nicholas Church) was the hanging tower for pirates, while the floor is covered with more than 100 tombs of Køge VIPs. Carved angels line the church's walls, but most have their noses cut off—a favorite pastime of drunken Swedish soldiers in the 1700s. *Kirkestræde, tel. 53/65–13–59. Admission free. Open Sept.–May, weekdays 10–12; June–Aug., weekdays 10–4.*

Nearby the **Køge Kunst Museet Skitsesamling** (Køge Art Museum) has changing exhibitions and an extensive permanent collection of Queen Margrethe's artistic works. Among them: silver spoons designed for Georg Jensen and porcelain figures for Royal Copenhagen, in addition to embroidery, watercolor paintings, and sketches. *Nørregade 29, tel. 56/26–24–14. Admission: DKr5 adults, DKr3 children. Open Tues.–Sun. 11–3.*

Near **Rødvig,** 24 kilometers (15 miles) south of Køge, are the
14 chalk cliffs of **Stevns Klint,** a third smaller than those farther south at Møn, but interesting because of the 13th-century **Højerup Kirke** (church) that was built on their plateau. As the cliffs eroded, first the cemetery, then the choir toppled into the sea. In recent years, the church has been restored and the cliffs below bolstered by masonry to prevent further damage. *Højerup Church, Stevns Klint, no tel. Admission: DKr5 adults, children free. Open Apr.–Sept., daily 11–5.*

Continuing south to the southeast tip of Sjælland, Route 59 east crosses a bridge to the island of **Møn,** bumped throughout with nearly 100 neolithic burial mounds, but most famous for
15 its dramatic chalk **Møns Klint** (Møn's Cliffs). Rimmed by a beech forest, the milky-white 75-million-year-old bluffs plunge 120 meters (400 feet) to a small, craggy beach—accessible by a path and 560 steps. Once there, Danish families usually spend their time hunting for blanched fossils of cuttlefish, sea urchins, and other sea life. The cliffs are an important navigational marker for ships, defining southern Sjælland's otherwise flat topography.

16 You can walk to a delightful folly of the 18th century, **Liselund Slot** (not to be confused with a hotel of the same name), which is 4 kilometers (2.4 miles) north of the cliffs. Antoine de la Calmette, the island's sheriff and a royal chamberlain, took his inspiration from Marie Antoinette's Le Hameau (the Hamlet) in Versailles and built the classical structure in 1792 for his beloved wife. The thatched palace, complete with English gardens, combines a Norwegian country facade with elegant Pompeian interiors. In this lovely setting, Hans Christian Andersen wrote his fairy tale *The Tinder Box*. The palace has been open to the public since 1938; visitors must wear the slippers provided to enter the house. *Tel. 55/81–21–78. Admission: DKr10 adults, DKr3 children. Tours May–Oct., Mon.–Sat. 10:30, 11, 1:30, and 2; Sun. 10:30, 11, 1:30, 2, 4, and 4:30. Tours are in Danish and German.*

17 The island's capital, **Stege,** received its town charter in 1268. Take time to explore its medieval churches, including **Stege, Elmelunde, Keldby,** and **Fanefjord,** which are famous for their naïve frescoes. Thought to have been completed by a collaborative group of artisans, the whimsical paintings include pedagogic and Biblical doodlings.

Connected to Møn by Route 59 is the tiny northeastern island of **Nyord** (New Word), which has a sanctuary for rare birds, including hen harriers, rough-legged buzzards, and snow buntings. The island has been divided among the same 20 farms, unchanged, for the past 300 years. Cars are not allowed in the island's central town. **Bogø** (Book Island) is southwest on Route 287. Relatively unchanged over the past few centuries, the islands are inhabited by a handful of families who continue to farm and sail.

Next is the island of **Falster,** accessible from Bogø directly on the E–47's striking Farø Bridge. Shaped like a tiny South America, the island has excellent blond beaches, especially
18 southeastern **Marielyst** and southernmost **Gedser.** The island is also one of the country's major producers of sugar beets.

West on the E–47 is the island of **Lolland,** which has a history going back more than 1,000 years when a man named Saxe sat at the mouth of the fjord and collected a toll. He later cleared the surrounding land and leased it. It became known as
19 Saxtorp, and eventually **Sakskøbing,** the island's capital. Though most people head straight for the beaches, the area has a few sights, including an excellent **car museum** in the 13th-century **Ålholm Slot** (castle), with more than 240 vehicles and a water tower with a smiling face. *Parkvej 7, Nysted, tel. 53/87–15–09. Admission to car museum: DKr40 adults, DKr20 children. Open mid-Apr.–May and early Sept.–mid-Oct., weekends and holidays; June–Aug., daily 10–6. Admission to castle: DKr40 adults, DKr20 children. Open June–Aug., daily 11–6.*

What to See and Do with Children

The **Knuthenborg Safari Park** on Lolland has a drive-through range, where you can rubber neck at tigers, zebras, rhinoceros, and giraffes, and pet camels, goats, and ponies. Besides seeing 20 species of animals, children can also play in Miniworld, which has a jungle-gym, a minitrain, and other rides. *Knuthenborg Safaripark, DK–4930 Maribo, tel. 53/88–80–89. Admission: DKr54 adults, DKr27 children. Open May–Sept. 15.*

Off the Beaten Track

West of Gilleleje, on the northwestern coast of Sjælland between Tisvilde and Liseleje, is the **Troldeskoven** (Trolls' Forest), where gnarled evergreens were planted 250 years ago to control the drifting sands. When you want to escape the beaches, this provides a magical respite.

Shopping

Shops are concentrated in the center of each town, along the pedestrian street. Between Roskilde and Holbæk is **Kirke Sonnerup Kunsthåndværk** (Art Handicrafts, Englerupvej 62, Såby, tel. 42/39–25–77), which has a good selection of pottery, glass, clothing, and woodwork produced by more than 50 Danish artists. Farther south in Næstved is the **Holmegaards Glassværker** (Holmegaards Glass Workshop, Glassværksvej 52, Fensmark, tel. 55/54–62–00), with seconds of glasses, lamps, and occasionally art glass and savings of up to 40% off the "perfect" cost. The **Danish Amber Gallery** (Skodsborgparken 21, Skodsborg, tel. 42/80–71–62), 18 kilometers (11 miles) north of Copenhagen, has a good selection of jewelry and a workshop.

Sports and Outdoor Activities

Bicycling Every town in Sjælland has a bicycle rental, and most roads have cycle lanes. Ask the tourist board for maps and local routes, especially along coastal roads.

Canoeing Though there aren't any rapids, there are several calm lakes north of Copenhagen, especially in the Lyngby area on the **Mølleå** (Mølle River) and the **Bagsværd, Lyngby,** and **Furesø** (Bagsværd, Lyngby, and Fur lakes). Contact **Frederiksdal Kanoudlejning** (canoe rental; Nybrovej, Lyngby, tel. 42/85–67–70), which offers hourly, daily, and package tours and rentals. In southern Sjælland, for trips on the **Suså** (Sus River), call **Susåen Kanoudlejning** (canoe rental; tel. 53/64–61–44).

Fishing Angling is free along Sjælland's east coast, north of Vedbæk. Elsewhere, along lakes, streams, and the ocean, check with the local tourism office for license requirements, which vary from area to area. Remember, it is illegal to fish within 500 meters (1,650 feet) of the mouth of a stream.

Golf There are more than 20 golf courses in Sjælland. Among them: the 18-hole **Korsør Course** (Ørnumvej 8, Korsør, tel. 53/57–18–36), the 18-hole **Sydsjælland Golf Klub** on Falster (Præstolandevej 39, Mogenstrup, tel. 53/76–15–03), **Roskilde's** 12-hole course (Kongemarken 34, tel. 42/37–01–80), and the 18-hole **Helsingør Golf Klub** (Gamle Hellebækvej, Helsingør, tel. 42/21–29–70).

Beaches

The beaches on the northern tip of Sjælland, especially **Hornbæk** and **Gilleleje,** are full of summer cottages, white dunes, and calm waters. **Tisvildeleje,** farther west, is quieter and close to woods; while **Sjællands Odde** (Zealand's Tongue), the tiny strip of land north of the Sejerø Bay, is marshier and more private. Inside the bay, the beaches are once again smooth and blond. **Nykøbing Falster,** especially around **Marielyst** and **Gedser,** is lined with woods and great beaches, but can get crowded. Almost everywhere, you'll find cafés, facilities, and water sport rentals.

Dining and Lodging

Dining and lodging throughout Sjælland is more moderately priced than in Copenhagen. Keep in mind, however, that many restaurants close early (some by 8 PM) and that some hotels expect you to check in before 7 PM.

Highly recommended establishments are indicated by a star ★.

Fredensborg
Dining and Lodging
★

Hotel Store Kro. Built by King Frederik IV, this magnificent Renaissance annex to Fredensborg Castle is the archetypal stately inn. Inside, it's appointed with European antiques and paintings, while outside glass gazebos and classical statues look over a lovely garden. The rooms are equally sumptuous, with delicate patterned wallpapers and antiques. *Slotsgade 6, DK–3480, tel. 42/28–00–47, fax 42/28–45–61. 49 rooms with* *bath. Facilities: restaurant, bar, sauna, room service, meeting rooms, parking. AE, DC, MC, V. Very Expensive.*

Frederiksborg
Dining

Slotsherrenskro. Under the shadow of the Frederiksborg Castle, this busy, family restaurant used to be the castle stables. Antique on the outside, it's bright orange inside, with prints and paintings of royalty and the castle. Popular with visitors who come to the castle, the Danish menu ranges from quick open-face sandwiches to savory stews, soups, and steaks. *Slotherrens Kro, tel. 42/26–75–16. Reservations advised. Dress: casual. DC, MC, V. No dinner Thurs., Nov.–Mar. Inexpensive.*

Helsingør
Dining

Bøf og Grønt. Across from the harbor, this arty restaurant has peach walls covered with old photos of Danish movie stars. In the summer there's outdoor seating in the square and inside, a hefty salad bar that comes with the steaks and a few vegetarian dishes. A Mexican and Chinese restaurant and a basement bar are under the same management. *Stengade 81 in Færgegaarden, tel. 49/21–39–46. Reservations advised. Dress: casual but neat. AE, DC, MC, V. Closed Mon.–Tues. Jan.–Feb. Moderate.*

Dining and Lodging
★

Marienlyst. Flashy neon, bolts of drapery, and glass architecture make this grown-up playground look airlifted from Atlantic City. A large casino, endless lounges, and two resident orchestras drive the point home, but when guests tire of gambling, there's a huge second-floor "Swinging Pool" with a water slide. The rooms are plush, done up in pastels, with every convenience. *Nordre Strandvej 2, DK–3000, tel. 49/21–18–01, fax 49/20–35–30. 209 rooms with bath, 12 suites. Facilities: 2 restaurants, 2 bars, nightclub, casino, indoor pool, sauna, solarium, room service, meeting rooms, parking. AE, DC, MC, V. Very Expensive.*

Hotel Hamlet. A few minutes from the harbor, this recently renovated hotel has lost some of its charm but makes an attempt at character with raw timbers and deep green walls. The rooms are furnished in rose schemes and dark wood modern, all comfortable, if nondescript. Downstairs there's a cozy bar and the Ophelia Restaurant, which serves traditional Danish seafood, steaks, and open-face sandwiches. *Bramstrædet 5, DK–3000, tel. 49/21–28–02. 36 rooms with bath. Facilities: restaurant, bar, small meeting room. AE, DC, MC, V. Closed Dec. 24–Jan. 1. Expensive.*

Klampenborg
Dining
★

Strandmollekroen. This 200-year-old beach-front inn is burnished with deep-green walls and filled with antiques and hunting trophies, but the best views are of the Øresund from the back dining room. The food is seafood and steaks served elegantly. For a bit of everything, try the seafood platter, with lobster, crab claws, and Greenland shrimp. *Strandvejen 808, tel. 31/63–01–04. Reservations advised. Dress: casual but neat. AE, DC, MC, V. Moderate.*

Lolland
Dining and Lodging

Lalandia. This massive water-park hotel has an indoor palm-studded pool, a beach-side view, and lots of happy families. Located on the southern coast of Lolland, about 27 kilometers (16 miles) southwest of Sakskøbing, its modern, white apartments, with full kitchen and bath, accommodate 2, 4, 5, 6 or 8 people. *Rødby Havn, DK–4970 Rødby, tel. 54/60–42–00, fax 54/60–41–44. 300 apartments. Facilities: restaurant, bar, health club, indoor-and-outdoor pool, tennis, golf, sauna, so-*

larium, meeting rooms, shops, parking, baker, hairdresser, playground. AE, DC, MC, V. Moderate.

Hotel Saxkjøbing. Behind its yellow half-timbered facade, this comfortable hotel doesn't offer character or frills, but the rooms are bright, sunny, and modern, if very simply furnished. Located in the center of town, it is convenient to everything. *Torvet 9, Saxkjøbing, DK–4990, tel. 53/89–40–39, fax 53/89–50–50. Facilities: restaurant, bar, nightclub, meeting room, parking. AE, DC, MC. Inexpensive.*

Møn
Dining and Lodging
★

Liselund Ny Slot. Set in a grand old manor on an isolated estate, this bright, modern hotel offers stately accommodations minus stodginess. The square staircase and painted ceilings have been preserved, while the renovated rooms are fresh and simple, with wicker and pastel schemes, half of which overlook a swan-filled pond and the forest. Downstairs there's an excellent restaurant that relies heavily on natural ingredients. *Liselund Ny Slot, DK–4791 Børre, tel. 55/81–20–81. 25 rooms with bath, 1 suite. Facilities: restaurant, meeting rooms. AE, DC, MC, V. Moderate.*

Nykøbing Falster
Dining

Czarens Hus. This stylish old inn dates back more than 200 years, when it was a guest house and supply store for area farmers and merchants. Deep green walls, gold trim, and chandeliers provide a background for antique furnishings. The specialty of the house is Continental Danish cuisine, which translates as creative beef and fish dishes, often served with cream sauces. Try the *Zar Beuf* (calf tenderloin in a mushroom-and-onion cream sauce). *Langgade 2, Nykøbing Falster, tel. 54/85–28–29. Reservations advised. Jacket advised. AE, DC, MC, V. Expensive.*

Stegepanden. The name of this family restaurant means frying pan, and nearly everything is grilled in small skillets in the open kitchen. The menu is Danish and German, with specialties like schnitzel, pepper steak, and fried salmon. Located in the middle of town, it's dimly lit, with high-back striped booths and benches and dark wood. *Torvet, Nykøbing Falster, tel. 54/85–82–82. Reservations not necessary. Dress: casual. MC. Closed Jan.; Sept.–Apr., Sun.–Mon.; May–Aug. Sun. Moderate.*

Lodging

Hotel Falster. This sleek and efficient hotel accommodates conference guests as well as vacationers, with an ambience that's comfortable and businesslike. Rustic brick walls and Danish antiques mix with sleek Danish-design lamps and sculpture, while the rooms are done up comfortably with dark wood and modular furniture. *Skovalleen, Nykøbing Falster, DK–4800, tel. 54/85–93–93, fax 54/82–21–99. 70 rooms with bath. Facilities: restaurant, bar, meeting room, whirlpool. AE, DC, MC, V. Moderate.*

Roskilde
Dining
★

Spise Loftet. Despite the name, Eating Loft, this charming restaurant is popular with locals who come for the mix-and-match menu: appetizer, entrée and dessert, and salad bar for DKr120. Choices range from vegetable quiche and steaks to Calvados or apple pie for dessert. The double-decker interior has two tables downstairs and a dozen upstairs beneath a gleaming white cathedral ceiling. *Algade 42, tel. 42/35–15–48. Reservations advised. Dress: casual. AE, DC, MC, V. Closed Sun. Moderate.*

Toppen. A half-hour walk from Roskilde Cathedral, this circular restaurant high above the water-tower looks frayed, with covered metal tables and dozens of round paper lamps hanging from the ceiling. The fish and steak menu, though somewhat institutional, includes a family Colorado Steak for up to four people. Ask to sit in the smaller dining room, overlooking the fjord. *Bymarken 37, tel. 42/36-04-12. Reservations advised. Dress: casual. DC, MC. No weekend lunch. Inexpensive.*

Dining and Lodging **Hotel Prindsen.** Centrally located in downtown Roskilde, this convenient hotel is popular with business guests. Built a hundred years ago, it's been recently renovated with an elegant dark wood lobby and nondescript rooms that are nonetheless homey and comfortable. Downstairs, the restaurant La Bøf serves up grill and fish fare, and next door there's a cozy bar. *Algade 13, tel. 42/35-80-10, fax 42/35-81-10. 38 rooms with shower. Facilities: restaurant, bar, meeting room. AE, DC, MC, V. Moderate.*

Roskilde Vandrehjem Hørgården. In front of a grassy yard, this youth hostel is perfect for families and budget travelers. In a former schoolhouse 2 kilometers (1.2 miles) east of the Roskilde Domkirke, everything looks straight out of third grade, and the rooms, with bunks, look like camp. *Hørhusene 61, DK-4000, tel. 42/35-21-84, fax 46/32-66-90. 21 rooms with four beds each, 8 showers. Facilities: kitchen. No credit cards. Open May-Sept., but call other times to check room availability. Inexpensive.*

The Arts and Nightlife

The Arts Sjælland's cultural center is Copenhagen; however, many towns do have free outdoor concerts and theater in the summer, most notably Roskilde, Køge, and Helsingør. Check with the local tourist offices for details. Some summers, **Kronborg Castle** is the site of outdoor performances of *Hamlet* by internationally renowned theater groups. The schedule varies from year to year, but check with the tourism board for current details.

Nightlife Outside of Roskilde and Helsingør, most islanders go to Copenhagen for a big night out. In the smaller towns, you'll find local bars, outdated discos, and quiet cafés and wine cellars. In Roskilde, the young head to **Gimle** (Ringstedgade 30, tel. 42/35-12-13) for live rock on the weekends, followed by the **Exima** disco (Algade 25A, tel. 46/32-06-92). **Kloster Kælderen** (Store Gråbrødrestræde 23, tel. 42/37-20-33) is a beer basement with a slightly older crowd. The **Bryggerhesten** (Algade 15, tel. 42/35-01-03) is where adults have a late supper and beer in cozy surroundings. During the summer, **Mullerudi** (Djalma Lunds Gord 7, tel. 42/37-03-25) is an arty spot with indoor and outdoor seating and live jazz. In Helsingør, **New Roxi** (Hovedvagtsstræde 2, tel. 49/21-06-58) draws the young to disco, while a more mixed crowd listens to jazz (on weekends) at **Underhuset** (Stengade 81, tel. 49/21-82-97).

Casinos The **Marienlyst Casino** (Ndr. Strandvej 2, tel. 42/20-10-42) is a big glitzy affair located in the Marienlyst Hotel, with several bars, blackjack, baccarat, and slot machines.

Fyn and the Central Islands

Introduction

Christened the Garden of Denmark by its most famous son, Hans Christian Andersen, Fyn (Funen) is the smaller of the country's two major islands. Lined with plumb-straight vegetable fields and flower gardens, the flat-as-a-board land is relieved by beech glades and swan ponds. Manor houses and castles that seem to pop up from the countryside like magnificent mirages include some of northern Europe's best-preserved: the 12th-century Nyborg Slot, travel pinup Egeskov Slot, and the lavish Valdemars Slot. The fairytale cliché often attached to Denmark really does spring from this provincial isle, where the only faint pulse emanates from Odense, its capital. Trimmed with thatched-roof houses and green parks, the city makes the most of the Andersen legacy, but surprises with a rich arts community at the Brandts Klædefabrik, a former textile factory turned museum compound.

It's quick and easy to reach the smaller islands of Langeland and Tåsinge—both are connected to Fyn by bridges. Slightly more isolated is Ærø, where the town of Ærøskøbing, with its painted half-timbered houses and winding streets, seems caught in a delightful time warp.

Important Addresses and Numbers

Tourist Information Most city tourism offices are open weekdays 10–4 and Saturday 9–noon during the fall and winter, and Monday through Saturday 9–6 in spring and summer. **Odense Tourist Office** (City Hall, DK–5000 Odense C, tel. 66/12–75–20) has information for all of Fyn, including the helpful "Tourist Information on Fyn" brochure. There are also offices in **Kerteminde** (Strandgade 5, tel. 65/32–11–21), **Svendborg** (Møllergade 20, DK–5700 Svendborg, tel. 62/21–09–80), **Nyborg** (Torvet 9, tel. 65/31–02–80), and **Ærøskøbing** (Torvet, tel. 62/52–13–00).

Emergencies For **police, fire,** or **ambulance** service, dial 000.

Hospital Emergency Room There is an emergency room at **Odense Hospital,** (J.B. Winsløws Vej, tel. 66/11–33–33).

Doctors and Dentists From 4 PM to 7 AM, call 66/14–14–33 or 0041 for a doctor. For dental or other emergencies, call **Falck** (tel. 66/11–22–22).

Late-night Pharmacy **Ørnen Apoteket** (Vestergade 80, Odense, tel. 66/12–29–70) is open late.

Arriving and Departing by Plane

Airport and Airlines **Odense Airport** (tel. 65/95–53–55), 11 kilometers (7 miles) north of Odense, is served by **Mærsk Air** (tel. 33/11–44–44) and **Muk Air** (31/53–44–33). There are nine daily flights between Copenhagen and Odense. The 25-minute flight costs DKr550.

Between the Airport and Center City Metered airport taxis charge DKr120 for the 15-minute drive downtown. Public bus No. 54 charges DKr9 for the half-hour trip and leaves 10 minutes after the hour weekdays; every hour, on the hour, weekends. A speedier **Mærsk Airbus** meets each flight and stops at the Grand Hotel, Hans Christian Andersen Hotel, and the main railway station. The fare is DKr40.

Arriving and Departing by Car, Train, and Bus

By Car From Copenhagen, take the E20 west to Korsør and drive aboard **Storebælt Færgen** (the Great Belt ferry; DKr245 per car, with up to five passengers and a reservation; unreserved tickets are DKr200, with a possible wait of several hours). For reservations, call **DSB** (tel. 33/14–88–00). The ferry departs hourly, every day. You'll arrive in Nyborg, which is a half hour from Odense or Svendborg.

By Train Trains from Copenhagen's main station depart for the 3-hour trip to Odense hourly, every day. Stations in both towns are central, close to hotels and sights. The one-way fare is DKr99 on Tuesday, Wednesday, Thursday, and Saturday; DKr124 Sunday, Monday, and Friday. A reservation is an additional DKr15 (tel. 33/14–17–01).

By Bus **DSB buses** depart daily from Nykøbing Falster (in South Sjælland) to the ferry at Tårs (on Lolland). In Spodsbjerg (on Langeland), they continue north, via bridges, to Odense. Tickets for the 3½-hour trip are DKr150 (tel. 33/14–17–01).

Getting Around

By Car The highways are excellent, while small roads meander beautifully on two lanes through the countryside. There is little traffic.

By Train and Bus Larger towns are served by intercity trains. These include a Nyborg–Odense–Middelfart and Odense–Svendborg route. The only other public transportation is by bus. Timetables are posted at all bus stops and central stations (rutebilstation). Passengers buy tickets on board and pay according to the distance traveled (tel. 66/11–71–11). For central Odense, the **Odense Eventyrpas** (Adventure Pass), available at the tourism office, affords admission to sights and museums and free city bus and train transport. Cost: DKr70 adults, DKr35 children, between April and October, half-price the rest of the year.

By Bicycle With their level landscape and short distances, Fyn and the central islands are perfect for cycling. Pick up maps from the tourism offices and rent bikes throughout the islands at **CykelCentret** (Allegade 72, Odense, tel. 66/13–88–94), **Cykelsmeden** (Nørregade 26, Odense, tel. 66/14–54–24), or **Fåborg Sportshandel** (Havnegade 40, Fåborg, tel. 62/61–28–22).

Guided Tours

The Odense Tourist Office (*see above*) oversees the **Odense City Tour** (3 hours), which includes a visit to the Hans Christian Andersen Museum and St. Knuds Cathedral, at 11 weekdays and at 2 Saturday from June 24 through August. Most other towns do not have organized tours, but check the local tourist office for step-by-step walking brochures. Full-day **Hans Christian Andersen** tours to Odense depart from Copenhagen's Rådhuspladsen May 13–September 16, Sunday at 9 AM, and cost DKr400. (Six out of 11 hours are spent in transit.)

Tour 1: Northern Fyn

Numbers in the margin correspond with points of interest on the Fyn and the Central Islands map.

1 Most visitors disembark from the ferry in **Nyborg,** a 13th-century town that was Denmark's capital during the Middle Ages. The city's major landmark, the moated 12th-century **Nyborg Slot** (castle), was the seat of the Danehof, the Danish parliament from 1200 to 1413. It was here that King Erik Glipping signed the country's first constitution, the Great Charter, in 1282. Besides geometric wall murals and an armory collection, the castle houses changing art exhibits. *Slotspladsen, tel. 65/31–02–02. Admission: DKr10 adults, DKr5 children. Open Mar.–May and Sept.–Nov., Tues.–Sun. 10–3; June–Aug., daily 10–5.*

Cross Gammel Torv and walk down the street to the **Nyborg Museum,** which is housed in a half-timbered merchant's house from 1601, for a picture of 17th-century life. Besides furnished rooms, there's a small brewery. *Slotsgade 11, tel. 65/31–26–19. Admission: DKr5 adults, DKr2 children. Open Mar.–May and Sept.–Oct., Tues.–Sun. 10–3; June–Aug., Mon.–Sun. 10–4.*

Take Route 160 northwest to the Avnslev junction and turn north to Route 165; then drive the 15 kilometers (9 miles) along
2 the coast to **Kerteminde,** an important fishing village and picturesque summer resort. On Langegade, walk past the neat half-timbered houses to Møllebakken and the museum of the Danish painter **Johannes Larsen** (1867–1961). Across from a crimson strawberry patch and a 100-year-old windmill, the artist built a modest country cottage that has been perfectly preserved, right down to the teacups. In front, there's a sculpture of a woman by Kai Nielsen. Local legend goes that one night, after a particularly wild party in Copenhagen, its legs were broken off. An ambulance was called, but once it arrived, the enraged driver demanded the artists pay a fine. A chagrined Larsen paid, and in return kept the wounded sculpture. *Møllebakken, tel. 65/32–37–27. Admission: DKr20 adults, DKr5 children. Open Mar. 25–May and Sept.–Oct., Tues.–Sun. 10–4; June–Aug., Tues.–Sun. 10–5.*

If you are a Viking enthusiast, head a few kilometers south to
3 the village of **Ladby** and the 1,100-year-old remains of the **Ladbyskibet,** a Viking chieftain's ship burial, complete with hunting dogs and horses for his trip to Valhalla—the afterlife. *Vikingsvej 12, tel. 65/32–16–67. Admission: DKr10 adults, DKr3 children. Open May–Sept., daily 10–6; Oct.–Apr., daily 10–3.*

Twenty kilometers (12 miles) southwest on Route 165 is
4 **Odense,** Denmark's third-largest city and birthplace of fairytale author Hans Christian Andersen.

Begin at the flourishing **Kongens Have** (King's Garden) and 18th-century Odense Castle, now a government building, and walk east on Stationsvej to Thomas B. Thriges Gade and Hans Jensens Stræde, where the **Hans Christian Andersen Hus** (H.C. Andersen Museum) stands in a manicured neighborhood of half-timbered houses and cobbled streets. Inside, the storyteller's life is chronicled through his photographs, drawings, letters, and personal belongings. There's also a library with

Fyn and the Central Islands

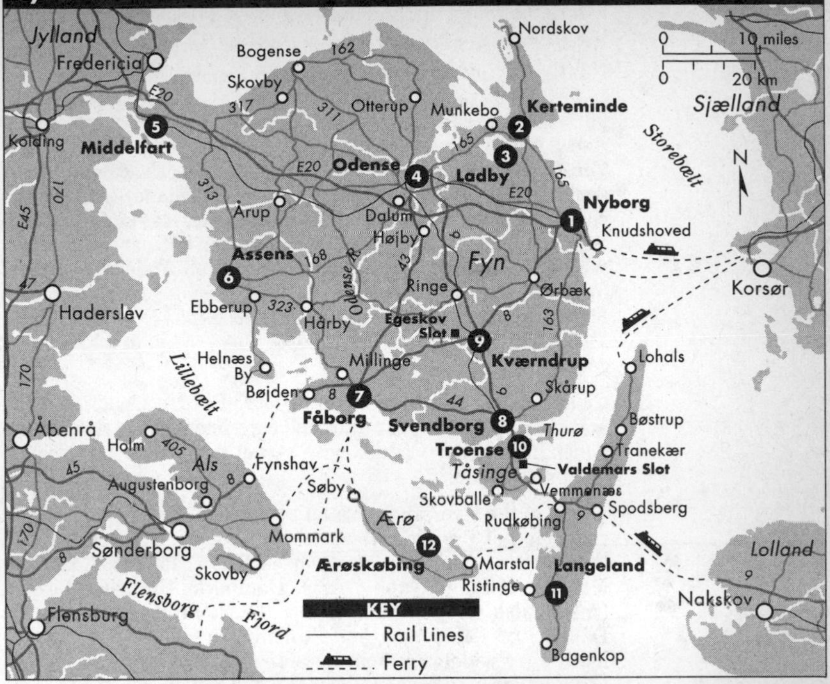

Andersen's works in over 100 languages, where you can listen to fairy tales on tape. *Hans Jensenstræde 37, tel. 66/13-13-72. Admission: DKr15 adults, DKr3 children. Open Apr.-May and Sept., daily 10-5; June-Aug., daily 9-6; Oct.-May, daily 10-3.*

At the end of Hans Jensens Stræde is the sleek **Carl Nielsen Museum,** which has multimedia exhibits of the life and work of Denmark's most famous composer (1865-1931) and of his wife, the sculptor Anne Marie Carl-Nielsen. *Claus-Bergs Gade 11, tel. 66/13-13-72. Admission: DKr10 adults, DKr2 children; free Thurs. 4-8 and Sun. Open daily 10-4, Sept.-May also Thurs. 10-8.*

Take a left on Claus Bergsgade to **Møntergården,** Odense's museum of urban history, which occupies four 17th-century row houses in a shady, cobbled courtyard. Exhibits range from interiors of the Middle Ages to Denmark's Nazi occupation to an impressive coin collection. *Overgade 48-50, tel. 66/13-13-72. Admission: DKr5 adults, DKr1 children. Open daily 10-4.*

Toward the pedestrian street on St. Knuds Kirkestræde, just in front of the Andersen Park, is the stately **St. Knuds Kirke,** built from the 13th to the 15th centuries, the only purely Gothic cathedral in Denmark. Inside, there's an intricate wooden altar covered with gold leaf, carved by German sculptor Claus Berg. Beneath the sepulcher are the bones of St. (King) Knud, who was killed during a farmers' uprising in 1086, and his brother. Continue west on St. Knuds Kirkestræde and take a left on Munkemøllestræde for a quick look at the diminutive **H.C.**

Andersens Barndomshjem (Andersen's Childhood Home), where the young boy and his parents lived in a room barely five by six feet.

Next, take a left from St. Knuds Kirkestræde on Filosofgangen to the takeoff point for the **Odense River Cruises** (tel. 65/95–79–96). Here you can catch a boat (May–September, daily 1 and 3, Sun. 11 also) downriver to the **Fruens Bøge** (the Lady's Beech Forest) and then walk down Erik Bøghs Sti (Erik Bøgh's footpath) to **Den Fynske Landsby** (the Fyn Village). Among the country's largest open-air museums, it includes 25 farm buildings and workshops, a vicarage, a water mill, and a theater, which in summer stages adaptations of Andersen's tales. *Sejerskovvej, tel. 66/13–13–72. Admission: DKr10 adults, DKr2 children. Open Apr.–May and Sept.–Oct., daily 9–4; June–Aug., daily 8–6:30; Nov.–Mar., Sun. and holidays 10–4.*

Cruise back to the town center or catch Bus No. 21, 22, 23, or 24 and walk down the boutique- and café-lined pedestrian street, which in summer is abuzz with street performers, musicians, and brass bands.

North of the river and parallel to Kongensgade is the artistic compound of **Brandt's Klædefabrik.** A former textile factory, the four-story building now houses **Museet for Fotokunst** (the Museum of Photographic Art), **Danmarks Grafiske Museum** (the Danish Graphics Museum), **Dansk Presse museum** (the Danish Press Museum), and **Kunsthallen** (an art gallery). Exhibits vary widely from national to international exhibits, but the Photography Museum and the art gallery especially show experimental work. *Brændt's Passage 37, tel. 66/13–78–97. Admission: DKr20 for each museum, DKr30 for all. Open Tues.–Sun. 10–5.*

Time Out The **Cafe Biografen** (Brændt's Passage, tel. 66/13–16–16) next door is a popular—and inexpensive—meeting place for locals to have a cup of coffee or snack.

If you continue west on E20, you'll reach the westernmost point
5 of Fyn, the town of **Middelfart,** where you can cross the country's only suspension bridge to Jylland, and the European continent.

Tour 2: Southern Fyn and the Archipelago

Continue south from Odense on Route 168 and you'll reach the
6 quiet town of **Assens.** The local gem is Tove Sylvest's sprawling **Seven Gardens,** just south on the Strandvej (Beach Road) off Route 323 in the town of Å. A privately owned botanical United Nations, the gardens represent the flora of seven European countries, including many plants rare to Denmark. *Strandvej 62, Å, Ebberrup, tel. 64/74–12–85. Admission: DKr25 adults, DKr10 children. Open May–Oct., daily 10–5.*

Thirty kilometers (18 miles) south of Odense on Route 43 is
7 **Fåborg,** a lovely 12th-century town whose surrounding beaches are invaded by sunseeking Germans and Danes in summer. Four times a day, you can hear the dulcet chiming of **Klokketårnet**'s (the Belfry's) carillon, the island's largest. In the center of town is the controversial **Ymerbrønden** sculpture

by Kai Nielsen, depicting a naked man drinking from an emaciated cow while it licks a baby.

On the more traditional side, the 18th-century **Den Gamle Gård** (the Old Merchant's House), of 1725, chronicles local history through furnished interiors, as well as exhibits of glass and textiles. *Holkegade 1, tel. 62/61–33–38. Admission: DKr10 adults, children free. Open May–Sept., daily 10:30–4:30.*

Next, follow Grønnegade and you'll pass the local **Familie og Ungdoms Vandre hjem** (Family and Youth Hostel), which is housed in a charming white half-timber building that used to be a poorhouse (tel. 62/61–12–03).

Next door, the **Fåborg Museum for Fynsk Malerkunst** (Art Gallery for Fyn Paintings) has a good collection of turn-of-the-century paintings and sculpture by the Fyn Painters, a school of artists whose work captures the dusky light of the Scandinavian sun. *Grønnegade 75, tel. 62/61–06–45. Admission: DKr10 adults, DKr5 children. Open Apr.–Oct., daily 10–4; Nov.–Mar., weekends 11–3.*

From Fåborg, take Route 44 east 25 kilometers (15½ miles) to
8 **Svendborg,** Fyn's second largest town. Svendborg celebrates its 800-year-old maritime traditions in July when old Danish wooden ships congregate in the harbor for the circular **Fyn rundt** (regatta). (There's even the chance to get on board and shuttle between towns. Contact the Tourist Board, or any agreeable captain.) With many charter boat options and good marinas, use Svendborg as a base to explore the hundreds of islands of the South Fyn Archipelago.

From the harbor, walk down Frederiksgade, cross Møllergade to Torvet, the market square. To the left on Fruestræde is the black and yellow **Anne Hvides Gård,** the oldest secular house in Svendborg and one of the four branches of **Svendborgs Omegns Museum** (the Svendborg County Museum). Inside you'll see 18th- and 19th-century interiors and glass and silver collections. *Fruestræde 3, tel. 62/21–02–61. Admission: DKr10 adults; DKr5 children, senior citizens, and students. Open May–Oct., daily 10–4.*

Take a left on Teatergade and cross Skolegade to **Bagergade,** (Baker's Street), which is lined with some of Svendborg's oldest half-timbered houses. On the left, at the corner of Grubbemøllevej and Svinget is the **Viebæltegård,** the headquarters of the Svendborg County Museum, a former poorhouse. You can wander through dining halls, washrooms, and the "tipsy clink," where inebriated citizens were left to sober up as recently as 1974. *Grubbemøllevej 13, tel. 62/21–02–61. Admission: DKr15 adults, DKr5 children, senior citizens, and students. Open May–Oct., daily 10–4; Nov.–Apr., daily 1–4.*

North of Svendborg 15 kilometers (9 miles) on Route 9 is the
9 town of **Kværndrup** and the moated Renaissance **Egeskov Slot,** one of the best preserved island-castles in Europe. Peaked with copper spires and surrounded by Renaissance, Baroque, English, and peasant gardens, the castle has an antique vehicle museum and the world's largest maze, designed by the Danish scientist-turned-poet Piet Hein. Visitors can see a few of the rooms, including the great hall, the hunting room, and the Riborg Room, where the daughter of the house was locked up from 1599 to 1604 after giving birth to a son out of wedlock.

Kværndrup, tel. 62/27-10-16. Admission: DKr40 for maze, gardens, car museum, and additional DKr40 for castle for adults; DKr20 for maze, gardens, car museum, and additional DKr20 for castle for children. Open June-Aug., daily 9-6; May and Sept., daily 10-5.

In the opposite direction, a few miles south of Svendborg, are the lilliputian islands of Thurø and Tåsinge. Admittedly, there are no major sights on **Thurø,** but it does offer a lovely embodiment of an unspoiled, provincial Danish isle. To the west, across the Svendborg Sound Bridge, is **Tåsinge,** where the local 19th-century drama involves Elvira Madigan (recall the movie?) and her married Swedish lover, Sixten Sparre. Preferring heavenly union to earthly separation, they shot themselves and are now buried in the central Landet churchyard. It's a tradition for brides to throw their bouquets on the lovers' grave.

With half-timbered buildings and hand-carved doors, the is-
10 land's main town of **Troense** is one of the country's best preserved maritime villages. South of town is **Valdemar's Slot,** dating from 1610, which is one of Denmark's oldest privately owned castles. Visitors have free passage to almost all the sumptuously furnished rooms (everything is under electronic surveillance), the libraries, and the candle-lit church. (There's also a saucy 19th-century cigar box that shouldn't be missed.) *Troense, tel. 62/22-61-06. Admission: DKr30 adults, DKr10 children. Open May-Sept., daily 10-5.*

11 Tåsinge is connected to nearby **Langeland** by a causeway bridge. The largest island of the southern archipelago, Langeland is rich in relics, and the beaches are worth scouting out. Bird-watching is excellent on the southern half of the island, where migratory birds roost before setting off on their cross-Baltic journey. To the south are **Ristinge** and **Bagenkop,** two towns with good beaches, where you can catch the ferry to Kiel, Germany.

From either Svendborg, Langeland, or Fåborg, you can take a car ferry to the island of **Ærø,** the "Jewel of the Archipelago," where country roads wend through fertile fields and past thatched farmhouses. About 27 kilometers (16 miles) southeast of Søby, the port town where the ferry from Fåborg arrives, is
12 the storybook town of **Ærøskøbing,** on the island's north coast. Established as a market center in the 13th century, it did not flourish until it became a sailing town in the 1700s, but every night when the gas lights illuminate the cobbled streets, time seemingly has stood still.

What to See and Do with Children

Fyn's **Terrarium** has all kinds of slippery and slithery creatures, including snakes, iguanas, alligators, and the nearly extinct blue frog. *Kirkehelle 5, Vissenbjerg, tel. 64/47-18-50. Admission: DKr25 adults, DKr10 children. Open daily 9-6.*

Off the Beaten Track

History is recorded in miniature at the **Flaskeskibssamlingen** (Bottle Ship Collection), thanks to curator Peter Jacobsen. A former ship's cook known as "Peter Bottle," he has built nearly 2,000 bottle ships in his day. *Smegade 22, Ærøskøbing, tel. 62/*

52–13–00. Admission: DKr10 adults; DKr5 children. Open May–Sept., daily 10–noon and 2–4; June–Aug., daily 9–5.

Covered wagons (which sleep two adults and two children), complete with a horse and feed, are available for a week of old-fashioned transportation, following preset routes and overnighting at designated camps, from **Destinations Langeland.** At DKr1,900 to 3,200 per week, it's an inexpensive and unique holiday. *DK–5935 Bagenenkop, tel. 62/51–14–44.*

Shopping

Antiques Many of Fyn's manor houses and castles now double as antiques emporiums. The largest is at **Hindemae** (near Rte. 315, 12 km/7 mi west of Nyborg, exit 46 or 47, tel. 65/35–22–05), with one of Fyn's most extensive European antiques collections. Smaller collections are available at **Hønnerup Hougård** (Hougårdsvej 6, Gelsted, tel. 64/49–13–00) and **Mullerup Slot** (Mullerupvej 22, Gudbjerg, tel. 62/25–32–25).

Crafts Studios and Shops As elsewhere in Denmark, crafts and handmade items in Fyn are well designed and functional. At the **Bjørnholt Keramik** (Risingevej 12, Munkebo, tel. 65/97–40–90), you can watch ceramics in the making. **Mogens Eigenbrod** (Adelgade 40, Bogense, tel. 64/81–18–81) produces endearing handmade wood carvings and Christmas ornaments. **Uromagerens Hus** (the mobile-maker's house, tel. 66/12–70–44) is in a half-timbered house across from the H.C. Andersen Museum. Inside, handmade mobiles range from simple paper hangings to intricate ceramic balloons. For hand-blown glass, visit **Glasmagerne** (Vemmenæsvej 10, Tåsinge, tel. 62/54–14–94).

Produce Markets Wednesday and Saturday mornings throughout the summer are market days in towns across Fyn. Often held in the central square, they offer fresh produce, flowers, and cheeses. Check for details with the local tourism office.

Sports and Outdoor Activities

Bicycling Flat and smooth, Fyn is perfect for bikes. Packages with bike rental, hotel accommodations, and half-board are available from **Hotel Svendborg** (Centrumpladsen, 5700 Svendborg, tel. 62/21–17–00). For maps and tips, contact local tourism boards (*see* Important Addresses and Numbers, *above*).

Fishing Angling anywhere on **Fyn's** 1,130-kilometer (680-mile) coast is free, though a license from the tourist bureau is required to fish the Odense River. **Langeland** has particularly rich waters, with cod, salmon, flounder, and gar. For package tours, contact **Erling Olsson** (Ristinge Fæled 4, DK–5932 Humble, tel. 62/57–20–23) or **Ole Dehn** (Søndergade 22, Lohals, DK–5953 Tranekær, tel. 62/55–17–00.

Golf Fyn has three 18-hole courses open to the public—**Odense, St. Knud**'s (in Nyborg), and **Svendborg.** For information, fees, and tee-off times, call the **Odense Golf Klub** (tel. 65/95–90–00).

Water Sports For smooth **windsurfing,** head to the Little Belt and southern shores; windier conditions can be found on the east and north coasts. The **Middelfart Tourism Office** (tel. 64/41–17–88) rents sailboards to windsurfers.

Beaches

The golden **beaches** of south Fyn are among the gentlest in Denmark and very popular with northern Europeans. Public facilities, kiosks, and cafés are always nearby.

Dining and Lodging

Fyn boasts a wide range of hotels, inns, and restaurants. Inquire about **Funen à la carte,** a flexible package of accommodations and meals. You can also make arrangements to stay in one of Fyn's many *kroer* (inns) by purchasing a packet of coupons valid at 66 inns (*see* Lodging in Before You Go, *above*). The islands also have numerous campsites and hostels, all clean and attractively located, but make your reservations early. Europeans book well in advance, leaving few rooms for last-minute travelers.

Highly recommended establishments are indicated by a star ★.

Ærøskøbing
Lodging

Ærøhus. A half-timbered building with a steep red roof, the Ærøhus looks like a barn on the outside, an old aunt's house on the inside. Hanging pots and slanted interiors fill the living areas, while pine furniture and cheerful duvets keep the guest rooms simple and bright. The garden's five cottages have small terraces. *Vestergade 38, DK–5970, tel. 62/52–10–03. 35 rooms, 12 with bath; 5 cottages. Facilities: restaurant, garden. AE, V. Closed Dec. 27–Jan. 20. Moderate.*

Fåborg
Dining

Vester Skerninge Kro. Midway between Fåborg and Svendborg, this traditional inn is cluttered and comfortable. Pine tables are polished from years of serving hot stews and homemade *mediste pølse* (mild grilled sausage) and *æggkage* (fluffy omelet made with cream, smoked bacon, chives, and tomatoes). *Krovej 9, Vester Skerninge, tel. 62/24–10–04. Reservations advised. Dress: casual. No credit cards. Closed Tues. Inexpensive.*

Dining and Lodging

★ **Falsled Kro.** Once a smuggler's hideaway, the 500-year-old Falsled Kro is now among Denmark's most elegant inns. A Relais et Châteaux member, it has appointed its cottages sumptuously with European antiques and stone fireplaces. The restaurant combines French and Danish cuisine, using ingredients from its garden and markets in Lyon. *Assensvej 513, DK–5642 Millinge, tel. 62/68–11–11, fax 62/68–11–62. 14 rooms with bath, 3 apartments. Facilities: restaurant, helicopter pad, 3-hole golf course, room service, sailing, horseback riding. AE, DC, MC, V. Closed mid-Dec.–Feb. Very Expensive.*

Steensgaard Herregårdspension. A long avenue of beeches leads to this 700-year-old moated manor that's tucked 7 kilometers (4½ miles) northwest of Fåborg. The rooms are elegant, with antiques, four-poster beds, and yards of silk damask. In the fine restaurant, wild game is served from the manor's own reserve. *Steensgaard 4, 5642 Millinge, tel. 62/61–94–90. 15 rooms, 13 with bath. Facilities: restaurant, tennis, horseback riding, helicopter pad. AE, DC, MC, V. Closed Jan. Very Expensive.*

Kerteminde
Dining

Rudolph Mathis. This busy harbor-side restaurant is topped by two chimneys venting open grills that broil popular fish dishes such as catfish with butter, fennel, and Pernod sauce, and grilled turbot in a green pepper and lime sauce. *Dossringen 13,*

Munkebo, tel. 65/32–32–33. Reservations accepted. Dress: casual. AE, MC, V. Closed Jan.–Mar.; Mon.–Sun. Sept.–Dec. Moderate.

Nyborg
Dining

Danehofkroen. Outside Nyborg Slot, this family-run restaurant does a brisk lunch, serving traditional Danish meals to tourists who enjoy a view of the castle and its tree-lined moat. The menu is meat-and-potatoes, featuring dishes like *flæskesteg* (sliced pork served with the crisp rind). *Slotsplads, tel. 65/31–02–02. Reservations required. Dress: casual but neat. No credit cards. Closed Mon. Moderate.*

Lodging

Hesselet. A Relais et Châteaux member, this modern hotel looks like a brick slab outside, a refined English-cum-Oriental sanctuary inside. The guest rooms are furnished with cushy, modern furniture, and most have a splendid view of the Storebælt (Great Belt). *Christianslundsvej 119, 5800 Nyborg, tel. 65/31–30–29, 46 rooms with bath and shower, 3 suites. Facilities: restaurant, room service, meeting rooms, indoor pool, sauna. AE, DC, MC, V. Very Expensive.*

Odense
Dining

Marie Louise. Near the pedestrian street, this elegant whitewashed dining room glitters with crystal and silver. The daily Franco-Danish menu typically offers specialties like salmon scallop with bordelaise sauce and grilled veal with lobster cream sauce. Business and holiday diners are treated to gratis extras—such as quail's egg appetizers or after-dinner drinks. *Lottrups Gaard, Vestergade 70–72, tel. 66/17–92–95. Reservations advised. Jacket and tie advised. AE, DC, MC, V. Closed Sun. Expensive.*

Under Lindetræt. Once a bakery, this award-winning restaurant is now done up in linen and lace and frequented by well-heeled tourists. Classic French cuisine, such as medallions of beef with lemon-mushroom sauce and poached smoked salmon with green herbs, are served in a private parlor atmosphere, in the glow of low-hanging lamps and a fireplace. *Ramsherred 2, tel. 66/12–92–86. Reservations advised. Jacket advised. DC, MC, V. Closed July. Expensive.*

Den Gamle Kro. Built within the courtyards of several 17th-century homes, this popular restaurant has an ancient stone decor sliced by a sliding glass roof. The Franco–Danish menu includes fillet of sole stuffed with salmon mousse, and chateaubriand with garlic potatoes, but there's also inexpensive smørrebrød. *Overgade 23, tel. 66/12–14–33. Reservations advised. Dress: casual. DC, MC, V. Moderate.*

★ **Frank A.** Guarded by a meter-tall wooden bulldog named Tobias, this merry meeting place is dominated by high kitsch curios and paintings and an enormous collection of bric-a-brac. Friendly waiters serve drinks and French-inspired Danish dishes such as ham schnitzel with creamed potatoes and pepper steak flambé to a mostly local crowd. *Jernbanegade 4, tel. 66/12–27–57. Reservations accepted. Dress: casual. DC, MC, V. Moderate.*

★ **Spisehuset.** This country-style restaurant gleams with lustrous frescoed walls and French posters. As with its sister restaurant Marie Louise, the menu changes daily, offering French and Danish dishes such as warm salad with veal sweetbreads and medallions of beef with port–wine sauce. *Pogstræde 31, tel. 65/91–55–35. Reservations advised. Dress: casual but neat. AE, DC, MC, V. Moderate.*

Målet. A lively crowd calls this sports club their neighborhood bar, and, next to steaming plates of schnitzel served in a dozen ways, soccer is the other delight of the house. *Jernbanegade 17, tel. 66/17–82–41. Reservations not accepted. Dress: casual. No credit cards. Inexpensive.*

Lodging

Sara Grand Hotel. A century old, with renovated fin-de-siècle charm, this imposing four-story brick-front hotel greets guests with old-fashioned luxury. Crimson carpets and chandeliers lead to a wide staircase and upstairs guest rooms that are modern, with plush furnishings and sleek marble bathrooms. *Jernabanegade 18, 5100 Odense C, tel. 66/11–71–71, fax 66/14–11–71. 138 rooms, 79 with bath, 59 with shower; 13 suites. Facilities: sauna, solarium, in-room movies, room service. AE, DC, MC, V. Expensive.*

★ **Hotel Ydes.** Newly remodeled, this bright, colorful hotel is a good bet for students and budget-conscious travelers tired of barrack-type accommodations. The plain, white hospital-style rooms are clean and comfortable. *Hans Tausensgade 11, 5000 Odense C, tel. 66/12–11–31. 30 rooms, 24 with shower. Facilities: café. MC, V. Inexpensive.*

Svendborg
Dining

★ **Sandig.** This austere white eatery near the harbor is spartan, but food, not decor, is owner-chef-waiter-dishwasher Volkert Sandig's priority. His daily changing French-Danish menu includes inventive fish and beef specialties. Try the cod served with mussel and garlic sauce or the roast veal in a creamy mushroom ragout. *Kullinggade 1b, Svendborg, tel. 62/22–92–11. Reservations advised. Dress: casual. DC, MC, V. Closed daily 2–6 and Sun. Oct.–May. Moderate.*

Æro. A dim hodgepodge of ship parts and maritime doodads, this harbor-side restaurant is peopled by brusque waitresses and serious local trenchermen. The menu is old-fashioned, featuring *frikadeller* (fried meatballs), fried *rødspætte* (plaice) with hollandaise sauce, and dozens of smørrebrød options. *Brøgade 1 ved Ærøfærgen, tel. 62/21–07–60. Reservations advised. Dress: casual. DC, MC, V. Closed Sun. Inexpensive.*

Lodging

Margrethesminde. The Fyn equivalent of a bed-and-breakfast, this manor house/art gallery is 16 kilometers (10 miles) west of Svendborg. Everything in the house—Oriental sculptures, European antiques, and owner Erleng Andersen's own arresting paintings and sculpture—is for sale. Sunlight fills the five guest rooms, which are mostly decorated in beige and overlook the surrounding countryside. *Fåborgvej 154, 5762 Vester Skerninge, tel. 62/24–10–44. 5 rooms with bath. Facilities: bicycle rental. MC, V. Moderate.*

Tåsinge
Dining

Restaurant Valdemars Slot. Beneath the castle, this domed restaurant is ankle-deep in pink carpet, aglow in candlelight. Fresh ingredients from France and Germany and wild game from the castle's preserve are the essentials for an ever-changing menu. Wild venison with cream sauce and duck breast à l'orange are typical of the French-inspired cuisine. A less expensive annex, Den Grå Dame, serves traditional Danish food. *Slotsalleen 100, Troense, tel. 62/22–59–00. Reservations advised. Jacket and tie advised. AE, DC. Closed Mon. Very Expensive.*

Lodging

★ **Thurø Røgeriet.** Set on the water's edge, this friendly family-owned and -run pension offers homespun hospitality and dramatic views of Tåsinge Sound. While the living room is full of antiques and paintings by grandfather Niels Hansen, the rooms are spare, with plain white beds and cane chairs; a few have balconies and slanted ceilings. *Måroddevej 22, Thurø, tel. 62/20-50-84. 16 rooms, 14 with bath. Facilities: restaurant. MC, V. Closed Dec.-Jan. Moderate.*

The Arts and Nightlife

The Arts **Castle Concerts** are held throughout the summer at **Egeskov, Nyborg,** and **Valdemar** castles and the rarely opened **Krengenrup** manor house, near Assens. Check with local tourism offices for schedules. In summer, the **Odense Street Theater**'s *Hans Christian Andersen Happenings* are presented daily at 4 and 5, with living history and fairy-tale performances just outside the Andersen Museum.

Nightlife Fyn nightlife revolves around the major towns of Odense and Svendborg, while the smaller towns make do with local bars and quiet nights.

Bars and Lounges Odense's central Arcade is an entertainment mall, with bars, restaurants, and live music, ranging from corny sing-alongs to hard rock. For a quieter evening, stop by **Café Biografen** (Brandts Passage, tel. 66/13-16-16). In Svendborg, the very mixed **Banjen Bar** (Frederiksgade 11C, tel. 62/22-25-46) often has live rock and blues.

Casinos Fyn's sole casino is in the slick glass atrium of the **Hans Christian Andersen Hotel** (Claus Bergs Gade 7, Odense, tel. 66/14-78-00), with blackjack, roulette, and baccarat.

Discos In Odense, the popular **All Night Boogie Dance Café** (Nørregade 21, tel. 66/14-00-39) plays pop, disco, and '60s music to a laid-back crowd. The **Atlantic Night Club** (Overgade 45, tel. 65/91-05-27) is more chic, with revolving mirror balls and strobe lights. Svendborg's **Chess** (Vestergade 7, tel. 62/22-49-69) is popular with a young crowd that comes for the live bands.

Jazz Clubs **The Cotton Club** (Pantheonsgade 5C, tel. 66/12-55-25) in Odense is a venue for old-fashioned jazz. Though Svendborg doesn't have a permanent jazz club, the **Orangi** (Jessens Mole, tel. 62/22-82-92), an old sailing ship that's moored in the harbor, is a popular summer restaurant where jazz musicians often perform.

Jylland

Introduction

Denmark's western peninsula is the only part of the country naturally connected to mainland Europe; its southern boundary is the frontier with Germany. Compared to the smooth, postcard-perfect land of Fyn and Sjælland, this Ice Age–chiseled peninsula is bisected at the north by the craggy Limfjord and spiked below by the Danish "mountains." Himmelbjerget, the zenith of this modest range, peaks at 438 feet, while farther south the Yding Skovhøj plateau measures 568 feet—modest hills just about anywhere else.

The first inhabitants of Denmark were hunters who lived in southern Jylland (Jutland) 250,000 years ago. You can see flint tools and artifacts from this period locked away in museums, but the land holds more stirring relics from a later epoch: After

1,000 years, Viking burial mounds and stones still swell the land, some in protected areas, others lying in farmers' fields, tended by grazing sheep.

The windswept landscapes filmed in *Babette's Feast,* the movie version of Isak Dinesen's novel, trace the west coast northward to Skagen, a luminous, dune-covered point (geographically not unlike the Outer Banks of North Carolina), while to the east coast, facing Fyn, lie deep fjords rimmed with forests. The center is dotted with castles, parklands, and the famed Legoland. Ribe, Denmark's oldest town, lies to the south, while the east coast is anchored by Århus and Aalborg, respectively Denmark's second- and fourth-largest cities, with nightlife and sights to rival Copenhagen's.

Important Addresses and Numbers

Tourist Information Tourism offices, open weekdays 10–4, Saturday 9–noon in winter and 9–6 weekdays and Saturday in the summer, are in: **Aalborg** (Østerå 8, tel. 98/12–60–22), **Århus** (Rådhuset, tel. 86/12–16–00), **Billund,** (c/o Legoland A/S, Åstvej, tel. 75/33–19–26), **Randers** (Hellingandhuset, Erik Menveds Plads 1, tel. 86/42–44–77), **Ribe** (Torvet 3–5, tel. 75/42–15–00), **Silkeborg** (Torvet 9, tel. 86/82–19–11), and **Viborg** (Nytorv 5, tel. 86/62–16–17).

Emergencies For **ambulance, fire,** or **police** emergencies, call 000.

Doctors After normal hours (4 PM–7 AM), in **Aalborg,** call 98/13–62–11. In **Århus,** call 86/15–00–44; day calls 86/12–72–11. Fees (DKr300–400) must be paid in cash. Elsewhere, call directory assistance at 0033 and ask for the local **night doctor** number.

Late-night Pharmacies Try **Århus** (Jernbaneapotek, Banegårdspladsen, tel. 86/12–02–44) or **Aalborg** (Budolfi Apotek, corner of Vesterbro and Algade, tel. 98/12–06–77). Pharmacies elsewhere rotate 24-hour emergency service and will only fill prescriptions called in by doctors.

Arriving and Departing by Plane

Billund Airport, 2 kilometers (1.2 miles) southwest of downtown, receives flights from London, Stockholm, Brussels, Amsterdam, and Stavanger on **Mærsk Air** (tel. 75/33–28–44), and the Norwegian carrier **Braathens** to Oslo, which continues to Århus. Several domestic airports, including **Aalborg, Århus,** and **Esbjerg,** are served by **Mærsk, Cimber Air** (tel. 74/42–22–77), and **SAS** (75/33–14–11), all with good connections to Copenhagen.

Arriving and Departing by Car, Train, and Ferry

By Car Two bridges link Middelfart on Fyn to Fredericia on Jylland. The older, lower bridge (1.7 kilometers/1 mile) follows Route 161, while the newer suspension bridge (1.2 kilometers/¾ mile) on E20 is faster.

By Train **DSB** (tel. 33/14–17–01) makes hourly links between Copenhagen and Fredericia. The 3½-hour trip includes train passage aboard the ferry, which crosses the Store Bælt between Korsør, on west Sjælland, and Nyborg, on east Fyn.

By Ferry Ferries from Hundested, Sjælland, to Grena in east Jylland take 2½ hours, while those from Kalundborg to Århus take 3 hours. For information, call **DSB** (tel. 33/14–17–01). **Scandinavian Seaways** (tel. in Esbjerg, 75/12–48–00; in Copenhagen, 33/15–63–00) also link Harwich and New Castle to Esbjerg, in the southwest. There are also ferries from Göteborg (3¼ hours), on Sweden's west coast and Oslo, Norway (10 hours) to Frederikshavn, in the northeast. Call **Stena Line** (tel. 98/42–43–66) for both.

Getting Around

By Car Although train and bus connections are excellent, sights and towns are widely dispersed, so this tour is best made by car. Whether you decide to take speedy, modern highways or winding old roads, traffic is virtually nonexistent.

By Train For long trips, the **DSB** (tel. 86/13–17–00) trains are fast and efficient, with great views of the countryside. Smaller towns do not have inner-city trains, so you'll have to switch to buses once you arrive.

By Bus Intercity buses are punctual but slower than trains. Passengers can buy tickets on the bus and pay according to destination. For schedules and fares, call **DSB** weekdays (tel. 86/12–67–03). For inner-city travel, schedules are posted at all bus stops and fares are usually under DKr10.

By Bicycle Jylland has scores of bike paths. In the west, the **Vestkyst-stien** (west-coast path) goes from Skagen in the north to Bulbjerg in the south. On the east, the **Vendsyssel-stien** (winding path) goes from Frederikshavn to the mouth of the Limfjord. The **Østkyst-stien** (east coast path) follows, and leads to the south of, the Limfjord. In the south, much of the 1,000-year-old **Hærvejen** (Old Military Road) has been converted into a network of picturesque cycling lanes. It's sign-posted for all 240 kilometers (145 miles) through the center of Jylland, from Padborg in the south to Viborg in the north. Many auto routes also have cycle lanes. Bike rentals are available in most towns from the tourism board, which can also supply maps and brochures. Among the tourist offices that can help with bike tips, call the Viborg and Silkeborg (*see* Tourist Information, *above*) and the Vejen tourist boards (tel. 75/36–26–96).

Guided Tours

Guided tours are few and far between, but check with the local tourism office for tips and reservations. Some carry brochures that describe walking tours. The **Århus Round the City** tour (2½ hours) begins at the tourist office and includes Den Gamle By, Domkirke, the concert hall, the university, and the harbor. **Aalborg's City Tour** (2 hours) departs from Adelgade and includes most of the town museums, the Budolfi Cathedral, Monastery of the Holy Ghost, the Town Hall, Jens Bang Stenhus, and Jomfru Ane Gade.

Exploring Jylland

Numbers in the margin correspond with points of interest on the Jylland map.

Nearly three times the size of the rest of Denmark, with long distances between towns, the peninsula of Jylland rewards several days or even weeks of exploring. If you are pressed for time, concentrate on one tour, or a couple of cities. Delightful as they are, the offshore islands are suitable only for those with plenty of time, as many require an overnight stay.

Tour 1: South Jylland

1 Most travelers arrive from **Middelfart** to **Fredericia,** Jylland's main rail junction, and 350 years ago a defense center. There's not much to see, so continue 20 kilometers (12 miles) southwest
2 to **Kolding** and the well-preserved **Koldinghus.** The massive stonework structure was a fortress and then a royal residence in the Middle Ages and is a historical museum today. In the winter of 1808, during the Napoleonic Wars, Spanish soldiers set fire to most of it as they tried to keep warm. *Rådhusstræde, tel. 75/50-15-00, ext. 5400. Admission: DKr22 adults, children free. Open May-Sept., daily 10-5; Oct.-Mar., Mon.-Sat. noon-3, Sun. 10-3.*

In the south of town is **Den Geografiske Have** (Geographical Garden) with more than 120 varieties of roses as well as some 2,000 plants arranged geographically by continent. *Christian Fjerde Vej, tel. 75/50-38-80. Admission: DKr30 adults, children free. Open June and Aug., daily 9-7; July, daily 9-8; Sept.-May, daily 10-6.*

About 60 kilometers (36 miles) southwest, but well worth the
3 extra driving time, is **Ribe,** the country's oldest town, whose medieval center is preserved by the Danish National Trust. From May to mid-September, a night watchman circles the town telling of its history and singing traditional songs. Visitors can accompany him nightly by gathering at the main square at 10 PM.

The **Ribe Domkirke** (Cathedral) stands at the site of one of Denmark's earliest churches, built around AD 860. The present structure dates from the 12th century, with a 14th-century bell tower. Note the Cat Head Door, said to be for the exclusive use of the devil. *Torvet, tel. 75/42-06-19. Admission: DKr5 adults, DKr1 children. Open May, Mon.-Sat. 10-5, Sun. noon-5; June-Aug., Mon.-Sat. 10-6, Sun. noon-6; Sept., Mon.-Sat. 10-5, Sun. noon-5; Oct.-Apr., Mon.-Sat. 11-3, Sun. noon-3.*

On Route 24, 23 kilometers (14 miles) to the northwest, is
4 **Esbjerg,** arrival point for ferries coming from Harwich and Newcastle, and terminus for the 20-minute ferry to the tiny island of **Fanø.** During the 19th century, the island had an enormous shipbuilding industry and a fleet second only to Copenhagen's. The shipping industry deteriorated, but the proud maritime heritage remains. From the ferry port in
5 Nordby, take a bus south to **Sønderho.** Along the tiny winding lanes are thatched cottages decorated with ships' relics, figureheads, painted doors, and brass lanterns. Even the traditional costume is still in use, especially on *Sønderhodag,* a town fest held the third Sunday in July.

6 Next in south-central Jylland is **Billund** and the famed **Legoland.** It's filled with scaled-down versions of cities and villages, working harbors and airports, a Statue of Liberty, a statue of Sitting Bull, Mount Rushmore, a safari park, and a Wild West saloon—all constructed from 35 million toy, plastic Lego bricks. There are also exhibits of toys from pre-Lego days, the most exquisite of which is **Tatania's Palace,** a sumptu-

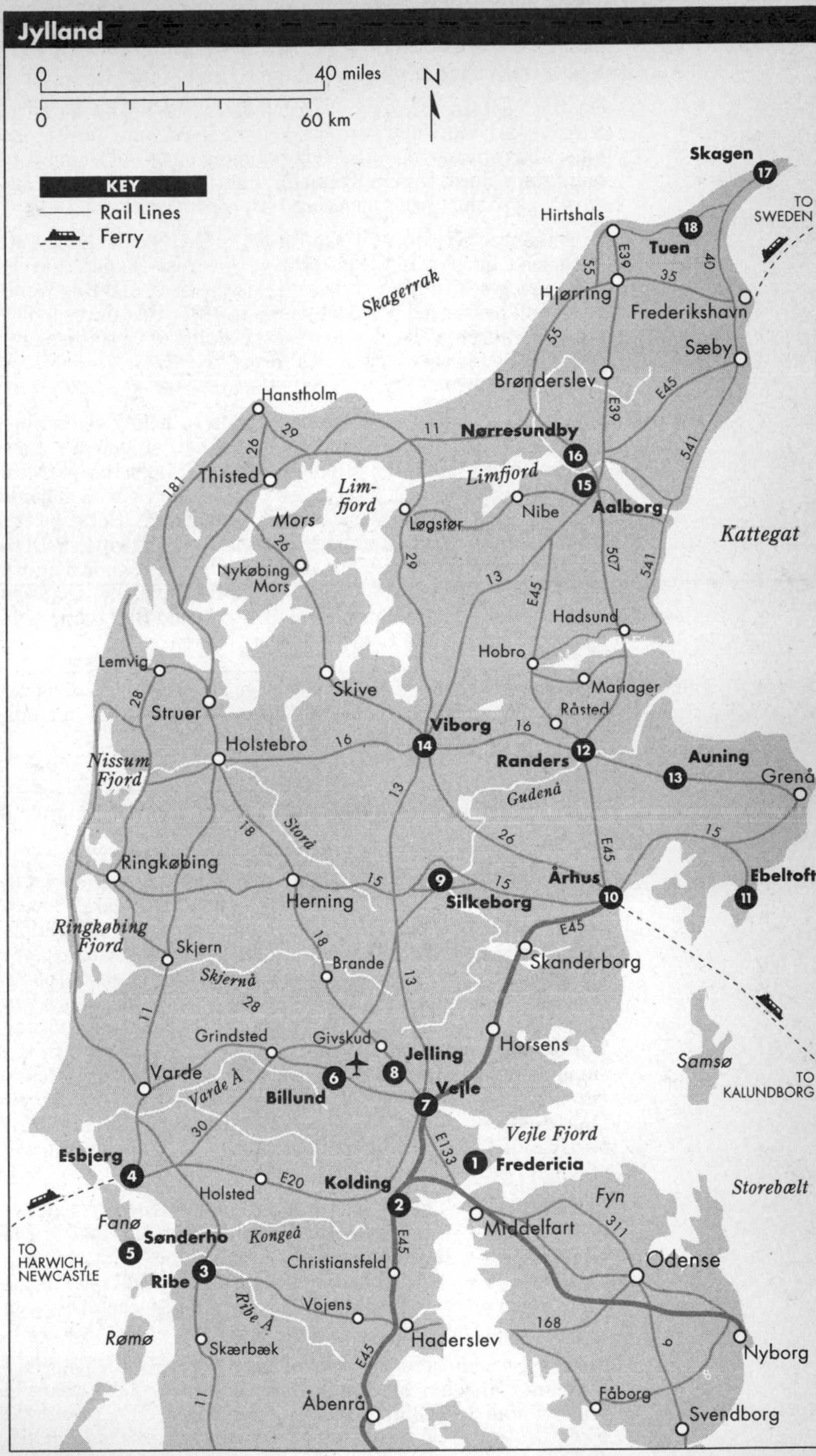
Jylland
0
40 miles
0
60 km
N
KEY
Rail Lines
Ferry
Skagen
17
TO SWEDEN
Hirtshals
18
Tuen
Skagerrak
Hjørring
Frederikshavn
Sæby
Brønderslev
Hanstholm
Nørresundby
16
Limfjord
15
Thisted
Lim-fjord
Aalborg
Nibe
Løgstør
Mors
Kattegat
Nykøbing Mors
Hadsund
Hobro
Lemvig
Mariager
Skive
Struer
Råsted
Viborg
14
Holstebro
Randers
12
Auning
13
Grenå
Nissum Fjord
Gudenå
Storå
Ringkøbing
Herning
9
Silkeborg
Århus
10
Ebeltoft
11
Ringkøbing Fjord
Skjern
Skanderborg
Brande
Skjernå
Horsens
Samsø
Grindsted
Givskud
Jelling
6
8
Varde
Varde Å
Billund
Vejle
7
TO KALUNDBORG
Vejle Fjord
Esbjerg
4
1
Fredericia
Kolding
Holsted
2
Fyn
Storebælt
Fanø
Middelfart
Sønderho
5
Kongeå
Odense
TO HARWICH, NEWCASTLE
Ribe
3
Christiansfeld
Vojens
Ribe Å
Haderslev
Rømø
Skærbæk
Nyborg
Fåborg
Åbenrå
Svendborg

ous doll house built in 1907 by Sir Neville Wilkinson for his daughter. *Billund, tel. 75/33–13–33. Admission: DKr44 adults, DKr22 children. Open May–Sept. 15, daily 10–8.*

7 On the east coast, **Vejle,** 20 kilometers (12 miles) north of Kolding, is beautifully positioned on the fjord, amid forest-clad hills. You can hear the time of day chiming on an old **Dominican monastery clock;** the clock remains, but the monastery long ago gave way to the town's imposing 19th-century city hall.

In the center of town, at Kirke Torvet, is **Skt. Nicolai Kirke** (St. Nicholas Church). In the left arm of the cross-shaped church, lying in a glass Empire-style coffin, is the body of a **Bog Woman,** found preserved in a peat marsh in 1835, that dates to 500 BC. The church walls also conceal the skulls of 23 thieves executed in the 17th century. *Kirke Torvet, tel. 75/82–41–39. Open May–Sept., Mon.–Fri. 9–5, Sat. 9–noon, Sun. 9–11:30.*

8 From Vejle, there's a **vintage steam train** to **Jelling** every Sunday in July and the first Sunday in August. Otherwise, take Route 18 10 kilometers (6 miles) north through the pastoral Grejs Valley to Jelling. There, two 10th-century burial mounds mark the seat of King Gorm and his wife, Thyra. Between the mounds are two **Runestener** (rune stones), one of which is Denmark's certificate of baptism, showing the oldest known figure of Christ in Scandinavia. The inscription explains that the stone was erected by Gorm's son, King Harald Bluetooth, who brought Christianity to the Danes in AD 960.

Time Out There are few eateries in Jelling, so go 2 kilometers (1.2 miles) west to **Skovdal Kro** (Fårupvej 23, tel. 75/87–17–81), a traditional inn that serves old-fashioned meals.

Tour 2: The Lake District and Central Jylland

9 North toward **Silkeborg,** on the banks of the river Gudena, is Jylland's **lake district.** Stretching from Silkeborg in the west to Skanderborg in the east, it contains some of Denmark's loveliest scenery, as well as some of the country's meager mountains, including the 438-foot Himmelbjerget. The best way to explore the area is by water, as the Gudena winds its way some 160 kilometers (100 miles) through lakes and wooded hillsides down to the sea. Take one of the excursion boats or, better still, the world's last coal paddle steamer, ***Hjejlen,*** which runs in the summer and is based in Silkeborg. *Havnen, Silkeborg. Reservations: tel. 86/82–07–66. Admission: round-trip tickets DKr29–66 adults; children half-price. Departs Silkeborg Harbor 10 and 1:45 Sun. in June, and daily mid-June–beginning of Aug.*

Since 1861, it has paddled its way through narrow stretches of fjord, where the treetops meet overhead, to the foot of the **Himmelbjerget** at Julsø (Lake Jul). From that point, you can climb the narrow paths through the heather and trees to the top, where an 80-foot tower stands sentinel, placed there on Constitution Day in 1875, in memory of King Frederik VII.

Silkeborg's main attractions are housed in the **Kulturhistoriske Museum** (Museum of Cultural History): the 2,200-year-old **Tollund Man** and **Elling Girl,** two more bog people, preserved by natural ingredients in the soil and water. *Hovedgådsvej, tel.*

86/82–15–78. Admission: DKr15 adults, DKr5 kr. children. Open Apr. 15–Oct. 23, daily 10–5; Oct. 24–Apr. 14, Wed. and weekends 12–4.

On the coast, 40 kilometers (24 miles) east of Silkeborg, is
10 **Århus,** Denmark's second-largest city. The town is liveliest during the 10-day Århus Festival in September, which combines everything from concerts, theater, and exhibitions, to beer tents and sports.

A good starting point is the **Århus Rådhus,** probably the most unusual city hall in Denmark. Built in 1941 by noted architects Arne Jacobsen and Erik Møller, the pale Norwegian-marble block building is controversial but cuts a startling figure when illuminated in the evening. *Park Allé, tel. 86/13–20–00. Free tours June–mid-Sept., weekdays at 4.*

Not to be missed is the town's open-air museum, known as **Den Gamle By** (the Old Town), which features 65 half-timbered houses, a mill, and a millstream, all carefully moved from locations throughout Jylland and meticulously re-created, inside and out. *Viborgvej, tel. 86/12–31–88. Admission: DKr30 adults, DKr12 children. Open Jan.–Mar. and Nov., daily 11–3; Apr. and Oct., Mon.–Sat., daily 10–4; May and Sept., daily 10–5; June–Aug., daily 9–6; Dec., Mon.–Sat. 10–3, Sun. 10–4.*

In a 250-acre forest in a park south of Århus is the indoor-outdoor **Mocsgård Forhistorisk Museum** (Prehistoric Museum), with exhibits on ethnography and archaeology, including the famed **Grauballe Man,** a 2,000-year-old corpse so well bog-preserved that scientists could determine his last meal. Also, take the **Forhistoriskvej** (Prehistoric Trail) through the forest, which leads past Stone- and Bronze-Age displays to reconstructed houses from Viking times. *Moesgård Allé, tel. 86/27–24–33. Admission: DKr20 adults, children free. Open Jan.–Mar. and mid-Sept.–Dec., Tues.–Sun. 10–4; Apr.–mid-Sept., daily 10–5.*

If you have time, drive northeast to the tip of what Danes call
11 Jylland's nose, to **Ebeltoft,** a town of crooked streets, sloping row houses, and local crafts shops. Danish efficiency is showcased beside the ferry, at the **Vindmølleparken,** one of the largest windmill parks in the world, where 16 wind-power mills on a curved spit of land generate electricity for 600 families. *Færgehaven, tel. 86/34–12–44. Admission free. Open daily.*

Tour 3: North Jylland

North 21 kilometers (15 miles) from Århus is the medieval town
12 of **Randers,** where in 1340 the Danish patriot Niels Ebbesen killed the German oppressor, Count Gert the Bald of Holstein, whose army was then occupying most of Jylland. To the east of Randers is the **Djursland Peninsula,** a popular vacation area, with fine manor houses open to the public.

If time permits, visit **Gammel Estrup Slot,** a grand 17th-centu-
13 ry manor in the tiny village of **Auning;** it's full of rich period furnishings, including an alchemist's cellar. *Randersvej 2, tel. 86/48–30–01. Admission: DKr20 adults, DKr5 children. Open Apr.–Sept., daily 10–5; Oct.–Mar., Tues.–Sun. 11–3.*

14 About 60 kilometers (36 miles) west of Randers is **Viborg,** whose history predates the 8th century, when it was a trading post and a place of pagan sacrifice. Later it became a center of Christianity, with monasteries and an episcopal residence. The 1,000-year-old **Hærvejen,** the old military road that starts near here, was once Denmark's most important connection with the outside world. Legend has it that in the 11th century, King Canute set out from Viborg to conquer England; he succeeded, of course, and ruled from 1016 to 1035. Today, you can buy reproductions of a silver coin minted by the king, embossed with the inscription, "Knud, Englands Kong" (Canute, King of England).

Built in 1130, Viborg's **Domkirke** (Cathedral) was once the largest granite church in the world. Today, only the crypt remains of the original building, which was restored and reopened in 1876. The dazzling early 20th-century biblical frescoes are by Danish painter Joakim Skovgard. *Mogensgade, tel. 86/62–10–60. Admission free. Open June–Aug., Mon.–Sat. 10–4; Sun. noon–5; Sept. and Apr.–May, Mon.–Sat. 11–4, Sun. noon–4; Oct.–Mar., Mon.–Sat. 11–3, Sun. noon–3.*

There's terrific walking country 8 kilometers (5 miles) south of Viborg, beside **Hald Sø** (Hald Lake) and on the heather-clad **Dollerup Bakker** (Dollerup Hills).

Another 80 kilometers (50 miles) north are the gentle waters of the **Limfjord,** the great waterway that severs Jylland.
15 Clamped to its narrowest point is **Aalborg,** Denmark's fourth-largest community, which celebrates its 1,300th birthday in 1992 with a year of festivities. The gateway between north and south Jylland, the city is a charming combination of new and old: twisting lanes filled with medieval houses and, nearby, broad modern boulevards. The only Fourth of July celebrations outside the United States annually blast off in nearby Rebild Park, a salute to the United States for welcoming 300,000 Danish immigrants that has continued since 1912.

Among the sights, the local favorite is the magnificent 17th-century **Jens Bangs Stenhus** (Jens Bang's Stone House), built by a wealthy merchant. Chagrined that he was never made a town council member, the cantankerous Bang avenged himself by caricaturing his political enemies in gargoyles all over the building and then adding his own face, its tongue sticking out at town hall. A five-story building dating from 1624, it has a vaulted Gothic stone beer and wine cellar (*see* Nightlife, *below*). *Østerä 9.*

A short walk to Gammel Torv, brings you to the Baroque cathedral, **Budolfi Kirke,** dedicated to the English saint Botolph, and the 15th-century **Helligandsklosteret** (Monastery of the Holy Ghost). One of Denmark's best-preserved monasteries—and perhaps the only one that allowed both nuns and monks—it is now a home for the elderly. During World War II the monastery was the meeting place for the Churchill Club, a group of Aalborg school boys who became world-famous for their sabotage of the Nazis.

In the center of the old town is **Jomfru Ane Gade,** named, as the story goes, after an aristocratic maiden who was accused of being a witch, then beheaded. Now the street's fame is second only to Copenhagen's Strøget. Despite the flashing neon and booming music of about 30 discos, bars, clubs, and eateries, the street remains old-fashioned, appealing to all ages.

16 Just north of the city, at **Nørresundby,** is **Lindholm Høje,** a Viking- and Iron Age burial ground, where stones placed in the shape of a ship enclose many of the site's 682 graves, and sheep often outnumber tourists. At its entrance, there's a brand-new museum that chronicles the Viking civilization, as well as recent excavations. *Hvorupvej, tel. 98/19–14–25. Museum admission: DKr20 adults, DKr15 children; Burial-ground admission free. Open Sept.–May, daily 10–5; June–Aug., daily 10–7.*

17 At the desolate northern tip of Jylland is **Skagen** (pronounced Skane), where long beaches and luminous light have inspired painters and writers alike. The 19th-century Danish artist Holger Drachmann (1846–1908) and his friends, including the very popular P.S. Kroyer, founded the Skagen School of painting, which captured the special quality of northern light; you can see their efforts on display in the **Skagen Museum.** *4 Brøndumsvej, tel. 98/44–64–44. Admission: DKr25 adults, children free. Open Apr. and Oct., Tues.–Sun. 11–4; May and Sept., daily 10–5; June–Aug., daily 10–6; Nov.–Mar., Wed.–Fri. 1–4, Sat. 11–4, Sun. 11–3.*

Danes say that here you can "stand one foot in the Kattegat [the strait between Sweden and eastern Jylland], the other in the Skagerrak [the strait between western Denmark and Norway]." The point is so thrashed by storms and clashing waters that the 18th-century **Tilsandede Kirke** (Sand Buried Church) 2 kilometers (1 mile) south of town, is completely covered by dunes. Equally dramatic is the west coast's **Råbjerg Mile,** a protected migrating dune that moves about 33 feet a year and is accessible on foot from the Kandestederne.

18 Another 30 kilometers (18 miles) south, at **Tuen,** is **Bindslev Ørne Reservat** (the Bindslev Eagle Sanctuary, the only place in the world where golden- and white-tailed eagles and large falcons are raised in close contact with people. In the summer, educational exhibits include feedings and aerial acrobatics. *107 Skagensvej, Tuen, tel. 98/93–20–31. Admission: DKr40 adults, DKr20 children. Showtimes June, Wed. 10, Sat.–Sun. 5; July, Tues. and Thurs.–Sun. 5, Wed. 10 and 5; Aug., Wed.–Thurs. 10, Fri.–Sun. 5; Sept., Wed. 10 and Sat. 3.*

What to See and Do with Children

Besides Legoland, there's the **Fårup Sommerland** (Summer Land) recreation center in Saltum, about 30 kilometers (18 miles) west of Aalborg, with a massive water park, moon buggies, trampolines, and rides. *147 Pirupvejen, tel. 98/88–16–00. Admission: DKr65–80. Opening times vary; call for current hours.*

Aalborg's **Tivoliland** has a boomerang roller-coaster, buggies, and gardens. *Karolinelundsvej, tel. 98/12–58–74. Admission: DKr30 adults, DKr20 children. Open May–Sept.; hours vary.*

Off the Beaten Track

A thousand years ago, the Vikings mined their chalk from the caves of **Mønsted Kalkgruber** (Chalk Mines), but now the cool, multipurpose grottoes store 220 tons of cheese, and a Museum of Bats. Occasional classical concerts are also held in the mine. *Kalkværksvej, Mønsted (15 km w of Viborg), tel. 86/64–60–02. Admission: DKr20 adults, DKr10 children. Open mid-May–mid-June and mid-Aug.–mid-Sept., Tues.–Sun. 10–5; mid-June–mid-Aug., daily 10–5.*

See exactly how small the world can be at the **Verdenskort** (World Map Garden), near Klejtrup Lake in the north of the peninsula. For 25 years, Søren Poulsen has been digging, moving and sculpting dirt along the southern shore of the lake into the exact shape of the continents. Leaps and bounds can take you around the world—and you can even putt on a miniature golf course. *Klejtrup Lake, 10 km (6 mi) southwest of Hobro and tip of Mariager Fjord, tel. 98/54–61–32. Admission: DKr12 adults, DKr6 children. Open Sept.–May, daily 9–6; June–Aug., daily 9–8.*

Shopping

Ask at the tourism offices about local potters, glassblowers, and craftspeople, as well as antiques dealers, and stroll through the central pedestrian streets, which are full of shops.

Sports and Outdoor Activities

Bicycling Package holidays range from island day-trips to eight-day excursions. Information is available from any tourism board or the **County of North Jylland** (Niels Bohrsvej, Box 8300, DK-9220 Aalborg, tel. 98/15–62–22). (*See* also Getting Around by Bicycle, *above.*)

Canoeing Canoe rentals (about DKr180 per day) are available in the lake district, Limfjord, and on almost all lakes and rivers. One- to three-day package tours are available with either camping or hostel accommodations. For more information, contact the **Randers Tourist Bureau.**

Fishing There's great angling (trout, perch, pike, and others), especially along the **Limfjord, Karup River** near Skive, and south along the **Lake District.** License requirements vary and package tours are also available; contact any tourism board for details.

Golf There are 21 18-hole courses, all of which are open to guests. For green fees and tee times, call **Holstebro Golf Club** near Randers (4 Brandsbjergvej, Råsted 7570 Vemb, tel. 98/48–51–55), the **Aalborg Golf Club** (Jægersprisvej 35, tel. 98/34–14–76), or the **Esbjerg Golf Club** (Sønderhedevej Marbæk, tel. 75/26–92–19).

Beaches

Jylland is famous among northern Europeans for its wide beaches and shifting dunes. Facilities and cafés almost always are nearby, and the beaches and water are clean. The east coast has calm waters, good for children and windsurfing, while western and northern waters are rougher, with expansive beaches. In these areas, you'll need to rent or buy a wind tarp as protection from the blowing sands.

Dining and Lodging

Dining in Jylland ranges from homespun kros serving huge country meals to snazzy restaurants offering French nouveau. As the area is mostly frequented by Danes, national specialties are almost always homemade, and prices tend to be substantially lower than in the rest of the country. As elsewhere in the Danish countryside, hotels, and especially family restaurants, expect guests to arrive early (say, by 7 PM). (For price category definitions, *see* Dining and Lodging in Staying in Denmark, *above.*)

Highly recommended establishments are indicated by a star ★.

Aalborg
Dining

Cafeen og Dufy. Light and bright on an old cobbled street, these are among the most popular eateries in town. Downstairs, bistro-style Cafeen has French-style ambience, with marble-topped tables, engraved mirrors, and windows over Jomfru Ane Gade, while upstairs, Dufy is more elegant and quiet. The French menu is the same in both, including lobster-and-cognac soup for two, sliced roast duck with Waldorf salad, and beef fillet. *Jomfru Ane Gade 8, tel. 98/16–34–44. Reservations advised. Dress: casual but neat. DC, MC, V. Moderate.*

★ **Spisehuset Kniv og Gaffel.** In a 400-year-old building parallel to Jumfru Ane Gade, this busy restaurant is crammed with oak tables, crazy slanting floors, and candlelight, while a year-round courtyard is a veritable greenhouse. Young waitresses negotiate the mayhem to deliver inch-thick steaks, the house specialty. *Maren Turisgade 10, tel. 98/16–69–72. Reservations advised. Dress: casual but neat. DC, MC, V. Closed Sun. Moderate.*

Dining and Lodging

Phønix. Centrally located in a sumptuous old mansion, this hotel is popular with international and business guests. The rooms are luxuriously furnished with plump chairs and polished dark wood furniture; the original raw beams are still intact in some. One of the three restaurants, the Halling, serves excellent French and Danish food. *Vesterbro 77, DK–9000, tel. 98/12–00–11, fax 98/16–31–66. 185 rooms: 120 with bath and shower, 57 with shower; 3 suites. Facilities: 3 restaurants, bar, café, sauna, solarium, room service, meeting center, parking. AE, DC, MC, V. Very Expensive.*

Århus
Dining

★ **Gammel Aabyhøj.** In an austere ivy-covered manor 2 kilometers (1.2 miles) west of Århus, this charming French restaurant is Jylland's only Relais Gourmand. Guests begin with appetizers in the library or garden, beneath walnut and chestnut trees. The traditional kitchen of chefs Michel and Annick Michaud specializes in seasoned meat, poultry, or fish dishes such as lemon sole with rich red wine sauce. The wine cellar is excellent, the desserts legendary. *Bakke Allé 1, tel. 86/15–77–33. Reservations advised. Jacket advised. AE, DC, MC, V. Closed Sun. Expensive.*

Lodging

Royal Hotel. Open since 1838, Århus's grand hotel has welcomed such greats as Artur Rubinstein and Marian Anderson. Well-heeled guests are welcomed into a stately lobby appointed in Chesterfield sofas, modern paintings, and a winding staircase that leads to the rooms above. The plush rooms vary in style and decor, but all boast rich drapery, velour and brocade furniture, and marble bathrooms. *Store Torv 4, 8100 Århus C,* *tel. 86/12-00-11, fax 86/76-04-04. 111 rooms with shower, 7 suites. Facilities: restaurant, bar, casino, sauna, solarium, business center. AE, DC, MC, V. Expensive.*

Ansgar Missions Hotel. This old hotel is simple and dated, with used Danish furniture, but the staff is agreeable and helpful. Despite drab halls and worn carpets, the rooms are adequate and comfortable, with laminated furniture, old-fashioned wallpaper, and bright lighting. Downstairs, there's a cafeteria-style restaurant where you can choose from a large smørrebrød table and nonalcoholic beverages. *Banegårdsplads 14, DK-8100, tel. 86/12-41-22, fax 86/20-29-04. 170 rooms, 137 with shower, 20 with shower and bath. Facilities: restaurant. DC, MC, V. Inexpensive.*

Fanø
Dining and Lodging
★

Sønderho Kro. Just 13 kilometers (8 miles) from Fanø's main town of Norrebro, this 270-year-old thatched-roof inn is one of Jylland's finest, its charm preserved with a beamed foyer, painted doors, and timbered ceilings. The rooms are gussied up with four-poster beds, elegant tapestries, and gauzy curtains. The Franco-Danish restaurant serves excellent seafood on its old tables. *Kropladsen 11, DK-6720, Sønderho, tel. 75/16-40-09. 7 rooms with bath, 1 suite. Facilities: restaurant, parking. AE, DC, MC, V. Closed Jan. 8-Feb. 7. Moderate.*

Kolding
Lodging
★

Hotel Garni. A 20-minute walk from town, this resplendent manor is a fine choice if you are a B&B and antiques enthusiast who likes grand old antiques, paintings, and curios. Owners Helene and Just Holst have skipped phones and TVs in the guest rooms, filling them instead with vintage photos, prints, and Danish antiques. Half the rooms have a shower, the others are among the cheapest in town. *Strandvejen 12, DK-6000, tel. 75/52-16-21. 6 rooms, 3 with shower. Facilities: parking. No credit cards. Inexpensive.*

Ribe
Dining

Sælhunden. This 300-year-old canal-side tavern barely accommodates a dozen tables, but its cozy atmosphere makes it popular with wayfarers and locals. Its name means "male seal"; the only seal mementoes left are a few skins and pictures, but you can still order a "seal's special" of cold shrimp, sautéed potatoes, and scrambled eggs or—an old Danish favorite—fat strips of bacon served with cream gravy and boiled potatoes. *Skibbroen 13, tel. 75/42-09-46. No reservations. Dress: casual. DC, MC, V. Inexpensive.*

Dining and Lodging
★

Hotel Dagmar. In the midst of Ribe's quaint center, this cozy half-timbered hotel encapsulates the charm of the 16th century—with stained-glass windows, sloping wood floors, and carved chairs. The lavish rooms are all appointed with antique canopy beds, fat armchairs, and chaises longues. The fine French restaurant serves such specialties as fillet of salmon in sorrel cream sauce and marinated foie gras de Canard. *Torvet 1, DK-6760, tel. 75/42-00-33, fax 75/42-36-52. 50 rooms with bath. Facilities: restaurant, bar, parking, meeting rooms. AE, DC, MC, V. Closed Dec. 24-Jan. 1. Expensive.*

Lodging

Ribe Family and Youth Hostel. Located in the center of town, this plain, red-brick hostelry is run by helpful wardens. Six- and four-bed dorm rooms are arranged in clusters of four, each sharing a shower, toilet, and small hallway. They are functional and child-proof, with pine bunks and industrial carpeting. *Ribehallen, Skt. Pedersgade 16, tel. 75/42-06-20, fax 75/42-42-88. 26 rooms, 12 communal showers and toilets. Facilities:*

cafeteria, kitchen, parking, sports hall. No credit cards. Closed Dec.–Jan. Inexpensive.

Silkeborg
Dining

Spisehuset Christian VIII. Divided from Silkeborg's center by a highway, this tiny crooked building seems transported from another time. Inside, it's elegant—and busy, with an international group of diners occupying the dozen cramped tables. The inventive menu includes such meat and poultry dishes as veal medallion stuffed with wild duck breast and lamb chops stuffed with feta cheese and rosemary. *Christian VIII Vej 54, tel. 86/82–25–62. Reservations advised. Dress: casual but neat. AE, DC, MC, V. Closed Sun. and 2 weeks in July. Moderate.*

Skagen
Dining and Lodging
★

Brøndums Hotel. A few minutes from the beach, this 150-year-old gabled inn is furnished with antiques and Skagen-School paintings. The 21 guest rooms in the main building, without TVs or phones, are old-fashioned, with wicker chairs and Oriental rugs, pine and four-poster beds. The 25 annex rooms are more modern. The hotel has a fine Danish-French restaurant with a lavish cold table. *Anchersvej 3, DK–9990, tel. 98/44–15–55. 46 rooms 11 with bath; 1 suite. Facilities: restaurant, conference rooms, parking. AE, DC, MC, V. Closed Dec. 24–Jan. 1. Expensive.*

Vejle
Dining and Lodging

Munkebjerg Hotel. Seven kilometers (4 miles) southeast of town, surrounded by a thick beech forest and majestic views of the Vejle fjord, this elegant hotel attracts guests who prefer privacy. The rooms overlook the forest and are furnished in blond pine and soft green, while the lobby is rustic. There are also two top-notch French-Danish restaurants and a swank new casino. *Munkebjergvej 125, DK–7100, tel. 75/72–35–00, fax 75/72–08–86. 145 rooms with bath, 2 suites. Facilities: 2 restaurants, casino, health club, indoor pool, tennis court, sauna, solarium, room service, business center, parking, heliport. AE, DC, MC, V. Closed Dec. 20–28. Very Expensive.*

Bredal Kro. North of Vejle 8 kilometers (5 miles), this street-side inn is an essential stop for travelers. Behind the green gables, the traditional menu of hearty Danish omelets and stews probably hasn't changed in 250 years, but, for the health conscious, there's a list of low-fat and cholesterol-free fish and game. Modest, motel-style rooms are in a separate annex. *Horsensvej 581, DK–7100, tel. 75/89–57–99. Reservations accepted. Dress: casual. AE, DC, MC, V. Closed Dec. 24–Jan. 1. Inexpensive.*

The Arts and Nightlife

The Arts

Cultural activities are concentrated in Århus and Aalborg, both of which have local symphonies and concert halls and free events throughout the summer. There's no better time to visit **Århus** than during the **10-day music festival** in September, when jazz, classical, and rock concerts are nonstop.

Nightlife

Nightlife in Århus, and especially Aalborg, is as glittery as anything in Copenhagen. Much of it is geared for young audiences, but there are late-night cafés and bars for an older crowd.

Bars, Lounges, and Discos

Besides dozens of bars on **Aalborg's** Jomfrue Ane Gade, **Duus Vinkjælder** (Østerä 9, tel. 98/12–50–56), the atmospheric wine cellar of the Jens Bangs Hus, is extremely popular. Among the discos, **Gaslight** (tel. 98/10–17–50), **New York** (tel. 98/16–45–

44), and **Over and Under the Clock** (tel. 98/10–30–22) on Aalborg's Jomfrue Ane Gade all draw young crowds, while **Ambassadeur** (Vesterbro 76, tel. 98/12–62–22), with four dance restaurants and live music, is popular with a more mature audience.

In **Århus, Café Mozart** (Vesterport 10, tel. 86/18–55–63) features classical music, while **Den Sidste Café** (Paradisegade 9, tel. 86/13–71–11) rocks until 5 AM. **Palæs** (Christiansgade 24, tel. 86/12–72–29) and **Down Town** (Store Torv 4, tel. 86/13–95–77) are packed with youngsters, but the new **Beach Club** in the Hotel Marselis (Strandvejen 25, tel. 86/14–44–11) attracts all ages for dancing to a trio every night except Monday and Thursday, when the music is classical. The **Alexis Night Club** (Frederiksgade 72, tel. 86/12–77–55) is all shiny neon, with a well-dressed crowd of all ages.

Casinos There are three new casinos on Jylland, all with blackjack, roulette, baccarat, and slot machines. They are in **Limsfjordshotellet** (Ved Stranden 14–16, **Aalborg,** tel. 98/16–43–33), **Munkebjerg Hotel** (Munkebjergvej 125, **Vejle,** tel. 75/72–35–00), and the **Royal Hotel** (Store Torv 4, **Århus** tel. 86/12–00–11).

Jazz Clubs In **Århus, Bent J's** (Nørre Allé 66, tel. 86/12–04–92) is a small club with free-admission jam sessions twice a week and occasional big-name concerts. On a larger scale there's **Glazz Huset** (Åboulevarden 35, tel. 86/12–13–12). **Aalborg** doesn't have a regular club, but local musicians get together at least once a week for **jam sessions.** Ask the tourist board for details.

Bornholm

Introduction

Called the Pearl of the Baltic for its natural beauty and winsomely rustic towns, Bornholm, 177 kilometers (110 miles) southeast of Sjælland, is geographically unlike the rest of Denmark. A temperate climate has turned this 363-square-kilometer (225-square-mile) jumble of granite bluffs, clay soil, and rift valleys into an extravagance of nature. Rich plantations of fir bristle beside wide dunes and vast heather fields, while lush gardens and meadows bear fig, cherry, chestnut, and mulberry trees—even grape vines. Denmark's third-largest forest, the Almindingen, crowns the center, while the southern tip is ringed with some of Europe's whitest beaches.

During the Iron and Bronze ages, Bornholm was inhabited by seafaring and farming cultures who dotted the land with their burial dolmens and engravings. From the Middle Ages to the 18th century, the Danes battled the Swedes for ownership of the island, protecting it with strongholds, battlegrounds, and fortified churches, many of which still loom over the landscape.

Today, Bornholmers continue to live from the land and sea—and increasingly from tourism. The towns are peaked with chalk-white chimneys, the harbors are abob with carefully painted fishing boats, and, in the spring and summer, the fields blaze with amber mustard and grain—all of which can best be seen from a bicycle.

Important Addresses and Numbers

Tourist Information Bornholm's tourism center in **Rønne** has brochures and maps that cover the entire island (Munch Petersensvej 4, tel. 56/95–95–00). Local tourist offices can be found in **Allinge** (Kirkegade 4, tel. 56/48–00–01), **Åkirkeby** (Jernbanegade 1, tel. 56/97–45–20), **Gudhjem** (Åbogade 9, tel. 56/48–52–10), **Nexø** (Åsen 4, tel. 56/49–32–00); and **Svaneke** (Storegade 24, tel. 56/49–63–50).

Emergencies For **ambulance, accident,** or **fire,** call 000.

Hospital Emergency Room **Bornholm's Central Hospital,** Sygehusvej, Rønne, tel. 56/95–11–65

Late-night Pharmacy The **Rønne Apotek** (Store Torvegade 12, Rønne, tel. 56/95–01–30) is open until 8 PM weeknights. At night, a phone number is left in the window for emergency calls.

Arriving and Departing by Plane

The airport is 5 kilometers (3½ miles) south of Rønne at the island's southwestern tip. **DanAir** (tel. 33/15–52–66) makes several daily flights only from Copenhagen.

Arriving and Departing by Car Ferry, Hydrofoil, and Bus

By Car Ferry and Hydrofoil The car ferry from Copenhagen's Kvæsthusbro harbor (near Nyhavn) departs at 8 AM year-round (except Wed.) and in July and August, daily at 11:30 PM. It takes 7 hours. To avoid delays, make a reservation. Comfortable sleeping bunks in a massive hall are also available for an extra cost. Additional summer ferries link Travemünde (10 hours) and Sassnitz (on the island of Rügen, 4 hours), in Germany. Call **Bornholms Traffiken** (tel. 33/13–18–66). A hydrofoil from Nyhavn goes to Malmö, Sweden, where it connects with a bus to Ystad and a ferry to Rønne. The daily, 4-hour voyage is at 9 AM and 4:30 PM.

By Bus A **Gråhund** (Greyhound) No. 866 bus from Copenhagen's Main Station travels to Dragør, boards a ferry to Limhamn, and then continues to Ystad where it connects with a ferry to Rønne. Buses depart twice daily, at 8:25 AM and 4:10 PM. Call **Bornholm Bussen** (tel. 44/68–44–00).

Getting Around

By Car There are excellent roads on the island, but be alert for cyclists and occasional wandering cows.

By Bus Bus service is good, with regular connections between towns. Schedules are posted at all stations, and you can usually pick one up on board. The fare is DKr7 per zone, or you can buy a *klip-kort* of 10 *klips* for DKr56 (tel. 56/95–21–21).

By Bicycle The island has a network of more than 600 kilometers (360 miles) of cycle roads, including an old railway converted to a cross-island path. There are more than 20 places to rent sturdy two-speeds and tandems, for about DKr50 a day. Rentals are available near the ferry, the airport, Allinge, Gudhjem, Hasle, Pedersker (near Åkirkeby), Rønne, Svaneke, and most other towns. Try **Bornholms Cykeludlejning** (Havnegade 11, tel. 56/95–13–59) and **Cykel-Centret** (Søndergade 7, tel. 56/95–06–04), both in Rønne.

Guided Tours

The **Bornholmrund** (Round Bornholm) bus tour (8½ hours), at 9:30 Tuesday and Thursday, includes Rønne, Hammershus, Allinge, Gudhjem, Østerlars Church, Svaneke, Nexø, Balka, Åkirkeby, and the Almindingen Forest. For a reservation call the Bornholm Tourist Center. An aerial tour in a Cessna or Piper plane (20–45 min.) covers either the entire coast or the northern tip. Call **Klippefly** (tel. 56/95–35–73 or 56/48–42–01). From mid-June to mid-September, boats to **Helligdomsklipperne** (the Sanctuary Cliffs) leave Gudhjem at 10:30, 1:30, and 2:30, with extra sails mid-June to mid-August. Call **Thor Båd** (tel. 56/48–51–65). Boats to **Christiansø** depart Svaneke at 10 daily; May to September daily at 10:20 from Gudhjem, 1 from Allinge. From mid-June to August, boats also leave Gudhjem weekdays at 9:40 and 12:15. Call **Christiansø Farten** (tel. 56/48–51–76).

Special-interest The **Kunst og håndværk** (Arts and Crafts) bus tour (5 hours) is Monday through Thursday at 10 and includes six glass and pottery studios. The **Pelle the Conqueror Tour** (6 hours), follows the history of Swedish immigrants as portrayed in Martin Andersen Nexø's novel *Pelle the Conqueror,* which was made into an Oscar-winning film. The tour is at 10 Wednesday and includes the Moseløkken Quarry Museum, Vang, Almindingen Forest, the Paradise Hills, and the Agricultural Museum at Melstedgård. For reservations, call 56/95–21–21.

Exploring Bornholm

Numbers in the margin correspond with points of interest on the Bornholm map.

1 The island's capital, port, and largest town is **Rønne,** a good starting point for exploring northward or southward on the island. East of the Nørrekås harbor on Laksegade, you'll find an enchanting area of rose-clad 17th- and 18th-century houses, among them the terra-cotta roofed **Erichsens Gård** (farm). The home of the wealthy Erichsen family, whose daughter married the Danish poet Holger Drachmann, it is preserved with paintings by Danish artist Kristian Zahrtmann, period furnishings, and a lovely garden. *Laksegade 7, tel. 56/95–87–35. Admission: DKr15 adults, DKr5 children. Open May–Sept., daily 1–4.*

Down the street, off Store Torv (Town Center), you'll come to the **Bornholm Museum,** which features local geological and archaeological exhibits, in addition to more than 4,500 pieces of ceramics and glass. Antiques and clock lovers shouldn't miss the 25 18th-century *Bornholmure* (Bornholm Clocks), which are as characteristic of the island as smoked herring. In 1744, a Dutch ship was wrecked on Bornholm, and the English grandfather clocks aboard it became the model for the island's clocks. There's also an annex of Bornholm paintings. *Skt. Mortensgade 29, tel. 56/95–07–35. Admission: DKr15 adults, DKr5 children. Open May–Oct., Mon.–Sat. 10–4; Nov.–Apr., Tues., Thurs., and Sun. 2–5.*

2 Another 14 kilometers (8½ miles) north is **Jons Kapel** (Jon's Chapel), where a medieval legend has it that a monk, Brother Jon, lived in a cave here and used the treacherous sea cliffs as a pulpit for his sermons. Wear rubber-soled hiking boots and

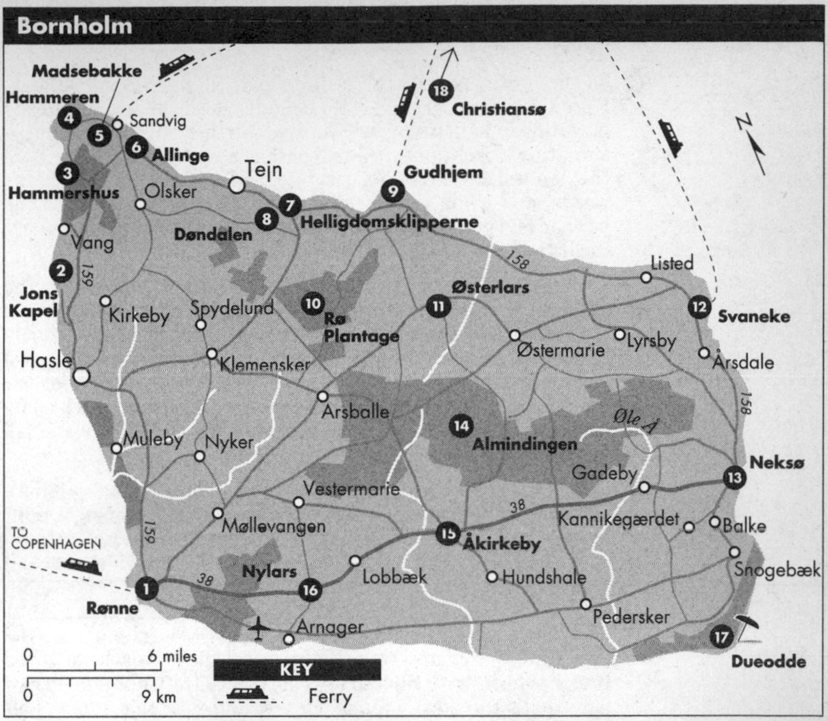

climb the stairs that lead to the pulpit, where the agile friar stood atop a dramatic 72-foot-high cliffs that loom over the crashing waves.

3 You can drive or bike northward on Route 159 to **Hammershus** fortress, but it's lovely (though mildly strenuous) to hike from the town of **Vang** up the rocky coast to the ruins of northern Europe's largest stronghold. The fortress, begun in 1255 by the archbishop of Lund (Sweden), became the object of centuries of struggle between Denmark and Sweden. In 1648, Danes under Jens Kofoed killed its Swedish governor, and the castle was given back to Denmark. Used until 1743, it became a ruin when it was quarried for stone to fortify Christiansø and that island's buildings. The government finally protected it in 1822, and now it's an impressive mass of snaggle-tooth walls and juggernaut-shaped towers atop a grassy knoll. During restoration work in 1967, 22 gold German guilders were found, though it's unsure where they came from. *No tel. Admission free.*

4 Bornholm's northern tip is called **Hammeren** (The Hammer) and is nearly separated from the island by a deep rift valley and the **Hammer Sø** (Hammer Lake). Despite constant Baltic winds, rare plants and trees grow on the warm, granite-scattered land, including bright anemone. Look over the water south of the tip to the stone formation called the Camel Heads.

5 South of the tip, outside the town of **Sandvig,** is **Madsebakke,** the largest collection of Bronze-Age rock carvings in Denmark. They are presumed to be ceremonial carvings, which ancient fishermen and farmers hoped would bring good weather and

bountiful crops. The most interesting of them depicts 11 ships, including one with a sun-wheel.

6 To the northeast are the twin towns of Sandvig and **Allinge.** Here you'll find centuries-old neighborhoods and, particularly in Allinge, half-timbered houses and herring smokehouses sprouting tall chimneys. Just south is a wood the islanders call the **Trolleskoe** (Troll Forest). Legend says trolls live in the woods, and when they brew fog, they escape the heat in the kitchen and go out looking for trouble. The most mischievous is the littlest troll, Krølle Bølle.

Another 8 kilometers (5 miles) south on the coastal path are the
7 grottoes and granite cliffs of **Helligdomsklipperne** (the Cliffs of Sanctuary), a well-known rock formation best seen from boats that ply the nearby waters in summer. There is also a pastoral
8 coastal path that leads to the tiny, preserved **Døndalen** forest. The fertile ground bears Mediterranean vegetation such as fig and cherry trees, and, during rainy periods, there's a waterfall at the bottom of the dale.

9 Southeast of the forest is the town of **Gudhjem** (God's Home). Tiny half-timbers with lace curtains and clay roofs are built atop steep stone streets that loop around the harbor and the island's first smokehouses, which still produce alder-smoked golden herring.

Time Out Gudhjem has bakeries and cafés; the favorite local snack is a Sol over Gudhjem (Sun Over Gudhjem): a slice of dark buttered bread, topped with filleted herring (that's the Gudhjem), a raw egg (that's the sun), onions, chives, and rock salt, from **Niels Hansens Rogeri** (Ejnar Mikkelsenf. vej 6, tel. 56/48–50–64) near the harbor. For something sweet, try the ice cream named after the impish **Krølle Bølle** that's available at cafés and kiosks.

Before you leave Gudhjem, walk down Brøddegade, which turns into Melstedvej. Here you'll find the **Landsbrugs Museum** (Agricultural Museum), and a working farm with cows, horses, sheep, and the house and garden of a 19th-century farm family. *Melstedvej 25, tel. 56/48–55–98. Admission: DKr15 adults, DKr5 children. Open mid-May–mid-Oct., Tues.–Sun. 10–5.*

10 Five kilometers (3 miles) inland is the **Rø Plantage** (Rø Plantation). A century ago, it was a heather-covered grazing area, but after stone dikes were erected to keep the cattle out, spruce, pine, larch, and birch were cultivated. The cool refuge now consists mostly of saplings and new growth—the result of devastating storms in the late '50s and '60s.

Southeast of the plantation 5 kilometers (3 miles) is the town of
11 **Østerlars,** and the **Østerlars Kirke** (Church). The largest of the island's four round churches, it was built about 1150; extensions, including the buttresses, were added later. Constructed from boulders and slabs of limestone, the whitewashed church was part spiritual sanctuary, part fortification, affording protection from enemy armies and pirates. Inside is the island's only painted tympanum, with a faded image of a cross and decorative foliage. Several Gothic wall paintings—including images of the Annunciation and the Birth of Christ—have survived from the 1300s. *Gudhjemsvej 28, tel. 56/49–82–64. Admission:*

DKr3 adults, children free. Open Apr.–mid-Oct., Mon.–Sat. 9–5.

12 The coastal town of **Svaneke,** Denmark's easternmost settlement, is an enchanting hamlet of 17th- and 18th-century houses, winding cobbled streets, and a harbor that was sliced from the rocky earth. Once a fishing village, it is now immaculately preserved and boasts a thriving artists' community.

13 Next is **Neksø,** 9 kilometers (5½ miles) south of Svaneke. Though it looks like a typical 17th-century town, it was rebuilt almost completely after World War II, when the Russians bombed it to dislodge stubborn German troops who refused to surrender—three days after the rest of Denmark had been liberated. The Russians also lingered on the island, until March 1946.

The **Neksø Museum** has a fine collection of fishing and local history exhibits, including photographs and memorabilia of Danish author Martin Andersen Hansen (1909–1955), who changed his last name to Nexø after his beloved town. A complicated and vehement socialist, he wrote, among other works, *Pelle the Conqueror,* which takes place in Bornholm at the turn of the century, when Swedish immigrants were exploited by Danish landowners. *Havnen, tel. 56/49–31–32. Admission: DKr10 adults, DKr5 children. Open mid-June–mid-Sept., Tues.–Sun. 9–noon.*

14 In the center of the island is the **Almindingen,** Bornholm's largest and Denmark's third-largest forest. Filled with ponds, lakes, evergreens, and well-marked trails, it blooms with lily of the valley in spring. Within it, the oak-lined **Ekkodalen** (Echo Valley) is networked with trails leading to smooth rock faces soaring up 72 feet. At the northern edge, near the road to Østermarie, is one of Bornholm's most famous sights: Seven evergreens growing from a single trunk.

15 South 5 kilometers (3 miles) is the town of **Åkirkeby,** the oldest town on the island, with a municipal charter from 1346. The town's church, **Åkirke,** is Bornholm's oldest and largest, dating from the mid-13th century. Though it is not a round church, both walls and tower were well suited for defense. The altarpiece and pulpit are Dutch Renaissance from about 1600, but the engraved sandstone font is as old as the church itself. *Torvet, tel. 56/97–41–03. Admission DKr5. Open daily 9–5.*

16 Next, 8 kilometers (5 miles) west is **Nylars,** and the **Nylars Kirke,** another round church. Like the Østerlars church, it dates from 1150, but the chalk paintings from the Old Testament on the central pillar are the oldest on the island, possibly dating to 1250. Even older are the runic stones on the church's porch. Both are of Viking origin. *Kirkevej, tel. 56/97–20–13. Donation: DKr3. Open mid-May–mid-Sept., Mon.–Sat. 9–5.*

17 At the southern tip of the island is the **Dueodde Strand,** which can be reached by walking through a pine, spruce, and wintergreen forest. The dunes crest up to 46 feet, and locals claim the sand, which was once used to fill hourglasses, is the finest in the world.

Before leaving Bornholm, take the 45-minute boat ride to the
18 island of **Christiansø.** It was originally a bastion, but only the Storetårn (Big Tower) and Lilletårn (Little Tower) remain of the fort, which was built in 1684 and dismantled in 1855. The

barracks, street, and gardens, for which the earth was transported in boats, have hardly changed since and remain under the jurisdiction of the defense ministry, making it a tiny tax-free haven for the 100 inhabitants. Nearby, the rocky, uninhabited island of **Græsholmen** is an inaccessible bird sanctuary—the only place in Denmark where the razorbill and guillemot breed.

What to See and Do with Children

Brændesgårdshaven is an old-fashioned amusement park with a rowboat pond, miniature golf, a toy factory, and Vandland (Waterland), with several water rides and swimming pools, about 6 kilometers (3½ miles) south of Svaneke. Bring a bathing suit and towel. *Ibsker, tel. 56/49–60–76. Admission: DKr35. Sept.–June, DKr40 July–Aug. Open May–June and Aug.–Sept., daily 10–6; July–Aug., daily 9–8.*

Bornholms Dyre og Naturpark (Deer and Nature Park) is filled with tame goats, donkeys, ponies, and fenced-in ostriches, llamas, camels, and others. *Borrelyngvej, 2 km (1 mi) south of Allinge in Hasle, tel. 56/48–15–65. Admission: DKr30 adults, DKr10 children. Open May–Sept., daily 10–5.*

Off the Beaten Track

At least one night, do as the Danes do: Climb the **Dueodde Fyr** (lighthouse) for a panoramic view, then watch the lingering indigo and purple sunset. Or just sit on a beach, near **Pedersker,** and watch the swallows dive. Afterward, trudge up the dunes to the beach-side kiosks—where children and grown-ups patiently queue up for bags of handpicked candy and jam-topped ice-cream cones.

Shopping

Bornholm is famous in Scandinavia for its craftspeople, especially the glassblowers and ceramicists, whose work is often pricier in Copenhagen and Stockholm. In the center of each town (especially Gudhjem and Svaneke), you'll find crafts shops and *værksteder* (workshops). When you're on the road, watch for *keramik* (ceramics) signs, which direct you to artists working from home.

Ceramics and Glass

The **Kampeløkken** (Havnegade 45, Allinge, tel. 56/48–17–66) gallery shop stocks the work of 24 potters and four glassblowers. Also stroll through the ateliers and boutiques in the central **Glastorvet** in Allinge. Among them is that of **Pernille Bülow**, one of Denmark's most famous glassblowers. Her work is sold in Copenhagen's best design shops. Even if you buy directly from her studio (Glastorvet, Brænderigænget 8, tel. 56/49–66–72), don't expect bargains, but do expect colorful, experimental work. **Baltic Sea Glass** (Melstedvej 47, Gudhjem, tel. 56/48–56–41) offers high-quality bright, imaginative decanters, glasses, candlesticks, and one-of-a-kind pieces. In Gudhjem, you can see the delicate porcelain bowls of **Per Rehfeldt** (Kastenievej 8, tel. 56/48–54–13) and the unique, hand-thrown pieces of **Julia Manitius** (Holkavej 12, tel. 56/48–55–99).

Specialty Stores A *Bornholmur* is a type of grandfather clock handmade on the island. Antique versions cost DKr5,000 to 9,000 and more. New clocks modeled from museum originals are custom-made by **Bornholmerure** (Torneværksvej 26, Rønne, tel. 56/95–31–08). The clocks often have round faces, but can be rectangular as well and are completely handmade and painted. On the hour, the modern clocks sound the hour with music—which ranges from Mozart and Verdi to Sondheim and Andrew Lloyd Weber. A handmade custom clock can cost as much as DKr25,000 ($4,166). For **leather,** visit **Askepot** (Postgade 5, Svaneke, tel. 53/99–70–42) for handmade hats, jackets, and wallets. For exquisite **woodwork,** see **Bernard Romain** (Rønnevej 54, Neksø, tel. 56/48–86–66), and for **hand-printed textiles, Bente Hammer** (Nyker Hovedgade 32, Rønne, tel. 56/96–33–35).

Street Markets There is a large vegetable and fruit market Wednesday and Saturday mornings in Stor Torv, the main square in **Rønne.**

Sports and Outdoor Activities

Bicycling *See* Getting Around, *above.*

Camping There are more than 15 excellent campsites on the island, including **Galløkken Camping** (Strandvejen 4, DK-3700 Rønne, tel. 56/95–23–20, **Sandvig Familie Camping** (Sandlinien 3, DK-3770 Allinge, tel. 56/48–00–01), and **Dueodde Camping** (Duegårdsvej 2, 3730 Neksø, tel. 56/48–81–49).

Fishing Cod, salmon, and herring fishing are excellent in season, though better from a boat than on shore. Licenses cost DKr15 to 35 per day. Contact the tourist board for details and information on charter trips. Among the handful of charter companies is **Per Andersen** (Holkavej 22, Gudhjem, tel. 56/48–55–54).

Golf There are three courses on the island: **Bornholms Golfbane** near Rønne (tel. 56/95–57–13), **Rø Golfbane** up north (tel. 56/48–42–00), and **Dueodde Golfbane** near the southern forest (tel. 56/49–24–04). Admission to each green is about DKr130.

Hiking Marked trails crisscross the island, including three 4-kilometer (2½-mile) hikes through the Almindingen forest and several more through its Ekkodalon. The northern coastline is beautiful, but a more strenuous walk and rocky. Ask for a map, routes, and tips from any tourism office. The *Bornholm Green Guide,* which is available in shops and tourism offices, is also very helpful with suggestions for walking and hiking tours.

Windsurfing The winds are strongest and most constant on the sandy southern coast, especially during spring and fall. The shores are rockier north of Neksø. There are several board rentals and classes on the island, including **Windsurfing ved Balke Strand** (tel. 56/95–00–77), south of Neksø.

Beaches

The northern beaches are rocky and narrow, better suited for hiking and walking, though some people like to dive from the rocks. On the road from Gudhjem to Svaneke on the east coast, there's a lovely rocky beach, but the swimming and sunning is best farther south, between Pedersker and Snogebæk, where the dunes are tall, the beaches wide. As elsewhere in Denmark, topless bathing is acceptable and nude bathing is tolerated.

Dining and Lodging

Most of the island's finest restaurants are in hotels, while inexpensive smokehouses and cafés provide Bornholm's "fast food." The island is popular with returning Europeans, who book accommodations up to a year in advance. In the summer, space is scarce and expensive, but if you arrive without a hotel, the tourist office can sometimes find a room or a campsite.

Highly recommended establishments are indicated by a star ★.

Allinge
Dining and Lodging
★

Strandhotellet. Completely renovated after a fire, this old hotel still has its romantic, Old World charm. Located on a corner across from the harbor, it has a white, arched entry into a stone-and-whitewashed lobby. The rooms are furnished in plain beech furniture with woolen covers and pastel colors. *Strandpromenaden 7, 3770, tel. 56/48–03–14, fax 56/48–02–09. 42 rooms with shower, 1 suite. Facilities: restaurant, bar, health club, sauna, solarium, steam room, parking. AE, DC, MC, V. Closed mid-Oct.–mid-Apr. Moderate.*

Dueodde
Dining and Lodging

Bornholm. In the midst of the Dueodde woods, this hotel has simple double rooms, apartments, and very sought-after bungalows, which have a living room, a terrace, two to three bedrooms, a kitchenette, and a shower. All are furnished in pre-1970 pivot chairs and formica. The entire compound faces the white beaches of the island's southern tip. *Pilegårdsvej 1, Dueodde, DK–3730, tel. 56/48–83–83, fax 56/48–85–37. 27 rooms, 16 apartments, 7 bungalows. Facilities: restaurant, laundry, sauna, solarium, indoor and outdoor pools, tennis, car and bicycle rental. No credit cards. Closed 1 week in mid-Feb. Expensive.*

Gudhjem
Lodging

Skt. Jørgens Gård Vandrehjem. In a 100-year-old former manor house, this half-timbered hostel in the middle of Gudhjem offers one- to eight-bed rooms with standard Danish hostel style: pine bunks and industrial carpeting. *Gudhjem Vandrehjem, 3760, tel. 56/48–50–35, fax 56/48–56–35. 52 rooms, 26 with bath. Facilities: restaurant, 6 kitchens. No credit cards. Inexpensive.*

Neksø
Dining and Lodging

Holms Hotel. The lobby of this old brick hotel overflows with bric-a-brac, toys, yellow vinyl furniture, and plaid carpets, while a breakfast café is elegantly laid with flowered table cloths and cut blossoms. The dated rooms have swivel armchairs and half-paneled walls. The cozy Martin Andersen Neksø restaurant serves excellent Danish seafood and traditional fare. *Torvegade 5, DK–3730 Neksø, tel. 56/49–20–45. 50 rooms, 33 with shower and toilet. Facilities: restaurant, bar. AE, DC, MC, V. Closed Dec. 23–Jan 2. Moderate.*

Pedersker
Dining

Bakkarøgeriet. In the middle of a quiet neighborhood, this smokehouse looks like a garage but has a brisk carryout herring business. On Thursday and Friday, burgers, cutlets, steaks, and *pølser* (sausages) are put out for guests to cook on tabletop grills in the garden. *Østre Sømarksvej 29, tel. 56/97–71–20. Reservations not accepted. Dress: casual. No credit cards. Closed Sept.–Apr. Inexpensive.*

Rønne
Dining

Rådhuskroen. With exposed timbers, comfortable armchairs, and close-set tables, this restaurant provides a softly lit change from Rønne's busy streets. The menu is Bornholm continental, with specialties such as poached Baltic salmon with salmon roe and lobster sauce, and grilled fillet of rosefish (redfish) with curry sauce. Beef choices include pepper steak with wine and cream sauce. *Nørregade 2, tel. 56/95–00–69. Reservations accepted. Dress: casual. AE, D, MC, V. Moderate.*

Dining and Lodging

Fredensborg. On a curve of forest near a small beach, this hotel sets the island's standard for luxury. The glass and clay-tile lobby is spare and sunny, the staff pleasant and eager. The dozen ample apartments have full kitchens, while the guest rooms are in pastel schemes, with modern furniture and balconies overlooking the sea. The timbered restaurant, De Fire Ståuerne, serves traditional Danish food. *Strandvejen 116, DK–3700, tel. 56/95–44–44, fax 56/95–03–14. 72 rooms with bath, 12 apartments. Facilities: restaurant, bar, whirlpool, tennis court, sauna, solarium, 24-hour room service, meeting rooms, parking. AE, DC, MC, V. Expensive.*

Hotel Griffen. Just off a busy street and the Rønne harbor, this is one of Bornholm's largest and most modern hotels. It's three stories tall with plenty of windows and views of the sea on one side, Rønne on the other. The rooms, done in deep brown tones, have every modern convenience. *Kredsen 1, DK-3700, tel. 56/95–51–11, fax 56/95–52–97. 140 rooms with bath, 2 suites. Facilities: restaurant, bar, disco, indoor pool, sauna, room service, meeting rooms, parking. AE, DC, MC, V. Closed mid-Dec.–Jan. 7. Expensive.*

Snogebæk
Dining
★

Den Lille Havefrue. This busy fish restaurant is lined with the paintings and ceramics of local artist Kirsten Kleman. Dine inside or out in the ample garden (with a play area for kids), which faces the Baltic. The menu includes steaks, soups, and salads, but the specialty is fresh, traditional fish, such as boiled or fried plaice, grilled cod with lobster gravy, and salmon with cream-and-chive sauce. *Hovedgaden 5, tel. 56/48–80–55. Reservations advised. Dress: casual but neat. AE, DC, MC, V. Moderate.*

Svaneke
Dining

Solskin. The name of this lunch café means sunshine, and everything is healthy—from hot veggie plates to occasional meat dishes, quiche, excellent brownies, and iced cappuccino. Like the food, the atmosphere is fresh, with posters and art on the walls and, true to its name, lots of sunlight. *Glastorvet 3, tel. 53/99–60–53. No credit cards. No dinner. Closed Oct.–Apr. Inexpensive.*

Dining and Lodging

Siemsens Gaard. Built in a 400-year-old merchant house, this U-shaped hotel with a gravel-courtyard café overlooks the harbor. Inside, it's cushy with Chesterfield sofas beneath severe black-and-white prints and antiques. The rooms differ, but all are done up in stripped pine and soft colors. The bright, modern restaurant serves Franco-Danish food, with a menu of 125 options—from club sandwiches to smoked Baltic salmon to smørrebrød. *Havnebryggen 9, DK–3740, tel. 56/49–61–49, fax 56/49–61–03. 50 rooms with shower. Facilities: restaurant, café, health club, sauna. AE, DC, MC, V. Moderate.*

Lodging
★

Hotel Østersøen. Across from the harbor, this newly renovated hotel has a provincial facade and a Key West courtyard with palm trees and a swimming pool. Industrial carpets and century-old beams line the modern lobby, and the stark apartments (rented by the week) are furnished with leather sofas, swanky teak dinette sets, and streamlined furniture. The hotel is well suited for families and couples traveling in pairs. *Havnebryggen 5, DK–3740, tel. 56/49–60–20, fax 56/49–72–79. 21 apartments. Facilities: outdoor pool, business facilities. AE, DC. Moderate.*

The Arts and Nightlife

The Arts Check with the tourist board for information on church and park concerts and special events at Hammershus.

Nightlife Bornholm nightlife is limited to a handful of discos and clubs in **Rønne.** The largest disco is **Annabelle's** (Kredsen 1, tel. 56/95–51–11) in the Griffen Hotel, which draws a mixed crowd, while **Sølvknappen** (Store Torv, tel. 56/95–48–01) is smaller, with lots of young locals. **Vise Vesth Huset** (Brøddegade 24, tel. 56/48–50–80) is popular for light meals and live folk music. For a rowdier time, there's **Sørens Værthus,** near the harbor in **Snogebæk** (Hovedgaden 1G, tel. 56/48–80–20), a popular pizza place with live rock, and a rowboat hanging from the ceiling—into which daring guests often climb.

Greenland

Introduction

When Eric the Red discovered Greenland (Kalaallit Nunaat in Greenlandic, Grønland in Danish) a thousand years ago, his Norsemen thought they had reached the edge of the world. After it, there was only *Ginnungapgap,* the endless abyss.

Greenland commands awe still from the handful of visitors who venture off the usual Scandinavian path to explore the world's largest island. Measuring over 1.3 million square kilometers (840,000 square miles), it's larger than Italy, France, Great Britain, unified Germany, and Spain, combined. The coastal regions are sparsely populated with 55,000 Danes and Inuits—the local people, whose roots can be traced to the people native to Canada's arctic. More than 80% of the land is eternally frozen beneath an ice cap that, at its deepest, reaches 3 kilometers (2 miles). If it melted, sea levels around the world would rise nearly 20 feet.

By its nature, Greenland is far more difficult to explore than dwarfed mother Denmark, but the southern and western towns, which are trimmed with building-block red-and-green houses and well-traveled harbors, have adequate hotels, airfields and helicopter pads, and summertime ferry service. (Greenland has no roads or railroads.) Man-made luxuries are few, but the rewards of nature are savagely beautiful. Below the Arctic Circle, the draws include Norse ruins, Ice-Age-gouged mountains, and jagged fjords, while farther north, dogsleds whip over icy plains and ferries glide past icebergs as big as city blocks.

Greenland's first inhabitants probably arrived 4,000 years ago from North America and left by 500 BC, when the climate grew colder. Recorded history began in AD 982, when Eric and his Norse settlers claimed the land, but, after 400 years of colonization, they mysteriously disappeared. During this period, Denmark and Norway joined under the Danish crown, a union that muddled ownership of Greenland until 1933, when the International High Court awarded Denmark complete sovereignty. (Because of this dual heritage, almost every town has a Greenlandic and a Danish name.) Geographically isolated, and increasingly politically independent, the Greenlanders are intent on redefining their Eskimo identity in a modern world. They refer to themselves as Inuits, in solidarity with those natives of Canada, Alaska, and the Soviet Union, and most people, particularly the youth, speak the native language, in addition to Danish.

In 1978 Denmark granted Greenland home rule, authorizing its tiny *Landsting* (Parliament), located in the capital, Nuuk/Godthåb, power over internal affairs. Though Denmark continues to transfer power, it still administers foreign policy and provides large doses of financial aid to bolster an economy based on fishing, animal husbandry, construction, and, increasingly, tourism.

With so few tourists (numbering under 10,000 annually), the ways of the isolated Greenlander can seem blissfully nonchalant. When things appear hopeless (as you will often be told they are), you'll do better if you remain calm and polite. Just be sure to do your research, arrange as much of your itinerary as possible before you leave home, and bring your own guidebooks.

When to Go

The loveliest time to visit is May to early August, when the sun hardly sets. Summer temperatures average 53°–65°F in the south (Nanortalik to Paamiut) and 50°–60°F in the center (Nuuk to Qeqertarsuaq), but it feels warmer due to low humidity. The temperature drops dramatically in the afternoon and evening, and the winds never completely die. Sudden ice, rain, and snow squalls are common in the central and northern regions. Winter is harsh, dark, and extremely windy, with temperatures dipping below 32° to 5°F in the south, −22°F and far below in the center and north, which also experiences polar night from November to March.

What to Pack

Pack light, as you'll have to tote your own luggage and because of cargo and weight considerations on small planes and helicopters.

Clothing Bring durable, wind- and waterproof sportswear, sturdy hiking boots or rubber-heeled walking shoes, a cap (one that won't fly off in the wind), and gloves or mittens. Wool sweaters, cotton T-shirts, and neat trousers are about as dressy as you'll need.

Miscellaneous The northern summer sun is blinding. Bring a pair of ultraviolet (UV) filter sunglasses and a waterproof sunscreen. Greenland's midges and mosquitoes are vicious, so pack a good repellent and carry it with you at all times. (An even better solution is a netted cap.) For your camera, bring a UV filter to compensate for the glare that will otherwise tint your photos blue.

Language

Take along a Danish-English phrase book. Though most Greenlanders speak Danish, English is not common.

Important Addresses and Numbers

Tourist Information There is a tourism office in almost every town, but brochures, maps, and specific information may be limited. The following are small, often mobile offices, so call first for an exact location: **Ilulissat/Jacobshavn** (Kussangajannguaq B 447, Box 272, DK–3952 Ilulissat, tel. 299/4–43–22, fax 299/4–39–33), **Narsaq** (Box 148, DK–3921 Narsaq, tel. 3–13–25), **Nuuk/Godthåb** (Box 199, 3900 Nuuk, tel. 2–27–00), **Qaqortoq/Julianehåb** (Box 128, 3920 Qaqortoq, tel. 3–84–44), **Qasigiannguit/Christianhåb** (Box 128, tel. 3–84–44). Tourist information offices in **Søndre Strømfjord** and **Narsarsuak** open when planes arrive. In Copenhagen, the staff at the **Greenlandic Travel Service** (Gammel Mønt 12, tel. 33/13–10–11) is helpful.

Emergencies Every community has its own fire, ambulance, and police numbers, and dentist and doctor, all of which are available from your hotel. The best way to handle emergencies is to avoid danger in the first place. Don't take risks, ask for advice, and give your travel agent and hotel your itinerary so that they can reach you in case of emergencies—or if you don't show up when you're due.

Hospital Emergency Room **Sana (Dronning Ingrids) Hospital,** DK–3900 Nuuk, tel. 299/2–11–01

Late-night Pharmacies If you are on a medication, bring enough to last. For emergencies, the local hospital can fill prescriptions.

Arriving and Departing by Plane and Helicopter

Icelandair has flights from New York, Baltimore, and Miami to Keflavik, Iceland, daily in summer. **Greenlandair** (Grønlandsfly in Danish) then makes two flights a week between Keflavik and Narsarsuak. It's more expensive to go by way of Copenhagen, with **SAS,** which flies four times a week to Søndre Strømfjord. Even pricier are connections through Canada, where you can catch an early morning flight from Montreal to Frobisher Bay on Baffin Island, then cross the Davis Strait to Nuuk on Greenlandair, which makes two flights a week. Because of Greenland's highly variable weather, delays are frequent. Helicopters and small planes connect airports to towns.

Getting Around

By Plane and Helicopter **Greenlandair** is the only airline licensed for domestic flights on the island. Its modest fleet of helicopters and small planes are booked year-round, so make reservations very early.

By Boat The most beautiful passage between towns is by water. Every town has a harbor, where private boats can be hired for connections or excursions. Two government-run ferries, the *Kununguak* and *Disko,* ply the waters of the west coast, making frequent stops, but space is limited and booked months in advance by locals. Again, reserve early. Contact **KNI** (Greenland Trade, DK–3900 Nuuk, tel. 299/2–52–11).

Guided Tours

Because transportation and accommodations are limited, have all details of your trip—connections, accommodations, sightseeing, and meals—arranged by an experienced travel agent, tour organizer, or airline. (It's also helpful to bring a copy of your tour contract and all confirmations.) Tour packages range from one-, three-, or four-day excursions from Reykjavík to month-long nature expeditions, which can include sailing, hiking, dogsledding (March to May), whale safaris, and iceberg watching. On-the-spot excursions are available in most towns and range from about DKr250 for a half day, to DKr350 for a full day. Among the travel agencies most experienced with Greenland are: **Bennett of Scandinavia** (270 Madison Ave., New York, NY 10016, tel. 212/532–5060), **Eurocruises** (303 W. 13th St., New York, NY 10014, tel. 212/691–2099), **Glace** (part of Greenlandair, tel. 612/473–9331), **Greenland Cruises** (10 Park Ave., New York, NY 10016, tel. 800/648–2544), **Icelandair** (610 5th Ave., New York, NY 10111, tel. 212/757–8585), **Society Expeditions** (3131 Elliott Ave., Suite 700, Seattle, WA 98121, tel. 206/285–9400), and **Travcoa** (4000 McArthur Blvd. E, Suite 650, Newport Beach, CA 92660, tel. 714/476–2800). In Denmark, contact **Arctic Adventure** (Åboulevarden 37, 1960 Frederiksberg C, tel. 31/37–12–33), **Greenland Travel** (*see* Tourist Information, *above*), and **Green Tours** (Kultorvet 7, DK–1175 Copenhagen, tel. 33/13–27–27).

Exploring Greenland

Numbers in the margin correspond with points of interest on the Greenland map.

Most museums and sights in Greenland do not have street addresses. To check for opening hours, ask at your hotel.

Tour 1: Southern Greenland

A convenient place to start exploring is near the island's southwestern tip, because most towns in this area have harbors and airstrips connecting them to the United States, Europe, and domestic routes.

1 If you begin in **Nanortalik,** take a stroll past the Ice Age granite, the old harbor, and the paint-box-color 19th-century buildings, a vestige of the Danish colonial past. During May and June, the normally quiet town bustles with local whale and seal hunters, who install themselves in tents and makeshift huts.

2 Northward 90 kilometers (54 miles) is **Qaqortoq/Julianehåb.** With a population of 3,000, this is the largest town in southern Greenland and one of the loveliest. In the town square, you'll see the island's only fountain, surrounded by half-timbered buildings and crayon-color houses. Though the oldest building in town is the cooper shop, which dates to 1797, the most interesting is the smithy, from 1871, which now houses the **Julianehåb Museum.** Inside are handmade hunting tools, kayaks, Inuit clothing, and a furnished sod house you can enter. A traditional dwelling, it remained cozy and warm even during the harsh winter. *Admission free. Open Mon.–Fri. 11–4.*

From this point, you can arrange to make the 14.5-kilometer (9-mile) sail to the well-preserved ruins of **Hvalsey Kirke,** where

Greenland

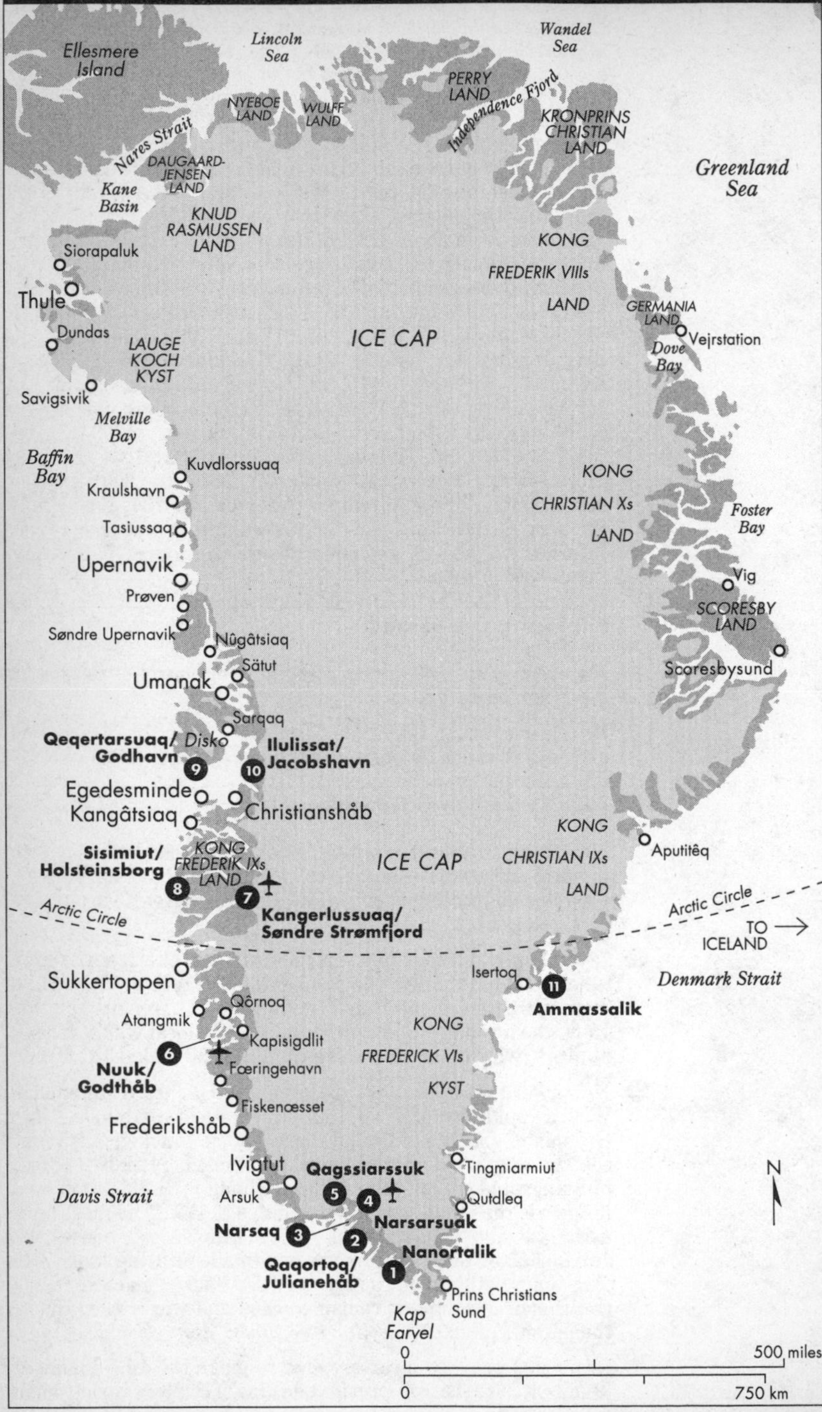
Lincoln Sea
Wandel Sea
Ellesmere Island
NYEBOE LAND
WULFF LAND
PERRY LAND
Independence Fjord
KRONPRINS CHRISTIAN LAND
Nares Strait
DAUGAARD-JENSEN LAND
Kane Basin
Greenland Sea
KNUD RASMUSSEN LAND
KONG FREDERIK VIIIs LAND
Siorapaluk
Thule
GERMANIA LAND
Vejrstation
Dundas
ICE CAP
LAUGE KOCH KYST
Dove Bay
Savigsivik
Melville Bay
Baffin Bay
Kuvdlorssuaq
KONG CHRISTIAN Xs LAND
Kraulshavn
Tasiussaq
Foster Bay
Upernavik
Vig
Prøven
SCORESBY LAND
Søndre Upernavik
Nûgâtsiaq
Scoresbysund
Sätut
Umanak
Sarqaq
Qeqertarsuaq/ Godhavn
Disko
Ilulissat/ Jacobshavn
9
10
Egedesminde
Christianshåb
Kangâtsiaq
KONG CHRISTIAN IXs LAND
Aputitêq
Sisimiut/ Holsteinsborg
KONG FREDERIK IXs LAND
ICE CAP
8
7
Arctic Circle
Kangerlussuaq/ Søndre Strømfjord
Arctic Circle
TO ICELAND
Sukkertoppen
Isertoq
11
Ammassalik
Denmark Strait
Qôrnoq
Atangmik
Kapisigdlit
KONG FREDERICK VIs KYST
6
Nuuk/ Godthåb
Færingehavn
Fiskenæsset
Frederikshåb
Ivigtut
Qagssiarssuk
Tingmiarmiut
Davis Strait
Arsuk
5
4
Qutdleq
Narsarsuak
Narsaq
3
2
Nanortalik
Qaqortoq/ Julianehåb
1
Prins Christians Sund
Kap Farvel
N
0
500 miles
0
750 km

in 1408 there was a large and well-attended Norse wedding—the community's last recorded activity before it mysteriously disappeared. As it is located close to a rocky beach, the hardy can opt for a frigid dip.

Another 25 kilometers (15 miles) across the Ericsfjord are the
3 mountains of **Narsaq.** A modern town of bright houses, with a hospital and fish-processing plant, it is also the starting point for excursions to the ice cap. Once you've reached the hump-backed glacier, you can have a picnic (packed by your hotel) and keep a lookout for the 150 pairs of white-tailed eagles, the world's largest, which are bred and protected in the area.

4 Next is **Narsarsuak,** Great Plain in Greenlandic, a name that aptly describes the wide, smooth land where the U.S. Air Force chose to build a military airport during World War II—one that survives as one of Greenland's largest civil airports. Not far is the edge of the glacier, the runoff of which is collected for Ice Cap Vodka. Also nearby is the point locals call **Hospitalsdalen** (Hospital Valley), a controversial area named for the alleged American Hospital where invalids of the Korean War were said to be hidden away, in order not to weaken morale back home. Though most history books deny the story, many locals swear it's true.

When exploring the area, don't neglect the 30-minute sail to **Brattahlid,** as well as the 1,000-year-old ruins of Eric the Red's farm and the remains of **Tjodhilde Kirke,** both of which are lo-
5 cated in the sheep-breeding village of **Qagssiarssuk.** It was from this point that Eric the Red's son, Leif Ericsson, began his expedition in AD 1,000 to discover *Vinland,* what modern archaeologists believe was Newfoundland. The first *Ting* (Outdoor Parliament) was also held here at about the same time.

Tour 2: Central and Northern Greenland

An hour or so by small plane, or 15 hours by ferry, north of
6 Narsarsuak is **Nuuk/Godthåb,** the capital of Greenland, which is beautifully situated on the peninsula between two fjords. It was founded in 1728 by the Norwegian missionary Hans Egede; his harborside home is now the private residence of the island's home-rule premier. The centrally located **Landsmuseet** (National Museum of Greenland) has a good permanent display that includes kayaks, costumes, and hunting weapons, an art exhibit, and the five 15th-century mummies of Qilakitsoq, one of Greenland's archaeological treasures. Among the most striking are a woman and child so well preserved that even their 500-year-old clothes are in pristine condition. *National Museum, tel. 299/22611. Admission free. Open weekdays and Sun. 1–4.*

7 Next (about one hour by plane from Nuuk) is **Kangerlussuaq/Søndre Strømfjord,** which is at the head of the longest and deepest fjord in the world. The airport, the island's most vital, lies just a few meters from the ice cap. Until World War II, nobody lived here permanently, but the Greenlanders would come in the spring to hunt reindeer. During the war, the U.S. Air Force chose its dry, stable climate for an air base, called Bluie West Eight. The military areas are now being dismantled.

8 Farther west, on the Davis Strait, is **Sisimiut/Holsteinsborg,** which means Burrow People. This hilltop town boasts many

Danish-style wooden houses, a local luxury, as all wood is imported. A favorite area for dogsledding, it is also the southernmost boundary for walrus hunting; the walrus is a popular game animal because of its valuable tusks.

Another 110 kilometers (70 miles) north is **Disko Bugt** (Bay) and the island of **Qeqertarsuaq/Disko,** where the main town is
9 **Qeqertarsuaq/Godhavn.** Until 1950 it was the capital of northern Greenland, while Nuuk/Godthåb was the southern capital. The task was divided because it was too difficult to rule the entire island from one town. Accessible by helicopter and ship, it's often booked to capacity by French and German tourists who come for the organized dogsled trips.

10 In the center of Disko bay is **Ilulissat/Jacobshavn,** which lies 300 kilometers (185 miles) north of the Arctic Circle. The tip of its fjord boasts the northern hemisphere's most productive iceberg, calving 130 million tons of floes each day. For a humbling experience, take one of the helicopter tours that circle the glacier. A violent land of floating ice giants and dazzling panoramas, it's been inhabited by the Inuit for as long as 4,000 years. The town was founded in 1741 by a Danish merchant, Jakob Severin. Today the largest industry is shrimping, though in the winter halibut is fished from dogsleds along the fjord. You can also visit the **Knud Rasmussens Fødehjem** (Childhood Home of Knud Rasmussen) (1879–1933). The Danish-Greenlandic explorer initiated the seven Thule expeditions, which enlarged the knowledge of arctic geography and Inuit culture. At the museum, you can follow his explorations through photographs, equipment, and clothing. *Open daily 10–2.*

The northern reaches of Greenland are sparsely populated, with few hotels. The American air base at Thule used for monitoring the northern hemisphere can be visited only by members of groups with special permits (check with the tourist office in Ilulissat). Much of the east coast is also empty, though a recent gold rush, along the southeast coast, has given rise to some makeshift accommodations. The only truly accessible
11 town on the east side is **Ammassalik,** 831 kilometers (470 miles) northwest of Reykjavík. It is a beautiful and wild land, but accommodations and facilities are sparse, as the only locals consist of a few hundred Inuit fisherfolk, polar bears, and seals.

Shopping

Clothing Most clothing is expensive and comparable to what is available in provincial Danish towns. The exception is the intricate—and expensive—**Greenlandic national costume.** Most often, it consists of a red pullover, a separate pearl and embroidery collar, sealskin embroidered trousers, and boots. Individual parts of the costume may be bought for prices starting at DKr2,200 (for the boots). Thick hand-knit wool turtlenecks, in traditional beige, brown, and gray patterns, are more common.

Furs **Seal** and **fox fur** are widely available. You can find both raw skins and finished coats, jackets, slippers, and other outerwear. It's expensive, but prices are half of what you'll find in Copenhagen. The tannery **Kalaallit Nunaata Ammerivia** in Julianehåb/Qaqortoq is a good place to watch the furs being sewn and to shop. Bargaining is not done.

Handicrafts In most towns, you can buy handmade folk art and crafts. Among the most unusual items are **tupilaks,** carvings the Inuit once believed would bring bad luck to enemies. These very collectible pieces were once made from fur, bones, peat, and other materials, but are now carved from wood, antler, tusk, and teeth. **Soapstone,** a soft, gray or green stone, is carved into small figures depicting humans and animals from Greenlandic mythology. Trees are scarce and precious in Greenland, so driftwood is often carved into utilitarian bowls and baskets.

Street Markets Every town has an outdoor market called *brædttet* (the plank, or board). Here locals buy and trade game, fish, and skins (a medium-size sealskin costs DKr500–600). Prices are set by the government, so there's no bargaining.

Sports and Outdoor Activities

Dogsledding The huskies that traverse the ice-covered land are only allowed north of the Arctic Circle. They are half-wild, so don't try to play with or pet them. For rides, contact the local tourist office or your hotel.

Fishing and Hunting The right to fish and hunt in Greenland is reserved for residents; however, visitors can buy fishing and hunting licenses from the local police, major hotels, and tourism offices. A fishing license costs DKr500, a small game license DKr1,000; and a large game license DKr3,000.

Hiking It's wiser to join an organized hike with an experienced guide than to attempt a solo expedition. (It's not uncommon for rescue crews to go out in search of lost hikers.) Organized excursions are available in Nuuk/Godthåb, Narsaq, and Narsarsuak for about DKr150 for a half day, DKr300 for a full day. The tourist offices of Qaqortoq/Julianehåb, Nanortalik and Sisimiut/Holsteinsborg arrange hikes upon request and charge according to the number of participants.

National Parks Most of Greenland's ice cap is protected as the world's largest national parkland and is closed to tourists.

Dining and Lodging

Good hotels are available with very plain rooms and few or no extras. Most restaurants are located in hotels and feature both Danish and Greenlandic fare. Expect a lot of fresh cod, flounder, salmon, and reindeer, as well as occasional whale and seal meat. Delicacies include large shrimp and the local lamb.

Ilulissat/Jacobshavn
Dining and Lodging

Hotel Arctic Ilulissat. This modern hotel is in the mountains just outside town, with adequate rooms, most of which have TV, phone, and views of the ice fjord and mountains. *Box 501, DK–3952, tel. 299/44153, fax 299/43924. 126 rooms. Facilities: restaurant. AE, DC, MC. Very Expensive.*

Hotel Hvide Falk. All rooms in this moderate-size two-story building have a magnificent view of the glacier and the Disko mountains. The restaurant, which offers Danish, Greenlandic, and French specialties, looks out over the bay and the Vistafjord, which is abob with icebergs. Unfortunately the hotel can be noisy at night. *Box 20, DK–3952, tel. 299/43343, fax 299/43508. 21 rooms with bath. Facilities: restaurant, guided tours. DC. Expensive.*

Narsarsuak
Dining and Lodging

Hotel Narsarsuak. Greenland's largest hotel boasts comfortable rooms, with functional Danish furniture, TVs, telephone, and private bath. The restaurant, which gets its ingredients from Denmark and has its own Danish chef, overlooks Eric the Red's Farm. A few hundred yards from the airstrip, the hotel organizes tours to the surrounding fjord and mountains and has its own excursion boats. *DK–3923, tel. 299/35253, fax 299/35370. 192 rooms with bath. Facilities: restaurant, bar, pub, sauna, solarium, laundry service. AE, DC, MC, V. Moderate.*

Nuuk/Godthåb
Dining and Lodging

Hans Egede. This hotel, built in 1986, is one of the best in Greenland. The rooms are plain and functional but have extras like mini-bars, TVs, videos, and phones. The sixth-floor Sky Top restaurant, known for its lovely view of the fjords and its inventive nouveau Greenlandic menu, combines local fish with French methods. *Aqqusinersuaq 1–5, Box 289, DK–3900, tel. 299/24222, fax 299/24487. 110 rooms with bath. Facilities: restaurant, conference rooms, discothèque, pub. DC, MC, V. Very Expensive.*

Qaqortoq/Julianehåb
Lodging

Hotel Qaqortoq. Built in 1987, this hotel is among the more modern on the huge island. Its glass and white facade atop a hill overlooks the surrounding fjord and picturesque center of town. The rooms are simple but comfortable, all with private bath. *Box 550, DK–3920, Sydprøve, Qaqortoq, tel. 299/38282, fax 299/37234. 21 rooms with bath. Facilities: restaurant. DC, MC, V. Very Expensive.*

Qasigiannguit/ Christianhåb
Lodging

Hotel Igdlo Qasigiannguit. This modern three-story wood and concrete hotel sits on a mountainside with views of the harbor and Disko Bay. *Box 160, DK–3951, tel. 299/45081, fax 299/45524. 15 rooms. Facilities: restaurant, café, discothèque, conference rooms. AE, DC, MC, V. Very Expensive.*

Nightlife

There's not much in the way of tourist nightlife, especially bars and discos, except in the finest hotels, and on weekends, even these get rowdy. Like many other indigenous peoples, the Greenlandic Inuits have had a difficult time assimilating 20th-century ways. Unfortunately, alcohol exacerbates these problems.

The Faroe Islands

Introduction

The 18 Faroe Islands (Føroyar in Færoese; Færørene in Danish) striate the North Atlantic in an extended knuckle of volcanic archipelago. All but one are inhabited, by 47,000 people and 80,000 sheep. Hospitable toward visitors, the inhabitants nevertheless are uninterested in seeing their home become a major tourist attraction. They live by fishing and shepherding and remain blissfully isolated from the outside world.

Located 290 kilometers (180 miles) northwest of Scotland, 419 kilometers (260 miles) southeast of Iceland, and 1,258 kilometers (780 miles) northwest of Denmark, the fjord-chiseled islands are sparsely vegetated, with a bristle of short grasses and moss. The climate is oceanic: humid, changeable, and stormy, with surprisingly mild temperatures—52°F in the summer, and 40°F in the winter, with a heavy annual rainfall of 63 inches.

Of its 870 square kilometers (540 square miles), 7% is fertile, the rest rough pasture—an Eden for 75 breeding and 200 migratory species of birds, among them thousands of guillemots, gannets, auks, and puffins. Beneath azure skies and rugged, mossy mountains, villages of colorful thatched houses cling to hillsides and harbors, while drying fish flap like laundry in the breeze. Religious and proud, the Faroese have built churches in nearly every settlement and practice voluntary prohibition.

Catholic monks from Ireland were the first to settle the islands but died out and were replaced by Norwegian Vikings who settled the land in about AD 800. It was here that the *Løgting* (Parliament) met for the first time in AD 1200 in Tórshavn—and still does. Though under the Danish Crown, the islands have had a home-rule government since 1948, with their own flag and language.

The roots of the Faroese language are in old west Norwegian. The young people know some English, but a Danish dictionary can be helpful to the visitor; Danish is the second language.

It's difficult for visitors to understand the isolation or the practical relationship the Faroese have with the natural world. Dubious outsiders, for example, accuse locals of cruelty during the traditional pilot whale harvests. An essential foodstuff, the islands' national sea mammals are killed in limited numbers and permit less dependence on imported meat. The hunt is also an important part of Faroese society, involving the youngest to the eldest.

Important Addresses and Numbers

Tourist Information In Copenhagen, call the **Faroese Government Office** (Højbroplads 7, tel. 33/14–08–66). Locally, the tourist offices are: **Strandferdslan Tourist Information** (á Stongunum, FR 700 Klaksvik, tel. 298/56006) and **Aldan Tourist Information** (Reyngøta 17, FR 100 Tórshavn, tel. 298/19391). The brochure *Around the Faroe Islands* is particularly helpful. The **Danish Tourist Board** (branches in Denmark and abroad) can also supply information.

Emergencies Dial 000 for any emergency.

Pharmacies Try **Tórshavn** (by SMS shopping center, tel. 298/11100), **Klaksvík** (Klaksvíksvegur, tel. 298/55055), or **Trøroyri** (tel. 298/71076).

Arriving and Departing by Plane

From Copenhagen there are daily connections to the western island of Vagar, which take about two hours. From there, count another 2½ hours to get to Tórshavn by bus and ferry. Delays due to heavy fog are common. For reservations on either **DanAir** or **Atlantic Airways,** call **SAS** (tel. 33/13–62–66) in Copenhagen, or DanAir (tel. 298/32755) in the Faroe Islands. Two weekly flights are also available from Reykjavík (tel. 91–25100) and one a week from Bergen, Norway (tel. 05/31–26–00), on **Icelandair.**

Arriving and Departing by Ferry

There is frequent ferry service to all islands, with the most remote areas served by helicopter as well. Once a week, in summer, there are car ferries from Esbjerg (33 hours) to Tórshavn. Call **DFDS** (tel. 33/11–22–55). Also in the summer, **Blue Water Shipping,** the Danish agent for the Faroes' **Smyril Line,** departs from Hantstolm, in northwest Jylland, to Tórshavn (36 hours), with connections in Norway, Iceland, and the Shetland Islands (tel. in Jylland, 97/96–22–44; in Tórshavn, 15900). Year-round ferries depart from Hirtshals, Jylland, on Friday and arrive in Tórshavn Monday (48 hours). Call **Faroeship** (tel. 31/29–26–88).

Getting Around

By Bus, Ferry, and Helicopter The main islands are connected by regular ferries, while smaller ones are linked by mailboat and helicopter. For ferries, call **Strandferdslan,** Tórshavn (tel. 298/14550 or 298/56006). **Helicopter Service** is in Tórshavn (tel. 298/16450). In towns, and between islands that are connected by bridges, there is regular bus service. For schedules and reservations, call **Bygdaleiðir** in Tórshavn (tel. 298/14366).

By Car Driving laws are the same as in Denmark. Car rentals are available in the larger towns, such as Tórshavn and Klaksvík. A network of two-lane asphalt roads has been built between towns, using tunnels and bridges. The roads are best on the nine main islands. Speed limits are 50 kilometers per hour (30 miles per hour) in urban areas, 80 kph (50 mph) outside. Once outside towns, beware of untethered animals. The islanders are extremely strict about drunk driving.

Guided Tours

There are two main tour operators on the islands: **Kunningarstovan** (Vaglid, Tórshavn, tel. 298/15788) and **Tora Tourist Travel** (N. Finsensgøta, Tórshavn, tel. 298/15505), which offer angling, city, and bird-watching tours. Among them: **Boat tours of Nolsoy and Hestur** (Kunningarstovan), leave from Tórshavn harbor (3 hours) and include coastal sails through the Kapilsund strait and Hestur's west coast to see puffins and other seabirds. Tora Tourist Travel organizes a tour to **Gjogy,** the northernmost village on Eysturoy (5 hours), including a view of mountains and a local village, and the **Vestmanna Birdcliffs Tour** (6 hours), which includes a look at bird colonies and nearby caves. Many hotels also offer tours within their vicinity.

Exploring the Faroe Islands

Numbers in the margin correspond with points of interest on the Faroe Islands map.

Most visitors who arrive by plane begin on the largest and most traveled island of **Streymoy,** which, though carved by sheer cliffs and waterfalls, has good roads and tunnels. On the northern end of the island are bird sanctuaries and a NATO base. On its southeastern flank is one of the world's tiniest capitals,
1 **Tórshavn,** named after the Viking god Thor.

The Faroe Islands

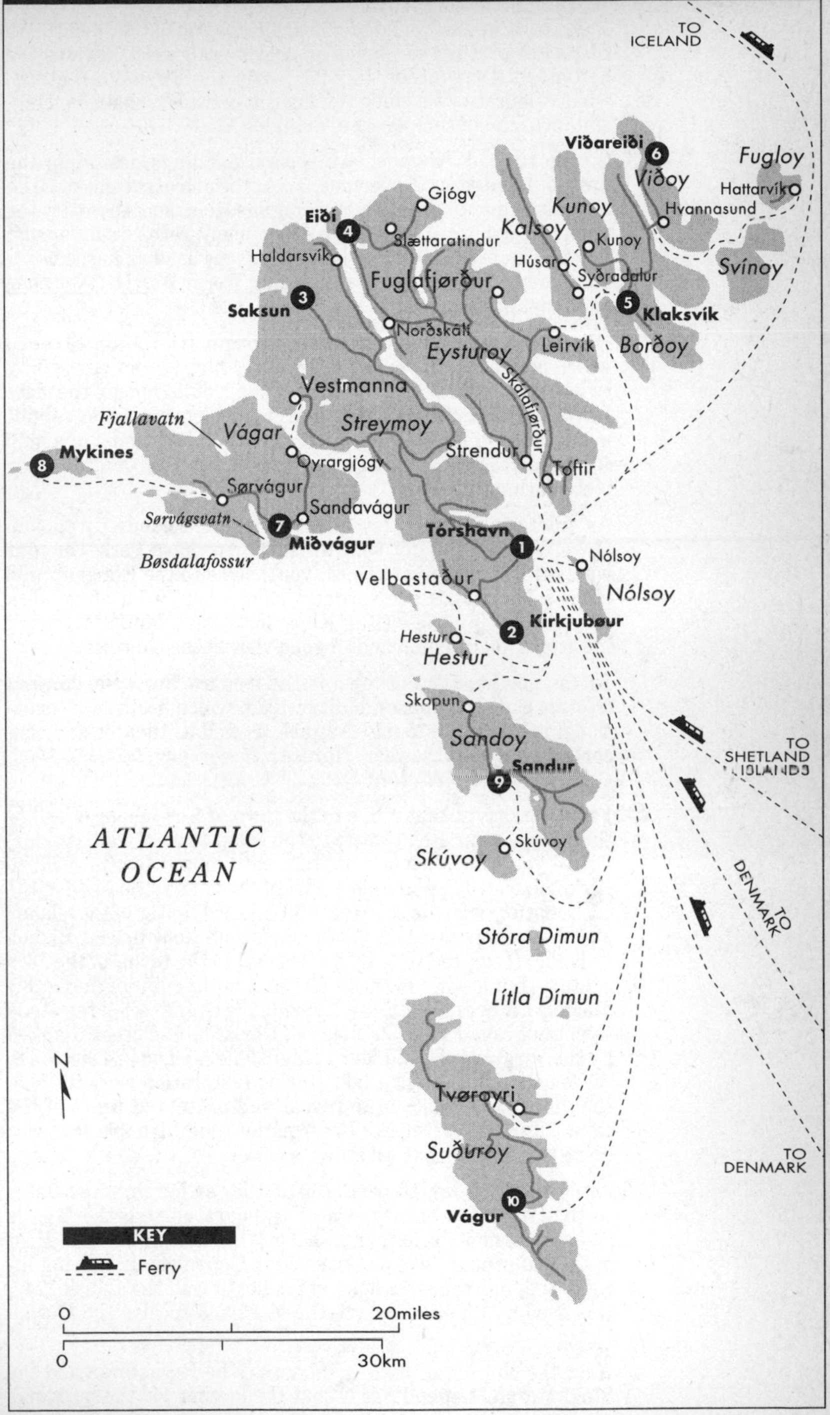

Centrally located among the islands, it has a population of 16,000. The Viking *Alting* (Parliament) met here on St. Olav's Day, AD 825, and founded the *Løgting* (legislative body). All that's left of it is the **Tinganes,** a rocky ridge that divides the harbor. St. Olav's Day, July 29, is now the Tórshavn Festival, when celebrations include rowing competitions, chain dancing, and, in a land of temperance, drinking.

On the rugged Tinganes are several buildings, including the present **Landsstýri** (Government). At the end of the docks is the **Skansin,** a fort built in 1580 by Magnus Heinason, to fortify the town against pirate attacks. After many reconstructions, it reached its present shape in 1790 and was used as Faroe headquarters by the British Navy during World War II. Two guns from that period remain.

Down from the Tinganes is the **Gongin** (Old Main Street), which is lined with small 19th-century houses and crossed by twisting streets. In the same direction, you'll come to the slate **Havnar Kirkja** (Tórshavn's Church), which has been rebuilt many times in its 200-year history. Inside is a model of a ship salvaged from an 18th-century wreck, its bell, and an altar piece dating to 1647.

As there are very few trees on the islands, walk up Hoyviksvegur and get your fill at the **Tórshavn Park.** On your way, off R.C. Effersøes Gøta, you'll come to the **Kongaminnid** (King's Memorial) on Nordrari Ringvegur, a basalt obelisk commemorating the visit of King Christian IX in 1874. Standing atop a hill, it commands a good view of the old town.

At the northern tip of town is the modern **Norðurlandahúsid** (Nordic Culture House), built in 1983, which hosts an international jazz festival in mid-August, as well as theater and concerts throughout the year. *Norðrari Ringvegur, tel. 298/17900. Call for event schedules.*

2 From Tórshavn, take a bus to the town of **Kirkjubøur** or follow the Landavegur Road west, to the small town of Velbastaøur, where you can follow a mountain path (opposite Rte. 536) to **Kirkjubøur.** On the southern part of the island, the town in the 12th century was the spiritual and cultural center of the islands and the bishop's seat. A particularly ambitious priest, Bishop Erland, attempted to build a cathedral in the town, in the 13th century, but it was never completed, and the ruins of the Gothic **Magnus Cathedral** still stand. Inside the church is a large stone tablet engraved with an image of Christ on the cross, flanked by the Virgin Mary and Mary Magdalene, and an inscription to St. Magnus and St. Thorlak. During restoration work in 1905, the tablet was removed to reveal well-preserved relics of the saints. In 1538, after the Reformation, the Bishop's seat was dissolved, and with it, the town's power.

Also in Kirkjubøur, the restored **St. Olav's Church,** which dates to the late-13th century, was a cathedral during the Middle Ages and is now the only church from that time still in use. Most of the sculptures have been moved to Copenhagen, leaving little to see, but there's a hole on the north wall that, until 1740, was used by lepers to watch the Mass and receive the Eucharist.

Near the church are two farmhouses, the **Roykstovan** and the **Stokkatovan.** Legend has it that the lumber for the buildings came drifting to the town, neatly numbered and bundled, from the Sogne Fjord in Norway. Inside, the two buildings give a good impression of traditional Faroese living in one-main-room cottages.

The northern end of the island is sliced by fjords. Within this
3 rugged setting is the tiny town of **Saksun,** 30 kilometers (18 miles) northwest by bus from Tórshavn, and one of the most popular excursions on the island. Set around a pastoral lake in the midst of a deep valley are scattered sod-roof houses and lovely views. The town also swarms with great skuas, a large brown sea-bird prone to low dives.

The next island, **Eysturoy,** is connected by bridge and buses to
4 Streymoy. The center of activity is the town of **Eiði,** which lies to the northwest, within a spectacular landscape of steep cliffs. Looking northwest, you can see two 250-foot cliffs, a part of local mythology: One night an Icelandic giant and his wife came to carry the islands to Iceland, but she dropped them, giving the islands their cracked geography. Once the sun rose, the giants were petrified and transformed into the bluffs.

Due east of the town is the highest point of the islands, the 2,910-foot **Slættaratindur** mountain. The island also has the longest fjord, the southern **Skálafjørður,** around which most of the population of 10,500 live.

The island of **Borðoy** is next, accessible by boat from eastern Eysturoy. On its southwest coast, nearly divided by two fjords,
5 is the Faroes' second-largest town, **Klaksvík.** Within this scattering of islands, Borðoy, Viðoy, and Kunoy are connected by causeways. The other three islands, Fugloy, Svinoy, and Kalsoy, are accessible by passenger boat or helicopter.

Klaksvík is the most important fishing harbor in the Faroes, with a fleet of sophisticated boats that harvest cod, haddock, herring, and other fish. The local church, **Christianskirkjan** (Christian's Church) has a 4,000-year-old granite baptismal font, thought to have had pagan origins in Denmark. Also under the church roof, you can see a 24-foot boat used by a former vicar to visit nearby towns.

The island of **Viðoy** is among the wildest, most alpine and beautiful of the islands, with mountains of 2,800 feet and sheer cliffs plunging into extremely rough, unnavigable waters. Amazing-
6 ly, 600 people live here. From the town of **Viðareði** (call Tora Tourist) you can take a boat tour to see many seabirds burrowed into cliff walls, including guillemots, kittiwakes, and puffins—endearing little black-and-white birds with enormous orange beaks. The Faroese have a remarkable relationship with the puffins, harvesting them by the thousand for food and yet not endangering their numbers.

To the west, the name of **Vágar,** the third-largest island, means fjords, and it is cut by three of them, as well as the **Fjallavatn** and **Sørvágsvatn** lakes, the last of which boasts the **Bøsdalafossur,** a 100-foot waterfall. The main town here is
7 **Miðvágur,** an excellent perch for auk- and gannet-watching.

West of the town, you can see a tall pointy cliff, called the **Trøllkonufingur** (Witch's Finger), which was only climbed once, in 1844, with tragic results. On the occasion of a royal visit, a young local climbed the monolith's sheer face to wave to

Crown Prince Frederik VIII. The second time he scaled it, to retrieve a glove, he slipped and fell to his death.

It's rough sailing to the tiny atoll of **Mykines,** and only manageable when weather permits. Accessible by helicopter or by traversing the island northward on foot about 2 kilometers (1.2 miles) from the boat landing is the isolated town of the same
8 name, **Mykines,** population 30, where the few dwellings are roofed with sod. The town was sited here to be close to the **Mykinesholmur,** a hill swarming with thousands of puffins, which are necessarily harvested for food.

Sandoy, the fifth-largest island, lies to the south. Relatively fertile, it's named for the sandy white beaches of the town of
9 **Sandur,** which lies in its bay. Amid green hills, sheep graze, while the lakes north and west of town swell with auks, purple sandpipers, and great skuas. Throughout, this is great land for walking or cycling (bike rentals are available in town).

The southernmost island, **Suðuroy,** is milder than the others, with cultivated green fields at its center and mountains along the coast. It is reachable by ferry from Tórshavn; the arrival
10 docks are in **Vágur,** and in the quieter village of **Tvøroyri.**

Dining and Lodging

Accommodations and hotels are minimal, though summer cottages are available through the Tora and Kunningarstovan tour operators (*see* Guided Tours, *above*). Most restaurants are located in hotels. Faroese cuisine consists mainly of fish, mutton, and lamb, and you can also find Danish open-face sandwiches. Because some islands have few shops and restaurants, it's a good idea to pack sandwiches and water when you go out exploring.

Eidi/Eysturoy
Dining and Lodging

Hotel Eidi. Perched on a hilltop village near the sea, about an hour by bus from Tórshavn, this slightly dated hotel is small and clean, with TVs and refrigerators in all rooms. *FR–470 Eidi, tel. 298/23456, fax 298/23200. 31 rooms. Facilities: restaurant. DC, MC, V. Moderate.*

Eysturoy
Lodging

Gjaargardur. This youth hostel, built in traditional Faroese style, is located in a beautiful area, on the north end of the island, near the ocean and the mountains. *FR–476, tel. 23171, fax 23505, 100 beds. No credit cards. Inexpensive.*

Klaksviik/Bordoy
Dining and Lodging

Klaksviikar Sjómans Heim. This big white sailors' hotel has comfortable rooms. *Vikavegur, tel. 55333. 68 beds. No credit cards. Moderate.*

Klaksviig Vandrehjem. This youth and family hostel, the only one in the northern islands, is in a former hotel, built in 1945. It is near a ferry slip and surrounded by hiking trails. *Gardavegur 31, FR–700 Klaksvík, tel. 55403 or 57555. 67 beds. No credit cards. Inexpensive.*

Nordoyggjar
Dining and Lodging

Hotel Nord. In a small town of 300 inhabitants on the northern end of the island, this simple business hotel has beautiful surroundings and great bird-watching. *FR–750 Vidareisi, tel. 51061, fax 51144. 10 rooms. No credit cards. Closed Oct.–May. Moderate.*

Sandoy
Dining and Lodging

Hotel Tvøroyri. In the middle of town, this old hotel has simple, clean rooms and minimal service. *FR–800 Tvøroyri, tel. 71171, fax 71394. 32 beds. AE. Moderate.*

Tórshavn/Streymoy
Dining and Lodging

Hotel Borg. Five minutes from the center of Tórshavn, this hotel has a view of the old town. The rooms all have TVs, refrigerators, and phones, and there's a good restaurant that features island specialties. *Oyggjarvegur, tel. 17500, fax 16019, 108 rooms with bath. Facilities: restaurant. AE, DC, MC. Expensive.*

Hotel Hafnia. Close to the walking streets of town, this modern business hotel offers a good buffet and big-city ambience. The rooms have TV, refrigerator, and phone. *Aarvegur 4, tel. 11270, fax 15250. 106 rooms with bath. Facilities: restaurant. AE, DC; MC. Expensive.*

Summarhotel. Open as a hotel from July to September, this is a school during the winter. *Vesturgøta 15, tel. 18900, fax 15707. 106 rooms with shower and toilet. AE, DC, MC. Moderate.*

Tilhaldshúsid Skansin. This modern, two-story guest house has only been open for a year, and it has already become a favorite among travelers and business guests. Showers are available on both floors, and breakfast is included in the price of a room. The obliging staff can also help with travel or tour arrangements. *Jekaragøta 8, Postbox 57, FR–110 Tórshavn, tel. 12242, fax 10657. 22 beds. No credit cards. Moderate.*

Tørshavnar Sjømans Heim. This sailors' hotel has comfortable rooms and a good restaurant. *Torsgøta 4, tel. 13515, fax 13286. 80 beds. Facilities: restaurant. No credit cards. Inexpensive.*

Vágur/Suðuroy
Dining and Lodging

Hotel Vagar. A standard small hotel, this one is modern. *FR–380 Sørvágur, tel. 32955, fax 32310. 54 rooms. Facilities: restaurant. AE, DC, MC. Moderate.*

Hotel Bakkin. This plain lodging is usually booked by fishermen and local workers. *FR–900 Vágur, tel. 73196. 24 beds. No credit cards. Inexpensive.*

3 Finland

Introduction

If you like majestic open spaces, fine architecture, and civilized living—and can afford the prices—Finland is for you. The music of Jean Sibelius, Finland's most famous son, tells you what to expect from this Nordic landscape. Both can swing from the somber nocturne of midwinter darkness to the tremolo of sunlight slanting through pine and birch, or from the crescendo of a blazing sunset to the pianissimo of the next day's dawn. The architecture of Alvar Aalto and the Saarinens, Eliel and son Eero, visible in many U.S. cities bespeaks the Finnish affinity with nature too, with soaring spaces evocative of Finland's moss-floored forests. In fact, Eliel and his family moved to the United States in 1923 and became American citizens—but it was to a lonely Finnish seashore that Saarinen had his ashes returned.

Until 1917, Finland was under the domination of its nearest neighbors, Sweden and Russia, who fought over it for centuries. After more than 600 years under Swedish rule and 100 under the czars, the country inevitably bears many traces of the two cultures, including a small (6%) Swedish-speaking population and a scattering of Russian Orthodox churches.

But the Finns themselves are neither Scandinavian nor Slavic. All that is known of their origins—they speak a Finno-Ugrian tongue, part Finnish, part Hungarian—is that they are descended from wandering tribes who probably originated west of Russia's Ural mountains before the Christian era and settled on the Gulf of Finland's swampy shores.

There is a tough, resilient quality to the Finn. Finland is one of the very few countries that shared a border with the Soviet Union in 1939 and retained its independence. Indeed, no country has fought the Soviets to a standstill, as the Finns did in the Winter War of 1939–40. This resilience, in part, stems from both the turbulence of the country's past and from the people's determination to work the land and survive the long, brutal winters. No wonder there is a poet-philosopher lurking in most Finns, one who sometimes drowns the darker melancholic side in a bottle. The Finn is in a constant state of confrontation—against the weather, the land, and the lurking Russian Bear. Finns are stubborn, patriotic, and self-sufficient, yet not aggressively nationalistic. On the contrary, rather than boasting of past battles, Finns are proud of finding ways to live in peace with the Soviet Union. They cling tenaciously to their country's neutrality and their personal freedom and will never relinquish either easily.

The average Finn volunteers little information, but that's due to reserve, not indifference. Make the first approach and you may have a friend for life. Finns like their silent spaces, though, and won't appreciate backslapping familiarity—least of all in the sauna, still regarded by many as a spiritual, as well as a cleansing, experience.

Finland

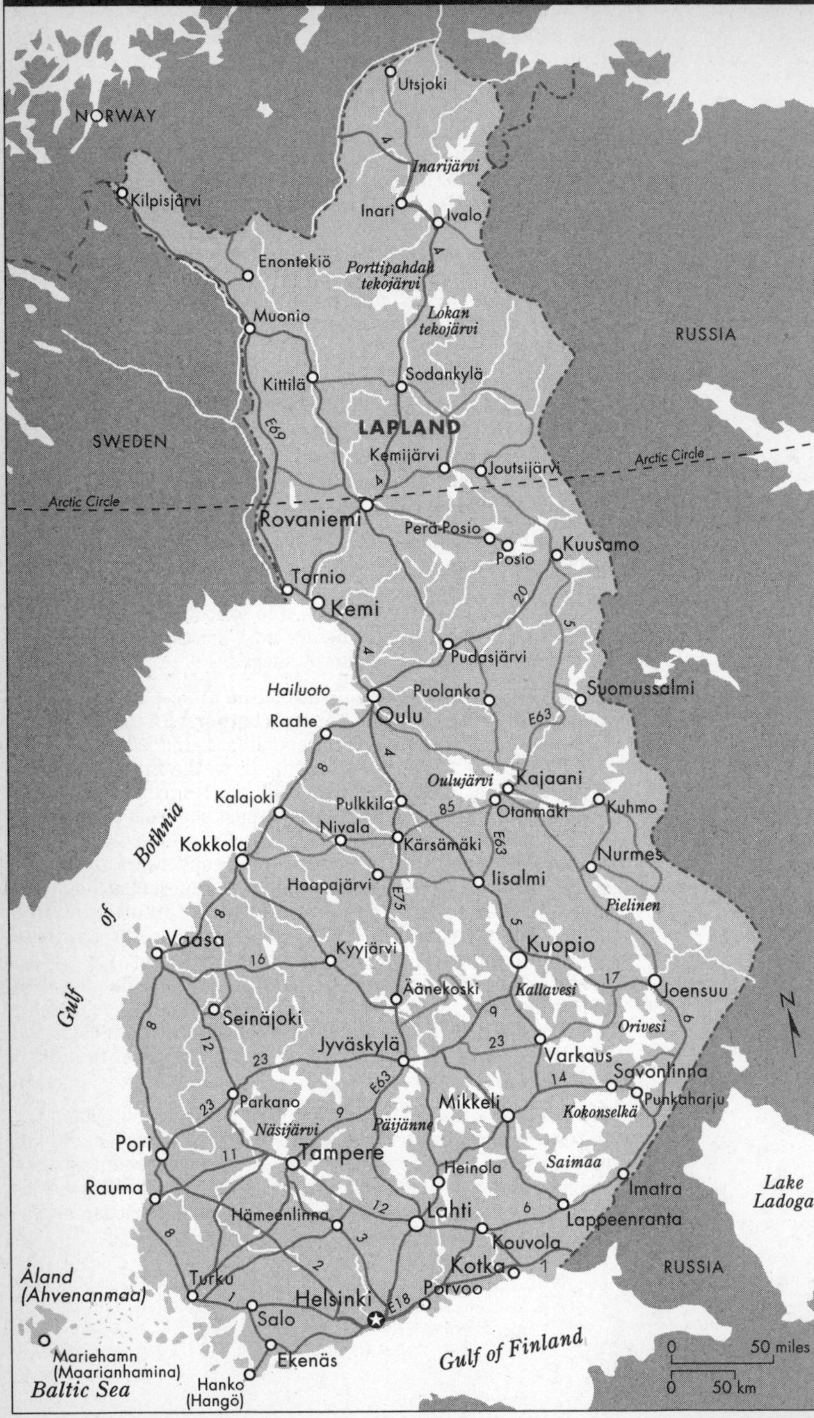
NORWAY
SWEDEN
RUSSIA
LAPLAND
Utsjoki
Inarijärvi
Inari
Ivalo
Kilpisjärvi
Enontekiö
Porttipahdan tekojärvi
Lokan tekojärvi
Muonio
Kittilä
Sodankylä
E69
Kemijärvi
Joutsijärvi
Arctic Circle
Arctic Circle
Rovaniemi
Perä-Posio
Posio
Kuusamo
Tornio
Kemi
20
5
4
Pudasjärvi
Hailuoto
Puolanka
Suomussalmi
Oulu
Raahe
E63
8
Oulujärvi
Kajaani
Kalajoki
Pulkkila
85
Otanmäki
Kuhmo
Nivala
Kärsämäki
E63
Bothnia
Kokkola
Nurmes
Haapajärvi
Iisalmi
E75
Pielinen
of
Vaasa
Kyyjärvi
Kuopio
16
17
Kallavesi
Joensuu
Äänekoski
Gulf
Seinäjoki
Orivesi
9
12
23
Varkaus
Jyväskylä
23
14
Savonlinna
E63
Punkaharju
Parkano
Mikkeli
Kokonselkä
Näsijärvi
Päijänne
Pori
11
Tampere
Saimaa
Heinola
Imatra
Lake Ladoga
Rauma
Hämeenlinna
12
Lahti
6
Lappeenranta
3
Kouvola
RUSSIA
Åland (Ahvenanmaa)
Turku
Kotka
1
Porvoo
Helsinki
E18
Salo
Gulf of Finland
Ekenäs
Mariehamn (Maarianhamina)
Baltic Sea
Hanko (Hangö)
0
50 miles
0
50 km
N

Before You Go

Government Tourist Offices

In the United States Finnish Tourist Board, 655 3rd Ave., New York, NY 10017, tel. 212/949–2333.

In Canada Finnish Tourist Board, 1200 Bay St., Suite 604, Toronto, Ont. M5R 2A5, tel. 416/964–9159.

In the United Kingdom Finnish Tourist Board, 66–68 Haymarket, London SW1Y 4RF, tel. 071/839–4048.

When to Go

Finland is delightful in the summer, with its clear clean air and phenomenally long sunny days. In the extreme north, the sun doesn't set at all during June and July, and even in Helsinki, where the sun often doesn't set before 10:30 PM, the night sky never becomes truly black. In the winter, not only is it very cold, but many of the tourist facilities are scaled down or even closed completely. The hotels are also less expensive in summer (and on weekends year-round), and so are domestic airfares. Finns tend to travel heavily during Christmas, Easter, and July—the peak summer vacation month—so book ahead if you must fly during these times.

Climate In summer, Finland is the warmest Scandinavian country. Summer temperatures are surprisingly high, often in the 80s and 90s. In winter, Helsinki averages about 25° F. Average temperatures in central Finland are 5° lower, and in Lapland, 10° lower. The following are average daily maximum and minimum temperatures for Helsinki.

Jan.	27F	- 3C	**May**	57F	14C	**Sept.**	59F	15C
	16	- 9		39	4		46	8
Feb.	25F	- 4C	**June**	66F	19C	**Oct.**	46F	8C
	16	- 9		48	9		37	3
Mar.	32F	0C	**July**	72F	22C	**Nov.**	37F	3C
	19	- 7		55	13		30	- 1
Apr.	43F	6C	**Aug.**	68F	20C	**Dec.**	30F	- 1C
	30	- 1		54	12		23	- 5

Festivals and Seasonal Events

January: The **Arctic Rally** gets into gear yearly in Rovaniemi, Lapland.

February: Shrove Tuesday Celebrations, throughout Finland, include skiing, skating, and tobogganing events; **Reppu-Finlandia** is a 40-kilometer (25-mile) Hämeenlinna–Lahti ski event.

March: The **International Ice Sculpture Contest** is held in Kemijärvi, as is the **Tar Skiing Race,** the oldest and longest (75-kilometer/47-mile) cross-country ski trek in the country; then there is the **Santa Claus Arctic Golf Tournament** in Rovaniemi.

April: April Jazz/Espoo features foreign and Finnish performers in a Helsinki suburb; the **Porokuninkuusravit Reindeer Races** are run in Ivalo; and the **Vermo Cup Horse Event** is held at the Helsinki trotting track.

May: Vapunaatto and Vappu (May Day Eve and May Day) celebrations occur nationwide and include bonfires, picnicking, and drinking; **Kainuu Jazz** means four days of listening to native and foreign musicians jamming in Kajaani.
June: The **Kuopio Music and Dance Festival** is on stage in Kuopio, while the **Naantali Music Festival** soothes the ears of classical music lovers; **Juhannus** (Midsummer Eve and Day) is celebrated nationwide with bonfires and all-night boat cruises.
July: The **Savonlinna Opera Festival,** on a grand scale and a month long, is a festival of international opera, ballet, and theater staged at Olavinlinna Castle, Savonlinna; **Pori Jazz,** Finland's premier international jazz festival, is set in Pori; the **Kuhmo Chamber Music Festival** means a week of chamber music in eastern Finland, and the **National Folk Music and Dance Festival** is based in Kaustinen.
August: The **Turku Music Festival** has Baroque to contemporary performances; the **Tampere Theater Festival** includes plays staged by Finnish and foreign troupes; the **Helsinki Festival** means two weeks of dance, music, drama, and children's shows in the capital and its environs.
September: Ålands Culture Festival is a time for arts performances and courses in Mariehamn.
October: The **Baltic Herring Festival** is the premier fishermen's fish market, for one weekend on the quayside in Helsinki.
November: Tampere Jazz, a modern jazz event, holds court in Tampere; the **Children's Festival** consists of performance art of all kinds for kids, in Helsinki; **Kaamos Jazz** is a festival of jazz in Lapland's winter twilight, at Inari.
December: Independence Day (December 6) means a parade to the candlelit Senate Square in Helsinki; the **International Jean Sibelius Violin Competition** is held every fifth year (next one is in 1995) in Helsinki; **New Year's Celebration** varies, but fireworks can be seen from Senate Square in Helsinki.

Finnish Currency

The unit of currency is the Finnmark (FM), also abbreviated as FMK and FIM. The Finnmark is divided into 100 pennies (penniä) in denominations of 5, 10, 20, and 50. Bills begin with the FM10 note progressing to FM50, 100, 500, and 1,000. At press time (fall 1991) the exchange rate was FM3.71 to the U.S. dollar, FM7.67 to the pound sterling, and FM3.65 to the Canadian dollar. There are exchange bureaus in most larger bank branches, post offices, the major airports, and also in the City Tourist Office in Helsinki during the summer months. Several large harbors have summer exchange bureaus, too, and any international ferry has an exchange desk. Banks give the best exchange rates. Extended exchange and banking hours at KOP bank booth at the Helsinki-Vantaa International Airport are 6:30 AM–11 PM daily.

What It Will Cost

With the plunge of the dollar against foreign currencies and Finnmark's continued strength, prices in the early '90s seem more outrageous here than ever before: Helsinki has now surpassed Tokyo as the most expensive city in the world, with food about 45% more expensive than in other Western nations. Still, people without scads of money can manage. If you camp or rent cabins rather than hotel rooms, and if you shop for meals carefully, you can cut costs way back. Helsinki is Finland's most expensive city for lodging. Food costs tend to be standardized across the country, however. Inflation was running just over 5% annually in the early 1990s.

Taxes There is a 17% sales tax on most consumer goods. Non-residents can get much of this back by going through the "tax-free for tourists" procedure (*see* Tax-Free Shopping, *below*). Restaurants and hotels include a 15% service charge in your bill.

Sample Costs Cup of coffee, FM5; soda, FM7; continental breakfast in hotel, FM32–60; bottle of beer FM12–36; 10-kilometer taxi ride, FM60.

Passports and Visas

Citizens of the United States, Great Britain, Canada, and most European countries need a valid passport to enter Finland; a visa is necessary only if your total stay in the Nordic countries will be longer than three months (*see* Chapter 1 for additional information).

Customs and Duties

On Arrival ★ Travelers age 20 years or over may bring in two liters of beer, one liter of alcohol under 21% volume and one liter of alcohol over 21% volume; or two liters of beer plus two liters of alcohol under 21% volume. Travelers between 18 and 20 cannot bring in any alcohol over 21% volume, but can bring beer or wine. Travelers 16 and older arriving from Europe may bring in 400 cigarettes or a little over a pound (500 grams) of tobacco. Travelers arriving from outside Europe have a 200-cigarette, ½-pound-plus (250-gram) tobacco limit. A permit for firearms and ammunition must be obtained on arrival from airport or harbor police.

On Departure A license is required to export the following: handicrafts and works of art more than 50 years old; any object over 50 years old with cultural or historic value; valuable Finnish coins, medals, or postage stamps.

Language

Finnish, the main language, is not a Scandinavian language, but a Finno-Ugric language related to Estonian and distantly to Hungarian. The country's second official language is Swedish, although only about 6% of the population speaks it. In the south, most towns have Finnish and Swedish names; if the Swedish name is listed first, it indicates more Swedish than Finnish speakers in that area. The third language is Saame, the language of the Laplanders. English is spoken in most cities and resorts.

Car Rentals

Car rental in Finland is not cheap, but a group rental might make it worthwhile. Be on the lookout for weekend and summer discounts. Regular daily rates range from FM120–FM350 ($34–$100), and per-kilometer surcharges from FM1.20–FM3.50 (4¢–10¢). Insurance is sold by the rental agencies. Some centrally located agencies are: **Avis** (Fredrikinkatu 67,

Helsinki, tel. 90/441–155; airport office, tel. 90/822–833), **Budget** (Fredrikinkatu 61A60, tel. 90/694–5300; airport office, tel. 90/870–1606), and **InterRent-Europcar** (airport office, tel. 90/826–677).

Rail Passes

The **Finnrail Pass** gives unlimited second-class travel within a set time; the eight-day pass costs $90, two-week pass $145, and three-week pass $181. These can be bought in North America and Britain, as well as inside Finland—the Finnish Tourist Board in your home country can tell you where to get them.

Finland also participates in the following rail programs: **EurailPass, Eurail Youth Pass** (for those under 26), **ScanRail Pass** (unlimited travel in Scandinavia for 21 days), **InterRail** (for those under 26 who are not residents of Scandinavia), and **Rail Europe Senior Card** (for men over 65 and women over 60). (*See also* Getting Around by Train, *below*).

Traveling with Children

Finland's is a child-oriented society. It is no problem finding things like changing rooms. Almost all hotels welcome children. Helsinki's city tourist office has a list of qualified babysitters in the capital area.

Farmhouse Holidays and Seaside Cabins

In Finland more than 150 farmhouses provide full board, half-board, or bed-and-breakfast accommodations; many also have children's rates and offer handicrafts classes, farm tours, and other organized activities for children.

In Finland, families of three or more traveling by bus over distances of at least 47 miles receive a 20% discount. **Finnrail** offers savings of 50% to all Finnrail Pass holders under 16, and savings of 20% to groups of three or more. Children ages two to 11 also get a 50% reduction on Finnair's Holiday Ticket, offering 15 days of unlimited air travel in Finland.

Young people ages 12 to 23 qualify for a **Finnish Youth Holiday Ticket** good for up to 15 days of unlimited air travel within Finland. For further information contact Finnair (tel. 800/950–5000). (*See also* Traveling with Children in Chapter 1.)

Hints for Disabled Travelers

In Finland, information on facilities for disabled visitors can be obtained from **Rullaten ry** (Vartiokyläntie 9, 00950 Helsinki, tel. 90/322–069), an organization specializing in assisting the disabled in planning their travel. Further information is available from the **Invalidiliitto ry** (Association of the Disabled) (Kumpulantie 1 A, 00520 Helsinki, tel. 90/718–466). A seven-day historical/architectural/cultural "Triangle Tour," beginning in Helsinki, for disabled travelers is available on request from the **Area Travel Agency** (Kaisanienmenkatu 13, 00100 Helsinki, tel. 90/18–551).

Hints for Older Travelers

Finland is a generally safe place with good public transportation, and visiting should be a pleasant experience for all. Carry some proof of your age whenever you buy tickets for events, museums, and especially for travel: There are significant discounts to be had for people over 65 years old—and sometimes for those over 60.

Arriving and Departing

From North America by Plane

Airports and Airlines All international flights arrive at Helsinki-Vantaa International Airport, 20 kilometers (12 miles) north of the city center. For arrival and departure information call 90/818–500 (6:15 AM–1:00 AM) or 90/821–122 (24 hours).

Finnair (tel. 800/950–5000) offers domestic and international flights, with daily direct service from New York and Los Angeles. **Delta** (tel. 800/221–1212) has direct service from New York. **British Airways** (tel. 800/247–9297), **Lufthansa** (tel. 800/645–3880), and **Scandinavian Airlines System** (SAS) (tel. 800/221–2350) also fly to Helsinki.

Flying Time Flying time from New York to Helsinki is about 8 hours, 9 hours on the return.

From the United Kingdom by Plane and Ship

By Plane **Finnair, British Airways,** and some charter companies fly from London to Helsinki. Ask the **Finnish National Tourist Board** at home for names of companies specializing in travel packages to Finland. All international flights land at Helsinki-Vantaa International Airport, 20 kilometers (12 miles) north of the capital. Finnair in the United Kingdom is located at 14 Clifford Street, London W1X 1RD (tel. 071/408–1222).

Flying Time Flying time from London to Helsinki is 2 hours, 45 minutes

By Ship **DFDS Scandinavian Seaways** (Scandinavia House, Parkeston Quay, Harwich, Essex, tel. 225/240–234) sails from Harwich to Göteborg, Sweden, with overland (bus or train) transfer to Stockholm; from there, Silja and Viking Line ships cross to the Finnish Åland Islands, Turku, and Helsinki. Traveling time is about two days (*see also* Getting Around by Boat, *below*).

Staying in Finland

Getting Around

By Plane Finland's flagship air carrier, **Finnair,** runs an extensive domestic service and a charter company, **KarAir.** Domestic flights are relatively cheap, and some planes have a set number of discount seats allotted so reserve early. "Red" flights in the Finnair timetable are the cheapest. Finnair's main office is at Mannerheimintie 102, 00250 Helsinki (tel. 90/81–881).

By Train **The Finnish National Railroad,** or VR, serves southern Finland well but connections in the central and northern sections are more scarce and are supplemented by buses (*see* Getting Around by Bus, *below*). Helsinki is the main junction, with Riihimäki to the north a major hub. You can get as far north as Rovaniemi by rail, but to penetrate further into Lapland, you'll need to rely on buses, domestic flights, or local taxis.

There are first- and second-class seats available on most trains. Children travel half-fare and there is a 20% reduction when three or more people travel together. You must make a seat reservation on special fast trains (FM15–FM25). For FM50, senior citizens (over 65) can buy a special pass entitling them to discounted train fares. Car and passenger trains leave for northern Finland daily. Passenger trains leave Helsinki twice daily for Leningrad (8 hours) and once daily on an overnighter to Moscow (15 hours). Travel to the Soviet Union requires a visa. To get to northern Sweden or Norway, you must combine train/bus or train/boat.

Inquiries on train travel can be made to the Finnish State Railways at the main railroad station in Helsinki, or to the **Information Service** at Vilhonkatu 13, PB 488, 00101 Helsinki (tel. 90/7071).

By Bus The Finnish bus network, **Matkahuolto** (Lauttasaareutie 8, 00200 Helsinki, tel. 90/692–2088), is extensive and the fares reasonable. You can also travel between Finland and Norway, Sweden, or the Soviet Union by bus. Full-time students can purchase a discount card for FM30 that translates into a 30%–50% discount on longer trips. Senior citizens will get good discounts with the **65 Card** for FM25; it's available at most Matkahuolto offices. Children and groups of three or more also get discounts.

A **Coach Holiday Ticket** (FM260) is good for up to 1,000 kilometers (650 miles) of travel for two weeks.

By Car Driving is pleasant on Finland's relatively uncongested roads. Gasoline costs FM3.50 per liter at press time. Driving is on the right. You must always use low-beam headlights outside of built-up areas. Seat belts are compulsory for all. You must yield to cars coming from the right at most intersections where roads are of equal size.

Speed limits range from 50 to 100 kilometers per hour (30 to 65 miles per hour), depending on road size and proximity to settled areas. Late autumn and spring are the most hazardous times to drive. Roads often are icy in autumn ("kelivaroitus" is the slippery road warning) and the spring thaw can make for *kelirikko* (heaves). The **Automobile Touring Club of Finland** (Kansakoulukatu 10, Helsinki, tel. 90/694–0022) has a wealth of information, including where to rent studded tires, mandatory from October through April.

Foreigners involved in road accidents should immediately notify the **Motor Insurers' Bureau** (tel. 90/19–251) and the police.

By Boat Finland is one of the world's largest shipbuilding nations, and the ferries that cruise the Baltic to the Finnish Åland islands and Sweden seem more like luxury liners. The boat operators make so much money selling duty-free alcohol, perfume, and chocolate, they spare no expense on facilities, which include saunas, children's playrooms, casinos, a host of bars and cafés, and often superb restaurants.

The Stockholm–Turku run takes about 10 hours; Stockholm–Helsinki takes about 14 hours, and all classes of sleeping accommodations are available on board. Other connections are Helsinki–Travemunde (Germany); Helsinki–Tallinn (Estonia, USSR), and Helsinki–Gdansk (Poland).

By Taxi Taxis travel everywhere in Finland. The meter starts at FM13, with surcharges at certain times and on certain days. In cities, people generally go to one of the numerous taxi stands and take the first available taxi. You can hail a cab, but most are on radio call. It is possible to order taxis by phone; look up "Taksi" in the white pages, then try to find one located nearby—they start the meter when leaving their station. Many taxi drivers take credit cards. Tipping is unnecessary; if you want to leave something, round up to nearest FM5–FM10. A receipt is a *kuitti*.

By Bicycle Finland is a wonderful place to bicycle, with its easy terrain, light traffic, and wide network of bicycle paths. You can get bike-route maps for most main cities. In Helsinki, cycling is a great way to see the main peninsula as well as some of the surrounding islands, linked by bridges. Rentals average FM30–FM60 per day. The brochure *Finland for Hostellers* suggests some long-distance cycling trips and is available from the **Finnish Youth Hostel Association** (Yrjönkatu 38B, 00100 Helsinki, tel. 90/694–0377); the youth hostel at the Helsinki Olympic stadium rents bikes for FM40 per day.

Telephones

Local Calls Public phones charge FM1.50–2 and take coins up to FM5. Kiosks often have phones. Airport and hotel phones take credit cards. Ringing tones vary, but are distinguishable from busy signals, which are always rapid. Most pay telephones have picture instructions on their operation, which varies.

Calls within Finland can be made from any phone. Remember that if you are dialing out of the immediate area, you must dial nine first, followed by the region code (example: 9–0 for Helsinki) then the number. Drop the nine when calling Finland from abroad.

International Calls The cheapest way to call overseas is to go to the post and telegraph office, to the "Lennätin" section, where you also may send faxes, telegrams, and telexes. In Helsinki, at Mannerheimintie 11B, the section is open weekdays 8 AM–10 PM, weekends 9–9. The *Finland Direct* pamphlet tells you how to reach an operator in your own country for collect or credit-card calls. Use any booth where there is a green light, and pay the cashier when you finish. You can also ask for a clerk to set up a collect call; when it is ready, the clerk will direct you to a booth.

The front of the phone book has overseas calling directions and rates. You must begin all direct overseas calls with 990 plus country code (1 for the United States/Canada, 44 for Great Britain). Finnish operators can be reached by dialing 92020 for overseas information or for placing collect calls.

Important Numbers For an operator in the United States, dial 9800–1–0010; in Canada, dial 9800–1–0011; and in the United Kingdom, dial 9800–1–0440. Other important numbers are as follows: 000, general emergency; 040, news in English; 0151, wake-up call; 012, Helsinki information; 020, information elsewhere in Finland; 92020, international information.

Mail

Post offices are open weekdays 9–5; stamps, express mail, registered mail, and insured mail service are available. There is no

Saturday delivery. Airmail letters to destinations outside Europe cost FM3.40; to central Europe and the United Kingdom, FM2.90; to other Scandinavian countries and within Finland, FM2.10. Postcards outside Nordic countries are FM2.90. You may receive letters care of the Poste Restante anywhere in Finland; the Poste Restante address in the capital is Mannerheimintie 11, 00100 Helsinki, at the side of the rail station. It is open Monday–Saturday 8 AM–10 PM, Sunday 11 AM–10 PM.

Tipping

Tipping is not the norm in Finland, but it is not unheard of, so use your own discretion. Finns normally do not tip cab drivers, but if they do they round up to the nearest FM5. Give FM5 to train or hotel porters, if you wish. Coat-check fees usually are posted, and tips above this amount are not expected. Restaurant and hotel bills include a 10%–15% service charge, so an additional tip is unnecessary unless you want to reward good service. For all other services, no tip or FM5 is acceptable.

Opening and Closing Times

Banks Most banks are open weekdays 9:30–4; the bank at Helsinki Airport has extended hours (*see* Where to Change Money in Helsinki, *below*).

Shops Stores generally are open weekdays 9–5, Saturday 9–1 or 2, and are closed Sunday. In Helsinki and other major cities, some large stores and malls remain open until 8. Kiosks, selling basic items like milk and toilet paper, are open daily—usually from 7 AM until midnight or later—and are found throughout the country.

Shopping

Finland is known for design—and prices are steep. Helsinki has the widest selection of goods and the highest prices. Most larger manufacturers and design firms set standard prices throughout the country. Furs, called *turkki* in Finland, are a good buy. You also might want to take home some of the delicious smoked or marinated fish found here—available vacuum-packed at Helsinki Airport.

Tax-free Shopping The total sales tax is 17%. You are entitled to a return of 13%, minus 2% processing fees, when you spend more than FM200 (cash or credit card) in a store.

When you ask for your tax rebate, you'll get a tax-free voucher and your goods in a sealed bag. Present the voucher and unopened bag at tax-free cashiers when leaving the country. These are located at most major airports, on board most long-distance ferries, and at major overland crossings into Sweden and Norway. You can get your money back in dollars, sterling, and other Scandinavian and major European currencies (depending on the cashier's supply).

Sports and Outdoor Activities

Bicycling Bicycling is popular as both transport and sport. Route maps are available from local tourist offices and from the **Finnish**

Youth Hostel Association (*see* Getting Around by Bicycle, *above*).

Boating Finns love all kinds of boating, and there are good facilities for guests' boats in most ports. Contact the **Finnish Yachting and Motorboating Association** (Radiokatu 20, 00240 Helsinki, tel. 90/1581).

Canoeing Lapland is one of the most popular canoeing areas. **Lapptreks** (Kiianpolku 2, 99870, Inari, tel. 9697/51–375) offers a combined canoeing/hiking/gold-panning trip, or contact the local tourist board or the **Finnish Canoe Association** (Radiokatu 20, 00240 Helsinki, tel. 90/158–2363).

Cross-country Skiing This is the most Finnish of all sports, and there are ski centers and resorts nationwide, many with equipment to rent. Any tourist board can advise you, or else contact **Suomen Latu** (Fabianinkatu 7, 00130 Helsinki, tel. 90/170–101). Finnair has fly/ski packages to the north; Vuokatti, Ylläs, Saariselkä, and Kiilopää are Lapland's leading ski centers.

Find out about ski events, including the February Hämeenlinna–Lahti Finlandia Race from the **Finlandia Ski Race Office** (Urheilukeskus, 15110 Lahti, tel. 918/49–811); the March Salpausselkä Ski Games and jumping events are also in Lahti.

Downhill Skiing The best skiing is in Lapland (*see* Cross-country Skiing, *above*).

Fishing The fish-rich waters of the Baltic archipelago and innumerable inland lakes and streams assure you will never run out of fishing opportunities. A recreational fishing license (FM30) is valid for one year. The Finnish Tourist Board has a *Finland Fishing* brochure and *A Guide to Angling*, with information on 600 fishing spots. The **National Board of Forestry** (Office for National Parks, Box 233, 00121 Helsinki) will provide guidance, too.

Hiking The country is full of hiking trails, both in the wilds and near the bigger towns. Most towns have a network of paths through the omnipresent forest. For those with rougher treks in mind, ask at local tourist boards or write to the National Board of Forestry (*see above*).

Orienteering This has a big following in Finland, and you can find out about routes and events from the **Finnish Orienteering Association** (Radiokatu 20, 00240 Helsinki, tel. 90/1581).

Waterskiing At both lake- and seaside there are many water-ski clubs; contact the **Finnish Water-Ski Association** (Radiokatu 20, 00240 Helsinki, tel. 90/158–2595).

Beaches For beaches with sand, you must look on the southern coastline and archipelago: for example, on the west coast of the Hailuoto Sands, a low, sandy island about 40 kilometers (25 miles) from Oulu. A car ferry runs there in summer. The nearly 40-kilometer-long (25-mile-long) Hankoniemi Cape is bordered by sandy beaches. The peninsula is part of the Salpausselkä ridge and forms Finland's southern tip.

Dining

Eating establishments in Finland run the culinary gamut from elegant restaurants to the humblest pubs, and it's easy to get a decent—though never cheap—meal.

Finnish food is known for freshness rather than variety, although recent years have seen major improvements in restaurant cuisine. Ironically, the hardest meal to find is the authentic Finnish meal—products from the forest, lakes, and sea. It is far easier to find pizza, which Finns prefer with many toppings.

However, search and you will find the stunning meals Finns make with game—pheasant, reindeer, hare, and grouse—accompanied by wild berry compotes and exotic mushroom sauces. The chantarelle grows wild in Finland, as do dozens of other edible mushrooms.

Other specialties are *poronkäristys* (reindeer casserole), *lihapullat* (meatballs in sauce), *uunijuusto* (oven cheese), and *hiilillä paistetut silakat* (charcoal grilled Baltic herring). *Voileipäpöytä,* the Finnish cousin to smorgasbord, is a cold table served at breakfast or lunch where you are free to take as little or much food as you want.

Fish is, of course, popular, especially smoked fish. Crayfish season begins on July 21. Finnish baked goods are renowned. *Mämmi,* a dessert made of wheat flour, malt, and orange peels and served with cream and sugar, is served at Easter. More nourishing are *karjalan piirakka,* thin, oval wheat-bread balls filled with rice or mashed potatoes and served warm with a mixture of egg and butter. *Kalakukko* is seen most often in Savolax and consists of wheat bread with small pieces of meat and onions baked inside the dough, served warm with melted butter.

Hearty meat dishes include *karjalan paisti,* in which pork, lamb, and beef are mixed and baked for many hours. *Maksalaatikko* is a dish combining liver, rice, and raisins, served with melted butter.

Helsinki and other cities offer a decent variety of foreign restaurants, the dominant ones being Russian and Chinese. Home-cooked meals tend to be beef or pork accompanied by potatoes. Yogurt and other dairy products are extremely good. The Finns like to make pizza at home Sicilian style—with thick, thick crusts. Filled pancakes, homemade bread, and sweet buns are other at-home favorites.

The prices of alcohol are legendary. A "cheap" bottle of wine (all wine is imported, though some is domestically bottled) will cost FM45 ($13) in a restaurant. The Finns make good beer, with a large brew costing around FM23 ($6.50). Cocktails usually start at about FM25 ($7). Spirits and liqueurs are pricey, too, but you'll fare a little better at **Alko,** the state liquor monopoly, open daily 9–5.

Category	**Helsinki***	**Other Areas***
Very Expensive	over FM250	over FM220
Expensive	FM200–FM250	FM180–FM220
Moderate	FM130–FM200	FM100–FM180
Inexpensive	under FM130	under FM100

**per person for dinner, excluding drinks and including appetizer, main course, dessert, and service charge.*

Lodging

Every class of lodging exists in Finland, from five-star urban hotels to rustic cabins on lake shores and in the forest. Cleanliness is the rule, as is modern decor and plumbing. The standard setup includes a bathroom in each room with toilet and shower; only exceptions to this standard (for example full bathroom with bathtub, shared bath) will be mentioned in reviews in this chapter.

The **Hotel Booking Center** in Helsinki, next to the train station, will make reservations for you anywhere in Finland for FM10. Some national hotel chains to contact are **Best Western Hotels Finland** (Annankatu 29, 00100 Helsinki, tel. 90/694–7755) or **Arctia Hotel Partners** (Annankatu 42D, 00100 Helsinki, tel. 90/694–8022).

Lomarengas (Museokatu 3, 00100 Helsinki, tel. 90/441–346) arranges stays at a range of facilities including *mökki* (cabin) holidays. **Suomen 4H Liitto** (Uudenmaankatu 24, 00120 Helsinki tel. 90/642–233) arranges farm vacations.

Bed-and-breakfasts **Lomarengas** and **Toyota Rent-a-Car** now have packages to Finland that include reasonably priced B&B accommodations and car rental plus six itineraries, detailed on route maps. The itineraries include handicrafts stops, sporting activities, and museum and church tours. Information and brochures are available from most offices of the Finnish Tourist Board (*see* Government Tourist Offices in Before You Go, *above*) or from Lomarengas (*see above*).

Summer Dormitories During the summer season (June 1–August 31) many university residence halls in Finland open their doors to visitors. Prices (from $30 per night) are much lower than those in ordinary hotels, and meals are generally available. Ask the Finnish Tourist Board for its brochure on budget accommodations.

Camping Finland is prime camping territory because of the great wealth of open space. If you camp outside authorized areas, you must get the landowner's permission if you are in a settled area, and must not camp closer than 300 feet to anyone's house. You may also swim anywhere that is not clearly marked as private property.

Finncamping Cheque is a coupon system for campers. For more information, contact the **Finnish Travel Association** (Camping Department, Mikonkatu 25, Box 776, 00101 Helsinki, tel. 90/170–868). The group also sells the National Camping Card, a useful ID card. The annually updated list of campsites, including classifications and English-language summary, is on sale at larger bookstores and at R-kiosks.

The price categories below are weekday prices. Larger discounts are available on weekends and in summer months, especially July, when prices are usually 30%–60% cheaper.

Category	Helsinki*	Other Areas*
Very Expensive	over FM850	over FM750
Expensive	FM600–FM850	FM500–FM750
Moderate	FM350–FM600	FM250–FM500
Inexpensive	under 350	under 250

**Prices are for two people in a double room and include service charge and taxes.*

Helsinki

Introduction

Helsinki is a city of the sea, built on peninsulas that stab into the Baltic. Streets and avenues curve around bays, bridges arch over to nearby islands, and ferries reach out to islands farther offshore.

Like other European capitals, Helsinki has expanded its boundaries, now absorbing about one-sixth of the Finnish population, and the suburbs sprawl from one peninsula to another. However, most of the city's sights, hotels, and restaurants cluster on one peninsula, forming a compact hub of special interest for the traveler.

Unlike most other European capitals, Helsinki is "new." About 400 years ago, King Gustav Vasa of Sweden decided to woo trade from the Estonian city of Talinn and thus challenge the monopoly of the Hanseatic League. To do this, he commanded the people of four Finnish towns to pack up their belongings and relocate at the rapids on the river Vantaa. This new town became Helsinki.

For three centuries, Helsinki had its ups and downs as a trading town. Turku, to the west, remained the capital and the country's intellectual center. Ironically, not until Finland fell under Russia's dominance did Helsinki's fortunes improve. Czar Alexander I wanted Finland's political center closer to Russia and, in 1812, selected Helsinki as the new capital. Shortly after the capital was moved from Turku, Turku suffered a monstrous fire. Such was the damage that the university was also moved to Helsinki. From then on, Helsinki's future was secure.

Fire was indeed fortuitous for the city's future. Just before the tsar's proclamation, a fire had gutted the town, permitting the construction of new buildings suitable for a nation's capital. The German-born architect Carl Ludvig Engel was commissioned to rebuild the city, and, as a result, Helsinki has some of the purest neoclassical architecture in the world. Add to this foundation the modern buildings designed by talented Finnish architects and the result is a European capital city that is as architecturally eye-catching as it is distinct from other Scandinavian and European capitals.

Important Addresses and Numbers

Tourist Information The **City Tourist Office** (Pohjoisesplanadi 19, 00100 Helsinki, tel. 90/169–3757) is open September 16–May 15, Monday 8:30–4:30 and Tuesday–Friday 8:30–4; and May 16–September 15, weekdays 8:30–6 and Saturday 8:30–1.

Embassies **U.S. Embassy,** Itäinen Puistotie 14A, 00140 Helsinki, tel. 90/171–931. **Canadian Embassy,** Pohjoisesplanadi 25B, 00100 Helsinki, tel. 90/171–141. **U.K. Embassy,** Itäinen Puistotie 17, 00140 Helsinki, tel. 90/661–293.

Emergencies The general emergency number is 000, which you can call for any emergency situation. Coins are not needed to make this call on pay phones (or any other calls beginning with 00).

Police Dial 002 or 000.

Ambulance Dial 006 or 000. Specify if the situation seems life-threatening, so medical attendants can begin immediate treatment in the ambulance.

Hospital Emergency Rooms **Töölön Sairaala** (Töölönkatu 40, tel. 4711) is a centrally located hospital (about 2 kilometers/1 mile from city center) with a 24-hour emergency room and first-aid service.

Doctors Dial 008 or 000.

Dentists Dial 90/736–166.

Where to Change Money Banks give the best exchange rates; banks with exchange facilities at the airport remain open late. The KOP bank booth at Helsinki Airport offers extended hours exchange and banking service and is open daily 6:30 AM–11 PM. Elsewhere banks are open weekdays 9–4. Major ferries, harbors, and rail stations have exchange facilities, too. You can also buy Finnmarks at the Post Restante in the main post office (on Railway Square, at the back of the Main Post Office at Mannerheimintie 11, Mon.–Sat. 8 AM–10 PM, Sun. 11 AM–10 PM). There is an automatic money-exchange machine in the ground floor of the Forum shopping center (corner Mannerheimintie and Simonkatu) but it does not offer the best rates. A passport is the preferred form of ID with traveler's checks.

English-language Bookstores **Akateeminen Kirjakauppa** (Academic Bookstore, Pohjoisesplanadi 39, tel. 90/12–141) and **Suomalainen Kirjakauppa** (The Finnish Bookstore, Aleksanterinkatu 23, tel. 90/651–855) both sell English-language books, newspapers, and magazines. Akateeminen is by far the larger of the two and is more expensive.

Late-night Pharmacy **Yliopiston Apteekki,** Mannerheimintie 5, tel. 90/179–092, is open daily 7 AM–midnight.

Travel Agencies **Area** (Pohjoisesplanadi 2, tel. 90/18–551), **Finnish Travel Association** (Mikonkatu 25, tel. 90/170–868), **FinnSov Tours Ltd.** (Eerikinkatu 3, 00100 Helsinki, tel. 90/694–2011), **Kaleva Travel** (Mannerheimintie 2, tel. 90/61–811), **Lomarengas** (accommodation service, Mikonkatu 25, tel. 90/170–611), and **Travela** (Mannerheimintie 5, 00100 Helsinki, tel. 90/624–101) are the leading agencies.

Arriving and Departing by Plane

Airports and Airlines All domestic and international flights to Helsinki use Helsinki-Vantaa International Airport, 20 kilometers (14 miles) north of the city. Helsinki is served by most major European airlines including: **SAS** (Pohjoisesplanadi 23, Helsinki, tel. 90/175–611), **Lufthansa** (Yrjönkatu 29A, Helsinki, tel. 90/694–9900), **Swiss-Air** (Mikonkatu 7, tel. 90/826–160), **British Airways** (Keskuskatu 7, Helsinki, tel. 90/650–677), **Air France** (Pohjoisesplanadi 27C, Helsinki, tel. 90/625–862), and several East European carriers. North American service is available from **Delta** (tel. 800/221–1212 in the U.S.; Helsinki information unavailable at press time).

Between the Airport and Downtown

By Bus A local bus, the 615, runs two to four times an hour between the airport and the main railway station. The fare is FM12. Local bus 614 runs one or two times an hour between the airport and the main bus station; the trip takes approximately 30 minutes and the fare is FM12. Finnair buses go two to four times an hour to and from the railway station (Finnair's city terminal) with a stop at the Hotel InterContinental. Request stops along the route are made, too. It takes approximately 35 minutes and the fare is FM18.

By Taxi There is a taxi stop at the arrivals building. A cab ride into central Helsinki will cost about FM130. Driving time is 20 minutes to 35 minutes, depending on time of day. Check if your hotel has a shuttle service, although this is not common here.

By Limousine **Pentti Lindfors Chauffeur Drive Ltd** (Alkutie 32H, 00660 Helsinki, tel. 90/744–577). A limousine ride into central Helsinki will cost about FM480.

Getting Around

The center of Helsinki is compact and best explored on foot. However, the City Tourist Office provides a free Helsinki route map that shows all public transportation. As far as public transportation tickets go, your best buy is the **Helsinki Card,** which gives unlimited travel on city public transportation, as well as free entry to many museums, a free sightseeing tour, and a variety of other discounts. It's available for one, two, or three days (adults FM70, FM100, and FM120; children FM40, FM50, and FM60) and can be bought at most hotels or at the City Tourist Office.

By Car Ring Roads One and Three are the two major highways that encircle the city. Mannerheimintie and Hämeentie are the major trunk roads out of Helsinki. Mannerheimintie feeds into highway E79, which travels west and takes you to the Ring roads. Hämeentie leads you to highway E4 as well as Roads 4 and 7. From either route, you will find directions for Road 137 to the airport. For specific route information, contact the **Finnish Automobile and Touring Club** (Kansakoulukatu 10, 00100 Helsinki, tel. 90/694–0022) or the City Tourist Office (*see* Tourist Information, *above*).

By Train Helsinki's suburbs as well as most of the rest of southern, western, and central Finland are well served by trains. Travel on trains within the Helsinki city limits costs the same as all public transport, FM7.5 or less if you use the 10-trip tickets (*see below*). A 10-trip **Helsinki Area Ticket,** or *Seutulippu,* for FM100 also provides a small discount for those who need to travel back and forth to adjacent areas such as Espoo and Vantaa.

By Bus, Tram, and Metro The bus and tram networks are extensive and service is frequent. Make sure to pick up a route map at the tourist office—many stops do not have them. If you have a one-trip ticket, or *Kertalippu,* (cost: FM7.5) or 10-trip ticket (*Kymmenen matkan kortti*) (cost: FM65), you must cancel it yourself. The metro system is small but has fast and frequent service from 6:30 AM–11:30 PM Monday through Saturday and infrequent service on Sunday. Cost is the same as for buses and trams.

By Taxi There are numerous taxi stands; central stands are at Railway Square on the west side of the station, the main bus station, and in the Esplanade. Taxis can also be flagged down but it can be difficult because many are on radio call.

Opening and Closing Times

Banks are open weekdays 9:30–4. Many offices and embassies close at 3 PM June–August. Stores are open weekdays 9–5 and Saturday 9–1 or 2 and are closed Sunday. Some stores in malls remain open until 8 PM on weekdays and until 4 on Saturday. In the Asematunneli (train station tunnel), stores are open weekdays 10–10 and weekends noon–10.

Guided Tours

Orientation Bus tours are a good way to get your orientation here. There is a 1½-hour tour of central Helsinki sights that comes free with the Helsinki Card; otherwise the cost is FM50 adults, FM25 children. The tour leaves from Railway Square (Asema-aukio) on Sunday at 11 AM throughout the year; it also runs Tuesday and Thursday in September. For more information contact **Suomen Turistiauto** (tel. 90/588–5166).

There is a year-round daily two-hour tour that leaves at 9:30 AM from the Olympic Harbor and Katajanokka Terminal. The cost is FM80 for adults and FM40 for children, not including lunch. For more information, call **Ageba Travel** (tel. 90/669–193). From April through October, Ageba also has a daily 2½-hour tour at 11 AM from the Olympic Harbor costing FM85 for adults, FM40 for children, excluding lunch).

Tram No. 3T around Helsinki, with a short recorded commentary in English, provides a good orientation to the city for the price of a regular tram ride (FM7.5 adults, FM3.5 children). You can get on board in front of the railway station on Kaivokatu for the 60-minute round-trip.

The Guide Booking Center (Lönnrotinkatu 7, 00120 Helsinki, tel. 90/601–966) will arrange tailor-made tours for you.

Boat Tours All boat tours depart from the Market Square. The easiest way to choose one is to go to the square in the morning and read the sandwich boards describing the tours. The city tourist office will have the most current information, however. Most tours run in the summer only. You can go as far afield as Porvoo (*see* Excursions from Helsinki, *below*) or take a short jaunt to the zoo.

A ferry to the Suomenlinna fortress island runs about twice an hour, depending on time of day. The ferry to the zoo island,

Korkeasaari, runs from the north harbor, just above the juncture of the Katajanokka peninsula to the mainland.

Walking Tours The city tourist office has an excellent brochure, "See Helsinki on Foot," with six walks covering most points of interest.

Highlights for First-time Visitors

Kaivohuone (Spa Restaurant) (*see* Tour 2)
Market Square (*see* Tour 1)
Senate Square (*see* Tour 3)
Seurasaari Island Outdoor Museum (*see* Tour 5)
Suomenlinna Fortress Island (*see* Tour 4)
Temppeliaukio Church (*see* Tour 5)
Uspenski Cathedral (*see* Tour 3)

Exploring Helsinki

Numbers in the margin correspond with points of interest on the Helsinki map.

Tour 1: From Market to Market

1 The **Kauppatori** (Market Square) outdoor market is a Helsinki institution—and a charming one. Wooden stands with orange and gold awnings bustle in the mornings when everyone, tourists and townspeople alike, comes to check out what's available. Fish, produce, flowers, hot coffee and doughnuts, and a plethora of possible souvenirs such as fur pelts are sold here Monday through Saturday between 7 AM and 2 PM. In the summer there is an evening market, too, from 3:30 to 8. In the square's center is Helsinki's first public monument—**Czarina's Stone,** an obelisk with a double-headed golden eagle symbolizing Imperial Russia. Erected in 1835, it was toppled during the Russian Revolution in 1917, but was fully restored in 1972.

Across from the market, on the other side of **Pohjoisesplanadi**
2 (north esplanade) is the **Presedentinlinna** (President's Palace). Originally built as a private residence for a German businessman, it was redesigned in 1843 as a palace for the czars. Now it is the home of Finland's President Mauno Koivisto, who will live there at least until the next election in 1994. The most interesting part of the house is said to be its hall of mirrors, but the uniformed guards will prevent you from entering. Next to the palace is **Kaupingintalo** (City Hall) and various administrative offices, and across from it is the waterfront, where ferries and sightseeing boats set out into the bay.

Cross the thoroughfare carefully (watching for trams) to the west, where you'll pass the **Kappeli European Café Brasserie.** Notice the restaurant's intricate lead-pane windows and the
3 towers that allow ample views of the **Havis Amandan Patsas** (Havis Amanda Statue and Fountain). The fountain's brass centerpiece, a mermaid-woman perched on rocks and surrounded by dolphins, was commissioned by the city fathers as a symbol for Helsinki. Sculptor Ville Vallgren completed her in 1908—using a Parisian girl as his model. Partying university students crown her with their white caps on the eve before Vappu, the May 1 holiday.

On the Pohjoisesplanadi between Unioninkatu and Fabianin-
4 katu is the **Kaupungin Matkailutoimisto** (City Tourist Office),

where you can stop in for information or to pick up a map. It was originally built in 1816 as a private house for a Russian businessman and was rebuilt—with the exception of the facade—in 1968. A few yards west is the entrance to the Art Nouveau **Jugendsali** (Helsinki Information Office). Originally designed as a bank in 1906, it now serves as a cultural information office and temporary exhibition hall for Finnish photography. *Pohjoisesplanadi 19, tel. 90/169–3757. Open Sept. 16–May 15, Mon. 8:30–4:30, Tues.–Fri. 8:30–4; May 16–Sept. 15, Mon.–Fri 8:30–6, Sat. 8:30–1.*

One block west along Pohjoisesplanadi (past the Arabia ceramics and Marimekko clothing stores) and across from the park is the elephantine **Gröngvistin Talo** (Grönqvist's block), designed by architect Theodor Höijer. Built in 1883, it was then Scandinavia's largest private apartment building.

Continue west on the Esplanade, which terminates at Mannerheimintie. On the right are Akateeminen Kirjakauppa and Stockmann's, respectively Finland's largest bookstore and department store (*see* Shopping, *below*). The bookstore was designed by Alvar Aalto, probably Finland's most famous architect.

Time Out The new **Aalto Café** (Pohjoisesplanadi 39) on the bookstore's mezzanine makes for a pleasant lunch or snack stop; you can also peer down at the tranquil hordes of book browsers.

5 The round **Svenska Teatern** (Swedish Theater) on Mannerheimintie at the head of the Esplanadi has been rebuilt many times since its creation in 1827. The original wooden theater was replaced by a stone building in 1866 because of its vulnerability to fire. Ironically, the stone building was nearly destroyed by a fire later on. The theater's last renovation was in 1936 by a group of architects that included Eero Saarinen and Jarl Eklund, but the red and gold auditorium dates back to the 19th century. The theater has its own company, which performs plays in Swedish year-round. *Pohjoisesplanadi 2, tel. 90/171–244. Box office open daily 10 AM–performance time.*

Turn left on Mannerheimintie and take a right onto broad, tree-shaded Bulevardi, passing **Vanha Kirkkopuisto** (Old Church Park), usually called Ruttopuisto (plague park), a tree-filled square that has a few 18th-century plague victims buried
6 under it. Continue on to the **Sinebrychoffin Taidemuseo** (Sinebrychoff Art Museum). Named after the Russian family who started the Sinebrychoff breweries, the museum houses a staid collection of Dutch and Swedish 17th- and 18th-century portraits, as well as a livelier collection of landscapes, miniatures, porcelain, and decorative furniture. The yellow and white neo-Renaissance mansion, built in 1840, looks over the once-private Punavuori park and its tower. In the summer, there are occasional outdoor concerts in the park. *Bulevardi 40, tel. 90/694–5933. Admission: FM5 adults, FM2 children. Open weekdays 9–5 (until 8 on Wed.), weekends 11–5.*

7 **Hietalahden Tori** (the Hietalahti Market) across the street sells fish, flowers, and produce outside and meat inside the brick market hall. Coffee and doughnuts as well as meat pies are sold in the market. A flea market (open year-round Monday through Saturday 8–noon and in summer also 4–8 PM) has tables piled

Ateneumin Taidemuseo, **19**
Cygnaeus Gallery, **13**
Finlandiatalo, **21**
Havis Amandan Patsas, **3**
Helsingin Taidehalli, **23**
Hietalahden Tori, **7**
Kaivohuone, **11**
Kauppatori, **1**
Kaupungin Matkailutoimisto, **4**
Mannerheim Museo, **12**
Merenkulkijoiden Muistomerkki, **10**
Mikael Agricolan Kirkko, **8**
Pörssi, **18**
Presedentinlinna, **2**
Senaatintori, **17**
Seurasaaren Ulkomuseo, **25**
Sinebrychoffin Taidemuseo, **6**
Suomenlinna, **20**
Suomen Kansallismuseo, **22**
Suomen Rakennustaiteen Museo, **15**
Svenska Teatern, **5**
Taideteollisuus-museo, **14**
Tamminiemi, **26**
Temppeliaukion Kirkko, **24**
Uspenskin Kirko, **16**
Villa Johanna, **9**

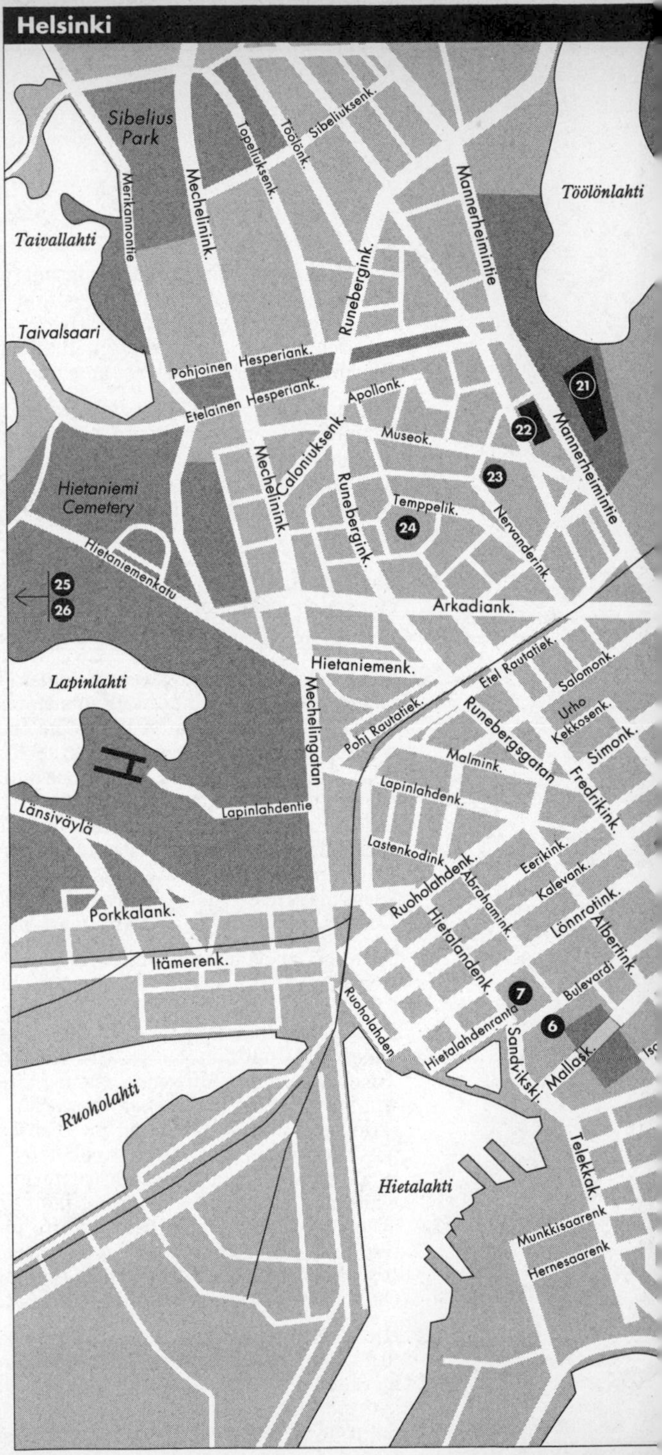

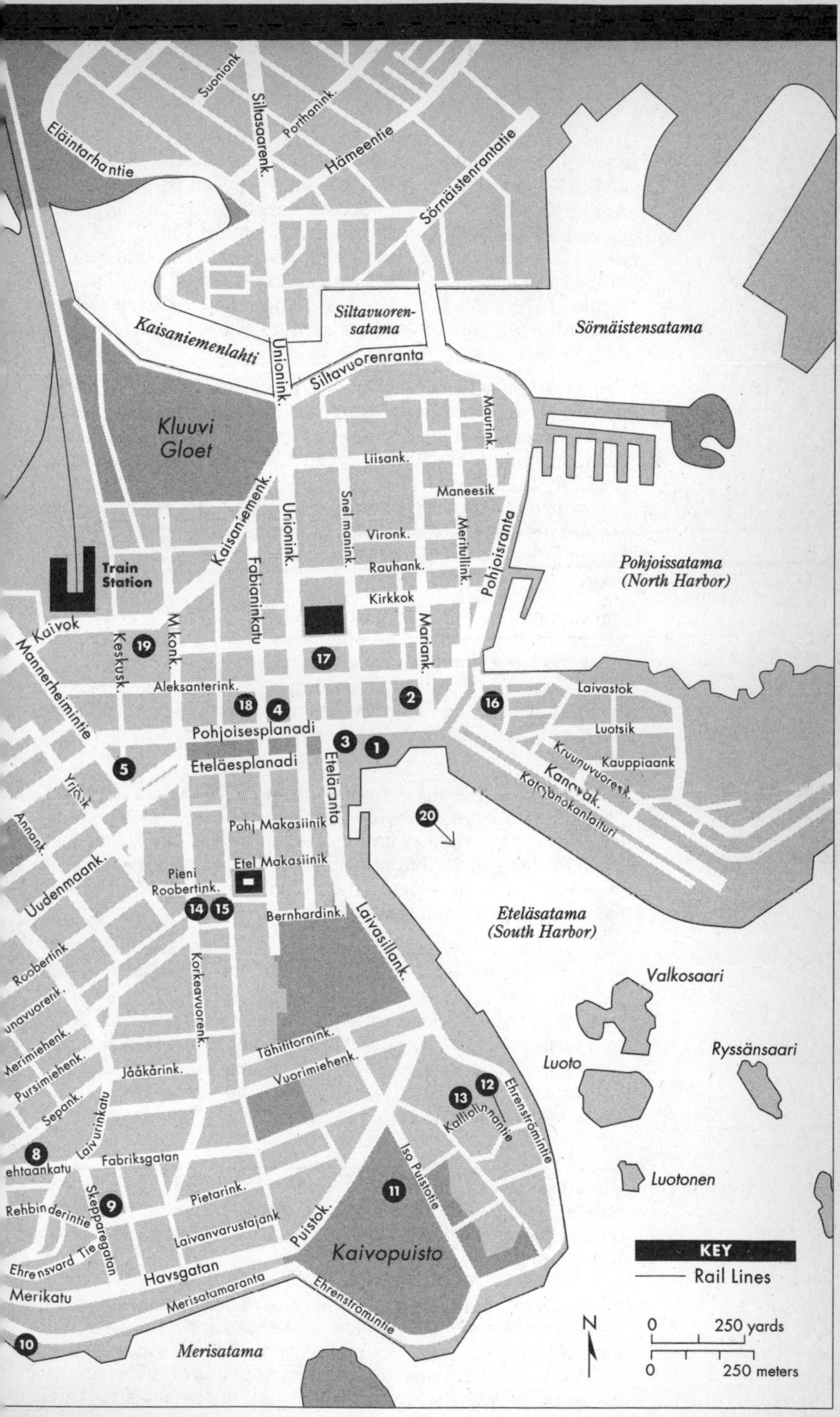

Suonionk
Siltasaarenk.
Porthanink.
Eläintarhantie
Hämeentie
Sörnäistenrantatie
Siltavuoren-
satama
Sörnäistensatama
Kaisaniemenlahti
Unionink.
Siltavuorenranta
Kluuvi
Gloet
Maurink.
Liisank.
Maneesik
Kaisaniemenk.
Unionink.
Snel manink.
Meritullink.
Pohjoisranta
Vironk.
Rauhank.
Kirkkok
Train
Station
Fabianinkatu
Pohjoissatama
(North Harbor)
Kaivok
Mannerheimintie
Keskusk.
Marjank.
Aleksanterink.
Laivastok
Pohjoisesplanadi
Luotsik
Eteläesplanadi
Eteläranta
Kauppiaank
Katajanokanlaituri
Pohj Makasiinik
Annank.
Etel Makasiinik
Uudenmaank.
Pieni
Roobertink.
Bernhardink.
Laivasillank.
Eteläsatama
(South Harbor)
Roobertink.
Valkosaari
Korkeavuorenk.
Merimiehenk.
Tähtitornink.
Ryssänsaari
Pursimiehenk.
Jääkärink.
Vuorimiehenk.
Luoto
Sepank.
Ehrenströmintie
Laivurinkatu
Fabriksgatan
Luotonen
Skepparegatan
Pietarink.
Iso Puistotie
Laivanvarustajank
Puistok.
Kaivopuisto
KEY
Rail Lines
Ehrensvärd Tie
Havsgatan
Merikatu
Merisatamaranta
Ehrenströmintie
N
0
250 yards
Merisatama
0
250 meters

with the detritus of countless Helsinki attics and cellars. The market is popular with the Soviet community.

Tour 2: Residential and Seaside Helsinki

From Bulevardi, turn south down Albertinkatu until you reach a small park, Tehtaanpuisto, where you'll see the sharp spire
8 and tall brick steeple of the **Mikael Agricolan Kirkko** (Mikael Agricola Church). Built in 1935 by Lars Sonck, this church was named for the man credited with promoting Finnish as a national language by translating the New Testament into Finnish in 1548 and by creating the first Finnish children's speller. The inside of the church is quite bare, and no visitors are allowed except during Sunday services. *Tehtaankatu 23A, tel. 90/638–663. Services Sun. 10–noon.*

From the opposite side of the park, cross Tehtaankatu and walk down Laivurinkatu past **Eiran Sairaala** (Eira Hospital), with its witch-hat towers and triangular garret windows. Just south
9 of the hospital is the Art Nouveau **Villa Johanna,** designed by Selim A. Lindqvist in 1906 and named after his wife. The villa is now privately owned by the Post Office Bank of Finland and is used for corporate dinners and events. You can't enter, but take a quick look at the carved roaring serpent over the front door.

Continuing south on the right side of Laivurinkatu, just before you reach Merikatu and an open view of the Baltic, is another Lindqvist creation (this time named after his daughter), the **Villa Ensi.** The white and pale gray structure is a private apartment building. The two bronze statues in front of it are *Au Revoir* and *La Joie de la Maternité* by J. Sören-Ring, dating from 1910.

As you come to the end of Laivurinkatu, with the sea surround-
10 ing you, the **Merenkulkijoiden Muistomerkki** (Seafarers Torch) will be on your right. The city commissioned the statue (finished in 1968) as a tribute to Finnish sailors and as a symbol of hope for their safe return. The eternal flame above this tall cement tripod is most dramatic at night.

Turn east to walk along **Merisatamanranta,** the seaside promenade. Out at sea is a handful of the thousands of islands that make up the Gulf of Finland archipelago. On your land side, the facades of the Eira and Kaivopuisto districts' grandest buildings form a parade of architectural splendor. One tradition that remains, even in this neighborhood, is rug washing in the sea. The process looks incredibly arduous, and you may also be astounded to see people leave their rugs to dry in the sea air without fear of theft.

Time Out Continue east along the shoreline to the **Ursula Café** (Kaivopuisto, tel. 90/652-817) a favorite among locals for coffee, ice cream, pastry, and light lunches; there is seating outdoors in the summer.

Kaivopuisto (Well Park) is a shady park with pleasant paths, surrounded by opulent private residences and embassies. The park was once the site of a popular spa that drew people from St. Petersburg, Tallinn, and all of Scandinavia until its popularity faded during the Crimean War. All of the spa structures

11 were eventually destroyed except one, which is now **Kaivohuone,** a renowned and refined bar-restaurant.

Take Kaivohuoneenrinne through the park past a grand Empire-style villa built by Albert Edelfelt, father of the famous Finnish painter who bore the same name. Built in 1839, it is the oldest preserved villa in the park. Follow the eastward loop of
12 Kalliolinnantie through the embassy district to the **Mannerheim Museo** (Marshal Mannerheim Museum). It exhibits the letters and personal effects of the great Finnish military leader Gustaf Mannerheim, who fought for Finnish freedom and later became president. The collection, set in his well-preserved family home, includes European furniture, Asian art, and military medals and weaponry. *Kalliolinnantie 14, tel. 90/635–443. Admission: FM15 adults, children free. Open Fri.–Sat. 11–3, Sun. 11–4.*

13 On the same street is the tiny **Cygnaeuksen Galleria** (Cygnaeus Gallery) with its lookout tower. Inside is a display of work by a variety of Finnish painters, sculptors, and folk artists. This cottage overlooking the harbor was once the summer home of the poet and historian Fredrik Cygnaeus (1807–1881). When he died, he left the cottage and all the art inside to the Finnish public. *Kalliolinnantie 8, tel. 90/656–928. Admission: FM6 adults, FM3 children. Open Thurs.–Sun. 11–4, Wed. 11–4 and 6–8.*

Follow Itäinen Puistotie to Tehtaankatu 1, where you'll see Finnish police guarding the enormous fenced-in Soviet Embassy complex. Then walk up Ullankatu and Ullanpuistikko to **Tähtitorninvuori,** the park named for the astronomical observatory on the hill. The observatory belongs to the astronomy department of Helsinki University and is closed to the public.

From here it is just a short hop (take any street to the left from the west side of the park, from Kasarmikatu to Korkeavuorenkatu) to one of Finland's finest museums, the
14 **Taideteollisuusmuseo** (Applied Arts Museum). All types of Finnish design can be seen here in permanent and temporary displays: furnishings, jewelry, and ceramics, as well as temporary exhibits of international design, frequently Italian and Japanese. *Korkeavuorenkatu 23, tel. 90/174–455. Admission: FM20 adults, FM10 children. Open Tues.–Fri. 11–5, weekends 11–4.*

15 From here you can go on to the **Suomen Rakennustaiteen Museo** (Finnish Architecture Museum). The exhibits include Alvar Aalto furniture, the language of wood, the home as art, and visiting collections. The museum also provides a list of buildings by Aalto in Helsinki (also available from the tourist board), the most famous of which is Finlandiatalo (*see* Tour 5, *below*). *Kasarmikatu 24, tel. 90/661–918. Admission free. Open Tues.–Sun. 10–4, also 4–7 Wed.*

Tour 3: Katajanokka and Senate Square

The Katajanokka headland (separated from the mainland by a canal) begins just east of the market square and is a charming residential quarter as well as a busy cargo and passenger ship port.

16 The first sight on Katajanokka is the **Uspenskin Kirkko** (Uspenski Cathedral) with its glistening onion domes. The

main cathedral of the Russian Orthodox religion in Finland, it was built and dedicated in 1868. The ornate interior of this imposing redbrick edifice was decorated by 19th-century Russian artists. *Kanavakatu 1, tel. 90/634–267. Open May 1–Sept. 30, Tues.–Fri. 9:30–4, Sat. 9–noon, Sun. noon–3.*

Time Out On the north flank of Katajanokka, near the end of Katajanokan Pohjoisranta you'll see the **Katajanokka Casino,** built in 1911. Set on its own headland, it was at first a warehouse, then a naval officers' casino. It has a summer terrace from which you can gaze across the North Harbor to the Kruunuhaka district while sipping cold beer.

Take a right onto Linnankatu and a left onto Pikku Satamakatu to the **Wanha Satama** (the "W" pronounced as a "V") (Old Harbor complex). From the outside it looks like nothing more than an old brick warehouse, but inside it's a small shopping center with several food stores, restaurants, and cafés; there's even an art gallery in the left (north) wing.

Turn right and continue to Ankkurikatu toward the seafront. On your left will be some of the giant liners bound for Stockholm. Cross the wooden bridge back over to Market Square and
17 take any street north to **Senaatintori** (Senate Square). The north side of the square is dominated by **Tuomiokirkko** (the Lutheran Cathedral of Finland), finished in 1852 and designed, as was most of the area, by C. L. Engel, a Berliner and the architect who designed much of Tallinn and St. Petersburg. The crypt of the church, at its rear, is a site for historic and architectural exhibitions.

On the square's west side is one of the main buildings of **Helsingin Yliopisto** (Helsinki University) and up the hill is the university library. On the east side is **Valtionneuvosto** (the Council of State building), completed in 1822 and once the seat of the autonomous Grand Duchy's Imperial Senate. At the lower end of the square are former merchants' homes now occupied by stores and restaurants, and the Senaatintori shopping hall. Many scenes from the film *Reds* were shot in and around this square.

Walk two streets west to Fabianinkatu to the Lars Sonck-de-
18 signed **Pörssi** (Stock Exchange), built in 1911. You'll be able to view the exchange floor (although active trading has now moved elsewhere) during regular hours; be sure to notice the bullet-shape chandeliers. *Fabianinkatu 14, tel. 90/650–133. Open weekdays 9–4.*

Time Out **Cafe Adlon** (Fabianinkatu 14, below the exchange, tel. 90/664–611) is a plush, busy bar that brings out Helsinki's yuppies—and friends.

---

19 Finish up this tour at the **Ateneumin Taidemuseo** (Atheneum Art Museum), which recently completed five years of renovation. Housed in a splendid neoclassical building adorned with Greek statues, it features some major European works, but the outstanding attraction is the Finnish art, particularly the art of Akseli Gallen-Kallela, inspired by the national epic *Kalevala.* The rustic portraits by Albert Edelfelt are enchanting, and many contemporary Finnish artists are well-represented. *Kaivokatu 2–4, tel. 90/173–361. Admission: FM40 adults,*

FM20 children. Open Tues. and Fri. 9–5, Wed. and Thurs. 9–9, weekends 11–5.

Tour 4: Suomenlinna

20 A former island fortress now taken over by resident artists, **Suomenlinna** (Finland's Castle) is a quirky, perennially popular collection of museums, parks, and gardens. In early summer it is engulfed in mauve-and-purple mists of lilacs, the trees introduced from Versailles by the Finnish architect Ehrensvard. In 1748 the Finnish army helped build this fortress, which grew so over the years that today Suomenlinna is a series of interlinked islands. The impregnable fortress was long referred to as the "Gibraltar of the North." While it has never been taken by assault, its occupants did surrender twice without a fight—once to the Russians in 1809 and then to the British in 1855, during the Crimean War.

There are no street names on the island, so be sure to get a map from the Helsinki tourist office before you go or make sure to buy one at the information kiosk on the island. From June 1 to August 31, there are guided tours in English that leave from the information kiosk daily at 12:30 and 2:30. To book a group tour, call 90/668–154. It is reached by public ferry (FM6.50) or private boat tour (FM30) from the Market Square.

Although the fortification of Suomenlinna involved six islands, the main attractions are concentrated on two, **Susisaari** and **Kustaanmiekka.** When you first land at Suomenlinna you will be facing the **Pohjoismainen Taidekeskus** (Nordic Arts Center) on Susisaari, with its changing exhibitions of contemporary Scandinavian art including sculpture, video art, painting, and more. *Suomenlinna (at ferry dock), tel. 90/688–143. Admission free. Open Tues.–Sun. 11–5.*

When you come out of the arts center, the church-lighthouse that you will see as you continue uphill through the archway is **Suomenlinna Kirkko** (Suomenlinna Church), built in 1854. The formerly Orthodox church is now a Lutheran church, open to the public on Sunday from noon to 4.

Walk past the church and pastel-colored private wood homes to explore Susisaari further. The **Ehrensvärd Museo** (Ehrensvärd Museum) is named for Augustin Ehrensvard who directed the fortification of the islands, and whose tomb is here also. The historical museum houses among its exhibits a model-ship collection and officers quarters that date back to the 18th century. *Tel. 90/668–154. Admission: FM6 adults, FM3 children. Open June–July daily 10–5; Sept. daily 10–3:30; Oct.–May weekends 11–3.*

On the coast of Susisaari island is the **Submarine Vesikko** which you'll be able to board. The submarine, which took part in World War II, was built in Turku in 1931–33. *Admission: FM5 adults, FM2.50 children. Open May 12–Aug. 31, daily 10–5; Sept. 1–30, daily 11–3.*

If possible, try to plan your visit around lunchtime so that after investigating the ramparts and visiting the museums you can make your way to the old fort near the historic King's gate for a meal at **Walhalla** (*see* Dining, *below*) located deep within the fort on Kustaanmiekka.

On Kustaanmiekka, visit **Rannikkotykistömuseo** (Coastal Artillery Museum), an arms museum set in a vaulted arsenal. The items on display here are from World Wars I and II. *Tel. 90/68–601. Open May 12–Aug. 31, daily 10–5; Sept. 1–30, daily 11–5.*

Five furnished rooms and a china collection make up the **Armfelt-Museo** (Armfelt Museum) in a reconstructed 19th-century upper-class home in a former barracks. *Tel. 90/668–132. Open May 12–Aug. 31, daily 11–5:30; Sept., weekends 11–5:30.*

The information kiosk alongside Tykistolahti Bay is open May 5 through August 31, daily 10–5. You can get general information on Suomenlinna year-round by calling 90/668–341.

Tour 5: Töölö and Seurasaari

A short walk up Mannerheimintie from the train station will
21 bring you to **Finlandiatalo** (Finlandia Hall), the concert hall that was one of Alvar Aalto's last creations. Its white, winged appearance is especially impressive on foggy days or at night. If you can't make it to a concert there, try to take a guided tour. *Karamzininkatu 4, tel. 90/40–241. Tickets cost: FM50–80. Concerts usually Wed. and Thurs. nights.*

Behind the hall lies the inland bay of Toolonlahti, and across the
22 street is the **Suomen Kansallismuseo** (National Museum). If you feel like you've seen it before, you probably have; its spired outline was the backdrop for televised reports on the 1990 U.S.-Soviet summit. The museum's exhibits take you from Finnish prehistory through medieval church art to contemporary Lapp exhibitions. One exhibit concentrates on Finland from the 16th century to the present, another on Finno-Ugric cultures. *Mannerheimintie 34, tel. 90/40–501. Admission: FM10 adults, FM5 children. Open May–Sept., daily 11–4, also 6–9 Tues.*

Take a left off Mannerheimintie on to Cygnaeuksenkatu (next street north), then a left on to Nervanderkatu, where you'll
23 reach the **Helsingin Taidehalli** (Helsinki Art Hall). Here you'll see the best of contemporary Finnish art, including painting, sculpture, architecture, and industrial art and design. *Nervanderinkatu 3, tel. 90/444–855. Admission varies according to exhibition, but usually FM10 adults, FM5 children. Open June–mid-Aug., weekdays 11–5, Sun. 12–4; mid-Aug.–May, Tues.–Sat. 11–6, Sun. 12–5.*

A few steps farther (take the small street directly across from
24 the art hall) is the modern **Temppeliaukion Kirkko** (Temple Square Church), carved into the rock cliffs at the square's center. Topped with a copper dome, it looks from the outside like a half-buried spaceship. The sun shines in from above, illuminating the stunning interior with its birch pews, tapestry seat cushions, modern pipe organ, and cavernous walls. Ecumenical and Lutheran services in various languages are held throughout the week. *Lutherininkatu 3, tel. 90/494–698. Open weekdays 9–5, weekends 9–6.*

25 The **Seurasaaren Ulkomuseo** (Seurasaari Outdoor Museum) is on an island about 3 kilometers (2 miles) northwest of the city center. You can walk there in about 30 minutes from the church (follow Lutherininkatu out of the square, turn left onto Runeberginkatu, right onto Arkadiankatu and follow to its

end; then follow the coast and signposts), or you can take the bus No. 24, which you can board downtown, in front of the Swedish theater at the west end of Esplanadi.

Seurasaari Island is connected to land by a pedestrian bridge and is a restful place to walk throughout the year, with its forest trails and ocean views. It was founded in 1909 with the intention of preserving Finnish rural architecture. The old farmhouses and barns that were brought to Seurasaari are mainly from Karelia in eastern Finland. Many are rough-hewn log buildings dating back as far as the 17th century; these were of primary inspiration to architects of the late 19th-century national revivalist movement in Finland. All exhibits are marked by signposts along the trails. Be sure not to miss the church boat and the gabled church. *Seurasaari. Admission: May–Aug., FM10 adults, FM5 children; free rest of year.*

The grand house overlooking Seurasaari from the mainland is
26 **Tamminiemi** (President Urho Kekkonen's Home), originally known as Villa Nissen. Inside are the scores of gifts to the late president donated by leaders from around the world. The house was built in 1904 and Kekkonen lived here from 1956 to 1986. His study is the most fascinating room, with its Hungarian pewter urn and gift from the United States of a cupboard full of *National Geographic* maps of the world. To assure an English-speaking guide, phone ahead (you cannot visit unguided). All large groups should call ahead. *Seurasaarentie 15, 00250 Helsinki, tel. 90/480–684. Admission: FM10 adults, FM5 children. Open Sept.–Apr., daily 11–3, also 6–8 Thurs.; May–mid-Sept., daily 11–4, also 6–8 Thurs.*

Time Out Tamminiementie, the road leading straight inland from the bridge to Seurasaari, has three cafés within five minutes' walk of each other.

Short Excursions from Helsinki

Tarvaspää/ Gallen-Kallela Estate This turreted brick-and-stucco mansion was the self-designed studio and home of the Finnish Romantic painter, Akseli Gallen-Kallela. It is set at the edge of the sea and surrounded by towering, windbent pines. Gallen-Kallela (1865–1931) lived in the mansion on and off from its completion in 1913 until his death. Inside, the tremendous open rooms of the painter's former workspaces make the perfect exhibition hall for his paintings. Also displayed are some of his posters and sketches of the ceiling murals he made for the Paris Art Exhibition at the turn of the 20th century. There is a café on the grounds. *Gallen-Kallelantie 27, tel. 90/513–388. Admission: FM25 adults, FM5 children. Open Mon.–Thurs. 10–8; Fri., Sat., and Sun. 10–5.*

Getting There To get to Tarvaspää from central Helsinki, take the No. 4 tram to Munkkiniemi and transfer to bus No. 33; request the Tarvaspää stop. If you prefer, walk the kilometer (⅔ mile) from Munkkiniemi.

Porvoo **Porvoo,** only 48 kilometers (30 miles) outside Helsinki, has much to offer. Visit the 15th-century stone and wood cathedral, where the diet of the first Duchy of Finland was held in the 1800s. There are a number of artisan boutiques around the Old Town Hall Square, and you'll want to be sure and take a stroll into the Old Quarter to see the multicolored old wood houses.

The **Walter Runebergin Kulttuuri, Kokoelma** (Walter Runeberg Sculpture Collection) (Aleksanterinkatu) and the **Porvoo and Edelfelt-Vallgren Museo** (Välikatu 11) feature exhibits of Edelfelt's art and the region's cultural history. Places of interest near Porvoo include the painter **Albert Edelfeltin Atelje** (Albert Edelfelt's studio) in Haikko, the nearby **Ruskis Luonnonsuojelualve** (Ruskis bird sanctuary), and the **Ilola Mākitupalaiskylā** (Ilola Village Open Air Museum).

Tourist Information Porvoo City Tourist Office, Rauhankatu 20, 06100 Porvoo, tel. 915/170–145, also at old Town Hall Square in summer, tel. 915/130–747.

Getting There The most pleasant way to travel to Porvoo is by boat. (There are also bus, road, and train connections.) In the summer, there are daily cruise departures from Helsinki's South Harbor (average round-trip cost is FM125; travel time is 1½ hours each way). You will be taken westward through dozens of islands before landing at Porvoo, which is small enough to see on foot.

Vantaa Although not remarkable as a city, **Vantaa,** the municipality just north of Helsinki proper (and home to the international airport) has some attractions well worth seeing. There is also a welcome surplus of open green space in Vantaa, and trails for biking, hiking, and jogging. It may also be a place to keep in mind as a base if your trip to Helsinki coincides with a convention and you can't find a room there. Vantaa is reached easily by public transport (a regional Helsinki ticket includes Vantaa and Espoo), and the airport is easily accessible.

The **Heureka Suomalainen Tiedekeskus** (Heureka Science Center) opened in 1989 and features exhibits on robotics, solar energy, and interactive computers; there is also the Jules Verne Planetarium; taped commentary is available in English. *Tiedepuisto 1, 01301, Tikkurila, Vantaa, tel. 90/85–799. Admission: FM45 adults, FM15 children. Open Fri.–Wed. 10–6, Thurs. 10–8. Closed first 2 weeks of Jan., Easter, first 2 weeks of Sept., December 20–25, and Dec. 30.*

Near the Myyrmäki train station on the Helsinki–Martinlaakso suburban line (M train) is the **Myyrmäki Kirkko,** an evocative example of Finnish contemporary church architecture. It has brilliant white walls, columns of tall windows, and vivid tapestries hung out to mark events in the Lutheran calendar.

The other Vantaa attractions are the 13th-century **Helsingin Pitajan Kirkko** (Parish Church Village; Kirkkoaukio, tel. 90/83–061), and the **Viherpaja Icelandic and Japanese Cactus Gardens** (Meirantie 1, 00300 Vantaa, tel. 90/822–628. Admission to Japanese Garden: FM5; Icelandic Garden free. Open June–Oct. weekdays 8–6, weekends 9–3; Nov.–May weekdays 8–7, weekends 9–5.)

Tourist Information City Hall (Asematie 7, 00130 Vantaa, tel. 90/839–2133).

Getting There Easiest access is by local bus; ask at airport information or the Vantaa Tourist Office (Unikkotie 2, 01300 Vantaa, tel. 90/839–3134).

Helsinki for Free

Several Helsinki parks, notably Kaivopuisto, have gigantic **outdoor chess boards** with life-size pieces you move around a grid painted on asphalt; games are free to all comers.

Also free are some of the **outdoor concerts** at the band shell (summertime) in Esplanadi at the side of the Kappelli restaurant, and in Kaivopuisto park, near the sea.

All cross-country ski trails around Helsinki are free, as are the many nature, bike, and jogging trails. The tourist board's Ulkoilukartta (outdoor activities map) shows you where to find these **outdoor trails.**

In winter, **Seurasaari,** the outdoor island museum, is free, mainly because access to the island is open to anyone who crosses the ice to get to it.

What to See and Do with Children

The two-week Helsinki Festival of performing arts in late-August–early September includes **children's shows** in Helsinki and environs.

The **Suomenlinna** fortress island makes a good excursion for travelers with children (*see* Exploring Helsinki, *above*), and includes a **Doll and Toy Museum** designed with children in mind.

The daily ferry to **Korkeasaari Elaintarha** (the zoo island), runs from the north harbor, just above the juncture of the Katajanokka peninsula to the mainland; the zoo is small and undergoing renovation, but children will like it anyway. You can also take the metro to the Kulosaari stop, cross under the tracks, and then follow the signs to the zoo (about a 20-minute walk). *Admission: FM15 adults, FM6 children 7–16, under 7 free. Open Jan.–Feb., daily 10–4; Mar.–Apr., daily 10–6; May–Sept., daily 10–8.*

Off the Beaten Track

The **Sadan Markan Villat** (Hundred Mark Villas), at the corner of Lastenkodinkatu and Ruoholahdenkatu, date from the 1880s and are a bastion of tranquil, country-style living right in central Helsinki. Walk through their tree- and flower-filled backyards (there are public walkways; go through arches on Lastenkodinkatu) and be transported away from city life.

To explore some of the wooded, residential islands of west Helsinki, take bus No. 20 from the Swedish theater (Esplanadi west end) to Katajaharjuntie (end stop on Lauttasaari). From here you have access via bridges, the ice (in winter), and shuttle boats (in summer) to the islands of **Kaskisaari, Lehtisaari,** and **Kuusisaari. Mustasaari,** east of Kaskisaari, is a tiny church-owned island with a café and community center in a charming wood-villa in the woods. Other access to these islands in summer is by boat direct from Taivalahti at the end of Pohjoinen Hesperiankatu.

Shopping

Helsinki's shopping facilities are improving all the time. Although many international stores are still missing, there are several malls and shopping districts where you can shop thoroughly and in comfort. Stores are generally open weekdays 9–5 and Saturday 9–1. The **Forum** (*see* Shopping Malls, *below*) and **Stockmann's** (*see* Department Stores, *below*) are open weekdays 9–8 and Saturday 9–4.

Kiosks remain open late and on weekends; they sell such basics as milk, juice, and tissues. Stores in **Asematunneli,** the train station tunnel, are open weekdays 10–10 and weekends noon–10.

Shopping Malls The three largest shopping complexes are the **Forum,** at the corner of Mannerheimintie and Simonkatu; **Kaivopiha,** at Kaivokatu 10 across from the train station; and **Kluuvi** shopping center at the corner of Kluuvikatu and Aleksanterinaktu. All have a good mix of stores plus several cafés and restaurants.

Shopping Districts **Pohjoisesplanadi** on the north side of the Esplanade has most of Helsinki's trademark design stores like Arabia, Marimekko, and Aarikka, and a wide array of other goods.

Senaatintori, the south side of Senate Square, has a host of crafts stores, open weekdays 9–5 and Saturday 9–2, with several antique and secondhand bookstores to be browsed on the adjoining streets.

There are many smaller boutiques in the streets **west of Mannerheimintie** (Fredrikinkatu and Annankatu for example), and there is one pedestrian shopping street a few blocks south of the Esplanade, on **Iso Roobertinkatu;** stores there are conventional, but the atmosphere is more relaxed, and there are several places to stop for shopping breaks.

Department Stores **Stockmann's** (tel. 90/1211), at the corner of the Esplanade and Mannerheimintie, is Helsinki's premier department store. **Aleksi 13** (Aleksanterinkatu 13, tel. 90/131–441) is more basic, but you can find some good deals on winter boots.

Street Markets The **Market Square, Hietalahdentori Market,** and **Hakaniemi** are the main street markets. They specialize in food, but all have some clothing (new and used) and household products. The Market Square also sells some fur products. Hours are Monday–Saturday 8–2; in summer they reopen from 3 until 6 or 8. **Hietalahti's flea market** is open Monday–Saturday 8 AM–noon; in summer it reopens 4–8.

Specialty Stores
Antiques The **Kruunuhaka** area (north of Senate Square) is the best bet for antiques. Some stores to try are **Antik Oskar** (Rauhankatu 7, tel. 90/135–7410), **Punavuoren Antiikki** (Mariankatu 14, tel. 90/662–682), and **Rahaliike Holmasto** (Snellmaninkatu 15, tel. 135–7500) if you are interested in coins, banknotes, medals, and silver. Other shops mix china, furniture, and art. Some of the old farm furniture is pretty but hard to find. Most stores are loaded with old china and cut glass, however. Also try **Kamppi** and **Punavuori districts,** between Eerikinkatu and Tehtaankatu; many here also sell secondhand books (usually a small selection in English).

Ceramics Firms like **Arabia** (Pohjoisesplanadi 25, tel. 90/170–005), **Pentik** (Pohjoisesplanadi 27C, tel. 90/625–558), and **Aarikka** (tel. 90/652–277) offer state-of-the-art contemporary ceramic design; the Arabia factory, at the end of the No. 6 tram line, also exhibits older designs.

Clothing **Marimekko** (Pohjoisesplanadi 31, tel. 90/177–944), on the Esplanade in Helsinki and with outlets in other cities, has bright, modern, unusual clothes for men, women, and children in quality fabrics, at a price. Take a look, even if you don't plan to spend.

Jewelry **Kalevala Koru** (Unioninkatu 25, tel. 90/171–520) is truly Finnish modern jewelry from Aarikka, and carries exotic ornamentation based on old designs.

Sports and Fitness

Bicycling Helsinki and environs make for good biking because there is a decent network of trails, many running through parks, forests, and fields. The free area sporting map (Ulkoilukartta) gives details of all trails. Daily rentals cost FM40 from the **Olympic Stadium Youth Hostel** (Pohjoinen Stadiontie 3B, tel. 90/496–071).

Golf For full information on golf in Helsinki and environs, contact the **Finnish Golf Union** (Radiokatu 20, 00240 Helsinki, tel. 90/1581). There are 18- and 9-hole courses in the Helsinki area, with green fees from FM50 to FM150.

Swimming The best place for public indoor swimming—and saunas—in Helsinki is the **Yrjönkadun Uimahalli** (Yrjönkatu 21B, tel. 90/60–981), a swimming hall from the 1920s. The three best beaches near central Helsinki are at **Hietaniemi, Lauttasaari,** and **Uunisaari.**

Tennis There are four tennis centers and 31 clubs in Helsinki. For specifics, contact the **Finnish Tennis Association** (Radiokatu 20, 00240 Helsinki, tel. 90/1581). It's best to bring your own equipment, although rentals are available.

Dining

Helsinki is home to some of the best Finnish eating establishments. Although the Russian restaurants are the star attraction, try to also seek out Finnish specialties such as game—pheasant, reindeer, hare, and grouse—accompanied by wildberry compotes and exotic mushroom sauces. The chanterelle grows wild in Finland, as do dozens of other edible mushrooms. Voileipäpöytä is a cold table served at breakfast or lunch—the Finnish version of smorgasbord.

Highly recommended restaurants are indicated by a star ★.

Very Expensive **Galateia.** The mirrored ceiling, white grand piano, and paintings of languid mermaids lend a cozy, underwater ambience to this seafood restaurant. Located on the top floor of the Hotel InterContinental, Galateia offers a nighttime panorama that takes in the city lights and an illuminated Finlandia Hall reflected in Töölo Bay. Tasty Caribbean dishes are the main event—Finnair flies in fresh fish daily from Miami. Caviar and roe specialties also are featured. If you are in Helsinki during the crayfish season, this is one of the best places to sample it. Attentive and knowledgeable waiters offer an impressive selection of appropriate wines. *Mannerheimintie 46 (Hotel InterContinental), tel. 90/405–5900. Reservations advised. Jacket and tie advised. AE, DC, MC, V. Closed July, Dec. 21–Jan. 2, and weekends. No lunch.*

★ **Ravintola Valhalla.** Set in vaulted rooms beneath the 18th-century fortress on Suomenlinna island, Valhalla recalls the bare dining halls of a medieval castle. Established in 1950, the restaurant has stripped wooden floors, brick walls, warm spotlighting and a spirit of dignified, elegant feasting. For an appetizer, try the clear perch soup or cold salmon with mustard sauce. Main course specials may include fresh fish, broiled or

Dining
Alexander Nevski, **30**
Bellevue, **32**
El Greco, **20**
Elite, **2**
Fatima, **20**
Galateia, **5**
Garlic Restaurant Kynsilaukka, **18**
Kaksi Kanaa, **33**
Lautasmatkat, **16**
Merimakasiini, **8**
Nygårds Restaurant, **23**
Parrilla Torni, **15**
Piekka Finnish Restaurant, **3**
Ravintola Valhalla, **34**
Ritarisali, **14**

Lodging
Academica, **6**
Anna, **19**
Clairet, **21**
Dipoli Summer, **1**
Finnapartments Fenno, **27**
Helka, **7**
Hesperia, **4**
Hotel Pilotti, **12**
Inter Continental, **5**
Irmala-Terminus-Pilvilinna, **29**
Lord, **17**
Olympia, **28**
Omapohja Teatterimajatalo, **22**
Palace, **31**
Rantasipi Airport Hotel, **11**
SAS Royal Hotel, **10**
Satakuntatalo, **9**
Seurahuone, **13**
Strand InterContinental, **25**
Torni, **14**
Ursula, **24**
Vantaa Hostel, **26**

Helsinki Dining and Lodging

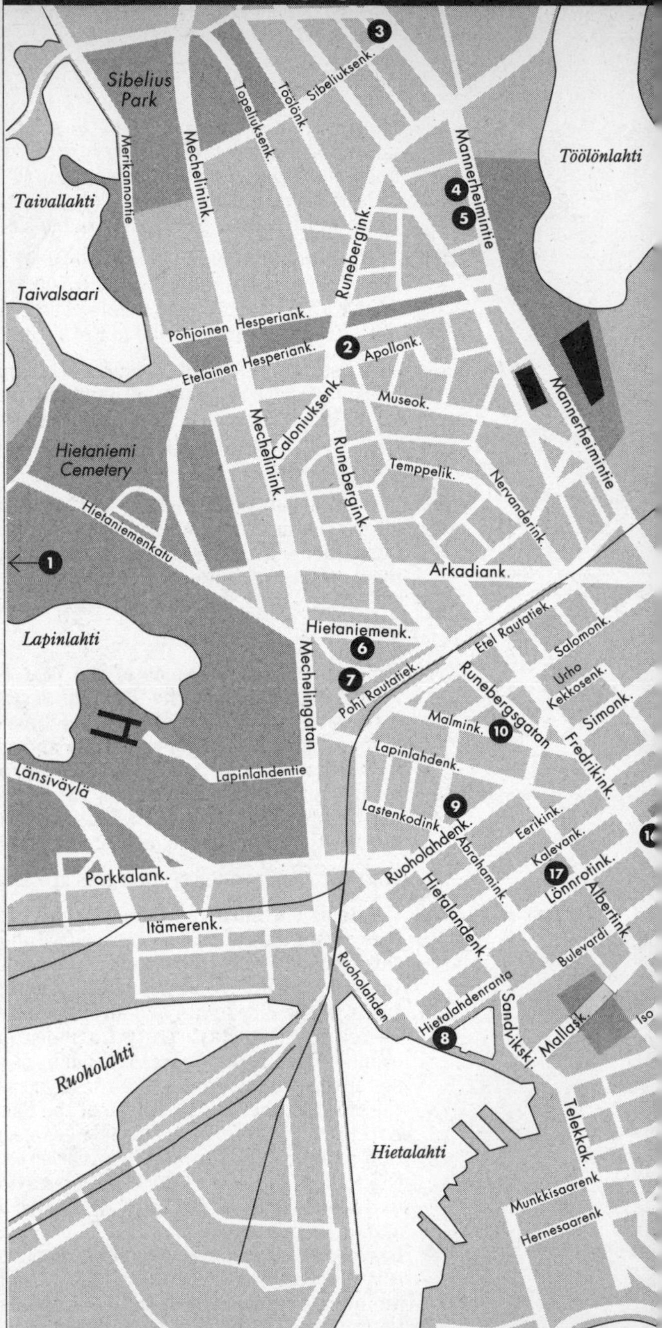

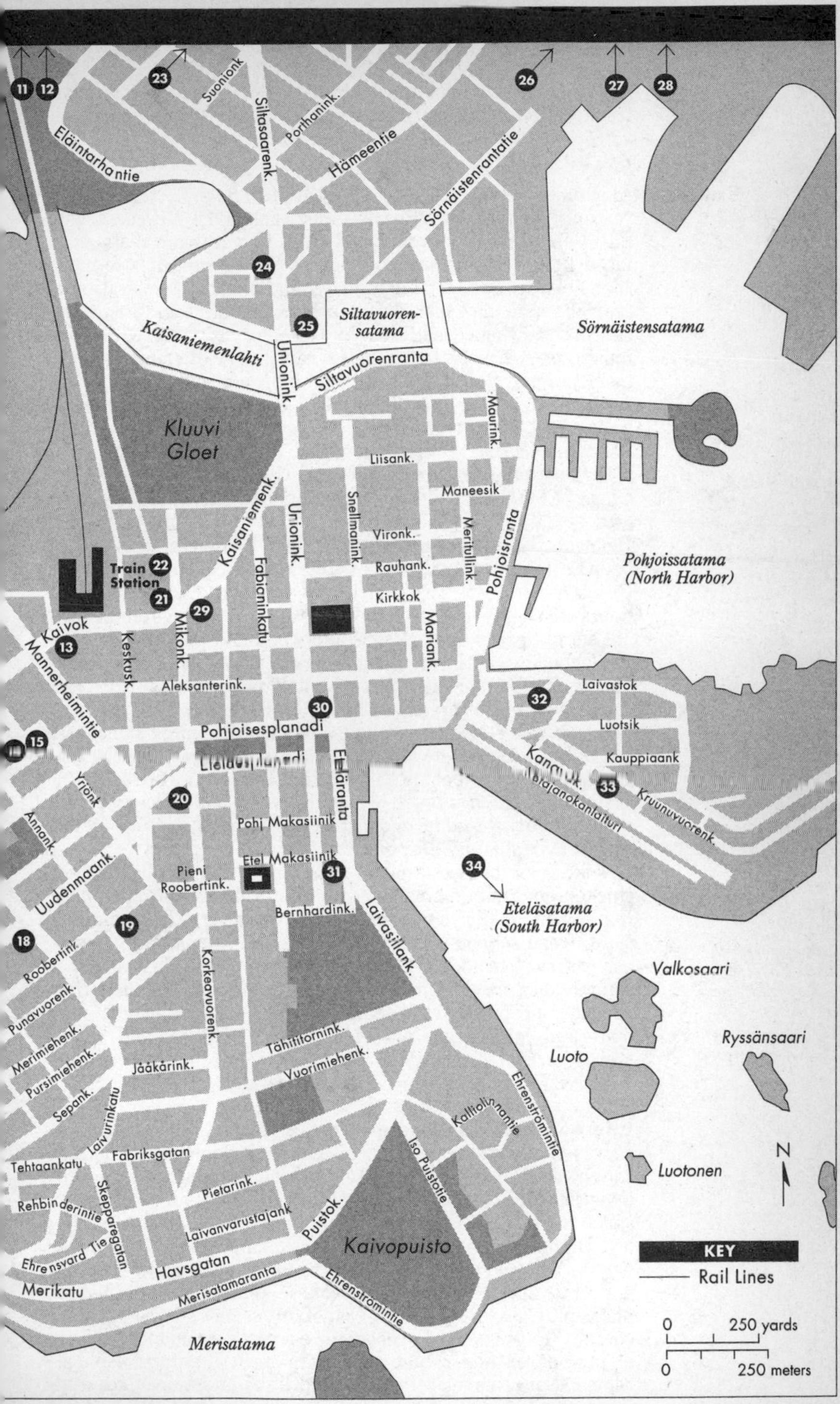

Eläintarhantie
Suoniionk.
Siltasaarenk.
Porthanink.
Hämeentie
Sörnäistenrantatie
Siltavuoren-satama
Sörnäistensatama
Kaisaniemenlahti
Unionink.
Siltavuorenranta
Maurink.
Kluuvi Gloet
Liisank.
Maneesik
Kaisaniemenk.
Fabianinkatu
Urionink.
Snellmanink.
Vironk.
Rauhank.
Kirkkok
Meritullink.
Pohjoisranta
Pohjoissatama (North Harbor)
Train Station
Mikonk.
Keskusk.
Mariank.
Kaivok
Mannerheimintie
Aleksanterink.
Laivastok
Luotsik
Pohjoisesplanadi
Eteläranta
Kauppiaank
Yrjönk
Annank.
Katajanokanlaituri
Kruunuvuorenk.
Pohj Makasiinik
Etel Makasiinik
Pieni Roobertink.
Uudenmaank.
Bernhardink.
Laivasillank.
Eteläsatama (South Harbor)
Roobertink.
Korkeavuorenk.
Valkosaari
Punavuorenk.
Merimiehenk.
Pursimiehenk.
Tähtitornink.
Vuorimiehenk.
Ryssänsaari
Jääkärink.
Luoto
Sepank.
Laivurinkatu
Kalliolinnantie
Ehrenströmintie
Fabriksgatan
Tehtaankatu
Iso Puistotie
Luotonen
N
Pietarink.
Rehbinderintie
Skepparegatan
Laivanvarustajank
Puistok.
Ehrensvard Tie
Kaivopuisto
Havsgatan
KEY
Rail Lines
Merikatu
Merisatamaranta
Ehrenströmintie
0
250 yards
0
250 meters
Merisatama
11
12
23
26
27
28
24
25
22
21
29
13
15
20
30
32
33
31
34
19
18

grilled; snow grouse with tarragon and peppers; and reindeer with honey marinated vegetables. For dessert you can savor oven-warmed cheese with cloudberry sauce, raspberry cream pudding, or white-chocolate parfait with mint sauce. There is a fresh daily special for vegetarians as well. *Suomenlinna, tel. 90/668–552. Reservations advised. Dress: casual but neat. AE, DC, MC, V. Closed Oct.–Apr.*

Expensive

★ **Alexander Nevski.** Helsinki is reputed to have better Russian restaurants than any Russian city, and until Moscow's new Savoy lured away its renowned chef, this Russian restaurant faced little competition from across the border. It still more than holds its own, setting high standards in the preparation of czarist-era dishes such as lamb steak in mint-and-rosemary sauce, traditional roe-filled blintzes, or ox fillet with wild mushrooms. Among the more extraordinary offerings is roast bear in a pot. Set at the edge of the harbor and marketplace, Nevski has all the trappings you'd expect to find in a czar's dining hall—heavy draperies, glistening samovars, and crisp linen tablecloths. *Pohjoisesplanadi 17, tel. 90/639–610. Reservations advised. Dress: casual but neat. AE, DC, MC, V. Closed Christmas, all national holidays except Easter, and Sun.*

Bellevue. The spare lines of Bellevue belie its real age—it has been around since 1922, serving imaginative dishes inspired by Russian cuisine of yore and Finnish country fare. The wood floors, skylights, and tremendous modern paintings on the wall are set off by pale table linens and wood-and-plush seats. Particularly noteworthy are the innovative meat dishes. The Bellevue is also famous for blinis—small pancakes topped with caviar and/or sour cream, or honey, and the like. The plush interior of this elegant town house has many shining samovars, but only some of them are functional. Appropriately, the restaurant is tucked behind the Russian Orthodox Uspensky Cathedral. *Rahapajankatu 3, tel. 90/179–560. Reservations advised. Jacket and tie advised. AE, DC, MC, V. Closed June 22–23, Christmas, Sun., and Easter Mon. No lunch Sat.*

Kaksi Kanaa. The name means two chickens, but oddly enough, chicken does not dominate the menu of this theater and music restaurant. While you listen to jazz, you can try the mushroom soup, fresh salmon tartare, vineyard-grown snails, feta-spinach pastry, tournedos Roquefort, or even pizza. There is a special advance order menu available featuring lobster and other specially prepared fresh seafood dishes. The interior is intimate and cabaret-like with new brick-tile floors and upholstered chairs. *Kanavakatu 3, tel. 90/669–260. Reservations advised. Dress: casual but neat. AE, DC, MC, V. Closed Sun., Christmas, and Easter Mon. No lunch Sat.*

Ritarisali. Based around a medieval theme, this restaurant serves a very hearty French cuisine influenced by locally caught seafood. The moderately priced set lunch includes an appetizer buffet, daily specials like veal meatballs with caper sauce or braised salmon with cucumber sauce, and dessert trolley. Dinners are grand. The "Menu du Chevalier" is a tremendous—and very expensive—gastronomic venture with a sole and crab starter and a main course featuring supremes of pheasant Catalan style with grapefruit sorbet served between courses. Regular dinner choices are expensive and include fillet of pike-perch and rabbit soup with horn chantarelle mushrooms. Large paned windows shed light on immaculate, embossed white table linens, wood paneling, warm creamy orange walls, and parquet floors with Oriental rugs. *Yrjönkatu 26 (Hotel Torni), tel. 90/131–131. Reservations advised. Dress: casual but neat. AE, DC, MC, V. Closed Sun. and Dec. 22–Jan. 8.*

Moderate

El Greco. In a bright room overlooking the Esplanade, this eatery offers an impressive array of Greek dishes with a slight Helsinki influence. The seafood on a skewer, for example, includes salmon, rainbow trout, whitefish, and shrimp served with spinach, rice, and garlic mayonnaise. There's also a fresh feta and spinach pie, fried eggplant with yogurt sauce, roast mutton, dolmades, and Samos-style liver cooked in wine. For smaller meals or snacks, the El Greco Cafe is downstairs at street level and has a summer terrace. *Etelä-esplanadi 22, tel. 90/607–565. Reservations advised. Dress: casual but neat. AE, DC, MC, V. Closed Dec. 23–26.*

★ **Elite.** Built in 1932, this restaurant is a Helsinki artists' hangout, but unless you know your Finnish actors, writers, and painters, it may be hard to pick them out. In any case, their presence makes for a very Continental atmosphere. The dark wood chairs, linen tablecloths, and carpeted floors that keep the noise level comfortable all add to the ambience, as well as the fine stained-glass window in the bar. The excellent Finnish and Continental fare includes noisettes of beef with fresh rose pepper, and *Vorschmack* (a Baltic specialty of richly spiced minced lamb laced with garlic, accompanied by chopped zucchini, beets, and potato with sour cream). Other specialties include gratineed reindeer in a pot and shrimp and feta casserole. *Eteläinen Hesperiankatu 22, tel. 90/449–625. Reservations advised. Dress: casual. AE, DC, MC, V. Closed Dec. 24–26.*

Fatima. This small, dark, exquisitely decorated Egyptian restaurant offers both vegetarians and meat eaters succulent, exotic dishes. Try the lentil soup or tahini baba ganoush appetizer, then the mushroom-stuffed beef, the grilled perch, or a selection from the "Cairo Table," a set meal that includes such dishes as falafel, beef, tahini, and marinated vegetables. Outdoor seating in summer. *Etelä-esplanadi 22, tel. 90/611–001. Reservations advised. Dress: casual. DC, MC, V.*

★ **Garlic Restaurant Kynsilaukka.** This is one of Helsinki's most imaginative new restaurants. Based on a garlic theme (there's even garlic beer), the food is fresh and beautifully presented, and often served by the three young owner-chefs themselves. The seafood bouillabaisse is superb, as is the cold marinated beef, the avocado salad, and the lamb pot. For dessert, the pancakes with cloudberry sauce and ice cream is a must. The decor is rustic and comfortable with a maritime theme. The set lunch menu is a good buy. *Fredrikinkatu 22, tel. 90/651–939. Reservations advised. Dress: casual but neat. AE, DC, MC, V.*

Merimakasiini. The nautical theme of this waterfront restaurant extends beyond the decor to its menu. However, in addition to dishes like Marseilles-style trout on a skewer and seafood casserole in garlic, olive oil, and white-wine sauce, there also are lamb, steak, chicken, and vegetarian dishes. For dessert, try the fried Camembert with cranberry sauce. There's a cozy bar and a terrace in the summer. *Hietalahdenranta 4, tel. 90/607–299. Reservations accepted. Dress: casual. AE, DC, MC, V.*

Nygårds Restaurant. In a gracious wood house on wide, tree-shaded lawns just outside the city, this spacious, beautifully furnished restaurant serves hearty entrées such as grilled pepper steak with oven-browned potatoes and vegetables; there's also a salad bar. Light, wide plank wood floors, Oriental rugs, comfortable Bentwood chairs, and old-style Finnish ceramic chimneys add extra warmth to rooms that are already large and sunny. There's a summer terrace that seats 40. *Uunirinne 2, Sotunki, Vantaa, tel. 90/876–1200. Reservations advised. Dress: casual but neat. DC, MC, V. Closed Dec. 24–26 and Midsummer Eve and Day.*

Parrilla Torni. The chef can speak Finnish, but he is a Spaniard from Galicia and the cuisine of his native region is well represented on the menu of this handsome restaurant. Along with its extensive Spanish wine list, Parrilla offers grilled chicken with chocolate sauce and chestnuts, herb-fried red snapper with garlic mayonnaise, olive chicken, paella marinara, and an assortment of omelets. Starters include a vegetable omelet and shrimp-and-garlic casserole. For dessert, try the almond surprise with figs. Small and intimate, the restaurant has an authentic Iberian atmosphere, with dark wood tables, leather seatbacks, iron grillwork, and a bull's head on the wall. *Yrjönkatu 26 (through Hotel Torni lobby), tel. 90/131–131. Reservations advised. Dress: casual but neat. AE, DC, MC, V. Closed Mon. and Dec. 24–26.*

★ **Piekka Finnish Restaurant.** One of the few restaurants in Finland that explicitly promotes the national cuisine, Piekka provides the perfect setting. Designed in birch wood from floor to ceiling, with handwoven table linens in rich blues, this restaurant offers delicately prepared reindeer and other game dishes in their season and makes a superb pork gravy. *Mannerheimintie 68, tel. 90/493–591. Reservations accepted. Dress: casual but neat. AE, DC, MC, V. No lunch.*

Inexpensive

Lautasmatkat. With marble tabletops and pale pink walls, this small but lively eatery specializes in steaks but has something for everyone. The Hungarian steak with creamy paprika and onion sauce is delectable; there are also several kinds of salad and pasta. The substantial children's menu includes grilled tuna, pasta, cheese dishes, and small-portion steaks. Order at the counter and the food is brought to you. *Lönnrotinkatu 13, tel. 90/601–031. No reservations. Dress: casual. Closed Dec. 24–26, Easter weekend, Midsummer's Eve and Day and Sun.*

Lodging

Helsinki's hotels are notoriously expensive, and most cater to the business traveler. The standards of cleanliness are high, though, and the level of service usually corresponds to the price.

Highly recommended hotels are indicated by a star ★.

Very Expensive

Hesperia. Enlarged and redecorated in 1986, the Hesperia is modern in the best Finnish tradition and close to the city center. The lobby's convenient semicircle of service booths includes a bank, an SAS check-in counter, a travel agent, a car rental service, and even an airport helicopter booth. The relatively spacious contemporary rooms are well equipped but unmemorable except for those with king-size beds—a rarity in Helsinki hotels. Some rooms overlook Töölö bay and the main avenue, Mannerheimintie; the back rooms face a quieter street. *Mannerheimintie 50, 00260, tel. 90/43–101. 376 rooms, 4* *suites. Facilities: restaurant, bar, café, cable TV, 24-hour room service, minibars, health club, saunas, indoor pool, solarium, golf-course simulator, rooms for nonsmokers and allergy sufferers. AE, DC, MC, V. Closed Dec. 24–26.*

★ **InterContinental.** This modern, centrally located hotel is the most popular hotel in the city—particularly with American business travelers. It's a virtual Helsinki institution—travelers en route to the Soviet Union usually spend the Finnish part of their trip here. Decor is pleasant and light—oatmeal carpets, birch paneling and closets, subtle floral print bedspreads and curtains. Services for business travelers are excellent. Galateia (*see* Dining, *above*) offers good seafood and a wonderful view. *Mannerheimintie 46, 00260, tel. 90/405–51. 555 rooms, 12 suites. Facilities: saunas, indoor pool, cable TV, 24-hour room service, rooms for nonsmokers and allergy sufferers. AE, DC, MC, V.*

Palace. A small hotel located on the ninth and 10th floors of a waterfront commercial building, the Palace has a splendid view of the South Harbor. The hotel attracts a faithful clientele of largely British, American, and Swedish patrons who appreciate the personal service that comes with its small size and such intimate touches as daily afternoon tea. The decor is nondescript, except for the wood paneling and plush carpet, and amenities in the guest rooms are few. The hotel's restaurants all have harbor views, as does the sauna. All rooms were renovated in 1991. *Eteläranta 10, 00130, tel. 90/134–561. 50 rooms, 6 suites. Facilities: restaurants, bar, saunas, cable TV, 24-hour room service. AE, DC, MC, V. Closed Dec. 24–26.*

SAS Royal Hotel. Helsinki finally got its own SAS Royal Hotel in the summer of 1991. This hotel was conceived and built much in the style of other SAS hotels worldwide, with high emphasis on servicing the business traveler; three check-in/out desks in a satellite-style reception area and a business center. Set in a residential section of the central city, the hotel is right on the metro line. Two floors are made up of Royal SAS Club rooms including several suites and conference areas. The decor varies with the rooms; some have bold primary colors, others are more traditional Scandinavian, and some are Oriental, set off by cream-color walls and light woods. *Runeberginkatu 2, 00101, tel. 90/6958–6500. 260 rooms, 7 suites. Facilities: restaurants, bar, business center, saunas, room service, conference and banquet rooms. AE, DC, MC, V.*

Seurahuone. This Viennese-style town house was built in 1914 and renovated in 1982, and has a loyal clientele won over by its ageless charm and cosmopolitan atmosphere. Well worn elegance emanates from the grand main stairway; the chandeliered Art-Nouveau café; the ornate, skylit Socis pub; and the traditionally furnished rooms (brass beds, high ceilings, chandeliers, teak cabinets) in the old section. The new section has sleek modern rooms, so specify your preference. Many of the rooms, even the modern ones, are furnished with Victorian antiques. Facing the railway station and housing a popular disco in addition to a café and pub, the lobby and public area are among the busiest in town. *Kaivokatu 12, 00100, tel. 170–441. 118 rooms, 5 suites. Facilities: restaurant, bar, café, saunas, cable TV. AE, DC, MC, V.*

★ **Strand InterContinental.** You will want for nothing at Helsinki's newest, and most expensive big hotel—from the tastefully furnished rooftop saunas and the large, crisply decorated rooms to the bathrooms with heated floors and the carwash service in the basement garage. The hotel's distinctive use of granite and Finnish marble in the central lobby is accentuated by a soaring atrium. Choose from a lobby bar and two restaurants. A whole floor is reserved for nonsmokers. Locals smile knowingly at the situating of this luxurious executive retreat in a traditionally socialist, working-class neighborhood; but the location is central, the waterfront vistas a pleasure. Five of the eight suites have panoramic views of the sea. *John Stenberginranta 4, 00530, tel. 90/39–351. 200 rooms, 8 suites. Facilities: restaurants, bar, saunas, indoor pool, cable TV, room service. AE, DC, MC, V.*

Expensive

Helka. A town house built in 1925, the Helka has been expanded and renovated in recent years. The unimaginative rooms and dreary corridors are compensated for by new facilities, however. The large, ultramodern sauna includes a Jacuzzi with skylight, a fireplace, and conference rooms. Rooms in the old section resemble motel accommodations; ask to be placed in the newer addition. Rooms on the street side get traffic noise on weekdays. Service is efficient and unpretentious, and the room price includes breakfast and a morning sauna, an unusual practice. The restaurant serves French cuisine. *Pohjoinen Rautatiekatu 23, 00100, tel. 90/440–581. 183 rooms with shower or bath; 1 suite. Facilities: restaurant, bar, saunas, Jacuzzi, rooms for nonsmokers. AE, DC, MC, V. Closed Dec. 21–Jan. 2.*

★ **Lord.** Located on a quiet side street, this latest arrival among the small luxury hotels already has set itself apart. The front section is a handsome stone castle, built in 1903, whose wood-beamed, medieval-style rooms have been converted into restaurants, lounges, a cavernous banquet hall, conference rooms, a sauna lounge, and an airy breakfast room. A walkway across a dreary inner court brings you to the modern building housing the guest rooms. Each of the 36 rooms (20 more are under construction) exhibits fine attention to detail: The desks and lighting are excellent; the contemporary style furnishings, in soothing pastel blue and gray tones, are comfortable; the storage space ample. For its rare combination of character, consistency, and service, this is a fine choice. There are discounts on weekends and in summer. *Lonnrotinkatu 29, 00180, tel. 90/680–1680. 36 rooms with shower or bath, 1 suite. Facilities: restaurant, bar, saunas, banquet hall, conference rooms, free parking. AE, DC, MC, V. Closed Dec. 24–Jan. 1.*

Rantasipi Airport Hotel. This fully equipped, modern accommodation statisfies Helsinki's need for an airport hotel that meets the highest international standards. Convenient for layovers, the hotel borders the airport commercial zone but has pleasant views of surrounding fields and forest. A standard room includes a large sofa and king-size bed and has soft touches like paisley bedspreads and wicker furniture; all are soundproof and air-conditioned. *Takamaantie 4, 01510 Vantaa, tel. 90/87–051. 300 rooms. Facilities: 3 restaurants, nightclub, conference center, minibar, TV, disabled access, indoor pool, free shuttle to airport, children's playroom, rooms for nonsmokers and allergy sufferers. AE, DC, MC, V.*

Torni. The older part was built in 1918, and its towers and internal details reflect some of the more fanciful touches of Helsinki's art deco period. The plainer "new" section dates from 1931. From this section, there are striking views of Helsinki from the higher floors—the Torni is one of the city's tallest buildings—and the rooms have large windows. As of mid-1991 all the rooms were to have been redone. The old-section rooms on the courtyard are recommended, however. They have high ceilings with original carved wood details and wood writing desks; many have little alcoves or other pleasing design oddities. Public areas have Oriental rugs and leather sofas. There is a conference room and bar atop the tower, with art exhibitions that change monthly. *Yrjönkatu 26, 00100, tel. 90/131–131. 155 rooms (36 with bath), 9 suites. Facilities: 2 restaurants, 2 bars, saunas, cable TV, room service, conference rooms. AE, DC, MC, V. Closed Dec. 22–Jan. 8.*

Moderate

★ **Anna.** Pleasantly situated in a central, residential location, the Anna is in a seven-story apartment building dating from the 1930s. The room fittings are modern, however, with light, comfortable furniture. The room price includes a buffet breakfast. *Annankatu 1, 00120, tel. 90/648–011. 60 rooms, 1 suite. Facilities: café, sauna, cable TV. AE, MC, V. Closed Dec. 24–26, Dec. 31–Jan. 1.*

Dipoli Summer. Built in 1952, the Dipoli was designed in part by Alvar Aalto. Its rooms are bright, and some overlook the sea. The hotel is five miles from Helsinki in the Espoo area, but there is frequent bus transport downtown. The room price includes breakfast. *Jämeräntaival 1, 02150, tel. 90/435–811. 241 rooms with toilet and shower. Facilities: saunas, indoor pool, use of health club and tennis courts. AE, DC, MC, V. Closed Sept. 1–June 1.*

Finnapartments Fenno. Finnapartments, located on a side street north of Hakaniemi Square, 10 minutes by tram to the city center, offers a break from Finland's sky-high prices; it's especially good if you are in town for a longer stay. This collection of guest apartments was built in 1989 and offers a choice in compact, modern apartments, each of which has a small kitchen with basic utensils. Variations include rooms with workspaces; some single and double studios are available, too. The walls are white and bedcovers and curtains are in primary colors. There is a self-service laundry room. The rooms on the courtyard are quietest; there's an outdoor café in the summer. *Franzeninkatu 26, 00530, tel. 90/773–1661. 100 apartments, 68 with bath. Facilities: cafeteria, TV, free parking, rooms for disabled. DC, MC, V.*

Hotel Pilotti. In a quiet suburban setting but within five minutes' drive of the airport, the Pilotti is also near the Science Center. Built in 1989, it is modern inside and out; each room has a large round porthole-style window. *Veromäentie 1, Tikkurila, 01510 Vantaa, tel. 90/870–2100. 112 rooms, 4 suites. Facilities: sauna, free shuttle to airport. No credit cards. Closed Dec. 23–Jan. 1.*

Olympia. There's fine ambience in the public areas of this hotel with their stone floors, dark walls, and sturdy furniture. By contrast, the rooms are light, with white walls and blue-green textiles and upholstery. The hotel dates from 1977; last redecoration was in 1990. *Läntinen Brahenkatu 2, 00510, tel. 90/750–801. 99 rooms, 1 suite. Facilities: restaurant, sauna, rooms for nonsmokers. AE, DC, MC, V.*

Omapohja Teatterimajatalo. Dating from 1906, this inn used to be a base for actors performing at the state theater next door. The rooms are cozily old-fashioned, with wood-paneled walls and handwoven bedspreads; they also have tremendous windows. You'll find this hotel at the bear sign in a mint-green

Jugend style building. *Itäinen Teatterikuja 3, 00100, tel. 90/666–211. 15 rooms, 4 with shower. Facilities: TV, breakfast served in room. MC, V. Closed Dec. 23–26, Easter, Midsummer holiday.*

Ursula. The furnishings in this hotel's rooms are much like those you'd find in a typical Finnish home: simple, clean lines, a plethora of wood tones, duvets with covers in bright, primary colors. Located in a traditional Helsinki working-class neighborhood but near the center and Hakaniemi market and Market Square, the Ursula is also near the airport bus stop and the Hakaniemi metro stop. *Paasivuorenkatu 1, 00530, tel. 90/750–311. 40 rooms, 3 suites. Facilities: AE, DC, MC, V. Closed Dec. 25–26.*

Inexpensive

Academica. This summer hotel is made up of what are, during the rest of the year, university students' apartments. Each floor has a small lounge; the rooms are sturdy, modern, and have their own small kitchens. Family rooms and extra beds are also available, and there are special family rates. Guests can eat reduced price meals at the nearby Perho restaurant. The central location is good for shopping and transport. *Hietaniemenkatu 14, 00180, tel. 90/402–0206. 217 rooms (115 with bath/shower, 102 with bath and use of hall shower). Facilities: sauna, pool, tennis court. AE, DC, MC, V. Closed Sept. 2–May 31.*

Clairet. Tucked away on a small street behind the state theater and a few steps from the train station, the Clairet suits the needs of the undemanding traveler who wants a great location. Room renovations in 1991 resulted in brighter, quieter quarters for guests. There is no elevator in this three-story hotel. *Itäinen Teatterikuja 3, 00100, tel. 90/669–707. 15 rooms with shared bath. Facilities: room for nonsmokers. V. Closed Dec. 24–26.*

Irmala-Terminus-Pilvilinna. In a turn-of-the-century building near the train station, this small hostelry prides itself on its individuality. The rooms are all of different sizes and appearances, and, the owner is constantly adding new touches. Some rooms have old-fashioned fixtures more in keeping with the exterior, others are filled with spare, contemporary furnishings. Some rooms have sleeping alcoves, some are hostel-style, with places for three or four guests. The rooms on the courtyard are the quietest. *Vilhonkatu 6, 00100, tel. 90/630–260 or 90/607–072. 65 rooms (5 with shower). Facilities: restaurant, coffee room, TV in some rooms, washing machine. MC, V.*

Satakuntatalo. The staffers here mainly are amiable university students, and the rooms are students' quarters during the year. Satakuntatalo, while bright and extremely well located, is definitely for guests with few demands; the rooms do not have their own bathrooms. *Lapinrinne 1, 00180, tel. 90/694–0311. 66 rooms. Facilities: saunas. AE, MC, V. Closed Sept. 1–May 31.*

Vantaa Hostel. This hostel was built in 1980 in conjunction with the adjoining sports center and, as hostels go, it is one of the cleanest and brightest you'll ever find. *Valkoisenlähteentie 52, Tikkurila, 01300 Vantaa, tel. 90/839–3310. 7 rooms with shared baths and showers. Facilities: use of sports center, washing machine. Closed Dec. 24–26.*

The Arts and Nightlife

The Arts For a list of events, pick up *Helsinki Today*, available in hotels and tourist offices. Two ticket agencies are **Lippupalvelu** (Mannerheimintie 5, in the Bio-Bio cinema arcade, tel. 90/643–043) and **Tiketti** (Yrjönkatu 29C, tel. 90/693–2255).

In the summer, there are many outdoor theaters where both plays and music are performed, at Suomenlinna, Mustikkamaa, and Seurasaari islands, and also at the Rowing Stadium. The Helsinki Festival Weeks, a performance and visual arts celebration set in venues around the city, are held yearly in early autumn.

Concerts **Finlandiatalo** (Finlandia Hall) (Karamzininkatu 4, tel. 90/40–241), the home of the Helsinki Philharmonic, also hosts many visiting world-class orchestras. Finland has produced many fine conducters and because many of them are based abroad—Esa-Pekka Salonen and Paavo Berglund, for example—it is an event when they come home. Concerts are generally held from September through May on Wednesday and Thursday evenings. A new opera house is being built at the other end of Hesperia park, but it's not expected to be ready until late 1992 or early 1993. In the meantime, there is the **Suomen Kansallisooppera** (National Opera) (Bulevardi 23–27, tel. 90/129–255); there is much original Finnish opera performed here, as well as international favorites. The ballet is in the same building. The rock-hewn **Temppeliaukio Kirkko** (Lutherinkatu 3, tel. 90/494–608) is a favorite venue for choral and chamber music.

Film There are 50 cinemas in Helsinki. Foreign films have Finnish and Swedish subtitles. Movie listings are in most daily papers, and posted at the kiosk near the east entrance of the main train station; there are weekly and monthly guides at the tourist office. Most cinemas have assigned seats. Tickets cost FM25–35.

Theater Finland's cultural institutions enjoy generous state financing. Private support of the arts is also strong—especially for the theaters, the best known of which are the **National Theater, City Theater, Swedish Theater,** and the **Lilla Teatern.** However, unless you are fluent in Finnish or Swedish, you're going to have a difficult time understanding the performances.

Nightlife At night, street life in restrained Helsinki consists mainly of youths hanging out at the train station or driving around in vintage American cars. The range of clubs is limited to quiet places for a chat, or discos and hotel nightclubs with loud music. Cover charges average FM15–FM50.

The Helsinki city tourist board has a "Clubs and Music Bars" listing of venues' music nights and cover-charge details.

Bars and Lounges A stylish crowd mingles in whimsical postmodern surroundings at the new **Alexia Bar** (Kluuvia Galleria, Aleksanterinkatu 9, 2nd floor, tel. 90/659–014). The **Socis Pub** (Kaivokatu 12, tel. 90/170–441) at the Seurahuone Hotel offers turn-of-the-century European ambience. **Sakkipilli** (Kalevankatu 2, tel. 90/605–607) is an English-style pub. Several other pubs, restaurants, and discos are located in the **Sakkipilli/Old Baker's complex** (Mannerheimintie 12, tel. 90/605–607), especially popular with young professionals after work. **Angleterre** (Fredrikinkatu 47, tel. 90/647–371), another English-style pub, attracts a fair share of foreigners, and the beer is slightly cheaper. **Robert** (Iso Roobertinkatu 28, tel. 90/616–4321) is a well-designed complex that includes a café, restaurant, bar, and dance area (which jumps on Sunday night).

Bar Restaurants with Music **Liberatore** (Kaivohuone, Kaivopuisto, tel. 90/177–881) features live soul and funk Sunday nights and live DJs Saturday nights; music every Wed.–Sun. 7 PM–3 AM. **Pariisitar** (Fabianinkatu 29, tel. 90/626–940), a relaxed French-style café, offers live music every Wednesday and Saturday, no cover charge on Wednesday.

Rock Clubs Friday and Saturday nights at **Botta** (Museokatu 10, tel. 90/446–940) are strictly disco, but Sunday evening sometimes is jam night and Tuesday is Latin night; on Wednesday there is a live DJ. **Tavastia** (Urho Kekkosenkatu 4–6, tel. 90/694–8322) is university-owned and one of the best clubs for top Finnish talent as well as some solid imports. A chic, mostly young crowd gathers in the bowels of the Helsinki Stock Exchange at the opulent **Cafe Adlon** (Fabianinkatu 14, tel. 90/664–611).

Nightclubs The **Hesperia Hotel Nightclub** (Mannerheimintie 50, tel. 90/43–101), Helsinki's largest and most famous club, occasionally hosts big-name acts. Enjoy gorgeous city views and the cabaret-style floor shows at the ninth-floor **Sky Bar** (Hotel Vaakuna, Asemaaukio 2, tel. 90/131–181). Also popular is the **Bar & Night Club Fizz** at the Hotel Marski (Mannerheimintie 10, tel. 90/68–061) and **Le Club Pressa,** at the Ramada Presidentti (Etelainen Rautatiekatu 4, tel. 90/6911).

Casinos At **Kappeli** (E. Esplanadi, tel. 90/179–242) the casino is set in the lower level of this well-known restaurant-café. The grand **Katajanokan Kasino** (Laivastokatu 1, tel. 90/653–401) sits on its own abutment out into the sea and has been the scene of many a great Helsinki party. In a city famous for beautifully situated casinos, **Kulosaaren Casino** (Hopeasalmenpuistotie 1, tel. 90/684–8201) is one of the most stunning. Five kilometers (3 miles) east of the city center by metro or taxi, it's on a marina. **Ramada Presidentti** (E. Rautatiekatu 4, tel. 90/6911) has several levels of casinos.

Jazz Clubs **Kuu** (Töölönkatu 27, tel. 90/443–308), a tiny supper bar, features local jazz artists every other Monday night. **Orfeus** (Eerikinkatu 2, tel. 90/640–378), one of the livelier jazz spots in Helsinki, offers live music Friday through Sunday, usually jazz or blues, from mostly local jammers; there are occasional out-of-town acts, too. **Studio Julius** (Keskuskatu 6, tel. 90/171–585) offers pleasant evenings of jazz, usually on Tuesday, Wednesday, and Friday. It's conveniently located in the railway-station tunnel. **Kaksi Kanaa** (Kanavakatu 3, tel. 90/669–260) is a bistro supper club with jazz Thursday through Saturday. The interior is cabaretlike but spanking clean. Reservations are advised.

Gay Bars **Botta** (*see* Rock Clubs, *above*) has occasional gay nights; for details contact the gay switchboard SETA (Wed.–Sun. 6–9 PM, tel. 90/769–642). **Gambrini** (Iso Roobertinkatu 3, tel. 90/644–391) is a laid-back café/bar where local gay/lesbian crowds gather; women-only the second Sunday and last Friday of the month (Gambrini is not strictly gay/lesbian); also **Vanhan Kellari, Vanha Yliopisto** (Mannerheimintie 3, tel. 90/174–357).

South Coast and Ålands

Introduction

Anyone with a weakness for islands will be thrilled to see the magic world of them stretching along Finland's coastline. There, in the Gulf of Finland and the Baltic, over 30,000 islands form a magnificent archipelago. The rugged and fascinating Åland Islands group rides westward from Turku, forming an autonomous province of its own. Turku, the former capital, was also the main gateway through which cultural influences reached Finland over the centuries.

The southwest is a region of flat, often mist-soaked rural farmlands. The larger villages are highly scenic because of their traditional wood houses, but apart from the summer when the cultural life of the region briefly comes alive, the southwest is pastoral and quiet.

Turku remains a busy harbor, from which you can sail for the Åland islands and points in Sweden. Historic seabound Naantali, with its 15th-century cloister and riot of boat harbors, makes a particularly pleasant detour from Turku.

The Ålands, a collection of small rocky islands, are inhabited in large part by families that fish or run small farms. Their connection with the sea is inevitable, and their tradition of being at sea is a revered one. Some of the greatest grain ships sailing the seas were built by the Gustav Eriksson family in Mariehamn.

Important Addresses and Numbers

Tourist Information The main tourist offices in the area are located at: **Åland** (Storagatan 11, Mariehamn, tel. 928/27–310), **Hanko** (Bulevardi 15, tel. 911/82–239), **Naantali** (Kaivotori 2, tel. 921/850–850), **Tammisaari** (Ekenäs) (Erottaja 16, tel. 911/14–600), and **Turku** (Kasityöläiskatu 3, tel. 921/336–366).

Emergencies The nationwide emergency number is 000; it can be used to call police and ambulance; local phone books, however, are the best sources of emergency information. These will also include medical emergency numbers.

Late-night Pharmacies Late-night pharmacies are in larger towns only. Look under *Apteekki* in the phone book; listings include pharmacy hours.

Arriving and Departing by Plane

The region's airports are at **Mariehamn** and **Turku.** Both have connections to Helsinki and Stockholm, with service by Finnair and its charter company Karair.

Arriving and Departing by Car, Train, Bus, and Boat

By Car The Helsinki–Turku trip is 165 kilometers (100 miles) on Route E3; signs on E3 will tell you where to turn off for the south-coast towns of Tammisaari and Hanko. Most of southwestern Finland is well served by public transport, so a car is not really necessary.

By Train Trains leave Helsinki for Turku several times a day; however, for most smaller towns, you must stop at stations along the Helsinki-Turku route and change to a local bus.

By Bus There is good bus service connecting the capital to the southwest from Helsinki's long-distance bus station, just west of the train station off Mannerheimintie. Information from **Matkahuolto** (Head office, Lauttasaarentie 8, 00200 Helsinki, tel. 692–2088).

By Boat Åland is most cheaply reached by boat from Turku. Call **Silja Line** in Turku (tel. 921/652–244), Mariehamn (tel. 928/12–120), or Helsinki (tel. 90/180–4422); or call **Viking Line** in Helsinki (tel. 90/12–351), Turku (tel. 921/63–311), or Tampere (tel. 931/11–051). Tickets can also be purchased at the harbor.

Guided Tours

Orientation Available through the Tammisaari tourist office is a **Tammisaari Archipelago Tour** (1½ to 3 hours), by boat, that takes in the national park and Kjällviken, the 19th-century home of Princess Dagmar of Denmark and her husband, Alexander III. The cost is FM50 adults, FM20 children.

Special-interest The Ukko–Pekka **steam locomotive tour** runs from Karjaa (on the road to Tammisaari) to Hyvinkää and back in summer; in Hyvinkää, the train stops at the Railway Museum. Arranged through **Ageba Special Travel Service** (Pohjoisranta 4, Helsinki, tel. 90/661–123). The round-trip cost is FM70 adults, FM50 children.

The **Seven Churches** 100-kilometer (65-mile) tour from Turku, taking in the area's major medieval churches and a country manor house, lasts 6½ hours and is arranged through **Varsinais-Suomen Matkailuyhdistys** (L. Rantakatu 13, Turku, tel. 921/517–333). The cost is FM90–FM125 adults, FM45–FM65 children.

United Travel Ltd. (Malminkatu 34, Helsinki, tel. 90/693–1477) also does a **Sibelius tour** in the southwest, originating in Helsinki and taking you to the composer's gracious home at Ainola, Tuusula.

Exploring the South Coast and Ålands

Numbers in the margin correspond with points of interest on the South Coast and Ålands map.

Turku and the Hanko Peninsula A trip to Turku via **Hanko** and Tammisaari will give you a taste of Finland at its most historic and scenic. Moving southwest from Helsinki along the Hanko road for about 77 kilometers (48
1 miles), you'll arrive in **Snappertuna,** a small farming town with a proud hilltop church, a charming homestead museum, and the handsome **Rasaseporin Linna** (Raseborg Castle), set in a small dale. The castle is believed to date from the 13th century. One 16th-century siege left the castle damaged, but restorations gave it a new face. In the summer, concerts, dramas, old-time market fairs, and mock medieval duels are staged here. *Tel. 911/34–015. Admission: FM4 adults, FM2 children. Open May 1–Aug. 31, daily 10–8. Guides arranged by Tammisaari tourist office (*see *Important Addresses and Numbers*, above).

The South Coast and Ålands

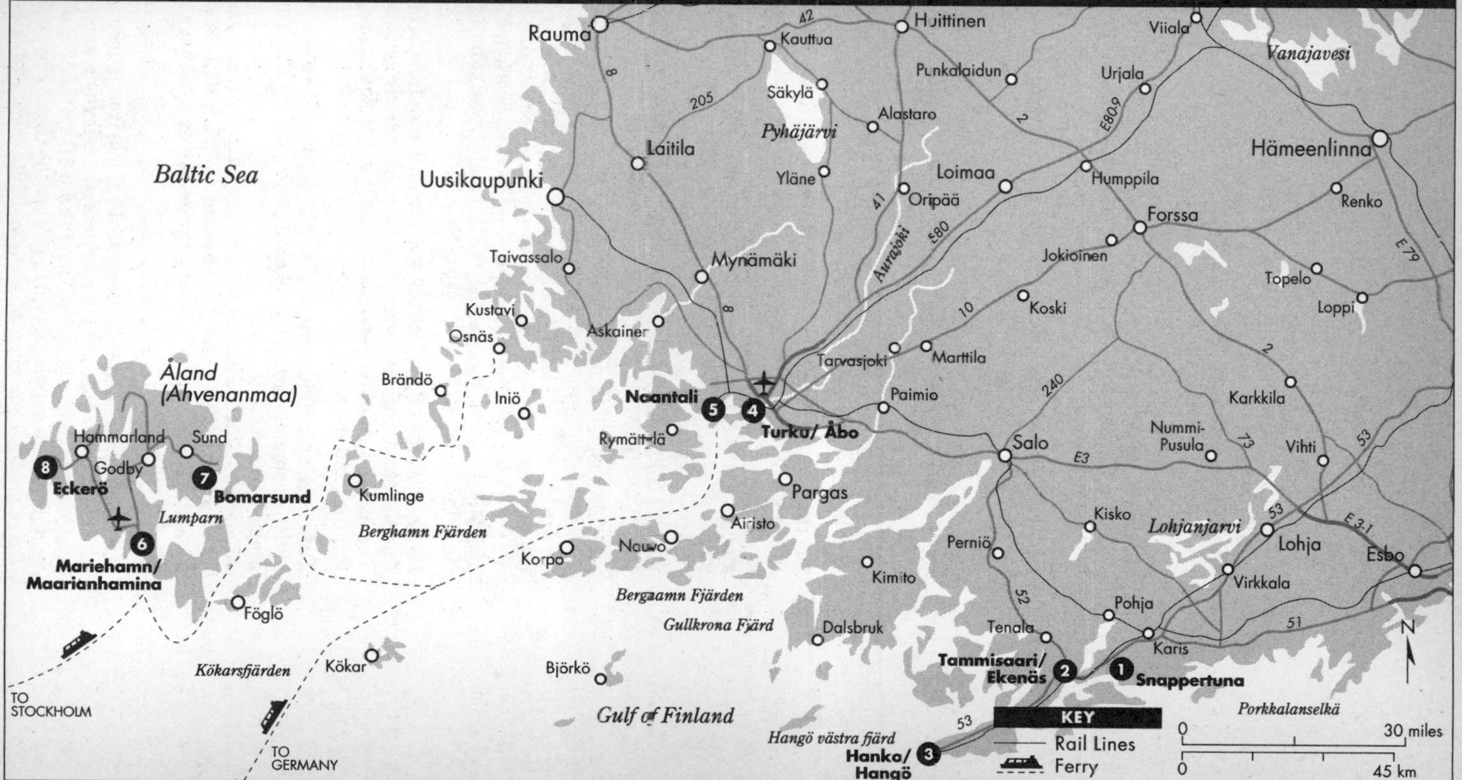

Continuing south for 16 kilometers (10 miles), you will find the
2 historic town of **Tammisaari** (Ekenäs), with its colorful old quarter, 19th-century buildings, and a lively marina. The scenery is dazzling in summer when the sun glints off the water and marine traffic is at its peak. The three-part **Tammisaaren Museo** (Ekenäs Commoners' Museum) provides a taste of its culture and history. *Kustaa Vaasan Katu 13, tel. 911/712–111. Admission: summer, FM5 adults; winter, FM3 adults; free for children under 16, senior citizens over 65, and full-time university students with ID. Open May 2–Aug. 15, Tues.–Sun. 12–4; Aug. 16–May 1, 6–8 PM, Fri.–Sun. 12–4.*

An hour's drive farther west is the popular seaside resort of
3 **Hanko** (Hango), with its long stretch of sandy beach. This customs port has some of the largest and most fanciful private homes in Finland. Their porches are edged with gingerbread ironwork and woodwork, and crazy towers sprout from their roofs. There are several beaches and good cycling paths, but the best pastime is a stroll along the main avenue past the great wood houses with their wraparound porches. A popular sailing center, Hanko has Finland's largest guest harbor. Hanko is historically rich, too. Fortified in the 18th century, the Hanko defense was destroyed by the Russians in 1854, during the Crimean War. It was later a popular spa town for Russians, then the port from which over 300,000 Finns emigrated to North America between 1880 and 1930.

4 Northwest of Hanko at the mouth of the Aura River is **Turku,** the center of Finland's southwest. Turku is the nation's oldest city, founded in the 13th century, and the original capital. With a population of more than 160,000, it is the third largest city and is often called "the cradle of Finnish culture." Commercially, its great importance lies in its year-round harbor; *turku* means trading post. It is also known for its shipyards and for being the site of the first Finnish university.

The 700-year-old **Turun Tuomiokirkko** (Turku Cathedral) remains the seat of the Archbishop of Finland. Although gutted by fire in 1827, the cathedral has been completely restored. In the choir can be seen R. W. Ekman's frescoes portraying Bishop Henry (an Englishman) baptizing the then-heathen Finns, and Mikael Agricola offering the Finnish translation of the New Testament to Gustav Vasa of Sweden.

Where the Aura flows into the sea stands **Turun Linna** (Turku Castle), one of the city's most important historical monuments. The oldest part of the fortress was built at the end of the 13th century, and the newer part dates to the 16th century.

Turku seems a staid town on first glance, but there is a lively artistic community here. It is most active during the August Music Festival.

Time Out The **Hamburg Börs Hotel** (Kauppiaskatu 6, tel. 92/637–881) has a pleasant German-style tavern for drinks or meals; it's near the market square.

A recommended stop 16 kilometers (10 miles) from Turku is the
5 coastal village of **Naantali,** an artists' town lining a snug harbor. Many of the buildings in Naantali date from the 17th century, following a massive rebuilding after the Great Fire of 1628. There are also a number of 18th- and 19th-century buildings,

and these form the basis of the Old Town, a settlement by the water's edge. These shingled wood buildings originally were built as private residences, and many remain so, although a few have been taken over by small galleries.

The town's extremely narrow cobblestone lanes gave rise to a very odd law. During periods when economic conditions were poor, Naantalians earned their keep by knitting socks and exporting them by the tens of thousands. Men, women, and children all knitted so feverishly that the town council forbade groups of more than six from meeting in narrow lanes with their knitting—and causing road obstructions.

A major attraction in the village is **Kultaranta,** the summer residence for Finland's presidents, with its more than 3,500 rosebushes. Guided tours can be arranged through the Naantali tourist board (*see above*) almost year-round, except when the presidential family is in residence. *Luonnonmaasaari. Call tourist board to check opening times; they vary greatly.*

Naantalin Luostarikirkko, Naantali's Vallis Gratiae/Order of St. Birgitta Convent, was founded in 1443. The convent, which alternately housed nuns then monks, operated under the aegis of the Catholic Church until it was dissolved by the Reformation in the 17th century. The church is all that remains of the convent. *Nunnakatu, Naantali, tel. 921/850–109. Admission free for nonguided visits. Open Apr. 16–30, daily 12–3; May 2–Aug. 15, daily 12–7; Aug. 16–Sept. 30, daily 12–3; Oct. 1–Apr. 15, Sun. 12–3. Group tours available through Naantali tourist office (*see *Tourist Information,* above*).*

Time Out When near Naantali's marina, a footbridge takes you to Kailo island where you'll find the art gallery/café **Taidehuone.** A playground, tennis courts, and park chess are all nearby.

The Åland Islands From Turku, there are air and sea connections to the **Åland** (Ahvenanmaa) Islands (approximately 6 hours by boat), where rural calm combines with striking coastal scenery. In all, there are over 6,500 islands and skerries; virtually all the inhabitants are Swedish-speaking and very proud of their largely autonomous status.

Åland is particularly well organized for cycling and fishing packages, motor tours (you can go island-hopping on the fleet of car or passenger ferries), farmhouse holidays, and rental cottages (there are over 7,000 scattered about the islands). These are also marvelous sailing waters for experienced sailors.

6 Nearly half the population lives in the tiny capital of **Mariehamn** (Maarianhamina), the hub of Åland life and the main port, on the main island of Åland. The **Pommern Museefartyget** (Pommern Museum Ship), situated in Mariehamn West Harbor at the center of town, is one of the last existing grain ships in the world. She belonged to the sailing fleet of the Mariehamn shipping magnate Gustav Erikson; the Pommern carried wheat from Australia to England from 1923 to 1939. *Tel. 928/531–421. Admission: FM10 adults, FM5 children. Open Apr.–Oct., daily.*

Time Out The marina café, just down the quay from the Pommern Museefartyget, lets you relax near the water.

In prehistoric times the islands were, relatively speaking, heavily populated, as shown by traces of no less than 10,000 ancient settlements, graves, and strongholds. One of the largest Viking cemeteries is near the 13th-century ruins of **Lembote Chapel,** one of the oldest known granite churches in Finland.

Also of interest are the scattered ruins of **Bomarsund Fort,** a huge naval fortress built by the Russians in the early 19th century and only half finished when it was destroyed by Anglo-
7 French forces during the Crimean War. It is in **Bomarsund,** about 30 kilometers (22 miles) north of Mariehamn on Rte. 2.
8 The fishing community of **Eckerö** (37 kilometers/23 miles northwest) and its small bathing beach also make for a good day's outing.

What to See and Do with Children

In Mariehamn, the **Pommern Museefartyget** (*see above*) is likely to fascinate children, big or small.

Through the telescope of **Vesitorni** (Hanko's Watch Tower), you can follow the comings and goings of the town's marine traffic and get a grander view of some of the very small islands sprinkled around the peninsula's edges. *Vartiovuori. Admission: FM5 adults, FM2 children. Open July 1–Aug. 31, daily 10–noon and 3–5.*

In Karjaa, **Lystiland** (Amusement Land) includes a miniature train tour on an enchanted forest path. *Karjaantie, tel. 911/36-565. Admission: FM40 adults. Open June–Aug., Wed.–Sun. noon–6.*

Off the Beaten Track

Ninety-two kilometers (57 miles) northwest of Turku is **Rauma,** the third oldest city in Finland. In 1992, Rauma will be celebrating the 550th anniversary of its incorporation. The city, which is widely known for its tradition of lacemaking and its annual event, Lace Week, held every year at the end of July, is also known for the beauty of its old wooden houses painted in distinctive 19th-century colors. The colors are so extraordinary, in fact, that no house can be repainted before the Old Rauma Association approves the color.

Shopping

If you are in the market for **nautical knickknacks,** this area has them in abundance. Otherwise, there are no products unique to the region, though the tendency among Finnish artists to summer in coastal towns probably accounts for an inordinate number of **galleries, art exhibitions,** and **handicraft boutiques.** In Naantali you'll find the workshop of a famous Finnish contemporary jewelry designer, **Karl Laine** (Mannerheiminkatu 10B, tel. 921/751–648). His use of brass and Lappish gold, and his combinations of starkly geometric and richly clustered metals, sometimes studded with tiny precious stones, are singular in their creativeness.

Sports and Outdoor Activities

Bicycling Most towns have bikes for rent from about FM20 per day. The fine scenery and the terrain, alternately dead flat and gently rolling, make for ideal cycling. The roads are not busy once you leave the highway. The **Finnish Youth Hostel Association** (Yrjönkatu 38B, 0100 Helsinki, tel. 90/694–0377) has bicycle trips varying in length from four days to two weeks (with overnight stops at hostels if you wish). For Åland bicycle routes, contact **Ålandsresor Ab** (PB 62, Storagatan 9, 22101 Mariehamn, tel. 928/28–040). Both organizations also rent bikes.

Boating A variety of boats can be rented through the Tammisaari, Hanko, and Mariehamn tourist offices (*see* Tourist Information, *above*); or at the guest harbor Info-Point in Hanko. The **Hanko Regatta** takes place yearly on a weekend at the end of June/beginning of July.

Tennis Both Mariehamn and Hanko have outdoor public tennis courts, many of which rent equipment. Contact local tourist offices for information.

Beaches

Hanko has Finland's best beaches, about 30 kilometers (21 miles) worth, some sandy and some with sea-smoothed boulders. The islands tend to have small but pleasant beaches, and Naantali has several bathing areas.

Dining and Lodging

Åland
Dining and Lodging

Arkipelag. Set on the bay and right in the middle of Mariehamn, Arkipelag Hotel is known for its fine marina and lively disco/bar. The rooms are modern and comfortable with huge picture windows. The restaurants, set in long, wood-paneled rooms with wide windows overlooking an ocean inlet, are a good place to sample Åland seafood at its best. Try the crayfish when it's in season. In the Terrace restaurant, the fresh shrimp sandwiches with dill mayonnaise are a treat. *Strandgatan 31, 22100 Mariehamn, tel. 928/24–020. 215 rooms, 8 suites. Facilities: 2 restaurants, nightclub, bar, casino, sauna, indoor/outdoor pool, solarium, conference rooms. DC, MC, V. Moderate–Expensive.*

Lodging

Björklidens Stugby. The appeal here are the snug, redwood cabins in the timeless style of Finnish summer cottages. They're small, but you are meant to be outdoors, enjoying the beach on Bomarsund Strait. Enjoy the free rowboats, grassy lawns, and trees with swings. It is 25 kilometers (17 miles) from Mariehamn. *Hammarland. 17 cabins. Facilities: beach, TV room, outdoor grill, fishing, playground, washing machines. MC, V. Closed late-Aug.–May. Inexpensive.*

Hanko
Dining and Lodging

Strand Hotel and Restaurant. Right in the heart of Tammisaari, this modern hotel stretches along the shoreline. The exterior is handsomely rendered in the style of turn-of-the-century wood manor houses. The rooms are modern, with sea-green carpet and spreads and old-fashioned nautical prints. The large restaurant in the round, with views over the sea, serves classic French style cuisine. Choose between the game bird dishes and the fresh seafood. There's a dance floor adjacent. *Pojogatan 2, 10600 Tammisaari, tel. 911/61–500. 20 rooms, 1 suite. Facili-*

ties: restaurant, bar, boat dock, sauna, cable TV, meeting rooms. AE, DC, V. Closed Dec. 24–26. Moderate–Expensive.

Ekenäs Stadshotell and Restaurant. This modern, airy feeling hotel is set amongst fine lawns and gardens. The rooms, each with its own balcony, have wide picture windows and comfortable modern furnishings, all in pale and neutral colors. The location, near the sea and the old town, is one kilometer (.6 miles from the town center. The restaurant offers Continental food and Swedish-Finnish seafood specialties prepared by a veteran chef. *Norra Strandgatan 1, 10600 Tammisaari, tel. 911/713–131. 18 rooms, 2 suites. Facilities: restaurant, bar, 2 cafés, cable TV, room service, indoor pool, dance floor. AE, DC, MC, V. Closed Dec. 24–25. Moderate.*

Lodging **Hanko Silversand Camping.** There are various facilities on the grounds, including eight-person cabins and full hook-ups for trailers, as well as trailers and tents for rent. *Hopeahietikko, 10600 Tammisaari, tel. 911/85–500. Facilities: cafeteria, store, cooking facilities, sauna, showers, bathrooms. Open June–mid-Aug. Inexpensive.*

Naantali
Dining **Tavastin Kilta.** This summer restaurant with a view of the boat harbor has a fresh cold table where the herring and marinated beef are especially good. Broiled steaks and fish are the featured hot dishes; vegetarian dishes are also offered. There is the Old World bishop's dining room, a nautical bar, and a tapas bar decorated in 19th-century style. Lemon pastries are a dessert specialty. *Mannerheimintie 1, tel. 921/751–066. Reservations advised. Dress: casual but neat. AE, DC, MC, V. Moderate.*

Stella. Pizzas come with every topping imaginable in this cafeteria-style restaurant decked out in Italian flags. *Tullikatu 8, tel. 921/752–988. No reservations. Dress: casual. MC, V. Inexpensive.*

Lodging **Naantali Spa.** The emphasis here is on pampering, with foot massages, shiatsu physical therapy, mud packs, and spa-water and algae baths. Activities include gymnastics and a special seven-day fasting program offered three times a year under medical supervision. All kinds of health packages can be arranged, including health-rehabilitation programs. It is set on a peninsula in a grandiose new building (1984) that replaced the original spa on the site. Stay three days or more on the basic plan and prices will be reduced by at least 15%. *Kalevanniemi, 21100 Naantali, tel. 921/857–711. Facilities: beauty salon, massage, physiotherapy solarium, Turkish bath, Roman pools, swimming pools. AE, DC, MC, V. Expensive.*

Päiväkulma Youth Hostel. The seclusion and charm of this sturdy wood house located on an arm of land 22 kilometers (14 miles) south of Naantali attracts families as well as backpackers. It has a general kitchen, a shoreline sauna, and rowboats and canoes. There is bus transport to Naantali and Turku. *21140 Rymättylä, tel. 921/521–894. No credit cards. Closed Oct.–Apr. Inexpensive.*

The Arts

Each town has concerts and art exhibitions in the summer; often set in outdoor venues. The best way to find out about arts happenings is through local tourist boards. The **Scandinavian**

Guitar Festival comes to Tammisaari on a rotating schedule in the summer.

Lapland

Introduction

Lapland is often called Europe's last wilderness, a region of endless forests, fells, and great silences. Often the arrival of settlers has obliterated all that came before, but here man has walked gently and left the virgin solitude almost unspoiled. Now easily accessible by plane, train, or bus, this Arctic outpost offers comfortable hotels and modern amenities, yet you won't have to go very far to find yourself in an almost primordial setting.

The oldest traces of human habitation in Finland have been found in Lapland, and hordes of Danish, English, and even Arabian coins indicate the existence of trade activities many centuries ago. The origins of the Lapps themselves are lost in the mists of history. There are only about 2,500 pure Lapps still living here; the remainder of the province's population of 220,000 are Finns. Until the 1930s, Lapland remained largely unexploited, a region where any trip was an adventure. Then the Canadian-owned Petsamo Nickel Company completed the great road that connects Rovaniemi with the Arctic Sea. Building activities increased along this route (later to be known as the Arctic Highway), the land was turned and sown, and a few hotels were built to cater to increasing numbers of visitors.

A few words should be said about the Lapps—a proud, sensitive, and intelligent people who prefer their own name for themselves, Saame (also spelled Sami or Same). Some of them can be resentful toward those visitors who regard them as only tourist attractions put there for photo opportunities. Modern influences (among them intermarriage) regrettably have changed many aspects of the Lapp's traditional way of life; for example, their attractive costumes are rarely seen, except on festive occasions. The young especially have been affected by the changes, and many of them are far more interested now in becoming teachers, lawyers, or engineers than in breeding reindeer or hunting from their remote homesteads. Some others profit from selling souvenirs to the tourists, but most prefer to go about their daily life minding their own business.

Summer has the blessing of round-the-clock daylight and often beautiful weather to go with it. In early fall the colors are so fabulous the Finns have a special word for it: *ruskaa*. If you can take the intense (but dry) cold, winter is a fascinating time in Lapland, not only for the northern lights but for such experiences as the reindeer roundups. Depending on how far north of the Arctic Circle you travel, the sun might not rise for several weeks around midwinter. But it is never pitch-black; light reflects from the invisible sun below the horizon even during midday, and there is luminosity from the ever-present snow.

But Finns are outdoors no matter what the light. Here, it is the wilderness that's the draw. For although the cities have fine facilities and much going on culturally, it is the lonely fells with the occasional profile of a reindeer herd crossing them, the gin-clear forest streams, and the bright trail of the midnight sun reflected on a lake's blackest waters that leave the indelible impressions.

Important Addresses and Numbers

Tourist Information The main offices are in **Ivalo/Inari** (Piiskuntie 5, bus station, tel. 9697/12521), **Kemijärvi** (Arctic Fells Tourist Office, Koillistunturit ry, Rovaniementie 6, tel. 9692/13777), **Oulu** (Torikatu 10, tel. 981/241–295), and **Rovaniemi** (Aallonkatu 1, tel. 960/16270; in summer at the railroad station also, tel. 960/22218).

Emergencies The nationwide emergency number is 000; it can be used for police and ambulance; local phone books, however, are the best source of emergency information, including medical emergency numbers for doctors and dentists.

Late-night Pharmacies You will find late-night pharmacies in larger towns only. Look under "Apteekki" in the phone book; the listings include pharmacy hours.

Arriving and Departing by Plane

The airports serving Lapland are at **Enontekiö, Ivalo, Oulu, Rovaniemi,** and **Sodankylä.** Finnair serves all these airports with flights from Helsinki; not all flights are nonstop, though. You also can fly to the north from most of southwest Finland's larger cities and from the lakes region.

Arriving and Departing by Car, Train, and Bus

By Car If you are driving north, follow Arctic Highway No. 4 (national highway) to Kuopio–Oulu–Rovaniemi, or go via the west coast to Oulu, then to Rovaniemi. From Rovaniemi, the national highway continues straight up to Lake Inari via Ivalo. The roads generally are good, but some roads in the extreme north may be rough.

By Train Train service will get you to Rovaniemi. From there you must connect to other forms of transport.

By Bus Bus service into the region centers on Rovaniemi; from there, you can switch to local buses.

Getting Around

By Plane There is daily service between Rovaniemi and Ivalo. You can also fly between Oulu or Rovaniemi to Ivalo, Enontekiö, and Sodankylä, all on Finnair domestic services. There are seasonal schedules.

By Car A car is necessary only for those who want to reach remote places.

By Bus Buses leave twice daily from Rovaniemi to Inari (six hours), and three times a day to Ivalo (five hours). You can take countryside taxis to your final destination; taxi stands are at most bus stations.

Guided Tours

Guided tours in towns are arranged through city tourist offices. The national tourist board's "Lappi à la Carte" booklet suggests gourmet trails through the north.

Orientation There is a large variety of Lapland tours, catering to both general and special interests. Finnair arranges many tours from Helsinki, including the Midnight Sun Flight Tour, one day, one night; the Arctic Safari to Lapland, one day, one night; and the Fantasy Tour to the Land of the Midnight Sun, seven days, six nights. Reservations and itinerary details are available from **Finnair** (Mannerheimintie 102, tel. 90/81–881, fax 90/818–8736). **Lapptreks** (Inari, tel. 9697/51375) arranges reindeer, canoe, and snowmobile safaris; ski treks; fishing trips; and Gold Trail tours. Lapland Experience, Lapland Express, and North Cape tours (Finland–Norway) are offered by **Area Travel** (Kaisaniemenkatu 13, tel. 90/18551). Other tour operators include: **Kaleva Travel** (Mikonkatu 6C, 00100 Helsinki, tel. 90/61–881) and **Finland Travel Bureau** (Kaivokatu 10A, 00101 Helsinki, tel. 90/18–261). Travel agencies also offer a variety of white-water rafting and nature-photography tours. For independent travelers, the **Finnish Youth Hostel Association** (*see* Staying in Finland in Essential Information, *above*) can suggest trekking routes and hostel/cabin/camping accommodations.

From Rovaniemi, the tourist board (*see* Important Addresses and Numbers, *above*) has a 2½-hour evening Arctic Circle tour. From Inari, **Feelings Unlimited** runs two-hour Lake Inari tours that leave from the Saame (Lapp) Museum and visit a Saame stone altar and burial island. Reservations are available from **Raimo Mustkangas** (Inari, tel. 9697/51352).

Exploring Lapland

Numbers in the margin correspond with points of interest on the Lapland map.

Your best base for traveling around the Arctic area is
1 **Rovaniemi,** where the Ounas and Kemi rivers meet almost on the Arctic Circle. Rovaniemi is the "Gateway to Lapland" and the administrative and communications center of the province.

If you're expecting an Arctic shantytown, you're in for a surprise. Rovaniemi nearly was razed by the retreating German army in 1944, and today is a modern city whose appearance is influenced strongly by Alvar Aalto's architecture. During rebuilding, the population rose from 8,000 to over 32,000, so be prepared for a contemporary city on the edge of wilderness. If the street layout seems capricious, it's because Aalto planned the town so it would look like reindeer antlers from the air.

One of the best ways to tune into the culture of Finland's far north is to visit **Lappia Talo** (Lappia House), which contains the **Lapin Maakuntamuseo** (Museum of the Province of Lapland). Its exhibit on Saame (Lapp) life is riveting, giving the full story of their survival. *Hallituskatu 11, tel. 960/322–2483. Admission: FM3. Open May–Aug., Tues.–Sat. 10–6; Sept.–Apr., Tues.–Sat. 10–4.*

Rovaniemi's real claim to fame, though, is that Santa Claus lives in its suburbs. Take the Arctic Highway (Highway E4) 10

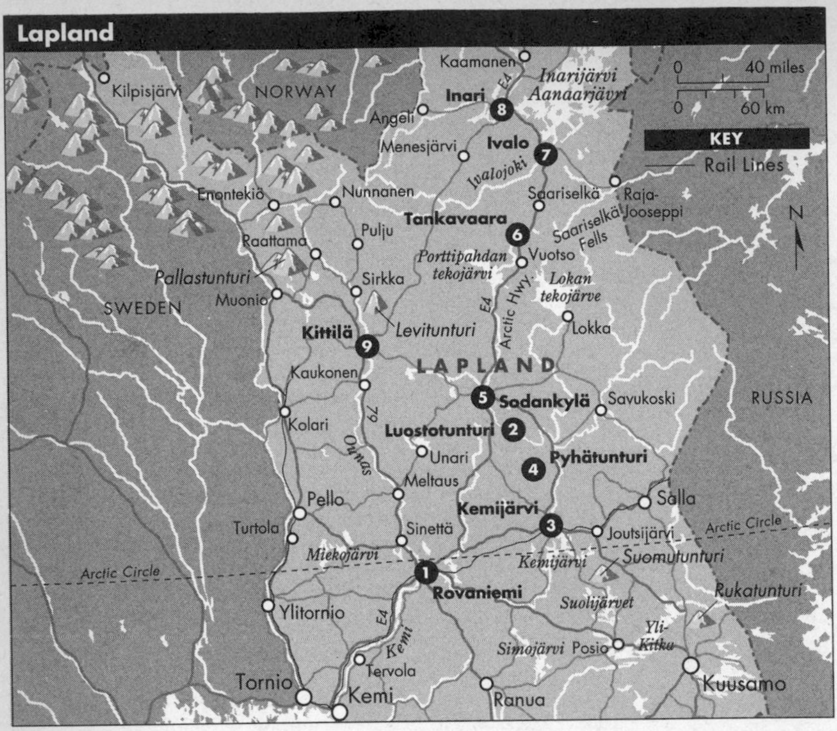

kilometers (7 miles) north toward the Arctic Circle to **Joulupukin Pajakylä** (Santa Claus Village). Lapps in native dress and reindeer hauling sleighs are here enhancing its authenticity. At Santa Claus's Workshop, gifts can be bought in midsummer for shipping at any time of year. For most visitors the main attraction is to mail postcards home from the special Arctic Circle post office. There's also a complete souvenir shopping complex, and the impressive sight of the mountains of mail that pour in from children all over the world. Yes, all of it gets answered! *Admission free. Open June–Aug., daily 9–8; Sept.–May, daily 9–5.*

Time Out Take the 3-kilometer (2-mile) hike to Ounasvaara hill for midnight sun viewing from on high, and stop at the **Sky Hotel** for coffee and pastries at the café.

2 After driving north for a couple of hours, you may want to take a short detour to the modern tourist center at **Luostotunturi,** in the fell district of southern Lapland. Turn right off the main road onto a secondary road about 16 kilometers (10 miles) south of Sodankylä, and follow it 22 kilometers (13 miles) to the center. 3 There is also a daily bus from **Kemijärvi** (reached via local 4 train from Rovaniemi) to the **Pyhätunturi** and **Luostotunturi** fell districts; these areas are superb hiking territory.

5 Back on the main road at **Sodankylä,** there is a Northern Lights Observatory (for professionals only) and an ancient wood church.

6 Continue north through the village of Vuotso to **Tankavaara**, 230 kilometers (143 miles) north of Rovaniemi and 60 kilometers (37 miles) south of Ivalo, the most accessible and the best developed of several gold-panning areas. The **Kultamuseo** (Gold and Prospectors' Museum) tells the century-old story of Lapland's hardy fortune seekers. For a small fee, authentic prospectors will show you how to pan gold dust and tiny nuggets from the silt of an icy stream. *Arctic Highway 4, Kultakylä, tel. 9693/46171. Admission: FM20 adults, FM5 children under 12, discounts for groups of 10 or more. Open June–Aug. 15, daily 9–6; Aug. 16–Sept. 30, daily 9–5; Oct.–May, daily 10–4.*

7 The village of **Ivalo** is the main center for northern Lapland. With its first-class hotel, airport, and many modern amenities, it offers little to the tourist in search of a wilderness experience, but the huge island-studded expanses of **Inarijärvi** (Lake Inari), north of Ivalo, offer vast possibilities for wilderness exploration with its seemingly limitless boating, fishing, hiking, and hunting opportunities. It is a beautiful 40-kilometer (24-
8 mile) drive northwest from Ivalo, along the lakeshore, to **Inari.** The **Saame Museum,** on the village outskirts, covers all facets of Lapp culture. *Inari, tel. 9697/51107. Admission: FM12 adults, FM5 children. Open June–Aug. 10, daily 8–10, Aug. 11–31, daily 8–8; Sept. 1–20, weekdays 9–3:30.*

The **Inarin Porofarmi** is a working **reindeer farm** 14 kilometers
9 (9 miles) from Inari in the direction of **Kittilä.** The farm trains racing reindeer. You can drive a reindeer sled or be pulled on skis by reindeer. From here, take Rte. 79 back to Rovaniemi. *Kaksamajärvi, Inari, tel. 9697/56512.*

What to See and Do with Children

Lapland abounds with possibilities for children. **Gold panning** (*see above*) is an activity children of all ages enjoy; most of Finland's gold comes from the region. A seven-hour trip up the Lemmenjoki River from Ivalo can be arranged by **Lemmenjoen Lomamajat** (Lemmenjoki, tel. 9697/57103).

Tunturikeskus Kiilopää (*see* Lodging, *below*) has a multi-activity center for children, including snow-castle building, centrifuge sled, special ski tracks, and reindeer and dogsled trips; there are summer activities, too.

Santa Claus Village (Highway E4, tel. 960/62096), 10 kilometers (6 miles) north of Rovaniemi, is closed when Santa is abroad on December 25. Accessible by car and bus, it is the most famed attraction in the region, and apart from all Santa's paraphernalia, it is likely to be the only place where your children will be able to pet a reindeer—the ones you'll see in the wild are shy. There is also a working reindeer farm near Inari (*see* Exploring Lapland, *above*) that is fun for everyone.

Off the Beaten Track

There are hundreds of hiking and skiing trails throughout the north that you could travel for days without seeing another soul. Thirty kilometers (18 miles) north of Tankavarra is **Saariselkä,** which has a variety of accommodations and makes a central base from which to set off on a trip into the true wilderness. There are marked trails through forests and over fells, where nothing much has changed since the last Ice Age. More than 1,556 kilometers (965 square miles) of this magnificent area has been named the **Urho Kekkonen National Park.**

Shopping

Lapp **handicrafts** are not only useful but artistically attractive. Keep an eye out for the **camping knives** with beautifully carved bone or wood handles; products made from **reindeer pelts;** colorful **weavings** and **embroidered mittens** and **gloves; felt shoes;** and **birchbark baskets** and **rucksacks.**

Sports and Outdoor Activities

Bicycling There are numerous planned cycling "safaris" offered in Lapland; for details contact the Finnish Youth Hostel Association (*see*, Staying in Finland in Essential Information, *above*).

Canoeing From canoe trips on Lake Inari to a foray over the rapids of the Ivalojoki River, choices for canoers are bountiful. Contact the **Finnish Canoe Association** (Radiokatu 20, Helsinki, tel. 90/158–2363).

Fishing Fly-fishing and combined canoe/fishing trips are readily available. Contact **Lapland Travel Ltd.** (Maakuntakatu 10, Rovaniemi, tel. 960/16052).

Golf Lapland's uncrowded courses offer such unusual experiences as snow golf and midnight-sun golf. Contact the **Finnish Golf Union** (Radiokatu 20, Helsinki, tel. 90/1581).

Hiking Maps of marked trails through Lapland's national parks can be ordered through **Karttakeskus Pasila** (Opastinsilta 12, Helsinki, tel. 90/154–3150). For organized hiking tours for families with children, as well as beginners, contact **Suomen Ladun** (Matkapalvelu, Fabianinkatu 7, Helsinki, tel. 90/170–101), or **Tunturikeskus Kiilopää** (*see* Dining and Lodging in Ivalo/Kiilopää, *below*).

Skiing Cross-country and downhill skiing, although found at numerous locales, are best at **Saariselkä** resort, 30 kilometers (20 miles) south of Ivalo, as well as **Tunturikeskus Kiilopää** (*see* Hiking, *above*). Note that Finland does not have any very long downhill trails.

Swimming Lapland's waters are exceptionally clean and good for swimming. Many hotels have pools, and **Kylpylä Hotel** at Ivalo/Saasriselkä features an indoor waterworld.

Dining and Lodging

Inari/Saariselkä
Dining and Lodging

Hotelli Riekonlinna. The pinewood and blue-textile decor of this contemporary Lappish hotel, built in 1987 and renovated in 1990, goes well with its natural setting. It has a meeting center, a multi-sport complex, and it is only 30 minutes from Ivalo airport. The restaurant serves fresh local specialties. *Saariseläntie, 99830 Saariselkä, tel. 9697/81601. 124 rooms, 2 suites. Facilities: restaurant, cable TV, pools, aerobics room, squash and tennis courts, massage. AE, DC, MC, V. Expensive.*

Ivalo
Dining and Lodging

Hotelli Ivalo. Modern and well-equipped for business travelers and families, it hugs the Lake Inari shore. The lobby has marble floors and there's a brick fireplace in the sauna lounge. The rooms are spacious and modern, with burlap woven wallpaper, oatmeal carpets, lots of blond birchwood trimming; ask for a room by the lake. It is 10 kilometers (six miles) from Ivalo airport. The restaurant offers local and Continental fare. *Ivalontie 34, 99800, tel. 9697/21911. 62 rooms. Facilities: restaurant, saunas, TV, baby-sitting, playroom, pool. AE, MC, V. Moderate.*

Ivalo/Kiilopää
Dining and Lodging

Tunturikeskus Kiilopää. This "Fell Center" is in the midst of a hikers' and cross-country skiers' paradise in the Urho Kekkonen National Park district, 45 kilometers (30 miles) south of Ivalo Airport. Accommodation is in beautifully crafted log cabins, apartments, or individual hotel rooms, all of wood and stone; cabins have huge picture windows and individual fireplaces. The casual restaurant serves reindeer and other game entrées. *Arctic Hwy. 4, 99800 Ivalo, tel. 9697/87101. 99 rooms. Facilities: restaurant, disabled access, ski rentals and trails, exercise rooms, gift store, tennis courts, baby-sitting, rooms for nonsmokers. MC, V. Inexpensive–Moderate.*

Rovaniemi
Dining and Lodging

Rantasipi Pohjanhovi. Stretched along the shore of the Kemijoki River, this hotel combines modern amenities with quick access to the fells. The rooms are large with low ceilings and big windows. The decor varies from white-walled rooms with autumn-toned upholstery and wood trim to black walls with light upholstery—for those who have trouble sleeping during the days of the midnight sun. *Pohjanpuistikko 2, 96200, tel. 960/33711. 216 rooms, 4 suites. Facilities: restaurant, bar, café, casino, tennis courts, fishing, saunas, boat rental, conference rooms. DC, MC, V. Expensive.*

Hotel Gasthof. Set in the center of Rovaniemi, the Gasthof has rooms that are extremely homey and bright, with parquet floors and soft subtle lighting; the furniture is modern, but with soft edges, especially the waterbeds. The saunas have skylights and the restaurant features Russian cuisine. *Koskikatu 41, 96100, tel. 960/31199. 142 rooms. Facilities: restaurant, saunas, indoor pool, seminar room, TV. MC, V. Moderate.*

Hotelli Oppipoika. Attached to one of Finland's premier hotelier and restaurateur schools, good service and an especially fine restaurant are prime attractions here. The modern rooms have pressed birch paneling and large windows. *Korkalonkatu 33, 96200, tel. 960/20321. 40 rooms. Facilities: restaurant, TV, indoor pool, gymnasium, sauna, conference room. MC, V. Moderate.*

Lodging

Ammattioppilaitos Summer Hotel. Just 2 kilometers (1 mile) from the railroad station, this hotel features small, contemporary rooms with their own shower and toilet; guests can use the sauna, too. *Kairatie 75, 96190, tel. 960/392–651. 36 rooms. Facilities: sauna, TV in lounge. MC, V. Closed Aug. 7–May. Inexpensive.*

Saariselkä
Dining

Riekonkieppi. This family restaurant has regional specialties as well as a Continental menu. Try the reindeer, prepared in various ways according to the restaurant's weekly theme. The fresh-trout is another specialty, as is the beef in garlic. *Saariseläntie, tel. 9697/81711. Reservations accepted. Dress: casual. AE, DC, MC, V. Closed Oct., May. Moderate.*

Riekonlinna. The restaurant's name means Snow Grouse's Castle, and this gives away one of the culinary delights to be had here. For dessert, try the traditional Lappish delight, Arctic cloudberries with cream or ice cream. There are other game dishes in season and there are Continental specialties as well. *Saariseläntie, tel. 9697/81601. Reservations advised. Dress: casual. AE, DC, MC, V. Moderate.*

Dining and Lodging

Kylpylä Spa Hotel. Finished in 1990, this hotel features a luxurious spa center. The glass-domed swimming area is crammed with foliage, fountains, waterslides, wave machines, and a Jacuzzi; the solarium, saunas, and Turkish baths are adjacent. The guestrooms' decor includes pressed blond and dark wood, slate blue carpet, and textile bedspreads in muted blues, purples, and pinks. Moderately priced cabin accommodations also are available. *Lutontie, 99830 tel. 9697/81440. 37 rooms, 1 suite. Facilities: restaurant, ski rental. DC, MC, V. Expensive.*

Lodging

Kisapesä Sports Complex and Hotel. This vacation center is decidedly for the athletically inclined with comfortable modern accommodations in pinewood lodge rooms offering tunturi views. The cabins, when shared by more than two, are in the moderate price range. Note that the breakfast and spa facilities of the Kylpylä Spa Hotel (*see above*) are included in prices. Children four–11 stay at half price; children under four stay for free. It's near the bus station. *Lutontie, 99830, tel. 9697/81555. 37 rooms, 36 apartments. Facilities: tennis, squash, bodybuilding gym, aerobics, dance, weight-lifting equipment, table tennis, field sports, golf course, conference rooms, ski trails nearby, sports equipment rental. DC, V. Moderate–Expensive.*

Hotelli Riekonkieppi. The piney comfort of the rooms and the quietude of the setting make this a good Lapland base. Rooms are in lodges or individual cabins. *Lutontie, 99830, tel. 9697/81711. 104 rooms. Facilities: saunas, health center, tennis and squash courts, pools. AE, DC, MC, V. Closed Oct., May. Moderate.*

Tankavaara
Dining

Wanha Waskoolimies. In the tradition of the old gold prospectors, the rustic simplicity of the three rooms hewn from logs makes a pleasant change. Daily specials "Fish in the Gold Pan" and "Prospectors Beef" will give you a taste of simple Lapland fare; the restaurant has received the Lappi à la Carte gourmet citation. *Arctic Hwy. 4, tel. 9693/46158. Reservations accepted. Dress: casual. DC, MC, V. Moderate.*

Dining and Lodging

Hotel Korundi. In a quiet setting just off the Arctic Highway, this hotel has cozy, contemporary rooms for two to five people, each with its own fireplace. The restaurant is in a separate building. *99695 Tankavaara, tel. 9693/46158. 13 rooms (8 with shower), 1 suite. Facilities: saunas. DC, V. Moderate.*

The Lakelands

Introduction

Nearly 200,000 lakes dimple Finland's gentle topography, according to recent counts. Nearly every lake, big or small, is fringed with tiny cabins. The lake cabin is a Finnish institution, and until the recent advent of cheap package tours abroad, nearly every Finnish family spent their vacation in the same way—in their cabin on a lake.

In general, the larger towns of this region are much less appealing than the smaller lake locales. But Savonlinna stands out among the towns, not only for its stunning, waterbound views—it is hugged by gigantic Lake Saimaa—but for its cultural life. The month-long Savonlinna Opera Festival in July is one of Finland's greatest. The quality of the opera, ballet, drama, and instrumental performance here during the annual festival weeks is world-class. Most events are staged at the 14th-century Olavinlinna Castle, splendidly positioned just offshore.

For centuries the lakeland region was a buffer between the warring empires of Sweden and Russia. After visiting the people of the Lakelands, you should have a basic understanding of the Finnish word *sisu* (guts), a quality that has kept Finns independent, fiercely guarding their neutrality.

Important Addresses and Numbers

Tourist Information The main offices are in **Heinola** (Torikatu 8, tel. 910/58444), **Hämeenlinna** (Palokunnankatu 11, tel. 917/202–649), **Imatra** (Keskusasema, tel. 954/24666), **Joensuu/North Karelia** (Koskikatu 1, tel. 973/201–362), **Jyväskylä** (Vapaudenkatu 38, tel. 941/624–903), **Kajaani** (Kirkkokatu 24, tel. 986/155–517), **Kuopio** (Haapaniemenkatu 17, tel. 971/182–584), **Mikkeli** (Hallituskatu 3A, tel. 955/151–444), **Savonlinna** (Puistokatu 1, tel. 957/13492), and **Tampere** (Verkatehtaankatu 2, tel. 931/126–652).

Emergencies The nationwide emergency number is 000; it can be used to call police and ambulance. Local phone books, however, are the best sources of emergency information, including medical emergency numbers.

Late-night Pharmacies Late-night pharmacies are in larger towns only. Look under "Apteekki" in the phone book; listings include pharmacy hours.

Arriving and Departing by Plane

Airports in the Lakelands are at **Tampere, Mikkeli, Jyväskylä, Lappeenranta, Savonlinna, Kuopio,** and **Joensuu.** Flight time to the Savonlinna area from Helsinki is 40 minutes. All the airports are served by Finnair's domestic service, including the KarAir charter company.

Arriving and Departing by Car, Train, and Bus

By Car The region is vast so the route you choose will depend on your destination. However, Finland has few highways so your choice will be limited. Consult the **Finnish Automobile Association** or tourist boards for route advice.

The Joensuu–Kuopio–Lahti–Tampere road belt will transport you quickly from one major point to the next, but if you are going to be taking a lake vacation you usually will finish your journey on small roads. The last stretch to the *mökki* (cabin) may be unpaved. You will need a detailed map to find most mökkis, which tend to be tucked away in well-hidden spots.

By Train Trains run from Helsinki to Imatra, Lappeenranta, Kuopio, Jyväskylä, and Joensuu. There is sleeping-car service to Joensuu and Kuopio, and in summer only, to Savonlinna. From Helsinki to Savonlinna is a 5½-hour trip.

By Bus Buses are the best form of public transport into the region, with frequent connections to lake destinations from most major towns. From Helsinki to Savonlinna is a six-hour ride.

Guided Tours

Orientation The Lakelands are well served by tours, most of which employ boat service. Try some of these boat tours: **Western Lakeland Silverline and Poets' Way Tour** (Verkatehtaankatu 2, Tampere, tel. 931/124–803), **Western Lakeland and Lake Päijänne Tour** (Lake Päijänne Cruises, Pellonpää, Haapaniemi, tel. 941/618–885), and **Saimaa Lakeland and Lake Pielinen** (Roll Ships Ltd., Matkustajasatama, Kuopio, tel. 971/126–744). There are dozens of other boat-tour companies operating in the Lakelands; contact the **Finnish Tourist Board Head Office** (Suomen Matkatoimisto, Helsinki, tel. 90/403–011) or local tourist offices in the region for a complete list as well as details of routes.

Special-interest Avid canoers should contact the **Finnish Canoe Association** (Radiokatu 20, Helsinki, tel. 90/158–2363), which will arrange guided tours; canoes are rented at about FM60 per day. **Lomaväline Ky** (Seminaarinraitti 9, Heinola, tel. 910/56555) arranges numerous lakeland canoe tours ranging in length from two to 15 days.

Two agencies that do white-water trips and canoe safaris in the region are **Ikaalinen Tourist Service** (Ikaalinen, tel. 933/801–355) and **Lieksan Matkailu Oy** (Pielisentie 7, Lieksa, tel. 975/20500).

Many sailing schools operate in the lakes region, with courses for sailors of all levels. Contact either the **Finnish Yachting Association** (Radiokatu 20, Helsinki, tel. 90/1581) or the **Nautic Center** (Itälahdenkatu 9, Helsinki, tel. 90/9670–271).

Nature-photography and fishing tours in North Karelia, are run by **United Travel Limited** (Malminkatu 34, Helsinki, tel. 90/693–1477); United also does architecture tours; agriculture tours; and culture-, nature- and sports-oriented tours.

Five- to six-day horseback-riding holidays are set up by **Messilän Lomakeskus** (tel. 918/86011), 7 kilometers (4 miles) from downtown Lahti. The fees include full board and a host of other sporting activities.

Exploring the Lakelands

Numbers in the margin correspond with points of interest on the Lakelands map.

Savonlinna The center of **Savonlinna** is a series of islands linked by bridges.
1 First, stop in at the tourist office for information; then cross the bridge east to the open-air market that flourishes alongside the main passenger quay. It's from here that you can catch the boat to Kuopio. In days when waterborne traffic was the major form of transportation, Savonlinna was the central hub of the passenger fleet serving Saimaa, the largest lake system in Europe. Now the lake traffic is dominated by cruise and sightseeing boats, but the quayside still bustles with arrivals and departures every summer morning and evening.

A 10-minute stroll from the quay to the southeast brings you to Savonlinna's most famous sight, the castle of **Olavinlinna.** First

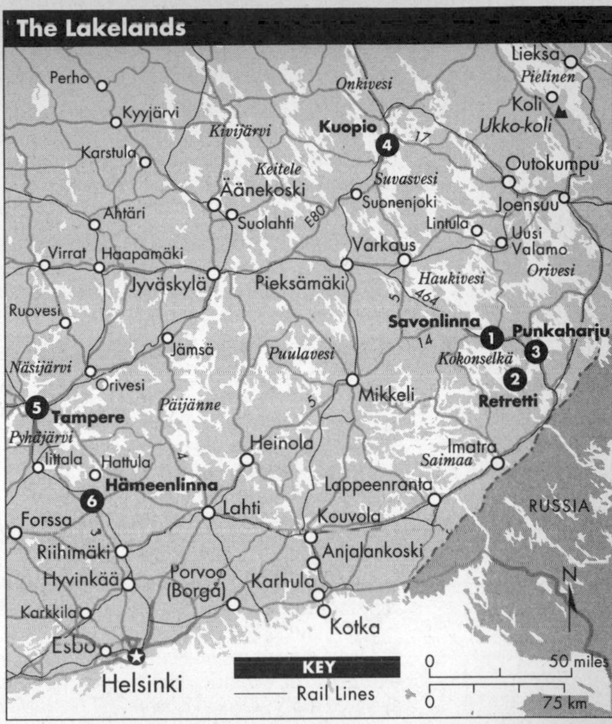

built in 1475 to protect Finland's eastern border, the castle retains its medieval character and is one of Scandinavia's best-preserved historic monuments. Still surrounded by water that once formed part of its defensive strength, the fortress rises majestically out of the lake. The International Opera Festival is held in the courtyard each July. The combination of music and setting is spellbinding. You will need to make reservations well in advance (tel. 957/514–700), both for tickets and hotel rooms, since Savonlinna becomes a mecca for music lovers. And music is not the only activity; arts and crafts are also strongly featured in exhibits around town. *Castle. Admission: FM15 adults, FM7 children; includes a guided tour. Open June–Aug., daily 9–5; Sept.–May, daily 10–3.*

Close to the castle is the 19th-century steam schooner, *Salama*, which houses an excellent museum on the history of lake traffic, including the fascinating floating timber trains that are still a common sight on Saimaa today. *Admission: FM10 adults, FM5 children. Open mid-June–mid-Aug., daily 10–8; off-season hours vary, check locally.*

2 The most popular excursion from Savonlinna is to **Retretti.** You can take either a 2-hour boat ride or a 30-minute, 29-kilometer (18-mile) bus trip. The journey by bus takes you along the 8-
3 kilometer (5-mile) ridge of **Punkaharju.** This amazing ridge of pine-covered rocks, which rises out of the water and separates the lakes on either side, predates the Ice Age. At times it narrows to only 25 feet, yet it still manages to accommodate a road and train tracks. Retretti itself is a modern art complex of unique design, which includes a new cavern section built into

Punkaharju ridge. It's also a magnificent setting for concerts in summer. *Admission: FM50 adults, FM45 senior citizens and students, FM20 children. Open summer, daily 10–8.*

Kuopio 4

The 12-hour boat trip from Savonlinna to **Kuopio** is probably the best opportunity you'll get to feel the soul of the Finnish Lakelands. Meals are available on board. The boat arrives at Kuopio passenger harbor, where you'll find a small evening market in action daily from 3 to 10.

The Kuopio tourist office is located close to the **Tori** (marketplace). The Tori should be one of the places you visit first, for it is one of the most colorful outdoor markets in Finland. *Open weekdays 7–3, Sat. 7–2.*

The **Orthodox Church Museum** has one of the most interesting and unusual collections of its kind in the world. When Karelia was ceded to the Soviet Union after World War II, the religious art was taken out of the monasteries and brought to Kuopio. The collection is eclectic and, of its type, one of the rarest in the world. *Karjalankatu 1, Kuopio, tel. 971/118–818. Open Tues.–Sun. 10–4.*

Visitors who are fascinated by the treasures in the museum will want to visit the Orthodox convent of Lintula and the **Monastery of Valamo.** The monastery is a center for Russian Orthodox religious and cultural life in Finland. The precious 18th-century icons and sacred objects are housed in the main church and in the icon conservation center. The Orthodox library is the most extensive in Finland and is open to visitors. Church services are held daily. *Uusi-Valamo, tel. 972/61911 (972/61959 for hotel reservations). Guided tours: FM15 adults, FM5 children. Open daily 10–6.*

The convent of Lintula can be reached by boat from Valamo, or you can visit both the convent and the monastery by boat on scenic day excursions from Kuopio, which run from June 10 through August 13. Tickets, available from the tourist office, cost FM170 for adults and FM85 for children.

Puijo Tower is best visited at sunset, when the lakes shimmer with reflected light. The slender tower is located 3 kilometers (2 miles) northwest of Kuopio. It has two observation decks and a revolving restaurant on top where you can enjoy the marvelous views. *Open in summer 8 AM–11 PM.*

Tampere 5

The 320-kilometer (192-mile) journey from Kuopio to **Tampere** will take four to five hours, whether you travel by car or bus. The train ride from Helsinki to Tampere takes about two hours.

Almost every guide will inform you that Tampere, the country's second largest city, is Finland's Pittsburgh. However, the resemblance begins and ends with the concentrated presence here of industry—the settings themselves have little in common.

From about the year 1000, this part of Finland was a base from which traders and hunters set out on their expeditions to northern Finland and even to Lapland. But it was not until 1779 that a Swedish king actually founded Tampere. Forty-one years later, Scotsman James Finlayson came to the infant city and established a factory for spinning cotton. This was perhaps the beginning of "big business" in Finland. The firm of

Finlayson exists today and is still one of the country's leading industrial enterprises.

Artful location is the secret of Tampere's many factories. An isthmus little more than half a mile wide at its narrowest point separates the lakes Näsijärvi and Pyhäjärvi, and at one spot the Tammerkoski Rapids provide an outlet for the waters of one to cascade through to the other. Called the "Mother of Tampere," these rapids provide the power on which the town's livelihood depends. Their natural beauty has been preserved in spite of the factories on either bank, and the well-designed public buildings of the city grouped around them enhance their general effect. Also in the heart of town is **Hämeensilta Bridge,** with its four statues by the well-known Finnish sculptor Wäinö Aaltonen.

Close to the Hämeensilta bridge, near the high-rise Hotel Ilves, are some warehouses that have been restored as shops and boutiques. Nearby, at Verkatehtaankatu 2, is the city tourist office.

Parts of the ridge of **Pyynikki** separating the two lakes form a natural park, including the Särkänniemi peninsula, about a 20-minute walk northwest of the city center. On the way there, visit one of Tampere's best small museums, **The Workers' Museum of Amuri.** It consists of a block of old timber houses, with descriptions and illustrations of how the original tenants lived; it is so well done that you half expect them to return at any minute. *Makasiininkatu 12. Admission: FM10 adults, FM3 children. Open June–early Oct., Tues.–Sun. noon–6.*

At Särkänniemi is Finland's tallest structure, the 560-foot **Nasinnuela Observation Tower** (open daily 10–8). There is an observatory on top, as well as a revolving restaurant. The views are magnificent, commanding the lake, forest, and town. The contrast between the industrial maze of Tampere at your feet and the serenity of the lakes stretching out to meet the horizon is unforgettable.

The same building complex houses the first planetarium in Scandinavia and a well-planned aquarium, which includes a separate dolphinarium. Near this complex is another striking example of Finnish architecture, the **Sarah Hildén Art Museum,** where the works of modern Finnish and international artists (including Miro, Leger, Picasso, and Chagall) are on display. *Joint admission: FM60 adults, FM40 children; Hildén Museum only: FM6 adults, FM1 children. Open daily 11–6.*

At the foot of the Pyynikki Ridge is the **Pyynikki Open Air Theater,** with a revolving auditorium that can be moved, even with a full load of spectators, to face any one of the sets.

On the east side of the town is the modern **Kaleva Church.** What may appear from the outside to be a grain elevator is in fact, as seen from the interior, a soaring monument to space and light. *Open daily 10–6.*

Most buildings in Tampere, including the cathedral, are comparatively modern. However, though the cathedral was built only in 1907, it is worth a visit to see some of the best-known masterpieces of Finnish art, including Magnus Enckell's frescoes, *The Resurrection,* and two works by Hugo Simberg, *Wounded Angel* and *Garden of Death.*

It was in Tampere that Lenin and Stalin first met, and this fateful occasion is commemorated with displays of photos and mementoes in the **Lenin Museum.** *Hallituskatsu 19. Admission: FM6 adults, FM2 children. Open Tues.–Sat. 11–3, Sun. 11–4.*

Just outside of town in Kaukajärvi, about 7 kilometers (4 miles) away, is the charming **Haihara Doll Museum.** The collection features dolls from different parts of the world. *Admission: FM15 adults, FM5 children. Open Apr. 15–Sept., daily noon–6; Oct.–Nov. and mid-Feb.–Mar., Sun. noon–4.*

One of the most popular excursions from Tampere is the **Poet's Way** boat tour along Lake Näsijärvi. The boat passes through the agricultural parish of Ruovesi, where J. L. Runeberg, Finland's national poet, used to live. Shortly before the boat docks at Virrat, you'll pass through the straights of Visuvesi, where many artists and writers spend their summers. *Finnish Silverline and Poet's Way, Verkatehtaankatu 2, 33100 Tampere, tel. 931/124–804. Round-trip fare: FM236.*

Not far north of Virrat is **Ahtari,** where Finland's first wildlife park has been established in a beautiful setting, with a holiday village, a good hotel, and recreation facilities.

Hämeenlinna
6

The Silverline's white motor ships leave Tampere for **Hämeenlinna** from the Laukontori terminal. If you're traveling by car, take Highway 3 and stop en route at the famous **Iittala Glassworks,** which offers guided tours and has a museum and shop. The magnificent glass is produced by top designers, and the "seconds" are bargains you won't find elsewhere. *Open Sept.–Apr., daily 9–6; May–Aug., daily 9–8. Guided tours weekdays at 11, 1, and 3.*

Hämeenlinna's secondary school has educated many famous Finns, among them composer Jean Sibelius (1865–1957). The only surviving timber house in the town center is the **birthplace of Sibelius,** a modest dwelling built in 1834. Here you can listen to tapes of his music and see the harmonium he played when he was a child. *Hallituskatu 11. Admission: FM3 adults, FM2 children. Open May–Aug., daily 10–4; Sept.–Apr., weekdays and Sun. noon–4.*

The much-altered medieval **Häme Castle,** on the lakeshore half a mile north of the town center, doesn't compare with Savonlinna's, but it has seen a lot of action in its time and has been used as a granary and a prison. *Admission: FM14 adults, FM7 children. Open May–Aug., daily 10–6; Sept.–Apr., daily 10–4.*

Hattula Church, 6 kilometers (3½ miles) to the north, is the most famous of Finland's medieval churches. The interior is a fresco gallery of biblical scenes whose vicious little devils and soulful saints are as clear and fresh as when they were first painted around 1510. There is a regular bus service from the town center. *Admission: FM10 adults, FM5 children. Open May 7–31, daily 9–6; June–Aug. 15, daily 10–6; Aug. 16–Sept. 3, daily noon–4.*

Rail and bus schedules to Helsinki are frequent. If you're traveling by car, take Highway 3. As you pass by **Riihimäki,** you'll see signs to the **Finnish Glass Museum.** Follow them! It's an outstanding display of the history of glass from early Egyptian times to the present, beautifully arranged in an old glass factory. *Admission: FM8 adults, FM4 children. Open Apr.–Sept., Tues.–Sun. 10–6.*

What to See and Do with Children

In **Outokumpu,** directly north of Savonlinna, is the **Vuoren Peikonmaa** (Land of the Mountain Troll) with an amusement park and mining museum and mineral exhibition. (For information, tel. 973/54795.)

Another good option is the **Messilä Summerland Children's Funpark** (near Lahti, tel. 918/86011) at **Hollola.**

The Retretti Art Center at Punkaharju near Savonlinna has over 40 different indoor and outdoor activities scheduled for children throughout the summer.

In **Mikkeli,** the **Visulahti Tourist Center,** 5 kilometers (3 miles) from town includes a waxworks and "Miniland"—a scale-model display of traditional buildings—and an amusement park with life-size models of prehistoric animals. Also near Mikkeli, the **Anja Hänninen Arboretum** (10 kilometers/6 miles from town) has extensive outdoor gardens as well as a small menagerie; get exact directions and/or bus information from the Visulahti Tourist office.

Shopping

Wild mushrooms and berries are abundant in this region and Finns make use of all of them. The various **preserves**—jams, compotes, and sauces included—are all delicacies and make good gifts; Finns eat them with thin pancakes.

Many towns in this region have **textile** workshops or factories, called *Tekstiilitehdas* or *Tekstiilimyymälä,* featuring woven **wall hangings** and **rya rugs** (*ryijy* in Finnish). **Ceramics** (*Keramiikkamyymälä*) works selling dishes and pottery are also scattered throughout the region; the soil here produces a rich clay.

If you want to go to the source of one of Finland's biggest manufacturers of **cross-country skis,** you'll find it right off Hartola's main street, at **Peltosen Suksitehdas** (Peltonen Ski Factory).

Many lake towns have traditional **outdoor markets,** usually on Saturdays. Most sell produce. In the autumn you'll find slightly larger markets when towns have their September fairs. These vestiges of harvest festivals are now mostly excuses to hold fun fairs and consume coffee and doughnuts.

Sports and Outdoor Activities

Canoeing The Finlandia Canoeing Relay is held in the Päijänne Lakes Region in the first half of June. Lasting five full days, it is a 545-kilometer (350-mile) endurance test and the race goes on day and night. Accommodations and suggestions for viewing spots are available from **Kymen Matkailu ry** (Varuskuntakatu 11, 45100 Kouvola, tel. 951/21763) (*see* Special-interest Tours, *above).*

Golf If you want to play on an 18-hole lakeside course, ask at Hämeenlinna's **Hotel Vaakuna** (Possentie 7, 13200 Hämeenlinna, tel. 917/5831).

Sailing Saimaa Sailing Oy has four-day courses for groups of four to five that are worked into all-inclusive vacation packages. The base is the handsome, historic coastal town of **Lappeenranta.** Contact **Saimaa Sailing** (Kimpisenkatu 22, Lappeenranta, tel. 953/18560). For other areas contact the **Finnish Yachting Association** (Radiokatu 29, Helsinki, tel. 90/1581). (*See* Special-interest Tours, *above.*) Europe's biggest inland sailing race, the Päijänne Regatta, takes place yearly in July. Details from the Finnish Yachting Association.

Windsurfing There are numerous windsurfing centers on the shores of Lakes Saimaa and Paijanne. Contact the **Finnish Windsurfing Association** (Tuohimäentie 86B, Helsinki, tel. 90/742–550).

Dining and Lodging

For details and price category definitions, *see* Dining in Essential information, *above.* Highly recommended establishments are indicated by a star ★.

Hämeenlinna
Dining

Hämeenlinna. Situated on the lake shore half a mile from the town center, Hämeenlinna (Castle) is sometimes the setting for medieval banquets. It also has a pleasant coffee house. *Linnantie 6, tel. 917/25928. Reservations required for banquets. AE, DC, MC, V. Restaurant: Expensive; coffee house: Moderate.*

Piiparkakkutalo. Located in a renovated old timber building, Piiparkakkutalo has a restaurant upstairs, a tavern downstairs. The menu offers fine Finnish fare. *Kirkkorinne 2, tel. 917/121–606. Reservations advised. AE, MC, V. Moderate.*

Lodging

★ **Rantasipi Aulanko.** One of Finland's top hotels sits on the lakeshore in a beautifully landscaped park 6.4 kilometers (2 miles) from town. *Aulanko, tel. 917/29521. 216 rooms. Facilities: nightclub, saunas, pool, squash, tennis, golf, riding, boating, swimming beach, tax-free shop. AE, DC, MC, V. Very Expensive (Moderate in July).*

Kuopio
Dining

Mustalammas. Located near the passenger harbor, Mustalammas has been attractively adapted from a beer cellar and features steaks and basic fish dishes. *Satamakatu 4, tel. 971/123–494. Reservations advised. AE, DC, MC, V. Expensive.*

Sampo. Situated in the town center, Sampo specializes in vendace *(muikku),* a kind of whitefish. Try the smoked variety. The atmosphere is unpretentious and lively. *Kauppakatu 13, tel. 971/114–677. MC, V. Inexpensive.*

Lodging

Rauhalahti. About 4.8 kilometers (3 miles) from the town center, Rauhalahti is set near the lakeshore and has a number of amenities catering to sportsmen and families. The hotel has three restaurants, including the tavern-style Vanha Apteekkari—a local favorite. *Katiskaniementie 8, tel. 971/311–700. 126 rooms. Facilities: saunas, swimming pool, solarium, gymnasium, children's playroom, disco, tennis, horseback riding, squash, boat rental. AE, DC, MC, V. Expensive.*

Rivoli. Completed in 1987, the Rivoli is the most modern and best equipped of local hotels. It has all the advantages of a lakefront location and is close to the center of town. *Satamakatu 1, tel. 971/195–111. 141 rooms. Facilities: sauna, swimming pool, Jacuzzi, solarium, tennis, boat rental. AE, DC, MC, V. Expensive.*

Sport Hotel Puijo. Located next to Puijo Tower, the Sport Hotel Puijo is only four years old but is built in the traditional timber style. The rooms are large and very quiet. *Puijo, tel. 971/114–841. 20 rooms. Facilities: saunas. AE, DC, MC, V. Moderate.*

Savonlinna
Dining

Rauhalinna. This romantic turn-of-the-century timber villa was built by a general in the Imperial Russian Army. From town it's 16 kilometers (10 miles) by road, 40 minutes by boat. Both food and atmosphere are old Russian, but some Finnish specialties are also available. *Lehtiniemi, tel. 957/523–119. Reservations required during festival season. AE, DC, MC, V. Closed Sept.–May. Expensive.*

Snellman. This small 1920s-style mansion is in the center of town. Meals are served against a quiet background of classical music. *Olavinkatu 31, tel. 957/13104. Reservations advised. AE, DC, MC, V. Expensive; Moderate lunch upstairs.*

Majakka. Centrally located, Majakka goes in for home cooking and a family atmosphere. *Satamakatu 11, tel. 957/21456. Reservations required during festival season. AE, DC, MC, V. Moderate.*

San Martin. A steak house with a pleasant open courtyard in summer. *Olavinkatu 46, tel. 957/13004. AE, DC, MC, V. Moderate.*

Musta Pässi. Located near the bus station, Musta Pässi serves fresh fish, meatballs, potatoes, and other homemade dishes in a tavern setting. *Tulliportinkatu 2, tel. 957/22228. AE, MC, V. Inexpensive.*

Lodging

Casino Spa. Built in the 1960s and renovated in 1986, the Casino Spa has a restful lakeside location on an island linked by a pedestrian bridge to the center of town. *Klypylaitoksentie, Kasinonsaari, tel. 957/22864. 79 rooms. Facilities: nightclub, saunas, pool, marina, spa treatment. AE, DC, MC, V. Expensive.*

Tott. This is an old favorite, located in the downtown area opposite the passenger harbor. It was completely renovated in 1987. *Satamakatu 1, tel. 957/514–500. 60 rooms. Facilities: nightclub, saunas, pool. AE, DC, MC, V. Expensive (Very Expensive in July).*

Seurahuone. This old town house is located near the market and passenger harbor. A new extension opened in 1989. Some older rooms are small. *Kauppatori 4, tel. 957/5731. 84 rooms. Facilities: disco, saunas. AE, DC, MC, V. Moderate.*

Vuoilinna Summer Hotel. Guests at this modern hotel use the facilities, including the restaurant, of the nearby Casino Spa Hotel. *Kasinonsaari, tel. 957/24908. 160 rooms, with shower for every 2 rooms. AE, DC, MC, V. Closed Sept.–May. Inexpensive (Moderate in July).*

Tampere
Dining

Finlayson Palatsi. Set in its own gardens about 1 kilometer (½ mile) from the town center, this elegant restaurant still has many of the original furnishings from the turn of the century, when it was a private residence. *Kuninkaankatu 1, tel. 931/125–905. Reservations advised. AE, DC, MC, V. Very Expensive.*

Natalie. Russian in atmosphere, cuisine, and background music, Natalie is housed in the old Workers' Theater near the center of town. *Hallituskatu 19, tel. 931/32040. Reservations advised. AE, DC, MC, V. Moderate.*

Salud. Salud has a well-earned reputation for Spanish specialties, though it also features some Finnish dishes. *Otava-*

lankatu 10, tel. 931/35996. Reservations advised. AE, DC, MC, V. Closed weekends in July. Moderate.

Silakka. Although its atmosphere is casual and unpretentious, Silakka has earned a great reputation for its Finnish fish specialties. *Vuolteenkatu 20, tel. 931/149–740. DC, MC, V. Closed Sun. in summer. Inexpensive.*

Lodging **Ilves.** The city's newest hotel soars above a newly gentrified area of old warehouses near the city center. It is favored by Americans. *Hatanpäänvaltatie 1, tel. 931/121–212. 336 rooms. Facilities: nightclub, saunas, pool, Jacuzzi, rooms for nonsmokers, nightclub. AE, DC, MC, V. Very Expensive.*

Cumulus. Overlooking the tamed rapids of Tammerkoski, Cumulus is central and modern. The Finnair terminal is in the same building. *Koskikatu 5, tel. 931/35500. 230 rooms with shower. Facilities: nightclub, saunas, pool. AE, DC, MC, V. Expensive.*

Domus Summer Hotel. About 1.6 kilometers (1 mile) from the center of town, in the Kaleva district, this hotel is a good value. *Pellervonkatu 9, tel. 931/550–000. 200 rooms, 85 with shower. Facilities: disco, saunas, pool. MC, V. Closed Sept.–May. Inexpensive.*

The Arts and Nightlife

The Arts These are limited in the Lakelands to the museums and galleries in the larger towns, and the occasional visiting exhibition or act in the summer. For more information, consult local tourist boards.

Nightlife Hotels and restaurants usually serve alcohol until midnight, and almost every town has its basic tavern or pub. In the larger towns, look for such chain restaurant establishments as **Rosso** and **HyvaYstava,** for a relaxed eating and drinking atmosphere.

4 Iceland

Introduction

by Jon Asgeir Sigurðsson

Born and educated in Iceland, Jon Sigurðsson is currently U.S. correspondent for Icelandic Broadcasting.

On the highway from Keflavík Airport into Iceland's capital, Reykjavík, the traveler is met by an eerie moonscape under a steel-gray sky. The flat terrain is barely covered by its thin scalp of luminescent green moss. Here and there the earth's floor splits open and narrow gasps of steam hiss forth. In lieu of trees, an occasional scrawny shrub clings to a rock outcropping. The very air smells different—sulphurous and wet—yet it's so clear here you can see for miles.

Welcome to Iceland, one of the most dramatic natural spectacles on this planet. It is a land of dazzling white glaciers and rugged black lava fields, of red sulfur, blue hot springs, and green, green valleys. This vast North Atlantic island offers insight into the ferocious powers of nature, ranging from the still-glowing lava of the Vestmannaeyjar volcanic eruption in 1973 to the chilling splendor of the Vatnajökull glacier. Generally the country is barren, with hardly a tree to be seen, but its few birches, wildflowers, and delicate vegetation are all the more lovely in contrast. Contrary to the country's foreboding name, the climate is surprisingly mild.

Located so far north—parts of the country lie inside the Arctic Circle—Iceland has the usual Scandinavian long hours of darkness in winter. This may be why Icelanders are such good chess players (Iceland played host to the memorable Fisher-Spassky chess match of 1972). These long nights may also explain why, per capita, more books are written, printed, bought, and read in Iceland than anywhere else in the world.

Another reason for this near-universal literacy may be Iceland's long tradition of participatory democracy, dating to AD 930, when the first parliament met at Þingvellír. Today it's a modern Nordic (most would find the term "Scandinavian" too limited) society with a well-developed social welfare system. Women have a unique measure of equality: Because children are given a surname created from their father's first name, Magnús, son of Svein, becomes Magnús Sveinsson, while Guðrún, daughter of Pétur, becomes Guðrún Pétursdóttir, and Guðrún keeps her maiden name even after she marries, though her children will bear her husband's name. Perhaps there is no connection, but it is interesting to note that Iceland also elected in 1980 the first woman president in Europe, Vigdís Finnbogadóttir.

Iceland was settled by Vikings and Celts, over a thousand years ago (the first Norse settlers arrived in AD 874, but there is some evidence that Irish monks landed even earlier). The Norse Sagas, describing the adventures of life in the Viking Era, were written by Icelanders, and modern Icelandic is remarkably close to medieval Norwegian. The Norsemen brought to the island sturdy ponies, robust cattle, and Celtic slaves, which is why you'll see so many redheads here today. These Irish settlers told their own stories, of *huldufólk*—humanlike supernatural elves—and even today some roads and construction projects may be changed to accommodate rocks and ridges where elves are thought to reside.

Iceland is the westernmost outpost of Europe, 800 kilometers (500 miles) from the nearest European landfall (in Scotland) and nearly 1,600 kilometers (1,000 miles) from Copenhagen, its administrative capital during Danish rule, from 1380 to 1944. Stranded in the middle of the North Atlantic, where the warm Gulf Stream from the south confronts the icy Arctic currents from the north, it also straddles the mid-Atlantic ridge where edges of two tectonic plates, the North American and the European, meet. As the plates slowly move apart, they create the volcanic activity by which Iceland is still being formed. (There has been an eruption in Iceland on an average of every five years during the last few centuries, the latest being in the Hekla volcano in January 1991.) Beneath the snowy glaciers are fires that heat hot springs and geysers all over the island, and the resourceful Icelanders have harnessed that thermal energy to heat their homes, power their industry, and warm their outdoor swimming pools year-round. Swift glacial rivers produce plentiful hydroelectricity.

Over 80% of the island's 65,000 square kilometers (16,000 square miles) remains uninhabited, and much of it is not arable. Surrounded by the sea, the Icelanders have become great fishermen, but most other foodstuffs and goods must be imported, adding to a cost of living that is high by any standard. For the last four decades the country was plagued by Europe's highest inflation rate, and though inflation was controlled by 1990, recession has hit the economy for a couple of years. Hotel and restaurant prices are relatively high, but you can always find a number of inexpensive alternatives for lodging, food, and travel—provided you look.

While the cosmopolitan capital, Reykjavík, is a good place to start your visit, any traveler who wants to know Iceland should venture out into the countryside, where rainbow-arched waterfalls drop from heath-covered mountains with great spiked ridges and snowcapped peaks. Climb mountains, ford rivers, watch birds, catch trout or salmon, even tend sheep and cattle at a typical Icelandic farm. The ocean here is always too cold for swimming, but the country is full of hot springs and naturally heated pools where Icelanders from all walks of life—from the prime minister on down—congregate for a soak or a swim all year round.

Before You Go

Government Tourist Offices

The main office of the **Icelandic Tourist Board** is at Gimli, Lækjagata 3, straeti, 101 Reykjavík (tel. 1/27488). For serious exploring or hiking, you can obtain good up-to-date maps from **Landmælingar Íslands** (the Icelandic Geodetic Survey) at Laugavegi 178, 105 Reykjavík (tel. 1/680999).

In the United States **Icelandic Tourist Board,** 655 3rd Ave., New York, NY 10017, tel. 212/949–2333, fax 212/983–5260.

In the United Kingdom **Icelandic Tourist Board,** 172 Tottenham Court Rd., 3rd floor, London W1P 9LG, tel. 017/388–5599.

When to Go

The best time to visit is in June, July, and August, since most travel services are geared to this period. During these months there is perpetual daylight—in Reykjavík the sun dips below the horizon for only a couple of twilight hours, and in the northernmost reaches of the island the sun never sets. The main drawbacks are that this is when everybody else is traveling—both Icelanders on vacation and foreigners visiting—and prices are higher.

If you visit in the winter, be prepared for long hours of darkness. In December, Iceland enjoys daylight for only three hours daily, but as a consolation you can watch a spectacular show of the aurora borealis, the northern lights.

Climate Considering how far north Iceland is, it has a surprisingly temperate climate—Reykjavík's average winter temperature is one degree Fahrenheit *above* that of New York. The warm Gulf Stream flows past the western and southern coasts, although this is counteracted by the Arctic current that circles along the northern and eastern coasts. As a result, conditions are very changeable and you can get a sampling of all types of weather in a single afternoon. Paradoxically, the climate is more stable in the north, with less rain and wind, and in summer it's often warmer there. June, July, and August can be expected to be partly sunny, breezy, with intermittent light showers. Summer temperatures seldom rise above 70°F (20°C). Winters can be windy and there is often rain or snow, which, compounded with the long hours of darkness, can be dismal. The following are average daily maximum and minimum temperatures for Reykjavík.

Jan.	36F	2C	**May**	50F	10C	**Sept.**	52F	11C
	28	-2		39	4		43	6
Feb.	37F	3C	**June**	54F	12C	**Oct.**	45F	7C
	28	-2		45	7		37	3
Mar.	39F	4C	**July**	57F	14C	**Nov.**	39F	4C
	30	-1		48	9		32	0
Apr.	43F	6C	**Aug.**	57F	14C	**Dec.**	36F	2C
	34	1		46	8		28	-2

Festivals and Seasonal Events

Shops, museums, and businesses are closed on national holidays: Maundy Thursday (April 16), Good Friday (April 17), Easter Monday (April 20), First Summerday (April 23), Labor Day (May 1), Ascension Day (May 28), Whitsun Monday (June 8), National Day (June 17), bank holiday (August 3), Christmas Day (December 25), Boxing Day (December 26), and New Year's Day.

January 24–mid-February: Þorri Banquets around the country feature medieval-style Icelandic food and drinks.
April 16–20: Easter Weekend sees skiing competitions in Akureyri and Isafjordur.
June: Reykjavík Arts Festival, a biennial event, brings summer music, theater, dance, and other events to the capital.
June 7: Sjómannadagur (Seamen's Day) is celebrated in many coastal towns; in Reykjavík there are rowing and swimming competitions, speeches, and an awards ceremony.
June 17: Iceland National Day is a nationwide party, with parades and outdoor dancing downtown in Reykjavík, Akureyri, and other towns.

August 1–3: Summer Weekend draws large crowds for outdoor celebrations throughout the country.
August 1–3: Þjóðhátið 1874 (Independence Festival) is celebrated in Vestmannaeyjar (the Westmann Islands).
August: Reykjavík Marathon sends world-class distance runners on their annual race around the city.

What to Pack

Clothing If you plan to hike in the mountains, be prepared for cooler temperatures—pack warm clothes and rainwear. Regular clothing will do anywhere in the lowlands. For hiking and extended walks, bring at least two pairs of water-resistant walking shoes. Rain comes mostly in drizzles or light showers, but it does not take long to soak a pair of sneakers when walking off the road. Umbrellas never caught on in breezy Iceland, but by all means bring a good waterproof coat and a sweater (or buy one of Iceland's famous hand-knit wool sweaters when you arrive).

Miscellaneous The standard current in Iceland is 220V (50 cycles) AC. Most hotels have built-in hair dryers. If you need a plug adapter or converter, buy it before leaving home.

Taking Money Abroad

You can bring in any amount of foreign currency and exchange it at any Icelandic bank, so don't go to the trouble of obtaining Icelandic currency before you go. Most hotels, shops, and restaurants accept common European currencies and U.S. dollars, but they may round off the daily exchange rate. VISA and MasterCard/Eurocard are widely accepted in Iceland. Most banks, hotels, and restaurants also accept other popular credit cards such as American Express and Diners Club. Gas stations do not accept credit cards.

Icelandic Currency

The unit of currency in Iceland is the króna (IKR). Icelandic notes come in denominations of IKr100, 500, 1,000, and 5,000. Coins are IKr1, 5, 10, and 50. The króna is divided into 100 *aurar*, which are as good as worthless. Icelandic money can be difficult to exchange back home, so exchange any last krónas you are carrying at the departure terminal in Keflavík.

The exchange rate of the króna has remained remarkably stable during the last three years, averaging IKr56 to the dollar, IKr103 to the pound sterling, and IKr53 to the Canadian dollar.

What It Will Cost

Until 1990 Iceland had the highest inflation rate in Europe, but prices are slowly coming down now. Iceland is still an expensive destination, but the effect can often be softened by shopping around. For instance, a cup of coffee costs IKr100 at a cafeteria but IKr120 at a fine restaurant. An imported German beer or Icelandic brew costs IKr120–150 at the state monopoly store (ÁTVR), but IKr420 at a bar. A can of soda costs IKr67 at the grocery, IKr150 at a restaurant or bar. A ready-made sandwich at the grocery costs IKr160. A short taxi ride within Reykjavík costs IKr500. A movie ticket costs IKr400.

Hotels and restaurants cost up to 50% more in Reykjavík than elsewhere in the country.

Taxes A 24.5% value-added tax (VAT) applies to most goods and services, with the exception of lodging and transportation. Usually the VAT is included in a price; if not, that fact must be explicitly stated.

On domestic flights and on flights to Greenland and the Faroe Islands, the airport tax is IKr150; for all other destinations the international departure tax is IKr1,150, payable when buying the ticket.

Passports and Visas

U.S., Canadian, and British citizens are required to have a valid passport to enter Iceland for a stay of up to three months. Visas and health certificates are not required.

U.S. Citizens For more information, contact the **Embassy of Iceland** (2022 Connecticut Ave. NW, Washington, DC 20008, tel. 202/265–6653).

British Citizens Contact the **Embassy of Iceland** (1 Eaton Terr., London SW1 W8EY, tel. 017/730–5131).

Canadian Citizens Contact the **Consulate General of Iceland** (200 Augusta Dr., Winnipeg, Manitoba R3T 4G5, tel. 204/275–0878).

Customs

On Arrival Tourists can bring in six liters of beer, one liter of beverages with an alcohol content of up to 21%, one liter of liquor not exceeding 47% alcohol, and 200 cigarettes. Laws regarding drugs are strictly enforced. Iceland also stringently prohibits any imports of fresh meat, poultry, or other farm produce, as well as live animals.

On Departure *See* Customs and Duties in Chapter 1.

Language

The official language is Icelandic, a highly inflected Germanic tongue, brought to the country by early Norse settlers. It has changed little over the centuries, enabling Icelanders to read the ancient manuscripts of the Sagas without difficulty. English is the second language, widely spoken and understood, particularly by the young.

The Icelandic alphabet contains two unique letters—þ, pronounced like the *th* in thin, and ð, pronounced like the *th* in leather.

Staying Healthy

Iceland has one of the best health care services in the world. All Icelandic physicians further their education in some specialty, usually at a teaching hospital abroad. There are hospitals in all corners of the island, and doctors in most communities. Due to reciprocal agreements, Scandinavian nationals and British subjects can stay at a hospital or get drug prescriptions at the same rates as Icelanders, meaning almost free of charge.

While there is little danger of disease, visitors should be careful of accidents when out in the countryside hiking, fishing, climbing, or pony trekking. Beware of the deceptive currents of Icelandic rivers, the covered cracks in the glaciers, or sudden shifts in the weather. When exploring the interior, travel with an organized tour or with a group that can request assistance if needed.

Car Rentals

Renting a car is expensive in Iceland. A compact car costs about IKr2,750 per day plus IKr28 per kilometer; a four-wheel-drive vehicle costs around IKr4,500 per day and IKr45 per kilometer. You must also pay for the gasoline, which is very expensive, IKr57 per liter ($3.50 per gallon) for regular unleaded. If you plan to explore the interior, it's a good idea to rent a four-wheel-drive vehicle.

Hertz (tel. 2/29577), **Avis** (tel. 2/50760), and **Icelandair** (tel. 1/690200) operate offices in the Leifur Eiríksson Terminal at Keflavík Airport. In other areas, rental agencies usually are close to airports.

Hints for Disabled Travelers

For information on provisions for the disabled in Iceland, contact the **Icelandic Tourist Board** in New York, or, in Iceland, the **Sjálfsbjörg** (Hátún 12, 105 Reykjavík, tel. 1/29133).

Further Reading

The Icelandic Sagas, the Nordic countries' most valuable contribution to world literature, have been translated into several languages. They tell of the lives, characters, and exploits of Icelandic heroes in the 10th and 11th centuries in an intricate combination of fantasy and history. The best known are the *Grettis Saga*, about the outlaw Grettir the Strong; *Laxdaela Saga*, a tragedy spanning four generations in which women play a prominent role; *Egil's Saga*, about the truculent Viking-poet Egill Skallagrimsson; and *Njal's Saga*, generally considered the greatest, about two heroes, one young and brave, the other old and wise. Told in simple language, with emphasis on dialogue, these epic poems are about love and hatred, family feuds and vengeance, loyalty and friendship, and tragic destiny.

Snorri Sturluson (1179–1241), esteemed the greatest historian of the Middle Ages, wrote the history of the kings of Norway up to 1184 in his *Heimskringla* (Orb of the World). His *Poetic Edda*, the only surviving document of the beliefs, cosmology, and outlook of the Germanic peoples in pre-Christian times, influenced Richard Wagner in writing his epic Ring Cycle of operas.

In 1936 two young poets, W. H. Auden and Louis MacNeice, summering in Iceland, wrote a series of letters in poetry and prose that were later collected in Auden's *Letters from Iceland*. Full of insights on the country, its people, and its politics, they are an unorthodox and witty introduction. Another modern work of at least peripheral interest to those traveling to Iceland is Jules Verne's classic science-fiction novel *Journey to the Cen-*

ter of the Earth, in which the heroes begin their subterrannean adventure with a descent into Iceland's majestic Snæfelljökull glacier.

More than 50 different volumes on Iceland—including poetry, biographies, travel guides, and picture books in English—can be ordered from *Iceland Review* (Box 8576, 128 Reykjavík, Iceland, tel. 1/84966, fax 1/674066). The review itself is a quarterly magazine with some of the best color photos from Iceland. It is well worth subscribing to *News from Iceland*, a monthly published by *Iceland Review*, prior to your trip.

Arriving and Departing

From the United States by Plane

Airports and Airlines All international flights originate from and arrive at **Keflavík Airport** (tel. 2/50600) in the southwestern corner of Iceland, 20 miles (35 kilometers) south of Reykjavík. On arrival you may spot some military aircraft, for Keflavík is also a NATO military installation, manned by the U.S. Navy. However, the ultramodern Leifur Eiríksson terminal is completely separate from the base.

Icelandair (610 5th Ave., New York, NY 10020, tel. 800/223-5500 or 212/967-8888) operates regular direct flights daily from New York City's JFK airport; service from Baltimore, Maryland, flies five times a week in summer, three times a week in winter; service from Orlando, Florida, runs twice a week in winter. The flight from New York to Keflavík takes less than five hours.

Discount Flights Iceland is a good destination to combine with a trip to continental Europe. The full round-trip fare from New York to Iceland in June 1991 was $1,316 mid-week (APEX fare $680), but the full round-trip fare from New York to Luxembourg only cost $879 midweek and allowed a stopover in Iceland for up to one week. If you stop over in Iceland for three days or less, the round-trip to Luxembourg would cost $778 mid-week (weekend fares are slightly higher). There may be substantial savings if you travel September through May, so check with Icelandair or your travel agent.

From the United Kingdom by Plane

Icelandair (172 Tottenham Court Rd., 3rd floor, London W1P 9LG, tel. 017/388-5599) flies daily from London Heathrow to Keflavík. There are two flights a week from Glasgow as well. The full round-trip fare from London in June 1991 was £658 (APEX fare £298). The flight from London is three hours.

From Scandinavia by Plane

Icelandair has several flights a week from Copenhagen (tel. 33/12-33-88), Stockholm (tel. 08/310240), and Oslo (tel. 02/42-39-75). **SAS** (tel. 33/13-62-66 in Copenhagen; tel. 1/622211 in Reykjavík) has a weekly flight to Keflavík from Copenhagen. Approximate flying time from Copenhagen to Keflavík is 3¼ hours.

From Scandinavia by Ship

It is possible, although not convenient, to sail directly from Scandinavia to Iceland on the car-and-passenger ferry *Norröna* operated by **Smyril Line** (Box 370, 3800 Tórshavn, Faroe Islands, tel. 1/5900; Engelgarden, Nye Bryggrn, N–5023 Bergen, Norway, tel. 5/320970; Aktionsgade 13, DK–7330, Hanstholm, Denmark, tel. 7961911; or in Iceland, **Norröna Travel,** Laugavegur 3, 101 Reykjavík, tel. 1/626362, fax 1/29450). From late May to early September, the *Norröna* sails from Bergen every Tuesday at 3 PM, making two stops—at Lerwick, in the Shetland Islands, and then at Tórshavn in the Faroe Islands—arriving in Seyðisfjörður on the eastern coast of Iceland. The total journey takes 41 hours. On the return trip, the *Norröna* leaves Seyðisfjörður only on Thursdays at noon, which makes a convenient connection to Denmark but entails a three-day wait for the boat to Bergen.

Staying in Iceland

Getting Around

By Plane Because so much of Iceland's central area is uninhabited, domestic air transport has been well developed to link the coastal towns. It isn't particularly cheap—round-trip fares range between IKr7,800 and IKr16,200—but there are various discounts available. The longest domestic flight takes just over an hour.

In summer, **Icelandair** (tel. 1/690200) schedules daily or frequent flights from Reykjavík to most of the large towns, such as Akureyri, Egilsstaðir, Húsavík, Höfn, Ísafjörður, Patreksfjörður, Sauðárkrókur, and Vestmannaeyjar. Icelandair provides bus connections between airports outside Reykjavík and nearby towns and villages.

Eagle Air (tel. 1/616060 or 1/28122) operates daily flights from the capital to Vestmannaeyjar, Siglufjörður, Bíldudalur, and Flateyri, and less frequently to some western villages. **Norlandair** (tel. 1/690200) serves the north from Akureyri, **Eastair** (tel. 1/690200) serves the east out of Egilsstaðir, and **Ernir Air** (tel. 1/24200) serves the western fjords from Ísafjörður. Local air fares range from IKr4,800 per round-trip to IKr10,500, depending on the distance.

By Bus An extensive network of buses serves most parts of Iceland; popular regions in the interior may be served only in summer. Fares range from IKr900 for a round-trip to Þingvellír to IKr6,600 for a round-trip to Akureyri. The bus network is operated by **Bifreiðastöð Íslands** (BSÍ, Vatnsmýrarvegur 10, tel. 1/22300, fax 1/29973); its terminal is located on the northern rim of Reykjavík Airport.

If you want to explore the island extensively, it's a good idea to buy the **Omnibus Passport,** which covers travel on all scheduled bus routes, with unlimited stopovers. A seven-day pass costs IKr23,200, a two-week pass IKr16,800, a three-week pass IKr21,600, and a four-week pass IKr24,600. The **Full Circle Passport,** which costs IKr11,400, is valid for a circular trip on the Ring Road mid-July to mid-September; you can take as long as you want to complete the journey, as long as you keep heading in the same direction on the circuit (detours into the interior must be paid for separately).

The **Air/Bus Rover** ticket provided by Icelandair and BSÍ allows you to fly one-way to any domestic Icelandair destination and by bus in the other direction, so you can save some time and still have a chance to explore the countryside. Prices range from IKr8,300 to IKr15,000.

By Car The Ring Road, which generally hugs the coastline, stretches almost 1,425 kilometers (900 miles) around Iceland. It is paved from Reykjavík beyond Hella in the south and in large stretches between the capital and Akureyri on the north coast; the rest of the road has a gravel surface, which can be quite smooth or full of potholes. In estimating driving times, allow as much as three hours per 100 kilometers (65 miles).

Service stations are spaced no more than half a day's drive from each other, on both main roads and side roads. Service stations in the Reykjavík area are open Monday through Saturday 7:30 AM to 8 PM; opening hours beyond Reykjavík vary, but gas stations often are open until 11:30 PM. For information on road conditions and availability of gas off the beaten track, call **Vegagerð Ríkisins** (Public Roads Administration; Borgartún 5–7, Reykjavík, tel. 1/21001).

Traffic generally is light outside Reykjavík, but roads have only one lane going in each direction, so stay within the speed limit: 70 kph (45 mph) on the open road, 50 kph (30 mph) in urban areas. Drivers are required by law to use headlights at all times. Seat belts also are required for all passengers.

Be cautious when driving in the interior in Iceland. The terrain can be treacherous, and many roads can only be traversed in four-wheel-drive vehicles; always drive in the company of at least one other car. Most mountain roads are so muddy that they remain closed until the beginning of July.

By Boat There is daily scheduled ferry service year-round between Reykjavík and Akranes on the ferry ***Akraborg*** (tel. 1/16050), and between Þorlákshöfn on the southern coast, and Vestmannaeyjar (the Westmann Islands) on the ferry ***Herjólfur*** (tel. 1/686464). The ***Baldur*** car ferry (tel. 3/81120 or 4/2020) sails twice daily in summer from Stykkishólmur, on the Snæfellnes peninsula, across Breiðafjörður bay to Brjánslækur in the Western Fjords.

Telephones

The international country code for Iceland is 354. The city code for Reykjavík is 1; other regions have one-digit codes. When calling between telephone regions within Iceland, dial 9 and the regional digit before the actual telephone number.

Local Calls There is one telephone directory for the whole country; names are listed alphabetically by first name, since so many Icelanders have the same surnames, as a result of the patronymic system (men add *-son* to their father's first name, women add *-dóttir*).

Public telephones are few and far between in Iceland. Pay phones usually are located indoors in post offices, hotels, or at transportation terminals. They accept IKr5 or IKr10 coins, which are placed in the slot before dialing. The dial tone is continuous. A 10-minute call between regions costs between IKr50 and IKr75.

International Calls You can dial direct or use an international calling card. Avoid charging overseas calls to your hotel bills, as the surcharge can double the cost of the call. New phones being installed in hotel lobbies, airports, and bus stations are designed for use with a special phone card, which you can buy at post offices and hotels; details of the new system were unavailable at press time, so inquire at your hotel upon arrival. For overseas calls, dial the operator 09 (or 08 for directory assistance).

Operators and Information For long-distance calls within Iceland, dial 02 for the operator or 03 for directory assistance.

Mail

Stamps for postcards to Europe cost IKr26, for airmail letters IKr31. Stamps for postcards to the United States cost IKr31, and airmail letters IKr47. Allow at least one week for international delivery to and from Iceland. Most post offices also have fax machines for public use.

English-language News

In June, July, and August, news in English is broadcast daily at 7:30 AM on FM 93.5 or 92.4. You can also call 1/693690 for a recording of the latest news bulletin in English.

Tipping

Tipping is not acceptable in Iceland and may even be frowned upon. Service charges of 15–20% are included in prices when applicable.

Opening and Closing Times

Museums and other attractions are generally open regular hours June–August. (Individual listings below state hours of opening.) If you wish to visit a site that's not regularly open September–May, call the listed telephone number and make an appointment for a private visit.

Banks All banks in Iceland are open weekdays 9:15–4.

Post Offices In most towns, post offices open at 8:30 or 9 and close at 4:30 or 5, weekdays only.

Shops Shopping hours are 9–6 weekdays, although some supermarkets stay open until 8 Thursday and Friday. On Saturday shops maintain differing hours between 10 and 4. Florists and kiosks stay open evenings and weekends in larger towns and villages. Beyond Reykjavík, most shops offering groceries and sundries for travelers are open seven days a week.

Restaurants Restaurants are usually open mid-morning until midnight. Lunch is generally served from noon to 2; dinner time is between 6 and 9.

Shopping

The classic gift to bring home from Iceland is the Icelandic sweater, hand-knit in traditional designs. Originally they were only available in natural wool colors—black, brown, gray, and white—but now they are also made from colored wool. These sweaters are mainly knitted at home by individuals who adjust the traditional designs to their own fancy, so no two sweaters are alike. In recent years, many Icelandic designers have returned from design institutes in the United States and Europe to create many new lines of sweaters, blankets, and shawls made from wool and other material as well.

The thick, soft Icelandic yarn makes a warm fabric that also breathes easily, just right for keeping sailors snug throughout long days at sea. The natural lanolin of the sheep is left in the yarn, which lightly mats its fibers for extra protection from cold and damp.

Like other Scandinavian countries, Iceland is renowned for its ales and spirits, the most famous being *brennivín*, an 80-proof liquor similar to aquavit. Other spirits include vodkas such as *Elduris*, from the state distillery, and *Icy*, which as sold well in the United States. The only stores where you can buy alcoholic beverages retail are the state alcohol and tobacco monopoly stores (*ÁTVR*) in Reykjavík and larger towns around the country; prices are lower there than at restaurants and hotels, and a number of good European wines are available at bargain prices, too.

Pickled herring and smoked salmon are the main delicacies from the sea. Choose between *graflax* (raw salmon pickled in a mixture of herbs served with mustard sauce), sliced smoked salmon, or whole fillets of smoked salmon or trout. Herring bits come packed in wine, garlic, and other sauces. You might also want to pick up a small jar of the red Icelandic caviar, or some *harðfiskur* (dried fish), which is best eaten in small bits. Icelandic lamb is another delicacy; you can buy it frozen or smoked.

Jewelry is also a popular souvenir of Iceland. For upwards of IKr600 you can buy silver replicas of Viking brooches, rings, necklaces, and religious symbols such as the *þórshamar* (Thor's hammer), runic letters, and pagan magical letters. A number of goldsmiths and silversmiths also design beautiful modern jewelry with Icelandic stones such as agate, jasper, and shiny black *hrafntinna*, as well as opals, diamonds, and other precious stones.

VAT Refund Foreign visitors can get a refund on the value-added tax (*virðisaukaskattur*, commonly called VSK), which accounts for 20% of the purchase price of most goods and services. Fifteen percent of the purchase price is refunded, providing you buy a minimum of IKr5,000 at that store. Souvenir stores issue "tax-free checks" that allow foreign visitors to collect the VSK rebates directly in the duty-free store when departing from Keflavík Airport. To qualify, keep your purchases in tax-free packages (except woolens), and show them to customs officers at the departure gate along with a passport and the tax-free check. If you depart the country from somewhere besides Keflavík, have customs authorities stamp your tax-free check, then mail the stamped check within three months to Iceland Tax-Free Shopping, Box 1200, 235 Keflavík, Iceland. You will be reimbursed in U.S. dollars at the current exchange rate.

Sports and Outdoor Activities

Fishing Iceland abounds with rivers and lakes where you can catch salmon, sea trout, brown trout, or char. The **trout** season normally runs April 1–September 20; permits can be bought on the spot for a number of lakes and rivers, at prices varying from a couple of hundred kronas up to several thousand per day, depending upon the quality of the fishing. *The Icelandic Fishing Guide* and a special fishing voucher book available from **Icelandic Farm Holidays** (Bændahöllin við Hagatorg, 107 Reykjavík, tel. 1/623640 or 1/19200) can be used in 50 river and lake locations around the country.

The normal **salmon** season runs June 10–September 10. At most rivers, guides are provided as well as accommodation. The most popular (and expensive) rivers must be booked at least a year in advance and you pay IKr51,000–120,000 per fishing rod per day, not including travel, accommodation, or food. For other rivers you must make reservations at least two months in advance and expect to pay IKr6,000–12,000 per rod per day. However, it is often possible to get salmon fishing permits during the summer at tackle shops or angling clubs. In Reykjavík, contact the **Angling Club** (Háaleitisbraut 68, tel. 1/686050), the **Icelandic Fishing Association** (Bolholt 6, tel. 1/31510), or the **Angling Club Laxa** (Laugavegur 51, tel. 1/23931). Reykjavík tackle shops include **Veiðihúsið** (Nóatún 17, tel. 1/84085), **Veiðivon** (Langholtsvegur 111, tel. 1/687090), **Veiðimaðurinn** (Hafnarstræti 5, tel. 1/16760), **Vesturröst** (Laugavegur 178, tel. 1/16770). **Þröstur Elliðason** (Laugarnesvegur 104, Reykjavík, tel. 1/82247) helps organizations and groups organize fishing permits and tours for longer or shorter periods, and will hire out fishing equipment and provide a guide if needed.

As befits a country that depends so much upon the ocean for its livelihood, several weekend deep-sea fishing competitions are held each year: in May in **Vestmanneyjar** (contact Elínborg Bernódusdóttir, tel. 8/11279); in July in **Ísafjörður** (contact Kolbrún Halldórsdóttir, tel. 4/3103); in August in **Siglufjörður** (contact Viðar Otteson, tel. 6/71514) or **Akureyri** (contact Július Snorrason, tel. 6/21173).

If you wish to bring your own fishing tackle, it must be disinfected, either at home (certificate needed) or by customs at Keflavík Airport.

Golf There are 27 golf courses in Iceland and two more under construction. Most are rather rough nine-hole courses, but there are five 18-hole courses, the best in Reykjavík and Akureyri. Green fees range IKr600–1,200 for nine-hole courses and IKr1,200–1,800 for 18-hole courses.

Hiking Many organized tours from Reykjavík and other towns include some days of hiking. You also can join special hiking tours popular among Icelanders, arranged by the touring clubs **Ferðafélag Íslands** (Touring Club of Iceland, Öldugötu 3, 101 Reykjavík, tel. 1/19533 and 1/11798) and **Útivist** (Touring Club Utivist Grófin 1, 101 Reykjavík, tel. 1/14606). In Akureyri contact **Ferðafélag Akureyrar** (Touring Club of Akureyri, Strandgata 23, 600 Akureyri, tel. 1/22720). If you choose to hike on your own, beware of the dangers. Lava covered with moss can be treacherous, with razor-sharp edges that can cut through clothes and skin. Around hot springs and sulphur springs, the ground may suddenly give way, leaving you standing in boiling water or mud. When hiking across country, follow paths made by sheep if footpaths are not available. Don't venture away from popular areas unless you have researched the territory in advance. Always let someone know of your hiking plans, and avoid hiking alone.

Horseback Riding The Icelandic horse is a purebred descendant of its ancestors from the Viking age, small but strong, exceptionally sure-footed, intelligent, and easy to handle. It's possible to ride without fatigue for days on end because of the horses' special smooth gait called *tölt*. A number of firms offer a variety of tours, from short one-day trips up to 12-day treks across various regions.

Skiing The winter season begins in January and usually lasts through April. There are about 90 ski lifts around the country, and at the larger resorts both alpine and cross-country skiing trails are available.

In summer, the **Kerlingarfjöll Ski School** west of the Hofsjökull glacier runs five- to six-day courses; you can also get lift tickets without taking lessons, and there is accommodation and food at the school. Contact Urval/Utsyn Travel Agency (Alfabakki 16, 109 Reykjavík, tel. 1/603060 or 1/26611).

Swimming Iceland has a good number of public outdoor swimming pools heated by thermal springs. Swimming is a required subject in elementary school and the country's most common sports activity.

Dining

The last decade saw a virtual revolution in Icelandic cuisine. The menu used to be very simple—boiled fish and roast leg of lamb. Now several restaurants offer gourmet cooking, and the best restaurants keep up with the latest culinary trends worldwide. Most offer menus that consist of a marriage of the best in traditional Scandinavian cooking and classic French cuisine.

You have not eaten in Iceland until you try the seafood: haddock, halibut, lobster, prawns, scallops, sole, monkfish, ocean perch, shrimp, turbot, *tindabikkja* (a type of skate), salmon, and trout caught in clear mountain rivers—the list can go on forever, and Icelandic cuisine now does justice to this bounty from the sea; gone are the days of simplistic overcooking.

Icelandic lamb is another delicacy, its distinct wild taste resulting from the sheep roaming free in the grasslands of the interior and feeding on highland herbs. Smoked lamb might be the traditional *hangikjöt* or lightly smoked London Lamb. Game such as duck and reindeer are popular at the more expensive restaurants. Local beef is also of high quality, much of it coming from the centuries-old domestic stock brought by the Vikings, which has not been hybridized out of all taste.

Part of the culinary revolution of the last decade included a proliferation of new domestic cheeses. *Gouda* remains number one, but there are many excellent types such as *Búri, Flóa Camembert, Dala-Brie,* and blue cheese. *Skyr,* a delicious yogurt-like food made from skim milk, is especially good with fresh fruit; one of its by-products is a cool drink called *mysa.*

There are fully licensed full-service restaurants in most larger towns, especially in summer when the Edda Hotels (boarding schools open to tourists as lodgings in summer) are open. It's wise to make reservations on weekends. Most establishments accept informal attire, casual but neat, but restaurants that feature dancing and entertainment usually require men to wear a shirt and tie.

The following chart defines the price categories used in the restaurant reviews below.

Category	**Cost***
Very Expensive	over IKr3,000
Expensive	IKr2,100–IKr3,000
Moderate	IKr1,200–IKr2,100
Inexpensive	under IKr1,200

**per person for a 3-course meal, including taxes and service charge and excluding wine*

About two-thirds of the country's restaurants participate in a tourist menu program, whereby set menus are available at low prices—IKr900–IKr1,000 for lunch, and IKr1,000–IKr1,500 for dinner for a three-course meal. The brochure "Dining, Wining and Dancing" is available free from the Icelandic Hotel and Restaurant Association (Garðastræti 42, 101 Reykjavík, tel. 1/27410 or 1/621410).

Wines and Spirits Most restaurants are licensed to serve the full range of alcoholic beverages—local or imported beer, German and French wines, cognac, and spirits. Wines, however, are very expensive. Like other Scandinavian countries, Iceland is renowned for its ales and spirits, the most famous being *brennivín*. Its nickname, "black death," alludes not only to the black labels on its bottles but also to the physical effects of drinking too much of it. Brennivín is associated with the midwinter celebrations of þorrablót, when it is drunk ice-cold and undiluted; more commonly, it is drunk mixed with cola. Icelandic vodkas, such as *Eldurís* and *Icy*, are also of high quality. Beer has only been legal since March of 1989, and because it was unobtainable for so long, Icelanders are still excited about it and willing to pay high prices for imported brands.

Lodging

The past few years have seen a concerted effort to upgrade the level of accommodations offered in Iceland; most of the better hotels were built or totally renovated in the last three to five years, and by 1992 strict standards for good mattresses will apply even to guest rooms at Icelandic farms. During the summer season, hotels or even youth hostels may be fully booked, so make reservations well in advance.

The following chart defines the price categories used in the hotel reviews below.

Category	Cost*
Very Expensive	over IKr12,000
Expensive	IKr9,600–IKr12,000
Moderate	IKr4,800–IKr9,600
Inexpensive	under IKr4,800

**Prices are for a double room with bath.*

Hotels and Guest Houses Hotels in Reykjavík and larger towns offer the usual amenities of all good hotels: hair drier, trouser press, telephone, and satellite TV in every room, with a Continental breakfast included in the room rate. Many travelers, however, find the simple guest houses adequate, while others prefer bed-and-breakfast at a private home. All types of lodging are regulated.

Farm Holidays An increasingly popular mode of lodging in Iceland, even among Icelanders themselves, farm holidays are a fun way to get to know the country and its people, and to explore the magnificent natural surroundings. You can choose from almost 130 locations around Iceland, about half of them real working farms. Know ahead of time what each farm offers, for they vary widely: You might stay in a separate cottage, in a bed in the farmhouse, or in a sleeping bag outdoors or in a barn. Breakfast is included in the price. Some farms have cooking facilities for guests, while others serve full meals if requested. Make reservations well in advance of your visit. An open voucher farm accommodation program offers accommodation for IKr1,850 a night including breakfast, for a minimum of five nights; sleeping-bag accommodation without breakfast costs IKr1,000 per night. Write to **Icelandic Farm Holidays** (Bændahöllinni við Hagatorg, 107 Reykjavík, tel. 1/19200 or 1/623640) for a booklet describing all farms and their facilities.

Campgrounds Organized camping grounds are available throughout the country. Some are located on private property, others are owned and operated by local communities, and still others are located in protected areas supervised by the Nature Conservation Council. Facilities may include primitive toilets, running water, showers, warm swimming pools, shopping, sleeping accommodation, snack bars, restaurants, sports facilities, and service stations and garages. Look for signs reading *Tjaldstæði bönnuð* (camping prohibited) or *tjaldstæði* (camping allowed). It is forbidden to use scrubwood for fuel; bring paraffin or gas stoves for cooking.

Camping equipment can be rented in Reykjavík at **Tjaldaleigan Rent-a-Tent** (tel. 1/13072). Write to the **Association of Leisure Site Owners** (c/o the Tourist Information Center, Bankastrætli 2, 101 Reykjavík, tel. (1/623045) for a comprehensive listing of campgrounds. Even the most complete campgrounds cost less than IKr350 per day for one person with a tent, trailer, or camper.

Mountain Huts You can also stay at one of 19 mountain huts owned by **Ferðafélag Íslands** (the Touring Club of Iceland; *see* Hiking, *above*) for IKr600–IKr900 depending on facilities. The huts are located in some of Iceland's most beautiful regions, such as Þórsmörk, Landmannalaugar, Herðubreiðarlindir, and Hveravellir.

Youth Hostels Youth hostels are inexpensive, about IKr1,140 per night, excluding breakfast. You get a bed, access to a kitchen and toilet, a pillow, and a blanket. Some hostels are crowded during summer, so call ahead. Hostels outside Reykjavík permit you to use your own sleeping bag. For information write to **Farfugladeild Reykjavíkur** (Sundlaugavegi 34, 105 Reykjavík, tel. 1/38110).

Edda Hotels, which operate as boarding schools during winter, offer sleeping-bag accommodation, in addition to regular rooms, around the country in the summer. You can sleep on a mattress in your own sleeping bag for IKr900 per night, and there usually is a restaurant offering good home-style cooking.

Reykjavík

The sprawling city of Reykjavík is the nation's nerve center, the seat of government, home to half of the island's population, and the main point of contact with the outside world. In the fall of 1986, with all of one week's notice, the capital hosted a hastily organized round of disarmament talks between U.S. President Ronald Reagan and Soviet leader Mikhail Gorbachev, with attendant aides, advisors, and sundry other camp followers, not to mention several thousand journalists. In its brief moment in the sun, Reykjavík surprised the world with its resourcefulness and efficiency, its culture and modern amenities, and, most of all, its offbeat charm. It's an egalitarian city, with no mansions and no slums. It's a relaxed casual city, where people enjoy having fun, even (or especially) throughout the dark days of winter.

Set on a fjord overlooked by proud Mount Esja, with its ever-changing hues, Reykjavík presents a colorful sight, its concrete houses painted in light colors and topped by vibrant red, blue, and green roofs.

Any part of town can be reached by city bus, but take a walk around to get an idea of the modern present and modest past. In downtown Reykjavík, uptown at the Árbær folk museum, or in other parts of the city, you'll see some preserved old-style wood homes, roofed with corrugated iron painted in bright colors. Stringent building codes now require earthquake-proof construction, so modern houses are built from reinforced concrete.

Reykjavík's name comes from the Icelandic words for steam, *reykur*, and for bay, *vík*. In AD 874, Norseman Ingólfur Arnarson saw Iceland rising out of the misty sea and came ashore at a bay eerily shrouded with plumes of steam from nearby hot springs. Today, most of the houses in Reykjavík are still heated by near-boiling water carried from the hot springs by two 10-mile-long insulated pipelines. As a result, the air is relatively smoke-free, but you may sometimes notice an odd sulfur smell in the bathrooms.

In contrast to the treeless countryside, Reykjavík has many tall Icelandic birches, rowans, and willows, and imported pines and spruces. At the Tjörnin lake, near the city center, you can observe many of the 17 species of ducks that nest in the country.

Reykjavík is the logical starting point for any visit to Iceland. Be forewarned, however, that it is considerably more expensive than the rest of this expensive country. Prices for hotel rooms, restaurant meals, and short tours are easily on a par with those of Amsterdam, Copenhagen, London, and Paris, although you can walk around its historic areas and visit most of its museums free of charge.

Important Addresses and Numbers

Tourist Information The Reykjavík **Tourist Information Center** (Bankastræti 2, tel. 1/623045), located a few yards up the street from Lækjartorg Square, is open June–August weekdays 8:30–6, Saturday 8:30–2, and Sunday 10–2; September–May it's open weekdays 10–4, Saturday 10–2. The **Iceland Tourist Board's** headquarters next door (Gimli, Lækjargata 3, tel. 1/27488) is open weekdays 9–5.

Embassies **U.S. Embassy:** Laufásvegur 21, tel. 1/29100. **U.K. Embassy:** Laufásvegur 49, tel. 1/15883. **Canadian Consulate:** Suðurlandsbraut 10, tel. 1/680820.

Emergencies Dial 1/11166 for **police** and 1/11100 for **ambulance** or **fire.**

Hospital Emergency Room The emergency ward at **Borgarspítalinn City Hospital** (tel. 1/696600) is open 'round the clock.

Doctors and Dentists Six health centers with officially appointed family doctors receive patients on short notice 8–5 weekdays. Call the **Reykjavík Health Centers** (tel. 1/22400) or look under *Heilsugæslustöð* in the phone book; for doctors' visits or house calls at other hours, call the **Medical Watch,** (tel. 1/21230).

Late-night Pharmacies Reykjavík pharmacies take turns at staying open around-the-clock. Signs are posted in all pharmacies indicating which one has the night watch (*næturvakt*). For information, call 1/18888.

Where to Change Money The **Tourist Information Center** at Lækjargata exchanges foreign currencies in June, July, and August 4:30–6 weekdays, 9–1 Saturday. At the **Hotel Loftleiðir,** a bank is open Monday–Saturday 8:15–4 and 5–7:15.

English-language Bookstores **Bókabúð Braga** (at Hlemmur bus station tel. 1/29311 or 1/624202) and **Sigfús Eymundsson** (Austurstræti 18, tel. 1/27077; also at Kringlan mall) carry foreign books as well as foreign newspapers and magazines, but these are usually several days old. **Mál og menning** (Laugavegur 18, tel. 1/24240), one of the largest bookstores in the city, has an extensive foreign section.

Travel Agencies Major agencies include **Atlantik** (Hallveigarstígur 1, tel. 1/625066), **Guðmundur Jónasson** (Borgartún 34, tel. 1/83222), **Iceland Tourist Bureau** (Skógarhlíð 18, tel. 1/25855), **Icelandic Highland** (Bankastræti 2, tel. 1/22225), **Icelandair** (Reykjavíkurflugvöllur, tel. 1/690100), **Samvinn-Travel** (Austurstræti 12, tel. 1/691070), **Úrval-Útsýn & Iceland Safari** (Álfabakki 16, tel. 1/603060), and **World Travel** (Austurstræti 17, tel. 1/622200).

Arriving and Departing by Plane

Airports and Airlines **Keflavík Airport** (tel. 2/50600), 50 kilometers (30 miles) south of the city, hosts all international flights. For reservations and information in Reykjavík, contact: **Icelandair** (tel. 1/690300) or **SAS** (tel. 1/622211).

Reykjavík Airport (tel. 1/694100) is the central hub of domestic air travel in Iceland. For reservations and information contact:

Icelandair (tel. 1/690200), **Eagle Air** (tel. 1/29577), or **Ernir** (tel. 1/624200).

Between the Airport and Downtown

By Bus

The **Reykjavík FlyBus** (tel. 1/621011) leaves Keflavík (from directly outside the terminal building) and arrives in Reykjavík at the **Loftleiðir Hotel** at Reykjavík Airport. From there, you can take a taxi or municipal bus to your destination. Buses run every 30 minutes during peak hours, but otherwise they await the arrival of each flight. For departures catch the FlyBus at the Saga, Esja, and Loftleiðir hotels and the Holiday Inn. The FlyBus also leaves the youth hostel in Laugardalur at 5 AM daily June–August The fare is ISK 400 per person. The drive takes 40–50 minutes.

From Reykjavík Airport, the No. 5 municipal (SVR) bus leaves from the Icelandair terminal on the western side of the airport. Other airlines operate from the east terminal (behind the Loftleiðir Hotel), which is served by the No. 17 bus.

By Taxi

A taxi from Keflavík to Reykjavík will cost IKr4,200, though if you share it with others you can split the cost. Taxi companies include **Aðalstöðin** (tel. 2/1515 or 2/52525) and **Ökuleiðir** (tel. 2/14141). From Reykjavík Airport, a taxi to your hotel will cost around IKr600; there are direct phones to taxi companies in the arrival hall.

Getting Around

The best way to see Reykjavík is on foot. Most of the interesting sights are in the city center, within easy walking distance of one another. There is no subway system.

By Bus

The municipal bus (**SVR**) system (tel. 1/12700) is extensive, cheap, and reliable. Buses run from 7 AM to midnight, every 15 minutes on the most frequently used routes, less often on others. Bus stops are marked by signposts with an "SVR" on top, or by a covered bench with a posted list of routes. The fare is IKr60 adults, IKr20 children, payable to the driver upon boarding. You can buy books of discounted tickets from the drivers or at the main terminals. The fare allows you to travel any distance in town; if you have to change buses, ask for *skiptimiða* (*skiff*-teah-meah-the), a trip extension ticket that you give the second bus driver. The SVR system connects to the bus systems in the Kópavogur, Garðabær, and Hafnarfjörður municipalities south of Reykjavík.

By Taxi

Most cabs are late-model fully equipped passenger sedans, including many Mercedes. They have small "Taxi" signs on top and can be hailed anywhere on the street; the sign "laus" indicates that the cab is available. All cars are radio-equipped and respond to calls within minutes. Some taxis accept major credit cards, but you must state that you want one when requesting the taxi. Fares are regulated by meter; rides around Reykjavík run between IKr200 and IKr600. Call **BSR** (tel. 1/611720), **Bæjarleiðir** (tel. 1/33500), or **Hreyfill** (tel. 1/685522). There is no tipping.

By Car

The excellent bus system and quick, inexpensive taxis make automobiles unnecessary for getting around town, doubly so considering how expensive car rentals and gasoline are. Gas stations are usually open 7:30 AM–8 PM, but they are closed on Sundays. Most have self-service pumps that accept IKr100, 500, and 1,000 notes. Some car rentals in Reykjavík: **Icelandair** (tel. 1/690500), **Geysir** (tel. 1/688888), **Avis** (tel. 1/624433), and **InterRent** (tel. 1/686915).

Opening and Closing Times

Even though many Reykjavík citizens like to stay up late, most of the capital closes down early on weekdays, and Sunday remains largely a sabbatical day. **Bars, discotheques,** and **dance clubs** stay open until 1 AM Mon.–Thurs. and 3 AM Friday and Saturday. **Bus service** stops at midnight, but **taxis** run around the clock.

Post offices are open weekdays 8:30–4:30; a post office at the BSÍ bus terminal is open 1:30–6 weekdays and 8:30–3 Saturday.

Museums are generally open Tues.–Sat. 11–4 and Sunday 2–6. Monday is the usual closing day.

Shops are open weekdays 9–6, although some supermarkets stay open until 8 on Thursday and Friday. Shops are usually open 10–4 on Saturday (though many are closed on Saturday in June, July, and August) and most are closed on Sunday year-round, with the exception of souvenir shops, florists, and kiosks.

Guided Tours

Orientation **Kynnisferðir** (Reykjavík Excursions), owned by the Icelandic Tourist Bureau, is the main tour operator in and out of Reykjavík. Kynnisferðir has offices at the Loftleiðir Hotel (tel. 1/621011) and at the Esja Hotel (tel. 1/688922). "Reykjavík City-Sightseeing" is a daily 2½-hour tour that includes commercial centers, folk museums, and art centers.

Personal Guides Many travel agencies offer English-speaking personal guides for tours of the city and outlying areas. Contact **Úrval-Útsýn Travel** (Pósthússtræti 13, tel. 1/26900), **Samvinn-Travel** (Austurstræti 17, tel. 1/691010), or **Atlantik-Tours** (Hallveigarstígur 1, tel. 1/625066).

Highlights for First-time Visitors

Alþingishús (House of Parliament), *see* Tour 1
Árbær byggðasafn (Open-Air Municipal Museum), *see* Tour 1
Árni Magnússon Institute, *see* Tour 2
Dómkirkjan (Lutheran Cathedral), *see* Tour 1
Hallgrímskirkja church, *see* Tour 2
Landsbókasafnið (National Library), *see* Tour 1
Þjóðminjasafn (National Museum), *see* Tour 2
Tjörnin Lake, *see* Tour 1

Tour 1: The Historic Downtown

Numbers in the margin correspond with points of interest on the Reykjavík map.

Most bus routes meet at the **Hlemmur** square, on the eastern edge of downtown. To the north is the tall, unimpressive central **Police Station** housing the **Ministry of Foreign Affairs** on the top floor. The building on the west side houses the
1 **Náttúrufræðistofnun** (Museum of Natural History), with an in-

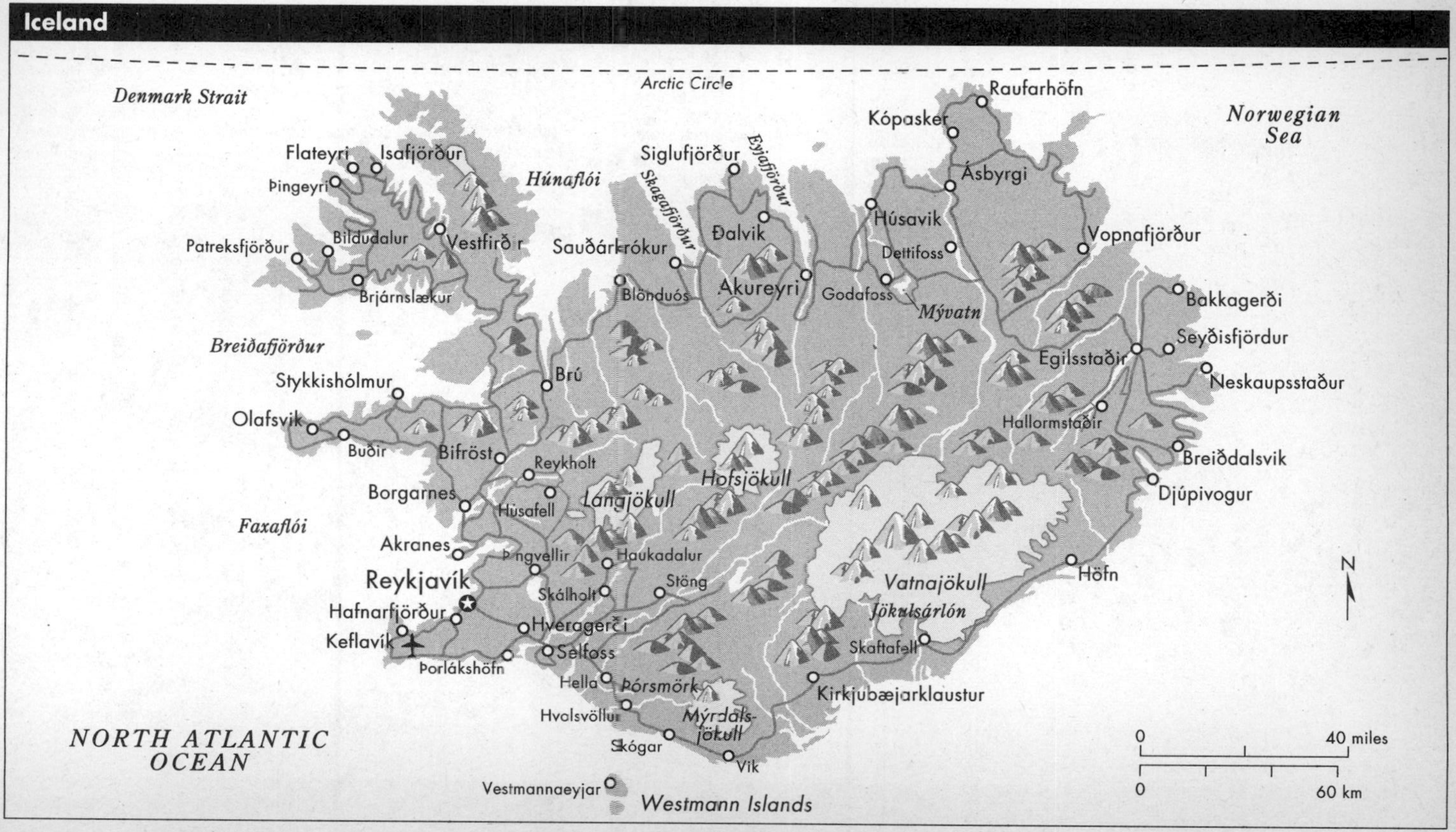
Iceland
Arctic Circle
Denmark Strait
Norwegian Sea
NORTH ATLANTIC OCEAN
Flateyri
Isafjörður
Þingeyri
Húnaflói
Patreksfjörður
Bildudalur
Vestfirð r
Brjárnslækur
Breiðafjörður
Stykkishólmur
Olafsvik
Buðir
Bifröst
Brú
Reykholt
Borgarnes
Húsafell
Faxaflói
Akranes
Þingvellir
Reykjavík
Hafnarfjörður
Keflavík
Þorlákshöfn
Hveragerði
Selfoss
Skálholt
Haukadalur
Stöng
Hella
Hvolsvöllur
Skógar
Þórsmörk
Mýrdalsjökull
Vik
Vestmannaeyjar
Westmann Islands
Langjökull
Hofsjökull
Siglufjörður
Skagafjörður
Eyjafjörður
Sauðárkrókur
Blönduós
Ðalvik
Akureyri
Godafoss
Mývatn
Húsavik
Dettifoss
Kópasker
Raufarhöfn
Ásbyrgi
Vopnafjörður
Bakkagerði
Seyðisfjördur
Egilsstaðir
Neskaupsstaður
Hallormstaðir
Breiðdalsvik
Djúpivogur
Höfn
Vatnajökull
Jökulsárlón
Skaftafell
Kirkjubæjarklaustur
N
0
40 miles
0
60 km

Reykjavík

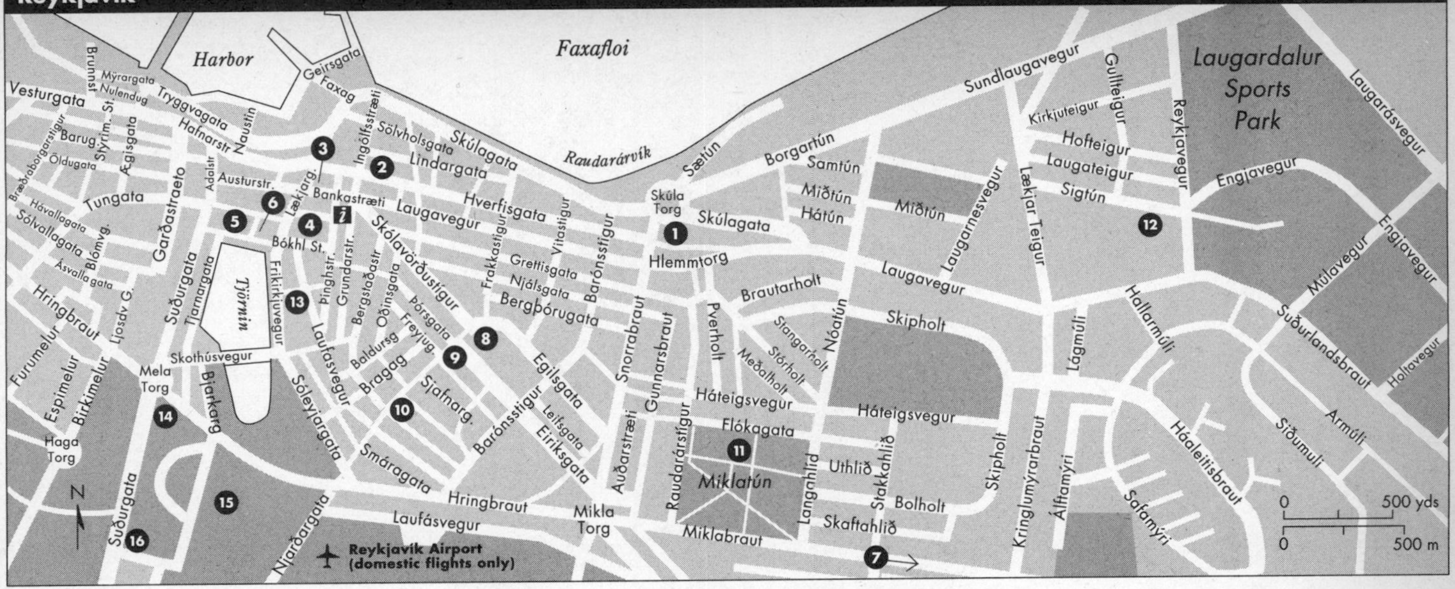

Alþingishús (Parliament), **5**

Arbæri byggðasafn (Open-Air Museum), **7**

Árni Magnússon Institute, **16**

Ásgrímur Jónsson Museum, **10**

Ásmundur Sveinsson Gallery, **12**

Dómkirkjan (Luthern Cathedral), **6**

Einar Jónsson Museum, **9**

Hallgrímskirkja, **8**

Kjarvalsstaðir, **11**

Landbóksasfnið (National Library), **2**

Listasafn Ríkisins (National Art Gallery), **13**

Menntaskólinn i Reykjavík, **4**

Náttúrufræðistofnun (Museum of Natural History), **1**

Norræna Húsið (Nordic House), **15**

Stjórnarráð, **3**

Þjóðminjasafn (National Museum), **14**

teresting, though small, collection. Exhibits include stuffed peacocks, giant sea turtles, and a specimen of the extinct great auk. *Hverfisgata 116, tel. 1/29822. Admission free. Open Sun., Tues., Thurs., Sat. 1:30–4.*

Walk west five blocks down Laugavegur, long the city's main shopping street (although it now meets stiff competition from the Kringlan shopping mall uptown—*see* Shopping, *below*). You'll pass high-fashion clothing stores, jewelry and record shops, bookstores, bars, and restaurants on the way downtown.

Time Out Stop in at the **Tíu Dropar** coffeehouse (Laugavegur 27), which serves a tantalizing selection of homemade cakes, a variety of coffees, and chocolate with lots of genuine whipped cream.

Turning right on Klapparstígur and left again on Hverfisgata, you'll be in an area housing many government ministries. On the right, past the Danish embassy, is the newly renovated **Þjóðleikhús** (National Theater), designed by architect Guîjón Bjarnason and built during the 1950s. Next door is the
2 **Landsbókasafnið** (National Library), an impressive early 20th-century structure testifying to this nation's universal literacy and great interest in the printed word. When ABC anchorman Peter Jennings was in Reykjavík, he got into a taxi and asked to be taken to the most interesting building in town; his driver took him to the National Library. The public reading room houses everything from current issues of *The New York Times Book Review* to myriad volumes on Icelandic genealogy. *In Safnahús, western end of Hverfisgata, tel. 1/16864 or 1/13080. Admission free. Open weekdays 9–7, Sat. 10–12.*

On the west side of the library, there is a grassy knoll known as Arnarhóll because it is topped by a **statue of Ingólfur Arnarson,** the first settler of Iceland and Reykjavík's founder. From here, there's a fine panorama of Reykjavík's architectural melange: 18th-century stone houses, 19th-century small wood houses, office blocks from the '30s and '40s, and, to the north, the ominously futuristic **Seðlabanki** (Central Bank), which still makes residents bristle because it restricts the view here.

Just past the hill, turn left on Lækjargata. On the left at the
3 corner of Bankastræti is the **Stjórnarráð,** a low white building originally used in the 18th century as a prison. Today it houses the offices of President Vigdís Finnbogadóttir (the first woman president in Europe) and Prime Minister Davíð Oddsson (formerly the mayor of Reykjavík). Continue along Lækjargata; on your left is the historic **Bernhöftstorfa** district, a small hill with colorful two-story wood houses from the mid-19th century. The
4 oldest educational institution in the country, **Menntaskólinn í Reykjavík** (corner of Amtmannsstígur and Lækjargata), is the largest building here; its graduates have from the early days dominated the country's political and social life. Turn right off Lækjargata onto Vonarstræti; to your left you can look out across **Tjörnin** lake. Thermal springs feed warm water into a corner of this pond, making it an attraction for birds year-round and a popular area for birdwatchers. It's also popular with ice skaters in winter. The new **Ráðhús** (Municipal Building), opened in 1991, is on the corner of Vonarstræti and Tjarnargata, overlooking the lake.

5 Head up Templarasund away from the lake. At the next corner, on your left you'll see the 19th-century **Alþingishús** (House of Parliament), one of Iceland's oldest stone houses. When Parliament is in session (October–May), you can view the proceed-
6 ings from the visitors' gallery. On your right is **Dómkirkjan** (the Lutheran Cathedral), a small, charming church erected in 1785. Directly ahead is **Austurvöllur,** the city's historic central square, with its **statue of Jón Sigurðsson** (1811–79), who led Iceland's fight for independence from Denmark. This is also where Ingólfur Arnarson built his residence back in the ninth century.

Time Out If it is late afternoon, visit one of the historic area's old pubs: **Café Hressó** (Austurstræti 20, tel. 1/14353), with its summery back garden; **Fógetinn** (Aðalstræti 10, tel. 1/16323), an intimate spot with low ceilings; or **Gaukur á Stöng** (Tryggvagata 22, tel. 1/11556), always bustling with the avant-garde crowd.

Leading west out of the square is Austurstræti, a pedestrian shopping street with the main post office on the right. From
7 here you can take bus No. 11 for a 20-minute ride to the **Árbær byggðasafn** (Open-Air Municipal Museum), a "village" of 18th- and 19th-century houses furnished in old-fashioned style, displaying authentic household utensils and tools for cottage industries. *Corner Höfðabakki and Rofabær, tel. 1/84094. Admission: IKr250 adults, IKr125 students, children under 16 and senior citizens free. Open June–Aug., Tues.–Sun. 10–6; Sept., Sat.–Sun. 10–6; Oct.–May, open by request only.*

Tour 2: Museums and the University

8 Take bus No. 1 to the large **Hallgrímskirkja** church, with its 210-foot stair-stepped gray stone tower that dominates the city's skyline. The church, which was completed in the late 1970s after more than 50 years of construction, is named for the 17th-century hymn-writer Hallgrímur Pétursson. From the church tower, the city's highest vantage point, you can enjoy a panoramic view; note the compactness of the city center to the west, compared to the suburbs that sprawled outward with a tenfold increase in population after World War II. *Tel. 1/10745. Admission to tower: IKr200 adults, IKr100 children under 12. Open daily 10–6.*

In front of the church is a **statue of Leifur Eiríksson,** the Icelander who discovered America 500 years before Columbus. (Leif's father was Eric the Red, who discovered Greenland.)

9 Across from the church is the **Einar Jónsson Museum** and **Sculpture Garden.** Jónsson (1874–1954) was Iceland's leading sculptor early in this century; his metal sculptures of the human figure explore a wide range of religious and mythical subjects. *Corner Njarðargata and Þórsgata. Admission: IKr100 adults. Open June–Sept., Tues.–Sun. 1:30–4; Feb.–May, weekends 1:30–4.*

From here, art lovers may want to visit three other art galler-
10 ies. Follow Njarîargata to Bergstaðastræti for the **Ásgrímur Jónsson Museum,** which features the works of the popular neo-impressionist painter Ásgrímur Jónsson (1870–1968). *Bergstaþastræti 74, tel. 1/32155. Admission free. Open June–Aug.,*

Tues.–Sun. 1:30–4; Sept.–May, Sat., Sun., Tues., and Thurs. 1:30–4.

11 **Kjarvalsstaðir,** a municipal art gallery named in honor of Jóhannes Kjarval (1889–1972), the nation's best-loved painter, features work by Kjarval and others. It's a 10-minute walk uptown from Hallgrímskirkja, in the spacious **Miklatún** public park. *Tel. 1/26131. Admission free, except for private exhibitions. Open daily 1–6.*

Go north to Laugavegur and catch the No. 4 bus to reach the
12 **Ásmundur Sveinsson Gallery.** Sveinsson (1893–1982), a social-realist sculptor, began his career in the 1920s. The surrounding garden, open at all times, contains several of his chunky, powerful sculptures. *Corner Sigtún and Reykjavegur, tel. 1/32155. Admission: IKr250. Open mid-May–Sept., daily 11–4; Oct.–mid-May, daily 1–4.*

From Hallgrímskirkja, walk on Þórsgata downhill (stay on it when it becomes Spítalastígur) to Þingholtstræti, where you turn left. Pass the **Borgarbókasafn** (City Library), which has a selection of books on Iceland in English on the second floor, and turn right onto Laufásvegur. The United States Embassy is to the right, an unimpressive building, but opposite it is the en-
13 trance to the **Listasafn Ríkisins** (National Art Gallery), which opened just a couple of years ago. Here you can view the works of Iceland's best painters, such as Gunnlaugur Scheving, Jóhannes Kjarval, and Tolli. *Frikirkjuvegur 7, tel. 1/621000. Admission free. Open Jan. 4–early Dec., Tues.–Sun. 12–6.*

Walk between the gallery and the **Fríkirkjan** church (corner of Frikirkjuvegur and Skálholtssígur) toward Tjörnin lake and turn left onto Lækjargata. Follow the lakeshore to the bridge on your right; cross the bridge and continue to the end of Skothúsvegur. On the right you see the oldest graveyard in Reykjavík, a peaceful spot with centuries of gravestones under the trees. On your left is a traffic circle, on the far side of which
14 stands the **Þjóðminjasafn** (National Museum). On display are Viking artifacts, national costumes, weaving, silver work, wood carvings, and some unusual whalebone carvings. *Suðurgata 41, tel. 1/28888. Admission free. Open mid-May–mid-Sept., Tues.–Sun. 11–4; Oct.–May, Tues., Thurs., and weekends 11–4.*

The museum is on the campus of the **University of Iceland,** founded in 1911. Leave the museum by walking between its main entrance side and **Félagsstofnun Stúdenta** (the Student Union). Continue along the sidewalk directly toward the main university building, in front of which is a large horseshoe-shaped lawn. On the lawn there is a **statue of Sæmundur Fróði,** a symbol of Icelandic students abroad (most Icelandic professionals pursue further studies in foreign universities). Legend has it that, after studying abroad, Sæmundur made a pact with the devil to change into a seal to carry him home. Just as they arrived, Sæmundur hit the seal on the head with the Bible and escaped unscathed.

15 Before you is the white-and-blue cultural center **Norræna Húsið** (Nordic House), designed by Finnish architect Alvar Aalto. There's a gallery in the basement, and lectures and concerts are often held upstairs. *Tel. 1/17030. Open daily 2–7.*

Time Out The **Nordic House cafeteria,** which offers a tempting selection of sandwiches and cakes, is a favorite haunt of university intelligentsia. A wide selection of Scandinavian newspapers is available.

Southwest of Nordic House, on Sturlugata, you pass the **Social Sciences Building** (the **University Art Museum** on the third floor is open daily 1:30–6; admission is free) and come to the Árnagarður building, behind the Social Sciences building, facing the street Suðurgata. The ground floor of Árnagarður

16 houses the **Árni Magnússon Institute,** which exhibits the most important national treasure, the original manuscripts of the Sagas. After years of dispute, Iceland signed a treaty with Denmark in 1965 that returned these manuscripts from Copenhagen to their rightful home here. *Tel. 1/25540. Admission free. Open mid-June–Aug., Mon.–Sat. 2–4; Sept.–early June, by request only.*

What to See and Do with Children

The most central supervised playgrounds are at **Njálsgata** (tel. 1/26568), **Vesturgata** (tel. 1/16830), **Frostaskjól** (tel. 1/23944), and **Dunhagi** (tel. 1/23918). Older children might want to visit one of the open-air, heated swimming pools, which have special shallow areas. All age groups would enjoy a visit to **Laugardalur,** a park in the northeastern suburbs (take the No. 2 bus east), with its large playground and swimming pool. It also features the **Icelandic Farm Animals** exhibit. The petting zoo includes goats, cows, horses, and other domestic animals; seals and fish are also on view in this handsomely laid-out park, opened in 1990. *Tel. 1/32533 or 1/32561. Admission: IKr200 adults, IKr100 students, senior citizens and children under 16 free. Open Mon.–Tues. and Thurs.–Fri. 1–5, Sun. 10–6.*

Just opposite the farm exhibit, also in Laugardalur, is the **Grasagarður** horticultural garden, with its extensive outdoor collection of plants from all over the world. *Tel. 1/38870. Admission free. Open June–Sept., weekdays 8 AM–10 PM, weekends 10–10.*

Off the Beaten Track

Visit the harborfront for an impression of the smells, sounds, and bustling activity of Iceland's basic export industry, fishing. Take the No. 2 bus to the end of its route at the beginning of Grandagarður and walk 15 minutes along that street out onto the **Örfirisey** peninsula. To the north you have a good view of **Esja,** mountain of a thousand hues. On the eastern side of Örfirisey is the city's largest and most modern fish-processing plant. Walking past it, you eventually end up at one of the two lighthouses at the entrance to the Reykjavík harbor.

Return walking along the waterfront, taking in the sights of a multitude of fishing vessels, pleasure boats, and freighters. On weekdays this is a bustling part of the city, with fishing boats coming in all the time. Beyond the bus stop, past another fish-processing plant, turn left on Mýrargata, heading downtown past small shipyards. Walk out along the landing ramps, where Icelandic youngsters like to hang out and do some serious fishing. Just past them is the ferry landing for the car-ferry to Akranes.

At the **Tollstöðin** (Customs House), you may want to detour around to the building's inland side, on Tryggvagata, where you can see Iceland's largest mosaic mural, a harbor scene by Gerður Helgadóttir. Return to the harbor's edge and walk north along the eastern pier, past more freighters and fishing vessels. Soon you come to **Ingófsgarður pier,** with its distinctive yellow lighthouse at the end. This is where the gray Icelandic Coast Guard vessels lie. Imagine these boats, each with one tiny cannon, scuttling between British trawlers and Royal Navy frigates on the high seas during the three so-called Cod Wars between 1958 and 1976, disputes over fishing grounds in the Arctic seas. Iceland won them all and succeeded in extending its fishing limit to 200 miles offshore, which consequently became the world standard.

At the end of the Coast Guard pier is a good view of Esja and of green **Viðey** island, accessible only by ferry (for ferry information call 1/681045 or 1/621632).

Shopping

The main shopping streets **downtown** are on and around Laugavegur, Bankastræti, Austurstræti, Aðalstræti, and Hafnarstræti. The **Kringlan** mall is on the east side of town (intersection of Miklabraut and Kringlumýrarbraut; take bus Nos. 3 or 6 from Lækjartog, or Nos. 8 or 9 from Hlemmur). The mall opened a couple of years ago and has drawn many customers, causing downtown merchants to become nervous. Visit the mall if only to observe the European-chic casual dress style of the average Icelander. There are also galleries and craft workshops all around town.

Street Markets In summertime, **Lækjartorg** square and the adjacent **Austurstræti** pedestrian shopping street fill with the stands of outdoor merchants offering anything from woolens, records, and books to vegetables, fruit, and bread.

Specialty Stores
Art Galleries **Gallery Borg** (Austurvöllur, tel. 1/24211, and Austurstræti 3, tel. 1/11664), and **Gallery FÍM** (Garðastræti 6, tel. 1/25060) display the latest work by contemporary Icelandic artists.

Coins and Stamps **Hjá Magna** (Laugavegur 15, tel. 1/23011) offers a wide selection. Due to the limited issues involved, a number of Icelandic stamps and coins are considered valuable items.

Crafts Long the staple purchase of visitors, woolens include both traditional hand knitted sweaters (a good sweater starts at around IKr2,000) and stylish, multicolored new designs. Lava ceramics, sheepskin rugs, and Viking-inspired jewelry are also popular souvenirs. Shop at **Rammagerðin** (Hafnarstræti 19, tel. 1/17910; at the Kringlan mall, tel. 1/68960), **Handprjónasamband** (Skólavörðustígur 19, tel. 1/21890), and **Íslenskur heimilisiðnaður** (Hafnarstræti 3, tel. 1/11785).

Sports and Fitness

Participant Sports
Golf At the southern tip of Seltjarnarnes, the westernmost part of the Reykjavík area, **Golfklúbbur Ness** (Suðurnes, tel. 1/611930) offers a well-kept 9-hole course with a great view in all directions. **Golfklúbbur Reykjavíkur** (Grafarholti, tel. 1/82815) is the granddaddy of them all, a challenging 18-hole course located just east of Reykjavík. **Keilir** (Vesturkoti, Hvaleyrarbraut, tel.

1/53360) is another well-established 18-hole course, located in Hafnarfjörður, south of Reykjavík.

Horseback Riding Two stables in the Reykjavík area rent horses by the hour or by the day. **Laxnes Pony Farm** (Mosfellsdalur, tel. 1/666179 or 1/621011 at Reykjavík Excursions) offers three-hour riding tours for IKr2,800, including guides and transportation to and from Reykjavík. **Icelandic Riding Tours** (Bæjarhraun 2, Hafnarfjörður, tel. 1/653044) offers one- to five-hour rides for IKr1,900–IKr2,800, which also includes guides and transportation from Reykjavík hotels.

Jogging In the crisp, clean air of the Reykjavík area, jogging is a pleasure on the wide sidewalks and in the parks. Favorite routes are around **Tjörnin** lake (*see* Tours 1 and 2, *above*), in **Laugardalur** park (*see* Swimming, *below*), and in **Miklatún** park (*see* Tour 2, *above*). For distance runners, there is the **Reykjavík Marathon** in August.

Skiing In wintertime, try the downhill and cross-country skiing at the **Bláfjöll** (tel. 1/78559) and **Skálafell** (tel. 1/666095) areas outside Reykjavík. Both are within a 30-minute drive of the capital and can be reached by BSÍ bus (tel. 1/22300).

Swimming There are nine swimming pools in the greater Reykjavík area, some with saunas. Rules of hygiene are strictly enforced—you must shower both before and after swimming. The pools of **Vesturbær** at Hofsvallagata (No. 4 bus) and **Laugardalur** (No. 2 bus going east) are favorite summer haunts. Both are open year-round, weekdays 7 AM–8:30 PM, Saturday 7:30–5:30, and Sunday 8–5:30. A locker and access to the swimming pool costs IKr100 or IKr50 for children (discount tickets available), but you must bring a towel or rent one. Use of the sauna is extra.

Spectator Sports

Soccer The national sport is played in summer before thousands of fans. A number of Icelandic soccer players are with professional soccer teams in Europe, and most come home to participate in international matches. The most important matches are played at **Laugardalsvöllur** arena (tel. 1/33527; take the No. 2 bus going east). Buy tickets at the box office just before the game, or inquire at downtown bookstores for advance sales.

Dining

Most of the better Reykjavík hotels have gourmet restaurants, belonging to the Chaine des Rotisseurs. There are also 11 fully licensed full-service restaurants with an international menu. In addition there are 20 combination pub/restaurants in the capital offering less extensive menus at reasonable prices.

Highly recommended restaurants are indicated by a star ★.

Very Expensive

Argentína. Come here for a change from seafood—there are 24 meat items on the menu. Located in a house set back off Barónsstígur, this recently opened steak house creates a South American atmosphere with white tiled walls, wood benches and beams. Argentinian wines are available and there are some distinctly Argentinian items on the menu, but Argentína also serves first-rate domestic Icelandic beef, basted with chicimurra sauce before being grilled. *Barónsstígur 11a, tel. 1/19555. Reservations advised. Dress: casual but neat. AE, DC, MC, V. No lunch.*

Grillið. Just off the university campus, atop the Saga Hotel, the

Grillið offers a spectacular view of the capital and the surrounding hinterlands. Seafood specialties include marinated ocean perch with mashed strawberries and lemon balm, baked in papillote. An excellent dessert is Akureyri blue cheese stirred with brown rum. *Hagatorg, tel. 1/25030. Reservations advised. Dress: casual but neat. AE, DC, MC, V.*

★ **Holt.** Located at the Holt Hotel, within walking distance of downtown, this restaurant is decorated with one of the finest collections of paintings by Icelandic masters; the bar features drawings by Jóhannes Kjarval. Holt has long been in the forefront of Icelandic restaurants, offering impeccable service and classic French cuisine: gravlax as appetizer, grilled halibut, rack of lamb, or reindeer steak as entrées. *Bergstaðastræti 37, tel. 1/25700. Reservations advised. Dress: casual but neat. AE, DC, MC, V.*

Expensive

Óðinsvé. Just east of downtown, this cozy restaurant is located on the first floor of the Óðinsvé Hotel. Decorated in pastel colors with pink tablecloths, half the dining area is under a covered porch. The chefs cook in a Scandinavian-French style, with an emphasis on seafood. Choice appetizers include the fish chowder; the best dessert is hot apfelstrudel. *Óðinstorg, tel. 1/25090. Reservations advised. Dress: casual but neat. AE, DC, MC, V.*

★ **Við Tjörnina.** This restaurant is simply the best in Iceland. The owner, epicure Rúnar Marvinsson, runs the kitchen himself, turning out classic Icelandic cuisine. Scallops in lobster sauce is a good choice for the appetizer; *tindabikkja* (fish with grapes, capers, and Pernod) is an unforgettable entrée. At lunchtime it's an incredible bargain—you can enjoy great salmon soup, a fish course, and a good cup of coffee for about IKr90. It's located just across Templarasund from the Parliament building and Dómkirkjan church, on the second floor of a typical corrugated-iron-clad early 20th-century house. The old-fashioned decor remains true to the house, with a hand-carved bar and chairs, embroidered tablecloths, and crocheted drapes. *Templarasund 3, tel. 1/18666. Reservations advised. Dress: casual but neat. AE, DC, MC, V.*

Moderate

Ítalía. Crisp Italian decor, a wine list that includes most Italian wines available in Iceland, and Parmesan cheese on every table helps this small eatery live up to its name. Scallops baked in garlic sauce are a good appetizer. The Italian cook makes excellent pork tortellini in cream sauce and lasagna Bolognese with blue cheese. For dessert, try Italian ice cream stirred with chopped fruit. *Laugavegur 11, tel. 1/24630. Reservations advised. Dress: casual but neat. AE, DC, MC, V.*

Þrír Frakkar hjá Úlfari. This fine little restaurant is located in a residential area not too far from downtown. Yellowish walls, wood paneling, wrought-iron tables, and comfortable chairs are set in a tasteful atmosphere. The menu features first-rate seafood as well as succulent beef dishes. Try the vegetable broth as an appetizer, butter-fried trout or Portuguese style bacalao (codfish stewed or fried with vegetables) as a main course, and apple pie for dessert. *Baldursgata 14, tel. 1/23939. Reservations advised. Dress: casual but neat. AE, DC, MC, V.*

Inexpensive

Bæjarins beztu. The most famous, most popular fast-food place in Iceland may easily escape you. Facing the harbor, set in a parking lot at the corner of Tryggvagata and Pósthússtræti, this is the home of the original Icelandic hot dog; one person serves about a thousand hot dogs a day out the window of a tiny hut—watch how fast his hands move. Ask for *ayn-ah-mud-lou* (pronounced quickly in monotone with stress on "mud"), which means "one with everything": mustard, tomato sauce, mayonnaise, and raw chopped onion. Eat standing up at one of the small outdoor tables. It's open from 10 AM until midnight. *Tryggvagata/Pósthússtræti, no tel. No reservations. Dress: casual. No credit cards.*

Kaffivagninn. Favored by cabdrivers, fishermen, and stevedores, this harborside restaurant serves traditional Icelandic fare. Sit at a table at the windows where you can have a nice view of the water. *Grandagarður 10, tel. 1/15932. No reservations. Dress: casual. No credit cards.*

Potturinn og pannan. Within walking distance of the uptown hotels, this is one of the city's best buys, though the cooking is unspectacular. There's an American-style open salad bar; fish or lamb entrées include juicy halibut steaks and lamb pepper steak with carrots and baked potatoes. Tile floors, copper light fixtures, and tables with benches create a cozy, intimate setting. Service is pleasantly brisk and efficient, but it's a popular spot, so you may have a wait during peak hours of lunch and dinner. *Brautarholt 22, tel. 1/11690. No reservations. Dress: casual. AE, MC, V.*

Lodging

Hotels and guest houses are spread all around Reykjavík, with the Holt and Óðinsvé hotels closest to downtown (at press time it was not certain whether the central but run-down Borg Hotel would remain open). Everything from modern, first-class Scandinavian-style hotels to inexpensive bed-and-breakfasts is available. Breakfast usually is included in the price, and free parking is available at all hotels. Inquire at the desk whether your hotel offers complimentary admission tickets to the closest swimming pool.

Highly recommended hotels are indicated by a ★.

Very Expensive

Holiday Inn. This international-class hotel built in 1987 is tastefully decorated in pastel colors with spacious rooms. Amenities include hair dryers, direct-dial telephones, minibars, and color TV. It's a 10-minute walk to the Laugardalur park and pool, and also is close to the Ásmundur Sveinsson Gallery. *Sigtún 38, 105, tel. 1/689000. 100 rooms with bath, 3 suites. Facilities: restaurant, coffee shop, bars. AE, DC, MC, V.*

Expensive

Holt. Excellent service and a gourmet restaurant make this quietly elegant hotel a favorite of business travelers. The main drawback is that the rooms are small, though luxuriously furnished, many with works by leading Icelandic artists. The location is in a pleasant residential suburb. *Bergstaðastræti 37, 101, tel. 1/25700. 50 rooms with bath, 4 suites. Facilities: restaurant, bar, lounge, conference room. AE, DC, MC, V.*

Loftleiðir. Recently redecorated in Scandinavian style, the hotel offers a wide range of amenities. The main drawback is its location at Reykjavík Airport, which means that you cannot walk anywhere and bus connections are difficult. *Reykjavík Airport, tel. 1/22322. 218 rooms with bath, 5 suites. Facilities: restaurant, cafeteria, bar, meeting rooms, pool, sauna, shops, bank, travel agency. AE, DC, MC, V.*

★ **Saga.** Popular with American business travelers, this first-class hotel was renovated in 1991 and has added a new wing. Located just off the university campus, it's a 10-minute walk to most museums, shops, and restaurants. All rooms are above the fourth floor and have spectacular views. *Hagatorg, 107, tel. 1/29900. 218 rooms with bath, 8 suites. Facilities: 2 restaurants, bars, nightclub, conference rooms, health club, shops, bank, travel agency. AE, DC, MC, V.*

Moderate **Höfði.** Formerly named the Geysir, this clean, recently renovated hotel offers simple but tasteful accommodations—light wood and neutral walls. Guests are usually budget-minded tourists. It's a 10-minute walk to the Hlemmur bus station and close to Miklatún park; the popular Potturinn og pannan restaurant is just around the corner, compensating for the lack of a restaurant in the hotel. *Skipholt 27, 105, tel. 1/623986. 36 rooms, 24 with bath. Facilities: breakfast room. AE, MC, V.*

★ **Lind.** Quietly unpretentious, decorated in light pastel colors, and located uptown close to the Hlemmur bus station, the Lind was fully renovated in 1987. Its clientele is largely Icelanders from the countryside, attending conferences or cultural events in Reykjavík. *Rauðarárstígur 18, 105, tel. 1/623350. 44 rooms with bath. Facilities: restaurant, conference rooms. AE, DC, MC, V.*

Inexpensive There are several guest houses around town, offering basic accommodations at low prices. The **Salvation Army** (Kirkjustræti 2, tel. 1/613203) charges IKr2,400 for a double room without bath or breakfast. The guesthouse at **Flókagata 1** (tel. 1/21155) charges IKr2,700 for the same. In private homes, such as **Ragna Björnsson's** (Ásvallagata 24, tel. 1/13481) guests get breakfast and access to a bath for around IKr4,100 per night. The **Reykjavík Youth Hostel** (Sundlaugavegur 34, tel. 1/38110) has 40 beds, without breakfast, for around IKr1,500 per night.

The Arts and Nightlife

Consult the monthly *Around Reykjavík* and biweekly *What's on in Reykjavík*, both available at hotels, for events of interest. Most hotels offer satellite TV channels from Europe and the United States, in addition to the countrywide Channel 1 and local Channel 2.

The Arts Theater, music, and opera are all popular in Iceland, but for the summer visitor the problem is that everything closes down during June, July, and August, except for the odd concert or two. In 1992, however, the biennial Arts Festival will liven things up. Call the tourist board for details if you plan to be in Reykjavík in June 1992.

Theater In winter, the **National Theater** (Hverfisgata, tel. 1/11200) and **City Theater** (Kringlumýri Center, tel. 1/680680) offer plays by Icelandic writers, such as Nobelist Halldór Laxness, as well as works by such diverse dramatists as Henrik Ibsen, Tennessee Williams, and Rodgers and Hammerstein.

Music Visiting musicians play everything from the classics to jazz, opera to rock. The **Icelandic Opera,** a resident company, performs in winter at its home on Ingólfsstræti.

Film The eight movie houses around the capital have up to six screens each and mostly show recent English-language films (with Icelandic subtitles). For listings, see the daily newspaper *Morgunblaðið*. The **University Cinemas** are on Hagatorg, near the university.

Folklore Traditional folklore entertainment in English, based on the Icelandic Sagas, is offered in summer by the **Light Nights** actors' show in various locations. Check with the Tourist Information Center (tel. 1/623045).

Nightlife Nightlife in Reykjavík is relegated mainly to weekends, beginning around 9 PM and ending at 3 AM. There are dozens of pubs and discos that charge a moderate entrance fee, but the high cost of drinks can make an evening out pricey. You may have to wait in line to get into the most popular places. The minimum drinking age is 18.

Púlsinn (Vitastígur 3, tel. 1/623137) is a great place for live music, even if conversation suffers for it. Jazz, rock, blues—anything goes here. **Gaukur á Stöng** (Tryggvagata 22, tel. 1/11556) is the mother of all pubs in Iceland. Opened well in advance of the end of beer prohibition in March 1989, it's always crowded and bustling with the avant-garde crowd. **L. A. Cafe.** (Laugavegur 45, tel. 1/626120), a cozy top-floor pub decorated with '50s and '60s movie themes, is frequented by people in their 20s. The service is friendly and inexpensive food is available. **Hótel Ísland** (Ármúli 9, tel. 1/687111), the largest restaurant and dance hall in Iceland, swallows over a thousand guests at a time. Offering live entertainment and music, it is popular with all ages.

Golden Circle Excursion

If you make only one foray beyond Reykjavík, take this popular day trip to the lakes, waterfalls, and hot springs just inland from the capital. You'll begin at Þingvellir, ancient seat of the world's first parliament; then you will see the original Geysir (whence the term geyser) hot spring, and stop to admire Gullfoss, the "Golden Waterfall" from which this tour takes its name.

Important Addresses and Numbers

Tourist Information General information is available in Reykjavík at the **Tourist Information Center** (Bankastræti 2, tel. 1/623045) or the **Iceland Tourist Board** (Lækjargata 3, tel. 1/27488).

In Hveragerði, contact the **South Coast Travel Service and Information Center** (Breiðumörk 10, tel. 8/34280).

Emergencies In Hveragerði the **police** can be reached at tel. 8/31154.

Getting There

By Car This circuit should take seven or eight hours by car, allowing time for stops at the various sights. At the farthest point, Gullfoss, you'll only be 125 kilometers (78 miles) from Reykjavík, and most of the drive is along paved main roads.

By Bus It is possible to explore this area by BSÍ bus, but you must allow plenty of time and perhaps stay overnight en route. **BSÍ Travel** (tel. 1/22300) serves Þingvellir twice daily (June–mid-Sept.) and Gullfoss/Geysir twice daily (June 15–Aug.).

Guided Tours

Kynnisferðir (Reykjavík Excursions, tel. 1/621011 or 1/6889 offers an eight-hour guided Golden Circle tour May–Septe ber, daily at 9 AM, and October–April, daily except Tuesda and Thursday.

Exploring the Golden Circle

After an hour's drive from Reykjavík, along Route 36 across the Mosfellsheiði heath, the broad lava plain of **Þingvellir** suddenly opens in front of you. Located at the northern end of Iceland's largest lake, Þingvallavatn, this has been the nation's most hallowed place since AD 930 when the settler Grímur Geitskór chose it as the site for the world's first thoroughly democratic parliament, the Icelandic *Alþingi* (Congress of All). In July of each year a large proportion of the population camped for two weeks at Þingvellir, meeting to pass laws and render judicial sentences. Iceland remained a sovereign nation-state, ruled solely by the people without a personal sovereign or central government, until 1262, when it came under the Norwegian crown; even then, the Alþingi continued to meet at Þingvellir until 1798, when the parliament was dissolved by Iceland's new Danish rulers. Nowadays campers' tents in the summer do, in a sense, carry on the tradition but in a much gentler form.

After you enter the Þingvellir park, but before you descend to the central plain, turn right at the sign for the **Almannagjá** gorge and follow a short road to the rim, where there is a fabulous view from the orientation marker. You can go down a path into the Almannagjá, which leads straight east to **Lögberg** (Law Speaker's Rock), where the person chosen as keeper of the laws would recite them from memory.

When Alþingi was established, the settlers diverted the Öxará River over the edge of Almannagjá, to attract the gods (who they believed inhabited waterfalls). In AD 1000 the Alþingi decided that Iceland should become a Christian country, but the old heathen gods were still worshiped in secret. Those Viking gods remain part of everyday English: Týr (as in Tuesday), Óðinn (as in Wednesday), Þór (as in Thursday), and the goddess Frigg (as in Friday). The **Öxaráfoss** waterfall is just north of Lögberg, with some beautiful, peaceful picnic spots north of it. Just below the waterfall in a deep stretch of the river lies the foreboding **Drekkingarhylur** pool, where unfaithful wives were drowned and adulterous husbands beheaded.

Besides its historic interest, Þingvellir has a special interest for naturalists: It is the geological meeting point of two continents. At Almannagjá, on the west side of the plain, is the easternmost edge of the American tectonic plate, which is otherwise submerged in the Atlantic Ocean. Over on the plain's east side, at the Heiðargjá gorge, you are at the westernmost edge of the Eurasian plate. In the 9,000 years since the Þingvellir lava field was formed, the tectonic plates have moved 231 feet apart. And they are still moving.

...e Out

The quaint **Valhöll Hotel and Restaurant** (in Þingvellir national park, tel. 8/22622) offers a fine menu. For a coffee break you might try the delicious *pönnukökur* (crepes filled with whipped cream and jam). Rather than the large common room, try to sit in one of the cozy corners of the restaurant, which are decorated with original Icelandic landscape paintings.

Seven kilometers (4 miles) east of the Þingvellir plain, Route 36 meets the road to **Laugarvatn** ("Lake for Bathing"), Route 365, which climbs 16 kilometers (10 miles) through the high country. If you keep a close lookout halfway along this road, you'll see on the left the large opening of a cave in which people lived in the early 20th century. True to its name, Laugarvatn is a lake warm enough for bathing, its water naturally heated by hot springs at the northern end. A cluster of buildings here houses a school in winter and Edda Hotels in summer. Drive around them to the lake's edge to a bathhouse where you can rent towels and take showers year-round. The entrance fee also covers a natural steam bath in an adjoining hut, where you actually sit atop a hissing hot spring.

A mile or so farther along Route 365, turn left onto Route 37, which leads 25 kilometers (16 miles) north to Route 35. A couple of kilometers east on Route 35 you'll come to the popular tourist spot Haukadalur, home of the **Geysir** and **Strokkur** geysers. Both are close to the road, near the Geysir restaurant and hotel (*see* Dining and Lodging, *below*). The famous Geysir hot spring nowadays only gives an occasional performance, gushing a column of scalding water 130 to 200 feet into the air (after being prodded by a generous amount of soap). Strokkur is a more reliable performer, having been drilled open in 1964 after a quiet period of 70 years; it throws up boiling water to as high as 100 feet at five-minute intervals. In the same area there are small boreholes from which steam arises, as well as beautiful pools of blue water. Always be careful when approaching hot springs or mud baths—the ground may be treacherous, giving way suddenly beneath you.

A couple of kilometers farther east along Route 35 you will come to thundering **Gullfoss,** the nation's most admired waterfall. It's named the Golden Waterfall both for the yellowish hue of the water and because popular legend has it that there is gold in waterfalls. Look at the end of the many rainbows reflected through the mist and you will indeed see a tantalizing shimmer of gold. Gullfoss, which is 105 feet high, really consists of a pair of waterfalls in the Hvítá River, set at right angles to each other. Below Gullfoss on the western bank of the river, where the steep walls begin to slant more, is a beautiful hidden spot a short steep climb from the road. Called **Pjaxi,** from the Latin *pax* meaning "peace," this is a restful nook of grassy knolls, natural springs, clear streams, and birch trees.

Return toward Reykjavík via Route 35 to the south. After 23 kilometers (14 miles), turn left onto Route 31, which takes you 5 kilometers (3 miles) past **Skálholt Church.** This ancient place of worship was established in 1056, soon after Iceland converted to Christianity; the present exquisitely simple building, with its modern altar piece, is the 11th church at this spot. Skálholt was the seat of the southern bishopric, the main center of learning and religion in Iceland until the 18th century. The modern memorial church at Skálholt houses some relics from the past, and a monument commemorates Roman Catholic bishop Jón Arason, who was beheaded at Skálholt in 1550 for resisting the Lutheran Reformation. Lutheranism is now the state religion.

Continue 10 kilometers (6 miles) along Route 31, then turn right to go south on Route 30, rolling through one of the most prosperous agricultural regions in Iceland. After 17 kilometers (11 miles), take a right onto Route 1, heading west toward Reykjavík. It's about 70 kilometers (43 miles) back to the capital, but if you have time, stop halfway along in **Hveragerði.** This floral wonderland of a town is home to a horticultural school, a large number of greenhouses heated by hot springs, and a fine swimming pool. From there it's a 40-kilometer (25-mile) drive to Reykjavík.

What to See and Do with Children

In Hveragerði the large **Skemmtigarðurinn** indoor amusement park is full of activities for kids, including go-carts and motorized inflatable boats. *Austurmörk 24, tel. 8/34115.*

Horse rentals in the area (*see* Horseback Riding, *below*) offer special tours for children.

Sports and Fitness

Boating At Þingvellir you can rent boats for rowing on Þingvallavatn (the rental facility is on the river by the Valhöll Hotel). Take extraordinary safety precautions; the shoreline drops off precipitously and the water is ice-cold.

Fishing Trout and char are plentiful in Þingvallavatn. Obtain fishing permits at the Valhöll Hotel at Þingvellir (tel. 8/22622).

Horseback Riding A number of stables offer guided trail rides in this area: **Íshestar** (Icelandic Riding Tours) at Miðdalur near Laugarvatn (tel. 8/61169); **Eldhestar** (Volcano Horses) in Hveragerði (Hveramörk 17, tel. 8/34212); the **Laxnes** Pony Farm (tel. 1/666179) on Route 36 to Þingvellir; and **Íshestar** in Hafnarfjörður (Bæjarhraun 2, tel. 1/653044) south of Reykjavík.

Swimming The swimming pool in Hveragerði (tel. 8/34113) is open Monday–Friday 7 AM–8:30 PM, Saturday 9–5:30, and Sunday 9–4:30.

Dining and Lodging

Haukadalur **Hótel Geysir.** Located at a popular tourist stop, beside the famous Geysir and Strokkur springs, this hotel is small and basic, but it has a large restaurant. *Tel. 8/68915. 10 rooms with shared baths. MC, V. Closed Sept.–May. Moderate.*

Hveragerði **Hótel Örk.** Recently built in the contemporary style, this white-concrete, blue-roofed hotel features a spa and swimming pool. The greenhouses, mud pools, and hot springs of Hveragarði are within a couple of blocks' walk. While accommodations are expensive, meals in the ground-floor restaurant are more moderately priced. *Breiðamörk 1, tel. 8/34700, fax 8/34775. 79 rooms with shower. Facilities: restaurant, pool, sauna, tennis. AE, MC, V. Expensive.*

Laugarvatn

Edda Húsmæðraskóli. This comfortable hotel and restaurant combination benefits from its location on the lake. *Tel. 8/61154. 27 rooms with bath or shower. MC, V. Closed Sept.–mid-June. Moderate.*

Edda Menntaskóli. This neighbor of the Edda Húsmæðraskóli also has a lakeside location, although conditions are a little less plush. *Tel. 8/61118. 88 rooms with bath or shower. MC, V. Closed Sept.–mid-June. Moderate.*

Þingvellir

Valhöll. This small, comfortable first-class hotel has an excellent location, right by the lake. Breakfast is included in the room rate. *Þingvellir National Park, tel. 8/22622, fax 1/621353. 37 rooms with bath or shower. Facilities: restaurant, fishing permits. MC, V. Closed Oct.–Apr. Expensive.*

The West and the Western Fjords

If you imagine the map of Iceland as the shape of a beast, two rugged western peninsulas—Snæfellsness and Vestfirðir—would be its proudly rearing head, jaws open wide around the huge bay of Breiðafjörður. The North Atlantic just off this coast is one of the country's prime fishing grounds. Busy fishing villages abound in Vestfirðir (the Western Fjords), but there also are remote cliffs thick with seabirds, tall mountains and deep fjords carved out of basaltic rock. Snæfellsness peninsula is crowned by the majestic Snæfells glacier.

Borgarfjörður, at the beast's throat, is an area of rich farmland that attracted many early settlers. Traces of the Viking past still fire visitors' imagination here today.

Important Addresses and Numbers

Tourist Information

In **Akranes,** the Tourist Information Center (Faxabraut 1, tel. 3/13327) is open 1–3 PM. In **Borgarnes,** the Hótel Borgarnes (Egilsgata 14–16, tel. 3/71119) provides information 24 hours a day year-round. In **Ísafjörður** the Tourist Bureau (Aðalstræti 11, tel. 4/3557) is open 9–noon and 1–5.

Emergencies

For local **police in** Borgarnes call tel. 3/71166, in Ísafjörður call tel. 4/4222, and in Stykkishólmur call 3/81008.

Arriving and Departing

By Plane

Air travel is the best way to visit the Western Fjords. You can fly to Ísafjörður on **Icelandair** (tel. 1/690200) and **Ernir Air** (tel. 1/24200 or 4/4200), and from there fly on Ernir Air to Bíldudalur, Flateyri, Ingjaldssandur, Patreksfjörður, Reykjanes, Suðureyri, and Þingeyri.

By Car

From Reykjavík and the north, you reach the West via the Ring Road (Route 1). Route 54 branches off to the Snæfellsness peninsula; Routes 60 and 68 branch off to the Western Fjords.

By Bus

BSÍ Travel (Reykjavík Airport, tel. 1/22300) runs frequent daily service to most towns in the region. It's a two-hour trip to Borgarnes, four hours to Stykkishólmur. Bus travel is not the best way to visit the Western Fjords; service to Ísafjörður runs a couple of days a week in summer only, and it's a 12-hour trip.

By Boat The **Akranes** car ferry, *Akraborg* (tel. 1/16050), sails three or four times daily year-round between Reykjavík and Akranes. In summer the **Baldur** car ferry (tel. 3/81120 or 4/2020) links Stykkishólmur, on the Snæfellsness peninsula, with Brjánslækur on the southern coast of the Western Fjords.

From Ísafjörður, you can travel by the ***Fagranes*** ferry (tel. 4/3155 or 4/4655) around the Western Fjords.

Guided Tours

The **Iceland Tourist Bureau** (tel. 1/25855) operates a 12-hour day trip from Reykjavík to the Western Fjords, flying to Ísafjörður and then sight-seeing by bus. The tour departs daily June–August.

Ísafjörður Travel Agency (Aðalstræti 11, tel. 4/3557) runs tours around the western fjords.

Boat Tours Speedboats tour Breiðafjörður Bay from **Stykkishólmur;** contact Eyjaferði (tel. 3/81450). One-day sightseeing tours of the Western Fjords run in the summers from Ísafjörður (tel. 4/3155 or 4/4655).

Exploring the West

The starting point for this tour is **Borgarnes,** 116 kilometers (72 miles) from Reykjavík along the Ring Road (the Reykjavík–Akranes ferry is a convenient shortcut).

Borgarfjörður Area Drive northeast from Borgarnes on the Ring Road 11 kilometers (seven miles) until you come to Route 53 leading eastward. Turn right onto Route 53 and pass the **Ferjukot** wild salmon farm; cross the one-lane bridge over the muddy glacial Hvítá River. Take the first left turn onto Route 52 and in 10 minutes you come to the **Laxfoss** waterfall in the Grímsá River, where salmon and trout leap the rapids. Continue across the Grímsá north on Route 50 a little more than 10 kilometers (6 miles) until you come to the **Kleppjárnsreykir** horticultural center, with its many greenhouses heated by thermal water from the region's hot springs. Many kinds of fruit and vegetables are available at the greenhouses.

Proceed eastward 8 kilometers (5 miles) on Route 518 to **Reykholt** where the writer and historian Snorri Sturluson lived from 1206 to 1241. Author of the *Snorra-Edda,* a textbook of poetics, and the *Heimskringla,* a history of Norway's kings, Snorri was also a wealthy chieftain and political schemer. He was murdered in Reykholt in 1241 on the orders of the Norwegian king. One may still view the underground passageway leading from the ruins of his residence to **Snorralaug,** the naturally heated pool where he bathed.

Continue for 15 minutes on Route 518 to the colorful **Hraunfossar** waterfalls. A multitude of natural springs under a birch-covered lava field above the Hvítá River creates a waterfall hundreds of feet wide, seemingly appearing out of nowhere. A little farther up the Hvíta (a few minutes along Route 518) is the **Barnafossar** (Waterfall of Children), which carves strange figures out of the rock. According to legend, a mother who long ago lost her two sons in the waterfall cast a spell on a stone arch over the river that no one shall cross the arch and live. A fatal accident at Barnafossar a few years ago convinced many people that the old spell still held sway.

The **Húsafell** park a few hundred meters up the road is a popular summer camping site, with its birch trees, swimming pool, and chalets. A large crowd gathers here for the large annual summer celebration on the first weekend in August.

Return past Reykholt to the Ring Road and go north about 10 kilometers (6 miles) to Bifröst. Right by the road is the **Grábrók** volcanic cone, which you can easily scale for a panoramic view of the area. Grábrók's lava field, covered with moss, grass, and birches offers many quiet spots for a picnic. Eight kilometers (five miles) north is the distinctive pyramid-shaped **Mount Baula,** a pastel-colored rhyolite mountain. In the 19th century, Icelanders enjoyed telling gullible foreign travelers fantastic stories of the beautiful green meadows and forests populated by dwarfs shepherding herds of fat sheep, at Baula's summit.

Snæfellsness Peninsula

The southern shore of this peninsula begins about 40 kilometers (25 miles) north of Borgarnes. Begin the journey north from Borgarnes on Route 54. As you drive farther west on the peninsula, you'll pass through the Staðarsveit district, with its beautiful mountain range. Many small lakes abound with flowers growing in the water, and there are many sparkling springs. At **Lýsuhóll,** a few minutes north of Route 54, you can bathe in the warm water of a naturally carbonated swimming pool. About 10 kilometers (6 miles) farther west is the **Búðahraun** lavafield, composed of rough, slaggy *apalhraun* lava. Its surface makes walking difficult, but it's more hospitable to vegetation than most Icelandic landscapes; flowers, trees, spices, and berries grow large here.

At **Búðir,** take a left turn onto the coastal road for a 50-kilometer (31-mile) drive circling the tip of the peninsula. On your right you'll see the majestic Snæfells glacier, **Snæfellsjökull,** which, like Mount Fujiama in Japan, covers a volcano. In the Viking past, great men made a final pilgrimage to the glacier to die; one such hero was the settler Bárður Snæfellsás, for whom the glacier is named. In more modern times, the glacier was featured in Jules Verne's novel *Journey to the Center of the Earth* as the spot where the explorers enter the depths of the world.

The coastal drive will take you past many beautiful villages, such as **Arnarstapi** and **Hellnar.** About an hour's walk from the road at the western tip of the peninsula lie the **Svörtuloft Cliffs,** home to multitudes of seabirds every year.

At **Ólafsvik,** you can stop at the Hotel Nes (*see* Dining and Lodging, *below*) to arrange snowmobile tours to the top of the glacier. The main highway (now numbered Route 57) begins again at Ólafsvik; from there it's 67 kilometers (42 miles) along the peninsula's north coast to **Stykkishólmur,** home of the scallops fishery. A ferry sails from here to the sparsely populated islands of the Breiðafjörður. The island **Flatey,** where the ferry stops over on the way to the western fjords, is worth a visit. The now sleepy vacation village was an important center of commerce and learning in the 19th century; some classic houses still stand today.

Vestfirðir (Western Fjords) From Stykkishólmur, follow Route 57 for another 80 kilometers (50 miles) to Route 60. From the Ring Road, pick up Route 60 about 10 kilometers (6 miles) past Bifröst and drive 43 kilometers (27 miles) to the intersection with Route 57. From there, it's a long drive north—340 kilometers (211 miles)—to **Ísafjörður**, the main airport and cultural center of the Western Fjords. Ísafjörður itself is one of the most important fishing villages in Iceland, but for visitors its main use is as a jumping-off point for tours of the splendid, peaceful, but desolate land north of the 66th parallel. Geologically the oldest part of Iceland, Vestfirðir offers spectacular views of mountains, fjords, and sheer cliffs. Hikers and mountaineers may want to hire guides to explore this unspoiled region, and anglers come here to catch trout in the rivers and lakes. The northernmost cliffs of **Hornbjarg** and **Hælavíkurbjarg** are home to large bird colonies; the largest colony, with millions of birds, is at **Látrabjarg**, an immense vertical cliff at Iceland's westernmost tip.

Sports and Fitness

Fishing There are nearly one hundred rivers and lakes that offer trout and salmon fishing. Ask at local hotels and service stations, or consult the *Icelandic Fishing Guide* (*see* Sports and Outdoor Activities *in* Staying in Iceland, *above*).

Golf There are courses at **Ólafsvík** (at Froða, east of town) and **Stykkishólmur** (a 9-hole course by the Hotel Stykkishólmur).

Horseback Riding To rent horses for exploring the Borgarfjörður area, call **Hotel Bifröst** (tel. 3/50000 or 3/50005, fax 3/50003).

Swimming There are swimming pools in **Borgarnes** (Skallagrímsgata, tel. 7/70027), **Ólafsvík** (Ennisbraut 9, tel. 3/61199), **Stykkishólmur** (tel. 3/81272), and **Ísafjörður** (Austurvegur 9, 4/3200).

Dining and Lodging

Bifröst **Hótel Bifröst.** Low white buildings with red roofs house this summer hotel beside the Ring Road in Borgarfjörður. *Hreðavatn, tel. 3/50000 or 3/50005, fax 3/50003. 26 rooms, 8 with bath. Facilities: restaurant, bar, horseback riding. MC, V. Expensive.*

Borgarnes **Hótel Borgarnes.** One of the biggest and most popular hotels on the west coast, this establishment offers both a cafeteria and an elegant restaurant. *Egilsgata 14–16, tel. 3/71119, fax 3/71443. 36 rooms, 20 with bath. AE, DC, MC, V. Moderate.*

Búðir **Hótel Búðir.** Under the magical glacier Snæfellsjökull, and close to a golden beach, this hotel has an excellent restaurant. *Tel. 3/56700. 10 rooms with shared bath. Facilities: restaurant, boats, fishing. AE, DC, MC, V. Closed Oct.–Apr. Moderate.*

Ísafjördur **Hótel Ísafjördur.** This is a good family hotel, located in the heart of town. The restaurant offers a great variety of tasty seafood, and breakfast is included in the room rate. Sightseeing tours and boat trips are offered in summer. *Silfurtorgi 2, tel. 4/4111, fax 4/4767. 32 rooms with shower. AE, MC, V. Moderate.*

Ólafsvík **Hótel Nes.** This functional hotel is close to the harbor. Its cafeteria offers good food at moderate prices. There are many hiking paths in the vicinity, and tours to the Snæfellsness glacier leave from here. *Ólafsbraut 19, tel. 3/61300. 38 rooms with shared bath. No credit cards. Inexpensive.*

Reykholt **Edda.** Located in a scenic part of Borgarfjörður, this comfortable, modern building is a secondary school in winter and a hotel in summer. *Tel. 3/51260. 60 rooms with bath. Facilities: restaurant, pool. MC, V. Closed Sept.–mid-June. Moderate.*

Stykkishólmur **Hótel Stykkishólmur.** This hotel makes a convenient jumping-off point for excursions to the islands of Breiðafjörður and for the ferry to the Western Fjords. It includes a good restaurant. *Vatnàsi, tel. 3/81330, fax 3/81579. 33 rooms with shower. DC, MC, V. Moderate.*

Youth Hostels
Borgarfjörður **Varmaland:** Stafholtstungum, tel. 3/51301. 82 beds. Closed Aug. 16–June 14.

Snæfellsnes **Stykkishólmur:** tel. 3/81095. 25 beds.

Western Fjords **Breiðavík:** Rauðasandi, tel. 4/1575. 40 beds. Closed Oct.–Apr.

The North

From the Hrútafjörður fjord, which gouges deeply into the western end of the coast, to Vopnafjörður on the east, Iceland's north is a land created by the interplay of fire and ice. Inland, you can find the largest lava fields on earth, some with plants and mosses, others barren and bare. Yet valleys sheltered by the mountains are lush with vegetation and rich in color, and the deeply indented coast offers magnificent views north toward the Arctic, especially spectacular under the summer's midnight sun.

The commercial and cultural center, Akureyri, is Iceland's second-largest city; from there, it's a pleasant drive to Lake Mývatn, where bird-watchers can spot vast numbers of waterfowl and hikers can explore weird lava formations. The weather is more stable here than in the south, and it's unusually mild around Mývatn, making it a pleasant outdoor destination.

Important Addresses and Numbers

Tourist Information In **Akureyri,** contact the Tourist Information Center (Coach Terminal, Hafnarstræti 82, tel. 6/24442); it is open June–Aug. weekdays 8:30–7 PM. In **Húsavík,** Húsavík Travel (Stórigarður 7, tel. 6/42100) is open weekdays, 9–noon and 1–5.

Emergencies To reach the local **police** in Akureyri, call 6/23222.

Arriving and Departing

By Plane **Icelandair** (tel. 1/690200) flies to Akureyri, Sauðarkrókur, and Húsavík. The flight to Akureyri takes about an hour. **Norlandair** and Icelandair (tel. 6/22000) share offices and operate flights from Akureyri to Grímsey, Húsavík, Kópasker, Ólafsfjörður, Raufarhöfn, Siglufjörður, Þórshöfn, and Vopnafjörður.

By Car It's a 432-kilometer (268-mile) drive from Reykjavík to Akureyri along the Ring Road (Route 1), a full day's journey. Branch off on Route 75 to Sauðárkrókur, or on Route 85 to Húsavík.

By Bus **BSÍ Travel** (tel. 1/22300) runs daily bus service from Reykjavík to the north. It's 5½ hours to Blönduós and eight hours to Akureyri. Bus service from Akureyri takes less than 1½ hours to Húsavík and four hours to Mývatn.

The **Akureyri Bus Company** (Gránufélagsgata 4, tel. 6/23510 or, at bus terminal, 6/24442) operates scheduled trips around the region, including a tour by bus and ferry to Hrísey Island, home of Galloway cattle, and to Grímsey Island on the Arctic Circle.

Guided Tours

The **Iceland Tourist Bureau** (tel. 1/25855) operates a 12-hour day trip from Reykjavík to Akureyri and Lake Mývatn, by plane to Akureyri and by bus to Mývatn. The tour departs daily June–mid-September.

Akureyri Travel Bureau (Ráðhústorg 3, tel. 6/25000) and **Nonni Travel** (Brekkugata 3, tel. 6/27922) run tours from Akureyri to Mývatn, historic sites, and the islands off the north coast.

Exploring the North

If you're driving the full Ring Road route, you'll enter the North at **Brú,** snuggled at the inland end of the long Hrútafjörður fjord. **Blönduós,** 90 kilometers (56 miles) farther west, makes a convenient stopping place. Another 50 kilometers (31 miles) west, Route 75 intersects the Ring Road. If you turn right and then take the next right a kilometer or so farther, you'll come to **Víðimýri,** where you can visit an 18th-century turf-roofed church. Returning north, cross the Ring Road and head north on Route 75 about 10 kilometers (6 miles) to the **Glaumbær Folk Museum.** Set in a turf-roofed farmhouse that originally belonged to affluent farmers, the museum provides a glimpse of 18th- and 19th-century living conditions in rural Iceland. *Tel. 5/38266. Admission: IKR 120. Open June–Aug., daily 10–noon and 1–7.*

Another 17 kilometers (11 miles) north on Route 75 will bring you to **Sauðárkrókur,** a large coastal town. In summer, boat trips from Sauðárkrókur to Drangey and Málmey islands provide some striking views.

From the junction with Route 75, it's another 95 kilometers (59 miles) along the Ring Road to **Akureyri.** Though not as cosmopolitan as Reykjavík, Akureyri is certainly more active than the villages around the coast. A century ago the farmers in the prosperous agricultural area surrounding Akureyri established KEA, a cooperative enterprise to combat the Danish businesses that dominated the area's economic life at the time; KEA still runs most stores and industries in Akureyri today.

Lying at the end of 64-kilometer-long (40-mile-long) Eyjafjörður fjord, Akureyri is sheltered from the ocean winds and backed by mountains on three sides. Late-19th-century wood houses give the city center a sense of history, while the twin spires of a simple ultramodern Lutheran church, rising on a green hill near the waterfront, provide a focal point. The church is named after Akureyri native Matthías Jochumsson, the poet who wrote Iceland's national anthem in 1874.

From the church, it's a short walk from the town center on Eyrarlandsvegur to the **Listigarðurinn** (Arctic Botanic Gardens), which has been planted with more than 400 species of Icelandic flora, including some rare arctic plants. At Eyrarlandsvegur 3 you'll pass **Matthíasarhús,** the house where Jochumsson once lived, now open as a museum (daily 2–4). Akureyri has two other museums honoring Icelandic writers: **Davíðshús,** the home of Davíð Stefánsson (Bjarkastígur 6, open weekdays 3–5), and **Nonnahús,** the boyhood home of Jón Sveinsson (Aðalstræti 54b, open daily 2–4:30).

Also near the church, on Hafnarstræti, is the **Náttúrugripasafnið** (Natural History Museum), which displays specimens of all the bird species that nest in Iceland. *Hafnarstræti 81. Open June and mid-Aug.–mid-Sept., Sun.–Fri. 1–4; July–mid-Aug., Sun.–Fri. 10–5; mid-Sept.–June, Sun. 1–3.*

The **Minjasafnið** (Folklore Museum) displays a large collection of old farm tools and fishing equipment. *Aðalgata 58, tel. 6/24162. Admission: IKr150. Open daily 1:30–5.*

During June and July, make a point of taking an evening drive north from Akureyri along Route 82. The midnight sun creates breathtaking views along the coast of Eyjafjörður.

From Akureyri you can see to the south the pyramid-shaped rhyolite mountain **Súlur** and, beyond it, **Kerling,** the tallest peak in Eyjafjörður. Head towards them for a taste of history. Drive 10 kilometers (6 miles) south on Route 821 to **Kristnes,** where the area's first settler, Helgi Magri ("Helgi, the thin one") from Ireland, lived on his farm, which is no longer intact. Proceed 5 kilometers (3 miles) along Route 821 to **Grund,** where you can visit an attractive turn-of-the-century church. Another 13 kilometers (8 miles) south on Route 821 will bring you to **Saurbær,** with a church built in the 1850s from wood and turf; it's typical of Icelandic dwellings through the centuries. From Saurbær, turn left onto Route 829, which runs north parallel to Route 821. A couple of kilometers along , you pass the historic **Möðruvellir** farm, the site of an historic Augustinian monastery from 1296 until 1550, when Catholicism was abolished in Iceland. The Möðruvellir church has an altar piece dating from the 15th century. This is the highest inhabited farm in the country, approximately 1,350 feet above sea level. From here it is 25 kilometers (16 miles) north to the Ring Road.

If you drive east from Akureyri on the Ring Road, passing farms left and right, you soon cross the Vaðlaheiði heath and enter the **Fnjóskadalur Valley,** formed by glaciers only a few thousand years ago. Go a few hundred meters past Route 833, which leads south into the western part of the valley, and turn right onto the next road, which takes you to the **Vaglaskógur** (Log Forest), one of the largest forests in this relatively treeless country. Vaglaskógur was probably even larger originally, but through the centuries trees were taken for building material and firewood. Its tallest birches today reach some 40 feet.

Return to the Ring Road and proceed east for about 12 kilometers (7 miles) to the beautiful **Goðafoss** (Waterfall of the Gods) in the Skjálfanda River. Its name derives from a historic event in AD 1000, when Þorgeir Ljósvetningagoði, ordered by the Icelandic Parliament to choose between paganism and Christianity, threw his pagan icons into the waterfall. (Þorgeir was less a saint than a pragmatist: He chose Christianity largely because the king of Norway held his son hostage until he converted!) Just before you reach Goðafoss, you'll pass the **Ljósavatn** church and farm where Þorgeir lived a millennium ago. Although the farm is long gone, you can visit the church, which houses among other relics some interesting runic stones recently unearthed. A new church and memorial will be built here before the year 2000, the millennial anniversary of Iceland's conversion to Christianity.

It's about 100 kilometers (62 miles) along the Ring Road from Akureyri to **Mývatn,** a gemlike lake set amid mountains and lava fields. This area deserves at least a day's exploration. Fed by cold springs in the lake bottom and from warm springs in the northeastern corner, the shallow lake, 15 square miles in area yet only three to 13 feet deep, teems with life—fish, birds, and insects, including the swarming midges for which the lake is named. Recent tallies indicate there are 150,000 ducks in the Mývatn area, including all 17 species found in Iceland, as well as thousands of geese and swans. The lake is one of the major breeding grounds for waterfowl in Europe.

Turning off the Ring Road at Route 848, you pass **Skútustaðir,** a village on the lake's southern shore. Proceed along the eastern shore to the 1,300-foot-high **Hverfjall** ash cone, a few hundred meters from the road. Several paths lead to the top, where you can take in a sweeping view of the lake and surroundings. The outer walls of this volcanic crater are steep but the ascent is easy. The walk around the top of the crater is about 4,300 feet. Southwest of Hverfjall is the **Dimmuborgir** (Dark Gulches) lava field, a labyrinth of tall formations where you can easily get lost, unless you bring a compass. Get out of your car and join the other vacationers wandering around this eerie landscape. Among its mysterious arches, gates, and caves, the best known is the **Kirkja** (Church), resembling a Gothic chapel (it's marked by a sign, lest you miss it).

Time Out At the northeastern corner of Mývatn, where Route 848 meets the Ring Road again, the modern **Reynihlíð Hotel** (tel. 6/44170) serves coffee and *kökur* (pastries), including traditional *kleinur* (deepfried twists) and *pönnukökur*.

Proceeding a few kilometers south from Mývatn on the Ring Road, you pass a factory processing diatoms (tiny skeletons of algae) sucked from the bottom of the lake, where they have been deposited through the centuries. Because the diatom content of the lake gives it a unique flora and fauna, the removal was strongly protested (to no avail) in 1970 by Halldór Laxness, who won the Nobel prize for literature in 1954. Indeed, materials from Mývatn soil have been put to industrial use for centuries.

In the **Námaskarð** mountain ridge, on the eastern side of the Ring Road, are bubbling mud and purple sulfur, boiling like a witch's cauldron in the strange red and yellow valleys. Hike around this fascinating area, but remember to step carefully and avoid the noxious gases.

Route 87 branches off the Ring Road to **Húsavík,** an attractive port on the north coast. (From Akureyri, the drive is 90 kilometers/56 miles.) From there, take Route 85 north along the coast to Tjörnes, ending up inland at the lush national park of **Ásbyrgi** (Shelter of the Gods). The forest here is surrounded by steep cliffs on all sides except the north, making it a peaceful shelter from the wind. Legend says this horseshoe-shaped canyon was formed by the giant hoof of Sleipnir, the eight-footed horse of Óðinn. Another 46 kilometers (28 miles) south on Route 864 will bring you to **Dettifoss,** Europe's highest waterfall.

Shopping

As Iceland's second-largest city, Akureyri offers better shopping than most towns outside of Reykjavík. **Álafoss** (Glerárgata 28, tel. 6/21900) is a factory store selling a wide selection of Icelandic sweaters, blankets, and other woolens. Woolens, ceramics, and other gift items are available at **París** (Hafnarstræti 96, tel. 6/27744).

Sports and Fitness

Bicycling The **Hótel Reynihlíð** (Mývatnssveit, tel. 6/44170) in Mývatn offers bicycle rentals for exploring the area around the lake.

Fishing Near Hrútafjörður, **Arinbjörn Jóhannsson** (Brekkulækur, tel. 5/12938) offers lake trout fishing and 7- to 13-day fishing trips on specified dates.

Golf In **Akureyri,** enjoy golf at the world's northernmost 18-hole course, at Jaðar on the outskirts of town. There also are golf courses in **Ólafsfjörður** and **Sauðárkrókur.**

Hiking **Akureyri Travel Bureau** (Ráðhústorg 3, tel. 6/25000) and **Nonni Travel** (Brekkugata 3, tel. 6/27922) run mountain hiking tours from Akureyri.

Horseback Riding The **Hotel Reynihlíð** (tel. 6/44170) in Mývatn offers pony treks around the lake. Near Hrútafjörður, **Arinbjörn Jóhannsson** (tel. 5/12938) in Brekkulækur also organizes horseback treks. In Akureyri, contact **Pólarhestar** (Grýtubakki 11, tel. 6/33179).

Swimming There are open-air pools in **Blönduós** (tel. 5/24451), **Sauðárkrókur** (tel. 5/35226), **Ólafsfjörður** (tel. 6/62363), **Akureyri** (Þingvallastræti 13, tel. 6/23260), and **Húsavík** (tel. 6/41144).

Dining and Lodging

Akureyri
Dining

Fiðlarinn. The view is fabulous from this rooftop restaurant and bar overlooking the Akureyri harbor and Eyjafjörður bay. The dining room is tastefully decorated in pale wood and paint. Danish gourmet cooking is featured. *Skipagata 14, tel. 6/27100. Reservations advised. Dress: casual but neat. AE, DC, MC, V. Expensive.*

Höfðaberg. Located in the KEA Hotel (*see below*), this fine restaurant sports modern maroon-and-mauve Scandinavian decor. The cuisine is both international and Icelandic. *Hafnarstræti 87–89, tel. 6/22600. Summer reservations advised. Dress: casual but neat. AE, DC, MC, V. Expensive.*

Lodging

Hótel KEA. Mauve-and-maroon decor with dark wood trim characterizes this recently renovated property, which is on a par with many of the capital's hotels. Besides the Höfðaberg Restaurant (*see* Dining, *above*), there is an inexpensive cafeteria on the ground floor. On weekends, the KEA is one of the city's main dancing spots. *Hafnarstræti 87–89, tel. 6/22200, fax 6/21009. 72 rooms with bath, 1 suite. Facilities: restaurant,* *bar, lounge, conference and banquet rooms. AE, DC, MC, V. Expensive.*

Hótel Norðurland. Completely renovated in 1989, with Danish modern furniture, this hotel features all the amenities of the better Reykjavík hotels. On the ground floor is the separately run Hlóðir Restaurant, where hotel guests get a hearty breakfast. *Geislagata 7, tel. 6/22600, fax 6/27833. 28 rooms with bath. Facilities: restaurant, bar, satellite TV, minibars, telephones. AE, DC, MC, V. Expensive.*

Brú
Dining

Staðarskáli í Hrútafirði. At the inland end of Hrútafjörður, this neat and clean restaurant offers good cooking—grilled lamb is a specialty—at reasonable prices. *Corner Rtes. 1 and 68, tel. 5/11150. Reservations not necessary. Dress: casual. Moderate.*

Húsavík
Dining and Lodging

Hotel Húsavík. Popular with skiers, this reputable hotel has a good restaurant and a practical cafeteria; breakfast is included in the room rate. *Ketilsbraut 22, tel. 6/41220, fax 6/42161. 21 rooms with shower. AE, DC, MC, V. Expensive.*

Mývatn
Dining and Lodging

Hotel Reynihlíð. This popular hotel has a helpful general information service for tourists and a restaurant. *Mývatnssveit, tel. 6/44170, fax 6/44310. 48 rooms with shower. Facilities: horseback riding, bicycle rentals. AE, DC, MC, V. Moderate.*

Hotel Reykjahlíð. Set in an exclusive location by the lake, this small hotel has a convenient restaurant. *Mývatnssveit, tel. 6/44142. 12 rooms with shared bath. AE, MC, V. Closed Sept.–May. Inexpensive.*

Sauðárkrókur
Dining

Dalakofinn. Reminiscent of a classic cozy American diner, complete with chrome chairs and plastic flowers, this restaurant serves somewhat standard food—overcooked Icelandic cuisine. *Aðalgata 15, tel. 5/36655. Reservations not necessary. Dress: casual. AE, MC, V. Inexpensive.*

Dining and Lodging

Mælifell. The restaurant serves good food at fair prices. There are six guest rooms for overnight stays. *Aðalgata 7, tel. 5/35265. 6 rooms with shared bath. AE, MC, V. Moderate.*

Youth Hostels

Akureyri: tel. 6/23657. 32 beds.
Húsavík: tel. 6/42220. 12 beds. Closed Jan.–May.
Lónkot: Skagafirði, tel. 5/37432. 20 beds. Closed Oct.–May 14.
Reykir: Hrútafjörður, tel. 5/10015. 20 beds.

The East

In 1974, when the final bridge was completed across the treacherous glacier waters pouring from the tongues of the Vatnajökull glacier, the eastern side of the island finally became accessible from Reykjavík. It is still a long journey by car, but you can watch miniature icebergs sliding toward the sea while the great skuas, predatory sea birds, swoop across weird black volcanic beaches. Egilsstaðir, on the shore of Lake Lögurinn, is the hub of the eastern fjords, and the Norröna ferry from Europe arrives at Seyðisfjörður 25 kilometers (16 miles) to the east.

Important Addresses and Numbers

Tourist Information

In **Egilsstaðir,** the Austurland Travel Bureau (Kaupvangur 6, tel. 7/12000) is open weekdays 9–noon and 1–5. In **Seyðisfjörður,** the Austfar Travel Agency (Fjarðargata 6, tel. 7/

21111) is open weekdays 9–noon and 1–5. In **Höfn,** the campsite (tel. 7/81701) is open July–August, daily, 8–11 and 5–11.

Arriving and Departing

By Plane **Icelandair** (tel. 7/12000) and **Eastair** (tel. 7/11122) operate scheduled flights from Reykjavík to Egilsstaðir. From there, there are connections to Bakkafjörður, Borgarfjörður, Breiðdalsvík, Fáskrúðsfjörður, Hornafjörður, Norðfjörður, and Vopnafjörður.

By Boat The **Norröna** car ferry from Norway or Denmark, via the Faroe Islands, arrives in Seyðisfjörður. Contact Norröna Travel, Laugavegur 3, 101 Reykjavík (tel. 1/626362, fax 1/29450).

By Car The region is accessible by car on the Ring Road (Route 1). The drive from Reykjavík to Egilsstaðir is about 700 kilometers (434 miles), and from Akureyri 273 kilometers (170 miles).

By Bus The East is so far from Reykjavík that bus travel is recommended only if you are making the entire circuit. From Akureyri the six-hour trip to Egilsstaðir runs daily in summer, three times a week the rest of the year. From Egilsstaðir there's frequent service around the region; it takes about 5 hours to get to Höfn.

Guided Tours

The **Iceland Tourist Bureau** (tel. 1/25855) operates a day trip from Reykjavík to Höfn by plane, with a snowmobile tour of the Vatnajökull glacier and a boat tour on the Jökulsárlón lagoon. The tour runs daily mid-June–Aug. **Austurland Travel Bureau** (Kaupvangur 6, Egilsstaðir, tel. 7/12000) specializes in adventure travel, including snowmobile tours of Vatnajökull.

Exploring the East

Egilsstaðir is located at the northern end of long, narrow lake **Lögurinn.** While the town itself has no particular sights to see, an easy 25-kilometer (15-mile) drive from town along the lake's southern shore, first on the Ring Road then onto Route 931, will take you to beautiful **Hallormsstaðaskógur National Park,** which contains the country's largest forest; more than 40 varieties of trees grow here, mostly spruce and larch. This area is one of Iceland's most accessible paradises, and a visit is strongly recommended. The Atlavík camping ground on the lake south of Hallormsstaðaskógur is a popular vacation spot, and legend has it that Iceland's version of the Loch Ness monster lives in the lake here. In the highlands west of Lögurinn you may be able to spot Icelandic reindeer. Though not native to the island (they originally were brought from Norway in the 18th century), the reindeer have thrived to the point that controlled hunting is allowed; some 600 animals can be killed every year.

Another excursion from Egilsstaðir will take you 71 kilometers (44 miles) north and east on Route 94 to **Bakkagerði,** a small village set on the Borgarfjörður fjord, cupped by mountains at Iceland's easternmost tip. The painter Jóhannes Kjarval lived here for a time, and Álfaborg, a hillock just outside the village, is the legendary home of elves.

Head east from Egilsstaðir on Route 92 and you'll have a breathtaking drive over the highest mountain pass in the country. You'll pass through **Eskifjörðor** (48 kilometers/30 miles from Egilsstaðir) and end up in **Neskaupsstaður,** which is 71 kilometers (44 miles) from Egilsstaðir. Both are large towns dramatically perched below steep crags on the rims of their respective fjords.

To continue along the Ring Road, drive south from Egilsstaðir 150 kilometers (93 miles) to the rugged stretch of coast indented by the inlets of **Álftafjörður** (Fjord of Swans) and **Hamarsfjörður.** Surrounded by majestic mountains, these shallow waters host myriad swans, ducks, and other birds that migrate from Europe in the spring and summer here.

Another 100 kilometers (62 miles) south is the town of **Höfn,** which is slowly being closed off from the ocean by silt washed by glacial rivers into the fjord. Spread out on a thin blanket of soil amid glacial puddles, Höfn offers a fine view of the awesome **Vatnajökull** glacier, which is not only Iceland's largest but is equal in size to all the glaciers on the European mainland put together. From Höfn you can arrange tours of the glacier (get information at the Hotel Höfn, *see* Dining and Lodging, *below*). About 50 kilometers (31 miles) west of Höfn, at the **Jökulsárlón** lagoon, you can see large chunks of the glacier tumble and float around in a spectacular ice show. For boat trips around the lagoon amidst the floating chunks of ice, call Fjölnir Torfason (tel. 7/81065). On the **Breiðamerkur sands** west of the lagoon is the largest North Atlantic colony of skua, large predatory sea birds with cruel, curved beaks.

Another 50 kilometers (31 miles) west of Jökulsárlón bordering on Vatnajökull is **Skaftafell,** the largest of Iceland's three national parks. The surrounding glacier shelters Skaftafell from winds, creating a verdant oasis, and farther up is the highest mountain in Iceland, **Hvannadalshnúkur,** rising to 2,119 meters (6,300 feet). The famous **Svartifoss waterfall** drops thinly over a cliff whose sides resemble the pipes of a great organ. In the park you can walk for an hour or a day on beautiful trails through a rare combination of green forest, clear water, waterfalls, sands, mountains, and glaciers.

Sports and Fitness

Fishing Near Seyðisfjörður, you can get fishing permits at Hotel Snæfell (Austurvegur 3, tel. 7/21460).

Horseback Riding Around Lake Lögurinn, you can rent horses at **Guesthouse Egilsstaðir** (tel. 7/11114). In Seyðifjörður, rent horses at **Hotel Snæfell** (Austurvegur 3, tel. 7/21460). To rent ponies near the Jökulsá Lagoon, call **Fjölnir Torfason** (tel. 7/81065).

Swimming There are swimming pools in **Egilsstaðir** (tel. 7/11467), **Neskaupstaður** (Miðstræti 5, tel. 7/71243), **Eskifjörður** (Lambeyrarbraut 14, tel. 7/61238), and **Höfn** (Harnarbraut, tel. 7/81157).

Dining and Lodging

Breiðsdalsvík **Hótel Bláfell.** Though it's only a few years old, this small hotel in a fishing village on Route 96 has a cozily rustic exterior and an award-winning restaurant. Fishing permits are available for the area. *Sólvellir 14, tel. 7/56770. 15 rooms with shared bath. AE, MC, V. Moderate.*

Djúpivogur **Hótel Framtíð.** In an old fishing village where 19th-century Danish merchant homes still stand, this small wood-frame hotel is right by the harbor. In the dining room, home-style food is served in a friendly atmosphere; seafood is a specialty. *Vogalandi 4, tel. 7/88887. 10 rooms with shared bath. Facilities: restaurant, sauna. AE, MC, V. Inexpensive.*

Egilsstaðir **Hótel Valaskjálf.** Large and practical, this hotel has a restaurant and a cafeteria. Breakfast is included in the room rate, and there is dancing on weekends. *Skógarland, tel. 7/11500, fax 7/11501. 66 rooms with shower. AE, MC, V. Moderate–Expensive.*

Guesthouse Egilsstaðir. This charming farmhouse hotel is on the outskirts of town. *Egilsstaðir 1, tel. 7/11114. 11 rooms with shared bath. No credit cards. Inexpensive.*

Hallormsstaður **Edda.** The hotel is adequate; the natural harmony of forest, lake, and quiet bays is the real attraction. The Edda has a good restaurant. *Hallormsstad, tel. 7/11705. 17 rooms with shared bath. AE, DC, V. Closed Sept.–mid-June. Moderate.*

Höfn **Hótel Höfn.** This newly built, modern-style hotel is clean and comfortable and has a good restaurant. The almond trout is excellent; fast food is also available at the grill. There's dancing on weekends. *Víkurbraut, tel. 7/81240, fax 7/81996. 40 rooms, 20 with shower. AE, MC, V. Expensive.*

Seyðisfjörður **Hótel Snæfell.** Set in an old wood house, this new hotel serves good food in a glassed-in restaurant by a dramatic fjord. *Austurvegur 3, tel. 7/21460. 13 rooms, 9 with shower and 4 with shared bath. AE, MC, V. Moderate.*

Youth Hostels **Bakkafjörður:** tel. 7/31694. 17 beds. Closed Sept.–May.
Djúpivogur: tel. 7/88788. 25 beds. Closed Sept. 2–May.
Höfn: tel. 7/81736. 30 beds. Closed Oct. 16–May 14.
Húsey: tel. 7/13010. 20 beds. Closed Sept. 16–May.
Seyðisfjörður: tel. 7/21410. 32 beds.

The South

The power of volcanoes is all too evident on this final leg of the Ring Road tour. At Kirkjubæjarklaustur, you can still see scars of the great Laki eruption of 1783. At Stöng, you can visit excavated ruins of a farmstead buried in 1104 by the eruption of Mount Hekla, which was known throughout medieval Europe as the abode of the damned; Hekla is still active, erupting most recently in 1991. Off the coast, the Vestmannaeyjar (Westmann) islands are still being formed by volcanic activity, and a 1973 eruption almost wiped out all habitation. The south also includes **Þórsmörk** (Thor's forest) a popular nature reserve.

Important Addresses and Numbers

Tourist Information In **Kirkjubæjarklaustur,** the Community Center (tel. 8/74621) is open June 15–August 15, daily 10–4. In **Vík,** the Camping Site and Víkurskáli (tel. 8/71345) will provide information.

Emergencies In **Kirkjubæjarklaustur,** contact the **police** at tel. 8/74694; in **Vík,** tel. 8/71176; in **Hvolsvöllur,** tel. 8/78434; and in **Selfoss,** tel. 8/21154.

Arriving and Departing

By Plane **Icelandair** (tel. 1/690200) and **Eagle Air** (tel. 1/616060 or 1/28122) fly daily from Reykjavík Airport to the Vestmannaeyjar (the Westmann Islands); flight time is about 30 minutes.

By Car Kirkjubæjarklaustur is 272 kilometers (169 miles) east of Reykjavík on the Ring Road. West from Höfn, it is 201 kilometers (125 miles) to Kirkjubæjarklaustur.

By Ferry The passenger and car ferry **Herjólfur** (tel. 8/11792 or 1/686464) sails daily to Vestmannaeyjar from Þorlákshöfn. Allow 3¼ hours for the journey. There are immediate bus connections to Reykjavík from the Westmann Islands ferry at Þorlákshöfn; the trip takes about 90 minutes.

By Bus **BSÍ** has daily service from Reykjavík, stopping in Hella, Hvolsvöllur, Selfoss, Vík, and Þorlakshöfn. The journey to Vík takes 4¼ hours; to Þorlakshöfn or Selfoss, one hour.

Guided Tours

The **Iceland Tourist Bureau** (tel. 1/25855) operates a 10-hour day trip from Reykjavík to the Vestmannaeyjar Islands by plane, running daily all year. Arrangements can also be made for a three-hour sightseeing flight over Heimaey in the islands. **Austurleið** bus company (Austurvegi 1, Hvolsvöllur, tel. 8/78197) operates tours to Þhórsmörk, Skaftafell, the eastern fjords, and the interior.

Exploring the South

Pick up the Ring Road in **Kirkjubæjarklaustur,** the site of an old convent from the 12th century to the Reformation. Just west of the village, turn right on the highland road leading north to see **Laka** volcano, with more than 100 craters dotting the landscape. The great lava field of the south coast was created by this volcano in a single eruption, in 1783–84. The worst in Iceland's history, it wiped out about 70% of the country's livestock and a fifth of the population. Jón Steingrímsson, then the priest at Kirkjubæjarklaustur, is said to have stopped the advance of the lava by prayer.

West from Kirkjubæjarklaustur 25 kilometers (15 miles) on Route 1, turn right onto Route 208 and continue for 20 kilometers (12 miles) on the mountain road Route F22 to **Eldgjá,** a 20-mile-long volcanic gulch. Historic records suggest it erupted in 934 with a ferocity similar to that of the Laka eruption. The northwestern part of the gulch is most interesting, with Ófærufoss, a waterfall cascading under a natural basalt bridge.

Proceeding west along the Ring Road, you cross the desert Mýrdalssandur and arrive at the village of **Vík,** with its vast population of arctic terns. Twelve kilometers (7 miles) past Vík, turn left toward the ocean to reach the southernmost point of the country, the **Dyrhólaey** promontory, with its lighthouse. The ocean has worn the black basalt rock here into the shape of an arch, 394 feet high; ships can sail through it in calm weather. This headland is also a bird sanctuary, so expect it to be closed during the nesting period in early summer.

Another 15 kilometers (9 miles) west on Route 1, turn right to the tiny settlement of **Skógar,** where you can visit a small museum of turf houses. Among the mementos of this region's primitive existence is one of the tiny, frail boats in which local fishermen once navigated this treacherous coast. *Tel. 8/78845. Admission free. Open May–Sept. 15, daily 9–noon, 1–6.*

Just west of Skógar is the impressive **Skógafoss waterfall,** which is over 197 feet high.

Another 30 kilometers (19 miles) along the Ring Road, you'll come to the powerful **Markarfljót River.** Route 249 on its east bank leads 15 kilometers (9 miles) east to some treacherous, dangerous streams into the **Þórsmörk** (Thor's forest) nature reserve, a popular vacation area bounded on its eastern and southern sides by the Eyjafjalla and Mýrdals glaciers. Nestled in a valley surrounded by mountain peaks, Þórsmörk enjoys exceptionally calm and often sunny weather, making it a veritable haven of birch trees and other Icelandic flora. There are many excellent trekking routes (*see* Hiking and Camping, *below*), such as a day's trip over the **Fimmvörðuháls mountain pass** (a compass is a necessity) down to Skógar, or a three-day hike into the interior to visit **Landmannalaugar,** where hot and cold springs punctuate a landscape rich in pastel, yellow, brown, and red rhyolite hills carved by glacial rivers.

The road on the west bank of the Markarfljót leads 10 kilometers (6 miles) north into Saga country, to the site of **Hlíðarendi,** the farm where Gunnar Hámundarson, one of the heroes of *Njál's Saga,* lived and died. Exiled by the Alþingi for murdering Þorgeir Oddkelsson, he refused to leave "these beautiful slopes." His direct descendants still own Hlíðarendi. In the lowlands to the southwest of the Markarfljót River (turn left off the Ring Road onto Route 252 and drive 20 kilometers/12 miles) is another famous place from *Njál's Saga:* **Bergþórshvoll,** where Njál's enemies surrounded his farmhouse and burned it to the ground, killing all within.

Continuing west on the Ring Road, you'll come to **Hella,** 100 kilometers (62 miles) west of Vík. About 10 kilometers (6 miles) past Hella, turn right on Route 26 and drive 40 kilometers (25 miles) or so until you see, on your right, the tallest peak in the region—the famous **Hekla volcano,** which has erupted nearly 20 times in recorded history and remains active. (It last erupted in 1991.) In the Middle Ages, Hekla was known throughout Western Europe as the abode of the damned. Some 25 kilometers (16 miles) farther, Route 26 intersects Route 32; turn left and go 15 kilometers (9 miles) to the right turn for **Stöng,** an ancient settlement on the west bank of the Þjórsá River, Iceland's biggest. The original farm here dates back almost 900 years; it was buried in 1104 when Hekla erupted, but you can visit the excavated ruins. A complete replica has been built, using the same materials as the settlers used, located just south of Stöng at Búrfell on Route 32. *Tel. 8/77713.*

From Hella, it's 93 kilometers (58 miles) along the Ring Road back to Reykjavík. At Hveragerði (*see* Golden Circle Excursion, *above*), take a left turn onto Route 38 and drive 20 kilometers (12 miles) to **Þorlákshöfn**—gateway to **Vestmannaeyjar,** the Westmann Islands.

Vestmannaeyjar (Westmann Islands) This tiny cluster of 15 islands off the south coast was named for the Irish slaves—called Westmen—brought to Iceland by the Viking settlers after AD 874. After an uprising in which some slaves killed their master Hjörleifur, brother of Reykjavík settler Ingólfur Arnarson, the Westmen fled to the islands. Ingólfur avenged his brother by killing most of the slaves or driving them off the cliffs in Vestmannaeyjar.

The islands were formed by volcanic eruptions only 5,000–10,000 years ago, and there is still much volcanic activity here. **Surtsey island,** the latest addition, was formed in November 1963 with an eruption that lasted 3½ years. In 1973, a five-month-long eruption on **Heimaey,** the only inhabited island in the group, wiped out part of the town of Vestmannaeyjar. The island's entire population was forced to flee in fishing boats, with only a few hours' notice. A few years later, however, the people of Vestmannaeyjar had removed tons of black lava dust from their streets and rebuilt everything. The lava, still hot, is used for heat by the resourceful islanders.

The main industry here is fishing, but another local occupation (nowadays more a sport than a job) is more unusual: egg-hunting. Egg-pickers dangle from ropes over the sheer black volcanic cliffs to collect eggs from the nests of seabirds. The islands are rich in birds, especially puffins, which are used for food.

Sightseeing tours from Reykjavík usually include a sail around Surtsey island and a stop at the multicolored sea cave **Kafhellir,** on the island of **Haena.** Every August, islanders celebrate the 1874 grant of Icelandic sovereignty with a huge festival in the town of Vestmannaeyjar, on Heimaey. The population moves into a tent city in the **Herjólfsdalur Valley** a short distance west of town for an extended weekend of bonfires, dancing, and singing.

Sports and Outdoor Activities

Golf The Svarfhólsvöllur course, in **Selfoss,** is on the banks of the Ölfusá River. There also is a golf course in **Hella.**

Hiking and Camping Both main Icelandic touring clubs, **Ferðafélag Islands** (Öldugata 3, Reykjavík, tel. 1/19533) and **Útivist** (Grófin 1, Reykjavík, tel. 1/14606) maintain large quarters with sleeping-bag accommodations in Þórsmörk; many long-distance hikes are organized from there.

Horseback Riding In Hvölsvollur, contact **Saga Hestar** (tel. 8/78138); in Hella call **Heklu Hestar** (tel. 8/76598).

Swimming There are swimming pools in **Hvolsvöllur** (tel. 8/78607), **Hella** (tel. 8/75334), **Þorlákshöfn** (tel. 8/33807), and **Selfoss** (Bankavegur, tel. 8/21227).

Dining and Lodging

Hvolsvöllur **Hótel Hvolsvöllur.** Facilities at this hotel include a restaurant, bar, and swimming pool. *Hlíðarvegur 7, tel. 8/78187. 28 rooms. AE, MC, V. Moderate.*

Kirkjubæjarklaustur **Edda.** Open year-round, this standard Edda facility in a modern building offers both a restaurant and a swimming pool. *Tel. 8/74799. 55 rooms with shower. AE, MC, V. Moderate.*

Skógar **Edda.** Close to the Skógarfoss waterfall, this hotel is beautifully located with views of the sea and the mountains and glaciers. It has a restaurant. *Skógum, tel. 8/78870. 36 rooms with shared bath. AE, MC, V. Closed Sept.–mid-June. Moderate.*

Youth Hostels **Fljótshlíð,** Fljótsdalur, tel. 8/78498. 15 beds. Closed Oct. 16–Apr. 14.

Mýrdalur, Reynisbrekka, tel. 7/71106. 25 beds. Closed Sept. 16–May.

Vestmannaeyjar, tel. 8/12915. 35 beds. Closed Sept. 16–May.

5 Norway

Introduction

by Melody Favish

Melody Favish is an American writer living in Oslo with her Norwegian husband and daughter.

Norway has some of the most dramatic scenery in the world. Perched at the very top of the globe, this northern land is mostly mountain, with fringes of fertile land along the coast and bordering the central valleys. Nowhere is this landscape more vivid than in the approach to Oslo's Fornebu Airport, most travelers' introduction to Norway. As your plane descends through the clouds, the snow-capped mountains of Norway's midsection rise to greet it. Treeless, barren, and blanketed with centuries of snow, they bask in the clean white light of the northern sun. This light emphasizes the cool colors of the landscape—ripples of blue water slice through sheer gray rock, and as the plane nears Oslo, bright green fields and deep green forests form patches of texture to contrast with the turquoise water of the Oslo fjord. Red cottages with white trim and tall flagpoles dot every island on the approach. Sailboats and seagulls speckle the water with white. Thanks to the Gulf Stream, the coastal regions enjoy a moderate, temperate climate in winter, keeping the country green, while the interior has a more typical northern climate.

Because the mountain landscape is so unyielding, vast areas of the country have remained untouched, and Norwegians intend to keep these intact. They have an almost reverential attitude toward nature and its wonders, which is reflected in their love of the outdoors. Norwegians yearn to retreat to their *hytter* (cabins), where they can forget the stresses of everyday life and enjoy nature's simple pleasures. They are experts at living off the land's bounty, and they avidly pick wild berries and mushrooms. They fish in the icy rivers and lakes, and they hunt in the dense fir forests. Once Norwegians don their knickers, parkas, and rucksacks, they truly are free people, ready to face the winter on skis or the summer in hiking boots. It is this resilience that has enabled them to survive years of brutal domination and wars, first with their neighbors and culminating with World War II.

Norwegians are proud of their Viking ancestors, whose travels and conquests are legendary. It was the Viking kings who first united Norway in the 8th century, but a millennium passed between that great era and Norwegian independence. Between the middle ages and 1905, Norway was always under either Danish or Swedish rule. Although the constitution was written in 1814, full independence was not achieved for another 91 years. The 19th century saw the establishment of the Norwegian identity and a sumptuous blossoming of culture. This romantic period produced the nation's greatest personalities, including composer Edvard Grieg, dramatist Henrik Ibsen, the expressionist artist Edvard Munch, the polar explorer Roald Amundsen, and the explorer/humanitarian Fridtjof Nansen. Many vestiges of this romantic period still survive in the buildings of the era, decorated with Viking dragonheads and scrollwork, symbolizing the rebirth of the Viking spirit.

True to their democratic nature, in 1905, when independence from Sweden became a fact, Norwegians held a referendum to choose a king. Prince Carl of Denmark became King Haakon VII. His baby son Alexander's name was changed to Olav, and father and son presided over the kingdom for more than 85 years. When King Olav died in January 1991, the normally re-

Norway

TO SVALBARD
North Cape
Vardø
Vadsø
Hammerfest
Kirkenes
ATLANTIC OCEAN
Alta
Karasjok
Tromsø
Kautokeino
VESTERÅLEN
Harstad
FINLAND
Narvik
LOFOTEN
Vestfjorden
Bodø
Fauske
Arctic Circle
Mo i Rana
Sandnessjøen
Mosjøen
Gulf of Bothnia
Brønnøysund
SWEDEN
Rørvik
Namsos
Steinkjer
Trondheim
Meråker
Støren
Kristiansund
Røros
Molde
Oppdal
Ålesund
Åndalsnes
Tynset
Østerdalen
Geiranger
Dombås
Gudbrandsdalen
Nord fjord
Otta
Koppang
Florø
Jostedalsbreen
Rena
Lillehammer
Sogne fjord
Lake Mjøsa
Hamar
Voss
Geilo
Eidsvoll
Baltic Sea
Bergen
Hønefoss
Hardangerfjord
Oslo
Drammen
Kongsberg
Fredrikstad
Oslofjord
Haugesund
Larvik
Halden
Porsgrunn
Stavanger
Arendal
Skagerrak
Sandnes
Evje
Kattegat
Grimstad
Mandal
Kristiansand
N
0
200 miles
0
300 km

served Norwegians stood in line for hours to write in the condolence book at the Royal Palace. Rather than just signing their names, they wrote touching letters of devotion to the man they called the "people's king." Thousands set candles in the snow outside the palace, lighting up the darkest time of the year and creating a cathedral of ice and flame for their beloved monarch. Norway has a new king now, Harald V, Olav's son, with continuity assured by Crown Prince Haakon, a high-school student.

Every Constitution Day, May 17, Norwegians salute their royal family with flag-waving and parades. This is no ordinary celebration but a huge street party, with people of all ages, many in national costume, converging on Karl Johans gate, Oslo's main avenue, which leads to the Palace. All day long, television broadcasts parades from around the country.

Norwegians are justifiably proud of their native land. Until the 1950s, Norway was a poor country, with little industrialization, its trade in raw materials, mostly fish and lumber. Shipping had always been important, but that sector was controlled by a few powerful families. Norway was just starting to develop when World War II and five years of German occupation ravaged the country.

The discovery of oil in the North Sea in 1968 is the most important single event in Norway's modern economic history. In the following 20 years, Norway became a wealthy country, with one of the world's highest standards of living, not just in numerical terms, such as per capita income and life expectancy, but also in those statistics that give an idea of just what kind of people Norwegians are—they read more newspapers than anyone else in the world, and they buy more English books than any other non-English-speaking people. On a less intellectual level, Norwegians buy VCRs, car phones, and car stereos more than any other national group and are at or near the top in ice-cream, chocolate, and soft-drink consumption.

Although it is a modern, highly industrialized country, Norway still has vast tracts of untamed but very accessible nature, a rare and appealing combination. It's a long, rangy country, 2,750 kilometers (1,700 miles) in length, with some 4 million people scattered over it. Norwegians like to say that if Oslo remained fixed and the northern part of the country were swung to the south, it would reach all the way to Rome.

Norway is a high-cost country, and many items, especially food and automobiles, are extremely expensive. Nevertheless, a low inflation rate and increased competition in the tourist industry have kept prices stable. During the summer season, Norway is a tourist's Eden of special offers, from hotels to airplane tickets, putting it within reach of most travelers. And its greatest attractions—the outdoors and breathtaking views—are free.

Before You Go

Government Tourist Offices

In the United States **Scandinavian Tourist Board,** 655 3rd Ave., New York, NY 10017, tel. 212/949–2333

In Canada **Scandinavian Tourist Board,** Box 115, Station N, Toronto, Ontario, M8V 3S4, tel. 416/823-9620

In the United Kingdom **Norwegian Tourist Board,** 20 Pall Mall, London SW1Y 4LR, tel. 071/839-6255

In Norway **NORTRA,** Nortravel Marketing, Pb 499, Sentrum, N-0105 Oslo 1, tel. 02/42-70-44

When to Go

Every season has its charm and its enthusiasts. Winter means skiing at resorts in the country's midsection, where snow is abundant and facilities are first-rate. Winter in Oslo means evenings at the theater or at the concert house. Skiing on the lit trails surrounding Oslo is almost as good as that farther afield. On the down side, winter means little daylight, few organized tours, restricted opening hours at museums, and higher hotel rates except on weekends. Avoid Easter, the traditional "last ski trip of the year" for many Norwegians. Christmas is similar, with families retreating to the privacy of their own homes for much of the holiday, which begins on December 24, and, for many, does not end until January 2 or 3. May is one of the best times to visit Norway, for the days are long and sunny, the cultural life in the city is still going strong, tourists are few, and *Syttende mai* (Constitution Day, May 17), with all the festivities, is worth a trip for its own sake. For enjoying the outdoors, September is a delightful time to hike in the hills. Most people come to Norway in the summer, and the months of July and August offer the most travel bargains. Hotels everywhere have special rates, and transportation packages of all kinds are available. In the far north, summer's main attraction is the midnight sun, visible at the North Cape from May 13 through July 29. In winter, the northern lights illuminate the sky.

Climate Coastal Norway enjoys mild winters, with more rain than snow in the southern areas. The temperature in Oslo seldom drops below 20°F, thanks to the Gulf Stream. It is dark, though, and if there's no snow, Oslo can look bleak. Summers in Norway are equally mild; days are relatively warm, but nights can be chilly. Inland and up north, winters are very long, cold, snowy, and dark, while summers are short, warm, intense, and endowed with an indescribably clear light.

What follows are average daily maximum and minimum temperatures for Oslo.

Oslo

Jan.	28F	-2C	**May**	61F	16C	**Sept.**	61F	16C
	19	-7		43	6		46	8
Feb.	30F	-1C	**June**	68F	20C	**Oct.**	48F	9C
	19	-7		50	10		37	3
Mar.	39F	4C	**July**	72F	22C	**Nov.**	37F	3C
	25	-4		55	13		30	-1
Apr.	50F	10C	**Aug.**	70F	21C	**Dec.**	32F	0C
	34	1		54	12		25	-4

National Holidays

The following are national holidays in 1992: January 1, Maundy Thursday and Good Friday (April 16-17), Easter Monday

(April 20), Labor Day (May 1), Constitution Day (May 17), Ascension Day (May 28), Whitmonday (June 8), December 25–27.

Festivals and Seasonal Events

1992: 250th anniversary of the city of Kristiansund N.
January: At the **Lillehammer Ski Festival** the sport's big names test the site of the 1994 Winter Olympic Games.
January: The **Northern Light Festival** features classical, contemporary, and chamber music in Tromsø.
February 22–24: The **Rørosmartnan Fair** has been held at Røros every year since 1854.
March 7–8: Speed Skating World Cup men's sprints, Savalen.
March 12–15: The **Holmenkollen Ski Festival** in Oslo features international Nordic events, including ski jumping.
March 22: The **Birkebeiner Race** commemorates a centuries-old cross-country ski race from Lillehammer to Rena.
April: The **Karasjok Easter Festival** features traditional Sami entertainment and folklore and reindeer racing.
May 17: Constitution Day brings out every flag in the country, and what seems like every school band in Oslo marches to the Palace to salute the royal family.
May 21–June 1: The **Bergen Music Festival,** customarily opened by the king, is the main annual music festival.
June: The **North Cape March** brings hikers from around the world to walk from Honningsvåg to the North Cape and back.
June: Den Store Styrkeprøven (Great Endurance Test) is a cycle race from Trondheim to Oslo.
Mid-June: Trollstigrennet, children's giant slalom race is held in Åndalsnes.
June 23: Midsummer Eve, called "Sankt Hans," is celebrated nationwide with bonfires, fireworks, and dancing outdoors.
July 3–5: The **Jarlsberg Grand International,** the **Scandinavian Grand Prix,** and the **Jarlsberg Grand Prix** feature international harness racing at Jarlsberg track in Tønsberg.
July 4: The **Bislett Games** attract the best international track and field stars to Bislet Stadium—where more world records have been set than in any other.
July 13–19: The **Molde International Jazz Festival** celebrates its 32nd year with 400 musicians and 30,000 spectators.
Mid-August: The **European Sea Fishing Championships** are held at Tananger, outside Stavanger.
Late-August: The **Norwegian Film Festival** celebrates its 20th year in Haugesund.
Early September: Kongsvingermarknen is an old-fashioned harvest fair in Kongsvinger.
October: The **Bergen Open** international draws some of the world's best tennis players.
December: Christmas concerts, fairs, and crafts workshops are held at museums and churches throughout the country.
December 1: Annual lighting of the Christmas tree at University Square in Oslo.
December 10: The **Nobel peace prize** winner is announced.

What to Pack

Clothing Casual clothing is the rule in Norway, although it is a good idea for men to pack a sport jacket for cool evenings. Women might want to bring a dress or suit, preferably with a jacket, for evenings, but it is possible to go just about anywhere in Norway in slacks. A windbreaker, good walking shoes and sunglasses are a must. Summer in Norway can be both chilly and rainy, so bring a raincoat (with lining for the fringe seasons) and an umbrella. Winter weather demands heavy outerwear but normal indoor clothing, as Norwegian buildings are well heated.

Miscellaneous Most hotels do not provide washcloths, so if you prefer them, bring your own. Many hotel bathrooms are equipped with converter outlets for shavers only, so if you bring a hair dryer, make sure that it is convertible. If you prefer decaffeinated coffee, bring some individual envelopes as many restaurants do not serve it.

Taking Money Abroad

Traveler's checks are the safest way to carry money. Major credit cards are accepted most places, with Visa and Mastercard (Eurocard) the most popular.

Norwegian Currency

The unit of currency in Norway is the *krone* (plural: *kroner*), which translates as "crown," written officially as NOK. Price tags are seldom marked this way, but rather read "Kr." and then the amount, such as Kr10. (In this book, the Norwegian Krone is abbreviated NKr.) One krone is divided into 100 *øre*, and coins of 10 and 50 øre, 1, 5 and 10 kroner are in circulation. The 10-øre coin, one of the world's smallest coins, will be withdrawn from circulation in 1992–93. Bills are issued in denominations of 50, 100, 500 and 1,000 kroner. As of August 1991, the exchange rate was NKr6.44 = $1, NKr11.15 = £1, and NKr5.70 = C$1. These rates fluctuate, so it is a good idea to check them when planning a trip.

What It Will Cost

Sample Prices Cup of coffee, from $1.20 in a cafeteria to $3.50 or more in a restaurant; a 20-pack of cigarettes, $5.15; a half-liter of beer, $4.50–$6.50; the smallest hot dog (with bun plus *lompe*—a Norwegian tortilla—mustard, ketchup, and fried onions) at a convenience store, $2.10; cheapest bottle of wine from a government store, $7; the same bottle at a restaurant, $15–25; urban transit fare in Oslo, $2.10; soft drink, from $2.75 in a cafeteria to $4 in a better restaurant; one adult movie ticket, $4–6; shrimp or roast beef sandwich at a cafeteria, $6; one-mile taxi ride, $6–7 depending upon time of day.

Passports and Visas

A valid passport is required for entry. Visitors planning to stay longer than 90 days are required to register with the police.

Customs and Duties

Any adult can bring in duty-free ¾ liter of alcohol (not exceeding 60% alcohol by volume) and one liter of wine (not exceeding 21% alcohol by volume). As most liquor is sold in 1-liter bottles, the allowance is flexible on that point. Two liters of beer also can be imported duty-free. Anyone over 16 years old can import 200 cigarettes or 250 grams of other tobacco products duty-free. Importing alcohol over the above limit is not recommended.

Language

Every Norwegian receives at least five years of English instruction, starting in the fourth grade. Norwegian has three additional vowels, *æ*, *ø* and *å*. *Æ* is pronounced as a short "a." The *ø*, sometimes printed as *oe*, is the same as *ö* in German and Swedish, pronounced very much like a short "u." The *å* is a contraction of the archaic aa and sounds like long "o." These three letters appear at the end of alphabetical listings.

There are two officially sanctioned languages, Bokmål and Nynorsk. Bokmål is used by 84% of the population and is the main written form of Norwegian, the language of books, as the first half of its name indicates. Nynorsk, which translates as "new Norwegian," is actually a compilation of older dialect forms from rural Norway, which evolved during the national romantic period around the turn of this century. All Norwegians have to study both languages.

The Sami (incorrectly called Lapp) people have their own language, which is more akin to Finnish than to Norwegian.

Staying Healthy

Norway has exceptionally high standards of hygiene. The water is not only potable but delicious and ice-cold straight from the tap. Norwegians have strict regulations regarding pollution and pesticides. All foodstuffs for sale have been thoroughly tested, so you can eat all fruits and vegetables.

Traveling with Children

Families visiting Norway in summer may enjoy renting an authentic *rorbu* (fisherman's shanty) at the seaside. Accommodations are simple yet adequate, and rowboats usually are available for rent. For more information contact **Borton Overseas** (5516 Lyndale Ave. S, Minneapolis, MN 55419, tel. 800/843–0602). Information on farming holidays in Norway is available from **Lille Norge** (Box 4, N–1353 Baerums Verk, Norway, tel. 02/51–14–27).

Hints for Disabled Travelers

The Oslo office of the Norwegian Tourist Board (H Heyerdahlsgate 1, Oslo 1) produces a *Travel Guide for the Disabled* as well as a leaflet detailing hotels with facilities for disabled visitors. Additional information is available from the **Norwegian Association of the Disabled** (Box 9217 Vaterland, N-0134, Oslo 1, tel. 02/17–02–55).

By Train In Norway, most express, InterCity, and long-distance trains have wheelchair compartments.

By Boat In Norway all ferries feature wide elevators and cabins to accommodate wheelchair users.

Hints for Older Travelers

Visitors over 67 are automatically entitled to a 50% reduction on all first- and second-class train tickets. Senior-citizen tickets can be purchased at all rail stations.

Arriving and Departing

From North America by Plane

SAS has daily nonstop flights to Oslo from New York, daily connections to Oslo via Copenhagen from Chicago, Los Angeles, and Seattle, and twice-weekly connections (also via Copenhagen) from Toronto and Anchorage. **TWA** serves Oslo from New York via Amsterdam. During the summer months, **Delta** has twice-weekly nonstop flights from New York to Oslo. **Icelandair** flies from New York to Oslo via Reykjavik. The best connection from Minneapolis/St. Paul to Oslo is via Amsterdam on **KLM.** A nonstop flight from New York to Oslo takes about 8½ hours.

Airports **Oslo Fornebu Airport** is the gateway to Norway for most visitors. Once called a "cafeteria with a landing strip," it is currently being transformed into a modern airport worthy of a capital city. Other international airports include **Bergen, Kristiansand S., Sandefjord, Stavanger,** and **Trondheim.**

From the United Kingdom by Plane

British Airways and **SAS** have three flights each daily between Heathrow and Oslo; on Saturdays, there are two flights each. SAS has two flights daily between Heathrow and Stavanger (one on Saturdays) and one flight daily between Aberdeen and Stavanger. **Braathens SAFE** has five flights a week between Newcastle and Stavanger and four a week between Newcastle and Oslo. **AirUK** has six flights weekly between Aberdeen and Stavanger and five between Aberdeen and Bergen. **DanAir** has five flights a week between Manchester and Stavanger. The flying time from London to Oslo is about 1¾ hours and to Stavanger, 1½ hours.

From the United Kingdom by Train and Boat

By Train Traveling from Britain to Norway by train is not difficult. The best connection leaves London's Victoria Station at noon and connects at Dover with a boat to Oostende, Belgium. From Oostende there is a sleeping-car-only connection to Copenhagen that arrives the next morning at 9:10. The train to Oslo leaves at 10:15 AM and arrives at 7:58 PM. A number of special discounted trips are available, including the **InterRail Pass,** which is now available for passengers of all ages.

By Boat Only one ferry line serves Norway from the United Kingdom, **Color Line** (Tyne Commission Quay, North Shields [near Newcastle] LEN29 6EA, tel. 091/296–1313, or Skoltegrunnskaien, 5000 Bergen, tel. 05/32–27–80), which has three departures a week between Bergen, Stavanger, and Newcastle during the summer season (May 3–Sept. 28), two during the rest of the year. Crossings take about 24 hours. Monday sailings stop first in Stavanger and arrive in Bergen six hours later, while the other trips stop first in Bergen. **Scandinavian Seaways** has crossing between Harwich and Göteborg, Sweden, a 4½-hour drive from Oslo.

Staying in Norway

Getting Around

The southern part of Norway can be considered fairly compact—all major cities are about a day's drive from one another (although Trondheim–Stavanger is pushing it). The distances make themselves felt on the way north, where Norway becomes narrower as it inches up to and beyond the Arctic Circle and hooks over Sweden and Finland to touch the Soviet Union. Because distances are so great, it is virtually impossible to visit the entire country from one base.

By Plane **SAS** (EuroClass tel. 02/17-00-10; Tourist tel. 17-00-20) serves most major cities, including Svalbard. **Braathens SAFE** (SAFE stands for the "South Asian and Far Eastern" routes of the parent shipping company; tel. 02/12-20-70) is the major domestic airline, serving cities throughout the country and along the coast as far north as Tromsø and Svalbard. It also has international routes from Oslo to Billund (Denmark), Malmö (Sweden), and Newcastle (England). **Widerøe** (tel. 02/73-65-00) serves smaller airports (with smaller planes), mostly along the coast, and in northern Norway. **Norsk Air** (tel. 02/73-65-00), a subsidiary of Widerøe, provides similar services in the southern part of the country. **Coast Air** (tel. 04/83-41-10) and **Norlink** (tel. 08/37-29-11), a SAS subsidiary, are commuter systems linking smaller and larger airports.

A number of special fares are available within Norway year-round, including air passes, family tickets, weekend excursions, youth (up to the age of 26), and senior (over 67). Youth fares are cheapest when purchased from the automatic ticket machines at the airport on the day of departure. All Norwegian routes have reduced rates from July through the middle of August, and tickets can be purchased on the spot. Outside of these times, a minifare during low traffic hours is probably the cheapest way to fly.

All flights within Scandinavia are nonsmoking, as are all airports in Norway, except for designated areas.

By Train **NSB,** the Norwegian State Railway System, has four main lines originating from the **Oslo S Station.** The longest runs north to Trondheim, then extends onward as far as Fauske and Bodø. The southern line hugs the coast to Stavanger, while the western line crosses some famous scenic territory on the way to Bergen. An eastern line through Kongsvinger links Norway with Sweden and the rest of Europe. Narvik, north of Bodø, is the last stop on Sweden's Ofot line, which runs from Stockholm via Kiruna, the world's northernmost rail system. It is possible to take a five-hour bus trip between Bodø and Narvik to connect with the other train.

NSB offers many kinds of passes, including the **Nordturist Card,** good for 21 days of rail travel (including some ferry and bus routes) in Norway, Sweden, Denmark, and Finland. The **Inter-Rail passes** offer one month and 22 countries and are now available for travelers of all ages. Discounted fares include family, senior citizen (including not-yet-senior spouses), and off-peak fares, which must be purchased a day in advance. NSB gives student discounts only to foreigners studying at Norwegian institutions.

NSB trains are clean, comfortable, and punctual. Most have special compartments for the handicapped and for families with children under two years old. Both first- and second-class tickets are available, but the view from second-class open-seating cars is better than that from the more enclosed first-class compartments. Both seat and sleeper reservations are required on long journeys.

Most trains have food service, ranging from simple sandwiches and beverages to a buffet car selling hot dogs, pizza, and perhaps an entree. Only the Oslo-Bergen route has a full-service dining car, where reservations are essential.

Train tickets can be purchased in railway stations or from travel agencies. NSB has its own travel agency (Stortingsgt. 28, tel. 02/83–88–50).

By Bus Every end station of the railroad is supported by a number of bus routes, some of which are operated by NSB, others by local companies.

Long-distance buses are another way to travel Norway, but they usually take longer than the railroad and fares are only slightly lower. Virtually every settlement on the mainland is served by bus, and for anyone with a desire to get off the beaten track, a pay-as-you-go open-ended bus trip is the best way to see Norway. **Nor-Way Bussekspress** (Karl Johans gate 2, 0154 Oslo 1, tel. 02/33–08–62) has more than 40 different bus services, covering 10,000 km (6,200 miles) and 500 destinations, in its organization and can arrange any journey. One of its participating services, **Feriebussen** (Østerdal Billag A/S, 2560 Alvdal, tel. 064/87–400) offers five package tours with English guides.

Discounted tickets are available for children, people over 60, families, students, and military personnel.

By Boat Ferries and passenger ships remain important means of transportation. Along west-coast fjords, car ferries are a way of life. Once you know your route, buy tickets for those ferries that allow advance purchase—this lets you drive to the front of the line.

More specialized boat service includes hydrofoil/catamaran trips between Stavanger, Haugesund, and Bergen. Other companies offer fjord cruises out of these cities, while others offer similar service in the north.

Norway's most renowned boat trip is the **Hurtigrute,** or Coastal Express, which departs from Bergen and stops at 36 ports in six days, ending with Kirkenes, near the Russian border, before turning back. Tickets can be purchased for the whole journey or for individual legs. Shore excursions are arranged at all ports. Tickets are available through travel agents or directly from the companies that run the service: FFR (9600 Hammerfest, tel. 084/11–655), OVD (8501 Narvik, tel. 082/44–090), Nordenfjeldske Dampskibsselskab A/S (Kjøpmannsgt. 52 7011 Trondheim, tel. 07/52–05–00, fax 07/52–05–15), and TFDS (9000 Tromsø, tel. 083/86–088).

By Car International driving licenses are required in Norway, except for license-holders from other Nordic countries.

All vehicles registered abroad are required to carry international liability insurance and an international accident report form, which can be obtained from automobile clubs. Collision insurance is recommended. One important rule when driving in Norway: Yield to the vehicle approaching from the right.

Dimmed headlights are mandatory at all times, as is the use of seatbelts and children's seats (when appropriate) in both front and rear seats. All cars must carry red reflecting warning triangles to be placed a safe distance from a disabled vehicle.

Four-lane highways are the exception and are found only around major cities. Outside of main coastal routes, roads tend to be narrow and sharply twisting, with only token guardrails and during the summer, always crowded. Along the west coast, waits for ferries can be significant.

Driving is on the right. Norwegian roads are well marked with directional, distance, and informational signs. Some roads, particularly those over mountains, can close for all or part of the winter.

The maximum speed limit is 90 kmh (55 mph) on major motorways. On other highways, the limit is 80 kmh (50 mph). The speed limit in cities and towns is 50 kmh (30 mph), and 30 kmh (18 mph) in residential areas.

Gas stations are plentiful, and unleaded gasoline and diesel fuel are sold virtually everywhere from self-service gas pumps. Those marked *kort* are 24-hour-a-day pumps, which take oil company credit cards or bank cards, either of which is inserted directly into the pump.

Norway has strict drinking and driving laws, and routine roadside checks, especially on Friday and Saturday nights, are common. The legal limit is a blood alcohol percentage of 0.05%, which corresponds to a glass of wine or a bottle of low-alcohol beer. If you are stopped for a routine check, you may be required to take a breath test. If that result is positive, you must submit to a blood test. No exceptions are made for foreigners, who can lose their licenses on the spot.

Speeding also is punished severely. Most roads are monitored by gray metal boxes equipped with radar and cameras. Signs warning of *Automatisk Trafikkontroll* (Automatic Traffic Monitoring) are posted periodically along appropriate roads.

Car Rental The major car rental companies operate in Norway. Avis (tel. 02/84–78–80 or 02/53–05–57), Budget (tel. 050/30–210 or 02/53–79–24), Hertz (tel. 02/12–55–55 or 02/53–36–47), and InterRent/Europcar (tel. 02/70–04–00 or 02/53–23–40) are located at Fornebu airport directly across the street from the Arrivals exit. When you reserve a car, be sure to specify if you need an automatic, as these are not always available.

By Taxi Even the smallest villages have some form of taxi service. Towns on the railroad normally have taxi ranks just outside the station. Look in the telephone book under "Taxi" or "Drosje." All city taxis are connected with a central dispatching office, so there is only one main telephone number, the taxi central.

Telephones

The telephone system is modern and efficient, and international direct service is available throughout the country. Phone numbers are six digits in the cities, five digits in small towns and in the country.

Public telephones are of two types. Push-button phones, which accept NKr1, 5, and 10 coins are easy to use: Lift the receiver, listen for the dial tone, insert the coins, dial the number, and wait for a connection. The digital screen at the top of the box indicates the amount of money in your "account."

Older rotary telephones sometimes have a grooved slope at the top for NKr1 coins, allowing them to drop into the phone as needed. Place several in the slope, lift off the receiver, listen for the dial tone, dial the number, and wait for a connection. When the call is connected, the telephone will emit a series of beeps, allowing coins to drop into the telephone.

Both types of telephones have warning signals (short pips) indicating that the purchased time is almost over.

Local Calls Local calls cost NKr2 (about 30 cents) from a pay phone and about NKr3 from hotel phones.

Long-distance Calls Norwegian area codes consist of two or three numbers, the first of which is always 0. Dial the code and then the number. Rates vary according to distance and time of day.

International Calls Dial the international access code, 095, then the country code, area code (omitting 0, if it is the first number), and number. All telephone books list country code numbers, including the United States and Canada (1), Great Britain (44), and Australia (61). Norway's code is 47. For operator-assisted calls, dial 0111 for national calls and 0115 for international calls. All international operators speak English.

Information Dial 0180 for information for Norway and the other Scandinavian countries, 0181 for international telephone numbers.

Mail

The letter rate for Norway and the other Nordic countries is NKr3.20 (48 cents), NKr4 (60 cents) for Europe, and NKr5 (77 cents) for outside Europe for a letter weighing up to 20g (¾ ounce). Postcards cost NKr3.20 within Scandinavia, NKr4 to all other destinations.

Tipping

Tipping is kept to a minimum in Norway, because service charges are added to most bills. It is, however, handy to have a supply of NKr5 or 10 coins for less formal service. Tip only in local currency.

Airport and railroad porters (if you can find them) have fixed rates per bag, so they will tell you how much they should be paid. Tips to doormen vary according to the type of bag and the distance carried—NKr5–10 each, with similar tips for porters carrying bags to the room. Room service usually has a service charge included already, so tipping is discretionary.

Round off a taxi fare to the next round digit, or anywhere from NKr5 to NKr10, a little more if the driver has been helpful with luggage.

All restaurants include a service charge ranging from 12 to 15% in the bill. It is customary to add an additional 5% for exceptional service, but it is not obligatory. Maître d's are not tipped, and coat checks have flat rates, ranging from NKr5 to NKr10 per person.

Opening and Closing Times

Banks are open weekdays 8 to 3:30, Thursday until 6. Most shops are open 9 or 10 to 5 weekdays, Thursday until 7, Saturday 9 to 2, closed Sunday. Some large shopping centers are open until 8 weekdays. Supermarkets are open until 8 or 10 weekdays and until 6 on Saturdays. During the summer, most shops close weekdays at 4 and at 1 on Saturday, while banks open at 8:15 and close at 3, with a Thursday closing at 5. Most post offices are open weekdays 8 to 5:30, Saturday 8 to 1.

Shopping

Good buys include handicrafts, handknitted sweaters, yarn, embroidery kits, textiles, pewter, rustic ironwork, silverware, wooden bowls and spoons, hand-dipped candles, and Christmas ornaments made from natural materials. *Husfliden* (home-craft) outlets are located in almost every city. The **classic knitting designs,** with snowflakes and reindeer, have been bestsellers for years and can be bought at most Husfliden and specialty stores, while more modern sweaters, made of combinations of brightly colored yarns, can be purchased from yarn shops. **Juleduk (Christmas tablecloths)** with typical Norwegian themes, are for sale year-round at embroidery shops. **High-fashion textiles** include coats and jackets in wool blanket material with nature motifs. Other handmade items include **candlesticks** of both pewter and wrought iron, **handblown glass,** and handturned **wood bowls** and **platters** made of birch roots. All Husfliden stores and many gift shops sell **Christmas ornaments** handmade from straw and wood shavings. Other, more off-beat, items include **cheese planes** (*osthøvel* in Norwegian) and graduated forms for making almond ring cakes (***kransekakeformer***). Hobby gardeners will appreciate the ***krafse,*** a practical tool somewhere between a spade and a hoe, while the outdoor person will like the ***supertrøye,*** a gossamer thin, insulated undershirt. Because Norwegian children spend so much time out of doors, practical clothing is a must, and good buys include **Helly-Hansen rain gear** and **insulated boots.**

Norwegian silver companies produce a wide range of patterns. At 830 parts to 1000, compared with 925 parts in sterling, Norwegian silver is stronger than English or American, and the price is very competitive.

Norwegian rustic antiques may not be exported. Even the simplest corner shelf or dish rack valued at $50 is considered a national treasure if it is known to be over 100 years old.

Value-added Tax Refunds

Value-added tax, MVA for short, but called *moms* all over Scandinavia, is a hefty 20% on all services and purchases except books; it is normally included in the prices of goods. All purchases of consumer goods totaling over NKr300 ($45) for export by non-residents are eligible for value-added tax refunds.

Shops subscribing to "Norway Tax-Free Shopping" provide customers with vouchers, which they must present, together with their purchases, upon departure in order to receive an on-the-spot refund of a percentage of the tax.

Shops that do not subscribe to this program have slightly more detailed forms, which must be presented to the Norwegian Customs Office along with the goods to obtain a refund by mail. This refund is closer to the actual amount of the tax.

It's essential to have both the forms and the goods available for inspection upon departure. Make sure that the appropriate stamps are on the voucher or other forms before leaving the country. If a form was not stamped upon departure, it can be stamped upon entry into the next country, or at the final destination.

Sports and Outdoor Activities

Norway is a sports lover's paradise. Outdoor sports have always been popular, while indoor facilities have been built nationwide. Close to 100 recreational and competitive sports are recognized in Norway, each with its own national association, 57 of which are affiliated with the **Norges Idrettsforbund** (Norwegian Confederation of Sports; Hauger Skolevei 1, 1351 Rud, tel. 02–51–88–00). Contact the confederation for the addresses of individual sports organizations.

Bicycling Most cities have marked bike routes and paths. Bicycling on country roads away from traffic is a favorite national pastime, but as most routes are hilly, this demands good physical condition. All cyclists are required to wear protective helmets.

Camping Norway offers more than 900 inspected and classified campsites, many with showers, bathrooms, and hookups for electricity. Most also have cabins or chalets to rent by the night or longer. For more information contact local tourist offices or the **Norwegian Automobile Federation** (Storgt. 2, N–0155, Oslo 1, tel. 02/42–94–00).

Fishing Whether it is fly-fishing for salmon or trout in western rivers or deep-sea fishing off the northern coast, Norway has all kinds of angling possibilities. Fishermen are required to buy an annual fishing tax card at the post office and a local license from the sporting goods store nearest the fishing site. Live bait is prohibited, and imported tackle must be disinfected before use.

Golf Golf came to Norway only recently, but the country has gone golf-crazy—there is even a course on arctic Spitsbergen! For information about guest privileges and greens fees, contact **Oslo Golfklubb** (Bogstad, 0740 Oslo 7, tel. 02–50–44–02); **Bergen Golfklubb** (Boks 470, 5001 Bergen, tel. 05–182077); **Stavanger Golfklubb** (Longebakken 45, 4042 Hafrsfjord, tel. 04–55–70–25); or **Trondheim Golfklubb** (Boks 169, 7001 Trondheim, tel. 07–53–18–85).

Hiking Every city has surrounding trails and many have cabins where guests can rest, eat, and even spend the night. **Den Norske Turistforening** (DNT, Boks 1963 Vika, 0125 Oslo 1, tel. 02–83–25–50) and affiliated organizations administer cabins and tourist facilities in the central and northern mountainous areas of the country and will arrange group hikes. They have English brochures that can be ordered by mail.

Horseback Riding Most cities and resort areas have stables, which rent chunky Norwegian fjord ponies and horses. **Steinseth Ridesenter** (Sollivn. 74, 1370 Asker, tel. 02–78–20–24), is a 30-minute drive from Oslo. Many resorts specialize in mountain pack trips; riding camps are in operation every summer.

Mountaineering The mountains of the Lofoten Islands and the Lyngen area of Troms County offer Alpine-class mountaineering. The **DNT** (*see* Hiking, *above*) has information. Oslo rock climbers practice on the Kolsås cliffs, a 20-minute drive west of the city, while the pros go to the Trolltindene peaks in Romsdal, near Åndalsnes.

Orienteering Norway's top mass-participation sport is based on running or hiking over territory with a map and compass to find control points marked on a map. Special cards can be purchased at sports shops to be punched at control points found during a season. It's an enjoyable, inexpensive family sport, and gear can be purchased at any sports shop.

Rafting Rafting excursions are offered throughout Norway. For more information, contact: **Flåte Opplevelser** (2050 Jessheim, tel. 062–35051); **Norwegian Wildlife and Rafting** (2254 Lundersæter, tel. 066–29724); **Oppdal Frilufts Senter** (Hotel Nor Alpin, 7340 Oppdal, tel. 074–22130); or **Schulstad Adventure** (Stabbursdal, 9710 Indre Billegjord, tel. 084–64746).

Running Grete Waitz and Ingrid Kristiansen have put Norway on the marathon runners' map in recent years. The first national marathon championships were held in Norway in 1897 and the Oslo Marathon always attracts a large following. For the recreational runner, **Norges Friidretts Forbund** (Tollbugt. 11, 0152 Oslo, tel. 02–20–53–20), has information about local clubs and competitions.

Sailing Both the late King Olav V and the present King Harald V won Olympic gold medals in sailing. Sailing in Oslo fjord and among the islands of the southern coast is a favorite summer pastime. Contact **Norges Seilforbund** (Hauger Skolevei 1, 1351 Rud, tel. 02–51–88–00) about facilities around the country; for the Oslo region, contact **KNS** (The Royal Norwegian Sailing Association; Huk Aveny 1, 0287 Oslo 2, tel. 02–43–74–10).

Skating Norway had one of the first indoor rinks in the world in the early 20th century. Some rinks have a few hours of public figure skating on weekends and just about every school in the country floods its playground in winter.

Skiing The ski is Norway's contribution to the world of sport. Norway's skiing season lasts from November to Easter. Preparations for the 1994 Winter Olympics are underway in Lillehammer, which, along with other Norwegian resorts, regularly hosts World Cup competitions as well. Cross-country skiing needs only basic equipment and rentals are readily available; every city has lit trails for evening skiing. **Skiforeningen** (Kongevn. 5, 0390 Oslo 3, tel. 02/92–32–00.) provides national snow condition reports. Ski centers in operation over the summer include: **Finse Skisenter** (Boks 12, 3590 Finse, tel. 05–52–67–11); **Galdhøpiggen Sommerskisenter** (2687 Bøverdalen, tel. 061–19711); and **Stryn Sommerskisenter** (6880 Stryn, tel. 057–71995).

Swimming Most towns have indoor swimming pools, while larger cities have heated outdoor pools. Many resorts also have swimming pools.

Tennis Municipal courts are usually booked in advance for a season at a time, while private tennis clubs have covered courts that are in use year-round. Many resorts have tennis courts.

Windsurfing The best windsurfing (a new sport here) is in western Norway. Centers include: **BT Brettseilerskole** (Nygårdsgt. 5/11, 5015 Bergen, tel. 05–21–45–00); **Selje Sjøsportsenter** (6740 Selje, tel. 057–56606); and **Stavanger Surfsenter** (Paradisvn. 33, 4012 Stavanger, tel. 04–52–31–08).

Sports for the Disabled Norway encouraged active participation in sports for the disabled long before it became popular elsewhere and has many Special Olympics medal winners. **Beitostølen Helsesportsenter** (2953 Beitostølen, tel. 063–41200), has sports facilities for the blind and other physically challenged people as well as training programs for instructors. Sports offered include skiing, hiking, running, and horseback riding.

Beaches

Many Norwegians enjoy bathing in the summer, but low water temperatures, from 14°C to 18°C (57°F to 65°F), are enough to deter all but the most hardy. The beaches around **Mandal** in the south and **Sola** near Stavanger are the country's finest, with fine white sand, while those around Oslo consist mostly of sharp pebbles and broken mussel shells, making rubber bathing shoes a necessity.

Dining

For centuries, Norwegians regarded food as fuel, and their dining habits still bear traces of this.

Breakfast is a fairly big meal, usually with a selection of crusty bread, herring, cold meat, and cheese. *Geitost* (a sweet, caramel-flavored whey cheese made wholly or in part from goats' milk) is on virtually every table. It is eaten in thin slices, cut with a cheese plane or slicer, a Norwegian invention, on buttered brown bread.

Lunch is simple, usually open-faced sandwiches. Most businesses have only a 30-minute lunch break, so unless there's a company cafeteria, most people eat home-packed sandwiches. Big lunchtime buffet tables, *koldtbord*, where one can sample most of Norway's special dishes all at once, are primarily for special occasions and visitors.

Dinner, the only hot meal of the day, is early, at four in the country, five in the city, so many cafeterias serving home-style food close by six or seven in the evening.

Traditional, home-style Norwegian food is stick-to-the-ribs fare, served in generous portions and blanketed with gravy. The most popular meal is *kjottkaker* (meat cakes), which resemble salisbury steaks, served with boiled potatoes and brown gravy. Almost as popular are *medisterkaker* (mild pork sausage patties), served with brown gravy and caraway-seasoned sauerkraut, and *reinsdyrkaker* (reindeer meatballs), served with cream sauce and lingonberry jam. Other typical meat dishes include *får i kål*, a great-tasting lamb and cabbage stew, and *stek* (roast meat), always served well-done. Fish dishes include poached *torsk* (cod) or *laks* (salmon), served with a creamy sauce called Sandefjord butter, *seibiff* (fried pollack and onions) and *fiskegrateng*, something between a fish souffle and a casserole, usually served with carrot slaw.

Norway is known for several eccentric, often pungent fish dishes, but these are not representative—both *rakfisk* (fermented trout) and *lutefisk* (dried cod soaked in lye and then boiled) are acquired tastes, even for natives.

Traditional desserts include the ubiquitous *karamellpudding* (creme caramel), and *rømmegrøt* (sour cream porridge served with cinnamon-sugar and a glass of raspberry juice). The latter, a typical farm dish, tastes rather like warm cheesecake batter—delicious. Christmas time brings with it a delectable array of light, sweet, and buttery pastries.

Norwegian restaurant food has undergone major changes in the last few years. Until recently, fine restaurants were invariably French, and fine food usually meant meat. Today, seafood and game have replaced beef and veal. Fish, from common cod and skate to the noble salmon, have a prominent place in the new Norwegian kitchen, and local cappelin roe, golden caviar, is served instead of the imported variety. Norwegian lamb, full of flavor, is now in the spotlight, and game, from birds to moose, is prepared with sauces made from the wild berries that are part of their diet. These dishes are often accompanied by native root vegetables.

Desserts, too, often feature fruit and berries. Norwegian strawberries and raspberries ripen in the long early summer days and are sweeter and more intense than those grown farther south. Red and black currants are also used. Two berries native to Norway are *tyttebær* (lingonberries), which taste similar to cranberries but are much smaller, and *multer* (cloudberries), which look like orange raspberries, but which have an indescribable taste. These wild berries grow above the tree line and are a real delicacy.

Category	**Cost***
Very Expensive	over NKr400
Expensive	NKr250–NKr400
Moderate	NKr100–NKr250
Inexpensive	under NKr100

**Prices are for a 3-course meal, including tax and 12½% service charge.*

Lodging

Norway is a land of hard beds and hearty breakfasts. Hotel standards are high, and even the simplest youth hostels provide good mattresses with fluffy down comforters and clean showers or baths. Breakfast, usually served buffet-style, is almost always included in the room price at hotels, while hostels often charge extra for the morning meal.

Norway has several hotel chains. **SAS,** which is a division of the airline, has a number of luxury hotels aimed at the business traveler. Many are above the Arctic Circle and are the "only game in town." **Rica** hotels, also a luxury chain, has expanded extensively in the last few years. The most interesting and individual hotel chain is **Home** hotels (Swedish-owned), which has successfully converted existing historic buildings into modern functional establishments in the middle price range. All Home hotels provide an evening meal, jogging suits, free beer, and other amenities designed to appeal to the single, usually business, traveler. As far as value for money is concerned, they are Norway's best buy. The **Farmers' Association** operates simple hotels in most towns and cities. These reasonably priced accommodations usually have **-heimen** as part of the name, such as Bondeheimen in Oslo. The same organization also operates cafeterias serving traditional Norwegian food, usually called **Kaffistova.** All of these hotels and restaurants are alcohol-free.

Many hotels offer summer rates, although some require advance booking or hotel passes that also must be purchased in advance. **Inter Nor Hotels** (Sommerservice, PB 150, 4891 Grimstad), a group of independently run hotels, offers a summer pass worth up to 50% off regular rates. It costs NKr60 (about $9) for two adults and two children and is valid at 50 hotels in Norway, 130 in the Nordic countries. **Fjord Pass** (Fjord Tours A/S PB 1752, 5024 Bergen, tel. 05/32-65-50, fax 05/31-86-56), which costs NKr50 (about $7) is valid at 298 establishments, from fancy hotels to simple mountain cabins.

Norway has 87 youth hostels, but in an effort to appeal to vacationers of all ages, the name has been changed to **vandrerhjem** (travelers' homes). Norwegian hostels are among the best in the world, squeaky clean and with excellent facilities—rooms sleep from two to six, and many have private showers. Membership can be arranged at any vandrerhjem, or you can buy a coupon book good for seven nights, which includes the membership fee. Linens are usually rented per night, so it's a good idea to bring your own—if you haven't, you can buy a lakenpose (sheet sleeping bag), at specialty stores. For more information and a list of vandrerhjem in Norway, contact **Norske Vandrerhjem** (Dronningensgt. 26, 0154 Oslo 1, tel. 02/42-14-10, fax 02/42-44-76).

Category	**Cost***
Very Expensive	over NKr200
Expensive	NKr150–NKr200
Moderate	NKr100–NKr150
Inexpensive	under NKr100

**All prices are for a standard double room, including service and 20% V.A.T.*

Oslo

Introduction

Although it is one of the world's largest capital cities in area, Oslo has only about 450,000 inhabitants, making it the smallest Scandinavian capital. Nevertheless, in recent years the city has taken off: shops are open late; pubs, cafés, and restaurants are crowded at all hours; and theaters play to full houses every night of the week.

Even without nightlife, Oslo has a lot to offer—parks, water, trees, hiking/skiing trails (2,600 km/1,600 mi in greater Oslo), and above all, spectacular views. Starting at the docks opposite City Hall, right at the edge of Oslo fjord, the city extends in great sweeps up the sides of the mountains that surround it, providing panoramic vistas from almost any vantage point.

Oslo has been Norway's center of commerce for 1,000 years and most major Norwegian companies are based in the capital. The sea has always been Norway's lifeline to the rest of the world: Oslo fjord teems with activity, from summer sailors and shrimpers to merchant ships and passenger ferries heading for Denmark and Germany.

Oslo is an old city, dating from the mid-11th century; under Danish and Swedish rule, it was renamed Christiania, after the 17th-century Danish king, Christian IV. An act of Parliament finally changed the name back to Oslo in 1925.

Important Addresses and Numbers

Tourist Information The main tourist office (Norway Information Center, tel. 02/83–00–50), located in the old Vestbanen railway station, is open weekdays 8:30–4; weekends 9–2. The office at the main railway station, **Sentralstasjon** (Jernebanetorget, tel. 02/17–11–24) is open daily 8 AM–11 PM. Look for the big round blue and green signs marked with a white **i.** Information about the rest of the country can be obtained from **NORTRA** (Nortravel Marketing; Postboks 499, Sentrum, 0105 Oslo 1, tel. 02/42–70–44).

Embassies **U.S. Embassy,** Drammensvn. 18, tel. 02/44–85–50. **Canadian Embassy,** Oscarsgate 20, tel. 02/46–69–66. **U.K. Embassy,** Thomas Heftyesgate 8, tel. 02/55–24–00.

Emergencies **Police:** tel. 002 or 02/66–90–50. **Fire:** tel. 001 or 02/11–44–55. **Ambulance:** tel. 003 or 02/11–70–70. **Car Rescue:** tel. 02/23–20–85.

Hospital Emergency Rooms **Oslo Legevakt** (Storgt. 40, tel. 02/20–10–90), near the Oslo S Station, is open 24 hours.

Doctors **Ring Medisinske Senter** (Sørkedalsvn. 33, tel. 02/46–68–95) is Norway's largest private clinic, located near the Borgen underground station. **Oslo Akutten** (N. Vollgt. 8, tel. 02/41–24–40) is an emergency clinic downtown, near Stortinget.

Dentists **Oslo Kommunale Tannlegevakt** (Kolstadgt. 18, tel. 02/67–48–46) is at Tøyen Senter. **Oslo Private Tannlegevakt** (Hansteens gt. 3, tel. 02/44–46–36) is a private clinic.

Late-night Pharmacies **Jernbanetorvets apotek** (Jernbanetorget 4B, tel. 02/41–24–82), across from Oslo S station, is open 24 hours.

Where to Change Money After normal banking hours money can be changed at the following places: The bank at **Oslo S station** is open June–Sept., daily 7 AM–11 PM; otherwise, weekdays 8 AM–8:30 PM, Saturday 8–2. The bank at **Fornebu Airport** is open weekdays 6:30 AM–9 PM, Saturday 7:30–7, Sunday 7 AM–10 PM. All post offices exchange money. **Oslo Central Post Office** is open weekdays 8–8, Saturday 9–3.

English-language Bookstores The best selection of English books can be found at **Tanum Libris** (Karl Johans Gate 43, tel. 02/42–93–10) and at **Erik Qvist** (Drammensvn. 16, tel. 02/44–03–26).

Travel Agencies **American Express/Winge Reisebureau** (Karl Johans Gate 33/35, tel. 02/41–20–30); **Bennett Reisebureau** (Skippergate 36, tel. 02/20–90–90); **Bordewick Reisebyrå** (Stenersgate 4, tel. 02/17–18–60); and **Univers Reiser** (Universitetssenteret, Blindern, tel. 02/45–32–00), for student travel.

Arriving and Departing by Plane

Airports and Airlines **Oslo Fornebu Airport,** 20 minutes west of the city, has international and domestic services under the same roof. Nevertheless the walks between international arrivals, baggage claim, and passport control are long.

SAS (tel. 02/17–00–20) is the main carrier, with both international and domestic flights. **Braathens SAFE** (tel. 02/12–20–70) and **Widerøe** (tel. 02/50–91–30) are the main domestic carriers. Other major airlines serving Fornebu include **British Airways** (tel. 02/33–16–00), **Air France** (tel. 02/42–10–45), **Finnair** (tel. 02/42–58–56), **Icelandair** (tel. 02/42–39–75), **KLM** (tel. 02/33–81–00), **Lufthansa** (tel. 02/83–65–65), **PanAm** (tel. 02/41–56–00), and **TWA** (tel. 02/83–44–28).

Gardemoen military airport, 35 kilometers (20 miles) north of Oslo, is the only one in the area that can handle 747s and DC10s. It is used primarily for charter traffic.

Between the Airport and Downtown Fornebu Airport is a 10–15-minute ride from the center of Oslo at off-peak hours. At rush hour (7:30–9 AM from the airport and 3:30–5 PM to the airport), it can take more than twice as long. None of the downtown hotels provides free shuttle service, although some outside the city do.

By Bus **Flybussen** (tel. 02/59–62–20; tickets: NKr25 adults, children 15 and under free; weekdays 6 AM–9:45 PM, Sat. 6 AM–7:45 PM, Sun. 6 AM–10 PM) departs from its terminal under Galleri Oslo shopping center, near Oslo S station, four times per hour and stops at Wessels plass, Nationaltheatret, Skøyen and Lysaker, before arriving at Fornebu approximately 20 minutes later. Another bus departs from the SAS Scandinavia Hotel 10 minutes after and 20 minutes before the hour and costs the same. Suburban bus No. 31, marked "Snarøya," stops outside the Arrivals terminal. On the trip into town, it stops on the main road opposite the entrance to the airport. Cost is NKr16.

By Taxi There is a taxi line to the right of the Arrivals exit. The fare to town varies from NKr80 to NKr100. All taxi reservations should be made through the **Oslo Taxi Central** (tel. 02/38–80–80) no less than one hour before pick-up time.

By Limousine **Bislett Limousine** (Hoffsvn. 10, tel. 02/73–28–55) can pick up six passengers from the airport and deliver them to one place in the Oslo area for NKr745.

Arriving and Departing by Car, Train, and Bus

By Car Route E18 connects Oslo with Göteborg, Sweden (by ferry between Sandefjord and Strömstad, Sweden), Copenhagen, Denmark (by ferry between Kristiansand and Hirtshals, Denmark), and Stockholm directly overland. The land route to Oslo from Göteborg is E6. A bypass under the city was finished in 1990 and has eliminated much of the through traffic. An electronic ring around Oslo requires all vehicles entering the city to pay NKr10.

By Train Long-distance trains arrive at and leave from **Oslo S** (tel. 02/17–14–00), while suburban commuter trains use **Nationaltheatret.** Tickets for long-distance travel can be purchased at railway stations or from travel agencies. Tickets for suburban commuter trains may be purchased at the station. Commuter cars reserved for monthly passholders are marked with a large black "M" on a yellow circle. If you have the correct amount in change, drive through one of the lanes marked "Mynt." If you don't, or if you need a receipt, use the "Manuell" lane.

By Bus Oslo has excellent bus connections with both suburbs and outlying districts. The terminal for local traffic, **Oslo M** (tel. 02/17–70–30), is located under the Galleri Oslo shopping center, across from the Oslo S station, while long-distance buses leave from the **Nor-Way Bussterminal** (tel. 02/33–01–91) on Havnegata, on the other side of Oslo S by the harbor. Long-distance tickets can be purchased at the Nor-Way Buss sales office (Karl Johans Gate 2, tel. 02/33–08–62), at travel agencies, and at the terminals. Local bus tickets can be bought at the terminal or on the bus.

Getting Around

Olso is a series of neighborhoods spread out over a relatively large area, with several, such as Bygdøy Peninsula and the area around Karl Johans Gate, containing a number of sights. It's easy enough to explore these sections on foot, but it is too time-consuming to walk to outlying parts of the city.

The center of the city is built on a grid, with Karl Johans Gate forming the spine. Most streets are one-way in alternating directions. Street numbers for the entire block are posted on corner buildings, making it easy to find the right address.

The **Oslo Card** offers unlimited travel on all public transport in greater Oslo as well as admission to museums, theaters, and cinemas and half-price fares on bus and boat sightseeing tours. The three-day adult card gives a 30% discount for trains to and from Oslo. A one-day Oslo Card costs NKr90, a two-day card, NKr130, and a three-day card NKr160.

Tickets on all public transportation within Oslo cost NKr14 without transfer, while tickets that cross communal boundaries have different rates. It pays to buy a pass or a multiple travel card, which includes transfers. A one-day pass costs NKr40 and a seven-day pass costs NKr130. A Flexicard is good for 10 trips with free transfer within one hour and costs NKr 100. Children 15 and under and senior citizens pay half price. These cards can be purchased at any post office, at tourist information offices, at subway stations, and on some routes. **Trafikanten** (Jernbanetorget, tel. 02/17–70–30), the information office for public transportation, is open weekdays 7 AM–8 PM, weekends 8–6.

Most public transportation starts running by 5:30 AM, with the last run just after midnight. On weekends, there is night service on certain routes.

By Subway Oslo has eight subway lines, which converge at **Stortinget** station. The four eastern lines all stop at **Tøyen** before branching off, while the four western lines run through **Majorstuen** before emerging above ground for the rest of their routes to the northwest suburbs. Tickets can be purchased at the stations.

By Bus About 20 bus lines, including four night buses on weekends, serve the city. Most stop at **Jernbanetorget** opposite Oslo S station. City buses have two-digit numbers. Tickets can be purchased from the driver.

By Tram/Streetcar Five tram lines serve the city. All stop at **Jernbanetorget** opposite Oslo S station. Tickets can be purchased from the driver.

By Ferry A ferry to **Hovedøya** and other islands in the harbor basin leaves from **Vippetangen,** behind Akershus castle (take Bus 29 from Jernbanetorget). From April through September, ferries run between **Rådhusbrygge 3,** in front of City Hall, and **Bygdøy,** the western peninsula, where several museums are located.

By Car **Oslo Card** holders can park for free at all parking places run by the city, but pay careful attention to time limits. Handicapped people with valid parking permits from their home country are allowed to park free and with no time limit in spaces reserved for the handicapped.

If you plan to do any amount of driving in Oslo, buy a copy of the *Stor Olso* map, availabe at book stores and gasoline stations. The center city section marks the direction of all one-way streets.

By Taxi All city taxis are connected with the central dispatching office (tel. 02/38–80–90), which can take up to 30 minutes to send one during peak hours. Cabs can be ordered from one to 24 hours in advance (tel. 02/38–80–80). Special transport, including vans and cabs equipped for the handicapped, can also be ordered (tel. 02/38–80–70). Taxi stands are located all over town, usually alongside Narvesen kiosks, and are listed in the telephone directory under "Taxi" or "Drosjer."

It is possible to hail a cab on the street. A cab with its roof light on is available, but cabs are not allowed to pick up passengers within 100 meters of a stand. Rates start at NKr17 for hailed or rank cabs, NKr30 to NKr40 for ordered taxis, depending upon the time of day.

Guided Tours

Tickets for all tours are available from Tourist Information at Vestbanen and at the Oslo S station. Tickets for bus tours can be purchased on the buses. All tours, except one, operate only during the summer.

Orientation All bus tours leave from the harborside entrance to City Hall (**Rådhuset**), while combination boat-bus tours depart from **Rådhusbrygge 3,** the wharf in front of City Hall.

H.M.K. Sightseeing (Hegdehaugsvn. 4, tel. 02/20–82–06) offers three bus tours. **Båtservice Sightseeing** (Rådhusbrygge 3, tel. 02/20–07–15) offers one bus tour, five cruises and one combination tour.

Special-interest

Forest Tours Tourist Information at Vestbanen can arrange four- to eight-hour motor safaris through the forests surrounding Oslo (tel. 02/83–00–50).

Sailing **Norway Yacht Charter** (Skippergate 8, tel. 02/42–64–98) can arrange sailing or yacht tours for groups of 5 to 200 people.

Sleigh Rides During the winter, it is possible to ride an old-fashioned sleigh through *Oslomarka*, the wooded area surrounding the city. **Vangen Skistue** (Laila or Jon Hamre, Fjell, 1404 Siggerud, tel. 09/86–54–81) or **Sørbråten Gård** (Helge Torp, Maridalen, tel. 02/42–35–79) can arrange this for you.

Street Train Starting at 11 AM and continuing at 45-minute intervals, the **Oslo Train** (tel. 02/42–23–64), which looks like a chain of dune buggies, leaves Aker Brygge for a 40-minute ride around the center of town (tel. 02/42–23–64).

Dogsled Tours For a faster and more exciting experience, tour the *marka* by dogsled. Both lunch and evening tours are available. Contact **Norske Sledehundturer** (Einar Kristen Aas, 1500 Moss, tel. 09/27–37–86).

Personal Guides Tourist Information at Vestbanen can provide an authorized city guide for your own private tour. **OsloTaxi** (Trondheimsvn. 100, tel. 02/38–80–00) also offers private sightseeing.

Walking Tours Organized walking tours are listed in *What's On in Oslo*, available from Tourist Information and at most hotels.

Highlights for First-time Visitors

Frogner Park (Vigeland Sculpture Park) (*see* Tour 3)
Holmenkollen (*see* Tour 3)
Kon-Tiki Museum (*see* Tour 4)
Munch Museum (*see* Tour 3)
Norsk Folkemuseum (*see* Tour 4)
Polar Ship *Fram* (*see* Tour 4)
Rådhuset (*see* Tour 1)
Viking ships (*see* Tour 4)

Exploring Oslo

Karl Johans Gate, starting with the Royal Palace and ending at Oslo S station, forms the backbone of downtown Oslo. Many of Oslo's museums and most of its historic buildings lie between the parallel streets of Grensen and Rådhusgata. Just north of the center of town is a historic area with a medieval church and old buildings. West of downtown is Frogner, the residential area closest to town, with embassies, fine restaurants, antiques shops, galleries, and the Vigeland sculpture park. Farther west is the Bygdøy Peninsula, with five museums and one castle. Northwest of town is Holmenkollen, with beautiful homes and a famous ski jump and restaurant. On the east side, home to many new immigrants, is the Munch Museum and the botanical gardens.

Numbers in the margin correspond with points of interest on the Oslo map.

Tour 1: Downtown, from the Royal Palace to the Harbor

Downtown Oslo has something for everybody—shops, museums, historic buildings, interesting architecture, restaurants, and clubs—all concentrated in a small area. In the evening, many buildings are illuminated.

1 Oslo's main promenade street, Karl Johans Gate, starts at **Slottet** (the Royal Palace). The neoclassical palace, completed in 1848, is closed to visitors, but the garden is open to the public. An equestrian statue of Karl Johan, King of Sweden and Norway, the street's namesake, stands in the square in front of the palace.

2 Down the incline and to the left are the three buildings of the old **universitet** (university). Matriculation of new students takes place here each fall. The great hall of the center building is decorated with murals by Norway's famed artist, Edvard Munch, and is the site of the Nobel peace prize award ceremony. *Aula, Karl Johans Gate 47, tel. 02/42–90–91, ext. 756. Admission free. Open July, weekdays noon–2.*

3 Around the corner from the university, with access from Universitetsgata, is the newly refurbished **Nasjonalgalleriet** (National Gallery). There are some excellent pieces in the 19th- and early 20th-century Norwegian rooms. Scandinavian impressionists, called the "Northern Light" artists, have recently been discovered by the rest of the world. The gallery also has an extensive Munch collection. *Universitetsgt. 13, tel. 02/20–04–04. Admission free. Open Mon., Wed., Fri., and Sat. 10–4; Thurs. 10–8; Sun. 11–3.*

4 Back-to-back with the National Gallery, across a parking lot, is a big, cream brick Art Nouveau-style building housing the **Historisk Museum** (History Museum). As well as Asian and African ethnographic displays, the museum features a collection of Viking and medieval artifacts, including many intricately carved stave church portals. *Frederiksgt. 2, tel. 41–63–00. Admission free. Open May 15–Sept. 14, Tues.–Sun. 11–3; Sept. 15–May 14, Tues.–Sun. noon–3.*

5 Continue along Frederiksgate to the university and cross Karl Johans Gate to **Nationaltheatret** (the National Theater) and **Studenterlunden Park,** a few steps from the train station. In front of the theater are statues of Norway's great playwrights, Bjørnstjerne Bjørnsen (who wrote the words to the national anthem and won a Nobel prize for his plays) and Henrik Ibsen, who wrote *The Doll's House* and *Hedda Gabler.*

Across the street on the other side of the theater is the **Hotel Continental,** owned by the same family since it was built in 1900. Take a quick tour around the lobby bar to see the collection of Munch graphics. The hotel's Theaterkafeen is one of Oslo's most fashionable restaurants.

6 Turn right on Universitetsgata to reach the red brick **Rådhus** (City Hall), dedicated during Oslo's 900-year jubilee celebrations in 1950 and a familiar landmark with its two block towers. It took 17 years to build, because construction was interrupted by World War II. Many sculptures outside, as well as murals inside, reflect the artistic climate in Norway in the 1930s—Socialist modernism in its highest form. *Rådhusplassen, tel. 02/*

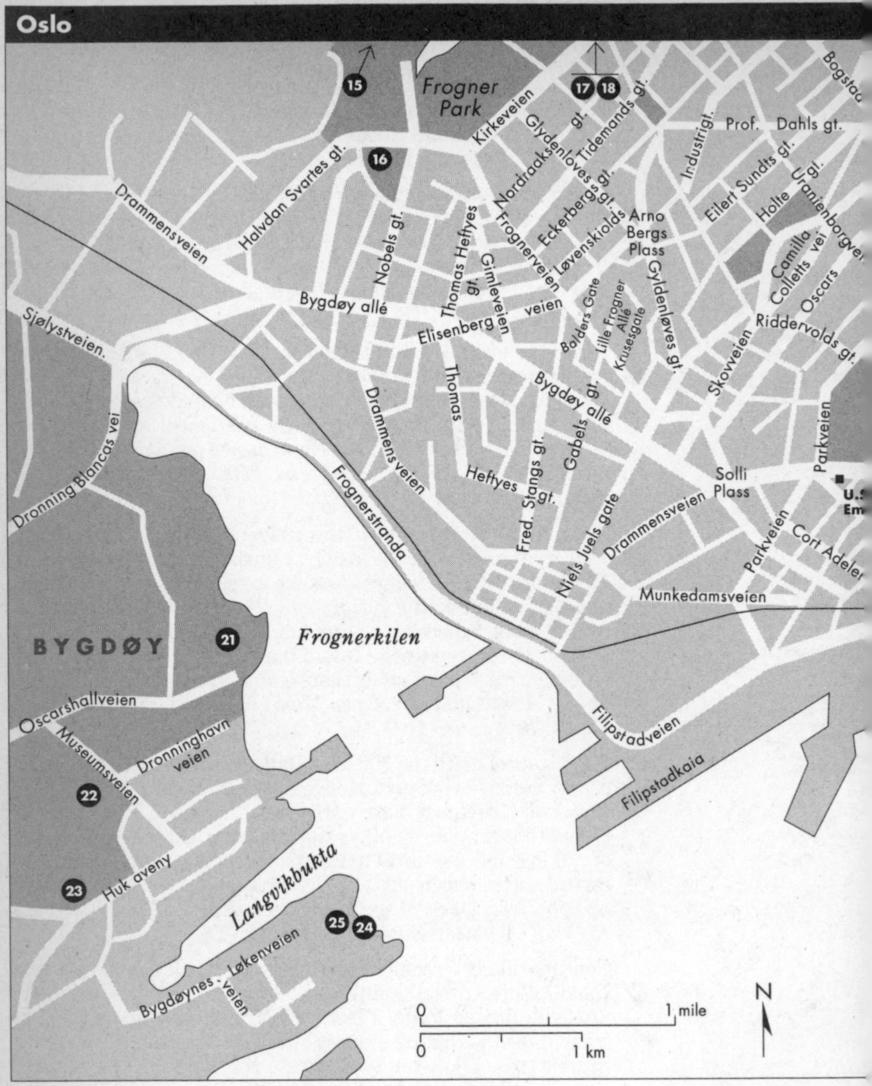

Akershus Slott, **11**
Domkirke, **8**
Fram-museet, **24**
Gamle Aker Kirke, **14**
Historisk Museum, **4**
Holmenkollbakken, **18**
Kon-Tiki Museum, **25**
Kunstindustri-museet, **13**
Mineralogisk-Geologiskmuseum, **20**
Munchmuseet, **19**
Museet for Samtidskunst, **9**
Nasjonalgalleriet, **3**
Nationaltheatret, **5**
Norsk Folkemuseum, **22**
Oscarshall Slott, **21**
Rådhus, **6**
Slottet, **1**
Skogbrand Insurance, **12**
Stortinget, **7**
Teatermuseet, **10**
Tryvannstårnet, **17**
Universitet, **2**
Vigelands anlegget, **15**
Vigelandsmuseet, **16**
Vikingskiphuset, **23**

Seilduksgt.
Helgesens gt.
Grüners gt.
Helgesens gt.
Sofienberggt.
Akerselva
Maridalsveien
Akersbakken
Waldemar Thranes gt.
Colletts gt.
Parkveien
Pilestredet
Holbergs gate
Ullevålsveien
Møllerveien
Nordregt.
Wessels gt.
Nordahl Bruns gt.
St. Olavsgt.
Akersveien
Hausmanns gt.
Trondheimsveien
Jens Bjelkes gt.
Frederiks Gate
Universitetsgt.
Rosenkrantz' gt.
Henrik Ibsens gt.
Grubbe gt.
Møllergt.
Torggt.
Youngs-torget
Karl Johans Gate
Drammensveien
Akersgata
Grensen
Stortorvet
Storgt.
Brugt.
Urtegt.
Norbygt.
Tøyengt.
Stortingsgt.
Munkedamsveien
R. Admurdsens gt.
Nedre Vollgt.
Oslo Spektrum
Oslo City
Grønlandsleiret
Lakkegata
Dokkveien
Rådhusgt.
Slottsgt.
Prinsens gt.
Nedre Tollbugata
Kirkegata
Dronningens gt.
Skippergt.
Fred Olsens gt.
Strandgt.
Central Station
Nylandsveien
Schweigaards gt.
Pipervika
Akershusstranda
Mynt gt.
Kongens Gate
Bispegt.
Bjørvika
Akerselva
Bispevika
Skippergt.
SØRENGA
Oslo gt.
Oslofjorden
Mosseveien
Ekebergsletta

86–16–00. Admission free. Open May–Sept., Mon.–Wed. and Fri.–Sat. 9–3:30; Thurs. 9–7; Sun. noon–3.

Return to Stortingsgata and walk past Tordenskioldsgate to Rosenkrantz' Gate, both lined with specialty shops. Cross over Stortingsgata and along the short end of the park back to Karl Johans Gate. On the left is a refurbished news kiosk from the early years of this century. Cross the street to the **Grand Hotel.** Many Norwegians rent street-facing rooms here on Constitution Day, May 17, for a good view of the parades. Its cafe was a favorite haunt of Ibsen and Munch.

Time Out Inside the Grand Hotel, just beyond the reception desk, is **Palmen,** an informal restaurant, where Oslo matrons take tea in the afternoon. Salads and light meals are served, as well as pastries and cakes.

Walk past the Lille Grensen shopping area and once again
7 across Karl Johan to **Stortinget** (the Parliament), built in the middle of the 19th century. *Karl Johans Gate 22, tel. 02/31–30–50. Admission free. Open July 1–Aug. 30, weekdays 11–2.*

Turn left on Kongens Gate from Karl Johans Gate to reach
8 **Stortorvet,** Oslo's main square. On its west side is **Oslo Domkirke** (Cathedral), completed in 1697, whose intricately carved Baroque pulpit merits a look. *Stortorvet, tel. 02/41–27–93. Admission free. Open June 1–Aug. 31, weekdays 10–3, Sat. 10–1; Sept. 1–May 31, weekdays 10–1.*

Behind the cathedral is a semicircular arcade housing many small artisans' shops, called **Kirkeristen** or Basarhallene. The building was constructed in the middle of the 19th century but was inspired by medieval architecture.

Time Out Order a cup of hot, foamy cappuccino at the **café** of the same name in the inner arcade. A copy of the *International Herald-Tribune* hangs from a rod inside for anyone to read.

From the Cathedral, follow Kirkegata left past Karl Johan to Bankplassen, and the 1902 Bank of Norway building, since
9 1990 the **Museet for Samtidskunst** (the Museum of Contemporary Art). The building, a good example of geometric Norwegian Art Nouveau, is itself is worth a visit, but the collection, housed mostly in small rooms built around a large core, is not outstanding. *Bankplassen 4, tel. 02/33–58–20. Admission free. Open Tues.–Fri. 11–7, weekends 11–4.*

Turn right onto Myntgata to reach Nedre Slottsgate, where the half-timbered buildings on the left stable police horses. This is Oslo's oldest neighborhood. At the corner of Nedre Slottsgate and Rådhusgata is the old city hall, housing **Gamle Rådhus** restaurant, which celebrated its 350th anniversary in
10 1991. Upstairs is **Teatermuseet** (the Theater Museum), a collection of old pictures and costumes, which sometimes holds an open house at which children can try on costumes and have makeup applied. The first public theater performance in Oslo took place here. *Nedre Slottsgt. 1, tel. 02/53–63–17. Admission: NKr5. Open Wed. 11–3, Sun. noon–4.*

Diagonally across Rådhusgata are two 17th-century buildings that house art galleries and a café. Turn left on Rådhusgata and
11 walk over the grassy hill to the entrance of **Akershus Slott** (cas-

tle) at Festningsplassen. It's a climb, but the views from the top are worth it. The oldest part of the castle was built around 1300. Today, it is used mainly for state occasions. A few rooms, including the recently restored chapel, are open to the public. The castle became German headquarters during the occupation of Norway in World War II, and many members of the Resistance were executed on the castle grounds. A memorial has been erected at the site, across the bridge at the harbor end of the castle precinct. In a building next to the castle, at the top of the hill, is **Norges Hjemmefrontmuseum** (the Norwegian Resistance Museum), which documents events during the German occupation from 1940 to 1945. *Akershus Slott, Festningsplassen, tel. 02/41–25–21. Admission to castle grounds and concerts free. Open weekdays 6 AM–9 PM, weekends 6 AM–7 PM; concerts in chapel, May 20–Oct. 21, Sun. at 2. Admission to castle: NKr10 adults, NKr5 children, students, senior citizens. Open May 2–Sept. 15, Mon.–Sat. 10–4; year-round, Sun. 12:30–4. Norges Hjemmefrontmuseum, Akershus Festning, tel. 02/40–31–38. Admission: NKr10 adults; NKr3 children, students, senior citizens. Open Apr. 15–Sept. 30, Mon.–Sat. 10–4; Sun. 11–4; Oct. 1–Apr. 14, Mon.–Sat. 10–4; Sun. 11–4.*

Walk back to Rådhusgata to see another interesting building,
12 **Skogbrand Insurance** (Rådhusgata 23B), in the block above the retaining wall. Architects Jan Digerud and Jon Lundberg have won awards for their innovative 1985 vertical addition to this 1917 building. Continue along to the harborside, where you can buy shrimp from one of the shrimpers docked opposite City Hall and enjoy them on a bench overlooking the water.

Tour 2: St. Olavs Gate to Damstredet

This quiet, old-fashioned district is particularly well preserved. It features artisans' shops and Oslo's most historic cemetery.

At the corner of St. Olavs Gate and Akersgata is
13 **Kunstindustrimuseet** (the Decorative Arts Museum), which houses a superb furniture collection as well as an entire floor of Norwegian decorative art. The most interesting collection is on the top floor—royal clothing, including Queen Maud's jewel-encrusted coronation gown from 1904. Her waist couldn't have been more than 18 inches. The clothes are worthy of any fairy tale. *St. Olavsgt. 1, tel. 02/20–35–78. Admission: NKr30 adults, NKr10 children, students, senior citizens. Open June 1–Sept. 15, Mon.–Sat. 10–6, Sun. noon–6; Sept. 16–May 31, Tues.–Sat. 10–4, Sun. noon–4.*

Diagonally across Akersgata is St. Olavs Kirke. Up the hill, on the right, is **Vår Frelsers Gravlund** (Our Savior's Cemetery), where many of Norway's famous, including Ibsen and Munch,
14 are buried. At its northeast corner is **Gamle Aker Kirke** (Old Aker Church), the city's only remaining medieval church, a stone basilica, which has undergone many changes since it was constructed around 1100. *Akersvn. 25, tel. 02/69–35–82. Admission free. Open Mon.–Sat. noon–2.*

Telthusbakken, on the south side of the church, is a well-preserved street with houses from the last century. Continue down Akersveien on the east side of the cemetery and veer left onto Damstredet, where many artisans live in old wood houses.

Tour 3: Frogner, Holmenkollen, and the Munch Museum

Catch the No. 2 "Majorstuen o/ Frogner" streetcar, which stops on Stortingsgatan at Nasjonalteatret and runs along the Drammensveien side of the Royal Palace.

Opposite the southwestern end of the Palace grounds is the triangular **U.S. embassy,** designed by American architect Eero Saarinen and built in 1959. At Solli Plass, the *trikk*, as Norwegians fondly call the streetcars, turns right onto Frognerveien. If you are interested in architecture, or if you would like to see what Oslo was like a century ago, leave the *trikk* and turn off Frognerveien onto **Krusesgate.** The old-fashioned wood houses here were built between 1890 and 1897 in the national romantic style (also called chalet style). It is the last well-preserved neighborhood in that style left in the city. Make a circle around Lille Frogner allé and return to Frognerveien. At this point, you can either catch the next *trikk* and ride to Frogner Park or walk the seven short blocks, following Balders Gate to Arno Bergs Plass with its central fountain. Turn left on Gyldenløves Gate (street of the golden lion) and walk through one of the city's most stylish neighborhoods. Most of the buildings were constructed in the early years of this century, and many have interesting sculptural decoration and wrought ironwork. Gyldenløves Gate ends at Kirkeveien. Turn right, past the Dutch embassy and cross the street at the light, which is next to the *trikk* stop. Frogner Park is just ahead.

15 There's nothing quite like **Vigelands anlegget** in Frogner Park anywhere else in the world. Sculptor Gustav Vigeland planned the layout as well as the figures, all of which represent stages in the cycle of life. Down the steps to the left of the bridge is the children's area, with figures from the embryo state to early childhood. Enter through the oversized wrought iron gates and cross the bridge, lined with bronzes of people of all ages.

Time Out Just before the sculpture bridge, on the left, is the park's outdoor restaurant, **Herregårdskroen,** where you can enjoy anything from a buffet lunch to a three-course dinner, depending on the time of day. It's a prime place for people watching.

Beyond the bridge is a fountain formed by six men carrying a large platter, symbolizing the artist's perception of the burdens men must bear. The corner granite groups represent the human struggle against evil, symbolized by the dragons. At the center of the park is a mosaic-paved area with 36 granite sculpture groups arranged on steps leading to a 52-foot-high monolith, another interpretation of man's struggle in life and the park's central axis. Beyond it are eight figural doors in wrought iron, and at the rear of the park, bordering a residential district, is a bronze "wheel of life."

Vigeland made the plaster models, while others did the carving and casting, all financed by the city. The figures are nude, but they're more monumental than erotic—bullet-headed, muscular men and healthy, solid women with flowing hair. Frogner Park is a living part of the city—people walk their dogs and babies here; they jog, ski, and sunbathe. The park complex also includes the City Museum, a swimming pool, an ice rink and skating museum (tel. 02/46–68–50), several playgrounds, and a restaurant. *Kirkeveien. Admission free.*

16 **Vigelandsmuseet** (the Vigeland Museum), across from the park, displays many of the plaster models for the sculptures, Vigeland's woodcuts and drawings, and mementoes of his life. *Nobelsgt. 32, tel. 02/44–23–06. Admission: NKr20 adults, NKr10 children, students, senior citizens. Open May 1–Oct. 31, Tues.–Sat. 10–6, Sun. noon–7; Nov. 1–Apr. 30, Tues.–Sat. noon–4, Sun. noon–6.*

Continue on Kirkeveien to Majorstuen underground station, up the steps on the left, and take the Holmenkollen line to Frognerseteren, a 15-minute ride.

Time Out **Frognerseteren Restaurant,** built in the national romantic style, dates from 1909, when newly independent Norway sought inspiration from its earlier history. The dragon heads on the eaves hark back to stave churches, while the log-cabin construction is reminiscent of the country cottages so dear to most Norwegians. On a clear day, the view is fantastic.

As if the view from Frognerseteren weren't spectacular
17 enough, **Tryvannstårnet** TV tower, offering the best panorama view of Oslo, is only a 15-minute walk away. Follow the signs. *Voksenkollen, tel. 02/14–67–11. Admission: NKr20 adults, NKr15 students, NKr10 children and senior citizens. Open July, daily 9 AM–10 PM; Aug. 1–19, daily 9–8; Aug. 20–31 and June, weekdays 10–7, weekends 10–6; May and Sept., weekdays 10–5, weekends 10–6; Oct.–Apr., weekdays 10–3, weekends 11–4.*

18 Downhill is **Holmenkollbakken** (the Holmenkollen Ski Museum and Ski Jump). The jump was built for the 1952 Winter Olympics and can be seen from many points in the city. Turn right at the statue of the late King Olav V on skis to enter the museum at the base of the jump. In addition to a collection of skis, the oldest dating to pre-Viking times, it displays equipment from the Nansen and Amundsen polar voyages and a model of a ski-maker's workshop. You can also climb (or ride the elevator) to the top of the jump tower. It's intimidating enough with a firm grip on the rail, but on skis and snow, it's mind-boggling. *Kongevn. 5, tel. 02/14–16–90. Admission: NKr30 adults, NKr20 students and senior citizens, NKr15 children. Open July, daily 9 AM–10 PM; Aug. 1–19, daily 9–9; Aug. 20–31 and June, daily 10–7; May, Sept. 10–5, and Oct.–Apr., weekdays 10–3, weekends 11–4.*

It's a 1-kilometer walk downhill to Holmenkollen Station to catch the train back to town. Leave the train at Majorstuen, cross the street, and catch the No. 20 bus, marked
19 "Galgeberg," which runs east to **Munchmuseet** (the Munch Museum). Edvard Munch, Scandinavia's leading artist, bequeathed an enormous collection of his work (about 1,200 paintings, 4,500 drawings, and 18,000 graphic works) to the city when he died in 1944. It languished in warehouses for nearly 20 years, until the city built a museum to house it in 1963. Munch was a troubled man, and his major works, dating from the 1890s, with such titles as *The Scream* and *Vampire*, reveal his angst. Women, violence, love, and death were his main themes. His extraordinary talent as a graphic artist emerges in the print room, where displays of lithographic stones and wood

blocks reveal his techniques. *Tøyengt. 53, tel. 02/67–37–74. Admission: NKr30 adults, NKr10 children, students, senior citizens. Open June 1–Sept. 15, Mon.–Sat. 10–6, Sun. noon–6; Sept. 16–May 31, Tues.–Sat. 10–4, Sun. noon–4.*

20 Nearby in Tøyen Park are the **Mineralogisk/Geologisk** Museum (Geological Museum) and the **Botanisk Hage** (Botanical Gardens). Geologists love Norwegian rocks because they are similar to those in North America and lend credence to the continental drift theories. *Sarsgt. 1, entrance also from Monradsgt., tel. 02/68–69–60, ext. 130. Admission free. Museum open Tues.–Sun. noon–3. Garden open May 1–Aug. 15, weekdays 7 AM–8 PM, weekends 10–8; Aug. 16–Sept. 30, weekdays 7–7, weekends 10–7; Apr., weekdays 7–6, weekends 10–6; Oct. 1–Mar. 31, weekdays 7–5, weekends 10–5.*

You can walk downhill past the Munch Museum to Tøyen Senter shopping area to catch the subway back to downtown.

Tour 4: Bygdøy

Oslo's most important historic sights are concentrated on Bygdøy Peninsula. Take the bus No. 30, marked "Bygdøy, " which stops on Stortingsgatan at Nasjonalteatret and runs along Drammensveien to Bygdøy Allé, a wide avenue lined with chestnut trees. Oslo's finest restaurant, Bagatelle, is on the right, at the beginning of the block, with the headquarters of Norsk Hydro, Norway's second largest corporation (after Statoil, the government-controlled oil company) across the street. The bus passes Frogner Church and old, stylish apartment buildings and several embassies to Olav Kyrres Plass, where it turns left, and soon left again, onto the peninsula. If you see some horses on the left, they come from the King's stables (the dark red building with the monogram); the summer palace, actually just a big white frame house, is on the right. Get off at the next stop, "Norsk Folkemuseum." Backtrack until you come to the narrow Oscarshallveien, which leads to
21 **Oscarshall Slott,** an eccentric neo-Gothic palace built in 1852 for King Oscar I as a site for picnics and other summer pursuits. *Oscarshallvn., tel. 02/43–77–49. Admission: NKr15 adults, NKr5 children. Open May 21–Oct. 1, Sun. 11–4.*

22 Next is the **Norsk Folkemuseum** (Norwegian Folk Museum), which consists of some 170 structures from all over the country that have been reconstructed on site. The best-known and most important building is **Gol stave Church** from around 1200. During summer and on weekends, guides in the buildings demonstrate various home crafts, such as weaving, sewing national costumes, and baking flatbread. On one side of the museum is a reconstructed 19th-century village, with shops and houses. Among its exhibits are a pharmaceutical museum and a dentist's office, complete with turn-of-the-century braces, a real mouthful of springs and bands. Indoor collections in the main building include toys, dolls and doll houses, a Sami (Lapp) collection, national costumes, and Ibsen's actual study. The museum puts on a special summer calendar of events, including daily activities from folk dancing to concerts with instruments from the museum's collection. *Museumsvn. 10, tel. 02/43–70–20. Summer admission: NKr35 adults, NKr25 students and senior citizens, NKr10 children. Winter: NKr20, NKr15, and*

NKr5. Open May 15–Sept. 14, daily 11–5; Sept. 15–May 14, daily noon–4.

23 Around the corner to the right is **Vikingskiphuset** (the Viking Ship Museum), Norway's best-known attraction. It looks like a cathedral from the outside, and inside the feeling of reverence is very real. It's hard to imagine that the three ships on display, all found buried along Oslo fjord, are nearly 1,200 years old. The richly carved *Oseberg* ship, thought to have been the burial chamber for Queen Åse, is the most decorative, while the *Gokstad* ship is a functional longboat, devoid of ornament. The small *Tune* ship has been left unrestored. Items found with the ships, including sleds with intricately carved decoration, tools, household goods, and a tapestry, are also on view. *Huk Aveny 35, tel. 02/43–83–79. Admission: NKr15 adults, NKr7 students, senior citizens, children. Open May 2–Aug. 31, daily 10–6; Sept., daily 11–5; Apr. and Oct., daily 11–4; Nov. 1–Mar. 31, daily 11–3.*

Time Out More fun than the collection of knots, model ships, and small boats at the nearby **Maritime Museum** is its outdoor café, **Najaden,** overlooking Oslo fjord.

---

24 Just beyond the Maritime Museum is the **Fram-museet,** an A-frame structure, in the shape of a traditional Viking boathouse. This museum, with its matter-of-fact displays of life on board ship, vividly depicts the history of polar exploration. The *Fram* (which means "forward") was constructed in 1892 by Scottish-Norwegian Colin Archer, a pioneer shipbuilder. Sometimes called the strongest ship in the world, the *Fram* has traveled farther north and farther south than any other surface ship. Fridtjof Nansen, led the first *Fram* expedition across the ice surrounding the North Pole; its most famous voyage took Roald Amundsen to Antarctica, the first leg of his successful expedition to the South Pole in 1911. Visitors board the ship by gangplank and are allowed to walk all over the vessel. Sled dogs can be heard on tape from the hold. The newest addition to the museum is a collection of hand-colored glass slides from Amundsen's expedition. Alongside the *Fram* is another famous Norwegian polar ship, the *Gjøa*, a tiny fishing boat that was stuck in Arctic ice for three years during Amundsen's journey through the Northwest Passage (1903-06). *Bygdøynes, tel. 02/43–83–70. Admission: NKr15 adults, NKr8 students, children, senior citizens. Open May 16–Aug. 31, daily 10–5:45; May 1–15 and Sept., daily 11–4:45; Apr. and Oct., weekdays 11–2:45, weekends 11–3:45; Nov.–Mar., weekends 11–3:45.*

25 Across the parking lot from the *Fram* is the **Kon-Tiki Museum,** which houses the famous raft, along with the papyrus boat, *Ra II*. Thor Heyerdahl continued the Norwegian tradition of exploration in his 1947 voyage from Peru to Polynesia on the *Kon-Tiki*, a balsa raft, to test his theory that the first Polynesians originally came from Peru. The *Kon-Tiki*, now showing its age, is suspended on a not-terribly convincing plastic sea. The *Ra II*, which sailed from Morocco to the Caribbean in 1970, is bigger and seems sturdier than the older raft. This museum is ripe for refurbishing, but it's still worth a short visit. *Bygdøynesvn. 36, tel. 02/43–80–50. Admission: NKr30 adults, NKr10 students, children, senior citizens. Open May 18–Sept. 31, daily 10–6; Apr. 1–May 16 and Sept. 1–Oct. 31, daily 10:30–5; Nov. 1–Mar. 31, daily 10:30–4.*

From April to October 31, you can take a 15-minute ferry ride from the dock in front of the *Fram* to the City Hall docks.

Short Excursions from Oslo

Numbers in the margin correspond with points of interest on the Oslo Excursions map.

The Henie-Onstad Center

It's been more than 20 years since Sonja Henie died, but she still skates her way through many a late-show movie (*Sun Valley Serenade* is a classic). The three-time Olympic gold medal winner was the first to realize the potential of the ice show, and her technical assistant, Frank Zamboni, has been immortalized in skating rinks around the world by the ice-finishing machine he developed just for her, the Zamboni. Henie had a shrewd head for money and marriage, and her third, to Norwegian
1 shipping magnate Niels Onstad, resulted in the **Henie-Onstad Center,** about 12 kilometers (7 miles) from Oslo. They put together a small but good collection of early 20th-century art, with important works by Leger, Munch, Picasso, Bonnard, and Matisse.

Buses 151, 153, 161, 162, 251, and 252 from the old university on Karl Johans Gate stop at the entrance to the museum grounds. To drive, follow E18 in the direction of Drammen, 12 kilometers (about 7 miles) from Oslo. There's plenty of parking. *Henie-Onstad Kunstsenter, 1311 Høvikodden (toward Drammen) tel. 02/54–30–50. Admission: NKr30 adults, NKr10 students, children, senior citizens. Open Mon. 11–5; Tues.–Fri. 9–9; also June–Aug. weekends 11–7 and Sept.–May weekends 11–5.*

The Cobalt Works

Blaafarveværket (the Cobalt Works), founded in 1776 to extract
2 cobalt from the Modum mines, is about 70 kilometers (45 miles) from Oslo, in Åmot i Modum. The mineral was used to make dyes for the world's glass and porcelain industries. Today the complex is a museum and national park with several attractions, visited by about 300,000 people every summer. The main building houses a one-man/woman show of works by a different Scandinavian artist every year. There is also a permanent collection of old cobalt blue glass and porcelain. For the children, there's a petting farm. Up the hill from the art complex is **Haugfossen,** the highest waterfall in eastern Norway. Beside the falls is an old-fashioned country store, with old metal signs and household goods on display, as well as a few newer items for sale, including gifts and jewelry made from local minerals. Restaurants serve Norwegian country dishes, including *rømmegrøt* (sour cream porridge topped with cinnamon sugar), while the Thranestua delicatessen specializes in cold food, such as *gravlaks* (marinated salmon), herring, and homemade liver pâté. Outdoor concerts are held throughout the summer on the grounds. Take E18 to Drammen, then E76 in the direction of Hokksund, over to Route 35 to Åmot, turning onto Route 287 to Sigdal. The road is well marked with signs for Blaafarveværket. Otherwise, take the bus to Modum, leaving from the old university on Karl Johan at 9:45 AM on Tuesday, Thursday, and Saturday. *Blaafarveværket, tel. 03/78–49–00. Admission to special exhibitions: NKr30 adults, NKr10 children. Open Apr. 5–May 31 and Sept. 2–30, daily 10–6; June 1–Sept. 1, daily 10–8.*

Hadeland

A day trip to **Hadeland** combines a drive along the Tyrifjord, with the best fjord views in eastern Norway, with a visit to a

Oslo Excursions

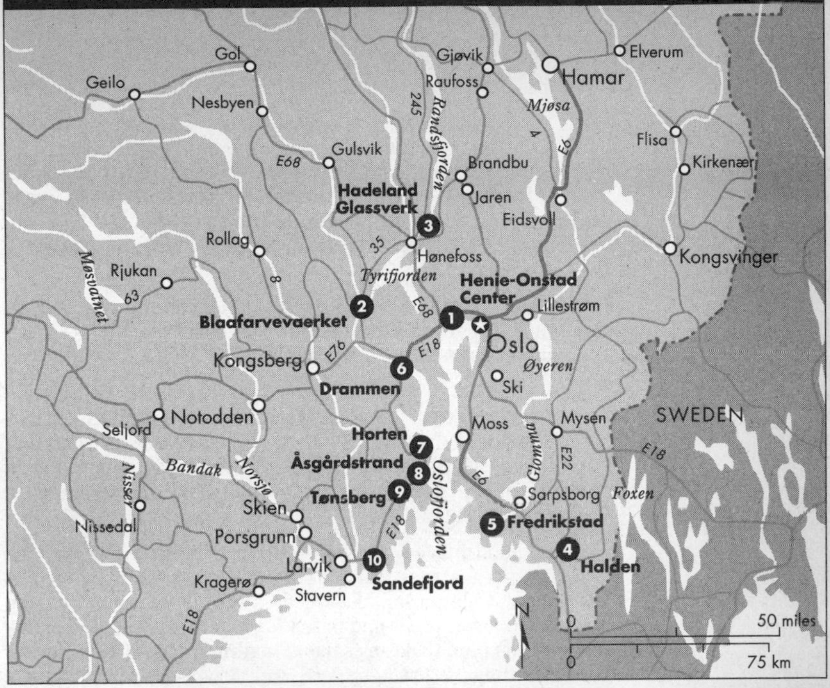

3 glass factory that has been in operation since 1762. **Hadeland Glassverk** (Rte. 245, toward Jevnaker) produces both practical table crystal and one-of-a-kind art glass. It is possible to watch artisans blowing glass, and their handiwork (first quality and seconds) is for sale at the gift shop. The museum and gallery have a collection of 15,000 items, with about 800 pieces on display.

The Kokkestua restaurant features local specialties and light meals. Another glass factory, **Randsfjord,** a bare-bones operation by comparison, is just a few minutes' drive away and is also worth a visit, especially for its reasonably priced gift items.

The only practical way to get to Hadeland is by car. Drive E18 west to Sandvika, turn right onto E68 and follow the signs to Hønefoss. At the Route 245 intersection, take the road to Jevnaker, which passes the glass factory. You can also take bus No. 71 marked Hønefoss, which leaves the old university on Karl Johan at seven minutes after the hour. Change in Hønefoss for the Jevnaker bus (no number). The total trip takes about two hours.

Oslo for Free

Many of the most interesting museums and important public buildings are free (*see* Tour 1, *above*), as well as Frogner Park (*see* Tour 2, *above*). Other free museums—mostly small and specialized—include:

Norsk Arkitekturmuseum (Norwegian Museum of Architecture) is located in a residential district from the 1850s, with some brilliant Gothic revival houses that are more interesting than the museum itself. *Josefinesgt. 32–34, tel. 02/60–22–90. Open May 16–Aug. 31, Tues.–Fri. 9–3; Sept. 1–May 15, Tues., Wed., and Fri. 9–3, Thur. 9–8.*

Forsvarsmuseet (Military Museum) at Akershus Castle traces Norwegian military history form the Vikings to the years immediately after World War II. *Akershus Castle, tel. 02/40–35–82. Open May 15–Sept. 15, Mon., Wed., and Fri. 10–3; Tues. and Thurs. 10–8, weekends 11–4; Sept. 16–May 14, weekdays 10–3, weekends 11–4.*

Postmuseet (Postal Museum) traces the history of the mail through 350 years and includes old mailboxes and signs as well as stamps. *Tollbugt, 17, tel. 02/40–80–59. Open Mon.–Fri. 10–3.*

For leisurely, free afternoon entertainment, watch the **changing of the guard** daily at 1:30 at the Royal Palace at the top of Karl Johans Gate. Follow the band down to the gazebo in **Studenterlunden Park** and listen to the music, weekdays when the king is in residence.

Another good place for people-watching is **Aker Brygge,** the shopping area across from the Tourist Information office at Vestbanen. **Oslomarka,** the woods and hills surrounding the city, has miles of trails and paths for hikers, skiers, and sightseers. If you plan to do any serious walking, stop at **Den Norske Turistforening** (Stortingsgt. 28, tel. 02/41–80–20) to buy a *turkart* (map), which concentrates on hiking and skiing trails, access roads, cabins, kiosks, and sights. Take virtually any subway or streetcar to its terminus and the marka is right at your feet. Wear good shoes and bring binoculars and camera when you climb to **Ringkollen Kikuttoppen** (Lookout Peak), for the views are breathtaking.

What to See and Do with Children

Bygdøy (*see* Tour 4, *above*) is a good place to take children. The Viking Ship, *Fram*, and *Kon-Tiki* Museums are obvious choices, but the **Norsk Folkmuseum** also has special exhibitions of old toys and dolls' houses. Live events, changing daily all summer, include old-fashioned bicycle races and sheep shearing.

The **Barnekunst** (Children's Art) **Museum** was the brainchild of Rafael Goldin, a Russian immigrant, who has collected children's drawings from more than 150 countries. Materials are provided for children to create on the spot. *Lille Frøensvn. 4, tel. 02/46–85–73. Admission: NKr25 adults, NKr15 children, students, senior citizens. Open June 25–Aug. 25, Tues.–Thurs., Sun. 11–5; Aug. 26–June 24, Tues.–Thurs. 9:30–2, Sun. 11–5.*

One stop closer to town on the subway is **Sporveismuseet** (the Transport Museum), with old buses and trains, including a horse-drawn streetcar. Take the subway to Majorstuen. *Gardevn. 15, tel. 02/34–49–71. Admission: NKr10 adults, NKr5 children. Open May–Sept. weekends noon–3; otherwise, Sun. noon–3.*

Oslo is proud of its brand new **Teknisk** (Technical) **Museum,** located about 20 minutes north of the city. Exhibits include the first airplane to fly over the North Sea, classic cars and motorcycles, and the development of computers, waterpower, and communication, all accompanied by demonstrations and films. *Kjelsåsvn. 143, tel. 22–25–50. Admission: NKr20 adults, NKr10 children. Open June–Aug., Tues.–Sun. 10–7; Sept.–May, Tues. 10–9, Wed.–Sat. 10–4, Sun. 10–5.*

Everyone enjoys **Tusenfryd,** Oslo's amusement park, a 20-minute ride east of the city. There are carnival rides, such as a merry-go-round, a ferris wheel, and a roller coaster with a loop, and a water slide. *Vinterbro, tel. 09/94–63–63. Admission (covers all attractions): NKr120 adults, NKr90 children. Open June 1–Aug. 20, daily 10–7:30; May and Aug. 21–Sept. 15, weekends 10–7:30.*

Off the Beaten Track

Most of the buildings of **medieval Oslo** are reduced to piles of rocks or foundations, but enough information is provided on site to enable anyone with a good imagination to visualize what it was like in days past. Take *trikk 9,* marked "Ljabru," to Bispegata (a few blocks behind Oslo S station), where signs point to the various ruins.

Oslo was founded by Harald Hårdråde in 1048, and the earliest settlements were here. The king and clergy usually occupied stone buildings, while the rest of the inhabitants lived in simple log houses facing narrow lanes on the incline down to the pier. Fires leveled the town several times, most recently in 1624, when it was rebuilt in the area around Akershus Castle. The ruins at **Minneparken** are all that are left of the city's former spiritual center: **Korskirken** (Cross Church; Egedes gate 2), a small stone church from the end of the 13th century; **Olavs kloster** (Cloister); St. Halvards plass 3, built around 1240 by Dominican monks; and the foundations of **St. Hallvards Kirke,** named for the patron saint of the city and dating from the early 12th century. The latter remained the city's cathedral until 1660. Stones from its walls were used to build Akershus Slott.

Next come the ruins of the old **Oslo Bispegård** (Bishop's seat) dating from around 1200. In 1725, **Oslo Ladegård** was built over its remains, and the vaulted ceilings of the earlier building can be seen in the cellar. Today, it houses displays of artifacts from medieval Oslo, and its reception rooms are used for official functions. *Oslo gate 13, tel. 02/19–44–68. Admission NKr20 adults, NKr10 children, students, senior citizens. Open May 2–Sept. 30; guided tours Wed. at 6, Sun. at 1.*

On the south side of Bispegata at Saxegaards Gate are the early 12th-century remains of **Clemens Kirke,** built of flat stones with a central row of columns down the nave. The bridge over Loenga partially covers it. The ruins at Sørenga, which include remains of the **Royal Precinct** and **Mariakirken,** are on the other side of the expressway, behind the freight-loading area (dodge past the containers and fork-lift tracks). A palace and a chapel were built here during the 12th century, first in wood, later in stone. They also included a large hall.

Shopping

Oslo is the best place to buy anything Norwegian. Prices of handmade articles, such as knitwear, are controlled, making comparison shopping unnecessary. Otherwise, shops have both sales and specials—look for the words *salg* and *tilbud*. Sales of seasonal merchandise, combined with the value-added tax refund, can save you more than half the original price. Although Norwegians are not particularly fashion conscious, they do like au courant skiwear and accessories, so there are plenty of bargains in last season's winter sportswear.

Two shopping districts stand out—downtown, in the area around **Karl Johans Gate;** and **Majorstuen,** starting at the subway station with the same name and proceeding down Bogstadveien to the Royal Palace.

Shopping Centers

Aker Brygge, the first major shopping center, is right on the water across from the Tourist Information office at Vestbanen. Once a shipyard, it now houses shops, restaurants, offices, apartments, and a theater complex. Shops are open until 8 most days, and some even on Sundays. Many are familiar chains, but one shop stands out. **Zig Zag** (Stranden 63, tel. 02/83–15–53), sells exquisite clothing that makes a fashion statement—exquisite embroidered and bejeweled creations for the slim and well-heeled.

Oslo City, at the other end of downtown, with access to the street from Oslo S station (Stenersgt. 1), is the largest indoor mall, but the shops are run-of-the-mill, the food is mostly fast, and the place has no pizzazz.

Paleet Karl Johan (Karl Johans Gate 39–41, between Universitetsgata and Rosenkrantz Gate), the newest downtown development, opens up into a grand atrium lined with supports of various shades of black and gray marble. Upstairs are familiar chain stores and specialty shops, while in the basement is a food court.

Department Stores

Christiania GlasMagasin (Stortorvet 9, tel. 02/11–40–80) is not a true department store, but it has a much more extensive selection of merchandise than a specialty shop. The best buys are glass and porcelain: Hadeland, Magnor, Randsfjord, and Severin glass and Porsgrunn and Figgjo porcelain and stoneware. Christmas decorations reflecting Norway's rural heritage are easily packed. There is also a wide selection of pewterware.

Steen & Strøm (Kongensgt. 23, tel. 02/41–68–00) is an old-fashioned, sprawling department store with a complete selection of Norwegian souvenirs.

Street Markets

The best flea market is Saturday at **Vestkanttorvet,** near Frogner Park.

Specialty Stores

Antiques

Norwegian rustic antiques cannot be taken out of the country, but just about anything else can with no problem. **Kaare Berntsen** (Universitetsgata 12, tel. 02/20–34–29) sells paintings, furniture, and small items, all very exclusive, and priced accordingly. **Blomqvist Kunsthandel** (Tordenskiolds Gate 5, tel. 02/41–26–31) has a good selection of small items and paintings, with auctions six times a year. **West Sølv** (Niels Juels Gate 27, tel. 02/55–75–83) has the largest selection of silver, both old and antique, in town. The residential area of Frogner is dotted with antiques shops, especially Skovveien and Thomas Heftyes Gate between Bygdøy Allé and Frogner Plass. **Esaias Solberg** (Dronningens Gate 27, tel. 02/42–41–08), behind Oslo Cathedral, has an exceptional selection of small antiques, including jewelry, silverware, and glass.

Books **Tanum Libris** (Karl Johans Gate 43, tel. 02/42–93–10) and **Erik Qvist** (Drammensveien 16, tel. 02/44–03–26) have the best selections of English books in Oslo. **Bjørn Ringstrøms Antikvariat** (Ullevålsvn. 1, tel. 20–78–05), across the street from the Museum of Decorative Art, has a wide selection of used books and records. For new and used paperbacks, go to **Pocketboka** (Ole Vigs Gate 25, tel. 02/69–00–18), at Majorstuen. The selection of paperbacks in English is enormous.

Embroidery **Husfliden** (*see* Handicrafts, *below*) sells embroidery kits, including do-it-yourself *bunader* (national costumes), while traditional yarn shops also sell embroidery. **Randi Mangen** (Jac Aalls Gate 17, tel. 02/60–50–59), near Majorstuen, sells only embroidery. It's an old-fashioned shop with a huge selection of already embroidered models, with emphasis on tablecloths, mats, and wall hangings.

Food Take back a smoked salmon or trout for a special treat. Most grocery stores sell vacuum-packed fish. **W. Køltzow** at Aker Brygge (Stranden 3, tel. 02/83–00–70) specializes in fish and can arrange for just about anything to be packed for export. Køltzow products also are for sale at Fornebu Airport.

Fur Look for the Saga label for the best quality farmed Arctic fox and mink. The most exclusive designs are found at **Studio H. Olesen** (Karl Johans Gate 31, tel. 02/33–37–50, and Universitetsgt. 20, tel. 02/42–99–49). Another shop with an excellent selection is **Hansson Pels** (Kirkevn. 54, tel. 02/69–64–20) near Majorstuen.

Furniture Norway is well-known for both traditional rustic furniture and for orthopedic, yet well-designed, chairs. Walk along **Møllergata,** the furniture street, to see both, or browse at **Tannum** (Stortingsgt. 28, tel. 02/83–42–95).

Glass, Ceramics, and Pewter If there's no time to visit a glass factory (*see* Short Excursions from Oslo, *above*), go to **Christiania GlasMagasin,** (Stortorvet 9, tel. 02/11–40–80) or to **Norway Designs** (Stortingsgt. 28, tel. 02/83–11–00) for the best items. The shops at Bazarhallene behind the Cathedral also sell glass and ceramics. Behind the Royal Palace is **Erik Abelson** (Skovvn. 27, tel. 02/55–55–94), with a shop crammed with the best modern designs.

Handicrafts **Heimen** (Rosenkrantz Gate 8, tel. 02/11–11–25) has a wide selection of small souvenir items as well as a specialized department for Norwegian *bunader* (national costumes). **Husfliden** (Møllergt. 4, tel. 02/42–10–75), behind Glasmagasinet, has an even larger selection, including pewter, ceramics, knits, handwoven textiles, furniture, handmade felt boots and slippers, handsewn loafers, sweaters, national costumes, wrought-iron accessories, and Christmas ornaments, all made in Norway. For individual pieces, visit Basarhallene, the arcade behind the Cathedral, where craftspeople have their studios and sales outlets.

Jewelry Gold and precious stones are no bargain, but silver and enamel jewelry, along with reproductions of Viking pieces, are. Some silver pieces are made with Norwegian stones, particularly pink thulite. **David-Andersen** (Karl Johans Gate 20, tel. 02/41–69–55) is Norway's best-known goldsmith and has the widest selection in Oslo. Other good jewelers are **Heyerdahl** (Fr. Nansens Place 6, tel. 02/41–59–18), near City Hall, and **ExpoArte** (Drammensvn. 40, tel. 02/55–93–90), who specialize in custom pieces. (*See also* Antiques, *above*.) All jewelers are required to be goldsmiths, and many make their own custom pieces, so virtually every shop has something exclusive.

Knitwear and Clothing Norway is famous for its handmade multicolored ski sweaters, but even mass-produced models are of top quality. The prices are regulated, so buy what you like when you see it. Sweaters are sold at Heimen and Husfliden (*see* Handicrafts, *above*) and at special sweater shops. **Maurtua** (Fr. Nansens Place 9, tel. 02/41–31–64), near City Hall, has a huge selection of both sweaters and blanket coats. **Oslo Sweater Shop** (SAS Scandinavia Hotel, Tullinsgt. 5, tel. 02/83–11–00) has one of the city's widest selections. **Siril** (Rosenkrantz Gate 23, tel. 02/41–01–80), near City Hall, is a small shop giving personal service. **Trønderstua** (Ruseløkkvn. 3, tel. 02/83–21–39) has a good selection of knitwear, yarn, and textiles. **William Schmidt** (Karl Johans Gate 41, tel. 02/42–02–88), founded in 1853, is Oslo's oldest shop specializing in sweaters and souvenirs.

If you prefer modern sweaters, or if you like to knit, head for yarn shops. The **Frost Shops** (Bygdøy Alle 27, tel. 02/44–56–66, and Valkyriegt. 13, near Majorstuen, tel. 02/69–58–53) have modern, multicolored, rather bulky sweaters, some based on traditional designs. **Grouff** (Grensen 15, tel. 02/42–96–82) has more conservative designs, as does **Garn og Vevstuen** (Karl Johans Gate 25, tel. 02/42–86–15) a block away.

Shoes **Aurlandssko** are handmade penny loafers in camel-color leather, very popular for informal occasions. The Sami of northern Norway make boots with upturned toes in the same color leather. Reindeer hide and handmade felt slippers are perfect for cold nights. All can be found at **Husfliden** (Møllergt. 4, tel. 02/42–10–75). Boots are also a good buy, from rubber boots to lined heavy boots for winter. **Grændsens Skotøimagazin** (Grensen 12, tel. 02/42–66–20) and **Agnar Hagen** (Bogstadvn. 20, tel. 02/46–50–36) have the best selections.

Sportswear Look for the Helly-Hansen brand. The company makes everything from insulated underwear to rainwear, snowgear, and great insulated mittens. **Sportshuset** (Ullevålsvn. 11, tel. 02/20–11–21, and Frognervn. 9C, tel. 02/55–29–57) has the best prices; **Gresvig** (Storgt. 20, tel. 02/17–39–80) and **Sigmund Ruud** (Kirkevn. 57, tel. 02/69–43–90), have the best choice.

Watches For some strange reason, Swiss watches are much cheaper in Norway than in many other countries. **Bjerke** (Karl Johans Gate 31, tel. 02/42–20–44, and Prinsens gt. 21, tel. 02/42–60–50) has the largest selection in town, with most of the familiar names.

Sports and Fitness

Bicycling **Den Rustne Eike** (The Rusty Spoke, Enga 2, tel. 02/83–72–31) rents bikes and equipment, including helmets (required by law). **Sykkeldelisk** (Fridtjof Nansens Place 7, tel. 02/42–60–20) and **Oslo Sykkelutleie** (Kjelsåsvn. 145, tel. 02/22–13–46) also rent a full range of bikes. The latter are located just on the edge of Oslo-marka, the wooded area surrounding the city, and they specialize in arranging routes covering that territory. **Syklistenes Landsforening** (National Organization of Cyclists; Maridalsvn. 60, tel. 02/71–92–93) sells books and maps for cycling holidays in Norway and abroad.

Fishing Oslo fjord and the many lakes in Oslo-marka provide many opportunities for fishing. Fishing licenses can be bought in post offices for NKr150.

Golf Until 1990, Oslo had only one international-level golf course, **Oslo Golfklubb** (Bogstad, tel. 02/50–44–02), but since then, one 18-hole and several nine-hole courses have opened, with expansions already planned. Oslo Golfklubb is private but will admit members of other golf clubs.

Health Clubs Aside from those in major hotels, few fitness centers are conveniently located to downtown. The newest, **Spektrum Trim & Helse** (Sonja Henie Place 4, tel. 02/17–98–00), welcomes visitors, as do **Trim Tram** (Akersgt. 16, tel. 02/17–08–05) and **Vika Gym & Trim** (Dronning Mauds Gate 11, tel. 02/83–38–80). Fees range from NKr40 to NKr70.

Jogging Head for the woods surrounding Oslo, the **marka**, for jogging; there are thousands of kilometers of trails, hundreds of them lit. Frogner Park has many paths, and you can jog along the Aker River, but a few unsavory types may be about late at night or early in the morning. **Oslo Turforening** (Oslo Hiking Association, Pilestredet 27, tel. 02/20–66–22) has numerous maps of trails around Oslo and can recommend individual routes.

Swimming **Tøyenbadet** (Helgesensgt. 90, tel. 02/67–18–89) and **Frogner Park** have large outdoor swimming pools, which are open from May 18 through August 25 (open weekdays 7–9 and 11–7, weekends 10–5). Tøyenbadet also has an indoor pool (open weekdays 7–7, weekends 10–5). All cost NKr35.

Tennis Like golf, tennis has become popular in Norway only recently. There are virtually no public courts with easy access. The courts at **Frogner Park** are generally rented out by the season, but it is possible to buy unused time. Ask at the kiosk at the Kirkeveien entrance to the park.

Beaches

Oslo has many beaches located a convenient distance from downtown. Oslo fjord is long, and it is well protected by the land masses surrounding it, so there's no real surf. The water temperature seldom exceeds 18° C (65° F). Few Norwegian women bother with bikini tops, and children under five seldom wear anything but shoes. While many beaches have toilet facilities and kiosks, none has mattresses or umbrellas for rent, nor are there lifeguards.

Drøbak This tiny community with clapboard houses and a wealth of small shops and restaurants, about 40 kilometers (25 miles) southeast of Oslo, has a typically Norwegian beach: rocks, shells, and a little bit of sand. There aren't enough parking spaces to accommodate the crowds on warm days.

Huk and Paradisbukta The Bygdøy beaches are the closest to Oslo and the most popular, especially after working hours on warm days. From about 3 PM, the two large parking lots fill rapidly. A small lagoon lined with broken shells and a few large photogenic rocks is backed by a grassy area for sunbathing.

Sognsvann The still water of the lake at Sognsvann, on the northern outskirts of the city, is even colder than that of Oslo fjord. It still manages to attract people of all ages, even a few who go swimming. The northeastern side of Svartkulp is set aside for nude bathing.

Dining

Food once was an afterthought in Oslo, but no longer. Its chefs are winning contests all over the world, and Norwegian cuisine, based on the products of its pristine waters and countryside, is firmly in the culinary spotlight. This does not mean that Oslo is packed with top-quality restaurants, however; eating out is a luxury for many Norwegians. Oslo also is a place where bad food is expensive and good food doesn't necessarily cost more—it's just a matter of knowing where to go. Highly recommended restaurants are indicated by a star ★.

Olso has many ethnic restaurants, most just so-so or worse, but several do stand out and provide alternatives just in case you become fished out.

Very Expensive

★ **Bagatelle.** Oslo's best restaurant is a short walk from downtown. Paintings by contemporary Norwegian artists accent the otherwise subdued interior. Internationally known chef/owner Eyvind Hellstrøm's cuisine is modern Norwegian with French overtones. His lobster lasagne, with big chunks layered among perfectly cooked noodles, napped with a velvety sauce, and the salmon with three kinds of caviar on a parsley coulis are extraordinary. Bagatelle has a wine cellar to match its food. *Bygdøy Allé 3/5, tel. 02/44–63–97. Reservations advised. Jacket and tie required. AE, DC, MC, V. Closed Sun., 1 week at Christmas and Easter, 3 weeks in July. Lunch Tues.–Fri. by prior arrangement.*

D'Artagnan. Freddie Nielsen's restaurant, right off Karl Johan, is marked with nothing more than a sign, a heavy door, and a bell. Inside, stairs lead to a comfortable lounge, while another floor up is the dining room. The decor is eclectic, but the food is classic and pure. The saffron-poached pike with asparagus is a good way to start a meal, while the boned fillet of salmon with lobster cream sauce seasoned with dill is attractive and flavorful. The dessert cart is loaded with jars of fruit laid down in liqueurs, which are served with various sorbets and ice creams. *Øvre Slottsgate 16, tel. 02/41–50–62. Reservations advised. Jacket and tie required. AE, DC, MC, V. Closed weekends and July. No lunch.*

De Fem Stuer. Located near the famous Holmenkollen ski jump, in the historic Holmenkollen Park Hotel, this restaurant has first-rate views and food. Bent Stiansen has won an assortment of prizes for his cooking; his modern Norwegian dishes have strong classic roots. Two of his signature offerings are a puff-pastry tart with mussels and leeks in a creamy mustard sauce and breast of ptarmigan with mushroom, apple, and shallot sauce. *Holmenkollen Park Hotel, Kongeveien 26, tel. 02/14–60–90. Reservations advised. Jacket and tie required. AE, DC, MC, V. No lunch.*

Holberg's Årstidene. Årstidene means "seasons," and both the decor and the menu change five times a year, to include Christmas. SAS Scandinavia Hotel's restaurant combines an open kitchen with a dark formal dining room, giving guests the opportunity to see award-winning Chef Lars Erik Underthun at work. His dishes are built up in layers, and they often feature a combination of sweet and sour, such as the fillet of reindeer with red onions and raisins. *SAS Scandinavia Hotel, Holbergsgate 30, tel. 02/11-30-00, ext. 2712. Reservations advised. Jacket and tie required. AE, DC, MC, V. Closed Sun., Mon., and 3 weeks in July. No lunch.*

Expensive
★

Feinschmecker. The name is German, but the food is modern Scandinavian. The atmosphere is friendly and intimate, with green rattan chairs, peach tablecloths, and floral draperies. Owner Bengt Wilson is one of Scandinavia's leading food photographers, so the food at Feinschmecker looks as good as it tastes. The roast rack of lamb with crunchy fried sweetbreads on tagliatelle and the chocolate-caramel teardrop with passion-fruit sauce are two choices on a menu that also makes fascinating reading. *Balchens gate 5, tel. 02/44-17-77. Reservations advised. Dress: casual but neat. AE, DC, MC, V. Closed Sun., 1 week at Christmas and Easter, and last 2 weeks of July. No lunch.*

Fiskekroken. This little restaurant, located beside a fish market near Majorstuen, is unpretentious, with 10 light tables and simple settings. The menu, which changes daily, is written on a chalkboard, and the fish of the day can be viewed in the case at the back. If you are bothered by smoke, go early, as the single room tends to fill up with both people and smoke quickly. Fish is the specialty, but there's always one meat dish, usually game, on the menu. Try the grilled gravlaks or the fish pâté for starters. The fish symphony, a medley of several fish, is a good main course. *Kirkeveien 57, tel. 02/46-86-47. Reservations advised. Dress: casual. AE, DC, MC, V. No lunch.*

Hos Thea. This gem has only 36 seats. It's located at the beginning of Embassy Row, a short distance from downtown. The decor is beige and blue, with a homey old-fashioned look. The small menu offers four or five choices in each category, but every dish is superbly prepared, from the fillet of reindeer in a sauce of mixed berries to the orange-flavored crème caramel. Owner Sergio Barcilon, originally from Spain, is one of the pioneers of the new Scandinavian cooking. The noise and smoke levels can be high late in the evening. *Gabels gate 11, entrance on Drammensveien, tel. 02/44-68-74. Reservations required. Dress: casual but neat. AE, DC, MC, V. Closed 1 week at Christmas and Easter, 3 weeks in July. No lunch.*

Sabroso. This cozy restaurant serving modern Scandinavian food is in the cellar of the Ambassadeur Hotel. It has one of the best bars in town, comfortable and well stocked. Huge swaths of fabric, dark colors, and baroque-style paintings of food, create a plush, cocoon-like ambience. The food stands in contrast to the decor—it's light, in both concept and color. The seafood salad in a light vinaigrette with plump mussels and shrimp is a winner, while the scallops in lemon buerre blanc are delicate and subtle. *Hotel Ambassadeur, Camilla Collets vei 15, tel. 02/55-25-31. Reservations advised. Dress: casual but neat. AE, DC, MC, V. Closed Sat., Sun., and July. No lunch.*

Moderate
★

Dinner. Though its name is not the best for a restaurant specializing in Szechuan-style cuisine, it's the only place for Chinese food, both hot and not so pungent. The mango pudding for des-

Oslo Dining and Lodging

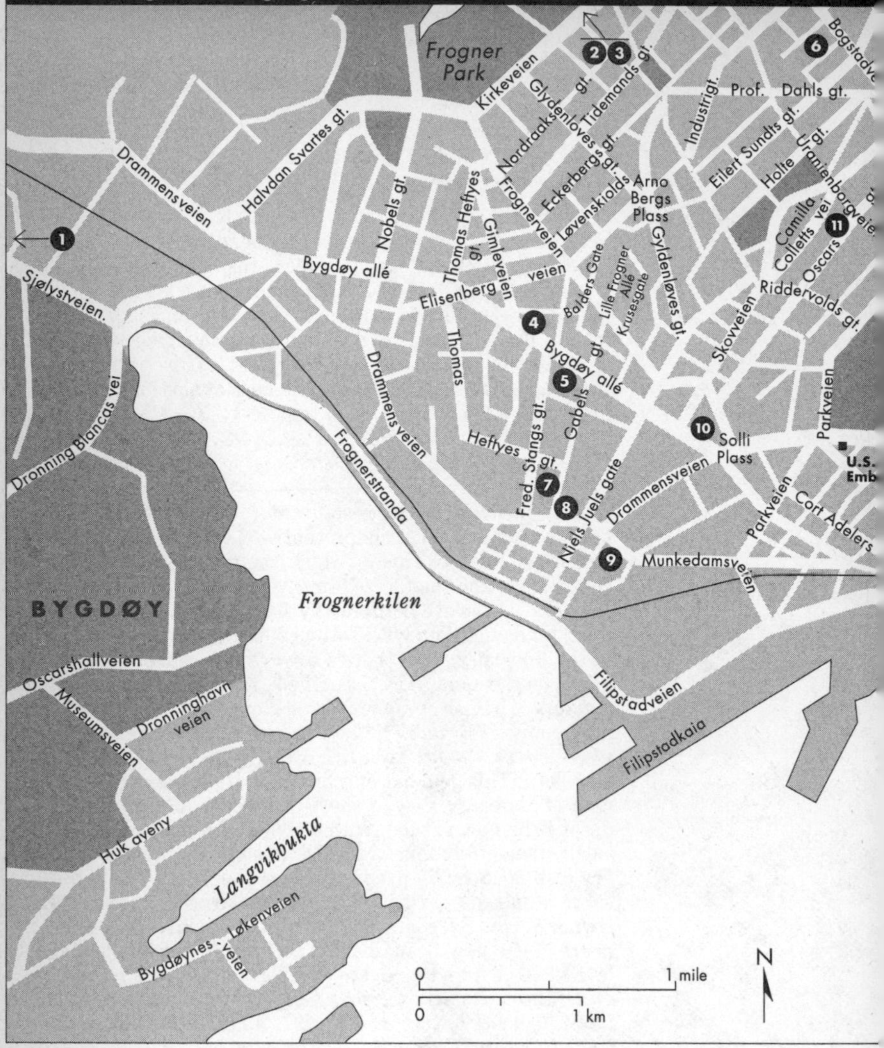

Dining
Bagatelle, **10**
D'Artagnan, **27**
De Fem Stuer, **2**
Den Grimme Ælling, **15**
Dinner, **19**
Dionysos Taverna, **30**
Feinschmecker, **4**
Fiskekroken, **3**
Fuji, **7**
Gamle Rådhus, **26**
Holberg's Årstidene, **13**
Hos Thea, **8**
Kaffistova, **22**
Kastanjen, **5**
LaMer, **9**
Sabroso, **11**
Shalimar, **33**
Stefan, **18**
Theatercafeen, **16**
Tysk City Grill, **29**
Vegeta Vertshus, **12**

Lodging
Ambassadeur, **11**
Bondeheimen, **23**
Bristol, **19**
Cecil, **20**
Gabelshus, **7**
Grand Hotel, **24**
Gyldenløve, **6**
Haraldsheim, **32**
Holmenkollen Park Hotel Rica, **2**
Hotel Continental, **16**
Munch, **17**
Oslo Plaza, **31**
Rica Victoria, **19**
Royal Christiania, **28**
SAS Park Royal, **1**
SAS Scandinavia, **13**
Stefan, **18**

Colletts gt.
Waldemar Thranes gt.
Akersbakken
Maridalsveien
Akerselva
Seilduksgt.
Helgesens gt.
Grüners gt.
Helgesens gt.
Sofienberggt.
Ullevålsveien
Parkveien
Pilestredet
gate
Møllerveien
Nordregt.
Wessels gt.
Nordahl Bruns gt.
Akersveien
Hausmanns gt.
Trondheimsveien
Jens Bjelkes gt.
Holbergs
St. Olavsgt.
Universitetsgt.
Frederiks Gate
Kristian IVs gt.
Henrik Ibsens gt.
Grubbe gt.
Møllergt.
Torggt.
Calmeyers Gate
Youngs-torget
Urtegt.
Lakkegata
Norbygt.
Tøyengt.
Drammensveien
Karl Johans Gate
Rosenkrantz' gt.
Akersgata gt.
Grensen
Storgt.
Munkedamsveien
R. Admundsens gt.
Stortingsgt.
Stortorvet
Stenersgt.
Brugt.
Grønlandsleiret
Nedre Vollgt.
Slottsgt.
Prinsens gt.
Central Station
Dokkveien
Rådhusgt.
Nedre Tollbugata
Kirkegata
Dronningens gt.
Skippergt.
Fred Olsens gt.
Strandgt.
Nylandsveien
Schweigaards gt.
Pipervika
Akershusstranda
Mynt gt.
Bispegt.
Kongens Gate
Bjørvika
Akerselva
Bispevika
SØRENGA
Skippergt.
Oslo gt.
Oslofjorden
Mossoveien
Ekebergsletta
12
13
14
15
16
17
18
19
20
21
22
23
24
25
26
27
28
29
30
31
32
33

sert is wonderful. Don't bother with the other Chinese restaurants. *Arbeidergata 2, tel. 02/42–68–90. Dress: casual. AE, DC, MC, V. No lunch.*

★ **Dionysos Taverna.** Nicola Murati gives his guests a warm welcome in this unpretentious little Greek restaurant. The hors d'oeuvre platter, which includes stuffed vine leaves, meatballs, feta cheese, tzatziki, tomatoes, and cucumbers, is a meal in itself. The souvlaki and moussaka are authentically prepared, as are the more unusual casserole dishes. A bouzouki duo provides live music on Friday and Saturday. *Calmeyersgate 11, tel. 02/60–78–64. Dress: casual. AE, MC, V. No lunch.*

Fuji. The sushi bar is upstairs, while downstairs is a more traditional Japanese restaurant with tatami rooms and regular tables. All the usual specialties, such as tempura, teriyaki, and sukiyaki are on the menu, along with unusual items, including glazed duck breasts and barbecued chicken livers. *Munkedamsveien 100, tel. 02/43–11–80. Dress: casual. AE, DC, MC, V. No lunch.*

Gamle Rådhus. Oslo's oldest restaurant, which celebrated its 350th birthday in 1991, is in the old City Hall. Don't let the beer signs and dirty windows put you off. The dining room is straight out of Ibsen, with dark brown wainscoting, deep yellow painted walls, old prints, and heavy red curtains. Famous for its lutefisk, a Scandinavian specialty made from dried fish that has been soaked in lye and then poached, the restaurant's menu allows ample choice for the less daring. The fried cod with bacon and root vegetables and the entrecôte (rib-eye steak) with rösti are both good and reasonably priced. *Nedre Slottsgate 1, tel. 02/42–01–07. Dinner reservations advised. Dress: casual but neat. AE, DC, MC, V.*

★ **Kastanjen.** This casual Frogner bistro is the kind every neighborhood needs. The style of food is new traditional, with modern interpretations of classic Norwegian dishes. The smoked lamb shoulder with parsley root sauce, which has its origins in western Norway, has survived numerous menu changes, while the fillet of beef in a red bell pepper sauce served with crunchy potato slices is a perfect blend of taste and texture. *Bygdøy Alle 18, tel. 02/43–44–67. Reservations advised. Dress: casual. AE, DC, MC, V. Closed Sun., 1 week at Christmas and Easter, 3 weeks in July. No lunch.*

Shalimar. This Pakistani restaurant is off the beaten track, but worth the trip, for the food, prepared by chefs imported from Karachi, is delectable. Try the tandoori mixed grill, which includes chicken, lamb, and kebab, or the chicken biryani with aromatic rice. Vegetarians have ample choices, and the naan bread is addictive. *Konghellegate 5, tel. 02/37–47–68. Dress: casual. AE, DC, MC, V. No lunch.*

★ **Stefan.** On the top floor of this downtown hotel is the best lunch buffet in town. Fish dishes are in abundance: the usual marinated and smoked salmon, pickled salmon with sour cream, and pâté of golden caviar. Smoked leg of moose and other cured meats, including reindeer, are equally popular. In the evening the Stefan has "early bird specials" from 4 to 6:30, which feature traditional Norwegian dishes, such as sauteed trout with sour-cream sauce, at very reasonable prices. *Rosenkrantz Gate 1, tel. 02/42–92–50. Lunch reservations required. Dress: casual but neat. AE, DC, MC, V. No Sun. lunch.*

Theatercafeen. This Oslo institution, on the ground floor of the Hotel Continental, is jammed day and night. Built in 1900, the last Viennese-style café in northern Europe retains its Art

Nouveau character. The menu is small and jumbled, with starters and main dishes interspersed; the only hint of the serving size is the price column. From 1 to 7, there's a reasonably priced two-course "family dinner." Go after 1 and order a starter, such as the game pâté, plus dessert. Pastry Chef Robert Brunn's *konfektkake* (a rich chocolate cake) and apple tart served with homemade ice cream are reasons enough to visit. *Stortingsgata 24–26, tel. 02/33–32–00. Reservations advised. Dress: casual. AE, DC, MC, V.*

Inexpensive

Den Grimme Ælling. Dane Bjarne Hvid Pedersen has recently opened a "branch" of his popular restaurant in the food court at Paleet. His *smørbrød* are the best buy in town: lots of meat, fish, or whatever on a small piece of bread. He also has daily dinner specials, such as roast pork loin with apples and prunes, or *frikadeller* (Danish meat cakes), all homemade. *Waldemar Thranes Gate 10, tel. 02/46–65–34, and Paleet, Karl Johans Gate 41B, tel. 02/42–16–16. Dress: casual. No credit cards.*

★ **Kaffistova.** Norwegian country cooking is served, cafeteria-style, at this downtown restaurant. Everyday specials include a soup and a selection of entrees, including a vegetarian dish. *Kjøttkaker* (meat cakes rather like salisbury steak) served with creamed cabbage is a Norwegian staple, and the steamed salmon with Sandefjord butter is as good here as in places where it costs three times as much. Low alcohol beer is the strongest drink served. *Rosenkrantz' Gate 8, tel. 02/42–99–74. Dress: casual. No credit cards.*

★ **Tysk City Grill.** In the midst of the Oslo City shopping mall's food court is a tiny, authentic German restaurant, complete with oompah music. The grilled bratwurst (with real German mustard and curry ketchup) with homemade potato salad is the best cheap meal in town, while the eisbein and the pea soup, both homemade, are hearty fare. *Stenersgata 8, tel. 02/17–04–70. Dress: casual. No credit cards.*

La Mer. This is Oslo's place for bouillabaisse. Fish prepared in the French manner is on the menu at this upstairs restaurnat near the SAS Scandinavia hotel. From 4 to 6:30, there is an inexpensive two-course dinner special. *Pilestredet 31, tel. 02/20–34–45. Dress: casual. AE, DC, MC, V. Closed Sun. No lunch.*

Vegeta Vertshus. Vegetarians and omnivores alike flock to the buffet, where the size of the plate determines the price. Atmosphere is nonexistent, but the food, especially the spicy dishes, is tasty and a great value. *Munkedamsveien 3B, tel. 02/83–42–32. Dress: casual. No credit cards.*

Lodging

Oslo gained over 1,000 hotel beds in 1989 and 1990 and more are being built. Most hotels are centrally located, a short walk from the top of Karl Johans Gate, the main street. The newest hotels are in the area around Oslo S station, at the bottom end of Karl Johan. For a quiet stay, choose a hotel in Frogner, the elegant residential neighborhood just minutes from downtown.

Lodging in the capital is expensive. Prices at downtown hotels are high, even for bed-and-breakfasts, although just about all have weekend, holiday, and summer rates. Taxes and service charges are included, and unless otherwise noted, a buffet breakfast as well.

Most hotels fall into different price categories during the summer. The very expensive ones tend to reduce their prices more than those on the lower end of the scale, so substantial bargains are available from the end of June to mid-August. Reductions range from 25% to 50%. As an example, summer rates for a double room at the Oslo Plaza are only NKr 35 more than those at the Cecil, surely one of the best buys in the city.

Oslo usually has enough hotel rooms to go around, but it's always a good idea to reserve a room at least for the first night of your stay, especially if you arrive late.

The hotel accommodations office at Oslo S station is open from 8 AM to 11 PM and can book you in anything from a luxury hotel to a room in a private home for a fee of NKr10 adults, NKr5 children.

If you are interested in renting rooms in private homes, contact **Bed & Breakfast** (Kirkevn. 68, Box 128, 1344 Haslum, tel. 02/53–51–07 or 02/59–05–35, fax 02/53–29–79; open weekdays 8:30–4). Most are located in the neighboring community of Bærum, 15 to 20 minutes from downtown Oslo. All addresses provided by the group are no more than a five-minute walk from public transport.

Highly recommended lodgings are indicated by a star ★.

Very Expensive

★ **Grand Hotel.** Located right in the center of Karl Johan, the Grand has been the premier hotel since it opened in 1874. Ibsen and Munch were regular guests, and since their time, the Grand has hosted many famous people and all recipients of the Nobel peace prize. The lobby gives no idea of the style and flair of the newly redecorated (1989–90) rooms. Even standard rooms are large, looking more like guest quarters in an elegant home than hotel rooms. Those in the new wing are smaller, cheaper, and not as nice. *Karl Johans Gate 31, 0159, tel. 02/42–93–90, fax 02/42–12–25. 290 rooms with bath, 50 suites. Facilities: 3 restaurants, nightclub, health club, pool, conference center, newsstand. AE, DC, MC, V.*

Hotel Continental. If it weren't for the Grand (*see below*), the Continental would be Oslo's top hotel. It came later and it tries harder, but it doesn't quite make it. It had a major facelift in 1989–90, but the rooms are still somewhat cold and austere. The Brockmann family, who have owned the hotel since it was built in 1900, strive for old-world comfort and elegance, but it can border on stuffiness and pretension, as in its paralyzingly formal restaurant, Annen Etage. Munch graphics from the family's own collection adorn the walls. *Stortingsgata 24–26, 0159, tel. 02/41–90–60, fax 02/42–96–89. 169 rooms with bath, 12 suites. Facilities: 3 restaurants, 2 bars, nightclub. AE, DC, MC, V.*

Oslo Plaza. Northern Europe's largest hotel, built in 1990, is a 10-minute walk from the heart of town. Every sitting area in this 37-floor giant is in a different style, from postmodernist to English library. Regular rooms are so small that diagonally placed beds have rounded corners to make enough room to walk past. The larger rooms on the top three floors cost more. The restaurants haven't quite gotten off the ground, but pastry chef Pascal Dupuy's cakes are world-class. *Sonja Henies Plass 3, 0107, tel. 02/17–10–00, fax 02/17–73–00. 685 rooms with bath, 20 suites. Facilities: 3 restaurants, 2 bars, nightclub,* *health club, pool, business/conference center, shops. AE, DC, MC, V.*

Royal Christiania. It started out as bare-bones housing for 1952 Olympians. Various additions made remodeling an architect's nightmare, but the job, finished in 1990, was well done. The original exterior has been retained, but inside, it's a whole new hotel, built around a central atrium. The rooms, decorated in soft colors with light furniture, are large. The California-style restaurant serves tasty, colorful food. *Biskop Gunnerus' Gate 3, 0106, tel. 02/42–94–10, fax 02/42–46–22. 456 rooms with bath, 100 suites. Facilities: 3 restaurants, 3 bars, nightclub, health club, pool, business/conference center, newsstand. AE, DC, MC, V.*

SAS Scandinavia Hotel. Oslo's only downtown business hotel, built in 1974, is getting some competition, but it still can hold its own: There's a business-class check-in in the lobby, and it has its own airport bus. The lower-level shopping arcade features high-fashion clothing and leather goods shops. All rooms were modernized in 1991 in four different styles, from high tech to Oriental. "Club rooms" cost more and have some special amenities, but standard rooms are spacious and light. The SAS is across the street from the palace grounds (but don't walk through them at night). *Holbergs Gate 30, 0166, tel. 02/11–30–00, fax 02/11–30–17. 500 rooms with bath, 15 suites. Facilities: 3 restaurants, 2 bars, nightclub, health club, pool, business center, shopping arcade. AE, DC, MC, V.*

Expensive

★ **Ambassadeur.** The most comfortable and elegant hotel in town hides behind a pale pink facade with wrought-iron balconies in a stylish residential area behind the Royal Palace, a few minutes from downtown. Originally built in 1889 as an apartment hotel, the Ambassadeur has practically no lobby, but the rooms make up for that. Apart from several singles, each room is individually furnished with thematic decors and good Norwegian art. The small, professional staff don't bother with titles, because everyone does whatever task presents itself, from laundering a shirt on short notice to delivering room service. *Camilla Colletts Vei 15, 0258, tel. 02/44–18–35, fax 02/44–47–91. 42 rooms with bath, 8 suites. Facilities: restaurant, bar, health club, pool, conference room. AE, DC, MC, V.*

Bristol. In the past few years, the Bristol has begun catering to people who want a classy but quiet hotel in the center of town. The lobby, decorated in the 1920s with a Moorish theme, is a tribute to style, and the library bar is Oslo's most comfortable. Some of the newly refurbished rooms are decorated with lightly colored painted Scandinavian furniture, while others have a Regency theme. The banquet rooms have true old-world elegance, and at the restaurant, the Bristol Grill, red meat has not gone out of style. *Kristian IV's Gate 7, 0130, tel. 02/41–58–40, fax 02/42–86–51. 141 rooms with bath, 4 suites. Facilities: 2 restaurants, 2 bars, nightclub, conference center, newsstand. AE, DC, MC, V.*

Holmenkollen Park Hotel Rica. The magnificent 1894 building in the national romantic style commands an unequaled panorama of the city and is worth a visit, even if you don't lodge there. The rather ordinary guest rooms are in a newer structure (1982) behind it. The ice-covered snowflake sculpture in the lobby is appropriate for a hotel that's a stone's throw from Holmenkollen ski jump. Ski and walking trails are just outside. *Kongeveien 26, 0390, tel. 02/14–60–90, fax 02/14–61–92. 191* *rooms with bath. Facilities: 2 restaurants, bar, nightclub, health club, pool, business/conference center. AE, DC, MC, V.*

Rica Victoria. Oslo's newest full-service hotel opened in May 1991, in a postmodern structure built around a center atrium. The rooms are furnished with Biedermeier reproductions and textiles in bold reds and dark blues, elegant and very stylish. Rooms with windows on the atrium may be claustrophobic for some. *Rosenkrantz' Gate 13, 0160, tel. 02/42–99–40, fax 02/42–99–43. 161 rooms with bath or shower, 5 suites. Facilities: restaurant, bar. AE, DC, MC, V.*

SAS Park Royal. Fornebu Airport's only hotel is somewhat anonymous, with long, narrow corridors and standard American-style motel rooms. The restaurant serves modern Scandinavian food. There are excellent business facilities, including a business-class check-in in the lobby, and the airport bus stops outside. *Fornebuparken, 1324 Lysaker, tel. 02/12–02–20, fax 02/12–00–11. 240 rooms with bath, 14 suites. Facilities: restaurant, bar, health club, tennis court, newsstand. AE, DC, MC, V.*

Stefan. Oslo's only first-class temperance hotel makes every aspect of a stay a positive experience, from hot welcome drinks for late arrivals to breakfast tables complete with juice boxes and plastic bags for packing a lunch. The top-floor lounge has books and magazines in English. The Stefan's kitchen still creates the best lunch buffet in town (*see* Dining, *above*). *Rosenkrantz' Gate 1, 0159, tel. 02/42–92–50, fax 02/33–70–22. 131 rooms with bath or shower. Facilities: restaurant, conference center. AE, DC, MC, V.*

Moderate

Bondeheimen. Founded in 1913 for country folk visiting the city, Bondeheimen, which means "farmers' home," still gives discounts to members of agricultural associations. The lobby and rooms are newly redecorated with pine furniture, handwoven rag rugs, soft blue textiles, and modern Norwegian graphics, just the way a Norwegian country home should look. Bondeheimen serves no alcohol, and the staff of country girls has a squeaky-clean look. *Rosenkrantz' Gate 8, 0159, tel. 02/42–95–30, fax 02/41–94–37. 76 rooms with shower. Facilities: restaurant, conference room. AE, DC, MC, V.*

★ **Cecil.** This bed-and-breakfast hotel one block from Parliament was built in 1989. The second floor opens onto an atrium: the hotel's activity center. In the morning, it's a breakfast room, with one of Oslo's best buffets, while in the afternoon, it becomes a lounge, serving coffee, juice, and fresh fruit, plus newspapers in many languages. The single rooms have double beds, while doubles have queen-size beds. *Stortingsgata 8, 0130, tel. 02/42–70–00, fax 02/42–26–70. 110 rooms with bath, 2 suites. AE, DC, MC, V.*

Gabelshus. With only a discreet sign above the door this ivy-covered brick house in an international residential area is one of Oslo's most personal hotels. It has been owned by the same family for 45 years. The lounges are filled with antiques, some in the national romantic style, but the rooms, renovated in 1989, are plain. It's a short walk to several of Oslo's best restaurants, and a seven-minute streetcar ride to the center of town. The Ritz Hotel, across the parking lot, is owned by the same family and takes the overflow at lower prices. *Gabels Gate 16, 0272, tel. 02/55–22–60, fax 02/44–27–30. 45 rooms with bath (plus 54 rooms with bath in Ritz). Facilities: restaurant. AE, DC, MC, V.*

Inexpensive

Gyldenløve. Located in the heart of a busy shopping area, this hotel, modernized in 1987, is one of the city's most reasonable bed-and-breakfast establishments. It is within walking distance of Vigeland sculpture park, and the streetcar stops just outside the door. Reproductions of Edvard Munch's paintings hang in every room and hall. *Bogstadveien 20, 0355, tel. 02/60-10-90, fax 02/60-33-90. 150 rooms with shower. AE, DC, MC, V.*

Munch. This modern bed-and-breakfast hotel, about a 10-minute walk from Karl Johans Gate, is unpretentious, well run, clean, and functional. The rooms, decorated in beiges and browns, are of a decent size. The lobby, with its Chinese rugs and oversized leather couches, contrasts markedly with the rest of the hotel. *Munchsgate 5, 0165, tel. 02/42-42-75, fax 02/20-64-69. 180 rooms with shower. Facilities: parking. AE, DC, MC, V.*

Haraldsheim. Oslo's newly refurbished youth hostel is one of Europe's largest. Most of the rooms have four beds, and all those in the new wing have showers. Nonmembers of the International Youth Hostel organization pay a surcharge. Bring your own sheet sleeping bag or rent one there. It is 4 kilometers (2½ miles) from city center. *Haraldsheimveien 4, tel. 02/15-50-43. No breakfast. No credit cards.*

The Arts and Nightlife

The Arts

The monthly *Oslo Guide* lists cultural events, as does section four of *Aftenposten*, Oslo's (and Norway's) leading newspaper. The information number at **Oslo Spektrum** congress and concert complex gives a rundown of all scheduled events (tel. 02/17-80-10). Tickets to virtually all performances in Norway, from a rock concert to a hockey game, can be purchased at any post office. Oslo's main theater and concert season runs from September through May, and tickets can be purchased directly from the theaters and concert halls or from the post office.

Nationaltheatret (*Stortingsgt. 15, tel. 02/41-27-10.*) performances are in Norwegian, but if you have always dreamed of experiencing Ibsen in the original, here's your chance. Bring along a copy of the play in translation, and you're all set.

Det Norske Teatret (Kristian IV's gate 8, tel. 02/42-43-44) is the national showcase for pieces in Nynorsk, the "other" Norwegian language. Many musicals are produced at this modern theater complex, along with performances by guest artists from abroad.

Bryggeteatret (*Aker Brygge, tel. 02/83-88-20*), Oslo's newest theater, features musicals and dance events.

The Norwegian Philharmonic Orchestra, under the direction of Mariss Janssons, is among Europe's leading ensembles. Its house, **Konserthuset** (*Munkedamsvn. 14, tel. 02/83-32-00*), was built in 1977 in marble, metal, and rosewood. Every Monday and Thursday in July and August, the folk dance group of Bondeungdomslaget (the Young Farmers' Association) performs folk dancing here.

Den Norske Opera (*Storgt. 23, tel. 02/42-94-75*) and the ballet perform at Youngstorvet.

Oslo Spektrum, (*Sonja Henies pl. 2, tel. 02/17-80-10*), a rounded brick building sprinkled with vignettes of glazed tile, is the most interesting piece of architecture in the area around Oslo S station. Sandwiched between Oslo City shopping mall and Oslo Plaza hotel, and minutes away from the Royal Christiania, the Spektrum is used as a congress/conference complex, a sports stadium, and a concert hall.

All **films** are shown in the original language with subtitles, except for some children's films, which are dubbed. If you plan to take children to see a film, check the age limits first. The Norwegian film censors set high and strictly enforced age limits on films they consider violent.

Nightlife

Oslo has recently become the nightlife capital of Scandinavia. At any time of the day or night, people are out on Karl Johan, and many clubs and restaurants in the central area stay open until 4 or 5 AM.

Bars and Lounges

Churchill Wine Bar (Fr. Nansens pl. 6, tel. 02/33–53–43) and **Fridtjof's** (Fr. Nansens pl. 7, tel. 02/33–40–88) are yuppie favorites for after-work imbibing. Both are near City Hall. For the serious connoisseur of beer, **Oslo Mikrobryggeri** (Bogstadvn. 6, tel. 02/56–97–76) is the place, with beer brewed on the premises; for variety, go to **Lorry** (Parkvn. 12, tel. 02/69–69–04); where they advertise 81 different brews. **Eilefs Landhandleri** (Kristian IV's gate, tel. 02/42–53–47) is a pub cum disco, with a piano player and a dance floor. For a more refined venue, go to **3 Brødre** (Three Brothers, Øvre Slottsgt. 14, tel. 02/42–39–00), with a beer and wine bar at street level and 1890-style wall paintings of forest maidens and cherubs on the ceiling. A more modern place for a pre-dinner drink is the **Summit,** at the SAS Scandinavia Hotel (Holbergsgt. 30, tel. 02/11–30–00). For more lounging than drinking, try the English-style bar at the **Bristol Hotel** (Kristian IV's Gate 7, tel. 02/41–58–40).

Cafés

For cappuccino and a quiet conversation, many cafés are open practically around the clock, and they're the cheapest places to eat. In the tony area around Frogner **Hilarios** (Niels Juels Gate 38, tel. 02/55–86–26) and **Clodion Art Café** (Bygdøy Allé 63, tel. 02/44–97–26), where the conversation is good and the art bad. Downtown, **Kafe Celsius** (Rådhusgt. 19, 02/42–45–39) in a half-timbered building from 1626, attracts an arty crowd, while **Sjakk Matt** (Haakon VII's Gate, tel. 02/83–41–56) appeals to postmodernists. If you prefer the '50s, go to **Teddy's Bar** (Brugt. 3, tel. 02/17–71–83), complete with vinyl stools and Formica countertops.

Discos and Nightclubs

Most discos open late, and the action doesn't really start until near midnight. There's usually an age limit, and the cover charge is around NKr50. Thursday is student disco night at **Comeback** (Rosenkrants' Gate 11, tel. 02/33–46–40) and **Rockefeller** (Torggt. 16, tel. 02/20–32–32). Oslo's beautiful people congregate at **Barock** (Universitetsgt. 26, tel. 02/42–44–20), part of a multilevel entertainment complex, **Humla,** which also houses a restaurant, nightclub, and theater. Most of the big hotels have discos that appeal to the over-30 crowd. **Sky Bar,** on the top floor of the Oslo Plaza (Sonja Henies Pl. 3, tel. 02/17–10–00), is the most fabulous or bizarre, accessible only from the glass elevator outside. **Grotten** (Wergelandsvn. 5, tel. 02/20–96–04) is a stylish restaurant with music and dancing, popular with well-heeled and well-dressed singles over 30.

Jazz Clubs Norwegians love jazz, and every summer the Oslo Jazz Festival, with a list of major international artists, attracts big crowds (check with the tourist office for dates and times). **Oslo Jazzhus** (Toftesgt. 69, tel. 02/38–59–63) is in an out-of-the-way location, but the music is worth it. **Stortorvets Gjæstgiveri** (Grensen 1, tel. 02/42–88–63) often presents New Orleans and ragtime bands. **Jegerhallen** (Akersgt. 38, tel. 02/42–97–44; closed June 20–Aug. 10) features the New Orleans Jazz Workshop. **Smuget** (Kirkegt. 34, 02/42–52–02) has live jazz, blues, and rock every evening.

Rock Clubs At Oslo's numerous rock clubs, the cover charges are low, the crowds young, and the music loud. **Rockefeller** (Torggt. 16, tel. 02/20–32–32), in old Torggata Bad (bathhouse), presents a good mix of musical styles, from avant-garde to Third World; Thursday is student disco night. Its only real competitor is **The Voice** (Chateau Neuf, Slemdalsvn. 7, tel. 02/69–80–50). There's always music at **Cruise Cafe** (Aker Brygge, tel. 02/83–64–30), but most of the acts are unknowns. If your taste leans toward reggae and calypso, the **Afro International Night Club** (Brennerivn. 5, tel. 02/36–08–04) has frequent Caribbean evenings.

Gay Bars For information about gay activities in Oslo, call **Homo-treffen** (tel. 02/07–80–08) or the information telephone (02/11–36–60), or read *Blikk*, the gay newsletter. **DNF-48** (The Norwegian Alliance of 1948), the nationwide gay association, has offices at St. Olavs Pl. 2, and operates **Apotheket Club St. Olavs Bar** at the same address. **Andy Capp Pub** (Fridtjof Nansens Pl. 4, tel. 02/41–05–65) is popular with gays, but it reeks of old smoke. **Joy's** (Kongensgt. 6, tel. 02/42–66–22), Oslo's oldest gay club, is a meeting place for lesbians and transvestites. **London Bar og Pub** (C.J. Hambros Pl. 5, tel. 02/41–41–26) won't win any awards for interior decorating, but it's still packed on weekends. **Why Not** (Teatergate 3, tel. 02/36–36–36) is the newest restaurant and discotheque in gay Oslo. A ticket to Why Not is also good for entry at **Den Sorte Enke** (The Black Widow, Møllergt. 23, tel. 02/11–05–60). **Kvinnehuset** (Women's House, Pilestredet 30B, tel. 02/36–09–83) is for women only.

Excursions from Oslo

Halden and Fredrikstad

Tourist Information **Fredrikstad:** Fredrikstad turistkontor (Turistsentret v/Østre Brohode, N–1630 Gamle Fredrikstad, tel. 09/32–03–30). **Halden:** Halden Reiselivskontor (Box 167, N–1751 Halden, tel. 09/18–24–87). **Moss:** Moss Turistinformasjon (Chrystiesgt. 3, N–1500 Moss, tel. 09/25–54–51).

Getting There

By Car Follow the E18 southeastward from Oslo and turn south at Mysen to reach Halden. Rte. E6 takes you north to Sarpsborg, where you can turn left to Fredrikstad.

By Train Trains for Halden leave from Oslo S station and take two hours to make the 136-kilometer (85-mile) trip. There are regular train connections between Halden and Fredrikstad.

Exploring Halden and Fredrikstad *Numbers in the margin correspond with points of interest on the Oslo Excursions map.*

A day's trip to this section of eastern Norway, between Oslo and the Swedish border, covers important historic ground.

4 **Halden** is practically at the Swedish border, a good enough reason to fortify the town; **Fredriksten festning** (fort), built on a French star-shape model in the late 17th century, is perched on the city's highest point. Norwegians and Swedes had ongoing border disputes, and the most famous skirmish at Fredriksten resulted in the death of King Karl XII in 1718. The entire area is well documented and marked, and maps of the precinct are available at the entrance. Few realize that slavery existed in Scandinavia, and until 1845, there were up to 200 slaves at Fredriksten, mostly workers incarcerated and sentenced to a lifetime of hard labor for the most trivial offenses.

Inside the fort itself is **Fredriksten Kro,** a good place to stop for lunch. Sit outside if the weather permits. *Tel. 09/18–24–87. Admission: NKr15 adults, NKr5 children. Guided tours June 18–Aug. 12, noon, 1:30, 6, 8:30.*

Just outside of Halden is **Rød Herregård,** a stately home built at the end of the 17th century. It was owned by one of the most powerful families in the country, who planted an impressive Baroque garden, complete with soil transported from England. *Tel. 09/18–54–11. Admission: NKr10 adults, NKr3 children. Open May–Sept., daily.*

5 North of Halden is **Fredrikstad,** at the mouth of the Glomma, Norway's longest river. The country's oldest fortified city, it has bastions and moat that date from the 1600s. The old town has been preserved, separate from the modern, industrialized part of town. Within the area are museums, art galleries, cafés, artisans' workshops, antiques shops, and old bookstores.

Just east is **Kongsten festning,** which mounted 200 cannons and could muster up to 2,000 men at the peak of its glory. The fort contains a museum that documents the history of the city. *Kongsten Fort, tel. 09/34–20–62. Admission free. Open 24 hours. Guided tours. Fredrikstad Museum, tel. 09/34–20–61. Admission: NKr10 adults, NKr5 children. Open June–Aug., Mon.–Sat. 10–4, Sun. noon–5; Sept.–May, weekends noon–5.*

A 5-kilometer (3-mile) ride outside **Moss,** at **Jeløy,** is **Galleri F15,** an art center set in an old farm. *Tel. 09/27–10–33. Admission free. Open daily 11–7.*

Dining and Lodging

★ **Refsnes Gods.** The main building dates from 1770, when it was a family estate, but it did not become a hotel until 1938. Behind the main building is a long, tree-lined promenade extending to the shores of the Oslo fjord. Refsnes has one of Norway's best kitchens and a wine cellar with some of the oldest bottles of Madeira in the country. Chef Frank Baer, a member of Norway's Culinary Olympic team, makes a meal here a memorable experience. *Jeløy, 1500 Moss, tel. 09/27–04–11, fax 09/27–25–42. 62 rooms. Facilities: restaurant, sauna, pool, beach, boats, function rooms. AE, DC, MC, V. Expensive.*

Drammen, Tønsberg, and Sandefjord

The towns lining the western side of Oslofjord are among Norway's oldest and wealthiest, their fortunes derived from whaling and lumbering. Although these areas no longer dominate, their influence remains in the monuments and in the wood architecture. This is summer vacation country for many Norwegians, who retreat to cabins on the water for all of July.

Tourist Information **Drammen:** Drammen Kommunale Turistinformasjonskontor (Radhuset, N–3017 Drammen, tel. 03/80–62–10). **Sandefjord:** Sandefjord Reiselivsforening (Torvet, N–3200, tel. 034/68–100). **Tønsberg:** tonsberg og Omland Reiselivslag (Storgt. 55, N–3100, tel. 033/14–819).

Getting There

By Car Route E18 south from Oslo follows the coast to within reach of the towns of this region. Sandefjord is 125 kilometers (78 miles) south of Oslo.

By Train Drammen is about 40 kilometers (25 miles) from Oslo. Take a suburban train from National Theater or trains from Oslo S to reach Horten, Tønsberg, and Sandefjord.

By Bus Because trains run infrequently to these towns, bus travel is the best alternative to cars. Check with Nor-Way Bussterminal (tel. 02/33–01–91) for schedules.

By Boat The most luxurious and scenic way to see the region is by boat: there are guest marinas at just about every port.

Exploring Drammen, Tønsberg, and Sandefjord

6 **Drammen,** an industrial city of 50,000 situated on the Simoa river at its outlet to a fjord, was a timber town and port for 500 years, the main harbor for silver exported from the Kongsberg mines. Today, cars are imported into Norway through Drammen. The city's main attraction, **Spiralen** (The Spiral), is a corkscrew road tunnel, which makes six complete turns before emerging about 600 feet above, on Skansen Plateau. It's open year-round and is free. The entrance is behind the hospital by way of a well-marked road.

Drammens Museum, formerly Marienlyst manor, is across the river. It recently won a prize for the use of concrete in its new addition, which looks like a small post-modernist temple set in the manor garden. Displays include glass from the Nøstetangen factory and a collection of rustic painted pieces. *Konnerudgt. 7, tel. 03/83–89–48. Admission: NKr20 adults, NKr10 senior citizens, NKr5 children. Open May–Oct., Tues. 11–7, Wed.–Sat. 11–3, Sun. 11–5; Nov.–Apr., Tues.–Sun. 11–3.*

7 Off the main route south, toward the coast, is **Horten,** which has some distinctive museums. The town used to be Norway's most important naval station, but after it was bombed heavily during World War II, a new base was built in Bergen. The city still retains the officers' candidates school and is the site of **Marinemuseet** (the Royal Norwegian Navy Museum), built in 1853. This old munitions warehouse has displays of relics from the nation's naval history. Outside is the world's first torpedo boat, from 1872, plus some one-man submarines from World War II. Look up at the trees—mistletoe thrives here, but don't pick it: It's protected by law. *Karl Johans Vern, tel. 033/42–081, ext. 452. Admission free. Open June–Sept., weekdays 10–3, weekends noon–4; Oct.–May, weekdays 10–3, Sun. noon–4.*

Redningsselskapets Museum (Museum of the Sea Rescue Association) traces the history of ship-rescue operations. The organization has rescued more than 320,000 people since it was founded, more than 100 years ago. *Strandpromenaden 8, tel. 033/47–066. Admission: NKr10 adults, NKr5 children. Open Apr. 1–Sept. 30, Fri.–Sun. noon–4.*

Preus Fotomuseum houses one of the world's largest photographic collections. Exhibits include a turn-of-the-century photographer's studio and a tiny camera that was strapped to a pigeon for early aerial photography. The excellent library is open by appointment only. *Langgt. 82, tel. 033/42-737. Admission: NKr10 adults, NKr5 children. Open weekdays 10–2, Sun. noon–2.*

Horten Bilmuseum (car museum), in an old brewery, houses a collection of 40 cars, 12 motorcycles, and several war vehicles, arranged both chronologically and thematically. Outside the museum is a working hand-operated gas pump from 1926. *Sollistrandsvn. 12B, tel. 033/42-601. Admission: NKr30 adults, NKr20 children. Open June 15–Aug. 15, daily noon–3; Aug. 16–June 14, Sun. noon–3.*

If you're not yet tired of museums, visit **Kihlegalleriet** (Kihle Gallery), which is dedicated to the works of local artist Harald Kihle, who specialized in horses. *Apenesgården, Falkenstensveien, tel. 033/44-013. Admission free. Open daily, noon–3, Tues., Thurs. also 6–8.*

Just beyond the town, between the road and the sea, is a Viking grave site, **Borrehaugene,** with five earth and two stone mounds. Continue past the 12th-century Borre church to
8 **Åsgårdstrand,** which was an artists' colony for outdoor painting at the turn of the century. Edvard Munch painted *Girls on the Bridge* here, and the house where he spent seven summers, **Munchs lille hus** (little house), is now a museum. *Munchs gate, no tel. Admission: NKr5. Open June–Aug., Tues.–Sun. 1–7; May and Sept., weekends 1–7.*

Continuing south, you pass the site where the Oseberg viking ship, dating from around AD 800 and on display in Oslo, was found at **Slagen,** on the road to Tønsberg, 105 kilometers (64 miles) from Oslo. Look for a mound where it was buried as you pass Slagen's church.

9 According to the sagas, **Tønsberg** is Norway's oldest settlement, founded in 871. Little is left of its early structures, although the ruins at **Slottsfjellet** (Castle Hill), by the train station, include parts of the city wall and citadel and the remains of a church from around 1150, and a 13th-century brick citadel. Other medieval remains are below the cathedral and near Storgata 17. Tønsberg lay dormant from the Reformation to the end of the 18th century, when shipping and later whaling brought it into prominence again. It is the birthplace of Svend Foyn, inventor of the explosive-powered harpoon, which revolutionized whaling. Another native son is the polar explorer Roald Amundsen.

Vestfold Fylkesmuseum (county museum), north of the railroad station, houses a small Viking ship, some whale skeletons, and Svend Foyn's inventions. There's an open-air section, too. *Farmannsvn. 30, tel. 033/12-919. Admission: NKr15 adults, NKr8 senior citizens. Open mid-May–mid-Sept., weekdays 10–5, Sun. noon–5.*

Time Out Take a break at **Seterkafe,** the museum's restaurant. Try *spekemat* (dried cured meats) served with sour cream and/or potato salad or *rømmegrøt* (sour-cream porridge) topped with cinnamon sugar.

Norwegian nobility literally died out in Tønsberg. Although the aristocracy was abolished in 1821 as a vestige of Danish domination, nobles could retain their titles until they died. Count Peder Anker Wedel Jarlsberg (no relation to the cheese) died in 1893, and his estate, Norway's largest, is still inhabited by his descendants. The manor house is not open to the public.

Continue 25 kilometers (16 miles) south of Tønsberg to
10 **Sandefjord,** which, in 1900, was the whaling capital of world, and possibly Norway's wealthiest city. Now the whales are gone, and all that remains of that booming trade is a monument to it. The city is still rich, thanks to shipping and other industry.

Kommandør Christensens Hvalfangstmuseum (The Whaling Museum) traces the development of the industry from small primitive boats to huge floating factories. An especially interesting display chronicles whaling in the Antarctic from the 1920s until the last expedition in 1968. *Museumsgt. 39, tel. 034/63–251. Admission: NKr10 adults, NKr5 children, senior citizens. Open May–Sept., Mon.–Sat. 11–4, Sun. 11–5, Thurs. also 4–7; Oct.–Apr., Sun. noon–4, Thurs. 4–7.*

Dining

★ **Edgar Ludl's Gourmet.** It took an Austrian chef to show the Norwegians that there's more in the sea than cod and salmon. Ludl is a champion of the local cuisine, and a recent "catch of the day" platter included salmon, ocean catfish, stuffed sole, a fish roulade, and lobster with two sauces. Ludl's desserts are equally good, especially the cloudberry marzipan basket or the honey parfait with nuts and wild berries. *Rådhusgt. 7, Sandefjord, tel. 034/62–741. Dress: casual but neat. AE, DC, MC, V. Expensive.*

Lodging

Rica Park Hotel. It *looks* formal for a hotel built right on the water in a resort town, but there's no dress code. The older rooms are nicer than the new. The decor is 1960s style, but it doesn't look passé. Summer rates (the hotel is also a member of Fjord Pass) make the Park more affordable. *Strandpromenaden 9, 3200 Sandefjord, tel. 034/65–550, fax 034/65–550. 160 rooms with bath, 6 suites. Facilities: 2 restaurants, 4 bars, 2 nightclubs, pool, health club, marina, business/conference center. AE, DC, MC, V. Moderate–Very Expensive.*

Atlantic. The Atlantic was built in 1914, when Sandefjord was a whaling center, and remodeled in 1990. The history of whaling is traced in exhibits in glass cases and in pictures throughout the hotel. There's no restaurant, but the hotel provides *aftens*, a supper consisting of bread and cold cuts plus a hot dish, as part of the room rate. *Jernbanealleen 33, 3200 Sandefjord, tel. 034/68–000, fax 034/68–020. 77 rooms with bath. Facilities: restaurant. AE, DC, MC, V. Inexpensive–Expensive.*

Sørlandet

Introduction

The coast bordering the Skagerrak is lined with small communities as far as Lindesnes, which is at the southernmost tip. Sørlandet (Southland) towns are often called "pearls on a string," and in the dusk of a summer evening, reflections of the white painted houses on the water have a silvery translucence.

The two chief cities of Norway's south, Kristiansand and Stavanger, differ sharply. Kristiansand is a resort town, scenic and relaxed, while Stavanger, once a fishing center, is now the hub of the oil industry, and Norway's most cosmopolitan city. Between the two is the coastal plain of Jæren, dotted with prehistoric burial sites and the setting for the works of some of the country's foremost painters.

Important Addresses and Numbers

Tourist Information The tourist information office in **Kristiansand** is at Dronningensgt. 2, Box 592, 4601, tel. 04/22–60–65, fax 04/22–52–55) and **Stavanger's** is at 158 Jernbanevn. 3, tel. 04/53–51–00, and at the marina, tel. 04/56–57–99).

Other tourist offices in the region are in **Horten** (Torget 6A, 3190, tel. 033/43–390), **Kvinesdal** (Vestre Vest-Agder Reiselivslag, N–4480, tel. 043/50–042), **Larvik** (Storgt. 20, 3250, tel. 034/82–623), **Mandal** (Mundalsregionens Reiselivslaj, Bryggegaten, N–4500, tel. 043/60–820), **Sandefjord** (Hjertnespromenaden, 3200, tel. 034/68–100), and **Tønsberg** (Storgt. 55, 3100, tel. 033/10–220).

Emergencies **Police,** tel. 002. **Fire,** in Kristiansand, tel. 042/21–010; in Stavanger, tel. 001. **Ambulance,** in Kristiansand, tel. 042/26–000; in Stavanger, tel. 003. **Car Rescue,** in Kristiansand, tel. 042/26–000 in Stavanger, tel. 04/58–29–00.

Hospital Emergency Rooms In Kristiansand, **Røde Kors** (Red Cross) **Legevakt** (Kirkegt. 3, tel. 04/22–52–20) is open weekdays 4 PM–8 AM *and* weekends 24 hours. In Stavanger, call **Rogaland Sentralsykehus** (tel. 04/51–80–00).

Doctors In Kristiansand, **Børsparken Legesenter** (Vestre Strandgt. 22, tel. 042/26–611) is open 8–4.

Dentists In Kristiansand, **Sentraltannklinikken** (Festningsgt. 40, tel. 042/21–971) is open 7–3. In Stavanger, the tourist office has a list of dentists available for emergencies.

Pharmacies **Elefantapoteket** (Rådhusgt. 12, Kristiansand, tel. 042/22–012) is open Monday through Saturday 8:20–8 and Sunday 4–8. **Løveapoteket** (Musegt. 3, Stavanger, tel. 04/52–06–07) is open daily 8 AM–11 PM.

Arriving and Departing by Plane

Kristiansand **Kjevik** Airport, 15 kilometers (10 miles) outside town, is served by **Braathens SAFE** (tel. 042/21–410), with nonstop flights from Oslo, Bergen, and Stavanger, and **SAS** (tel. 042/63–033) with nonstop flights to Copenhagen. **MUK Air** serves Aalborg, Denmark, while **Agder Fly** serves Göteborg, Sweden, and Billund, Denmark. Tickets on the latter two can be booked with Braathen or SAS.

The airport bus (tel. 042/21–410) departs from the Braathens SAFE office, Vestre Strandgate, approximately one hour before every departure and proceeds, via downtown hotels, directly to Kjevik. Tickets cost NKr30 for adults, NKr15 for children.

Stavanger **Sola Airport** is 14 kilometers (9 miles) from downtown. **Braathens SAFE** (tel. 04/53–60–70) has nonstop flights from Oslo, Sandefjord, Kristiansand, Haugesund, Bergen, and

Trondheim. **SAS** (tel. 04/65–89–00) has nonstop flights from Bergen, Oslo, Copenhagen, Aberdeen, Göteborg, and London. **Dan Air** (book with Braathens), **Air France** (tel. 04/65–60–00), and **British Airways** (tel. 04/65–15–33) have nonstop flights to Stavanger from Billund, Paris, and London respectively.

The **SAS bus** (tel. 06/07–22–42) to town takes 20 minutes and stops at hotels and outside the railroad station. Tickets cost NKr30.

Arriving and Departing by Car, Train, Bus, and Boat

By Car From Oslo, it is 329 kilometers (203 miles) to Kristiansand and 574 kilometers (352 miles) to Stavanger. Route E-18 parallels the coastline but stays slightly inland on the eastern side of the country and even farther inland in the western part. Although seldom wider than two lanes, it is easy driving because it is so flat. Count on eight hours on the road to Stavanger.

By Train The **Sørlandsbanen** leaves Oslo S station four times daily for the approximately five-hour journey to Kristiansand and three times daily for the 8½ to nine-hour journey to Stavanger. Two more trains travel the 3½-hour Kristiansand–Stavanger route. Kristiansand's train station is at V. Strandgata (tel. 042/27–000 or 21–443). The information number for trains out of Stavanger is 04/52–61–37.

By Bus **Aust-Agder Trafikkselskap** (tel. 041/26–500), based in Arendal, has two departures daily in each direction for the 5½- to six-hour journey between Oslo and Kristiansand.

Sørlandsruta (042/24–380), based in Mandal, has two departures in each direction for the 4½-hour trip from Kristiansand to Stavanger. All buses depart from Strandgate 33.

For information about both long-distance and local bus services in Stavanger, call 04/52–26–00; the bus terminal is outside the train station.

By Boat *Stavanger* **Color Line** (Strandkaien, tel. 04/52–45–45) has four ships weekly on the Stavanger–Newcastle route. High-speed boats to Bergen are based at **Hurtigbåtterminalen** (tel. 04/52–20–90).

Getting Around

By Car Sørlandet is flat, so it's easy driving throughout. All the water makes the center of **Stavanger** difficult to maneuver by car. One-way streets are the norm downtown. Parking is limited, and streets are very crowded on Saturday.

By Bus Bus connections in Sørlandet are infrequent; the tourist office can provide a comprehensive schedule. Tickets on **Stavanger's** excellent bus network cost NKr12.

By Taxi All **Kristiansand** taxis are connected with a central dispatching office (tel. 042/32–700). Journeys are charged by the taximeter within the city, otherwise by the kilometer.

Stavanger taxis are also connected to a central dispatching office (tel. 04/52–60–40). The initial charge is NKr19, with NKr9 per kilometer during the day, NKr11 at night.

Passes *Kristiansand* A **Sommerpass Kristiansand,** which costs NKr50 for adults and NKr30 for children, gives free admission to many sights and a 25% discount on tickets to the zoo and the M/S *Maarten.* It can be purchased at the tourist office, the zoo, and at all hotels. If you stay three nights at any hotel in the city, the pass is free.

Stavanger The **Stavanger card,** available free at hotels and guest houses, gives discounts of up to 50% on sightseeing tours, museums, buses, car rentals, and other services and attractions.

Guided Tours

Kristiansand Tours of Kristiansand run only in the summer. The **City Train** (Rådhusgt. 11, tel. 042/30–524) runs a 15-minute tour of the center. The M/S *Maarten* (Fiskebrygga, tel. 042/26–065) offers two-hour tours of the eastern archipelago (June 14–Aug. 18) and a three-hour tour of the western archipelago (July 1–July 31).

Stavanger A two-hour bus tour, which includes Old Stavanger, Breidablikk Mansion, and Ullandhaug Tower leaves from the Marina at **Vågen,** daily at 1 from June 1 to August 31.

Rødne Clipperkontoret (Skagenkaien 18, tel. 04/52–02–67) offers three different tours.

Exploring Sørlandet

Numbers in the margin correspond with points of interest on the Sørlandet map.

Tour 1: The Coast 1 **Larvik** is the last of the big whaling towns, 19 kilometers (12 miles) south of Sandefjord. It's still a port, but now the traffic is in passengers to Fredrikshavn, Denmark. Near the ferry quays is **Kong Haakon VIIs kilde** (King Haakon VII's spring), also called Farris kilde, Norway's only natural source of mineral water. A spa was built there in 1880, but now people drink the water rather than bathe in it. *Fjellveien, Open June 25–Aug. 3, weekdays 10–3.*

Larvik is the site of **Herregården,** a large estate once owned by the noble Gyldenløve family. The main building was finished in 1677. Note the furnishings: Scandinavian nobility had to make do with furniture painted to look like marble or carving, rather than the real thing. *Herregaardssletta 1, tel. 03/48–60–00. Admission: NKr15 adults, NKr5 children. Open June 17–Aug. 12, daily 3–7; May 27–Sept. 2, Sun. 1–7.*

From Larvik, it's only 8 kilometers (5 miles) along the coast to **Stavern,** now a popular sailing center. On the water east of town is **Fredriksvern,** named after King Fredrik V and Norway's main naval station from 1750 to 1850; 17 buildings from that period still stand. The church is a fine example of Scandinavian Rococo. The benches were designed so their backs could be folded down to make beds in case the church had to be used as a field hospital in time of war. *Fredriksvern Verft. Open June 20–Aug. 8, 10–2.*

Farther down the coast about 35 kilometers (22 miles) comes
2 **Kragerø,** a picturesque town with its own small archipelago. The **Berg museum,** a former country estate, is right on the beach at Hellefjorden, about 4 kilometers (3 miles) from town. In addition to a collection of furniture and glass, it features an old country store. *Lovisenbergvn. 45, tel. 03/98–14–53. Admission: NKr20 adults, NKr10 children. Open June 20–Aug. 15,*

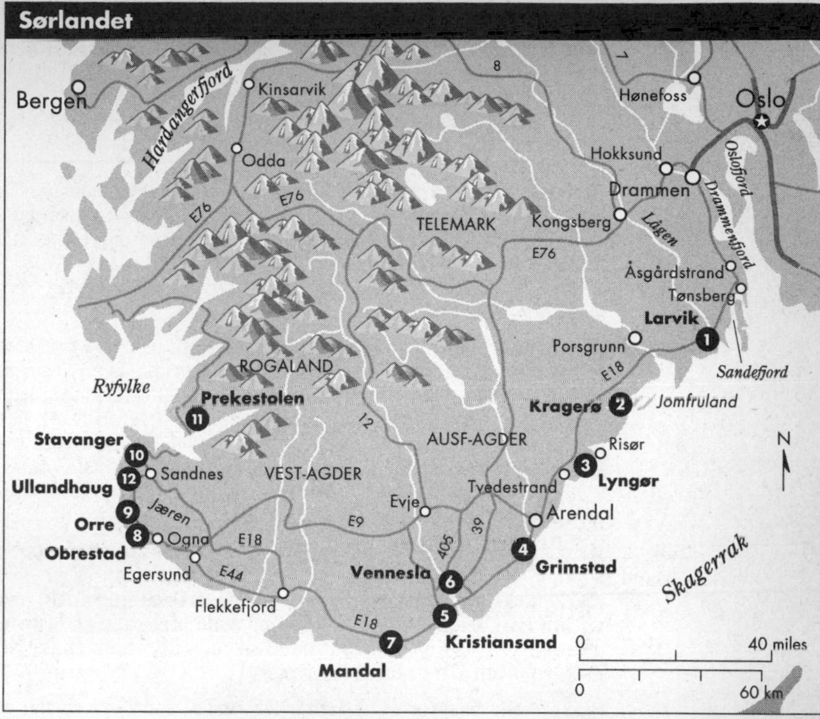

Tues.–Fri. noon–3, Sun. noon–5; May 17–June 20 and Aug. 15–Sept. 15, Sun. noon–5.

Theodor Kittelsen (1857–1914), famous for his drawings of trolls and illustrations of Norwegian fairy tales, lived in Kragerø, and his birthplace is now a museum. *Th. Kittelsens v. 5. Admission: NKr20 adults, NKr10 children. Open June 15–Aug. 15, weekdays 11–3.*

The next pearl on the southern string is **Risør,** east from E18 on the coast. On the first weekend in August the town holds a wooden boat festival, when the harbor is packed with beautiful antique boats.

3 **Lyngør,** four tiny rocky islands off the coast, was recently chosen Europe's best-preserved village. In winter the population is 110, but every summer thousands descend upon it. Hardly changed since the days of sailing ships, it's idyllic and romantic: white painted houses, window boxes full of pink and red flowers, and carless. To get there, follow E18 to the sign for "Sørlandsporten" (Gateway to the South). Turn off just after the sign and drive 26 kilometers (16 miles) to Lyngørfjorden Marina, where you can take a five-minute watertaxi (tel. 041/66–888) ride to the island. The only hotel books most of its rooms by the year to large firms, so don't count on staying overnight.

Lyngør Seilmakerverksted (sailmaker's workshop) is still a thriving business. The old-fashioned shop is a reminder of what the sailing life was like in bygone days.

Time Out **Den Blå Lanterne** (tel. 041/66–480) is Lyngør's only restaurant, housed in a historic 100-year-old white house with blue trim. Eat as much of their famous fish soup as you like for one price. There's often live music; it's pricey, but also the only game in town. Be sure to reserve a table. While you're there, ask about organized "island wandering."

Arendal, a little farther south, has more tidy white houses. On the island of **Merdøy,** a 30-minute boat ride from Arendal's Langbrygga (wharf), is an early 18th-century sea-captain's home, now a museum, **Merdøgaard.** *Tel. 041/22–422. Admission: NKr10 adults, NKr5 children. Open June 24–Aug. 15, weekdays 9–3, Sat. 9–1, Sun. noon–3.*

4 As you move southward, you reach **Grimstad.** Its glory was also in the days of sailing ships, when Ibsen worked as an apprentice pharmacist here for six years. Grimstad Apotek, the apothecary shop, in what is now **Ibsenhuset** (Ibsen House), has been preserved with its 1837 interior intact. Ibsen wrote his first play here. *Henrik Ibsensgt. 14, tel. 04/14–46–53. Admission: NKr15 adults, NKr5 children, senior citizens. Open May 15–Sept. 15, Mon.–Sat. 11–5, Sun. 1–5.*

Tour 2: Kristiansand

5 **Kristiansand,** with 65,000 inhabitants, is one of Sørlandet's leading cities. According to legend, King Christian IV in 1641 marked the four corners of the city with his walking stick, and within that framework, the grid of wide streets was drawn. The center of the city, called the **Kvadrat,** still retains that grid pattern, even after numerous fires.

Start at the **fisketorvet** (fish market) on the southern corner of the grid right on the sea. Follow Strandpromenaden to **Christiansholm festning** (Fortress), on a promontory opposite Festningsgata. Completed in 1672, it has played a more decorative than defensive role.

Six blocks inland is the Gothic Revival **Cathedral** from 1885. Its best feature is the organ. Check to see if there's a concert soon. *Kirkegata, tel. 042/24–789. Admission free. Open June 1–Sept. 1, Sun.–Fri. 10–2.*

Several interesting sights lie on the other side of the Otra River. To reach them take bus No. 22, marked "Gimle Gård," from Henrik Wergelandsgate at 10 minutes past the hour, or drive to Route E-18 and cross the bridge over the Otra to Parkveien. Turn left–the street changes names to Ryttergangen. Drive to Gimleveien and turn right to get to **Gimle Gård** (Gimla Manor), built by a wealthy merchant/shipowner around 1800 in the Empire style, with period furnishings and decoration, including hand-blocked wallpaper. *Gimleveien 23, tel. 043/92–132 or 043/90–228. Admission: NKr10 adults, NKr5 children (free with Summerpass). Open July 1–Aug. 15, Tues.–Sun. noon–4; June 1–31 and Aug. 15–Sept. 15, Sun. noon–4.*

Eastward on Gimleveien is **Oddernes Church,** one of the oldest dedicated to St. Olav. The runestone in the cemetery tells that Øivind, godson of St. Olav, built this church on property he inherited from his father. The altar and the pulpit are both in the Baroque style, decorated with acanthus leaves and richly gilded. *Oddernesveien, tel. 042/90–187. Admission free. Open May 1–Sept. 1, Sun.–Fri. 9–14.*

Continue to **Vest-Agder Fylkesmuseum** (County Museum), just south of Vigeveien. Here you can visit two *tun* (farm buildings traditionally constructed in clusters around a common area, which suited the extended families). A reconstructed city street features dwellings and workshops, including a tobacco mill and a cabin used by the Resistance during World War II. *Vigevn., Kongsgård, tel. 042/90–228. Admission: NKr10 adults, NKr5 children (free with Summerpass). Open June 20–Aug. 20, Tues.–Sat. 10–6, Sun. noon–6; May 19–June 19 and Aug. 21–Sept. 10, Sun. noon–6.*

Excursions from Kristiansand

6 **Setesdalsbanen** (the Setesdal Railway) at **Grovane i Vennesla,** 20 kilometers (13 miles) north of Kristiansand, is a 4.7-kilometer- (3-mile-) long stretch of narrow-gauge track featuring a steam locomotive from 1894 and carriages from the early 1900s.

Follow Route 12 to Mosby, veer right onto 405, and continue to Grovane, or catch bus No. 30, marked "Setesdalsbanen, Grovane," from Kristiansand's Festningsgate at 9:40 or 12:40 on Sunday or No. 31, same markings, at 4:10 or 4:40 on Wednesday. The travel time is about 40 minutes. *Grovane, tel. 042/56–482. Admission: NKr40 adults, NKr20 children (50% discount with Summerpass). Open June 9–Aug. 25, Sun. at 11:30, 1, 2:30; July, Wed. at 6.*

Many rockhounds head for **Evje,** about 60 kilometers (36 miles) north of Kristiansand, to look for beryl, aquamarine, and amazonite. At **Evje Mineralsti,** you can hunt for blue-green amazonite. *No tel. Admission: NKr34, NKr70 family. Open daily 10–5:30. At other times, visitors pay by honor system.*

If you don't find any amazonite, you can visit **Fennefoss Museum** just south of Evje in Hornnes and look at the mineral collection. *No tel. Admission: NKr15 adults, NKr5 children. Open daily 10–2.*

Tour 3: The South

7 From Kristiansand you can go 28 kilometers (17 miles) southwest to **Mandal,** with its historic core of well-preserved wooden houses and its beautiful long beach, Sjøsanden, considered Norway's finest.

Lindesnes Fyr, Norway's oldest lighthouse, was built on the southernmost point of the country. The old coal-fired light dates from 1822. The marker indicates that it is 2,518 kilometers (1,561 miles) from the North Cape.

Follow E-18 inland to **Kvinesdal,** the heart of the Bible Belt. The Pentacostalists have built the country's largest mission and media center which seats 4,000, but up to 50,000 people come to the meetings.

Route E-18 continues northward now along the coastal plain of **Jæren,** painted by many Norwegian artists, and a rich agricultural area. The landscape has a Danish feel, with low buildings covered by sloping roofs. In the region ancient monuments are still visible, notably the **Hå gravesite** below the Hå parsonage
8 near **Obrestad** light on coastal Route 44, which connects with Route E18 by way of Route 504. It consists of about 60 mounds including two star-shaped and one boat-shaped, dating from around AD 500, all marked with stones. **Hå parsonage,** built in the 1780s, is now a cultural center. *Admission: NKr15. Open May 1–Sept. 30, Sun.–Fri. noon–7, Sat. noon–5; Oct. 1–Apr. 30., Sat. noon–5, Sun. noon–7.*

9 Continue northward on Route 507 to **Orre,** site of a medieval stone church. Near Orre pond, slightly inland, is a bird-watching station.

Tour 4: Stavanger

10 **Stavanger** has always prospered from the riches of the sea. During the 19th century, huge harvests of brisling and herring established it as the sardine capital of the world. A resident is still called a Siddis, from S(tavanger) and *iddis,* which means sardine label, and the city symbol, fittingly enough, is a sardine-can key.

During the past two decades, a different product from the sea has been Stavanger's lifeblood—oil. Since its discovery in the late 1960s, North Sea oil has transformed both the economy and the lifestyle of the city. In the early days of drilling, expertise was imported from abroad, chiefly from the United States. Although Norwegians have now taken over most of the projects, the foreign influence is still strong, making Stavanger the country's most cosmopolitan city. Though the population is only about 100,000, the city has all the bustle of one many times its size.

In the center, next to a small pond called Breiavatnet, is **Stavanger Domkirke** (the cathedral), the country's best-preserved large medieval church. It was begun around 1100 by Bishop Reinald of Winchester, probably assisted by English craftsmen, and dedicated to St. Svithun. Though it is a patchwork of old and not-so-old, the church still retains much of its original style. Every Thursday at 11 there is an organ recital, with coffee served in the crypt afterward. *Ved Breiavatnet. Admission free. Open May 15–Sept. 15, Mon.–Sat. 9–8, Sun. 1–6; Sept. 16–May 14, Mon.–Sat. 9–2.*

Next to the cathedral is the **Kongsgård,** former residence of bishops and kings, but now a school and not open to visitors. A few streets to the left, on Eiganesveien, is an old patrician residential district. As the road angles to the left, it's only one long block to **Breidablikk** (manorhouse). This outstanding example of what the Norwegians call the "Swiss style" of architecture was built in 1881 for a shipowner. In spite of the label, it is uniquely Norwegian, inspired by national romanticism. *Eiganesveien 40A, tel. 04/52–60–35. Admission: NKr10 adults, NKr5 children. Open June 15–Aug. 15, Tues.–Sun. 11–3; Aug. 16–June 14, Sun. 11–4.*

Across the road and through the park is **Ledaal,** a stately house built by the Kielland family in 1799 but now the residence of the royal family when they visit Stavanger. The second-floor library is dedicated to the writer Alexander Kielland, a social critic and satirist. *Eiganesveien 45, tel. 04/52–60–35. Admission: NKr10 adults, NKr5 children. Open June 15–Aug. 15, Tues.–Sun. 11–3; Aug. 16–June 14, Sun. 11–4.*

Exit toward Alexander Kiellands Gate, turn right, and walk around the stadium complex, and several blocks farther, until you reach Øvre Strandgate, which, along with Nedre Strandgate, forms the periphery of old Stavanger, where there are small, white wood houses with many-paned windows, ceramic roof tiles, and narrow cobblestone streets.

Norsk Hermetikkmuseum (Canning Museum) is a former canning factory, which documents the production of brisling and sardines, the city's most important industry for nearly 100 years. *Øvre Strandgate 88A, tel. 04/52-60-35. Admission: NKr10 adults, NKr5 children. Open June 1–Aug. 31, Wed.–Sun. 11–3; Sept. 1–May 31, Sun. 11–4.*

Walk along Strandkaien to **Sjøfartsmuseet** (the Maritime Museum), in the only two shipping merchants' houses that remain completely intact. The warehouses face the wharf, while the shops, offices, and apartments face the street on the other side. Inside, the house is just as it was a century ago, complete with office furniture, files, and posters, while the apartments show the standard of living for the mercantile class at that time. *Nedre Strandgate 17–19, tel. 04/52–60–35. Admission: NKr10 adults, NKr5 children. Open June 15–Aug. 15, Tues.–Sun. 11–3; Aug. 16–June 14, Sun. 11–4.*

From all along the quay you can see **Valbergtårnet** (Valbergjet 4, tel. 04/52–21–95) built on the highest point of the old city. Once a fire watchtower, it is now a lookout point and craft center.

If you are of Norwegian stock, you might want to visit **Det Norske Utvandrersenteret** (Emigration Center) to search for your ancestors. *Bergjelandsgate 30, tel. 04/50–12–67. Open weekdays 9–3.*

Excursions from Stavanger

11 **Prekestolen** (Pulpit Rock) is a huge cube of rock with a vertical drop of 600 meters (2,000 feet); if you are afraid of heights, forget it. You can take a tour there (*see* Guided Tours, *above*) or you can do it on your own from June 16 to August 25 by taking the ferry from Fiskepiren to Tau and then to Jøssing. It takes 1½ to 2 hours to walk to the rock—the well-marked trail crosses some uneven terrain, so good walking shoes or boots are vital. There are both food and lodging near the trail.

12 About 5 kilometers (3 miles) west of Stavanger is **Ullandhaug,** a reconstruction of an Iron-Age farm. Three houses have been built around a central garden, and guides wearing period clothing demonstrate the daily activities of 1,500 years ago, spinning thread on a spindle, weaving, and cooking over an open hearth. *Ullandhaug, tel. 04/53–41–40. Admission: NKr10 adults, NKr5 children. Open June 15–Aug. 15, daily noon–5; May 8–June 14 and Aug. 16–Sept. 16, Sun. noon–5.*

What to See and Do with Children

Kristiansand

East of town 11 kilometers (6 miles) on E-18 is **Dyreparken,** Norway's largest zoo and recreational park. Besides Julius the chimp, who has appeared on TV and in picture books, there are 700 other animals, from pettable bunnies to rare birds, and rides galore. The newest attraction is **Kardemomme By** (Cardamom Town), an actual re-creation of the setting of a beloved children's book by the popular Norwegian writer and illustrator Thorbjørn Egner. *Dyreparken, tel. 04/24–62–00. Admission: NKr120 adults, NKr100 children (25% discount with Summerpass). Open June 22–Aug. 18, daily 9–7; May 9–June 21 and Aug. 19–Sept. 15, daily 10–6; Sept. 16–May 16, daily 10–3.*

Stavanger

At **Vestlandske Skolemuseum** (West Norway School Museum), located in an old school building, children can see what it was like to go to school in olden days. *Veumveien, Hillevåg, tel. 04/58–53–72. Admission: NKr10. Open June 25–Aug. 6, daily 11–15; Aug. 7–June 24, Mon.–Tues. 9–noon.*

Kongeparken Amusement Park has an 85-meter-long figure of Gulliver as its main attraction, and all the usual rides. *Ålgård, tel. 04/61–71–11. Admission: NKr25; rides and activities, NKr5–20. Open June 16–Aug. 12, daily 11–7; May 1–June 16, weekends 11–7.*

Shopping

Porsgunn Outside Porsgrunn, 27 kilometers (17 miles) west of Larvik, is **Porsgrunn Porselænfabrik** (porcelain factory) (Porselensgt. 12, tel. 03/55–00–40), where you can take a factory tour and visit the seconds shop.

Stavanger Shops in **Stavanger** are open Monday through Wednesday and Friday from 9 to 5, Thursday from 9 to 8 and Saturday from 9 to 2. Kvadrat Mall, on E-18 between Stavanger and Sandnes, is open weekdays from 10 to 8 and Saturdays from 10 to 5. Outside of town are a ceramics factory and two outlet stores:

Figgjo Ceramics (Rte. E18, Figgjo, tel. 04/67–00–00) turned 50 years old in 1991; it was started during World War II, when Norway was occupied by German forces. A museum documents the history of the factory; the seconds shop has discounts of around 50% (and accepts Visa).

Polaris (Orstad i Klepp, tel. 04/67–31–99) sells pots and pans in stainless steel, copper, and cast iron. The small stainless-steel coffee pots, modern versions of traditional Norwegian ones, are a useful souvenir.

Skjæveland Strikkevarefabrikk (Ålgård, tel. 04/61–85–06) has a huge selection of men's and women's sweaters in both Norwegian patterns and other designs for around NKr200 less than in the shops.

Sports and Fitness

Southern Norway is an outdoor paradise, with a mild summer climate and terrain varying from coastal flatland to inland mountains and forests. There's plenty of fish in the rivers and lakes, as well as along the coast. The region is particularly well suited to canoeing, kayaking, and rafting, as well as hiking. Southern Norway is home to some 5000 beavers, as well as deer, fox, and forest birds, so bring binoculars if you like to see them more closely.

Bicycling **Kristiansand** has 70 kilometers (43 miles) of bike trails around the city. The tourist office can recommend routes.

Golf At Randesund, southeast of **Kristiansand,** is a nine-hole golf course. The season is from May to October. Contact **Kristiansand Golfklubb's** secretary (042/12–986) for details. **Stavanger** has an 18-hole course. Contact **Stavanger Golf klubb** (tel. 04/55–70–25) for details. Equipment can be rented.

Hiking
Kristiansand West of **Kristiansand** is **Ravnedalen** (Raven Valley), a national park and recreational area developed in the late 1870s, with gardens, lakes with swans and a 100-meter-high cliff with 200 steps to the top, plus narrow, winding trails.

Stavanger **Stavanger Turforening** (Musegt. 8, tel. 04/52–75–66) can plan a hiking tour through the area. They also oversee cabins for members (you can join on the spot) to use on their hikes.

Water Sports
Kristiansand

Kuholmen Marina (Rolighcdcn Camping, tel. 042/96–635) arranges rentals of boats, water skis, and water scooters. **Sail Scandinavia** (Tollbodgt. 8, tel. 042/70–749) rents sailboats by the day, weekend or week, with or without captain, while **Hamresanden Båtutleie** (Kirsti Stabel, Moneheia 4, tel. 042/46–825) rents out kayaks and rowboats.

Anker Dykkersenter (Randesundsgt. 2, Kuholmen, tel. 042/97–909) rents out scuba equipment, while Blomberg Sport (Kongensgt. 8, tel. 042/21–709) rents out windsurfers and holds classes.

Stavanger

Diving is excellent all along the coast. **Siddis Dykkerskole** (Peders gt. 50, tel. 04/52–28–30) rents equipment. There's a special weekend rate.

Spectator Sports

Stavanger's Viking soccer team (Holbergs gate, tel. 04/52–89–34) plays at their home stadium every other Sunday all summer. Matches start at 6PM.

Beaches

Kristiansand

Kristiansand has some excellent bathing places. Stretch out on a *svaberg* (a smooth boulder that has been warmed by the sun). The bathing spots closest to the city are **Galgenbergtangen** and Blomsbukta east of the Otra river.

Stavanger

Møllebukta at Madla and **Solastrand,** a 2½ kilometer (1½ mile) long sandy beach near the airport, are easiest to reach. Take bus No. 143, marked "Sola" to get to Madla. For Sola beach, take No. 143 to Sola, then change to No. 149 to get to the beach.

Dining and Lodging

Dining

Coastal Sørlandet is seafood country. Restaurants in this resort area are casual and unpretentious, and the cooking is simple. Better restaurants are usually in the hotels, especially in small towns.

Stavanger has many more good restaurants than other cities of comparable size, thanks to the influx of both foreigners and money to the city.

Lodging

Hotels in the small towns along the coast are either modern and impersonal or quaint and old-fashioned. Prices are about the same, regardless of style.

Most of Kristiansand's big hotels look alike, and all cost within NKr100 of one another in summer.

Highly recommended establishments are indicated by a star ★.

Bryne
Dining

Thime Station. It's a 40-minute train ride from Stavanger to Bryne and the restaurant is next to the station. The specialty of the house is a seafood platter with salmon, monkfish, ocean catfish, mussels, and ocean crayfish in a beurre blanc sauce. For dessert, try the *krumkake*, a Norwegian cookie baked on an iron, wafer thin, and filled with blackberry cream. *Bryne Station, tel. 04/48–22–56. Reservations required. Dress: casual but neat. Closed Sun. No weekday lunch. AE, DC, MC, V. Moderate.*

Kristiansand
Dining

Sjøhuset. Built in 1892 as a salt warehouse, this red-painted building with white trim is furnished with comfortable leather chairs and accented with maritime antiques. The specialty is seafood, and the monkfish with Newburg sauce on green fettuccine is both colorful and delicious. *Østre Strangt. 12, tel. 042/26–260. AE, DC, MC, V. Moderate–Expensive.*

Petters Kjøkken. One kitchen serves both a cafeteria and a restaurant at this restaurant on the eastern shore by the small boat harbor. The self-service side offers simple, nicely prepared Norwegian food with no fuss, while dishes on the other side are more elaborate. Main courses include ocean catfish in red-wine sauce. For dessert try the warm apple cake topped with homemade vanilla ice cream. *Framnesveien 10, tel. 042/91990. Dress: casual. AE, MC, V. Inexpensive–Moderate.*

Mållaget Kafeteria. The Association for the Advancement of Nynorsk (Norway's second language) runs this cafeteria, where, according to the cook, everything is homemade except for the gelatin dessert. That includes such dishes as meatballs, brisket of beef with onion sauce (highly recommended), and trout in sour-cream sauce. It's the best deal in town, but it closes right around the time most people think about eating dinner. *Gyldenløves Gate 11, tel. 042/22–293. Dress: casual. No credit cards. Inexpensive.*

Lodging

Ernst Park. It was modernized in 1988, but a few clumps of chairs and sofas are left in nooks and crannies. Wall paintings along some halls attest to its former brilliance. The rooms are decorated in light furniture, with chintz bedspreads and drapes. The corner rooms have a tower nook at one end. *Rådhusgt. 2, 4611, tel. 042/21–400, fax 042/20–307. 113 rooms with bath or shower, 3 suites. Facilities: 3 restaurants, 2 bars, nightclub, conference rooms. AE, DC, MC, V. Moderate–Expensive.*

Hotel Norge. Another recently refurbished hotel in the heart of town, this one has an entrance a bit more modern than that of the Ernst Park, but upstairs, the difference is negligible. Here the rooms are furnished in bright colors and dark woods. Get up for breakfast to taste the homemade breads and rolls. This hotel honors the Fjord Pass. *Dronningens Gate 5, 4610, tel. 042/20–000, fax 042/23–530. 115 rooms with bath or shower. Facilities: restaurant, conference rooms. AE, DC, MC, V. Inexpensive–Moderate.*

Stavanger
Dining
★

Jans Mat & Vinhus. The cellar setting is rustic, with old stone walls and robust sideboards providing a nice counterpoint to the refined menu. Saddle of Rogaland county lamb is boned and rolled around a thyme-flavored stuffing, and the fillet is topped with a crunchy mustard crust. For dessert, there's a nougat parfait dusted with cocoa or a chocolate mousse tart with vanilla sauce. *Breitorget, tel. 04/52–45–02. Reservations required. Jacket and tie required. AE, DC, MC, V. Closed Sun. No lunch. Expensive.*

Straen. The city's only fish restaurant, right on the quay, has two old-fashioned dining rooms. The three-course dinner of the day is always the best value. The house fish soup and the tournedos of monkfish with lobster sauce and a garnish of mussels and shrimp are excellent. No meat dishes are served. *Nedre Strandgate 15 (Strandkaien), tel. 04/52–62–30. Reservations advised. Dress: neat but casual. AE, DC, MC, V. Dinner only. Closed Sun. Expensive.*

City Bistro. This turn-of-the-century frame house with tiled roof is furnished with massive oak tables and benches. Choose from reindeer medallions with rowanberry jelly, deer fillet with lingonberries and pears, or halibut poached in cream with saffron, garnished with shrimp, crayfish and mussels. The dish of the day is NKr99, served from 5 to 6. *Madlaveien 18–20, tel. 04/53–31–81. Reservations required. Dress: casual but neat. AE, DC, MC, V. No lunch. Moderate.*

Galleien Bistro. It used to be a sardine cannery, and the pictures on its wall illustrate the early history of the building. Ask for a window table, for you're right at seaside. Back in the kitchen, which you can visit, are tanks filled with cod, flounder, oysters, mussels, crabs, and lobster. Simple preparation emphasizes the natural flavor of the fish. *Hundvågvn. 27, tel. 04/54–91–44. Reservations advised. Dress: casual but neat. V. Closed Sun. No lunch. Moderate.*

Cafe Sting. It's a restaurant–gallery–concert hall–meeting place day and night. All food is made in-house and is less stodgy than most inexpensive fare in Norway. There's a skillet dish with crisp fried potatoes and bacon, flavored with leek and topped with melted cheese, and a meat loaf with mashed potatoes and sprinkled with cheese. The chocolate and almond cakes are good. By late evening, the place is smoky. *Valberggt. 3, tel. 04/52–75–20. Dress: casual. AE, DC, V. Inexpensive.*

Lodging

SAS Royal. Room styles include Scandinavian, American, Japanese, and Italian, but the chairs in the gray and yellow Italian rooms are uncomfortable. The swimming pool is big enough for a good swim. The Chicago Bar & Grill serves prime steaks. *Løkkeveien 26, 4000, tel. 04/56–70–00, fax 04/56–74–60. 204 rooms with bath, 8 suites. Facilities: 2 restaurants, bar, 24-hour room service, pool, fitness center, business/conference center. AE, DC, MC, V. Moderate–Very Expensive.*

Skagen Brygge. The city's newest hotel incorporates three rehabilitated old seahouses. Almost all rooms are different, from modern to old-fashioned maritime with exposed beams and brick and wood walls; many have harbor views. Even the smallest rooms have upholstered chairs with ottomans. There's no restaurant, but the hotel has an arrangement with 15 in the area—they make the reservations and the tab ends up on your hotel bill. *Skagenkaien 30, 4006, tel. 04/53–03–50, fax 04/52–02–26. 110 rooms with bath, 2 suites. Facilities: bar, pool, fitness center, conference center. AE, DC, MC, V. Moderate–Expensive.*

Hummeren. Built in 1986 in the style of old harborside buildings, Hummeren (The Lobster) is 5 kilometers (3 miles) from the airport and 15 kilometers (9 miles) from Stavanger, at Tananger harbor. Boats dock immediately outside, and it even has showers for people who otherwise live on their boats. The personal touch is evident in this small hotel with big rooms. Many rooms face the harbor, and some have balconies. The restaurant is good. *4056 Tananger, tel. 04/69–93–90. 32 rooms with shower or tub. Facilities: restaurant, bar, conference rooms. AE, DC, MC, V. Inexpensive–Moderate.*

Victoria. The ads for this hotel are real eye-catchers—Queen Victoria as a sardine label. This remodeled Victorian brick building downtown looks great from the outside, but inside, it falls apart; the rooms are a disappointment—standard, boring, and not a bit Victorian. *Skansegaten 1, 4000, tel. 04/52–05–26, fax 52–71–48. 110 rooms with bath or shower. Facilities: res-*

taurant, bar, conference rooms. AE, DC, MC, V. Inexpensive–Moderate.

The Arts and Nightlife

The Arts *Stavanger* **Stavanger Konserthus** (Concert Hall, Bjergsted, tel. 04/56–17–16) features local artists. Stavanger has several movie theaters; all films are shown in the original language with Norwegian subtitles.

Nightlife *Kristiansand* As in most smaller cities, Kristiansand's nightlife centers around hotels.

Stavanger People are out at all hours, and sidewalk restaurants stay open until the sun comes up. Walk along **Skagenkaien** and **Strandkaien** for a choice of pubs and nightclubs—nightlife is the focus here or, in winter, in the hotel nightclubs.

Bergen

Introduction

Hansa merchants from northern Germany settled in Bergen during the 14th century and made it one of their four major overseas trading centers. The Hanseatic buildings on Bryggen (the quay) still remain and are on the UNESCO World Heritage list. During the Hanseatic period, this active port was Norway's capital and largest city. Boats from northern Norway brought dried fish to Bergen to be shipped abroad by the Dutch, English, Scottish, and German merchants who had settled there. By the time the Hansa lost power, the city had an ample supply of wealthy merchants and shipowners to replace them. For years Bergen was the capital of shipping, and until well into the 19th century, it remained the country's major city.

Norway's first great international cultural figures came from Bergen, starting with dramatist Ludvig Holberg—although the Danes claim him as their own, all Bergensers know better. Norway's musical geniuses, Ole Bull and Edvard Grieg, both came from the city of the seven hills.

About 200,000 people live in the greater metropolitan area now, versus nearly 500,000 in Oslo. Even though the balance of power has shifted to the capital, Bergen remains a strong commercial force, thanks to shipping and oil, and it remains the cultural capital, with an international music and arts festival every spring. The downside to Bergen: It has about 300 rainy days a year.

Important Addresses and Numbers

Tourist Information The **tourist information office** at Torgalmenningen (tel. 05/32–14–80), in the center of the city, has brochures and maps and can arrange for accommodation and sightseeing. There is also a currency exchange.

Emergencies **Police,** tel. 002. **Fire,** tel. 001. **Ambulance,** tel. 003. **Car Rescue,** tel. 05/29–22–22.

Hospital Emergency Rooms The outpatient center at Lars Hillesgate 30 (tel. 05/32–11–20), near Grieghallen, is open 24 hours.

Dentists The dental emergency center, also at Lars Hillesgate 30 (tel. 05/32–11–20), is open daily 10–11 AM and 7–9 PM.

Pharmacies **Apotek Nordstjernen** (tel. 05/31–68–40), by the bus station, is open daily from 8:30 AM to midnight.

Where to Change Money Outside normal banking hours, the tourist information office at Torgalmenningen can change money. Post offices exchange money and are open Monday through Wednesday 8 to 5, Thursday and Friday 8–6, and Saturday 9 to 2.

Arriving and Departing by Plane

Flesland Airport is 20 kilometers (12 miles) south of Bergen. **SAS** (tel. 05/23–63–00) and **Braathens SAFE** (tel. 05/23–23–25) are the main domestic carriers. **British Airways** and **Lufthansa** also serve Flesland.

Between the Airport and Downtown

By Bus Flesland is a 30-minute ride from the center of Bergen at off peak hours. The **airport bus** departs twice per hour from the SAS Royal Hotel via Braathen SAFE's office at the Hotel Norge and from the bus station. Pick-up prior to departure can be arranged. Tickets are NKr36.

By Taxi A taxi rank is outside the arrivals exit. The trip into the city costs around NKr150.

By Car Driving from Flesland to Bergen is simple, and the road is well-marked. Bergen has an electronic ring surrounding it, so any vehicle entering the city weekdays between 6 AM and 10 PM has to pay NKr5. There is no toll in the other direction.

Arriving and Departing by Car, Train, Bus, and Boat

By Car Bergen is 485 kilometers (300 miles) from Oslo. Route 7 is good almost as far as Eidfjord (320 kilometers/198 miles) at the eastern edge of the Hardangerfjord, but then deteriorates considerably. The road through Måbydalen, just before Eidfjord, used to have 124 switchbacks, with many hairpin turns, but now tunnels have been blasted through much of the mountain. It still can be difficult in places. The ferry along the way, crossing the Hardanger fjord from Main to Bruravik, runs continuously from Brimnes 5 AM to midnight and takes 10 minutes. For a slower voyage, you can cross from Kinsarvik to Kvanndal. (Reserve a place, if possible—waiting can take longer than the crossing, especially in summer. With a reservation, you go to the front of the line.) E-68 from Kvanndal to Bergen hugs the fjord part of the way for some spectacular scenery.

Driving from Stavanger to Bergen involves from two to four ferries, a long journey in "fits and starts," packed with breathtaking scenery. The Stavanger tourist information office can help plan the trip and reserve ferry space.

By Train The **Bergensbanen** has four departures daily, plus one more on Friday and two on Sunday, in both directions on the Oslo–Bergen route. Trains leave from Oslo S station for the 7½- to 8½-hour journey. For information about trains out of Bergen, call 05/31–96–40.

By Bus The summer-only bus from Oslo to Bergen, **Geiteryggekspressen** (literally, "Goat-Back Express"—does it refer to speed, comfort, or terrain?) leaves the Nor-Way bus terminal (Havnegate, at Oslo Station, tel. 02/33–01–91) at 8 AM and arrives in Bergen 12½ hours later, after covering 524 km (325 mi). Buses also connect Bergen with Trondheim and Ålesund. Western Norway is served by several bus companies, which use the station at Strømgaten 8 (tel. 05/32–67–80).

By Boat Boats have always been Bergen's lifeline to the world. **Color Line** (Skuteviksboder 1–2, 5023, tel. 05/32–27–80) ferries serve Newcastle. Others connect to the Shetland and Faroe islands and Iceland. All dock at Skoltegrunnskaien.

Express boats between Bergen and Stavanger run three times daily on weekdays, twice daily on weekends, for the four-hour trip. All arrive and depart from **Munkebryggen.**

Getting Around

The best way to see the small center of Bergen is on foot. Most sights are within walking distance of the marketplace.

By Bus Yellow city buses are marked with destination and route number from 1 to 19. Tourist tickets for 48 hours of unlimited travel within the town boundaries cost NKr45 payable on the bus. All buses serving the Bergen region depart from the central bus station at Strømgaten 8 (tel. 05/32–67–80). A 24-hour ticket, good for travel with five different bus companies in Bergen and the surrounding area, costs NKr60 at the information office on Torgalmenningen or at the bus station.

By Taxi Taxi ranks are located in strategic places downtown. All taxis are connected to the central dispatching office (tel. 05/99–09–90). Minibuses, station wagons, handicapped transport, and children's seats can be ordered, and taxis also can be booked in advance (tel. 05/99–13–00). Sightseeing can be booked through central dispatch for NKr250 per hour.

By Car Downtown Bergen is enclosed by an inner ring road consisting of Christies Gate, Småstrandgaten, Kaigaten, Jon Smørs Gate, Håkonsgaten, and Nygårdsgaten. The area within is divided into three zones, which are separated by one-way and do-not-enter signs. To get from one zone to another, return to the ring road and drive to an entry point into the desired zone. The object is a relatively car-free center, but the system is both confusing and frustrating, as drivers cruise around trying to find an entry point or parking. Parking garages and lots, furthermore, are not conveniently located.

Opening and Closing Times

Shops are open Monday through Wednesday plus Friday from 9 to 4:30. On Thursday, and for some shops also on Friday, the hours are 9–7. On Saturday, shops are open 9–2. The shopping centers, Galleriet and Bystasjonen, are open weekdays 9–8 and Saturday 9–4.

Guided Tours

Bergen is the guided-tour capital of Norway, because it is the starting point for most fjord tours. Tickets for all tours are available from the tourist information office.

Orientation **Unitur** (Strandgaten 191, tel. 05/23–88–88) offers two tours departing from Hotel Norge. **De Gule Bussene** (yellow buses, tel. 05/91–57–70) offers three tours departing from Torggaten by the Hotel Norge. **Bryggen Guiding** (1½ hours, June 1–Aug. 31) offers a historic tour of the buildings at Bryggen, as well as entrance to Bryggens Museum, the Hanseatic Museum, and Schøtstuene after the tour. **Bergens-Expressen** (tel. 05/18–10–19), an old-fashioned "train on tires," leaves from outside the tourist information office at Torgalmenningen for a one-hour ride around the center of town.

Fjord Tours Ask at the tourist office for tours to Sogne, Hardanger, and other fjords. A leading operator is **Fjord Sightseeing** (tel. 05/31–43–20), which offers boat tours, leaving from Fisketorget. Tickets are sold at the tourist information center or at the quay. Students receive a 25% discount.

Fylkesbaatane (County Boats) **i Sogn og Fjordane** (tel. 05/32–40–15) has several combination tours.

If you don't have time to get to Geiranger or don't feel like dealing with the hassle of cars and buses, a two-day minicruise to Nordfjord, offered from May 23 to Sept 12, leaving Bergen Monday and Wednesday at 3:30 for Stryn, is the next best thing. It's an advantage to travel by boat, because the contrasts between the fjords and mountains are greatest at water level, and the boats are comfortable and stable (remember, the water is practically still), so seasickness in rare. Stops are frequent, and all the sights are explained. This is only one of many small cruises on the fjords.

Highlights for First-time Visitors

Bryggen (*see* Tour 1)
Bryggens Museum (*see* Tour 1)
Fantoft Stave Church (*see* Tour 3)
Fisketorget (*see* Tour 1)
Fløibanen (*see* Tour 1)
Hanseatisk Museum (*see* Tour 1)
Lysøen (*see* Tour 4)
Troldhaugen (Edvard Grieg's home) (*see* Tour 3)

Exploring Bergen

Numbers in the margin correspond with points of interest on the Bergen map.

Many of Bergen's sights are concentrated in a small area, so walking tours are the best way to see the city.

Tour 1: Historic Bergen

1 Start at **Torget,** Bergen's marketplace, also called **Fisketorvet** (fish square). At the turn of the century, pictures of this active and smelly square, with fishermen in Wellington boots and mackintoshes and women in long aprons, were popular postcard subjects. Times haven't changed. *Open Mon.–Sat. 8–3.*

2 Look over toward **Bryggen,** the row of wood buildings with pointed gables facing the harbor. These houses were first built during the Hansa period in the 14th century and are on UNESCO's World Heritage List. The buildings are mostly reconstructions, with the oldest dating from 1702, for several fires, the latest in 1955, have destroyed the original structures.

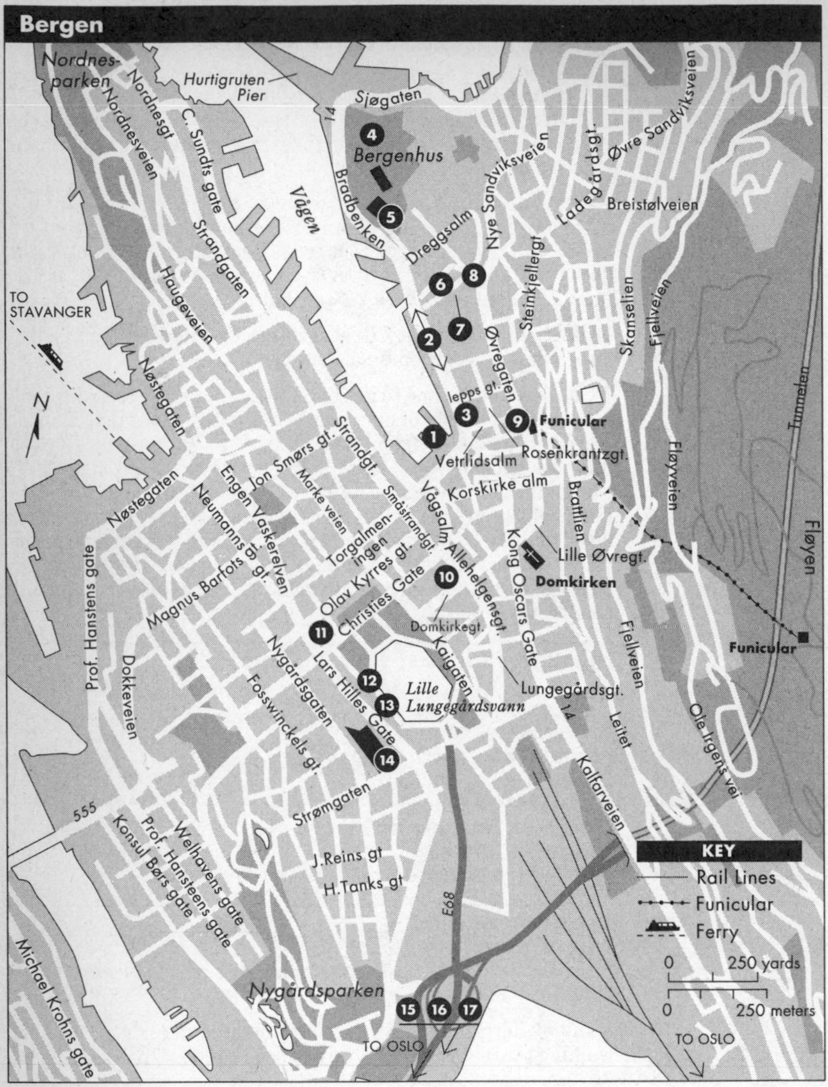

Bergenhus Festning, **4**
Bryggen, **2**
Bryggens Museum, **6**
Fantoft Stavkirke, **16**
Fløibanen, **9**
Gamle Rådhuset, **10**
Grieghallen, **14**
Hanseatisk Museum, **3**
Lysøen, **17**
Mariakirken, **8**
Rasmus Meyers Samlinger, **13**
Rosenkrantztårnet, **5**
Schjøtstuene, **7**
Stenersen Collection, **12**
Torget, **1**
Troldhaugen, **15**
Vestlandske Kunstindustri-museum, **11**

The Hanseatic League was a German trading monopoly that dominated northern Europe during the Middle Ages. As Bergen was one of the league's main ports, the city achieved an early prominence; Bryggen was the site of Hansa headquarters.

If it is in port, you may also see *Statsråd Lehmkuhl*, the Norwegian navy's tall-masted training ship.

3 Follow the pier to the **Hanseatisk** (Hanseatic) **Museum** at Finnegården. It was both office and home to an affluent German merchant. Apprentices lived upstairs, in boxed-in beds with windows cut into the wall, so the tiny cells could be made up from the hall. Although claustrophobic, they retained body heat, practical in these unheated buildings. *Bryggen, tel. 05/31–41–89. Admission: NKr10 adults, NKr5 children. Open June–Aug., daily 9–5; May and Sept., daily 11–2; Oct.–Apr., Sun., Mon., Wed., and Fri. 11–2.*

4 Past the historic buildings, at the end of the Holmen promontory is **Bergenhus Festning** (fort), dating back to the mid-13th century. **Håkonshallen,** a royal ceremonial hall used as early as 1261, was badly damaged by a wartime explosion and fire in 1944, but was restored by 1961. *Bergenhus, tel. 05/31–60–67. Admission: NKr10 adults, NKr5 children. Open May 15–Sept. 14, daily 10–4; Sept. 15–May 14, daily noon–3, also Thurs. 3–6. Closed during Bergen International Festival.*

5 Nearby, **Rosenkrantztårnet** (Rosenkrantz tower), damaged in the same explosion as Håkonshallen, was built in the 1560s by the Danish governor of Bergenhus, Erik Rosenkrantz, as a fortified official residence. It is furnished in the same formal, rather austere style as the hall. *Bergenhus, tel. 05/31–43–80. Admission: NKr10 adults, NKr5 children. Open May 15–Sept. 14, daily 10–4; Sept. 15–May 14, Sun. noon–3.*

6 Retrace your steps to the SAS Royal Hotel. Nearby is **Bryggen Museum,** which houses artifacts found during excavations on Bryggen, including 12th-century buildings constructed on site from the original foundations. The collection gives a good picture of daily life before and during the heyday of the Hansa, down to a two-seater outhouse. It also has displays of runic inscriptions. *Bryggen, tel. 05/31–67–10. Admission: NKr10. Open May 1–Aug. 31, Mon., Wed., and Fri. 10–4; Tues. and Thurs. 10–8; weekends 11–3; Sept. 1–Apr. 30, weekdays 11–3, Sat. noon–3, Sun. noon–4.*

7 On one side of the museum are the **Schjøtstuene,** three old guild halls, built by the Hanseatic merchants in the 16th century. These were the local men's clubs, where the foreign community met. *Øvregaten 50, tel. 05/31–60–20. Admission: NKr10 adults, NKr5 children. Open June–Aug., daily 10–4; May and Sept., daily 11–2; Oct.–Apr., Tues., Thurs., and weekends 11–2.*

8 The 12th-century **Mariakirken** (St. Mary's Church) is next door. Bergen's oldest building began as a Romanesque church but has gained a Gothic choir, richly decorated portals, and a splendid Baroque pulpit over the centuries. Organ recitals are held daily during the summer (June 25–Aug. 31). *Dreggen, tel. 05/31–59–60. Admission free. Open May–Aug., weekdays 11–4; Sept.–Apr., Tues.–Fri. noon–1:30.*

From Øvregaten, the back boundary of Bryggen, you can look down toward the wharf along the narrow passages where the

citizens of the city lived. Walk about four blocks to the popular
9 **Fløibanen,** the funicular (a cable car that runs on tracks on the ground) to **Fløyen,** a lookout point 1,050 feet above the sea. Several marked trails lead from Fløien into the surrounding wooded area, or you can walk back to town on Fjellveien. Fløibanen is Bergen's most popular attraction and in Norway is second only to Holmenkollen in the number of visitors per year. *Admission: NKr26 adults, NKr12 children; one-way tickets are ½ price. Rides every ½ hour from early morning to 11 PM.*

On Lille Øvregaten, Bergen's antiques shopping street, you can drop in at Professor Willy Dahl's secondhand bookstore, which specializes in mystery books—in English, too. On your left at the intersection with King Oscars Gate is Bergen **Domkirke** (the Cathedral), another church with a profusion of styles. The oldest part dates from the late 12th century. *Tel. 05/31-05-70. Open weekdays 11-2.*

Walk down Domkirkegaten to Allehelgensgate, past the police
10 station, and turn right. Across the street is **Gamle Rådhuset** (the old City Hall), built in the 16th century as the residence of Kristoffer Walckendorff, the governor. The city council still meets there.

To its side, on Christies Gate, is the fire station, built in 1888, bright red, and complete with a tall tower.

You can return to the tourist information center at Torgalmeningen along Rådhusgaten.

Tour 2: For Art Lovers

From Torgalmeningen, walk to Nordahl Bruns Gate and turn
11 left for the **Vestlandske Kunstindustrimuseum** (West Norway museum of Decorative arts). Seventeenth- and 18th-century Bergen silversmiths were reknowned throughout Scandinavia for their heavy, elaborate Baroque designs. Tankards embossed with flower and acanthus motifs or inlaid with coins form a rich display. *Permanenten, Nordahl Bruns Gate 9, tel. 05/32-51-08.*

Follow Christies Gate along the park and turn left to reach the
12 **Stenersen Collection,** which concentrates on such early 20th-century European artists as Edvard Munch, Max Ernst, Paul Klee, Vassily Kandinsky, and Joan Miró. *Rasmus Meyers Allé, tel. 05/32-14-60. Admission: NKr10. Open May 15-Sept. 15, Tues.-Fri. noon-4, Thurs. also 6-7, weekends noon-3; Sept. 16-May 14, Tues.-Sun. noon-3.*

13 Just beyond is **Rasmus Meyers Samlinger** (collections). Meyer, a businessman who lived from 1858 to 1916, assembled a superb collection, with many names that are famous today but were unknown quantities when he invested in them. You'll see the best Munchs outside Oslo, as well as major works by Scandinavian impressionists and Postimpressionists. *Rasmus Meyers Allé 7, tel. 05/97-80-00. Admission: NKr10. Open May 15-Sept. 15, Mon.-Sat. 11-4, Sun. noon-3; Sept. 16-May 14, Wed.-Mon. noon-3.*

14 Next is **Grieghallen** (the concert hall), named for the city's favorite son, Edvard Grieg (1843-1907), the composer of the *Peer Gynt Suite* and other orchestral music, as well as choral and piano works. Built in 1978, this home of the Bergen Philharmonic

Orchestra is a tribute to the architectural decadence of the 1970s, but the acoustics are marvelous. It is the main stage for the annual International Festival. Contact the tourist office for information about summer concerts.

Tour 3: Troldhaugen and Fantoft

Take any bus marked Fana (gates 18–20) from the main bus station to Hopsbroen, about a 15-minute ride. From the bus stop, follow the signs to Troldhaugen, another 10 to 15 minutes. To drive, follow E-68 (Nesttun/Voss out of town about 5 kilometers (3 miles). Turn left at the second pedestrian bridge over the main road, marked Fantoft Studentby. Then follow signs to Troldhaugen.

Composer Edvard Grieg and his wife Nina moved to a villa by Nordåsvannet, about 8 kilometers (5 miles) from downtown Bergen, in 1885. The main building is white clapboard with restrained green gingerbread trim. Although Grieg traveled ex-
15 tensively, he always returned to **Troldhaugen** (Troll Hill), and he and his wife are buried here. The house is cluttered with memorabilia. In 1985, an addition, **Troldsalen** (Troll Hall), which can hold 200 people, was built for concerts. *Tel. 05/91–17–91. Admission: NKr10 adults, NKr5 children. Open May 2–Oct. 1, daily 9:30–5:30. Check with tourist information center for concert listings.*

16 On the return trip, visit **Fantoft Stavkirke** (Stave Church). It was built in the early 12th century in Sognefjord but was later moved to its present site. Stave churches are unique to Norway. These medieval wood buildings combine pagan and Christian elements in their structure and fanciful ornamentation. *Paradis, tel. 05/28–07–10. Admission: NKr7. Open May 15–Sept. 15, daily 10:30–1:30 and 2:20–5:30.*

Tour 4: Lysøen

17 Getting to violinist Ole Bull's villa, **Lysøen,** is a trek, but it's worth the effort. The "Lysefjordruta" bus (tel. 05/32–67–80) leaves from the bus station (gate 20) for the 50-minute ride. By car, take E-68 or Route 553 to Fana, over Fanafjell to Sørestraumen. Follow signs to Buena Kai. The ferry, *Ole Bull*, leaves on the hour, (Monday–Saturday noon–3 and Sunday 11–4). The last ferries leave Lysøen Monday–Saturday at 4 and Sunday at 5. Return fare is NKr 25 adults, NKr 10 children.

This Victorian dream castle, built in 1873, has to be seen to be believed. Inside, the music room is a frenzy of filigree carving, fretwork, braided and twisted columns, and gables with intricate openwork in the supports, all done in knotty pine. *Tel. 05/30–90–77. Admission: NKr15, adults, NKr5 children. Open May 19–Sept. 2, Mon.–Sat. noon–4, Sun. 11–5.*

What to See and Do with Children

Akvariet (the aquarium) has 50 tanks with a wide variety of fish, but the main attractions are penguins—several kinds, one of which has a blond feather "hairdo," strangely appropriate in this land of blonds—and seals. Whenever a seal pup is born, names are chosen from children's suggestions. So far, there are

Selius, Selma, and Selina (*sel* is Norwegian for *seal*). It's on Nordnes peninsula, a 15-minute walk from downtown, or take bus No. 4. *Nordnes, tel. 04/32-04-52. Admission: Nkr 22 adults, Nkr 10 children. Open May–Sept., daily 9–8; Oct.–Apr., daily 10–6. Feeding times: 11, 2, and 6.*

Off the Beaten Track

Bergen has several museums that appeal to special interests:

Buekorpsmuseet (Crossbow Drill Corps Museum). Drum and crossbow drill teams are unique to Bergen. Their museum is at "Muren," built in 1562. The exhibits include medals, banners, drums, and pictures. *Wall Gate. Admission free. Open Sat. 11–4, Sun. noon–3. Consult the tourist office for opening times, which vary.*

Lepramuseet—St. Jørgens Hospital. St Jørgen (George) was the patron saint of lepers. Dr. G.H. Armauer Hansen, who discovered the leprosy bacteria, was Norwegian. This dusty little museum, a two-story wood building with a wide dark central hall, dates from 1754. Water-stained pictures adorn the walls of the tiny rooms, and the doctor's microscope is on display. *King Oscars Gate 59, no telephone. Admission: NKr 15 adults, NKr 4 children. Open May–Aug., daily 11–3.*

Shopping

Sundt & Co (Torgalmenningen 14, tel. 05/38-80-20) and **Kløverhuset** (Strandkaien 10, tel. 05/32-17-20) are traditional **department stores** with a wide selection of Norwegian sweaters and gifts. **Galleriet,** on Torgalmenningen, and **Bystasjonen,** by the bus terminal, are downtown **malls** with small shops and lots of windows.

Shops specializing in Norwegian **crafts** are either near Torgalmenningen, on Bryggen, or just behind it. **Antiques** shops are concentrated in the area around Fløibanen.

Outdoor Activities

Hiking The area surrounding Bergen has many possibilities for walking tours. Special maps are available from bookstores and from **Bergens Turlag** (touring club) (C. Sundtsqt. 3C, tel. 05/32-22-30), which arranges walking tours and maintains cabins for hikers.

Beaches

Nordnes sjøbad (seabath), near the aquarium, is a seaside resort with an outdoor heated pool. Take bus No. 4. Bergen does not have sandy beaches, and although it is possible to get to some swimming places by bus, they are not worth the trip.

Dining

Bergen is known more for its sights than for its food, but certain dishes have become synonymous with the city. *Bergensk fiskesuppe* (Bergen fish soup) is so well known that packets of dehydrated soup are even labeled "Bergen-style." Walk among the stalls at Fisketorget (fish market) and look for the heart-shaped fish cakes unique to Bergen. There's plenty to eat here, such as shrimp or smoked salmon rolls. Top it off with another local specialty, a *skillingsbolle*, a big cinnamon roll, sometimes with a custard center, but most authentic without. Highly recommended restaurants are indicated by a star ★.

Very Expensive

Bellevue. Established in 1899, this restaurant is on a hill overlooking the city; it has an elegant and formal dining room, with 18th-century-style furnishings. Poached salmon in the traditional manner is a specialty, along with fillet of deer with chantarelle mushrooms, but more modern dishes are also on the menu. There's a limited choice at lunch. In good weather, the patio is open for less formal meals. *Bellevuebakken 9, tel. 05/31–02–40. Reservations required. Jacket and tie required. AE, DC, MC, V. Closed weekends.*

Lucullus. The decor is not particularly inspiring, in spite of all the good art on the walls. Old-fashioned lace tablecloths don't go with chairs that look like they belong in a board room. But the food is always good. Sautéed monkfish with lobster sauce and rack of reindeer with blueberry sauce are two among many superb dishes. *Hotel Neptun, Walckendorfsgate 8, tel. 05/90–80–00. Reservations required. Jacket and tie required. AE, DC, MC, V. No lunch. Closed weekends.*

Expensive

Fiskekrogen. It's right on Fisketorvet, and in good weather you can sit outside for lunch. The fish soup is a meal in itself, and the appetizer plate is a sampling of specialties, from smoked shrimp to marinated moose. The most popular dish is the fish symphony, with two or three kinds of fish with lobster sauce and a garnish of shellfish. Meat-lovers should try the grilled moose or deer rib-eye steak with herb butter. *Zachariasbryggen, Fisketorget, tel. 05/31–75–66. Reservations required. Dress: casual. AE, DC, MC, V. No lunch Sept. 16–Apr.*

To Kokker. The name means two cooks, and that's what there are. It's on Bryggen, in a 300-year-old building complete with crooked floors. Try the aquavit-marinated reindeer with lingonberry sorbet or the sauteed monkfish with spinach and tomato sauce. Desserts feature local fruit and berries. *Enhjørningsgården, tel. 05/32–28–16. Reservations required. Dress: casual but neat. AE, DC, MC, V. Closed Sunday. No lunch.*

Moderate

Bryggestuen & Bryggeloftet. It's always full, upstairs and down. The menu's the same in both places, although only the first floor is authentically old. Poached halibut served with boiled potatoes and cucumber salad, a traditional favorite, is the specialty, but there's also sauteed ocean catfish with mushrooms and shrimp, as well as grilled lamb fillet. *Bryggen 6, tel. 05/31–06–30. Reservations advised. Dress: casual. AE, DC, MC, V.*

Munkestuen Cafe. With its five tables and red-and-white-check tablecloths, this mom-and-pop place looks more Italian than Norwegian. Try the monkfish with hollandaise sauce or the fillet of roedeer with morels. *Klostergaten 12, tel. 05/90–21–49. Reservations required. Dress: casual. AE, DC, MC, V. Closed Sat. and 3 weeks in July. No lunch.*

Inexpensive

Augusta and **Augustus.** You can't beat these two cafeterias under the same management for lunch or for cake and coffee in the afternoon. Vegetarians will be impressed by the number of salads and quiches, in addition to pâté and open-face sandwiches.

Augusta: C. Sundtsgate 24, tel. 05/23–00–25. No reservations. Dress: casual. Augustus: Galleriet, tel. 05/32–35–25. No reservations. Dress: casual. No credit cards.

Banco Rotto. The fanciest café in town used to be a bank. Depending upon the time of day, it changes its identity from café to restaurant to piano bar; it functions best at either end of the scale—as a lunch restaurant and a place to have a cup of coffee and cake in the afternoon, and as an evening spot with music and dancing Friday and Saturday nights. *Vågsalmenning 16, tel. 05/32–75–20. No reservations. Dress: casual. AE, DC, MC, V.*

Børskafe. What began as a beer hall in 1894 is now more of a pub, with hearty homemade food at reasonable prices. The corned beef with potato dumplings is served only on Thursday and Friday, while meat cakes with stewed peas and fried flounder plus the usual open-face sandwiches are always on the menu. Go somewhere else for dessert. *Strandgate 15, tel. 05/32–47–19. No reservations. Dress: casual. No credit cards. Closed Sun.*

Lodging

From June 20 through August 10, special summer double-room rates are available in 19 different Bergen hotels. Rooms can be reserved up to 48 hours in advance. All include breakfast. Highly recommended hotels are indicated by a star ★.

Moderate–Very Expensive

Hotel Admiral. This dockside warehouse from 1906, right on the water across Vågen from Bryggen, was converted into a hotel in 1987. The building is geometric Art Nouveau, but the small rooms are ordinary and don't live up to the potential of the building. The harborside restaurant, Emily, has a small but good buffet table. *C. Sundts Gate 9–13, 5004, tel. 05/32–47–30, fax 05/23–30–92. 95 rooms with bath or shower, 12 suites. Facilities: restaurant, bar. AE, DC, MC, V.*

Hotel Norge. Other hotels come and go, but the Norge stays. It's a traditional luxury hotel in the center of town, right by the park. The architecture is standard modern, with big rooms. Braathens SAFE's ticket office is on the premises, as well as the airport bus terminal. Many tours start here. *Ole Bulls Plass 4, 5012, tel. 05/21–01–00, fax 05/21–02–99. 348 rooms with bath, 12 suites. Facilities: 4 restaurants, 2 bars, nightclub, pool, fitness center, conference center, shops. AE, DC, MC, V.*

SAS Royal Hotel Bryggen. The hotel is behind the famous buildings at Bryggen, one story taller, with the same width and roof pitch, and very well designed. Finished in 1982, the smallish guest rooms, with their subdued woven spreads and dark wood beds, are beginning to look dated. More expensive rooms, on the top floor, have been refurbished. *Bryggen, 5003, tel. 05/31–80–00, fax 05/32–48–08. 267 rooms with bath, 7 suites. Facilities: 2 restaurants, 2 bars, nightclub, pool, fitness center, conference center. AE, DC, MC, V.*

Inexpensive–Moderate

Augustin Hotel. This small, family-run hotel, one block from the harbor, is just off the main pedestrian shopping street. The rooms are small but newly refurbished, and some overlook the harbor. The first-floor bistro offers simple meals, and the coffee shop, Augusta (*see* Dining, *above*), serves wonderful cakes. *Sundts Gate 24, 5004, tel. 05/23–00–24, fax 05/23–31–30. 38* *rooms with shower. Facilities: 2 restaurants, conference room. AE, DC, MC, V.*

Hotell Dreggen. Restored in 1990, this hotel is between Bergenshus Fortress and Bryggen Museum. It's basically a bed and breakfast, but other meals can be arranged. Virtually every room is a different size or shape, but all are furnished in light wood and pale-color textiles. The airport bus stops next door at the SAS Hotel. *Sandbrugt. 3, 5003, tel. 05/31–61–55, fax 05/31–54–23. 21 rooms with bath. Facilities: restaurant, bar, conference room. AE, DC, MC, V.*

Hotel Park. Near the university, this small family-run hotel is in a well-kept Victorian building. Both the public rooms and the guest rooms are furnished with antiques. The only disadvantage is that it's a 10-minute walk to downtown. *Harald Hårfagres Gate 35, 5000, tel. 05/32–09–60, fax 05/31–03–34. 21 rooms with bath. Facilities: restaurant, conference room. AE, V.*

Inexpensive

Fantoft Sommerhotell. This student dorm, 6 kilometers (3½ mile) from downtown, becomes a hotel from May 15 to August 20. Family rooms are available. Accommodation is simple but adequate. Take bus No. 18, 19, or 20 from the bus station to Fantoft. *5036 Fantoft, tel. 05/28–29–10, fax 05/28–07–70. 72 rooms with shower. Facilities: restaurant. AE, DC, MC, V.*

The Arts and Nightlife

The Arts

Bergen is known for its **Festspillene** (International Festival), held each year during the last week of May and the beginning of June. It features famous names in classical music, jazz, ballet, the arts, and theater. Tickets are available from the Festival Office at **Grieghallen** (Lars Hillesgate 3, 5015, tel. 05/32–04–00).

During the summer, the **Bjorgvin folk dance group** performs a one-hour program of traditional dances and music from rural Norway at Bryggens Museum. Tickets are sold at the tourist information center and at the door. *Bergen Folklore, Bryggen, tel. 05/24–89–29. Cost: NKr70. Performances June 24–Aug. 21, Mon. and Wed. at 8:30.*

A more extensive program is offered in an evening of folklore, with traditional wedding food, dances, and folk music, plus a concert, at the 800-year-old Fana Church. Tickets are sold at A/S Kunst (the Art Association, Torgalmenning 9) or at your hotel. Inquire about additional dates in May and September. The NKr160 cost includes dinner. *Fana Folklore, tel. 05/91–52–40. June 5–Aug. 31., Mon., Tues., Thurs., and Fri.*

Concerts are held at **Troldhaugen**, home of composer Edvard Grieg (*see* Tour 3, *above*), all summer. Tickets are sold at the tourist information center or at the door. Performances are given June 26–August 4, Wednesday and Sunday at 8; and September 1–October 15, Sunday at 1.

All movie theaters show films in the original language with subtitles.

Nightlife

Most nightlife centers around the harbor area. **Zachariasbryggen** is a restaurant and entertainment complex right on the water. **Kjøbmandsstuen** is a piano bar with a crowd on weekends. Otherwise, **Banco Rotto** (*see* Dining, *above*) is a popular place for Bergen's beautiful people. There's always live music on Friday and Saturday nights. The over-35's patronize the piano bar and club at the Hotel Norge and at the SAS Royal Hotel.

Bergensers love jazz, and a major jazz festival is held there in the third week in August. During the winter, **Bergen Jazz Forum** (Georgernes Verft 3, tel. 05/32–09–76) is the place, but it's closed much of the summer. For rock, **Hulen** (The Hole, Olav Ryesvei 47, tel. 05/32–32–87) has live music on weekends.

Bergen has an active gay community with clubs and planned events. **Homofil Bevegelse** (Movement Fosswinckels Gate 42 tel. 05/31–21–39) is open weekdays 7–10 PM.

Mountains and Valleys of the Interior

Introduction

Norwegians have a reputation for being independent and self-reliant, fostered by the isolation of small farming communities—usually extended families—on remote outposts with little communication. This also encouraged the development of dialects—each tiny area has its own speech patterns. Even with urbanization, weekenders from Oslo, and the concentration of population around industries, small farms remain, but now, many are worked part-time.

The southern part of the interior, around Hardangervidda, is prime vacation land for wilderness sports lovers, with fishing, canoeing, rafting, hiking, and horseback riding over the plateau in the summer, and skiing in the winter. The northern part turns to rolling hills and leafy forests, and the principal town, Lillehammer, attracts skiers from around the world to its slopes and trails; in 1994 it hosts the Winter Olympics. Next comes Peer Gynt country, Jotunheimen. The other-worldly quality of oblique northern light against wildflower-covered hills has inspired centuries of folk tales, and artists from Ibsen to Wagner. At the northern end of the region is the copper-mining town of Røros, which is on UNESCO's World Heritage List.

Important Addresses and Numbers

Tourist Information The main tourist offices of the region are in: **Geilo** (tel. 067/86–300); **Hamar** (Rådhuset, Strandgata 23, tel. 065/27–660); **Kongsberg** (Schwabes gate 1, tel. 03/73–15–26); **Lillehammer** (Jernbanegate 2, tel. 062/59–299); **Lom** (tel. 062/11–286); **Notodden** (Heddal Stave Church, tel. 036/12–022); **Øyer** (tel. 062/77–950); **Rjukan** (Torget 2, tel. 036/91–290); **Røros** (Bergmannsplassen, tel. 07/91–722) and **Skien** (Turistkontor, Henrik Ibsensgt. 2, tel. 03/52–82–27).

Arriving and Departing by Car, Train, and Bus

By Car On Route E18 from Oslo, the drive southeast to Kongsberg (84-kilometers/52-miles) takes a little over an hour. The wide, two-lane Route E6 north from Oslo passes through Hamar and Lillehammer. Route 3 follows Osterdalen (the eastern valley) north to Røros from Oslo, or Route 3 and E6 connect Røros with Trondheim, 156 kilometers (97 miles) farther north.

By Train The train from Oslo S to Kongsberg takes 1 hour and 25 minutes. There are good train connections between Oslo and the major interior towns to the north.

By Bus The many bus lines that serve the region are coordinated through Nor-Way Bussekspress in Oslo (Karl Johansgate 2, 0154 Oslo 1, tel. 02/33–08–62).

Getting Around

By Car Roads in the southern part of the interior region are open and flat, while those to the north become increasingly hilly and twisty as the terrain roughens into the central mountains. E18, E76, and 37 are the chief routes of the south; the northern end of the region is threaded by Routes E68, 51, E6, and 3.

By Train The only train service in the southern part of the region is the Oslo–Bergen line. The northern part is served by the Oslo–Trondheim line and two others.

By Bus Buses rarely run more than twice a day in the region, so get a comprehensive schedule from the tourist office or Nor-Way Bussekspress and plan ahead. There are good bus connections between Kongsberg and Notodden, Heddal, and Rjukan.

Exploring Mountains and Valleys of the Interior

Numbers in the margin correspond with points of interest on the Mountains and Valleys of the Interior map.

Tour 1: Central Norway The central part of the interior is outdoor country. Sports enthusiasts flock year round to Hardangervidda, Norway's great central plateau.

1 **Geilo** is the country's most popular winter resort, with miles of downhill slopes and cross-country trails. It has more recently become popular as a summer destination, with fishing, boating, hiking, and riding, although it still looks like a winter resort minus the snow, with wide, naked slopes and lonely lifts.

2 Geilo is the gateway to **Hardangervidda,** Europe's largest mountain plateau and Norway's biggest national park—10,000 square kilometers of unique scenery, with the largest herd of wild reindeer in Europe, and home to many birds and animals on the endangered list. It also has rich and varied flora, about 450 different species, partly due to the two different climates on the plateau—coastal on the western side, and inland to the east. The entire plateau is above the tree line, so Artic plants can be found here, in addition to some varieties of small pine trees from an earlier, warmer period in the swamps. Otherwise, it's mostly scrubby plants, still water, and rock. The moss from which the anti-rejection drug cyclosporin was developed was discovered on Hardangervidda. Many tourists use Geilo as their departure point for tours of the plateau, either on horseback or on foot. The area is marked with trails for all levels of proficiency, and along them, the Norwegian Touring Association (DNT) has built cabins at strategic intervals.

3 The western vidda settlement of **Finse** (which is on the Bergen railroad) is one of the most frigid places in southern Norway. Polar explorers Nansen and Scott tested their equipment here, and the snow scenes in the *Star Wars* movies were filmed in Finse. It, too, is a good starting point for tours of the vidda.

Mountains and Valleys of the Interior

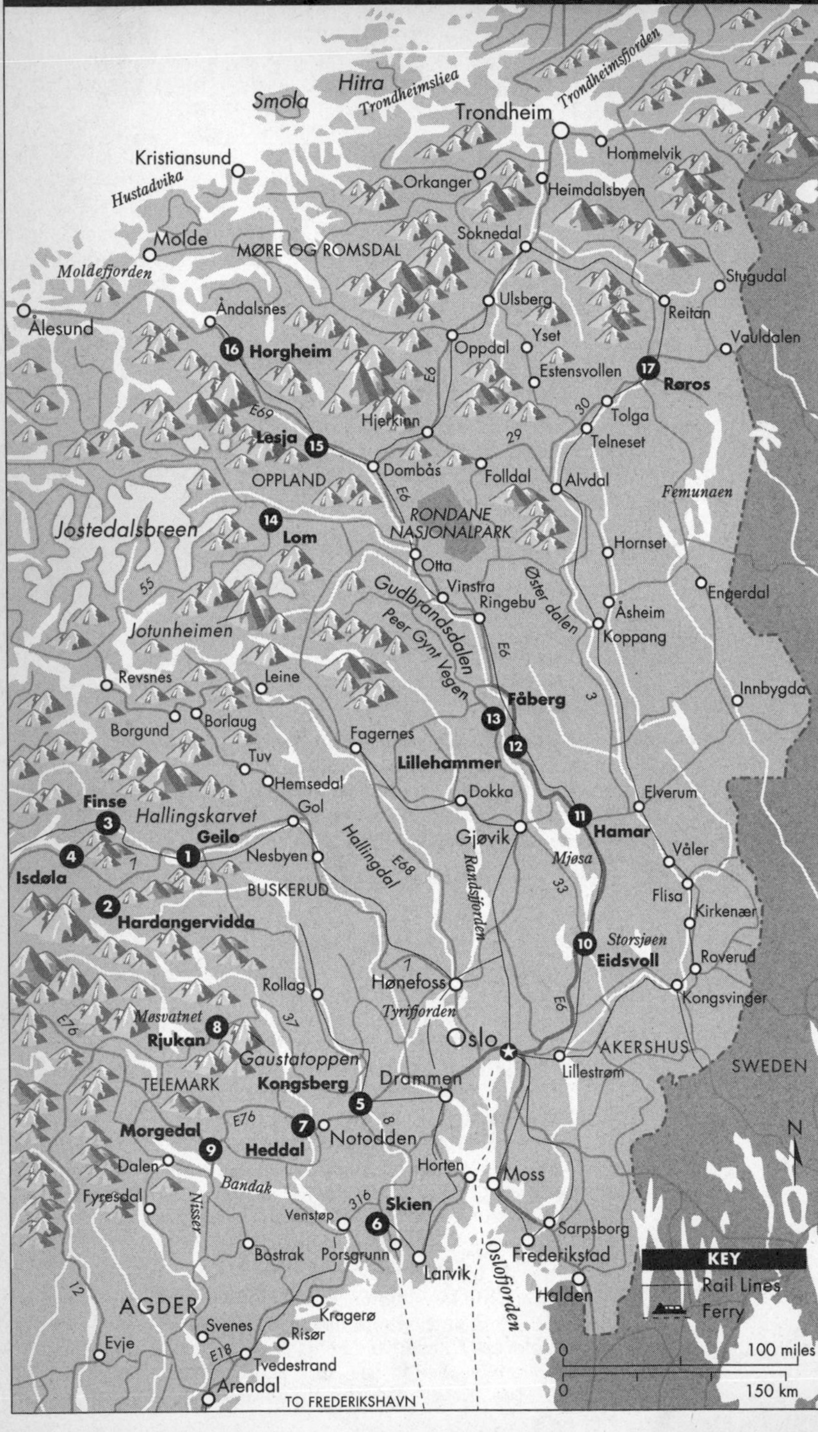

4 At the western end of vidda, 72 kilometers (44 miles) beyond Geilo, is **Isdøla,** at the junction of the 1-kilometer (it seems like 10) road to Fossli and Vøringfossen (falls), with a 145-meter vertical drop. The road down to the valley of Måbødalen was blasted into the mountain early in the century and had many hairpins and tunnels. It has been improved steadily, and now most of the difficult parts are tunneled. Cyclists and hikers can go down the side of the mountain to the base of the falls on the original trail, with 124 swings and 1,300 steps—it takes about 30 minutes—but it's not for amateurs.

At the base is the innermost arm of the **Hardangerfjord.** It's the least exciting, but still beautiful, with royal blue water and lush apple orchards.

Tour 2: Historic Kongsberg and Telemark

Kongsberg, Norway's first industrial town, rose to prominence because of the discovery there of silver in its purest form. The town of Rjukan was the site of the country's entrance into modern technology, in the form of hydroelectric power. Telemark is the birthplace of skiing as we know it today, as well as the birthplace of many ancestors to Norwegian-Americans, for the poor farmers of the region were among the first to emigrate to the United States during the 19th century.

5 **Kongsberg,** with 20,000 people, was Norway's silver town for more than 300 years. The world's largest deposits of pure silver have been found here, but now the mines are closed, although the Royal Mint is still going strong.

Norsk Bergverksmuseum (Norwegian Mining Museum) in the old smelting works, documents the development of silver mining and exhibits the pure silver along with gold, emeralds, and rubies from other Norwegian mines. The Royal Mint museum, in the same building, is a treasure trove for coin collectors, with a nearly complete assemblage of Norwegian coins. Children can pan for silver all summer. *Hyttegt. 3 tel. 03/73–12–75. Admission: NKr20 adults, NKr10 children, NKr15 senior citizens. Open May 18–June 30, Aug. 16–31, daily 10–4; July 1–Aug. 15, weekdays 10–6, weekends 10–4; Sept. 1–30, daily noon–4; Oct. 1–May 17, Sun. noon–4.*

The **Gruvene** (mines) are 8 kilometers (5 miles) outside town, toward Notodden. Guided mine tours include a 2.3-kilometer ride on the mine train into Kongensgruve (the King's mine) and a ride on the first personnel elevator. The temperature in the mine is about 7°C (43°F), so dress accordingly. *Admission: NKr30 adults, NKr20 children, NKr25 senior citizens. June–Aug. 15 departing daily at 11, 12:30 and 2; May 18–31 and Aug. 16–31, daily at 12:30. tel. 036/20–250.*

Kongsberg Kirke (church), finished in 1761, was built during the heyday of the silver mines, with an impressive gilded Baroque altar, organ, and pulpit all on one wall. It seats 3,000. The royal box and the galleries separated the gentry and mineowners from the workers. *Admission free. Open May 18–Aug. 31, guided tours lasting 45 min. on the hour, weekdays 10–4, Sat. 10–1. Sunday services at 11 with tours afterward until 1:30. Organ concerts Tues. and Fri. at 11 during July.*

Time Out

Peckels Resept (Peckels gt. 12), in the center of town, is a restaurant with a personality. It serves sandwiches and hot dishes, along with delicious cakes for lunch.

---

6 South of Kongsberg on Rte. 8 is **Skien,** the capital of the Telemark region. This town of 50,000 is best known as the birthplace of playwright Henrik Ibsen. The **Fylkesmuseet** (county museum), a manor house from 1780, has a collection of Ibsen memorabilia, including his study and bedroom and the "blue salon" from his Oslo flat (other interiors are at the Norsk Folkmuseum in Oslo). The museum also has an English garden from 1815 and a display of Telemark-style folk art, including rose painting and wood carving. *Ovregt. 41, tel. 03/52–35–94. Admission: NKr10 adults, NKr5 children. Garden open mid-May–Sept. daily 11–8. Museum open mid-May–mid-June, Tues.–Sat. 10–2, Sun noon–6; mid-June–Sept., Mon–Sat. noon–4, Sun. noon–6.*

Venstøp, 5 kilometers (3 miles) northwest of the city, looks just as it did when the Ibsen family lived there from 1835 to 1843. The attic was a setting in *The Wild Duck*. It is part of Skein's county museum. *Tel. 03/52–35–94. Admission: NKr10 adults, NKr5 children. Open June, Tues.–Sat. 10–2, Sun. noon–6; July–Sept., Tues.–Sat. noon–4, Sun. noon–6.*

7 **Heddal,** site of Norway's largest stave church, is 35 kilometers (20 miles) west of Kongsberg. The church dates from the middle of the 13th century and has exceptional animal-style ornament, along with grotesque human heads on the portals. *Tel. 036/20–250. Admission: NKr12. Open June 21–Aug. 20, Mon.–Sat. 6–7, Sun. 1–7; May 15–June 20, Aug. 21–Sept. 15, 10–5, Sun. 1–5. Sunday services at 11. July 1–Aug. 10, organ concerts Tues. and Fri. at 11.*

Route 37 northwest from Kongsberg to Rjukan passes the 6,200-foot **Gaustatoppen** mountain, a looming, snowstreaked
8 table of rock popular with hikers. The town of **Rjukan** may not ring a bell, but mention "heavy water," and anyone who lived through World War II or saw the film *The Heroes of Telemark* knows about the sabotage of the "heavy water" factory there, which thwarted German efforts to develop an atomic bomb.

Rjukan's history actually began in the decade between 1907 and 1916, when the population grew from a few hundred to 10,000, because of a different kind of water, hydroelectric power. Norsk Hydro, one of Norway's largest industries, which uses hydroelectric power for manufacturing chemicals and fertilizer, was started here.

It is also the site of northern Europe's first cable car, **Krossobanen,** built in 1928 by Hydro to transport people to the top of the mountain, where the sun shone year-round. After being closed for six years, it was reopened with new machinery in 1991. *Admission: NKr20 adults, one way, NKr10 children, senior citizens. Open June 30–Aug. 25 daily 10–7; May 1–June 30, Aug. 26–Sept. 30, daily 10–5; Oct. 1–Apr. 30, Fri.–Sun. 10–5.*

Heavy water was produced as a byproduct in the manufacture of fertilizer at **Vemork,** 6 kilometers (4 miles) west of town. A museum has been built at the site. Exhibits document both the development of hydroelectric power and the action that took place there during World War II. The first Saturday in July, the path of the saboteurs is retraced as a special event, but the 8-kilometer (5-mile) trail, starting at Rjukan Fjellstue (mountain lodge) and finishing at the museum, is marked and can be followed at any time. *Tel. 036/95–153. Admission: NKr 30* *adults, NKr 15 children. Open June 15–Aug. 24, daily 10–6; May 1–June 14, daily 10–4; Aug. 15–Sept. 30, weekdays 10–4, weekends 10–6; Oct. 1–31, weekends 11–4.*

9 Farther into the heart of Telemark is **Morgedal,** the birthplace of modern skiing. A hundred years ago, skiers used one long pole, held diagonally, much like high wire artists. Eventually, the use of two short poles became widespread, although purists feel that the one-pole version is the "authentic" way to ski.

The **Bjaaland Museum** in Morgedal is named for Olav Bjaaland, who was chosen for Amundsen's expedition to Antartica because he could ski in an absolutely straight line. The museum collections illustrate the development of the Telemark style of skiing. Also on display are Bjaaland's streamlined polar sled and his photographs of the expedition. One of Bjaaland's descendants runs the museum. *Opposite Morgedal Turisthotell, tel. 036/54156. Admission: NKr10 adults, NKr5 children. Open June–Aug. daily 10–5.*

Tour 3: Gudbrandsdal

The Gudbrandsdal (Gudbrand's valley) is one of Norway's longest, extending from Lake Mjøsa, north of Oslo, diagonally across the country to Åndalsnes. At the base of the lake is
10 **Eidsvoll,** where Norway's constitution was signed on May 17, 1814. Mjøsa was once thought to have a monster on the order of Loch Ness, and it's pictured on old maps.

11 E6 follows the lake halfway to **Hamar.** During the Middle Ages, Hamar was the seat of a bishopric, and part of the cathedral wall, with four Romanesque arches, remains the symbol of the city. During recent summers, Oslo University has sponsored digs around the cathedral precinct just outside town and have found thousands of artifacts, which are displayed nearby at **Hedmarkmuseet og Domkirkeodden** (the Hedmark Museum and Cathedral ruins). One of the museum's divisions is the Utvandrermuseum (Emigration museum), with two cabins brought back from Minnesota and North Dakota, along with letters and photographs documenting that period. *Tel. 065/21-304 and 31-166. Admission: NKr20 adults, NKr10 children. Open June 15–Aug. 18, daily 10–6; May 20–June 14, Aug. 19–Sept. 8, daily 10–4.*

12 The winter sport center of **Lillehammer,** with 22,000 inhabitants, is next. It will host the 1994 winter Olympics, a big challenge for such a small town. Lillehammer's facilities were no match for the demands of the games, and construction of arenas, as well as accommodation, is in full swing.

A highlight of Lillehammer's ski year is the Birkebeiner cross-country ski race, which commemorates the trek of two warriors, whose legs were wrapped in birchbark (hence *birkebeiner*—birch legs), across the mountains from Lillehammer to Osterdalen in 1205 to save the 18-month-old prince Håkon Håkonsson from his enemies. The race attracts 6,000 people annually.

Lillehammer claims fame as a cultural center as well. Sigrid Undset, who won the Nobel prize in literature, lived in the town for 30 years, and it is also the site of **Maihaugen,** Norway's oldest open-air museum, founded in 1887. In addition to more than 120 buildings from all over Norway, it has a main building with reconstructed artisan's workshops and the dental clinic of the museum's founder, Anders Sandvig. *Maihaugveien 1, tel.*

062/50–135. Admission: NKr35 adults, NKr15 children. Open June–Aug. 10–6; May, Sept. 10–4. Ticket includes guided tour.

13 At **Fåberg,** just north of Lillehammer, you can turn onto a scenic route, **Peer Gynt Vegen** (well marked), named after Ibsen's character. Peer traveled along the rolling hills sprinkled with old farmhouses and rich with views of the mountains of Rondane, Dovrefjell and Jotunheimen. The road is only slightly narrower and just 3 kilometers (1 mile) longer than the main route and passes two major resorts, **Skeikampen/Gausdal** and **Golå/Wadahl** before rejoining E6 at Vinstra.

From Vinstra, the road continues along the **Gundbrandsdal,** famous for goat cheese. If the sun is shining, the views of red farmhouses and lush green fields extending from the banks of the river valley up the sides of the mountains is impressive.

At Otta, Route 15 turns off for the 62-kilometer (38-mile) ride
14 to **Lom,** in the middle of **Jotunheimen** national park. It is a picturesque, rustic town, with log cabin architecture, a stave church from 1170, and plenty of decorative rose painting.

Lom stave church is on the main road. It is a mixture of old and new construction. The interior has a Baroque feel, for the pulpit, a large collection of paintings, pews, windows, and the gallery all date from that period. *Open May 1–Sept. 30, Mon.–Sat. 10–5, Sun. noon–5.*

Upper Gudbrandsdal has breathtaking scenery. The area
15 around **Lesja** is trout-fishing country; Lesjaskogvatnet, the lake, has a mouth at either end, so the current changes in the middle. The landscape becomes more dramatic with every mile, as jagged rocks loom up from the river, leaving the tiny settlement of **Marstein** without sun for five months of the year.

16 **Horgheim** used to have a gingerbread hotel for elegant early tourists to view **Trollveggen,** the highest overhanging vertical rockface in Europe. Now the tourists have been replaced by expert rock climbers from around the world. Åndalsnes, the end station on the railroad, is the perfect departure point for tours of Central Fjord Country.

Tour 4: Røros

At the northern end of the Østerdal, the long valley to the east
17 of Gudbrandsdalen, lies **Røros,** for more than 300 years a company town: Practically everyone who lived there was connected with the copper mines. The last mine in the region closed in 1986, but Norway's only mountain town has managed to survive, thanks to other industries, including tourism, especially after it was placed on UNESCO's World Heritage List.

The main attraction is the **old part of town,** with its 250-year-old workers' cottages, slag dumps, and managers' houses, one of which is now City Hall. Descendants of the man who discovered the first copper ore in Røros still live in the oldest of the nearly 100 protected buildings.

The tourist office has 75-minute guided tours of this part of town, starting at the information office and ending at the church. *Admission: NKr24 adults, NKr18 senior citizens and students, NKr12 children. Tours: June 1–21 and Aug. 19–Sept. 29, Mon.–Sat. at 11; June 22–Aug. 18, Mon.–Sat. at noon and 3, Sun. at 3.*

The **church,** which towers over all the other buildings in the town, is an eight-sided stone structure from 1784, with the mines' symbol on the tower. Inside, it can seat 1,600, impressive in a town with a population of only 3,500 today. Seating in the old days was according to rank, with a gallery to separate the managers from the masses. *Admission: NKr12 adults, NKr10 senior citizens, and students, NKr6 children. Open June 1–21 and Aug. 19–Sept. 29, weekdays 2–4, Sat. 11–1; June 22–Aug. 18, Mon.–Sat. 10–5.*

Olavsgruva (Olaf's mine), outside town, is now a museum. From June 30 to August 11, a bus leaves Røros daily except Saturday at 1 (Saturday at 10) and arrives at the mine about 25 minutes later. The trip back to town leaves at 2:30 (11:30). Bus tickets cost NKr50 adults, NKr25 children.

The guided tour of Olavsgruva takes visitors into the depths of the mine, complete with sound and light effects. Remember to bring warm clothing and good shoes, as the temperature below ground is about 5°C (41°F) year-round. *Admission: NKr32 adults, NKr24 senior citizens and students, NKr16 children. Guided tours June 1–21 and Aug. 19–Sept. 29, Mon.–Sat. at 1 and 3, Sun. at noon; June 22–Aug. 18, daily at 10:30, noon, 1:30, 3, 4:30, 6.*

Back in town, in the old smelting plant, is **Rørosmuseet** (the Røros museum), which documents the history of the mines, with working models in ¹⁄₁₀th scale demonstrating the methods used in mining. *Admission: NKr25 adults, NKr20 senior citizens, students, NKr12 children. Open May 1–June 9, Aug. 19–Dec. 31, weekdays 11–3:30, weekends 11–2; June 10–Aug. 18, weekdays 11–6, weekends 11–4.*

What to See and Do with Children

Eidfjord From Eidfjord, on the road to Bergen 18 kilometers (10 miles) beyond Isdøla, it's only 6 kilometers (4 miles) to **Sima power station,** built 700 meters into the mountain rock, completely hidden from view. It's as big as a 14-story building and generates 2.7 billion KwH of electricity per year. The plant tour, which includes a slide show, is especially interesting for children and gives understandable explanations about electricity. *Admission Free. Open June 20–Aug. 20. Guided tours daily at 10, noon, and 2.*

Hamar **Jernbanemuseet** (the Railway museum) documents the development of rail transportation in Norway, with locomotives and rolling stock on both normal and small gauge track. *Tertittoget,* NSB's last steam locomotive, gives rides from mid-May to mid-August. The oldest locomotive on display, "Caroline," was built by Robert Stephenson in 1861. Videos are shown in an old passenger car, and there's a café in Norway's oldest dining car. *Strandveien 132, tel. 065/21–560. Admission: NKr20 adults, NKr10 children. Open June 16–Aug. 18, daily 10–6; May 18–June 15, Aug. 19–Sept. 15, daily 10–4.*

Lillehammer **Hunderfossen park,** 13 kilometers (8 miles) north of Lillehammer, has rides and a petting zoo for small children, plus an energy center, with Epcot-influenced exhibits about oil and gas (big business in Norway) and a 5-screen theater for everyone. There's also the world's biggest troll. *2638 Fåberg, tel. 062/77–222. Admission: NKr adults, NKr80 children, senior citi-*

zens. Open June 22–Aug. 18, daily, 10–8; June 1–21, daily 10–4.

Two kilometers beyond Hunderfossen is **Lilleputthammer,** a miniature version of Lillehammer as it looked at the turn of the century, complete with animated figures in period dress. There are also rides, a swimming pool, and Europe's only water discothèque. *Øyer Gjestegård, 2636 Øyer, tel. 062/77–335. Admission to Lilleputthammer: NKr30. Open June 22–Aug. 18, daily 10–7. Admission to swimming complex: NKr40. Open daily 10–9.*

Off the Beaten Track

Geilo About 35 kilometers (21 miles) northeast of Geilo on Rte. 7 is **Torpo,** site of a stave church dating from the late 12th century. It is known for its colorful painted ceiling, decorated with scenes from the life of St. Margaret. *Open June–Aug., daily 9:30–5:30.*

South of Geilo on Route 8, in the little town of Dagali, is an 1850 wood church designed by Hans Ditlev Linstow (1787–1851) architect of the Royal Palace in Oslo. The Dagali Museum has assembled a collection of farm buildings typical of the mid-18th century. *3588 Dagali, tel. 067/87–722. Open June 28–Aug. 20, daily 10–3.*

Lillehammer The composer of Norway's national anthem and the 1903 Nobel prize winner in literature, Bjørnstjerne Bjørnson lived at **Aulestad,** in Gausdal, 18 kilometers (11 miles) northwest of Lillehammer, from 1875 until he died in 1910. After his wife, Karoline, died in 1934, their house was opened as a museum. He was a central literary, cultural, and political figure in Scandinavia, and his home is representative of the lifestyle of the cultural elite at the turn of the century. *2620 Follebu, tel. 062/20–326. Admission: NKr20 adults, NKr10 children, senior citizens. Open July, daily 10–5:30; June, Aug., daily 10–3:30; Sept., daily 11–2:30.*

Hamar Take a ride on the world's oldest paddleboat, 130-year-old ***Skibladner,*** also called the "white swan of the Mjøsa," which connects the towns along the lake. The schedule is complicated, with only three stops a week in Eidsvoll and Lillehammer, but three stops daily three times a week in Gjøvik. Ask for a schedule from tourist information or the *Skibladner* office. *Grønnegt. 11, 2, 300 Hamar, tel. 065/27–085. June 15–Aug. 10.*

The childhood home of Wagnerian opera star **Kirsten Flagstad,** who died in 1963, is now a museum, with pictures, costumes, and a sound-studio where her recordings can be heard. *Strandgt. 23, tel. 065/27–660. Admission: NKr10 adults, NKr5 children. Open June 15–Aug. 18, Tues.–Sun. 10–4, closed Mon.*

Skien From Skien, you can take boat tours on the **Telemark waterways,** a combination of canals and natural lakes between Skien and either **Dalen** or **Notodden.** (For trips to Dalen, contact Telemarkreiser, tel. 03/52–95–05; Notodden is served by Telemarksbåtene, 3812 Akkerhaugen, tel. 03/95–82–11, fax 03/95–82–96.)

The trip to Dalen takes you through **Ulefoss,** the center of the ice block trade before the days of refrigeration, and also the site of **Ulefoss Jernverk** (iron foundry), started in 1657. The boats go through multiple locks to pass the falls at Ulefoss. You can leave the boat and visit **Ulefoss Manor,** which dates from 1807, and is considered the finest example of neoclassical architecture in Norway. It has recently been restored and is open to the public. *Ulefoss, tel. 03/94–44–36.*

Shopping

Kongsberg **Bergkrystallen** (Kirkegt. 21, tel. 03/72–45–45) has a good selection of minerals, along with Kongsberg silver and standard souvenirs.

Lillehammer At **Reidun's Rosemaling og Brukskunst** (Storgt. 84A, tel. 062/58–450) you can watch Reidun at work in her studio. In addition to her own rosepainted articles, she sells local wood carving, ceramics, and knitwear.

Sports and Outdoor Activities

Telemark country is a popular destination for summer sports—**horseback rides** over Hardangervidda, **canal rides, fishing, hiking,** and **boating.** Contact Rjukan Tourist Office or **Telemarkreiser** (tel. 03/52–92–05).

Skiing **Telemark** is famous as the cradle of skiing, and the region is a center for ski touring. Just to the north, **Geilo** (24 km/15 mi of Alpine pistes, 130 km/81 mi of cross-country trails; 18 ski lifts) and **Hemsedal** (34 km/21 mi of Alpine slopes, 175 km/108 mi of cross-country trails; 12 ski lifts), together with several nearby areas, offer hundreds of miles of Alpine and cross-country trails along with comfortable, modern facilities. **Lillehammer,** north of Oslo, the 1994 Winter Olympics town, is another major skiing center (20 km/12 mi of Alpine, 400 km/248 mi of cross-country trails; 7 ski lifts). **Beitostolen,** on the southern slopes of the Jotunheim range, has everything from torchlit night skiing to paragliding (9 km/5 mi of downhill slopes, 150 km/93 mi of cross-country trails; 7 ski lifts). At the northern end of the region is **Oppdal** (45 km/27 miles of Alpine pistes, 186 km/115 mi of cross-country trails; 10 ski lifts), another World Cup venue. Like most other areas, it has lighted trails and snowmaking equipment.

Dining and Lodging

Highly recommended establishments are indicated by a star ★.

Elveseter
Dining and Lodging
Elveseter Hotell. Staying at this family-owned hotel is like living in a museum. Imagine a swimming pool in a barn dating from 1579. Every room has a history, and doors and some walls have been painted by local artists. In the public rooms are museum-quality paintings and antiques. There's no place like it. *2687 Bo[accent]verdalen, tel. 062/12–000, fax 062/12–101. 90 rooms with bath or shower. Facilities: 2 restaurants, bar, swimming pool, conference rooms, parking. No credit cards. Closed Sept. 25–May 31. Inexpensive.*

Geilo
Dining and Lodging
Dr. Holms Hotell. Others cost more and are fractionally more elegant, but the decisive factor in choosing a mountain hotel is the food. Dr. Holms wins hands down, thanks to the chef, Jim Weiss, who trained at the Stanford Court in San Francisco, and

who has made the gourmet restaurant (not to be confused with the dining room) worth a special trip. His game sausages are full of flavor, and his butterscotch pudding with crunchy topping is sensational. *3580, tel. 067/85–622, fax 067/86–620. 110 rooms with bath or shower, 14 suites. Facilities: 2 restaurants, 2 bars, nightclub, fitness room, swimming pool, conference center, garage. AE, DC, MC, V. Moderate.*

Kongsberg
Dining and Lodging

Grand. A statue of Kongsberg's favorite son, Olympic ski-jumper Birger Ruud, stands in the park in front of this modern, centrally located hotel. All rooms were refurbished in 1990. *Kristian Augustsgate 2, 3600, tel. 03/73–20–29, fax 03/73–41–29. 92 rooms with bath or shower, 2 suites. Facilities: 2 restaurants, 2 bars, nightclub, fitness room, swimming pool, conference rooms, parking. AE, DC, MC, V. Inexpensive–Moderate.*

Lillehammer
Dining and Lodging

Hammer Hotel. The Home Hotel chain opened their newest property near Maihaugen open-air museum in August 1991. It's named after the old Hammer farm, which first opened its doors to guests in 1665. The rooms are furnished in shades of green with oak furniture, both modern and rustic. As at other Home Hotels, free beer, waffles, and an evening meal are included in the price. *Storgt. 108, 2600, tel. 062/63–500, fax 062/63–730. 71 rooms with shower. Facilities: fitness room, conference center, garage. AE, DC, MC, V. Moderate–Expensive.*

Lillehammer Hotel. A 5-minute walk from Maihaugen, the hotel has the prime location for the Olympics—next door to Olympic Park, the hub of the games. The rooms are big but anonymous. *Turisthotellun. 27B, 2600, tel. 062/54–800, fax 062/57–333. 166 rooms with bath or shower. Facilities: 2 restaurants, bar, nightclub, fitness room, 2 swimming pools, parking. AE, DC, MC, V. Moderate–Expensive.*

Lom
Dining and Lodging

Fossheim Turisthotell. Arne Brimi's cooking has made this hotel famous. He's a self-taught champion of the local cuisine, whose dishes are based on nature's kitchen, with liberal use of game, wild mushrooms, and berries. Anything with reindeer is a treat in his hands, and his thin crisp wafers with cloudberry parfait make a lovely dessert. *2686, tel. 062/11–105, fax 062/11–510. 54 rooms with bath or shower. Facilities: restaurant, bar, parking. AE, DC, MC, V. Inexpensive–Moderate.*

Oppdal
Dining and Lodging

Oppdal Hotell. The 1970s-style concrete and glass sloped-front addition blights a fine brick building, but inside, it improves. The public rooms are overdecorated, but the bedrooms are understated, small but tastefully furnished, with light wood and pale woven textiles. It's basically a resort, with sports year-round. *O. Skasliens v., 7340, tel. 074/21–111, fax 074/20–824. 75 rooms with bath or shower. Facilities: 2 restaurants, bar, nightclub, fitness center, conference center, parking. AE, DC, MC, V. Inexpensive–Moderate.*

Øyer
Dining and Lodging

Hafjell Hotell. The largest hotel between Oslo and Trondheim, near the Olympic alpine facilities, opens in the spring of 1992. It is built in a modern, yet rustic Norwegian style. Stig Søvik, one of Norway's finest chefs, will prepare updated versions of Norwegian classics at the restaurant. *2636, tel. 062/77–777. All rooms with bath. Facilities: restaurant, bar, parking. AE, DC, MC, V. Moderate–Expensive.*

Rjukan
Dining and Lodging

Gaustablikk Høfjellshotell. Built at the foot of Gaustadtoppen mountain 15 kilometers (9 miles) from Rjukan, this modern timber hotel is a popular ski resort, with seven downhill slopes and 80 kilometers (50 miles) of cross-country trails. In the summer, these marked trails are perfect for walks and hikes. *3660, tel. 036/91–422, fax 91–975. 78 rooms with bath or shower, 13 suites. Facilities: restaurant, bar, nightclub, fitness room, swimming pool, parking. AE, DC, MC, V. Moderate.*

Park Hotell. This newly refurbished hotel is in the center of town. The rooms are tastefully decorated in light colors. *Sam Eydes gt. 67, 3660, tel. 036/90–288, fax 036/90–505. 39 rooms with bath or shower. Facilities: restaurant, bar, nightclub. AE, DC, MC, V. Moderate.*

Røros
Dining and Lodging

Bergstadens Turisthotel. The rooms have dark wood furniture and somewhat outdated brown and beige textiles. The lobby is big but anonymous, but when there's a fire in the stone fireplace, it can be cozy. The main draw here is the dining room: Chef Kjell Sund recently was praised for his menu during a royal visit. He sticks to local traditions and products—fish from mountain streams and berries from the nearby forest. *Osloveien 2, 7460, tel. 07/41–11–11, fax 07/41–01–55; 76 rooms with bath or shower, 2 suites. Facilities: 2 restaurants, bar, nightclub, pool, conference center. AE, DC, MC, V. Moderate.*

Skien
Dining

Boden Spiseri. In the 1970s, Norwegians began their love affair with pepper steak, with crushed black pepper and maybe some green peppercorns in the sauce. Boden serves an excellent version, but it also has Norwegian-style food, such as medallions of reindeer. For dessert, the cream-puff swan filled with ice cream and covered with chocolate sauce is a delight. *Landbrygga 5, tel. 03/52–61–70. Dress: casual. AE, DC, MC, V. No lunch. Moderate.*

Kaffestove. For a homey meal, served cafeteria-style (no service charges), the Farmers' Organization's restaurants always give good value. The menu at all restaurants of this type features Norwegian standards, like *kjøttkaker* (meat cakes), and *medisterkaker* (pork patties) served with *surkål* (Norwegian-style sauerkraut with caraway seeds). *Prinsessegt. 7, tel. 03/52–00–30. Dress: casual. No credit cards. Inexpensive.*

Dining and Lodging

Rica Ibsen. Built in 1979, it's an early (for Norway) adventure into postmodern design. Standard rooms are of medium size, but some of the textiles are ghastly. Its excellent restaurant, Suzannah, serves modern Norwegian food. *Kongensgt. 33, 3700, tel. 03/52–49–90, fax 03/52–61–86. 119 rooms with bath. Facilities: 2 restaurants, 2 bars, nightclub, pool, business/conference center. AE, DC, MC, V. Inexpensive–Expensive.*

Lodging

Høyers Hotell. Near the market square, the old-fashioned character of its "Grand Hotel" exterior, all cornices and pedimented windows, extends into the Hoyers's lobby, which is an incongruous mixture of old and new. The rooms are modern and light, thanks to the big old windows. *Kongensgt. 6, 3700, tel. 03/52–05–40, fax 03/52–26–08. 69 rooms with bath, 1 suite. Facilities: restaurant, bar, nightclub, conference center. AE, DC, MC, V. Inexpensive–Moderate.*

The Arts

Bø i Telemark

During the second week in August Bø holds its annual **Telemarksfestival** for international folk music and dancing, featuring musicians and dancers from distant lands as well as Norwegian and Sami artists.

Nearly every weekend during the summer there's entertainment at **Telemark Sommanlier** in Bø—everything from gospel singers to jazz.

Kongsberg Every June, jazz fans descend on Kongsberg for its annual **jazz festival.**

Skien Henrik Ibsen's home town celebrates its favorite son every August with the **Ibsen-kultur-festival,** which includes concerts as well as drama (Box 608, 3701, Skien, tel. 03/58–1000).

Central Fjord Country

Introduction

To many, the word *fjord* is synonymous with Norway. Three things are needed to create a fjord: a mountain range, a river bed, and an Ice Age. These three elements came together in Norway a million years ago. Near the coast, the ice cap was relatively thin, while inland, it was proportionately thicker and much heavier. Where rivers had already dug valleys, the weight of the ice continued to burrow deeper, sometimes as far beneath sea level as the rocky mountains towered above it. That's why the mouths of the fjords are shallow, while in the interior, they can be 4,000 feet deep. Although they sometimes look like wide rivers or lakes, fjords are arms of the sea and are made up of salt water, so that except for the remotest branches, with brackish water, they don't freeze. Because fjords extend so far inland and are relatively narrow and always very deep, they appear to be still, like deep blue mirrors. There's no tide worth mentioning, so the water line seldom changes and trees grow right at water level. The abrupt change from bright green vegetation or the vertical drop from the mountains to the absolutely flat and unmoving surface of the water adds to the dramatic effect.

Fjord Norway is more than just water and snow-capped mountains. It also encompasses islands and deep valleys with isolated farms, for some of the most fertile land lies along the water. Sheep and goats graze on the scrubby plants higher up the sides of the mountains.

The farther north one travels, the more rugged and wild the landscape. Sognefjord is the longest, extending 190 km (110 mi) inland and the deepest, at 1220 meters (4000 feet). It's so deep and still that the water appears almost black. Some sections are so narrow, with gray rock looming on either side, that they look as if someone had sliced through the mountains with a giant knife. Branching off the Sognefjord are the narrow Nærøyfjord and the Aurlandsfjord, with an austere mountain setting.

At the top of Sogn and Fjordane county are a succession of fjords referred to as Nordfjord, with Jostedalsbreen, mainland Europe's largest glacier, to the south. Sunnfjord is the coastal area between Nordfjord and Sognefjord, with Florø, the county seat on an island close to Norway's westernmost point.

The mountains of Møre ag Romsdal county are treeless moonscapes of gray rock, stone cliffs that hang out over the water far below. It also has some of the highest waterfalls in the country, feeding into cold lakes and fjords. Geirangerfjord is the most spectacular, with a road zig-zagging all the way down from the mountaintops to the water alongside a famous waterfall.

Tourists have been visiting central fjord country ever since the English "discovered" the area some 150 years ago in their search for the ultimate salmon. One of these tourists was Kaiser Wilhelm, who spent every summer but one, from 1890 to 1913, in Molde, and who contributed to the rebuilding of Ålesund after its disastrous fire in 1904, which left 10,000 people homeless. That's why one of the city streets bears his name.

Important Addresses and Numbers

Tourist Information **Ålesund** (Rådhuset, tel. 071/21–202); **Åndalsnes** (corner Nesgata/Romsdalsvn., tel. 072/21–622); **Balestrand** (dockside, tel. 056/91–255); **Flåm** (railroad station. tel. 056/32–106); **Geiranger** (dockside, tel. 071/63–099); **Hellesylt** (dockside, tel. 071/65–052); **Loen** (tel. 057/77–677); **Lærdal** (tel. 056/66–509); **Molde** (Storgata 1, tel. 072/54–330); **Olden** (tel. 057/73–126); **Stryn** (tel. 057/71–526); **Ulvik** (dockside, tel. 05/52–63–60); **Voss** (Voss Tinghus, tel. 05/51–17–16).

Emergencies *Ålesund* **Police,** tel. 071/21–321. **Ambulance,** tel. 001. **Hospital Emergency Rooms**/Doctors/Dentists, tel. 071/23–348. **Car Rescue,** tel. 071/41–833.

Late-night Pharmacies *Ålesund* **Nordstjernen** (Kaiser Wilhelmsgt. 22, Ålesund, tel. 071/25–945) is open Wednesday until 6 and Saturday and Sunday from 6 to 8.

Arriving and Departing by Plane

Ålesund's **Vigra** airport is 15 km (9 mi) from the center of town. Braathens SAFE (tel. 071/25–800 Ålesund, 071/83–245 Vigra) has nonstop flights from Oslo, Bergen, Trondheim and Bodø. It's a 25-minute ride from Vigra to town with Flybussen, which stops at the Braathens SAFE office and at the main bus terminal. Tickets cost NKr50. Buses are scheduled according to flights—they leave the airport about 10 minutes after all arrivals and leave town about 60 or 70 minutes before each flight.

Arriving and Departing by Car, Train, and Bus

By Car From Oslo, it is 570 kilometers (353 miles) via route E6 to Dombås and then E69 via Åndalsnes to Ålesund. The well-maintained two-lane road is inland to Åndalsnes and then follows the coastline out to Ålesund.

The 340-km (210-mi) drive from Bergen to Ålesund covers some of the most breathtaking scenery in the world. Roads are narrow two-lane much of the time; Passing is difficult, and during the height of summer, the line of campers seems endless.

By Train The **Raumabanen** between Oslo S and **Åndalsnes** runs three times daily in each direction for the 6½-hour ride. At Åndalsnes, buses wait outside the station to pick up passengers for points not served by the train. The 124-km (76-mi) trip to Ålesund takes close to two hours.

By Boat **Hurtigruten** (the coastal steamer) stops at Skansekaia in **Ålesund,** northbound at 12:30 PM, departing at 2:15, and stops southbound at midnight, departing at 1. A catamaran runs between Ålesund and Molde at least twice daily.

Getting Around

By Car Ferries are a way of life in western Norway, but they seldom are big enough or run often enough during the summer, causing built-in delays. In high season, the lines of cars waiting for ferries can be long. Some hassle can be eliminated by reserving ahead, as cars with reservations get to board first.

By Bus Every place worth visiting is on a bus route. The tourist office has information about do-it-yourself tours by bus to the outlying districts. Three local bus companies serve **Ålesund;** all buses depart from the terminal on Kaiser Wilhelms gate.

By Boat In addition to regular ferries to nearby islands, boats connect Ålesund with other points along the coast. Excursions by boat are available through the tourist information office.

Guided Tours

Orientation A one-hour guided stroll through **Ålesund,** concentrating mostly on the art nouveau buildings, departs from Skansekaia (coastal steamer dock) Saturday at 12:15 and Tuesday at 4 from June 15 to August 10.

Special-interest
Cruises The ***M/S Geirangerfjord*** (tel. 071/63–007) offers 105-minute guided mini-cruises (at 10, 1, 3, 5 and 8) on the Geirangerfjord. Tickets are sold at the dock in **Geiranger.**

Flying Firdafly A/S (tel. 057/65–388), based in **Sandane,** offers air tours over Jostedalsbreen. Hotel Alexandra in Loen (*see* Lodging, *below*) arranges group flights.

Hiking **Aak Fjellsport** (mountain sport) Center, in **Åndalsnes** (tel. 072/26–444) specializes in walking tours of the area, from rambling in the hills for beginners and hikers, to full-fledged rock-climbing, along with rafting in the Rauma river. These are the guys who hang out of helicopters to rescue injured climbers, so they know what they're doing. Out of season, they train oil rig personnel.

From Easter through September, **Jostedalen Breførerlag** (5828 **Gjerde,** tel. 056/83–273) offers a number of glacier tours, from an easy 1½-hour family trip on the Nigard branch (equipment is provided) to advanced glacier courses with rock and ice climbing.

Rafting **Hans J. Starheim** (tel. 071/25–305) offers deep-sea rafting tours around **Ålesund,** to the islands in the outer fjord, and to the bird island of Runde.

Exploring Central Fjord Country

The best way to see fjord country is to make an almost circular tour—from Oslo to Åndalsnes, out to the coastal towns of Ålesund, Molde, and Kristiansund, then over Trollstigveien to Geiranger, a ferry to Hellesylt, down to Stryn, around Loen and Olden and through the sub-glacial tunnel to Fjærland, a ferry to Balestrand, connecting to another ferry down to Flåm, where the railroad connects to Myrdal on the Bergen line (*see*

Excursions from Bergen, *above*). Then the trip can either continue on to Bergen or back to Oslo.

Numbers in the margin correspond with points of interest on the Central Fjord Country map.

Tour 1: Åndalsnes and the Coast

1 **Åndalsnes,** a town with about 3,000 people, has three things going for it—as the last stop on the railroad, it is a gateway to fjord country; **Trollstigveien** (the Trolls' Path), one of Europe's most fantastic zig-zag roads, starts here; and **Trollveggen** (the Trolls' Wall), the highest sheer rock wall in Europe (1,000 meters, 3,300 feet), which attracts climbers from around the world, is just outside of town.

The view from anywhere in Åndalsnes is spectacular: the mountains—the King, the Queen, the Bishop and Romsdalshorn—form a gray rock landscape against the sky. Trollveggen, with jagged points straight up, is just behind them.

2 While Åndalsnes is the closest town to the fjords, **Ålesund,** 124 kilometers (76 miles) west along the coast, is the nearest city, with 35,000 inhabitants. Built on three islands between two bright blue fjords, it is worth a visit in its own right for its art nouveau core. Nearly 800 buildings in the center of town were destroyed by fire in 1904, and that area was rebuilt in the prevailing style, art nouveau, but with a Nordic/Germanic character, less sinuous, more solid, with turrets and dragonhead decoration. The walking street, Kongensgate, which starts near the coastal steamer dock, and Løvenvoldgata, the last intersecting street before St. Olavs Plass on the eastern side of Brosundet, are both lined with important examples of the style.

Ålesund also has one of Norway's largest harbors for exporting both dried and fresh fish and is a center for fish processing, as the majority of the country's salmon farms are in the area.

You can drive or ride a bus (tel. 071/26–582) up nearby Aksla mountain to a vantage point, **Kniven** (the knife), for a splendid view of the city.

Time Out **Fjellstua,** a modern lodge at the very top of the mountain, has a terrace with a cafeteria, where the view is especially good.

Near Ålesund is **Runde,** Norway's southernmost major bird rock, one of the largest in Europe, and a breeding ground for some 130 species, including puffins, gannets, and shags. The island is otherwise known for the "Runde Hoard," 1,300 kg of silver and gold coins, which were retrieved from a Dutch ship that sank in 1725. The catamaran leaves from Skateflua quay (on the other side of the coastal steamer dock) for the 25-minute trip to Hareid, where it connects with a bus for the 50-kilometer (31-mile) trip to Runde. There is a path from the bus stop to the nature reserve. It is also possible to sail around the rock on the yacht *Charming Ruth,* which leaves from Ulsteinvik at 11 on Wednesday and Sunday.

3 North of Ålesund, **Molde,** often called the "city of roses," is best known for the yearly jazz festival at the end of July, when big names from around the world get together for a huge jam session. Tickets can be purchased at all post offices in Norway.

Central Fjord Country

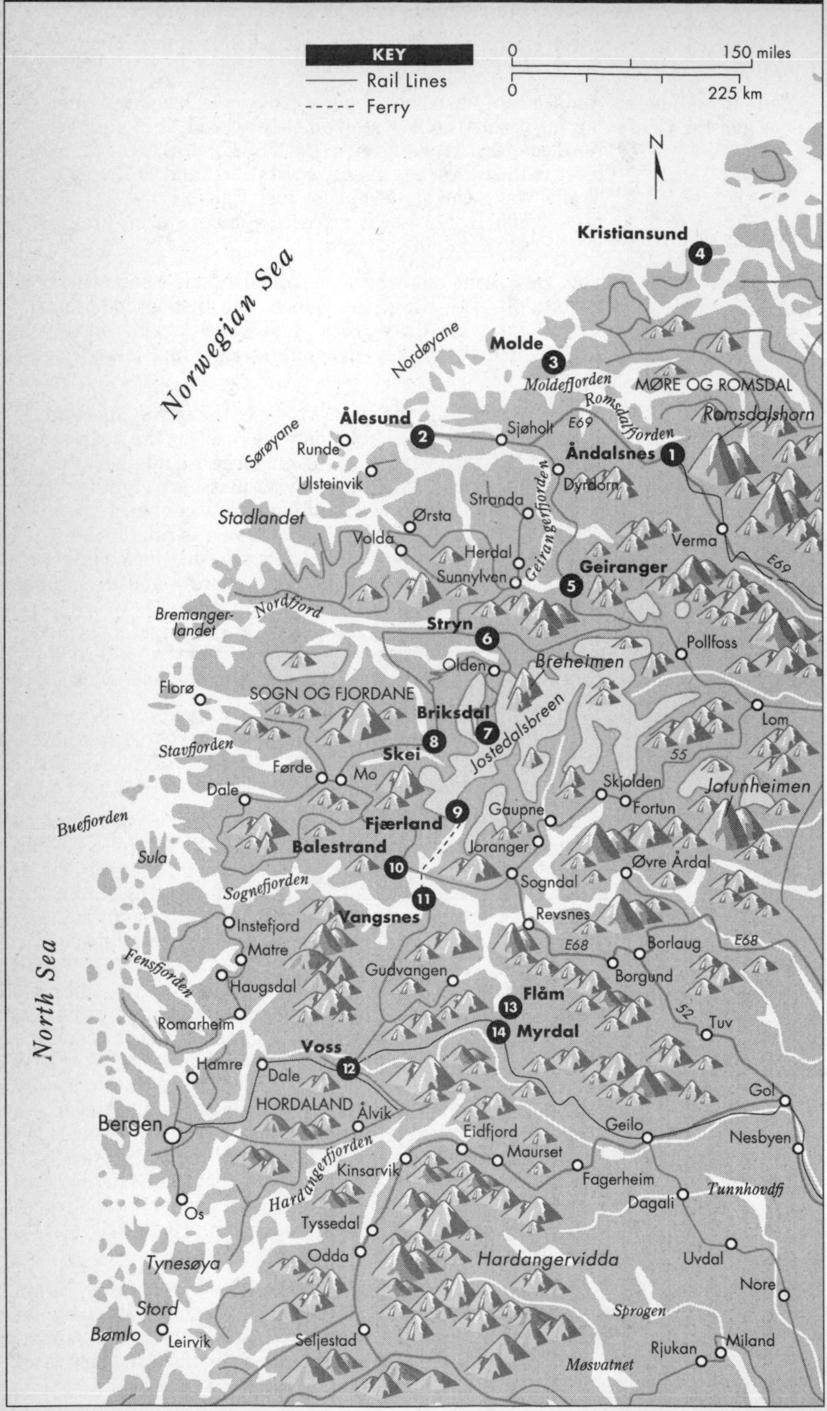

While Molde is a modern town, rebuilt almost entirely after it
4 was bombed during World War II, **Kristiansund** lives more in tune with the past and celebrates its 250th birthday in 1992. Although much of Kristiansund also was destroyed during the war, the historic area around Vågen, the harbor, was spared. Many buildings have been preserved intact, including **Woldbrygga,** a cooper's (barrelmaker) workshop from 1875 to 1965, with its original equipment still operational. *Admission: NKr10 adults, NKr5 children. Open weekdays 2–4, Sun. 1–4.*

Tour 2: Geirangerfjord to Sognefjord

Geiranger is the ultimate fjord, Norway at its most dramatic, with the finest sightseeing in the wildest nature compressed into a relatively small area. The mountains lining the Geiranger fjord tower 2,000 meters above sea level. The most scenic route to Geiranger is the two-hour drive along routes 63 and 58 over **Trollstigen** (the Troll path) from Åndalsnes. This road took 100 men 20 summers (from 1916 to 1936) to build, in a constant fight against rock and water. Trollstigveien and Ørneveien (at the Geiranger end) zig-zag over the mountains separating two fjords. They're open only during the summer, but there's enough snow for skiing well into July. Trollstigveien has 11 giant hairpin turns, each one blasted from solid rock. Halfway up, the spray from **Stigfoss** (Stig falls) blows across the bridge.

Time Out

Trollstigen Fjellstue, near the top of Trollstigveien, is a good place to stop for a snack. The countryside is barren and treeless, but inside the lodge, it's cozy and rustic. The *medisterkaker* with *surkål* (mild sausage cakes with sauerkraut flavored with caraway) is a good, hearty meal—be sure to pick up a little tub of *tyttebær* (lingonberry jelly).

---

5 Ørneveien (the Eagles' Road), down to **Geiranger,** completed in 1952, with 11 hairpin turns, leads directly to the fjord. The 16-kilometer-long, 300-meter deep Geirangerfjord's best-known attractions are its waterfalls—the Seven Sisters, the Bridal Veil and the Suitor—and the abandoned farms at **Skageflå** and **Knivsflå,** which are visible (and accessible) only by boat (*see* Guided Tours, *above*). No wonder the farms were abandoned—imagine carrying everything needed in a household from a boat practically 250 meters straight up to get to Skageflå!

If you continue on to Stryn, take the ferry across Geiranger fjord to Hellesylt, a 75-minute ride. It's about 50 km (30 mi) from Hellesylt to Stryn on Route 60. Stryn, Loen, and Olden, at the eastern end of Nordfjord, were among the first tourist
6 destinations more than 100 years ago. **Stryn** is famous for its salmon river, and now there's a summer ski center, while Loen and Olden are starting points for expeditions to branches of Europe's largest glacier, **Jostedalsbreen.**

7 **Briksdal** is the most accessible arm of the Jostedal glacier. Take a bus (from Stryn, Loen or Olden) or drive to Briksdalsbre Fjellstove. The glacier is a 45-minute walk from the end of the road, or you can ride there with pony and trap, as tourists did 100 years ago. Local guides lead tours (*see* Guided Tours, *above*) over the safe parts of the glacier. These perennial ice masses are more treacherous than they look, for there's always the danger of calving (breaking off), and deep crevasses are not always visible.

Time Out **Briksdalsbre Fjellstove** celebrates its 100th anniversary in 1992. Stop at the gift shop and cafeteria (delicious homemade cakes), or spend the night at the modern lodge.

It is also possible to visit the **Kjenndal** arm of the glacier on the *M/B Kjenndal* (tel. 057/77–660), which departs from Sande, near Loen. It sails down the 14-kilometer (9-mile) arm of the lake under mountains covered by protruding glacier arms and past Ramnefjell (Ramne mountain), scarred by rock slides, to **Kjenndalsbreen Fjellstove.** A bus runs from the lodge (which serves excellent trout) to the glacier.

For many years, **Olden** was the home of American landscape artist William H. Singer (d. 1943), scion of a Pittsburgh steel family. A philanthropist, he paid for the road and the regional hospital (and administered it), and his American-style frame house is now a nursing home. His **studio** (open July and August, weekends, 12–2) can be visited.

From Olden it's 62 kilometers (37 miles) of easy driving, but
8 boring terrain, to **Skei,** at the base of Lake Jølster, from where the road goes under the glacier for more than 6 kilometers of
9 the journey to **Fjærland,** which, until 1986, was without road connections altogether. In 1991, the **Norsk Bremuseum** (Norwegian Glacier Museum) opened just north of Fjærland. It has a huge screen with a film about glacier trekking and a fiberglass glacial maze, complete with "blue ice," and special effects, courtesy of the *Star Wars* movies set designer. *Tel. 056/93–101. Admission NKr55 adults, NKr30 children, senior citizens. Open May–Sept. daily 10–6; Apr., Oct. daily 10:30–5.*

By 1996, Fjærland should have road connections with Sogndal, but until that time, the only way to travel is by ferry, which
10 stops at both **Balestrand,** one of the famous destinations of old,
11 and **Vangsnes** across from it on the southern bank of **Sognefjord,** the longest and deepest fjord in the world, snaking 200 kilometers (136 miles) into the heart of the country. Along its wide banks are some of Norway's best fruit farms, with fertile soil and lush vegetation. Ferries are the life line and main transportation in the region.

12 From Vangsnes, it is 80 kilometers (50 miles) south to **Voss,** birthplace of football hero Knut Rockne, and a good place to stay the night, either in the town itself, or 36 kilometers (23 miles) away at Stalheim. The road to Stalheim, an old resort, has 13 hairpin turns in one 1½-kilometer (1-mile) stretch of road and it's 550 meters (1,800 feet) straight down. Voss is connected to Oslo and Bergen by train and by 118 kilometers (73 miles) of some of the worst roads in Norway.

13 It is also possible to take a ferry from Balestrand: to **Flåm,**
14 where you can ride a train from Flåm to **Myrdal**—Norway's most exciting railway journey. Only 20 kilometers (12 miles) long, it takes 40 minutes to travel 2,850 feet up a steep mountain gorge, even longer on the way down. Don't worry about the brakes. The train has five separate systems, any one of which is able to stop it. A masterpiece of engineering, the line includes 21 tunnels. From Flåm it is also an easy drive back to Oslo along the Lærdal river, one of Norway's most famous salmon streams—King Harald's favorite.

Off the Beaten Track

Halfway across the southern shore of Lake Jølster (about a 10-minute detour from the road to Fjærland) is **Astruptunet,** the farm of artist Nicolai Astrup (1880–1928). The best of his primitive, mystical paintings sell in the $500,000 range, making him second only to Edvard Munch among Norwegians. His home and studio, a cluster of small turf-roofed buildings on a steep hill overlooking the lake vividly show what it was like to live in a remote, isolated area. Stop at the tiny cafeteria and have a *svele* (a raised pancake rolled with sugar or brown cheese) while watching the video about Astrup. *Tel. 057/27–782. Admission NKr30 adults, NKr15 children, senior citizens. Open May 19–June 9, Aug. 12–Sept. 1, weekdays, Sun. noon–5, Sat. noon–3; June 10–Aug. 11, weekdays, Sun. 10–6, Sat. 10–4.*

Shopping

Skei in Jølster **Audhild Vikens Vevstove** (Skei, tel. 057/28–125, Førde, tel. 057/20–084) specializes in the handicrafts, particularly woven textiles, of the Jølster region as well as handicrafts from neighboring areas, including brass, porcelain, and leather goods.

Stryn **Strynefjell Draktverkstad** (6890 Oppstryn, tel. 057/77–220) is a women's workshop, started in 1988, which specializes in stylish knickers, trousers, and skirts from heavy wool fabric. There's also a cafeteria serving homemade lefser and a dish of the day. It's a 10-minute drive east of Stryn on route 15.

Voss **Norsk Strikk** (5700 Voss, tel. 05/51–25–18) offers sweaters made in Voss that feature geometric longships—beautifully designed, thoroughly Norwegian, yet fashionable and with none of the kitsch of many traditional styles.

Sports and Outdoor Activities

Fishing The lakes and streams inland offer salmon and trout. Licenses are available at post offices and campgrounds.

Hiking Walks and hikes are especially rewarding in this region, with spectacular mountain and water views everywhere. Be prepared for abrupt weather changes in spring and fall.

Skiing **Voss** is an important Alpine skiing center in western Norway (40 km/25 mi of alpine slopes; 1 cable car, 8 ski lifts; 8 illuminated and 2 marked cross-country trails).

Dining and Lodging

Dining Outside of some roadside snack bars and simple cafeterias, restaurants are few in fjord country. Most visitors dine at the hotels, where food is often more abundant than imaginative. Most feature a cold table at either lunch or dinner.

Lodging Highly recommended establishments are indicated by a star ★.

Ålesund
Dining
Gullix. The decor is a bit much, with stone walls, plants hanging from the ceiling, musical instruments, and even the odd old-fashioned record player, but you can't fault the food, which ranges from sauteed monkfish garnished with shrimp, mussels and crayfish to grilled marinated filet mignon of lamb.

Rådstugt. 5B, tel. 071/24-606. Dress: neat casual. Reservations advised. AE, DC, MC, V. Moderate.

Sjøbua. Within walking distance of the new hotels, this fish restaurant is typical Ålesund art nouveau. The mixed fish and shellfish platter is the most popular dish on the menu. The lobster soup is excellent, too, but leave room for the raspberry ice cream with nougat sauce. *Brunholmsgt. 1, tel. 071/27-100. Reservations advised. Dress: neat casual. AE, DC, MC, V. Closed Sun. Moderate.*

Brosundet Cafe. Hotel Atlantica's coffee shop is the most popular restaurant in town. It has its own bakery, so there's always homemade bread and rolls. The *sirupsnipper* (spice cookies) are very popular. You can order anything from *bløtkake* (cream cake) and coffee, with free refill, to peppersteak. *R. Rønnebergsgate 4, tel. 072/29-100. No reservations. Dress: casual. AE, DC, MC, V. Inexpensive.*

Vesle Kari. This tiny maritime-theme cafe serves typical Norwegian fare—open-face sandwiches and hot dishes like *kjøttkaker* (meat patties), predictable but tasty. *Apotekergaten 2, tel. 071/28-404. No reservations. Dress: casual. No credit cards. Inexpensive.*

Lodging

Scandic. The newest Ålesund hotel is a large post-modernist building complex next to the Exhibition Hall. It's decorated with a maritime theme. The rooms are both spacious and tastefully decorated. *Moloveien 6, tel. 071/28-100. 120 rooms with bath. Facilities: restaurant, bar, nightclub, swimming pool, fitness center. AE, DC, MC, V. Moderate.*

Bryggen. The Home hotel chain specializes in restoring old buildings with a vivid past and maintaining the theme in their decoration. Bryggen, right on Brosundet, formerly a turn-of-the-century fish warehouse, was finished in early 1990. The decor in both lobby and guest rooms illustrates the importance of the fishing industry to Ålesund. A hot meal is included in the room price, and waffles and coffee are always available. *Apotekergate 1–3, tel. 071/26-400, fax-071/21-180. 76 rooms, 6 suites. Facilities: Fitness room, conference rooms, fishing, parking. AE, DC, MC, V. Inexpensive–Moderate.*

Rica Parken. This modern business hotel near Aksla offers panoramic views from most of the small but well-appointed rooms, which were redecorated in 1990 with rattan furniture and pastel colors. *Storgata 16, tel. 071/25-050, fax 071/22-164. 132 rooms with bath, 6 suites. Facilities: restaurant, bar, nightclub, fitness center, conference rooms, parking. AE, DC, MC, V. Inexpensive–Moderate.*

Hotel Scandinavie. The impressive building with towers and arches dates from 1905, but the rooms are newly refurbished, with dark modern Scandinavian furniture, while some textiles pay a token tribute to art nouveau. *Løvenvoldgate 8, tel. 071/23-131, fax 071/29-488. 75 rooms with bath, 2 suites. Facilities: 2 restaurants, bar, fitness room, conference room, garage. AE, DC, MC, V. Inexpensive–Moderate.*

Åndalsnes

Lodging

Grand Hotel Bellevue. It looks like a white stucco apartment building from the 1950s. The rooms are spare but adequate, all with a view of either the mountains or the fjord. *Åndalsgate 5, N-6300 tel. 072/21-011, fax 072/26-038. 46 rooms with bath or shower. Facilities: 2 restaurants, bar, conference room, parking. AE, DC, MC, V. Moderate.*

Balestrand
Lodging

Kvikne's Hotel. This huge wooden gingerbread house at the edge of the Sognefjord has been a landmark since 1913. It is fjord country's most elaborate old hotel, with rows of open porches and balustrades. The rooms are comfortable—those in the old section have more personality, but the view's the best part. *Balholm, N-5850, tel. 056/91-101, fax 056/91-502. 190 rooms with bath or shower. Facilities: restaurant, nightclub, fitness room, fishing. AE, DC, MC, V. Moderate.*

Fjærland
Lodging

Hotel Mundal. This small, old-fashioned yellow-and-white gingerbread hotel celebrated its 100th anniversary in 1991. All rooms are individually and simply decorated. The dining room is rather dreary, but the food is good. *N-5855, tel. 056/93-101, fax 056/93-179. 36 rooms with bath. Facilities: 2 restaurants, bar, conference rooms, fishing, parking. No credit cards. Moderate-Expensive.*

Flåm
Lodging

Fretheim Hotell. With the fjord at the front and mountains at the back, the setting is perfect. The hotel is an anonymous, white, functional building typical of Norwegian resorts. The inside has comfortable lounges, but the rooms won't win any prizes for interior decoration. *N-5743, tel. 056/32-200, fax 056/32-303. 56 rooms with bath or shower, 28 without. Facilities: 2 restaurants, bar, fishing. AE, MC, V. Moderate.*

Geiranger
Lodging

Union Turisthotel. This family-owned hotel celebrated its 100th anniversary in 1991. The old building was torn down, but the present hotel is a tribute to the old style. It is modern and comfortable, with lots of windows facing the famous view, and light furniture in the relatively large rooms. *N-6216, tel. 071/63-000, fax 071/63-161. 145 rooms with bath or shower, 10 suites. Facilities: restaurant, bar, nightclub, fitness room, indoor and outdoor swimming pools, parking. AE, DC, MC, V. Expensive.*

Grande Fjord Hotell. Idyllically situated at the edge of the fjord, this small hotel and cabin complex has more charm than the big hotels in the area. The rooms are simple but comfortable. *N-6216, tel. 071/63-067 (Apr.-Oct.), 071/46-111 (Nov.-Mar.). 10 rooms with bath, 5 without, 18 cabins with bath. Facilities: restaurant, parking. No credit cards. Inexpensive.*

Kristiansund N.
Lodging

Grand. Practically every Norwegian town has a Grand Hotel. This one's primarily a conference hotel, but the rooms are nicer than most (certainly much nicer than the lobby), with brass beds and light wood furniture. *Bernstorffstredet 1, N-6500, tel. 073/73-011, fax 073/72-370. 130 rooms with bath/shower. Facilities: 2 restaurants, bar, nightclub, fitness room, conference center, parking. AE, DC, MC, V. Moderate-Expensive.*

Loen
Dining and Lodging

Alexandra. It looks like a huge white hospital, about as big as all the houses in this tiny fjordside settlement put together. More than 100 years ago, wealthy English and German tourists came to Loen by steamer, and the Alexandra was the most luxurious hotel in the area. That is still true, even though the original dragon-style building exists only in pictures in the lobby. The facilities are first rate, but the food is the best part. Chef Knut Solberg was recruited from Oslo's Annen Etage, and he has revamped both the dining room and the menu. Because most guests don't have time for a big lunch, Alexandra offers a dinnertime smorgåsbord. *N-6878, tel. 057/77-660, fax 057/77-770. 200 rooms with bath. Facilities: 2 restaurants, bar, night-*

club, swimming pool, fitness room, gift shop, tennis, boating, conference center. AE, DC, MC, V. Expensive.

Molde
Dining and Lodging

Alexandra Molde. Spisestuen, the restaurant of Molde's premier hotel, is worth a special trip. Kåre Monsås uses the classic kitchen as his departure point, with starters such as pepper-marinated veal fillet. The orange cake is an excellent dessert. The rooms, many of which overlook the water, are nondescript but comfortable, with dark brown wood furniture and textiles in shades of blue. *Storgata 1–7, N–6400, tel. 072/51–133, fax 072/51–133, line 704. 139 rooms with bath/shower, 11 suites. Facilities: 2 restaurants, 2 bars, swimming pool, fitness room, conference rooms, garage. AE, DC, MC, V. Moderate–Expensive.*

Runde
Lodging

Christineborg Turisthotel. This modern hotel faces the sea and the bird rocks. It's surprisingly comfortable and civilized, a welcome place to unwind out in the wild. *N–6096, tel. 070/85–950, fax 070/85–972. 31 rooms with shower. Facilities: restaurant, fishing boat. MC, V. Inexpensive.*

Stalheim
Lodging

Stalheim Hotel. A large, rectangular building, much like other Norwegian resort hotels, it has been painted dark red and blends into the scenery better than most. One of the most luxurious hotels in the region, it has an extensive collection of Norwegian antiques and even its own open-air museum with 30 houses. *N–5715, tel. 05/52–01–22, fax 05/52–00–56. 127 rooms with bath or shower, 3 suites. Facilities: Restaurant, bar, fishing, shop. AE, DC, MC, V. Expensive–Very Expensive.*

Stryn
Lodging

King Oscar's Hall. After remodeling a dozen houses in the Washington, DC, area, Mike and Møyfrid Walston took on the project of bringing back to life a derelict but magnificent hotel from the heyday of the dragon style, 1896, complete with a tower with dragonheads on the eaves. The Great Hall gives new meaning to the word "great" and the number of royal guests, both present and past is impressive. *6880 Stryn, tel. and fax, 057/71–953. 5 suites. Facilities: restaurant, parking. AE, DC, MC, V. Expensive.*

Voss
Lodging

Fleischers Hotel. The modern addition along the entire front detracts from the turreted and gabled charm of this old hotel. Inside, the old style has been especially well maintained, particularly in the restaurant. Ask for a room in the old section—comfortable and pleasantly old-fashioned compared to the boring rooms in the new motel wing. *Evangervegen 13, tel. 05/51–11–55, fax 05/51–22–89. 101 rooms with bath or shower. Facilities: restaurant, bar, nightclub, indoor pool, fitness room, parking. AE, DC, MC, V. Moderate.*

Trondheim and the North

Introduction

Trondheim, Norway's third-largest city, with about 135,000 people, marks the border between "southern" and "northern" Norway. The city is dominated by Nidarosdomen, the rebuilt Gothic cathedral where the kings of Norway have traditionally been crowned. Norway's second-oldest city (after Tønsberg), Trondheim was founded in 997 by the Viking king Olav Tryggvason.

Northern Norway's appeal lies in its seemingly endless miles of wilderness uninhabited save for the odd lonely cabin or herd of reindeer. Views are often exquisite: glaciers, fjords, rocky coasts, and the celestial displays of the midnight sun in summer and the northern lights (aurora Borealis) in winter. Nordkapp (the North Cape) has a special mystique: Beyond this rocky plateau lie only water and ice (and the Norwegian islands of Svalbard) before you reach the North Pole.

Important Addresses and Numbers

Tourist Information **Trondheim** (Trondheim Torg, tel. 07/52–72–01). Other tourist offices in the region: **Bodø** (Sjøgt. 21, 8000, tel. 081/26–000); **Harstad** (Rikard Kaarbøsgt. 20, 9400, tel. 082/63–235); **Lofoten Reiselivslag** (8300 Svolvær, tel. 088/71–053); **Mo i Rana** (8600, tel. 087/50–421); **Narvik** (Kongensgt. 66, 8500, tel. 082/43–309); **Tromsø** (Storgt. 61, 9000, tel. 083/10–000); and **Vesterålen Reiselivslag,** (8400 Sortland. tel. 088/21–555).

Emergencies *Trondheim* **Police,** tel. 002. Fire, tel. 001. **Ambulance,** tel. 003. **Car rescue,** tel. 07/96–82–00 or 07/59–88–00. **Doctors,** tel. 07/59–88–00. **Dentists,** tel. 07/52–25–00.

Other Towns **Bodø:** tel. 002; **Harstad:** tel. 082/62–010; **Narvik:** tel. 082/41–060; **Tromsø:** tel. 002.

Late-night Pharmacies *Trondheim* **St. Olav Vaktapotek** (Kjøpmannsgt. 65, tel. 07/52–31–22), in the first building at Bryggene, is open Monday through Saturday 8:30 AM–midnight and Sunday 10 AM–midnight.

Tromsø **Nordstjernen Apotek** (Strandskillet 2, tel. 083/85–628, open daily, 6–9.)

Arriving and Departing by Plane

Airports and Airlines Trondheim's **Værnes airport** is 35 kilometers (22 miles) northeast of the city. **SAS** (tel. 07/82–49–22), **Braathens SAFE** (tel. 07/82–60–22), and **Widerøe** (tel. 07/82–56–88) are the main domestic carriers. SAS also has one flight between Trondheim and Copenhagen daily, except Sunday. The airport bus departs 75 minutes before every SAS and Braathens SAFE flight from the **main bus terminal** (Leuthenhaven, Erling Skakkes Gate 40, tel. 07/52–44–74), with a stop at Braathens SAFE's office at the Royal Garden Hotel. Tickets are NKr40 for the 45-minute ride.

A taxi rank is outside the arrivals exit. The trip downtown costs around NKr350.

Driving on the new highway (E-6) by way of Hommelvik costs NKr20 and takes about 30 minutes. The old road, which follows the coastline and is more scenic, is free, but the ride takes a bit longer.

With the exception of Harstad, all cities in northern Norway are served by airports less than 5 kilometers (3 miles) from the center of town. Tromsø is a crossroads for air traffic between northern and southern Norway and is served by Braathens SAFE, SAS and Widerøe. SAS flies to eight destinations in northern Norway, including Bodø, Tromsø, Alta, and Kirkenes. Braathens SAFE flies to five destinations, including Bodø and Tromsø. Widerøe specializes in northern Norway and flies to 19 destinations in the region, including Honningsvåg, the airport closest to the North Cape.

Arriving and Departing by Car, Train, Bus, and Boat

By Car **Trondheim** is about 500 kilometers (310 miles) from Oslo: seven to eight hours of driving. Speed limits are 80 kmh (50 mph) much of the way. There are two alternatives, E-6 through Gudbrandsdalen, or Route 3 through Østerdalen.

The biggest barrier to driving to **northern Norway** is the distance. Roads are decent, for the most part, but can become heavily traveled with campers during midsummer, sometimes making the going slow. It's 734 kilometers (455 miles) from Trondheim to Bodø on route E6, which goes all the way to Kirkenes.

By Train The **Dovrebanen** has five departures daily, four on Saturday, in both directions on the Oslo–**Trondheim** route. Trains leave from Oslo S station for the seven- to eight-hour journey. Trondheim is the gateway to the North, and two trains run daily in both directions on the 11-hour Trondheim–Bodø route. For information about trains out of Trondheim, tel. 07/52–64–69.

The **Nordlandsbanen** has two departures daily in each direction on the Bodø–Trondheim route, an 11-hour journey. The **Ofotbanen** has one departure daily in each direction on the Stockholm–Narvik route, a 21-hour journey.

By Bus Buses run only from Oslo to Otta, where they connect with the train to Trondheim. Buses connect Bergen, Molde, Ålesund, and Røros with Trondheim.

The easiest way to get to northern Norway by bus is through Sweden. The roads are better and the route is straighter.

Nor-Way Bussekspress (tel. 02/33–08–62) can help you to put together a bus journey to the North. The Express 2000 travels three times a week between Oslo, Kautokeino, Alta, and Hammerfest. The journey, via Sweden, takes 24, 26, and 29 hours, respectively.

By Boat **Hurtigruten** (the coastal express boat, which calls at 35 ports from Bergen to Kirkenes) stops at Trondheim, southbound at St. Olav's Pier, Quay 16, northbound at Pier 2, Quay 7.

Getting Around

The center of **Trondheim** is small, and the only way to see it is on foot. The few sights that are not right downtown are reached easily by public transport.

By Plane Northern Norway has excellent air connections through SAS, Braathens SAFE and Widerøe. SAS and Braathen even fly to Svalbard, the islands off the northern coast. Widerøe, however, has the most complete network. They fly from Bodø to Kabelvåg (near Svolvær), Leknes, Sørværøy (by Værøy) and Røst in the Lofotens and Stokmarknes and Andenes in Vesterålen, as well as to Narvik, Tromsø, Alta, Hammerfest, Honningsvåg (closest airport to the North Cape), Kirkenes, and many others. Getting from the airport to town is never a problem in northern Norway, because no airport is more than 5 km from town.

By Bus

Trondheim Most local buses in **Trondheim** stop at the Munkegata/Dronningens Gate intersection. Some routes end at the bus terminal (Skakkes Gate 40, tel. 07/52–44–74). Tickets cost NKr12 and allow free transfer between buses and streetcars (**Gråkallbanen,** tel. 07/55–21–63). For bus information, call 07/54–71–00.

The North North of **Bodø** and **Narvik** (a five-hour bus ride from Bodø), beyond the reach of the railroad, buses go virtually everywhere, but they don't go particularly often. Get a comprehensive bus schedule from a tourist office or travel agent before making plans. Local bus companies include **Saltens Bilruter** (Bodø, tel. 081/25–025), **Ofotens Bilruter** (Narvik, tel. 082/46–480), **Tromsbuss** (Tromsø, tel. 083/70–233), **Tromsøexpressen** (Tromsø, tel. 083/72–787), and **Finnmark Fylkesrederi og Ruteselskap** (Alta, tel. 084/35–211, Hammerfest, tel. 084/11–655).

By Boat Boat is the ideal transportation in Nordland. The **Hurtigruten** stops twice daily (north and southbound) at 20 ports in northern Norway. It is possible to buy tickets between any harbors right on the boats. **Saltens Dampskibsselskab** (Bodø, 081/21–020) has express boats, between Bodø and Hamarøy and Svolvær, while **OVDS** (Narvik, tel. 082/44–090) has ferries between Bodø and Værøy, Røst, and Moskenes and express boats between Bodø and Sortland, Svolvær, and Narvik, as well as other places in Nordland. **TFDS, Troms Fylkes Dampskibsselskap** (Tromsø, tel. 083/86–088) operates various boat services in the region around Tromsø.

By Car The roads aren't a problem in northern Norway—most are quite good, although there are always narrow and winding stretches, especially along fjords. Traffic can be surprisingly heavy, especially during midsummer, when campers line the roads. Distances are formidable. From Bodø to Narvik, it's 306 kilometers (189 miles), including the 126 kilometers (78 miles) round trip on route 80. From Narvik to Alta is 522 kilometers (323 miles), while from Alta to Kirkenes, it's another 569 kilometers (353 miles), all on E6. To get to Tromsø and the North Cape involves additional driving on narrower roads, off E6, round trips of 146 kilometers (90 miles) and 340 kilometers (210 miles), respectively. The road from Alta to Kirkenes is excellent, straight much of the way across the treeless, marshy Finnmark plateau.

A better though more expensive idea than making the long trek across the northern reaches of the country is to fly the big distances and then rent a car for sightseeing within the area. There's no better way to see the Lofoten and Vesterålen islands than by car. Book a rental car as far in advance as possible, as only a limited number are available in the islands. Nordkapp is another excursion best made by car. Take the plane to Honningsvåg, but make sure to book the car well in advance.

By Taxi Taxi ranks are located in strategic places in downtown **Trondheim.** All taxis are connected to the central dispatching office (tel. 07/52–76–00). The initial charge for a taxi from a rank is NKr17 during the day, NKr21 at night and on weekends. Kilometer charges run from NKr6 to NKr8, depending upon the time of day.

Taxi numbers in other towns are: **Harstad,** tel. 082/64–900; **Narvik,** tel. 082/46–500; **Røst,** tel. 088/96–338; and **Tromsø,** tel. 083/88–020.

Guided Tours

Tromsø The tourist information office sells tickets for **City Sightseeing** (Dampskipskaia) and ***M/S Polstjerna,*** an original Arctic vessel that offers a fishing tour in the waters around Tromsø island.

Trondheim The Trondheim Tourist Authority offers a number of tours. Tickets are sold at the tourist information office or at the start of the tour.

Svalbard **Svalbard Polar Travel** (9170 Longyearbyen, tel. 080/21–971) arranges combination air-sea visits, from three-day mini-cruises to 12-day trekking expeditions on the North Pole rim. **Spitsbergen Travel** (9170 Longyearbyen, tel. 080/21–160) offers specialized "exploring" tours, which focus on the plant and animal life of the region.

Exploring Trondheim and the North

Numbers in the margin correspond with points of interest on the Trondheim and the North map.

Tour 1: Trondheim

1 **Trondheim**'s original name, Nidaros (still the name of the Cathedral), is a composite word referring to the city's location at the mouth of the Nid River. Center city is a triangular piece of land bordered by the river and a canal. After a particularly savage fire in 1681, the wooden town was rebuilt according to the plan of General Cicignon, a military man from Luxembourg, who also designed its fort. The wide streets of the city center are still lined with brightly painted wood houses and picturesque warehouses.

Start at the tourist information office at Torget, the town square, with the statue of St. Olav in the middle. South on Munkegate is one of the finest collections in Scandinavia, the **Kunstindustrimuseum** (Decorative Arts Museum). It has superb period rooms from the Renaissance to 1950s Scandinavian modern. The Tiffany windows are also magnificent. *Munkegt. 5, tel. 07/52–13–11. Admission: NKr15 adults, NKr5 children. Open June 20–Aug. 15, Mon.–Sat. 9–5, Sun. noon–5; Aug. 16–June 19, Mon.–Sat. 10–3, Thurs. 10–5, Sun. noon–4.*

Continue on Munkegate to **Nidaros domen** (Nidaros Cathedral), built on the grave of St. Olav, who introduced Christianity to Norway. Although construction was begun in 1070, the oldest existing parts date from around 1150. During the Catholic period, it attracted crowds of pilgrims, but after the Reformation, its importance declined and fires destroyed much of it. The 1814 constitution decreed that Norway's kings should be crowned at the cathedral. Restoration began around 1870 and the interior was completed in 1930. The facade is still being rebuilt, and the western front, with twin towers and a rose window, has been finished in the last 60 years. The first king of modern Norway, Haakon VII, and Queen Maud, daughter of Edward VII of England, were crowned in the cathedral in 1906. Two years later, the constitution was altered to eliminate the coronation ceremony, but in 1957, King Olav, and in 1991, King Harald and Queen Sonja, were formally blessed there. The

Trondheim and the North

crown jewels are on display. *Kongsgårdsgt. 2, tel. 07/50–12–12. Castle admission: NKr10 adults, NKr5 children, senior citizens, students. Ticket also permits entry to Erkebispegården* (see below). *Open June 15–Aug. 20, weekdays 9:30–5:30, Sat. 9:30–4, Sun. 1–4; May 1–June 14 and Aug. 21–Sept. 30, weekdays 9–2:30, Sat. 9–2, Sun. 1–4; Oct. 1–Apr. 30, weekdays noon–2:30, Sat. 11:30–2, Sun. 1–3. Belfry admission: NKr3. Open June 15–Aug. 20, daily every ½ hour during regular opening hours. Organ recitals: Sat. at 1; June 15–Aug. 20, weekdays at 3.*

Next door is Scandinavia's oldest secular building (actually two buildings connected by a gatehouse), from around 1160, **Erkebispegården** (the Archbishop's Palace), the residence of the archbishop until the Reformation. After that, it was a Danish governor's palace, and later a military headquarters. *Tel. 07/50–12–12. Admission: NKr10 adults, NKr5 children, senior citizens, students. Ticket also permits entry to cathedral. Open June 1–Aug. 20, weekdays 9–3, Sat. 9–2, Sun. noon–3.*

Within the Erkebispegården is **Forsvarsmuseet** (the Army Museum), with displays of uniforms, swords, and daggers. The Resistance Museum, also there, documents the occupation of Norway during World War II through objects and photographs. *Tel. 07/51–51–11, ext. 182. Admission NKr 5 adults, NKr 2 children. Open June 1–Aug. 31, weekdays 9–3; year-round, weekends 11–4.*

Walk to Bispegate and turn right, following the curve of the river and passing Gamle Bybro (the old city bridge), first built in 1681 to connect with Kristiansten Fort on the opposite bank. At each end was a customs and guard's house (the house on the western side now is used as a day-care center). The present bridge, with its decoratively carved portals, was built in 1859.

Walk up Kjøpmannsgata and turn left on Kongensgate. Behind the **Biblioteket** (the library) (Kongensgate 2) are the remains of St. Olavskirke (St. Olav's Church). The crypt of another medieval church can be seen inside Trondhjems og Strindens Sparebank (a savings bank building at Sondregate 2) during normal banking hours.

Time Out Two short blocks farther is Nordregate, a pedestrian mall. Pop into **Erichsens** restaurant-coffee shop (Nordregt. 10.) for a quick lunch, cake, and coffee, or a three-course meal. It's popular with university students. The fish sandwiches, poached haddock mixed with mayonnaise (Norwegian mayo is a treat) and lemon, are delicious, as is the fish soup and the walnut-marzipan cake.

Between Nordregate and Torvet is a small, narrow alley lined with wood houses, called *veite*, that were once typical for Trondheim. There is another by the tourist information office.

Continue on Nordregate and turn left on Dronningens Gate. On the left is **Stiftsgården,** Scandinavia's largest wood building, built in 1778 as a private home. Today, it is the king's official residence in Trondheim. The interior is sparsely furnished in threadbare Rococo, Empire, and Biedermeier. *Tel. 07/52–24–73. Admission: NKr10 adults, NKr5 children. Guided tours, June 1–Aug. 31, Mon.–Sat. every ½ hour 11–2.*

The street on the far side of Stiftsgården is Munkegate. To the right is **Ravnkloa Fiskehall** (fish market), by the water, where you can see an immense variety of seafood offered for sale. Past the railroad station and the quay across the water is **Sjøfartsmuseet** (the Maritime Museum), in a former prison. Inside there are galleon figureheads, ship models, a harpoon cannon from a whaling boat, and a large collection of seafaring pictures. *Fjordgt. 6A, tel. 07/52–89–75. Admission: NKr10 adults, NKr5 children, senior citizens. Open Mon.–Sat. 9–3, Sun. noon–3; closed Sat. in winter.*

The museum is at the top of Kjøpmannsgata; partway down is **Olavskvartalet,** a modern shopping mall and cultural center built in 1989.

Time Out In the center of Olavskvartalet is **Torgcafeen,** run by the Grand Hotel Olav, which serves sandwiches, salads, and cakes. The pound cake with chocolate chunks and hazelnuts is great with a cup of strong coffee.

Across the street is the Royal Garden Hotel, built in the same Hansa style as the buildings that line the wharf. Farther down are the oldest buildings on the river, dating from the 1700s.

For an unusual museum visit, you can take bus No. 1 marked LADE to Fagerheim, a 30-minute ride. Here you will find **Ringve Music Museum** at Ringve Gård, the childhood home of the naval hero Admiral Tordenskiold. It was started as a private collection but was opened to the public in 1952 as a living museum. Guides (music students) demonstrate the instruments on display and tell about their use and role in the history of music. Concerts, featuring period instruments played by musicians in period costume, are held regularly in the antiques-filled house and in the auditorium in the converted barn. *Lade Allé 60, tel. 07/92–24–11. Admission: NKr 30 adults, NKr 20 senior citizens and students, NKr 10 children. Open May 20–June 30 and Aug. 11–31, guided tours in English daily at 11, 12:30, 3; July 1–Aug. 10, daily at 11, 12:30, 2:30, 4:30; Sept. 1–31., daily at noon, 2; Oct. 1–May 19, Sun. at 1:30. Tour lasts approximately 75 minutes.*

At the other end of town, **Trøndelag Folkemuseum** has a collection of rustic houses and buildings from the turn of the century, including a dental office and a lace-and-ribbon-maker's workshop. *Sverresborg, tel. 07/53–14–90. Admission: NKr20 adults, NKr10 children, senior citizens. Open May 20–Sept 1, daily 11–6.*

Tour 2: Trondheim to Narvik

As the country stretches up north of Trondheim, toward the Arctic Circle, cities and towns give way to small fishing settlements and tiny farms. Rural Norway, always sparsely settled, becomes even less populated up north. Green, well-tended fields and thick evergreen forests disappear, and scrubby bushes and wildflowers take over.

Few tourists ever see much of the 738 kilometers (458 miles) between Trondheim and Bodø. Nord Trøndelag, above Trondheim, is largely agricultural. Taken on its own, it's beautiful, with farms, mountains, rock formations and clear blue water, but compared with the rest of Norway, it somehow falls short—the landscape is too gentle—so many tourists just sleep through it on the night train, or fly over it on their way to the North.

The first town of any size is **Steinkjer,** a military base, boot camp for 3000 Norwegian army recruits every year. Industrial towns lining the climb up to the Arctic Circle include Namsos, once exclusively a timber port, and Mosjøen, where the aluminum plant dominates the town. **Mo i Rana** is a center for iron and steel production using ore from nearby mines.

On a bleak stretch of treeless countryside 80 kilometers (50
2 miles) north of **Mo i Rana** is the Arctic Circle. **Polarsirkelsenteret** (The Arctic Circle Center), on the E6 highway, presents a multiscreen show about Norway using 12 projectors. The post office has a special postmark, and you can get your Arctic Circle Certificate stamped. There's also a cafeteria and gift shop. *8242 Polarsirkelen, tel. 087/66–066. Admission: NKr30. Open May 1–Sept. 30 (Apr., Oct., cafeteria only).*

3 **Bodø,** a modern city of about 37,000 just above the Arctic Circle, is best known as the end station of the Nordlandsbanen railroad and the gateway to the Lofoten Islands and the North. From here, other kinds of transportation take over. At Bodø, the Midnight Sun is visible from June 2 to July 10. Like many other coastal towns, it began as a small fishing community, but today it is a commercial and administrative center.

4 **Saltstraumen,** 33 kilometers (20 miles) southeast of Bodø on Route 80/17, is a 3-kilometer- (2-mile-) long and 500-foot-wide section of water between the outer fjord, which joins with the sea, and the inner fjord basin. During high tide, the volume of water rushing through the strait and into the basin is so great that whirlpools result, the legendary mælstrøm. Sometimes as many as four separate whirlpools can be seen, and the noise made by these "cauldrons" can be both loud and eerie. All that rush of water brings enormous quantities of fish, making the mælstrøm a popular fishing spot.

Time Out **Saltstraumen Hotel** (tel. 081/87–685) is practically on top of the mælstrøm. The restaurant to the left of the entrance serves delicious steamed halibut in butter sauce with new potatoes in season.

---

5 During the 19th century, the trading center of **Kjerringøy,** 40 kilometers (25 miles) north of Bodø on Route 834, was one of the most prosperous in northern Norway. Fifteen buildings have been preserved with interiors intact, including the bakery, the stables, the smithy, and a guesthouse. Norwegian novelist Knut Hamsun used the settlement as a model for "Sirilund" in his book, *Benoni og Rosa.* It was one of the last stops for fishermen bound for the Lofoten Islands, which extend from the coast north of Bodø. During the summer, Kjerringøy has its own postmark. (A bus leaves from Bodø station at 1:10 for the 40-km/25 mi trip, which includes one ferry. After 2⅓ hours at Kjerringøy, the bus returns, arriving at Bodø at 6:30.)

6 **Narvik,** 296 kilometers (183 miles) to the North, is more easily reached by rail from Stockholm than from most places in Norway, as it is the end station on the Ofotbanen, the Norwegian railroad that connects the Swedish railroad's northernmost

line. It was originally established as the ice-free port for exporting Swedish iron ore mined around Kiruna.

On May 9, 1940, the German army invaded Norway through Narvik. Although the Allies won the battle for the city—the only one the Germans lost in the first three years of the war—they could not keep troops stationed there, as they were needed farther south. So the German occupying forces moved in and stayed for more than five years. After the war, Narvik had to be completely rebuilt. **Krigøminnemuseet** (the War Memorial Museum) documents wartime events with artifacts, models, and pictures, including glimpses of civilian life, how the Resistance movement operated, and the conditions of prisoners of war. *Torget, tel. 082/44–426. Admission: NKr20 adults, NKr10 children, senior citizens. Open June 15–Sept. 15, daily 10–10; Sept. 16–June 14, daily 10–2.*

Tour 3: The Lofoten Islands ❼

Extending out into the ocean north of Bodø are the **Lofoten Islands,** a 190-kilometer (118-mile) chain of jagged peaks, mountaintops rising from the bottom of the sea, looking like sharp molars in an animal's lower jaw. The Midnight Sun is visible here from May 26 to July 17. In the summer, the idyll of farms, fjords, and fishing villages makes it a major tourist attraction, while in the winter, the coast facing the Arctic Ocean is one of Europe's stormiest.

Until about 40 years ago, fishing was the only source of income. Cod and haddock were either dried or salted and sold on the Continent. Up to 6,000 boats with 30,000 fisherman would mobilize between January and March for the Lofotfiske, the annual cod fishing "event." Many small individual fishermen still participate. During the season, they fished in open boats and took shelter during stormy nights in *rorbuer,* simple cabins built right on the water. Today, many rorbuer have been converted into lodgings, and much of the fishing has been taken over by year-round factory ships, but many fishing villages, still with the wooden racks set out in the open air for drying fish, remain.

Svolvær, the main town, connected with the other islands by ferry and by coastal steamer and air to Bodø, has a thriving summer art colony. A drive on Route 19, from Svolvær to the outer tip of the Lofotens (130 kilometers, 80 miles)—the town with the enigmatic name of Å—is an opportunity to see how the islanders really live. Now that all the islands are linked by bridges, it's an easy trip on excellent roads. Scenic stops include **Nusfjord,** a 19th-century fishing village on the UNESCO list of historic monuments; **Sund,** with its smithy; and **Reine,** another picturesque village.

Time Out

Gammelbua, in Reine, serves excellent steamed halibut, homemade fish soufflé, and some of the most inspired desserts and cakes in Norway. Sit at a long oak table under the eaves upstairs or at the counter with the locals.

Off the tip of Moskenesøy, the last island with a bridge, is **Moskenesstraumen,** another mælstrøm, not quite as dramatic as Saltstraumen, but inspiration to both Jules Verne, who wrote about it in *Journey Beneath the Sea,* and Edgar Allan Poe, who described it in his short story, "A Descent into the Mælstrom."

8 North of the Lofotens are the **Vesterålen Islands,** with more fishing villages and rorbuer and more diverse vegetation.

Tour 4: Harstad to the North Cape

Harstad, east of Vesterålen on Hinnøya, Norway's largest is-
land, has around 22,000 people and is known for its cultural fes-
9 tival every June, which attracts about 20,000 people to
concerts, theater, and dance, and its deep-sea fishing festival
in July.

10 **Tromsø,** the most important city north of the Arctic Circle, with about 50,000 people, is 318 kilometers (197 miles) northeast. The Midnight Sun is visible from May 21 to July 23. The 13,000 students at the world's northernmost university are one reason why the nightlife is better than in many other northern cities. **Ishavskatedralen** (the Arctic Cathedral), more striking than beautiful, was built in 1965. It is also the site of the **Nordnorsk Kunstmuseum** (the Art Museum of Northern Norway), which has exhibits of paintings, drawings, photography, sculpture, and applied arts. Tromsø has been known to call itself the "Paris of the North," but "Gateway to the Arctic" is more accurate and descriptive, as most polar expeditions started here.

Polarmuseet (the Polar Museum), in an 1830s customs warehouse, documents the history of the polar region, with skis and equipment from Roald Amundsen's expedition to the South Pole and a reconstructed Svalbard hunting station from 1910. *S. Tollbugt. 11b, tel. 083/84–373. Admission: NKr20 adults, NKr5 children. Open May 15–Sept. 15, daily 11–5; Sept. 16–May 14, 11–3.*

It's 409 kilometers (253 miles) to Alta on coastal road most of the way. Kautokeino Sami spend the summer in turf huts at **Kvænangsfjellet,** so you might see a few reindeer. **Øksfjordjøkelen,** the only glacier in Norway that calves into the sea, is 13 kilometers (8 miles) west of Alteidet.

11 **Alta** is the last marker on the way to the North Cape, a place to
12 spend the night before making the final ascent. At **Hjemmeluft,**
southwest of Alta, four groupings of **prehistoric rock carvings,** the largest in northern Europe, range from 2,500 to 6,000 years old and are on the UNESCO World Heritage List. The pictographs, featuring ships, reindeer, and even a man with a bow and arrow, were discovered in 1973. *Tel. 084/35–997 (Alta Museum). Admission: NKr10 adults, NKr5 children. Open July 1–31, daily, 8–8; June 15–30, Aug. 1–15, 10–6.*

A detour on the way to the North Cape is to the world's north-
13 ernmost town, **Hammerfest,** an important fishing center 145 ki-
lometers (90 miles) from Alta. In 1891, Hammerfest became the first city in Europe with electric street lamps.

The final part of the journey, from Alta to the Cape, is 217 ki-
lometers (134 miles) and includes a 45-minute ferry ride from
14 Kåfjord to **Honningsvåg,** the last village before the Cape. In
Honningsvåg you can visit **Nordkappmuseet** (the North Cape Museum), on the third floor of Nordkapphuset (the North Cape House), which documents the history of the fishing industry in the region as well as the history of tourism at the North Cape. *9750 Honningsvåg, tel. 084/72–090. Admission: NKr15 adults, NKr5 children. Open June 15–Aug. 15, Mon.–Sat. 11–8, Sun. 3–8; Aug. 16–June 14, weekdays 11–3, closed weekends.*

15 From Honningsvåg, it's 34 kilometers (21 miles) to **Nordkapp,** on the only stretch of the journey featuring truly Arctic landscape and vegetation so far—treeless tundra, with crumbling mountains and sparse dwarf plants. The contrast between this near-barren territory and the new **North Cape Hall** is striking. This "experience center" was blasted into the interior of the plateau and includes a panorama restaurant, which serves champagne and Norwegian golden caviar. A tunnel leads past a small chapel to a grotto with a panoramic view of the Arctic Ocean and to the cliff wall itself, passing exhibits that trace the history of the Cape, from Richard Chancellor, an Englishman who drifted around it and named it in 1533, while looking for the Northeast Passage, to Oscar II, king of Norway and Sweden, who climbed to the top of the plateau in 1873, and King Chulalongkorn of Siam (now Thailand), who visited the Cape in 1907. There's also a multi-screen film about Finnmark, a gift shop, and a post office. Out on the plateau itself, a hollow sculptured globe is illuminated by the Midnight Sun, which shines from May 11 to August 31. *9764 Nordkapp. Admission: NKr90 adults, NKr30 children.*

All the time spent getting to the North Cape reinforces the perception that it is indeed at the end of the earth (though Knivsjellodden, slightly west and much less dramatic, is actually closer to the Pole).

Tour 5: Samiland

Everyone has heard of Lapland, but few know its real name, Samiland. The Sami recognize no national boundaries, as their territory stretches from the Kola Peninsula in the Soviet Union through Finland, Sweden, and Norway. These indigenous reindeer herders are a separate ethnic group, with a language related to Finnish. Although still considered nomadic, they no longer live in tents or huts, except for short periods during the summer, when their animals graze along the coast. They have had to conform to today's lifestyles, but their traditions survive through their language, music, art, and handcrafts. Norwegian Samiland is synonymous with the communities of Kautokeino and Karasjok in Finnmark.

16 **Kautokeino,** 129 kilometers (80 miles) from Alta, is the site of the Sami theater and the Nordic Sami Institute, dedicated to the study of Sami culture. It is a center for Sami handcrafts and education, with even a school of reindeer herding.

Guovdageainnu (Kautokeino in the Sami language) **Gilisillje,** the local museum, documents the way of life of both the nomadic and the resident Sami of that area prior to World War II, with photographs and artifacts, including costumes, dwellings, and art. *9520 Kautokeino, tel. 084/56–203. Admission: NKr15 adults, NKr5 children. Open weekdays 8:30–3, weekends closed.*

17 **Karasjok,** on the other side of the Finnmark plateau, is the seat of the 39-member Sami Parliament and capital of Samiland. It's often mentioned in winter weather reports as the coldest place in the country—it has a typical inland climate, with the accompanying temperature extremes, for it also can be unusually warm in the summer.

Samid Vuorku-Davvirat (the Sami Collections), is a comprehensive museum of Sami culture, with emphasis on the arts, reindeer herding, and the status of women in the Sami community.

Museumsgt. 17, tel. 084/66–305. Admission: NKr15 adults, NKr5 children. Open Mon.–Sat. 9–3, Sun. 12–3.

For a more active experience of Sami life, **Berit Gaup** (tel. 084/66–442) can initiate you in the ways of reindeer herding.

Tour 6: The Finnish-Russian Connection

At its very top, Norway hooks over Finland and touches the Soviet Union for 122 kilometers (75 miles). The towns in east Finnmark have a more heterogeneous population than those in the rest of the country. A century ago, during hard times in Finland, many industrious Finns settled in this region, where their descendants keep the language alive.

18 A good way to visit this part of Norway is to fly to **Kirkenes** and then explore the region by car. Only Malta was bombed more than Kirkenes during World War II, so virtually everything has been built within the last 40 years.

From Kirkenes, it's about 60 kilometers (37 miles) to **Grense Jakobselv,** the Russian border. As a protest against constant Russian encroachment in the area, King Oscar II built a chapel
19 right at the border in 1869. Just south of Kirkenes is **Storskog,** the only official land crossing of the border between Norway and the Soviet Union, where anyone with a visa can cross.

The southernmost part of Finnmark, a narrow tongue of land
20 tucked between Finland and Russia, is **Øvre Pasvik** national park. This subarctic evergreen forest is the western end of Siberia's *taiga* and supports many varieties of flora found only here. The area is surprisingly lush, and in good years, all the cloudberries make the swamps shine orange.

Tour 7: Svalbard

North of the North Cape are the islands of **Svalbard,** the largest
21 of which is Spitsbergen. Officially part of Norway only since 1925, they might have remained wilderness, with only the occasional visitor, if coal had not been discovered late in the 19th century. Today, both a Norwegian and a Russian coal company have operations there, parts of which can be toured by visitors. Two Russian coal miners' communities on Spitsbergen give a glimpse of Soviet life. There are ample opportunities for exploring the islands on skis, dogsleds, and skidoos.

The best way to experience Svalbard is by ship, as accommodations on the islands themselves are sparse. The capital, **Longyearbyen,** is 90 minutes by air from Tromsø. It was named for an American, John Monroe Longyear, who established a mining operation there in 1906. Only three species of land mammals—polar bear, reindeer, and Arctic fox—and one species of bird—ptarmigan—have adapted to Svalbard winters, but during the summer months, more than 30 species of birds nest on the steep cliffs of the islands, and white whales, seals, and walruses also come for the season.

Because Svalbard is so far north, it has four months of continuous daylight, from April 21 to August 21. Summers can be lush, with hundreds of varieties of wild flowers. The season is so compressed that buds, full-blown flowers and seed appear simultaneously on the same plant.

What to See and Do with Children

Tromsø

Take bus No. 28 to the mainland to ride Fjellheisen cable car to **Storsteinen** (the Big Rock) 420 meters above sea level, for a great view of the city. *Tromsdalen, tel. 083/35–121. Admis-*

sion: NKr40 adults, NKr20 children. Open May 1–Sept. 30, daily 10–5, also June 1–Aug. 31, 9 PM–12:30 AM when sunny.

Nordlysplanetariet, the Northern Lights Planetarium, at Breivika, is a 10- minute bus ride (No. 37) from town. Inside, 112 projectors guarantee a 360-degree view of programs, which include a tour through the Northern Lights, the Midnight Sun, and geological history, as well as a film and multimedia show about the city. *Breivika, tel. 083/76–000. Admission: NKr40 adults, NKr20 children, NKr30 senior citizens.*

Tromsø Museum, at the southern end of the island, includes seven divisions (geology, botany, zoology, archaeology, Samiethnography, modern social history, and marine biology). An open-air museum, with more than 40 buildings, including reconstructed 18th-century farm and trading post, is on the same grounds. *Folkeparken, tel. 083/45–000. Admission: NKr10 adults, NKr5 children. Open June 1–Aug. 20, daily 9–6; Aug. 21–May 31, weekdays, 8:30–3:30, Wed. also 7–10; Sat. noon–3, Sun. 11–4. Aquarium only: Open June 1–Aug. 20, daily 10–5; Aug. 21–May 31, Sun. only 11–2.*

Off the Beaten Track

Kirkenes From mid-June to mid-August, the ***FRR Hammerfest*** (tel. 084/14–334) operates visa-free day-cruises to Murmansk on a high-speed catamaran. Booking is required two weeks in advance.

St. Georgs kapell, 45 kilometers (28 miles) west of Kirkenes, is the only Russian-Orthodox chapel in Norway, where the Orthodox Skolt-Sami had their summer encampment. It's a tiny building, and services are held outside, weather permitting. On the last Sunday in August, there is a pilgrimage to the Chapel, where a Greek Orthodox priest blesses the waters of the Neiden River.

Lofoten Islands From Moskenes, just north of Å, (or from Bodø), you can take a ferry to the bird sanctuaries of **Værøy** and **Røst.** Hundreds of thousands of seabirds inhabit the cliffs of the islands, in particular, the eider ducks, favorites of the local population, who build small shelters for their nests. Eventually the down collected from these nests ends up in *dyner* (feather comforters).

Mo i Rana **Sætergrotta** and **Grønligrotta** are two of around 200 caves, 26 kilometers (16 miles) northwest of Mo i Rana. Sætergrotta, with 2400 meters of charted underground paths, many narrow passages, natural "chimneys," and an underground river, is for serious cave explorers. A certain amount of agility is required, as is a pair of rubber boots. Tickets for the guided tour, which cover rental of hardhat with light and protective clothing, can be purchased from the tourist office. *Tel. 087/50–421. Admission: NKr 140. Two-hour guided tours daily at 11 and 2.*

Grønligrotta, Scandinavia's best known show-cave, even has electric lights. The 20-minute tour, which is suitable for the whole family, goes deep into the limestone cave to the underground river. Tickets can be purchased at the entrance. *Admission: NKr 30 adults, NKr 15 children. Tours daily on the hour 10–7. Open June 15–Aug. 15.*

Svartisen **Saltens Dampskibsselskap** (tel. 087/21–020) offers seven-hour boat tours from Bodø to Svartisen, the second-largest glacier in Norway, near Mo i Rana. The name means literally "black ice." This is the easiest way to get to the glacier. From Mo, it is 32 kilometers (20 miles) by car (no public transport) to Svartisvatn lake. A boat crosses the lake every hour (June 20–Sept. 20, daily 10–8) to within 2½ km of the Østerdal arm of the glacier. If you plan to get to the glacier on your own, you should inquire at the tourist office about connecting with a guide. Glacier walking is extremely hazardous and should never be done without a professional guide, because even though a glacier may appear fixed and static, it is always changing, melting from below and accumulating new snow above. There's always the danger of crevasses.

Shopping

Harstad **Trastadsenteret** (Rik. Kaarbøsgt. 19) sells pottery, weavings, and textile prints by local artists.

Kåfjord **Grenbu** (tel. 089/16–273) at Løkvoll in Manndalen on E6 about 15 kilometers (9 miles) west of Alta is a center for Coastal Sami weaving, on vertical looms. Local weavers sell their rugs and wall hangings along with other regional crafts.

Karasjok The specialties of the region are Sami crafts, particularly handmade knives. In **Sameland Senter** (084/66902) is a large collection of shops featuring northern specialties, including **Knivsmed Strømeng** (tel. 084/67–105) has a good selection.

Kautokeino Frank and Regina **Juhls** silver gallery (tel. 084/56–189) is a rather sophisticated shop for this out-of-the-way place. They sell Sami crafts as well as their own modern jewelry.

Lofoten Lofoten is a mecca for artists and craftspeople; a list of galleries and crafts centers, with all locations marked on a map, is available from tourist offices.

Probably the best-known craftsperson in the region is Hans Gjertsen, better known as **Smeden i Sund** (the blacksmith at Sund; tel. 088/93–629). Watch him make wrought iron cormorants in many sizes, as well as candlesticks and other gift items.

Tromsø The city has two major shopping centers: **Veita** (Storgaten 102, tel. 083/58755) and **Pyramiden** (Solstrand veien 47, tel. 083/38200).

Trondheim Trondheim has an extraordinary number of high-quality art and handicraft stores. In addition to **Husfliden** (Olav Tryggvasonsgt. 18, tel. 07/52–27–62), **Håndlaget** (Kjøpmannsgt. 63, tel. 07/53–53–22) sells handicrafts from 340 different artists in the area. **Yvonne Verkstedutsalg og Galleri** (Ørjaveita 6, tel. 07/52–73–27) also sells works of local artists. Modern arts and crafts are at **K** (Dronningens Gate 29, tel. 07/51–68–03). **Gullsmed** (Goldsmith) **Moller** (Munkegt. 3, tel. 07/52–04–39) sells jewelry with the Trondheim rose, similar to the Tudor rose. **Olavskvartalet,** across from the Royal Garden Hotel, is a shopping center with many specialty stores.

Sports and Outdoor Activities

Trondheim *Fishing* **Nidelven** (Nid River) is one of Norway's best salmon and trout rivers. You can fish right in the city, but you need a license. Ask at any sports store.

Skiing **Bymarka** and **Estenstadmarka,** the wooded areas on the periphery of the city, are popular areas for cross-country skiers. At **Skistua** (ski lodge) in Bymarka, and at **Vassfjellet** south of the city, there are downhill runs.

Beaches The island of Munkholmen, easily reached by ferry from Ravnkloa, has a popular sandy beach.

The North Northern Norway is a sports-lover's delight, with tremendous opportunities to fish, raft, hike, and ski. Ask at any tourist information office.

Dining and Lodging

Dining **Trondheim** is known for several dishes, including *surlaks* (pickled salmon), marinated in a sweet-and-sour brine with onions and spices, and served with sour cream. A sweet specialty is *tekake* (teacake), which looks like a thick-crust pizza topped with a lattice pattern of cinnamon and sugar.

If you visit northern Norway between May and August, try the specialty of *måsegg* and *Mack-øl*, more for curiosity value than for taste. *Måsegg* (seagulls' eggs), are always served hard-boiled and halved in their shells. They're larger than chicken eggs, and they look exotic, with greenish-gray speckled shells and bright orange yolks, but they taste like standard supermarket eggs. *Mack-øl* (similar to pils), is brewed in Tromsø at the world's northernmost brewery. Otherwise, as in the rest of provincial Norway, most better restaurants are in hotels.

Lodging Most Trondheim hotels have summer rates, but for some, a hotel pass or special booking method is required. Unless otherwise noted, breakfast is included.

At times, it seems as though the SAS and Rica hotel chains are the only ones in northern Norway, and often that is true. These are always top standard, usually the most expensive hotel in town, with the best restaurant and the most facilities. Rustic cabins and campsites are also available everywhere, as well as independent hotels.

In the Lofoten and Vesterålen islands, *rorbuer* (old fishermen's cabins), which have been converted into lodgings or modern versions of these simple dwellings, are the most popular form of accommodation. These rustic quayside cabins, with mini-kitchens, bunk beds, living room (seldom with TV), and showers are reasonably priced, and they give an authentic experience of the region. *Sjøhus* (seahouses) are larger, usually two or three-storied buildings similar to rorbuer.

Highly recommended establishments are indicated by a star ★.

Alta
Dining and Lodging **SAS Alta Hotell.** This new postmodernist hotel does everything it can to make you forget that you are in a place where it is dark a lot of the time. Everything is light, from the reflectors on the ceiling of public rooms to the white furniture in the rooms. *Tel. 084/35–000, fax 084/35–825. 155 rooms with bath or shower, 2 suites. Facilities: 2 restaurants, 2 bars, nightclub, conference center, parking. AE, DC, MC, V. Expensive.*

Bodø
Dining **Løvolds' Kafeteria.** Freshly caught fish (the Løvolds also sell fishing gear) and traditional Norwegian dishes are featured at this upstairs cafeteria with a harbor view. It's a good place for

coffee and cake, too, for all pastries are made in-house. *Tollbugt. 9, tel. 20–261. No reservations. Dress: casual. No credit cards. Moderate.*

Dining and Lodging

Bodø Hotell. This pale blue-gray postmodernist building has an identity of its own yet fits well into the Bodø street scene. The facade is more interesting than the rooms. *Professor Schyttesgt. 5, tel. 081/26–900, fax 081/25–788. 63 rooms with bath or shower, 3 suites. Facilities: restaurant. AE, DC, MC, V. Moderate.*

Diplomat. This new hotel near the harbor is a short walk from the shopping district. The rooms are large, but soberly decorated. The restaurant has live entertainment six days a week, but the food could be a little more imaginative. *Sjøgt. 23, tel. 081/27–000, fax 081/22–460. 104 rooms with shower (no bathtubs). Facilities: 2 restaurants, bar, nightclub, fitness room, conference center, garage. AE, DC, MC, V. Moderate.*

Hammerfest

Dining and Lodging

Rica Hotel Hammerfest. The entire hotel was redecorated in 1989. Rooms are small, but at least the furniture is light. Like so many other hotels up north, it lacks character. *Sørøygt. 15, tel. 084/11–333, fax 084/11–311. 88 rooms with bath or shower. Facilities: restaurant, bar, nightclub, fitness center, conference center, parking. AE, DC, MC, V. Moderate–Expensive.*

Harstad

Dining

Røkenes Gård. This large, white wooden house with an intricately carved portal was built in 1750 as a commercial trading house and inn. Recently, it was restored by the ninth generation of descendants, and it is now a cozy restaurant serving regional specialties, such as reindeer and cloudberry parfait. *9400 Harstad, tel. 082/17–465. Reservations required at least 24 hours in advance. Dress: casual but neat. Closed Sun. AE, DC, MC, V. Expensive.*

Dining and Lodging

Grand Nordic. It's a neat brick red building in the Bauhaus style, with Norwegian 1970s-look leather furniture in the public rooms. Bedrooms are no bigger than necessary and furnished with dark woods. The restaurant and conference rooms are lighter and more modern. *Strandgt. 9, tel. 082/62–170, fax 082/67–730. 85 rooms with bath or shower, 3 suites. Facilities: 2 restaurants, bar, nightclub, parking, conference center. AE, DC, MC, V. Moderate–Expensive.*

Kirkenes

Dining and Lodging

Rica Arctic Hotel. Do not confuse this new hotel with the Rica Hotel Kirkenes, an older establishment, which ends up costing the same during the summer. Rooms are spacious and pretty, with white painted furniture and light printed textiles. *Kongensgt. 1–3, tel. 085/92–929, fax 085/91–159. 80 rooms with bath. Facilities: restaurant, bar, nightclub, fitness room, swimming pool, conference center, shopping center, parking. AE, DC, MC, V. Moderate–Very Expensive.*

Lofoten Islands

Dining

Fiskekrogen. This quayside restaurant in the fishing village of Henningsvær will prepare your own catch. Chef-owner Otto Asheim's specialties include smoked *gravlaks* (smoking the dill-marinated salmon gives it extra depth of flavor) and sautéed ocean catfish garnished with mussels and shrimp. *8330 Henningsvær, tel. 088/74–652. Reservations required. Dress: casual. AE, DC, MC, V. Moderate.*

Skipperstua. Part of the Nyvågar dockside complex, this rustic restaurant serves specialties from the "Arctic" kitchen, such as almond-breaded Arctic char fillets, steamed cod with shellfish, and an excellent fish soup. *8300 Svolvær, tel. 088/78–900. Res-*

ervations advised. Dress: casual. AE, DC, MC, V. Inexpensive–Moderate.

Dining and Lodging

Nyvågar. Built in 1990, this hotel and recreation complex is a 15-minute drive from the airport. It looks old, but it's brand new. Activities are well organized, with fishing boat tours, eagle safaris, and deep-sea rafting, plus planned evening entertainment. *8310 Kabelvåg, Solvær, tel. 088/78–900, fax 088/78–950. 60 rooms with shower. Facilities: 2 restaurants, conference rooms. AE, DC, MC, V. Moderate–Expensive.*

Henningsvaær Rorbuer. This small group of renovated turn-of-the-century rorbuer, all facing the sea, is just outside the center of Lofoten's most important fishing village. Breakfasts can be ordered from the cafeteria/reception, where there's a fireplace and TV. Reservations are essential for July. *8330 Henningsvær, tel. 088/74–600. 14 one or two-bedroom rorbuer with shower. Facilities: cafeteria, sauna, laundry, grill. MC, V. Inexpensive.*

Narvik

Dining and Lodging

Grand Royal. It looks like an office building from the outside, but inside it is a comfortable top-class hotel, with big, rather formal rooms. The main restaurant is also quite formal. *Kongensgt. 64, tel. 082/41–500, fax 082/45–531. 112 rooms with bath or shower. Facilities: 2 restaurants, 2 bars, fitness room, conference center. AE, DC, MC, V. Moderate–Expensive.*

Tromsø

Dining

Brankos. Branko and Anne Brit Bartolj serve authentic Yugoslavian food, including *cevapcici* and *raznici*, accompanied by their own imported Yugoslavian wines, in their art-filled dining room. *Storgt. 57, tel. 083/82–673. Reservations required. Dress: casual but neat. AE, DC, MC, V. No lunch. Moderate–Expensive.*

Compagniet. An old wooden trading house from 1837 is now a stylish restaurant serving modern Norwegian food. Chef Morten Lønstad, formerly of Oslo's Feinschmecker, prepares sauteed shrimp with garlic and mussels baked in an herb sauce for starters, while main dishes include grilled monkfish with Dijon mustard hollandaise sauce. *Sjøgt. 12, tel. 083/55–721. Reservations required. Dress: casual but neat. AE, DC, MC, V. No lunch. Moderate–Expensive.*

Dining and Lodging

SAS Royal Hotel. It's a new, modern hotel with splendid views over the Tromsø shoreline, but standard rooms are tiny, and even the costlier "Royal Club" rooms aren't big enough for real desks and tables, so modular ones have been attached to the walls. *Sjøgt. 7, tel. 083/56–000, fax 083/85–474. 193 rooms with bath, 6 suites. Facilities: 3 restaurants, bar, nightclub, business center, parking. AE, DC, MC, V. Moderate–Very Expensive.*

Hotel With. This newly constructed building on the waterfront in the dock area has spacious rooms decorated in shades of gray with the occasional colorful accent. The sauna/relaxation room on the top floor has the best view in town. As a Home hotel, it offers free beer, a hot meal included in the room price, and waffles and coffee at all times. *Sjøgt. 35–37, tel. 083/87–000, fax 083/89–616. 76 rooms with shower. Facilities: fitness room, conference rooms, parking. AE, DC, MC, V. Moderate–Expensive.*

Polar Hotell. This no-frills hotel gives good value for money in the winter, when none of the bigger hotels have special rates. Rooms are small, and the orange/brown color scheme is a bit dated, but it's a pleasant, unassuming place to stay.

Grønnegaten 45, tel. 083/86–480, fax 083/89–136. 64 rooms with shower (no bathtubs). Facilities: restaurant, bar, conference room. AE, DC, MC, V. Inexpensive–Moderate.

Trondheim
Dining

★ **Bryggen.** The furnishings are in bleached wood, with dark-blue and red accessories, and the atmosphere is intimate. The menu features a reindeer fillet salad with cranberry vinaigrette and an herb cream soup with both freshwater and ocean crayfish for starters. Meat dishes include breast of chicken with a red-wine sauce and lamb medley. *Øvre Bakkelandet 66, tel. 07/53–40–55. Reservations required. Dress: casual but neat. AE, DC, MC, V. Closed Sun. No lunch. Expensive.*

Havfruen. "The Mermaid" has a maritime dining room with an open kitchen at street level, while in the cellar, 200-year-old stone walls from the original building frame the setting. Fish soup is the most popular starter, while summer main dishes include poached halibut. Desserts are simple—the citrus parfait is especially good. *Kjøpmannsgata 7, tel. 07/53–26–26. Reservations advised. Dress: casual but neat. AE, DC, MC, V. Closed Sun. No lunch. Moderate–Expensive.*

Hos Magnus. The price/value ratio is excellent at this old-fashioned, cozy restaurant in the new part of Bryggen. The menu ranges from such modern dishes as cognac-marinated moose fillet with mustard dressing to the old local specialty, *surlaks* (pickled salmon), for appetizers. The grilled, marinated spiral pork chop and the fillet of beef with mushrooms and onions are featured on the meat menu. There are ample fish dishes and vegetarian choices, too. *Kjøpmannsgata 63, tel. 07/52–41–10. Reservations advised. Dress: casual but neat. AE, DC, MC, V. Moderate.*

Lian. Into the heights above the city, Lian offers scenery and Norwegian standards. The oldest part of the restaurant dates from 1700, but the round section, from the 1930s, commands the best view. The food is solid, honest, and hearty, with roast beef, reindeer, smoked pork loin, and the old standby, *kjøttkaker* (Norwegian meat cakes). *Lian, tel. 07/55–90–77. Dress: casual. No credit cards. Closed Mon. Moderate.*

Palmehaven. It's been an "in" place for nearly 100 years, and judging from old pictures, it looks the same as it did at the turn of the century, with lots of pillars and palms and a fountain in the middle. Purposely pretentious, it is fine for lunch, but at night, it's overwhelming and overpriced. The hot dishes of the day are reasonably priced and well prepared, but the cakes are the big draw. *Brittania Hotel, Dronningens Gate 5, tel. 07/53–00–40. Jacket and tie required. AE, DC, MC, V. Closed Sun. Moderate.*

★ **Tavern på Sverresborg.** This big, yellow, wood former ferryman's house at the Trondelag Folkemuseum has been an inn since 1739. The food is authentic Norwegian, including meat and fish prepared with old methods—pickled, salted, and dried. Choices include a plate with four different kinds of herring, roast lamb ribs, trout, meat cakes, and rømmegrøt. Homemade oatmeal bread and rolls accompany all dishes. *Sverresborg Allé, tel. 07/52–09–32. Dress: casual but neat. MC, V. No lunch Sept. 2–May 19. Moderate.*

De 3 Stuer. This small bistro chain serves everything homemade, and the daily special features dishes like fish soufflé, fried fish with sour-cream sauce, split-pea soup with sausage, boiled beef, and lamb stew, all served with dessert and coffee. For lunch, there's smørbrød, crescent rolls, salads, and cakes.

Sundl (department store), Torvet, tel. 07/52–92–20; Leuthenhaven, tel. 07/52–43–42. Dronningens Gate, tel. 07/52–63–20. No reservations. Dress: casual. No credit cards. Dronningens Gate closed Sun. Inexpensive.

Lodging **Prinsen.** Rooms in this recently remodeled hotel in the center of the city are light, monochromatic to the point of being dull, and decorated with classic furniture. Teatergrillen, named after a nearby theater, serves a good early dinner. *Kongensgt. 30, 7002, tel. 07/53–06–50, fax 07/53–06–50. 65 rooms with bath or shower, 1 suite. Facilities: 3 restaurants, 3 bars, nightclub. AE, DC, MC, V. Moderate–Very Expensive.*

Royal Garden. The city's showcase hostelry, right on the river, was built in the same style as the old warehouse buildings that line the waterfront, only in glass and concrete. It's a luxury hotel, with big rooms, light wood furniture, and predominantly blue textiles. *Kjøpmannsgata 73, 7010, tel. 07/52–11–00, fax 07/53–17–66. 297 rooms with bath, 8 suites. Facilities: 3 restaurants, bar, pool, fitness room, shops. AE, DC, MC, V. Moderate–Very Expensive.*

Augustin. Remodeled in 1987, the rooms in this central hotel are small, but they have flair, with textiles in vibrant colors and lacquered furniture. The bathrooms are pristine white, and plenty of towels are provided. Minibars have soft drinks only (this is a dry hotel), but they're on the house. *Kongensgt. 26, 7011, tel. 07/52–83–48, fax 07/51–55–01. 75 rooms with bath or shower. Facilities: conference room. AE, DC, MC, V. Inexpensive–Moderate.*

★ **Bakeriet.** Built as a bakery in 1863, Trondheim's newest hotel opened in March 1991. There's no restaurant, but a hot evening meal is included in the room rate. You can borrow a track suit, and there's free beer in the lounge by the sauna. Every room has a VCR and a window thermometer. Few rooms look alike, but all are large, with natural wood furniture, beige-and-red-stripe textiles, and stylish in their simplicity. *Brattørgata 2, 7000, tel. 07/52–52–00, fax 07/50–23–30. 91 rooms with bath or shower, 1 suite. Facilities: sauna. AE, DC, MC, V. Inexpensive–Moderate.*

Trondheim. If you've always wanted to try mead, the fermented honey drink of the Vikings, you can do it here—it's produced on the premises. The building is old on the outside, with a curved corner and wrought-iron balconies, but inside, it's completely remodeled. The rooms are big and light, with what is now considered classic Scandinavian bentwood furniture. *Kongensgt. 15, 7013, tel. 07/52–70–30, fax 07/51–60–58. 140 rooms with shower or bath. Facilities: restaurant, bar, conference room. AE, DC, MC, V. Inexpensive–Moderate.*

Singsaker Sommerhotell. A student dorm that becomes a hotel from June 15 to August 20, it is not much cheaper than many downtown hotels. It's good for the single traveler, though, as the lounge fills up in the evening with other loners. Take bus No. 63, marked JERNBANE to Johnsensgaten. *Rogertsgt. 1, 7016, tel. 07/52–00–92. 100 rooms, 15 with bath. Facilities: bar, fitness room. AE, DC, MC, V. Inexpensive.*

The Arts and Nightlife

The Arts
Trondheim

Olavshallen (Kjøpmannsgt. 44, tel. 07/53–61–00), a concert and cultural center built in 1989, is the home of Trondheim's symphony and the nearly 3,000 music students in the city. The auditorium seats 1,300. The concert and entertainment season is from September through May.

During the last week in July, the *St. Olav Play* is performed at the outdoor amphitheater in **Stiklestad,** 98 km (60 mi) from Trondheim. The play, with a cast of 300, commemorates the life of King Olav Haraldsson, who united and brought Christianity to Norway, and was killed in battle here on July 29, 1030. Tickets are available from any post office or from Trondheim or Stiklestad tourist information offices (tel. 076/71–200, open June 20–Aug. 20).

Tromsø Every year in January the city celebrates **Nordlysfestivalen** (the Northern Lights Festival) with a series of concerts by distinguished visiting artists at Kulturhuset (the Culture House) (Grønnegata 87, tel. 083/82064). For concert information and reservations, contact the festival at Box 966, N–9000 Tromsø, tel. 083/80863, or fax 083/80109.

The North Nature takes precedence over the arts in northern Norway, but Harstad hosts the yearly **Northern Norway Festival** in June.

From June 15 to August 15, **Beaivas Sami Theater** (9250 Kautokeino, tel. 084/56–811) offers summer programs of traditional Sami folk songs and modern works.

Nightlife

Trondheim **Olavskvartalet** is the center of much of the city's nightlife, with a disco, a jazz and blues club, and a bar and beerhall in the cellar. **Hotell Prinsen** has a summer restaurant, **Sommer'n,** open from mid-May to the end of August, with live music and dancing. **Restauranthuset Norrein** (Dronningens Gate 12, tel. 07/52–24–23) is an entertainment complex with the **Sunset Club,** a piano bar, and **Beverly,** a postmodern café straight out of California. On the top floor is a disco for the younger crowd.

Tromsø Tromsø brags that it has 12 nightclubs, not bad for a city of 50,000 at the top of the world. **Compagniet,** (*see* Dining, *above*) has the classiest nightclub; **Charly's** at the SAS Royal Hotel and **Papagena** at the Grand Nordic Hotel are also popular.

6 Sweden

Introduction

by Chris Mosey

Chris Mosey is an English journalist who for 12 years lived in Sweden, where he was correspondent for the London newspapers The Times *and* The Observer. *He now lives in southern France.*

Sweden requires the visitor to travel far, in terms of both distance and attitude. In distance you head to the forested fringes of northernmost Europe to a land where nature dominates: vast tracts of pine, spruce, and birch, tens of thousands of lakes, and acre upon acre of wild, desolate moorland littered with great granite boulders and spliced by wild, tumbling rivers.

In attitude this is a more silent, reserved, brooding, and specifically Scandinavian world than that of its neighbors. Once the dominant power of the region, Sweden has traditionally looked mostly inward, seeking to find its own, Nordic, solutions. During the Cold War, it tried with considerable success to steer its famous "Middle Way" between the two superpowers, both economically and politically. Its citizens were in effect benignly subjected to a giant social experiment aimed at creating a perfectly just society, one that adopted the best aspects of both socialism and capitalism.

As it slips into worsening economic crisis, it must make adjustments at home that will eventually lessen the role of its all-embracing welfare state in the lives of its citizens. As a result, the mostly blond, blue-eyed Swedes may now be more open to the outside world than at any other time in their history.

The country possesses stunning natural assets. Nature is a real part of life here, not just something glimpsed between freeways and airports. In the forests, moose, deer, bear, and lynx roam, coexisting with the whine of power saws and the rumble of automatic logging machines as mankind exploits a natural resource that remains the country's economic backbone. Fish abound in sparkling lakes and tumbling rivers, sea eagles and ospreys soar over myriad pine-clad islands in the archipelagoes off the east and west coasts.

The population is thinly spread, with 8.5 million people inhabiting a country 173,731 square miles in area, Europe's fourth largest. If, like Greta Garbo, one of its most famous exports, you want to be alone, you've come to the right place. A law called *Allemansrätt* guarantees freedom of access to the countryside; you'll seldom encounter signs warning NO TRESPASSING.

Sweden stretches 977 miles from the barren, Arctic north to the fertile plains of the south. Contrasts abound, but they are neatly tied together by a superbly efficient infrastructure, embracing air, road, and rail. You can catch salmon in the far north, justly claimed to be "Europe's last wilderness," and, thanks to the excellent domestic air network, have it cooked by the chef of your luxury hotel in Stockholm later the same day.

The seasons contrast savagely: Sweden is usually warm and exceedingly light in the summer, then bitterly cold and dark in the winter. The sea may freeze and, in the north, iron railway lines may snap.

Sweden also is an arresting mixture of ancient and modern. The countryside is dotted with rune stones recalling its Viking past: trade beginning in the 8th century eastward to Kiev and as far south as Constantinople and the Mediterranean, expansion to the British isles in the 9th through 11th centuries, and

Sweden

N
0 50 miles
0 75 km
Norwegian Sea
Kiruna
Luleälven
Jokkmokk
Arjeplog
Tärnaby
Kalix
Torneå
Arvidsjaur
Sorsele
Luleå
Piteå
Storuman
Lycksele
Skellefteå
Umeälven
Åsele
Umeå
Strömsund
Åre
Östersund
Tännäs
Sundsvall
FINLAND
NORWAY
Ljungan
Gulf of Bothnia
Idre
Hudiksvall
Bollnäs
Söderhamn
Mora
Klarälven
Falun
Borlänge
Avesta
Fagersta
Uppsala
Karlstad
Västerås
Stockholm
Mälaren
Gulf of Finland
Mellerud
Örebro
Strömstad
Vänern
Gotska Sandön
Uddevalla
Trollhättan
Norrköping
ESTONIA
Vättern
Linköping
Göteborg
Baltic Sea
Jönköping
Borås
Visby
Gulf of Riga
Nässjö
Falkenberg
Värnamo
Oskarshamn
Gotland
Halmstad
Växjö
Kalmar
Öland
LATVIA
Helsingborg
Karlskrona
Kristianstad
Malmö
DENMARK
LITHUANIA
Trelleborg
Ystad

settlement in Normandy in the 10th century. Small timbered farmhouses and Maypoles around which villagers still dance to folk music at Midsummer in their traditional costumes evoke both the pagan early history and the more recent agrarian culture.

Its cities are sci-fi modern, their shop windows filled with the latest in consumer goods and fashions, but Swedes are reluctant urbanites: Their hearts and souls are in the forests and the archipelagoes, and there they faithfully retreat in the summer and on weekends to take their holidays, pick berries, or just listen to the silence. The skills of the woodcarver, the weaver, the leatherworker, and the glassblower are all highly prized. Similarly, Swedish humor is earthy and slapstick. Despite the praise lavished abroad on introspective dramatic artists such as August Strindberg and Ingmar Bergman, it is the simple trouser-dropping farce that will fill Stockholm's theaters, the scatological joke that will get most laughs.

Again, despite the international musical success of the rock groups Roxette and Abba, the domestic penchant more often is for the good old-fashioned dance band. Gray-haired men in pastel-shaded sweaters playing saxophones are more common on TV than heavy-metal rockers. Strangely, in ultramodern concert halls and discos, it is possible to step back in time to the 1950s, if not the 1940s.

It is also a respect for tradition, in this case the Lutheran religion, that has led to Sweden's strained relationship with alcohol. In the "bad old days," when the country was one of the most backward agrarian societies in Europe, spirits were used by impoverished peasants to dull the trials of everyday life. The labor movement and political parties saw alcohol abuse as an evil and over the years imposed restrictions on the sale and consumption of strong drink.

As a consequence, in preference to living it up, Swedes favor quiet nights at home, having what they call a *mysig* time. The word is difficult to translate but "cozy" comes closest.

Despite the much-publicized sexual liberation of Swedes, the joys of hearth and home are most prized in what remains in many ways an extremely conservative society. Conformity, not liberty, is the real key to the Swedish character: The good of the collective has always come before that of the individual, and this is why socialism has had such a strong appeal here.

Sweden was the first country in the world to peacefully and freely elect a socialist government (in 1920) and the Social Democratic Party has mostly held power since. Sometimes, to the outsider, political attitudes can seem quaintly askew, but appearances deceive. Swedes will point accusing fingers at U.S. policies in Latin America or the Middle East that can infuriate the unsuspecting visitor. The next minute, your interlocutor will joyously tell you how much he or she enjoys watching *Dallas* or *Twin Peaks*, oblivious to any contradiction.

Again, while democratic socialism firmly established itself, Swedes remain devoted royalists and patriots, avidly following the fortunes of King Carl XVI Gustaf, Queen Silvia, and their children in the media and raising the blue-and-yellow national flag each morning on the flag poles of their country cottages. Few nations, in fact, take as much effort to preserve and defend their natural heritage. It is sometimes difficult in cities such as Stockholm, Göteborg, or Malmö to realize that you are in an urban area. Right in the center of Stockholm, thanks to a cleanup program in the 1970s, you can fish for salmon or go for a swim. In Göteborg's busy harbor, you can sit aboard a ship bound for the archipelago and watch fish jump out of the water; in Malmö hares hop around in the downtown parks. It is this pristine quality to life that can make a visit to Sweden a step out of time, a relaxing break from the modern world.

Before You Go

Government Tourist Offices

In the United States **Swedish Tourist Board,** 655 3rd Ave., 18th floor, New York, NY 10017, tel. 212/949–2333.

In Canada Sweden has no tourist office in Canada. For information write to the U.S. office.

In the United Kingdom **Swedish Tourist Board,** 29–31 Oxford St., 5th floor, London W1R 1RE, tel. 071/437–5816.

Tour Groups

General-interest **Cole Travel Service Inc.** (310 W. State St., Geneva, IL 60134, tel. 312/232–4450) can arrange bed-and-breakfast holidays at 200 hotels, inns, and guest houses at 130 locations in Sweden. **Scantours Inc.** (1535 6th St., Suite 205, Santa Monica, CA 90401, tel. 213/451–0911) can fix independent packages, escorted tours, and group travel. **Scandinavian American World Tours, Inc.** (795 Franklin Ave., Franklin Lakes, NJ 07417, tel. 201/891–6641) offers "deluxe, first-class" and escorted tours. **Bennett Tours** (270 Madison Ave., New York, NY 10016, tel. 800/221–2420) offers tours of Scandinavia. **Watling Sweden** (91–93, Cranbrook Rd., Ilford, Essex, England, tel. 081/553–3883) and **Swedish Chalets** (28 Hillcrest Rd., Orpington, Kent, BR6 9AW, England, tel. 689/24958) offer chalet holidays for the family. **Star Tour of Scandinavia** (209 Edgware Rd., London W2 1ES, tel. 71/706 25–20) and **Scanscape Holidays** (Hillgate House, 13 Hillgate St., London W8 7SP, tel. 071/221–3244) offer low-cost charter flights from the United Kingdom. **Anglers World** (46 Knifesmith Gate, Chesterfield, Derbyshire, England, tel. 246/221717) runs holidays for fishermen in Sweden.

Cruises **EuroCruises** (Box 30925, New York, NY 10011, tel. 212/691–2099) offers cruises to Sweden from Amsterdam, Helsinki, Leningrad, Newcastle, North Cape, Tallinn, and Turku. **Scandinavian Seaways** (Crown Place, Suite 212, 6499 N.W. 9th Ave., Ft. Lauderdale, FL 33309, tel. 800/533–3755, and Parkeston Quay, Harwich, England, tel. 0255/240–240) offers overnight crossings to Sweden from England and Holland.

When to Go

The best time to visit Sweden is in the summer, from mid-May through August, when temperatures are usually high and the days exceptionally long. However, remember to pack some warm and rainproof clothing, just in case. The winters are usually long, dark, and hard, the country covered with snow and ice. January is too dark for skiing but in February the days start to lengthen and the trails are in prime condition. A word of warning: Temperatures will be far lower than those of central Europe. The following are average daily maximum and minimum temperatures for Stockholm.

Jan.	30F	-1C	**May**	57F	14C	**Sept.**	59F	15C
	23	-5		43	6		48	9
Feb.	30F	-1C	**June**	66F	19C	**Oct.**	48F	9C
	23	-5		52	11		41	5
Mar.	37F	3C	**July**	72F	22C	**Nov.**	41F	5C
	25	-4		57	14		34	1
Apr.	46F	8C	**Aug.**	68F	20C	**Dec.**	36F	2C
	34	1		55	13		28	-2

Festivals and Seasonal Events

January 13: Knut signals the end of Christmas festivities and "plundering" of the Christmas tree: Trinkets are removed from the tree, edible ornaments eaten, and the tree itself thrown out.

February (first Thursday, Friday, and Saturday): A **market** held in the small town of Jokkmokk, above the Arctic Circle, features both traditional Lapp artifacts, modern bric-a-brac, and plenty of reindeer with a herd usually driven down the main street.

Shrove Tuesday: Special buns called *semlor* are eaten; lightly flavored with cardamom, filled with almond paste and whipped cream, they traditionally are placed in a dish of warm milk and topped with cinnamon.

March (first Sunday): The **Vasaloppet 55-mile ski race** from Sälen to Mora in Dalarna attracts entrants from all over the world.

Maundy Thursday: Small girls dress up as witches and hand out "Easter letters" for small change. *Påskris*, twigs tipped with brightly colored chicken feathers, decorate homes.

April 30: For the **Feast of Valborg,** bonfires are lit to celebrate the end of winter. The most lively celebrations involve the students of the university city of Uppsala, 60 kilometers (37 miles) north of Stockholm.

May 1: Labor Day marches and rallies are held nationwide.

June 6: National Day is celebrated, with parades, speeches, and band concerts nationwide.

June: Midsummer's Day celebrations are held on the Saturday that falls between June 20 and 26. Swedes decorate their homes with flower garlands, raise Maypoles, and dance round them to folk music.

August 7–16: Stockholm Water Festival celebrates crayfish eating next to the Royal Palace, accompanied by fireworks.

August (second Wednesday): Crayfish are considered a delicacy in Sweden and on this day, the **Crayfish premiere,** friends gather to eat them at outdoor parties.

November 11: St. Martin's Day is celebrated primarily in the southern province of Skåne. Roast goose is served, accompanied by *svartsoppa*, a bisque made of goose blood and spices.

December: For each of the four weeks of **Advent,** leading up to Christmas, a candle is lit in a four-prong candelabra.

December 10: Nobel Day sees the presentation of the Nobel prizes by King Carl XVI Gustaf at a glittering banquet held in Stockholm City Hall.

December 13: Santa Lucia Day officially commemorates a Sicilian saint but most likely has its roots in pagan times. Young girls (preferably blondes) are selected to be "Lucias," and ceremonies are held in which the Lucias wear candles (today usually electric substitutes) in their hair and sing hymns along with their handmaidens and "stablelads."

December 24: Christmas Eve is the principal day of Christmas celebration in Sweden. Traditional Christmas dishes include ham, rice porridge, and *lutfisk* (ling that is dried and then boiled).

What to Pack

Take a warm sweater and something rainproof with you, even in summer, just in case. In winter, make sure you have lots of warm clothing and a hat or cap with protection for ears. The emphasis should be on sensible clothing. Mosquitoes can be a nuisance in the countryside from June through September, so pack an effective repellent.

Swedish Currency

The unit of currency is the krona (plural kronor), which is divided into 100 öre and is written as SKr. The 10-öre coin was phased out in 1991, leaving only the 50-öre and SKr1 coins. However, sometime in the next three years these will be joined by a SKr10 coin. Banknotes are at present: SKr10, 50, 100, 500, 1,000, and 10,000. However, the SKr10,000 note ceased to be legal tender in 1991 because of problems with counterfeiting, and the SKr10 note is to be phased out, replaced by the new coin, sometime in the next three years. At the same time a new SKr20 note will be introduced. At press time (summer 1991), the exchange rate was 5.97 to the dollar, 10.35 to the pound, and 5.30 to the Canadian dollar.

Bank Cards

There is an American Express cash and traveler's check dispenser at Arlanda, Stockholm's international airport, and outside the American Express office at Birger Jarlsgatan 1, Stockholm. The 1,000 or so blue Bankomat cash dispensers nationwide are being adapted to take some foreign cards by the autumn of 1991. For more information, contact Bankomat Centralen, tel. 08/7257240.

What It Will Cost

The short answer is a lot! Special tourist rates usually apply in the summer and some hotel chains give discounts. For details, contact the **Swedish Tourist Board,** Box 7473, 103 92 Stockholm, tel. 08/7892000. Some sample prices: Cup of coffee SKr12; strong beer SKr42–SKr55, mineral water, SKr11–SKr17; cheese roll, SKr16; pepper steak, à la carte, SKr160, cheeseburger, SKr30; pizza, SKr52.

Passports and Visas

American, British, and Canadian citizens are required to have a valid passport to enter Sweden, but no visa is needed unless they are planning to stay for more than three months.

Customs and Duties

Tourists entering Sweden are allowed to bring with them duty-free one liter of spirits, one liter of wine (includes aperitifs), and two liters of strong beer (exceeding 2.8% alcohol by weight). Travelers from Europe may bring in 200 cigarettes or 250 grams of other tobacco products. Other travelers are allowed to bring in 400 cigarettes or 500 grams of other tobacco products duty-free. More than 13,000 shops are part of a tax-free shopping service for visitors. When you buy goods, you are given a voucher for the value-added tax (VAT) paid on them that you can cash in when leaving the country. Look for the blue and yellow TAX FREE sign. For more information, including a brochure listing shops that are part of the plan, contact: **Sweden Tax-free Shopping,** Information Dept., Box 128, 231 22 Trelleborg, tel. 0410/19560.

Language

Swedish is closely related to Danish and Norwegian and derives primarily from German. After "z," the Swedish alphabet has three extra letters, "å,","ä," and "ö," something to bear in mind when using the phone book. Most Swedes speak English.

Car Rentals

All major companies are represented in Stockholm, many with branches nationwide. For local firms, look in the yellow pages under *Biluthyrning*. Many car rentals have special weekend rates off-season.

Rail Passes

A special pass called **Scanrail** allows for cheaper travel either for four days within a two-week timespan, nine days within three weeks, or 14 days within one month. The passes are available for both first- and second-class travel and can be purchased abroad through travel agents. (*See also* Chapter 1, Essential Information.)

The **Eurail** and **InterRail** passes are both valid in Sweden. **Statens Järnvägar** (SJ, the Swedish state railway company) also organizes reduced-cost package trips in conjunction with local tourist offices. Details are available at any railway station or from **SJ** (Vasagatan 22, 102 34 Stockholm, tel. 08/762–2000).

Student and Youth Travel

To and from Stockholm, those under 26 years of age can fly SAS for Skr150 to Skr200 one-way, and farther for Skr300. Such tickets cannot be reserved in advance, however, and are offered only if there is room. Airport buses, boat trips, and tourist tickets in Stockholm are free for children under seven years of age, free on weekends for children ages seven to 11 when riding with an adult, and half-price ages seven to 18.

Only Swedish students are given a discount by **SJ.** However, young people up to 26 years old can buy **Transalpino** tickets when traveling between Scandinavian countries that give 20% to 30% discounts on ordinary prices. Further information on student travel can be obtained from the **Swedish National Student Travel Bureau,** Kungsgatan 4, 103 87 Stockholm, tel. 08/234515.

Accommodations In addition to youth hostels, young visitors to Sweden will find low-cost, comfortable accommodations at any bed-and-breakfast establishment displaying the BILTUR-LOGI sign. For further information contact the **Swedish Tourist Board** or **Biltur-Logi** (S–79303 Tallberg, Sweden, tel. 247/50925).

Traveling with Children

On Swedish trains, up to two children under 12 years old can travel with an adult free, except for a small fee to make a reservation. In summer, families traveling with at least one child under 16 can receive a 50% discount for trips over 140 kilometers (87 miles) in second-class seats. Tickets can be bought only in Sweden. There are special family cars equipped with toys for children on the Stockholm–Malmö and Stockholm–Göteborg lines. Ask for this service when you are making reservations.

Hints for Disabled Travelers

Sweden has made great efforts to make life as easy as possible for disabled travelers. There are lifts and ramps for wheelchairs, specially adapted public toilets, and a host of other aids. The Swedish Tourist Board produces a free 265-page booklet titled *Holiday Guide for the Disabled*, which gives details of the many services available nationwide. These include special taxi and bus services, help for disabled travelers to board trains, and a list of camping sites, youth hostels, and hotels with special facilities for the disabled. One annual guide, "Hotels in Sweden" lists hotels with rooms adapted for disabled visitors. **Swiss Chalets** (28 Hillcrest Rd., Orpington, Kent BR6 9AW, England) offers holidays in Sweden designed for the disabled.

Getting Around
By Rail **Swedish State Railways (SJ)** offers special "transport chairs" to help physically disabled passengers get into trains and reach their seats. Most InterCity and other long-distance trains have wide carriages and large toilets, and a new kind of second-class carriage being introduced on the Stockholm–Malmö and Sundsvall–Stockholm–Göteborg routes allows passengers to sit in their own wheelchairs for the entire journey.

By Bus With advance notice, most bus companies in Sweden will gladly provide special assistance to disabled travelers. In addition, **Sirius Travel Service** (Stockholm, tel. 08/749–1900) operates taxis and mini-buses—complete with lifts and wheelchair mountings—for disabled passengers. **SHT** (Stockholm, tel. 08/528100) provides special coaches for group and individual travel.

By Taxi Information on **Fardtjänst,** a Swedish taxi service for the disabled, is available from local tourist offices in Sweden. Short trips are priced on an hourly basis, longer trips, according to distance.

Hints for Older Travelers

In Sweden during summer, travelers over 50 can buy a first-class train seat for only SKr50 more than a second-class seat. The Swedish **SARA** hotel chain offers a *SeniorPass* for those 65 and over, with rooms at half price (SeniorPass, SARA Hotels, Svarspost, Kundnr. 31598113, 18201–Denderyd, Sweden).

SAS offers discount tickets to and from Stockholm for those over 65, depending on distance, at a price of up to SKr400. Tickets may be reserved in advance.

Further Reading

One of the easiest and certainly most entertaining ways of finding out about modern Swedish society is to read the Martin Beck detective series of thrillers by Maj Sjöwall and Per Wahlöö, all of which have been translated into English. One of these, *The Terrorists*, was even prophetic, containing a scene in which a Swedish prime minister was shot dead, precursor to the murder of Olof Palme in 1986.

Similarly, an entertaining insight into how life was in the bad old days when Sweden was one of the most backward agrarian countries in Europe may be obtained from Vilhelm Moberg's series of novels on poor Swedes who emigrated to America: *The Emigrants*, *Unto a Good Land*, and *The Last Letter Home*.

One Swedish writer of genius was August Strindberg (1849–1912), whose plays greatly influenced modern European and American drama. Perhaps the most enduringly fascinating of these, *Miss Julie*, mixes the explosive elements of sex and class to stunning effect.

Another major talent was the novelist Selma Lagerlöf, first Swedish writer to win the Nobel Prize for Literature, whose works are rooted in local legend and saga. Best for providing insights on things specifically Swedish are the collection, *Tales of a Manor* (1899) and the children's book, *The Wonderful Adventures of Nils* (1906).

One of the most exhaustive and comprehensive studies in English of the country published in recent years is *Sweden: The Nation's History*, by Franklin D. Scott (University of Minnesota Press). The author's own *Cruel Awakening, Sweden and the Killing of Olof Palme* (C. Hurst, London 1991) seeks to provide an overview of the country and its recent history seen through the life and assassination of its best-known politician of recent times and the farcical hunt for his killer.

Arriving and Departing

From North America by Plane

Airports and Airlines Stockholm's **Arlanda** airport and Göteborg's **Landvetter** airport are served by **SAS** (tel. 800/251–2350), **British Airways,** and other major international airlines.

From the United Kingdom by Plane, Car, Ferry, Train, and Bus

By Plane The major airlines flying to Sweden from the United Kingdom include **SAS** (52–53 Condute St. W1R OAU, London, tel. 071/734–4020) and **British Airways (tel. 081/897–4000).**

By Car and Ferry There are excellent links between Harwich and Göteborg and Newcastle and Göteborg aboard **Scandinavian Seaways** ferries (Scandinavian Seaways, DFDS Ltd., Scandinavia House, Parkeston Quay, Harwich, Essex, CO12 4QG, England, tel. 0255/240–240). An alternate approach is through Denmark using ferry crossings to Malmö or Helsingborg.

By Train From London, the **British Rail European Travel Center** (Victoria Station, London, tel. 071/834–2345) can be helpful in arranging connections through to Sweden's **SJ** (Statens Jarnvagar).

By Bus Bus travel is the least expensive alternative, although it is slower and less comfortable.

Staying in Sweden

Getting Around

By Plane All major cities and towns are linked with regular flights by **Scandinavian Airlines System** (SAS) and the associated domestic airline, **Linjeflyg.** Most Swedish airports are located a long way from city centers but are linked to them by fast and efficient bus services. SAS also operates a limousine service at leading airports. For more information, contact SAS, Inrikes (Flygcity, Klarabergsviaducten 72, 111 64 Stockholm, tel. 08/240000).

By Train **SJ,** the state railway company, has a highly efficient network of comfortable, electrified trains. On nearly all long-distance routes, there are buffet cars, and, on overnight trips, sleeping cars and couchettes in both first and second class. A high-speed train was recently introduced on the Stockholm–Göteborg route. Look for so-called *röda avgångar* (red departures), which offer 50% reductions. Children under 16 travel at half fare. Up to two children under 12 may travel free if accompanied by an adult. There is a supplementary fare on trains designated as City Express. A "go as you please" ticket costing a little over SKr500 is available between June and August on the scenic *Inlandsbanan* (Inland Railway), which runs for more than 1,290 kilometers (800 miles) from Gällivare in the far north to Kristinehamn in the south. The ticket gives discounts on overnight accommodations and restaurants en route. For more information, contact **SJ** (Vasagatan 22, 105 51 Stockholm, tel. 08/762–2000).

In Sweden you can take your car onto the train. SJ car-trains go from Malmö, Göteborg, and Västerås to Luleå and Kiruna. You can also rent a car upon arrival by reserving a *tågbil* (train-car) when you buy your train ticket. These cars can be rented at all the larger stations by the day or weekend.

By Bus There is excellent bus service between all major towns and cities. Consult the yellow pages under *Bussresearrangörer* for telephone numbers of the companies concerned. Recommended are the services offered to different parts of Sweden from Göteborg by **GDG Continentbus** (Gullbergs Strandgatan 34, 411 04 Göteborg, tel. 031/735525). The state railway company, **SJ,** also operates bus services.

By Car There are few expressways, but roads are well maintained and relatively traffic free. Major car rental companies such as **Avis, Hertz, Europcar, Bonus, Budget, OK,** and **InterRent** have facilities in all major towns and cities and at airports. It is worth shopping around for special rates. See the yellow pages under *Biluthyrning* for telephone numbers and addresses.

By Boat An excellent way of seeing Sweden is from its many ferry boats, which ply the archipelagoes and main lakes. In Stockholm, visitors should buy a special *båtluffarkort*. This gives unlimited travel on the white archipelago ferry boats for a 16-day period and is available at the ferry ticket offices. Highly popular four-day cruises are available on the Göta Canal, which makes use of rivers, lakes, and, on its last lap, the Baltic Sea. This lovely waterway, which links Göteborg on the west coast with Stockholm on the east, has a total of 65 locks, and you travel on fine old steamers, some of which date back almost to the canal's opening in 1832. The oldest and most desirable is the *Juno*, built in 1874. Prices start at SKr4,300 for a bed in a double cabin. For more information, contact the **Göta Canal Steamship Company** (Box 272, S–401 24 Göteborg, tel. 031/806315).

Telephones

Post offices do not have telephone facilities, but there are plenty of pay phones, and long-distance calls can be ordered at special telegraph offices called *Telebutik*, or marked "Tele."

Local Calls The new orange pay phones, which are rapidly replacing the old green models, take 50-öre, SKr1, and SKr5 coins. A local call costs a minimum of SKr2. For calls outside the locality, dial the area code.

International Calls The foreign dialing code is 009 followed by the country code, then the number you require.

Operators and Information For directory inquiries, dial 07975 for information concerning Sweden, 0013 for the Nordic Area, and 0019 for other foreign inquiries. For operator-assisted foreign calls, dial 0018 on green pay phones; the orange pay phones cannot be used for such calls.

Mail

Postal Rates Letters up to 20 grams and postcards cost SKr2.50 to send inside the Nordic Area, SKr3.80 to elsewhere in Europe, and SKr4.60 to the United States and the rest of the world by air. Surface mail costs SKr3.80.

Tipping

A service charge of 15% is usually included in hotel bills; it is not necessary to tip unless you have received extra services. Similarly, a service charge of 13% is included in restaurant bills. It is a custom, however, to leave small change when buying drinks. Taxi drivers and hairdressers expect a tip of around 10%.

Opening and Closing Times

Banks **Banks** are open from 9:30 to 3. In the larger cities some stay open until 5:30. All banks are closed on Saturdays. The bank at Arlanda Airport, Stockholm, is open daily between 7 AM and 10 PM. There is also a bank at Landvetter Airport, Göteborg, which is open daily from 8 to 8. There are "Forex" **currency exchange** offices at the Central Station in Stockholm (8 AM–9 PM), Stockholm City Terminal (9 AM–6 PM), Göteborg Central Station (8 AM–9 PM), and at the Malmö tourist office (Hamngatan 1; 8 AM–9 PM).

Museums Most **museums** are open Tuesday through Sunday 10–5, though some have other hours. A free guide is available from tourist offices.

Stores Shopping hours vary, but most businesses are open 10–6 on weekdays and 9–1 (and sometimes 4) on Saturday. Some grocery shops are open until 9 PM, sometimes even 11 PM, though these are rare.

Shopping

Sweden produces expensive, high-quality handicraft goods, which are available at special *Hemslöjd* shops and in leading department stores such as **NK, Åhléns,** and **Pub.** Swedish crystal is a traditional favorite, the leading brands being Orrefors and Kosta Boda. At the glass factories themselves in the south, "seconds" shops provide bargain buys; otherwise expect to pay heavily for the craftsmanship, design, and reputation.

Sports and Outdoor Activities

Bicycling As there are separate bicycle tracks through most cities, and Swedish roads are usually not congested, bicycling is an increasingly popular way of getting around. Rental costs average around SKr80 per day. Tourist offices and Sveriges Turist förening (STF; the Swedish Touring Association) in Stockholm (tel. 08/790–3100) have information about cycling package holidays that include bike rentals, overnight accommodations, and meals. The bicycling organization, **Cykelfrämjandet** (tel. 08/321680), publishes an English-language guide to cycling trips.

Boating and Sailing STF, in cooperation with Televerket (Sweden's PTT—Postal, Telephone, and Telegraph authority), publishes an annual guide in Swedish to all the country's marinas with telephone numbers. It is available from STF (tel. 08/790–3250) or in your nearest PTT "Telebutik." The **Swedish Canoeing Association** (Svenksa Kanotförbundet, Idrottens Hus, 123 87 Farsta, tel. 08/605–6000), publishes a similar booklet for canoers.

Camping There are 760 registered campsites nationwide, many located close to uncrowded bathing places and with fishing, boating, or canoeing; they may also offer bicycle rentals. Prices range from SKr60 to SKr110 per 24-hour period. Many camping places also offer accommodations in log cabins at various prices, depending on the facilities offered, and some have special facilities for the disabled. Most are open between June and September, but about 200 remain open in winter for skiing and skating enthusiasts. An annual catalogue in English is available from tourist bureaus. For additional information, contact **Sveriges Camp-**

ingvärdarnas Riksförbund (Box 255, S-45117 Uddevalla, tel. 0522/38345).

Golf Sweden has 283 golf clubs, and the sport is exceptionally popular. You can even play by the light of the midnight sun at Boden in the far north. A booklet in English titled *Swing in Sweden* was published in 1986 and is available from the **Swedish Tourist Board** (tel. 08/789–2000). The **Swedish Golfing Association** (Svenska Golfförbundet, Box 84, 182 11 Danderyd, tel. 08/753–0265) publishes an annual guide in Swedish with current information; it costs around SKr60, plus postage.

Hiking There are countless trails nationwide, but **Kungsleden** (The King's Trail) through the mountains of Lappland, including Kebnekaise, at 7,000 feet the country's highest peak, is especially rewarding. Information on walking routes and overnight accommodations is available from **STF** (Box 25, S–101 20 Stockholm, tel. 08/790–3100).

Skiing There are plenty of both downhill and cross-country facilities. The best known resorts are in the country's western mountains: **Åre** in the north, with 29 lifts; **Idre Fjäll,** to the south of Åre, offering accommodation for 10,000; and **Sälen** in the folklore region of Dalarna. You can ski in summer at **Riksgränsen** in the far north. A new center called the **Discover Sweden Shop** (Stureplan 9, Stockholm, tel. 08/611–7430) has information on skiing and winter sport activities and will advise on equipment and clothing needed.

Tennis Since the time when Björn Borg won Wimbledon with almost monotonous regularity, Sweden has become a force in world tennis. There are indoor and outdoor courts throughout the country. The **Swedish Tennis Association** (Svenska Tennisförbundet, 12–13 Lidingövägen, 115 30 Stockholm, tel. 08/667–9770) can supply more information.

Water Sports Windsurfing and water-skiing are extremely popular in Sweden. One can learn the basics and rent equipment at many locations nationwide.

Beaches

There are relatively few sand beaches but thousands of unspoiled "bathing places" or *bad.* These are more likely to be grassy or rocky areas by the lakeside than sandy beaches, though these too can be found along both the east and west coasts and on the Baltic resort islands of Gotland and Öland. However, there is little need for the tourist to seek these out when it is possible to swim in clear, clean waters close to most urban centers.

Dining

In August look for *kräftor* (crayfish), which are boiled with dill, salt, and sugar, then cooled overnight. Swedes eat them with hot buttered toast, caraway seeds, and schnapps or beer. Later in the fall come an exotic assortment of mushrooms and wild berries.

Regional specialties include *spettekaka,* a cake of eggs and sugar made in Skåne, and *Gotlandsflundror,* a smoked flat fish from the island of Gotland. *Husmanskost* (home-cooking) recipes are often served in restaurants as a *dagens rätt* (the daily special). Examples are *pytt i panna* (literally, "put in the pan"—beef and potato hash topped with a fried egg), or pea soup with pancakes, a traditional meal on Thursday.

Sweden is known for its coffee. Jealous Danes theorize that foreigners like their coffee weak and therefore prefer Swedish varieties; Swedes just say it tastes better.

The nation's cuisine is basically peasant—sausages, potatoes, and other hearty foods to ward off the winter cold. However, it also has produced the *smörgåsbord,* a generous and artfully arranged buffet featuring both hot and cold dishes. You start with the herring, then eat your way through salads, vegetable dishes, meats, cheeses, and breads, winding up with a slice of *tårta* (cake) or some fruit. Fish—fresh, smoked, or pickled—is a Swedish specialty; herring and salmon both come in a myriad of traditional and innovative preparations.

The hotel breakfast is usually an extremely well-stocked *smörgåsbord*-style buffet. Lunches are markedly less expensive than dinner. Even in Stockholm, it is still possible to eat the *dagens rätt* (dish of the day) between 11:30 AM and 2 PM for under SKr50, with bread, salad, and either a light beer or a cup of coffee.

Dinner is a different matter entirely. An indifferent steak and potatoes can set you back SKr160, and a bottle of mediocre wine with the meal will cost at least that much again. Dinner for two with wine in one of the better Stockholm restaurants could easily cost SKr600 or more.

Category	**Cost***
Very Expensive	Over SKr500
Expensive	SKr250–SKr500
Moderate	SKr150–SKr250
Inexpensive	under SKr150

**per person, for a two-course meal, including service charge and tax but not wine.*

Lodging

While usually extremely clean and efficient, hotels are very expensive all over the country. However, in the summer months there are usually price breaks available.

Your travel agent or the Swedish Tourist Board will have full details, but some of the better buys are as follows: The **SARA** hotel chain offers the **Scandinavian BonusPass,** which costs about $25 and entitles the holder to discounts of between 15% and 30% from June 1 to August 31. The **Scandic Hotel** check plan enables you to pay for your accommodation in advance, with a weekend check costing SKr230 (SKr275 in the summer) with a supplement of SKr150 at city center hotels. **Sweden Hotels** offer a "hotel pass" costing SKr170 that gives a 50% discount at hotels throughout the country from mid-May to mid-September.

Some 50 hotels offer the **"Stockholm Package,"** providing accommodations for one night, breakfast, and a card giving free admission to museums and travel on public transport. Costs run from SKr380 to SKr610. Details are available from tourist bureaus or from the **Stockholm Information Service** (Box 7542, S–103 93 Stockholm).

Vandrarhem (youth hostels), also scrupulously clean and well-run, are more expensive than elsewhere in Europe. **Sveriges Turistförening** (STF; the Swedish Touring Association, Box 25, S–101 20 Stockholm, tel. 08/790–3100) has 280 nationwide, most with 4- to 6-bed family rooms and 80 with running hot and cold water in the rooms. They are open to anyone irrespective of age. Prices are SKr66 to SKr85 per night for members of STF or organizations affiliated to the International Youth Hostel Federation. For nonmembers, there is an extra charge of SKr32 per night. A hostel handbook is published annually by STF.

Category	**Cost***
Very Expensive	over SKr1,500
Expensive	SKr1,200–SKr1,500
Moderate	SKr1,000–SKr1,200
Inexpensive	under SKr1,000

**All prices are for a standard double room, including tax.*

Stockholm

Introduction

Set at the point where the waters of Mälaren (Lake Mälar) rush into the Baltic, Stockholm is one of Europe's most beautiful capitals. Nearly 1.6 million people now live in the greater Stockholm area, yet it remains a quiet, almost pastoral city.

Built on 14 small islands among open bays and narrow channels, Stockholm is a handsome, civilized city, full of parks, squares, and airy boulevards, yet it is also a bustling, modern metropolis. Glass-and-steel skyscrapers abound, but you are never more than five minutes' walk from twisting, medieval streets and waterside walks.

The first written mention of Stockholm dates from 1252, when a powerful regent named Birger Jarl built a fortified castle and city here. King Gustav Vasa took over the city in 1523, and King Gustavus Adolphus made it the heart of an empire a century later.

During the Thirty Years' War (1618–48), Sweden gained importance as a Baltic trading state, and Stockholm grew commensurately. But by the beginning of the 18th century, Swedish influence was waning, and Stockholm's development had slowed. It did not revive until the Industrial Revolution, when the hub of the city moved north from the Old Town area.

Nowadays most Stockholmers live in high-rise suburbs dotted in the pine forests and by lakesides around the capital, linked to it by a highly efficient infrastructure of roads, railways, and one of the safest subway systems in the world. Air pollution is minimal and the city streets are relatively clean and safe.

Important Addresses and Numbers

Tourist Information The main tourist office in the center of the city at **Sverigehuset** (Sweden House; Kungsträdgården, Stockholm, tel. 08/789–2000) is open every day. Here you will find information on current events, sightseeing, one-day tours, and so on. Bookings can be made for tours. Maps, postcards, books, and souvenirs are on sale.

The free publication *Stockholm This Week* is available at most hotels and tourist centers. Also worth buying is the Saturday edition of the daily newspaper *Dagens Nyheter* for its current listing of events, films, restaurants, and museums (in Swedish, of course).

Embassies **U.S. Embassy:** Strandvägen 101, tel. 08/783–5300. **Canadian Embassy:** Tegelbacken 4, tel. 08/237920. **U.K. Embassy,** Skärpögatan 6–8, tel. 08/6670140.

Emergencies Dial 90000 for emergencies. This covers police, fire, ambulance, and medical help, and sea and air rescue services.

Doctors There is a 24-hour national health service emergency service (tel. 08/449200) and private care via City Hälsocentral (tel. 08/206990).

Dentists There is an emergency clinic at St. Erik's Hospital, open 8 AM–7 PM, with provision for acute cases up until 9 PM (tel. 08/541117). The emergency number is 08/459200.

English-language Bookstores Nearly all bookshops stock English-language books. The best selections are at **Hedengren's** (Sturegallerian shopping complex, tel. 08/611–5132) and **Akademibokhandeln** (Mäster Samuelsgatan 32, near city center, tel. 08/214890). For English-language newspapers and magazines, try the **International Presscenter** (Regeringsgatan 12, tel. 08/723–0191) or one of the newsstands at the central station.

Late-night Pharmacies **C. W. Scheele** (Klarabergsgatan 64, tel. 08/218934 or 08/218280) is open all night.

Travel Agencies **American Express** is at Birger Jarlsgatan 1 (tel. 08/235330) and **Thomas Cook** at Vasagatan 22 (tel. 08/204990). **SJ,** the state railway company, also has a travel bureau at Vasagatan 22 (tel. 08/148915 for train travel, 08/148910 for air travel). For other travel agencies, see the yellow pages under *Resor-Resebyråer*.

Arriving and Departing by Plane

Airport Stockholm's **Arlanda** Airport was opened in 1960 at first solely for international flights, but it now also contains the domestic terminal. Arlanda is 41 kilometers (26 miles) from the center of Stockholm and is linked to it by freeway.

Between the Airport and City Center

By Bus Buses leave both the international and domestic terminals every 10 to 15 minutes from 7:10 AM to 10:30 PM and run to the city terminal at Klarabergsviadukten next to the central railway station. The trip costs SKr40. For more information, tel. 08/236000.

By Taxi A taxi from the airport will cost at least SKr300, but SAS operates a shared limousine to any point in central Stockholm. This will cost between SKr185 and SKr280, depending on distance. If two or more people travel together in a limousine to the same address, only one pays the full rate; all others pay half price. For more information and bookings, call 08/797–3700.

Arriving and Departing by Car, Train, and Bus

By Car You will approach the city by either the E3 highway from the west or the E4 from the north or south. The roads are clearly marked and well sanded and plowed during winter.

By Train All trains arrive at Stockholm Central Station on Vasagatan in downtown Stockholm (tel. 08/762–2000). From here regular commuter trains serve the suburbs, and an underground walkway leads to the central subway station.

By Bus Buses arrive at various points, all close to the central railway station. There are numerous companies, but the principal ones, with services to most parts of the country, are run by **SJ,** the state railway company (tel. 08/762–2000), and **GDG Continentbus** (tel. 08/234810).

Getting Around

The most effective way to get around the city is to purchase a *Stockholmskort* (Key to Stockholm) card. Besides giving unlimited transportation on city subway, bus, and rail services, it offers free admission to 50 museums and several sightseeing trips. The card costs SKr125 for 24 hours, SKr250 for two days, and SKr375 for three days. It is available from the tourist center at Sweden House in Kungsträdgården and from the Hotellcentralen accommodations bureau at the central station.

Otherwise, tickets may be bought on buses or at the subway barrier. The minimum fare is SKr10. It is cheaper to buy a discount coupon from one of the many Pressbyrån newsstands. A one-day ticket for the city center alone, valid for both subway and buses, costs SKr28. A ticket covering the entire Greater Stockholm area costs SKr50 for 24 hours or SKr95 for 72 hours. People under 18 or over 65 pay half.

Maps and timetables for all city transportation networks are available from the SL information desks at Norrmalmstorg or Sergels Torg. Information is also available by phone (tel. 08/236000).

By Car Rental cars are readily available in Sweden and relatively inexpensive. Because of the availability and efficiency of public transport, there is little point in using a car within the city limits. However, if you are traveling elsewhere in Sweden, roads are uncongested and well marked, but gasoline is expensive (SKr7 per liter at press time). All major car rental firms are represented, including **Avis** (Ringvägen 90, tel. 08/449980) and **Hertz** (Vasagatan 26, tel. 08/240720.)

By Bus and Subway Stockholm has excellent bus and subway service. The subway stations are marked by a blue-on-white T (short for *Tunnelbanan,* or subway). They are decorated with modern art (and, increasingly, graffiti). The subway covers more than 60 route miles, and trains run frequently between 5 AM and 2 AM. There are also several night buses.

By Taxi Stockholm's taxi service is both inefficient and overpriced. To order a cab, telephone 08/150000 or 08/150400 if you need to reserve one well in advance. However, be warned: You are most likely to encounter an automatic answering service asking you (in Swedish) to be patient and wait. There is an immediate charge of SKr19 if you hail a taxi, SKr40 if you order by phone. A trip of 10 kilometers (6 miles) costs SKr58.8 between 6 AM and 7 PM, SKr67 at night, and SKr77 on weekends. There is an additional charge if you book in advance.

Opening and Closing Times

Banks **Banks** are open weekdays 9:30 AM to 3 PM but some, notably the SE-Banken branch in Sergels Torg, stay open until 5:30 most days. The bank at Arlanda airport is open every day with extended hours and the Forex currency exchange offices also have extended hours.

Museums The opening times for **museums** vary widely but most are open from 10 AM to 4 PM weekdays and over the weekend but closed on Monday. Consult the guide in *På Stan*, the entertainment supplement published in *Dagens Nyheter's* Saturday edition.

Stores **Shops** are generally open weekdays from 9 AM, 9:30 AM, or 10 AM until 6 PM and Saturday from 9 AM to 1 PM or 4 PM. Most of the large department stores stay open later in the evenings and some open on Sunday. There are several supermarkets open Sunday and there is a reasonable number of late-night food shops.

Guided Tours

Orientation A bus tour in English and Swedish of all the main points of interest leaves each day starting at 11 AM from outside the Tourist Center at Sverigehuset and costs SKr100. Other more comprehensive tours, taking in museums, the Old Town, and City Hall, cost SKr200. Tickets are available at the Tourist Center (Kungsträdgården).

City Sightseeing (tel. 08/117023) runs several tours, including a three-hour "Stockholm in a Nutshell" combined boat and bus tour and a 50-minute introductory "mini-tour." These leave from in front of the Royal Opera House in Gustav Adolfs Torg.

Stockholm Sightseeing (tel. 08/240470) also runs combined boat and bus tours from outside the Grand Hotel and City Hall.

Boat Tours **Strömma Sightseeing** (Skeppsbron 22, tel. 08/233375) runs boat trips from various locations, including a 9 PM candlelight cruise from Nybroplan, the quay in front of the Royal Dramatic Theater.

Personal Guides Individual city guides may be hired from Stockholm Information Service's **Guide Centralen** (Box 7542, S–10393 Stockholm, tel. 08/789–2431), but be sure to book well in advance. Costs average SKr700 for a three-hour tour.

Walking Tours There is a walking tour of the Old Town every evening at 6:30 from June to mid-September, starting from the Obelisk, Slottsbacken (Palace Hill).

Highlights for First-time Visitors

Djurgården (*see* Tour 4)
Drottningholm Palace (*see* Tour 3)
Gamla Stan (Stockholm's Old Town) (*see* Tour 2)

Kungliga Slottet (Royal Palace) (*see* Tour 2)
Stadshuset (City Hall) (*see* Tour 3)
Skansen (*see* Tour 4)
Vasa Museum (*see* Tour 4)

Exploring Stockholm

The center of Stockholm is Sergels Torg, a modern, sunken square dominated by Kulturhuset (the House of Culture). A short walk south down Drottninggatan takes you past the Parliament building on Helgeands Holmen (Holy Ghost Island) over the tumbling Strömmen (the Current), where Lake Mälar empties into the Baltic, and into the superbly well preserved medieval Gamla Stan (Old Town).

Behind the island of Skeppsholmen there is another stretch of water where fine old sailing boats rest at anchor along Strandvägen, the waterfront for Östermalm, the upscale residential area. At the end of Strandvägen, a bridge takes you over to Djurgården.

Directly south of Gamla Stan is Södermalm (known as Söder), the south island, traditionally a working-class neighborhood though today much sought after by all and with several art and handicraft galleries.

Numbers in the margin correspond with points of interest on the Stockholm map.

Tour 1: Modern Stockholm

The heart of the city, **Sergels Torg,** named after Johan Tobias Sergel (1740–1814), one of Sweden's greatest sculptors, is dominated by modern, functional buildings that include
1 **Kulturhuset** (the House of Culture), a combined library and exhibition center, with an excellent restaurant. Make a slight detour to visit the Åhléns department store, then walk north, along the pedestrian street Sergelgatan in the shadow of five identical concrete-and-glass skyscrapers to **Hötorget** (the Hay
2 Market), where you'll find **Konserthuset** (the Concert House), a colorful fruit and vegetable market, and the PUB department store. You might also like to visit **Hötorgshallen,** an underground, old-fashioned food hall, with inexpensive restaurants.

Head east over Sveavägen, where you can make a brief detour to see the spot where Olof Palme was assassinated in 1986 and to visit his grave in Adolf Fredrik's Churchyard nearby.

Next, walk down **Kungsgatan,** Stockholm's main shopping street, to Stureplan. In **Stureplan,** you'll find Sturegallerian, a fine modern shopping precinct, and Hedengrens, the best English bookshop in town. South along **Birger Jarlsgatan,** a street named after the nobleman generally credited with founding Stockholm around 1252, there are still more interesting shops and restaurants. When you reach Nybroplan, take a look at
3 **Kungliga Dramatiska Teatern** (the Royal Dramatic Theater), an imposing building with a gilded roof that faces out over the Baltic harbor. Here productions by Ingmar Bergman, the country's leading director, provoke the imagination.

4 Heading west up Hamngatan, drop in at **Hallwylska Museet** (the Hallwyl Museum), a private turn-of-the-century palace, with large imposing wood-panel rooms, housing a collection of

furniture, paintings, and musical instruments in a bewildering mélange of styles assembled by the Countess von Hallwyl, who left it to the state on her death. *Hamngatan 4, tel. 08/666–4499. Admission: SKr30. English guided tour June–Sept., daily 1 PM; Sept.–May, Sun. 1 PM.*

Not far along Hamngatan you find **Kungsträdgården,** a park since 1562 but previously the royal kitchen garden. There are usually public concerts and events here in the summer.

5 On the park you will find **Sverigehuset** (Sweden House), with its excellent tourist center, and on the opposite side of the street the NK department store.

If you have time, head down Kungsträdgårdensgatan to the Blasieholmshamnen quay, passing the **Grand Hotel** (where No-
6 belists are accommodated each year) and visit the **National Museum,** with its fine collection of old masters, including some of Rembrandt's major works. *Södra Blasieholmshamnen, tel. 08/666–4250. Admission: SKr30, free Fri. Open Wed., Fri., Sat., Sun. 11–5; Tues., Thurs. 11–9.*

Cross the footbridge to the idyllic island **Skeppsholmen,** where
7 you'll find two museums. **Östasiatiska Museet** (the Museum of Far Eastern Antiquities), has an arresting collection of Chinese and Japanese Buddhist sculptures and artifacts. *Skeppsholmen, tel. 08/666–4250. Admission: SKr30, free Wed. Open Tues. 11–9, Wed.–Sun. 11–5.*

8 A little farther along, **Moderna Museet** (the Modern Museum) features a good selection of contemporary art, including works by Picasso, Dali, and Modigliani. The museum is also the venue for numerous important touring exhibitions and a popular rendezvous for local art lovers, with a fine, health-food-oriented canteen and a workshop for children. *Skeppsholmen, tel. 08/666–4250. Admission: SKr30, free Thurs. Open Tues.–Fri. 11–9; Sat., Sun., 11–5.*

9 The adjoining island, **Kastellholmen,** is a pleasant place for a stroll, especially on a summer evening, with fine views of Gamla Stan's seafront, across the Baltic harbor.

Tour 2: Gamla Stan (The Old Town)

Gamla Stan sits on a cluster of small islands between two of Stockholm's main islands and is the site of the medieval city. The narrow twisting cobbled streets are lined with superbly preserved old buildings.

10 Start at the refurbished stone **Riksdagshuset** (Parliament building) on **Helgeandsholmen** (Holy Ghost Island). It dates from the end of the 19th century. *Admission free. English guided tours Oct.–May, weekends 12:30 PM; June–Aug., weekdays 12:30, 3.*

11 Cross the bridge to **Kungliga Slottet** (the Royal Palace), a magnificent granite edifice designed by Nicodemus Tessin and completed in 1760. There is a fine view here of the Baltic harbor, with the *af Chapman* sailing-ship youth hostel and the Grand Hotel and National Museum in the background. The **State Apartments** feature fine furnishings and Gobelins tapestries. **Livsrustkammaren** (the Royal Armory) boasts an outstanding collection of weaponry and royal regalia while **Skattkammaren** (the Treasury) houses the crown jewels, which

Stockholm

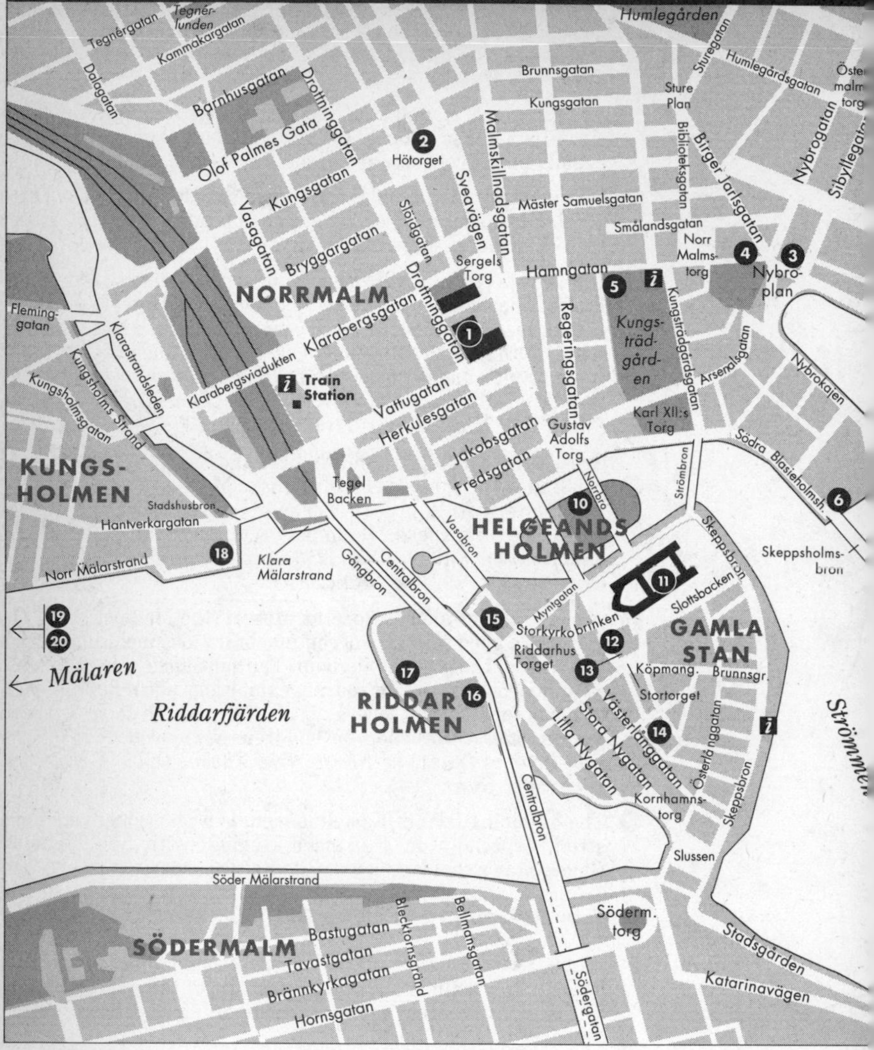

Biologiska Museet, **25**
Drottningholms Slott, **19**
Drottningholms Slottsteater, **20**
Gröna Lund, **23**
Hallwylska Museet, **4**
Historiska Museet, **28**
Kaknästornet, **27**
Kastellholmen, **9**
Konserthuset, **2**
Kulturhuset, **1**
Kungliga Dramatiska Teatern, **3**
Kungliga Slottet, **11**
Moderna Museet, **8**
National Museum, **6**
Nordiska Museet, **22**
Östasiatiska Museet, **7**
Riddarholmskyrkan, **16**
Riddarhuset, **15**
Riksdagshuset, **10**
Skansen, **24**
Stadshuset, **18**
Stockholms Fondbörs, **13**
Storkyrkan, **12**
Svea Hovrätt, **17**
Sverigehuset, **5**
Tyska Kyrkan, **14**
Vasa Museet, **21**
Waldemarsudde, **26**

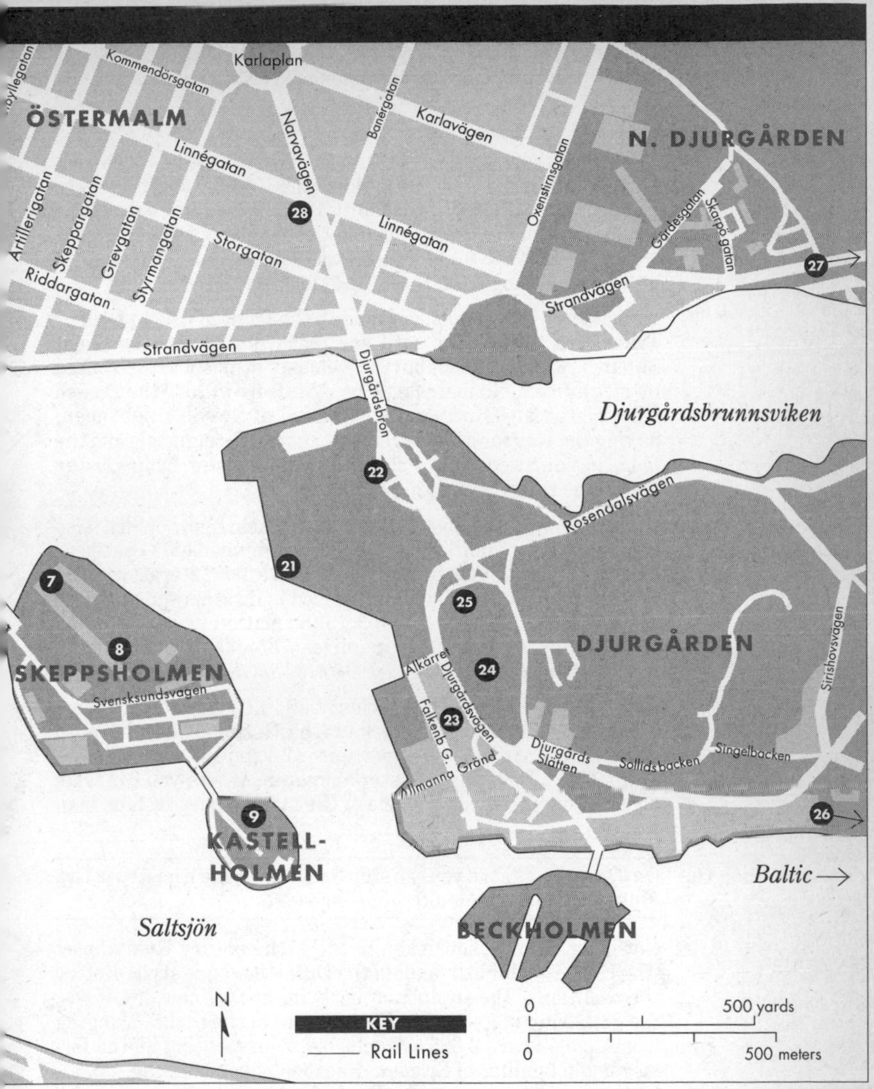
Karlaplan
Kommendörsgatan
ÖSTERMALM
Linnégatan
Narvavägen
Banérgatan
Karlavägen
Oxenstirnsgatan
N. DJURGÅRDEN
Artillerigatan
Skeppargatan
Grevgatan
Styrmangatan
Storgatan
Riddargatan
Strandvägen
Gärdesgatan
Skarpögatan
Djurgårdsbron
Djurgårdsbrunnsviken
Rosendalsvägen
DJURGÅRDEN
Sirishovsvägen
SKEPPSHOLMEN
Svensksundsvägen
Alkärret
Djurgårdsvägen
Falkenb G.
Allmanna Gränd
Djurgårds Slätten
Sollidsbacken
Singelbacken
KASTELL-HOLMEN
Baltic
Saltsjön
BECKHOLMEN
N
KEY
Rail Lines
0
500 yards
500 meters
7
8
9
21
22
23
24
25
26
27
28

are no longer used, even on ceremonial occasions, in this self-consciously egalitarian country. *Admission: State apartments SKr25; treasury and royal armory SKr25; treasury and armory open Mon.–Sat. 11–3, Sun. noon–4. State apartments open Tues.–Sun. noon–3.*

It is only a short walk from the palace to Stockholm's 15th-cen-
12 tury Gothic cathedral, **Storkyrkan** (the Great Church), where Swedish kings were crowned until 1907. It contains a dramatic wood statue of St. George slaying the dragon, carved by Bernt Notke of Lübeck in 1489, and the *Parhelion,* a painting of Stockholm dating from 1520, the oldest in existence.

Walk a few yards on Källargränd to the front of Storkyrkan or Trångsund to the rear until you reach **Stortorget** (the Great Square), which is small but marvelously atmospheric, fronted by magnificent old merchants' houses. Here in 1520 the Danish King Christian II ordered a massacre of Swedish noblemen, paving the way for a national revolt against foreign rule and the founding of Sweden as a sovereign state under King Gustav Vasa, who ruled from 1523 to 1560.

13 In **Stockholms Fondbörs** (the Stock Exchange), which also fronts onto the square, the Swedish Academy meets each year to decide the winner of the Nobel Prize for Literature. The Stock Exchange itself is computerized and rather quiet. There are no tours in English, but an information center is being established to deal with inquiries. *Stockholms Fondbörs, Källargränd 2, Stockholm, tel. 08/613–8800.*

Enjoy the spectacle of the ancient buildings as you walk down
14 Svartmangatan to **Tyska Kyrkan** (the German Church), with its magnificent oxidized copper spire and airy interior. Then go down Tyska Brinken to Västerlånggatan, where you can walk north, stopping to shop in one of the many pricey fashion boutiques.

Time Out On Västerlånggatan you can stop for a coffee and a pastry in **Grå Munken** (the Gray Monk) coffee house.

15 Cut down Storkyrkobrinken to the 17th-century **Riddarhuset** (the House of Nobles), built in the Dutch Baroque style. Before the abolition of the aristocracy early in the 20th century, it was the gathering place for the First Estate of the realm. Hanging from its walls are 2,325 escutcheons, representing all the former noble families of Sweden. Because of the building's excellent acoustic properties, Riddarhuset is often used for concerts. *Riddarhuset, tel. 08/105682. Admission free. Open weekdays 11:30–12:30.*

A short walk takes you over the Riddarholmen bridge to **Riddarholmen** (the Island of Knights), on which stands
16 **Riddarholmskyrkan,** an old Greyfriar monastery dating from 1270. The second-oldest structure in Stockholm, it has been the burial place for 17 Swedish kings over four centuries. The most famous figures buried here are King Gustavus Adolphus, hero of the Thirty Years' War, and the warrior king Karl XII, renowned for his daring invasion of Russia, who finally fell in Norway in 1718. The latest king to be put to rest here was Gustav V, in 1950. The church normally is not used for services. The various rulers' sarcophagi, usually embellished with their monograms, are visible in the small chapels given over to the

various dynasties. The redbrick structure is distinguished by its delicate iron fretwork spire. *Admission: SKr10. Open May–Aug. 10–3, Sun. 1–3.*

17 Riddarholmen is also the site of the white 17th-century palace that houses the **Svea Hovrätt** (Swedish High Court). The quiet and restful quayside here is an excellent place to end an afternoon's sightseeing, sitting by the water's edge, watching the boats on **Riddarfjärden** (Bay of Knights) and beyond it, Lake Mälar. It affords a fine view of the lake, the magnificent arches of **Västerbron** (the West Bridge) in the distance, the southern heights, and above all the imposing profile of Stadshuset (the City Hall), which appears to be almost floating on the water. At the quay you may see one of the Göta Canal ships.

Tour 3: Stadshuset and Drottningholm

Stockholm's city hall and Drottningholm Palace, outstanding embodiments of Swedish architecture and sensibilities from different centuries, share access from Mälaren.

18 Start at **Stadshuset,** arriving at 10 AM if you want a guided tour (there is also one at noon on weekends). The redbrick building is a powerful symbol of Stockholm, generally reckoned to be among the most impressive pieces of modern architecture in Europe. Completed in 1923, it was created by Rangnar Östberg, one of the founders of the National Romantic movement. It is both functional (headquarters for the city council) and ornate (its immense Blue Hall is the venue for the Nobel prize dinner each December, Stockholm's principal social event). The Golden Hall is striking: Its 180-foot walls are covered with gold-leaf mosaic designs by Einar Forseth, which, in a highly stylized way, illustrate events in Stockholm's history. A trip to the top of the 348 foot tower, most of which can be achieved by elevator, is rewarded by a breathtaking panorama of the city and Riddarfjärden. *Ragnar Östbergs Plan, tel. 08/785–9000. Admission: SKr30. Tower open May–Sept., daily 11–3.*

Time Out After climbing the tower, relax on Stadshuset's fine grass terraces, which lead down to the bay, or perhaps have lunch in **Stadshuskällaren** (the City Hall Cellar, tel. 08/505454), where food comes from the same kitchen that prepares the annual Nobel banquet.

Walk the short distance over Stadshusbron (City Hall Bridge) to the quayside at **Klara Mälarstrand,** from which boats leave
19 regularly for **Drottningholms Slott** (Queen's Island Castle), a miniature Versailles dating from the 17th century on an island in Mälaren some 45 minutes from the city center. The royal family once used it as their summer residence. Tiring of the immensity of the Royal Palace, they moved permanently to one wing of Drottningholm in the 1970s. Drottningholm is one of the most delightful of European palaces, embracing all that was the best in the art of living practiced by mid-18th-century royalty. The interiors are from the 17th, 18th, and 19th centuries, and most are open to the public. *Drottningholms Slott, tel. 08/789–8690. Admission: SKr30. Open May–Aug., Mon.–Sat. 11–4:30; Sun. 12–4:30.*

The lakeside gardens of Drottningholm are its most beautiful
20 asset, containing **Drottningholms Slottsteater** (The Court Theater), the only complete theater to survive from the 18th century anywhere in the world. It was built by Queen Lovisa Ulrika in 1766 as a wedding present for her son Gustav III. It fell into disuse after his assassination at a masked ball in 1792, but in 1922 it was rediscovered. There is now a small theater museum here as well. To obtain tickets for a performance, you must book well in advance, but the effort is worthwhile. A word of caution: the seats are extremely hard—take a cushion. *Tel. 08/759-0406. Admission: SKr25. Open May–Aug., weekdays 11:30–4:30, Sun. 12:30–4:30; Sept. 12:30–3.*

Tour 4: Djurgården and Skansen

Djurgården is Stockholm's pleasure island. On it you will find the outdoor museum Skansen, the Grona hund amusement park, and the *Vasa*, a 17th-century warship raised from the bottom of the harbor in 1961, as well as other delights.

You can reach **Djurgården** by sea aboard the small ferries that leave from **Slussen** at the southern end of Gamla Stan or from **Nybrokajen** (the New Bridge Quay) in front of the **Kungliga Dramatiska Teater.** Alternatively, starting at the theater, stroll down the **Strandvägen** quayside, taking in the magnificent old sailing ships permanently anchored here and the fine views over the harbor, and then cross **Djurgårdsbron** (the Djurgården Bridge) to the island. Your first port of call should
21 be the **Vasa Museet,** where you can see the *Vasa*, a warship that sank on its maiden voyage in 1628, was forgotten for three centuries, then located in 1956, and raised from the seabed in 1961. Its hull was found to be largely intact, because the Baltic's brackish waters do not support worms that otherwise eat ship's timbers. Now largely restored to her former, if brief, glory, the man-of-war resides in a handsome new museum. *Galärvarvet, Djurgården, tel. 08/666-4800. Admission: SKr25 adults, SKr10 children. Open daily 10–5.*

22 Close by is the **Nordiska Museet** (the Nordic Museum), housed in a splendid late-Victorian structure, worth a quick visit for an insight into Swedish folklore. Its collection includes peasant costumes from every region of the country and exhibits on the Sami (pronounced **sah**-mee; Lapps), formerly seminomadic reindeer herders who inhabit the far north. *Djurgårdsvägen 6–16, tel. 08/666-4600. Admission SKr20. Open Tues.–Fri. 10–4, weekends 11–4.*

23 Just down the road is **Gröna Lund,** an amusement park that features a range of carnival rides, though on a smaller scale than both Copenhagen's Tivoli and Göteborg's Liseberg. *Djurgårdsvägen, tel. 08/665-7000. Admission: SKr25 adults, SKr15 children. Open Apr. 20–Aug. 31.*

24 Cross Djurgårdsvägen to **Skansen,** a must for any visitor to Stockholm. The world's first open-air museum, it was founded by philologist and ethnographer Artur Hazelius (who is also buried there) in 1891 to preserve traditional Swedish architecture, including farmhouses, windmills, barns, a working glassblower's hut, and churches, which have been brought here from all parts of the country. Not only is Skansen a delightful trip out of time in the center of a modern city, it also provides an easily assimilated insight into the life and culture of Sweden's

various regions. In addition, the park contains a zoo, a circus, an aquarium, a theater, and cafés. It is worth a day's visit in itself. *Djurgårdsslätten 49–51, tel. 08/663–0500. Admission: SKr20 adults, children under 14 free. Open May–Aug., daily 9–10; Sept.–Apr., daily 9–5.*

Time Out For a snack with a view, try the **Solliden Restaurant** at Skansen. The museum also offers a selection of open-air snack bars and cafés; Gröna Lund has four different restaurants.

25 The charmingly archaic **Biologiska Museet** (Biological Museum), in the shadow of Skansen, is worth a visit, with its collection of stuffed animals in various simulated environments. *Hazeliusporten, tel. 08/661–1383. Admission: SKr6. Open daily 10–3.*

26 Djurgården's treasure is **Waldemarsudde,** the beautiful turn-of-the-century home of Sweden's Prince Eugen, an accomplished painter, who died in 1947. His mansion, bequeathed to the Swedish people, maintains an important collection of Nordic paintings from 1880 to 1940 in addition to the prince's own works. Its grounds are a delight. You can get there on the 47 bus. *Prins Eugens väg 6, tel. 08/662–1833. Admission: SKr30. Open Tues.–Sun. 11–4.*

27 Finally, eastward on Norra Djurgården is **Kaknästornet,** the radio and television tower, completed in 1967 and, at 511 feet the highest building in Scandinavia. Here you can eat a meal in a restaurant 426 feet above the ground and enjoy panoramic views of the city and the archipelago. *Mörkakroken, off Kaknäsvägen, tel. 08/667–8517. Admission: SKr15. Open Apr. 15–Sept. 15, daily 9 AM–10:30 PM.*

Cross the Djurgården bridge and proceed up Narvavägen to
28 **Historiska Museet** (the Museum of National Antiquities), which houses important collections of Viking gold and silver treasures. **Myntkabinettet** (the Royal Cabinet of Coin), in the same building, boasts the world's largest coin. *Narvavägen 13–17, tel. 08/783–9400. Admission to both: SKr40. Open Tues., Wed., and Fri.–Sun. noon–5; Thurs. noon–7.*

Short Excursions from Stockholm

Numbers in the margin correspond with points of interest on the Excursions from Stockholm map.

Skärgården **Skärgården** (the archipelago) is Stockholm's greatest natural asset: more than 25,000 islands and skerries, many uninhabited, spread across an almost tideless sea of clean, clear water. To sail lazily among these islands aboard an old steamboat on a summer's night is a timeless delight.

Regular ferry services depart from the quayside in front of the Grand Hotel. Cruises on a variety of boats leave from the harbor in front of the Royal Palace or from Nybrokajen, across the road from the Royal Dramatic Theater.

For the tourist with limited time, one of the simplest ways to get a taste of the archipelago's delights is to take a one-hour
1 ferry trip to **Vaxholm,** an extremely pleasant, seaside town of small, red-painted wood houses. It is the site of a fortress guarding the approaches to Stockholm. The fortress, **Vaxholms Kastell,** houses a small museum, **Vaxholms Kastell Museum,**

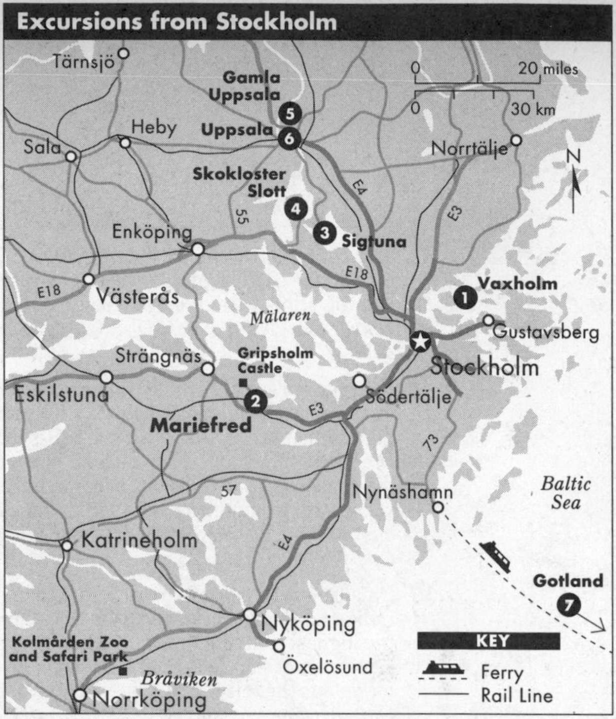

showing the defense of Stockholm over the centuries. *Tel. 0764/30107. Admission: SKr10 or SKr25 including boat fare. Open May 15–Aug. 31, daily noon–3:45. Group admission also at other times by arrangement.*

A more authentic way of getting to know the archipelago is to seek out the ***Blidösund.*** A coal-fired steamboat built in 1911 that was in regular service for 50 years, it is now run by a small group of enthusiasts, who take parties of around 250 merry-makers on cruises. The *Blidösund* leaves from a berth close to the Royal Palace in Stockholm. *Blidösund, Ångfartyg, Roslagens Skeppslag AB, Skeppsbron 4, tel. 08/117113 or 08/202186.*

The finest of the other steamboats is *Björkfjärden,* which leaves from Nybrokajen, close to the Strand Hotel. *Björkfjärden, Ångfartyget, St. Nygatan 45, tel. 08/236935.*

Mälaren Boats plying the lake leave from a quay close to City Hall. There are regular services and excursions to various points, but the most delightful way to experience the true vastness of
2 Sweden's third-largest lake is the trip to **Mariefred** aboard the coal-fired steamer of the same name, built in 1903 and still going strong. *Round-trip fare, SKr140; one-way, SKr90. Limited service from May, regular sailings from June, daily 10 AM, arriving Mariefred 1:30. Lunch served on board. Return trip 4:30 PM.*

The principal attraction in Mariefred, an idyllic little town of mostly timbered houses, is the 16th-century **Gripsholm Slott** (castle), which contains fine Renaissance chambers, a superbly atmospheric theater dating from the late-1700s, and Sweden's royal portrait collection. *S–64700, tel. 0159/10194. Admission: SKr25. Open May–Aug., daily 10–4; Mar. Apr., Sept., and Oct., Tues.–Fri. 10–3 and weekends 12–3; Nov.–Feb., Sat. and Sun. 12–3.*

You can also travel by narrow-gauge steam railway from Mariefred to a junction on the main line to Stockholm, returning to the capital by ordinary train.

Sigtuna

3 This extremely picturesque and restful little town of 5,000 is idyllically located some 30 kilometers (20 miles) from Stockholm on a northern arm of Lake Mälar. **Sigtuna** was the principal trading post of the Svea, the tribe that settled Sweden after the last Ice Age. After it was sacked by Estonian pirates, its merchants founded Stockholm sometime in the 13th century. Little remains of Sigtuna's former glory, beyond parts of the principal church, which escaped the Estonian onslaught. However, the town hall dates from the 18th century, the main part of town from the early 1800s, and there are two houses said to date back to the 15th century. Sigtuna can be reached by taking a commuter train from Stockholm's central station to Märsta, where you change to either the 570 or 575 bus. From June to August it can also be reached by boat from the quay near the City Hall. The fare is approximately SKr60.

Skokloster Slott

4 About 20 kilometers (12 miles) to the northeast of Sigtuna on the E18 highway, lies **Skokloster Slott,** a Baroque castle that was the home of a celebrated Swedish soldier, Field Marshal Carl Gustav Wrangel. It is exquisitely furnished with the spoils of his successful campaigns in Europe in the 17th century. *S–14800 Bålsta, tel. 018/386077. Admission: SKr10. Open May–Sept., daily noon–4.*

What to See and Do with Children

In addition to **Skansen** and the **Gröna Lund** amusement park, (*see* Tour 4, *above*) the **Stockholms Leksaksmuseet** (Toy Museum) features a collection of toys and dolls from all over the world and has a playroom for children. *Mariatorget 1, Södermalm, tel. 08/416000. Admission: SKr20 adults, SKr7 children. Open Tues.–Fri. 10–2, Sat.–Sun. 12–4.*

See also the Saturday *Dagens Nyheter* newspaper for details of children's events at other museums.

Off the Beaten Track

Hidden away over a grocery store, **Strindbergsmuseet Blå Tornet** (Strindberg Museum, Blue Tower) is dedicated to Sweden's most important author and dramatist (1849–1912). This was actually August Strindberg's home from 1908 until his death, and the interior has been lovingly reconstructed with authentic furnishings and other objects (including his pen). It also has a library, a press, and picture archives and arranges literary, musical, and theatrical events. *Drottninggatan 85, tel. 08/113789. Admission: SKr15. Open Tues.–Sat. 10–4, Sun. noon–5.*

Millesgården is another home that has become a museum dedicated to its former owner, in this case American-Swedish sculptor Carl Milles (1875–1955). His works and his collection of the works of other artists are displayed in the house, and his sculptures top columns on terraces in a magical garden high above the harbor and the city. *Carl Milles väg 2, Lidingö, tel. 08/731-5060. Admission: SKr25. Open: May–Sept., daily 10–5; Oct.–Apr., weekdays 11–3 and Sat.–Sun. 11–4.*

Shopping

Shopping Districts The three main department stores are situated in the central city area, as are the **Gallerian** and **Sturegallerian** shopping malls. However, there are interesting boutiques and galleries in **Västerlånggatan,** the main street of the Old Town, and some excellent handicraft and art shops line the raised sidewalk at the start of **Hornsgatan** in Söder.

Department Stores Sweden's leading department store, **NK** (the initials, pronounced ***enn-koh***, stand for *Nordiska Kompaniet*), is located in Hamngatan, just across the street from Kungsträdgården (tel. 08/762–8000). It sells a wide range of quality goods and has both a special Swedish crystal department and a "very Swedish shop" for visitors from abroad. The **Åhléns** department store (tel. 08/246000) is only a short distance up Hamngatan at Klarabergsgatan. **PUB** (the initials of founder Paul U. Bergström) is at Hötorget (tel. 08/791–6000). Greta Garbo worked here before she went into films.

Street Markets There is a **flower and fruit market** every day at **Hötorget** and a **fleamarket** at **Skärholmen,** a suburb that can be reached on the subway. The best streets for **bric-a-brac** and **antiques** are **Odengatan** and **Roslagsgatan** (nearest subway station Odenplan).

Specialty Stores

Antiques The principal local auction houses are **Bukowski** (Wahrendorffsgatan 8, tel. 08/102595), **Beijers Auktioner** (Birger Jarlsgatan 6, tel. 08/248590), and **Stockholms Auktionsverk** (Jakobsgatan 10, tel. 08/142440).

Books Both **Hedengrens** (Sturegallerian, tel. 08/611–5132) and **Akademibokhandeln** (Mäster Samuelsgatan 32, tel. 08/214890) have excellent selections of English-language and Swedish books. **Hemlins** (Västerlånggatan 6, in the Old Town, tel. 08/106180) has the latest foreign titles and antique books in the basement.

Crystal Swedish crystal is available at a number of stores, among them **Nordiska Kristall** (Kungsgatan 9, tel. 08/104372), **Svenskt Glas,** (Birger Jarlsgatan 8, tel. 08/142305), and **New Scandinavian Design** (Tegelbacken 4, tel. 08/219211). All feature everything from small bowls to major art works at prices that range from SKr144 to SKr88,000; they also supply a packaging and postal service that guarantees to get it to you intact.

Handicrafts Swedish handicrafts from all over the country are available at **Svensk Hemslöjd** (Sveavägen 44, tel. 08/232115). **Stockholms Läns Hemslöjdsförening** (Drottninggatan 14, tel. 08/117549) also has an excellent selection. Prices are high but so is the quality. Wood is the principal material used for kitchen implements, model birds, and the renowned small red horses from the province of Dalarna. Knitwear is also of a high caliber.

Men's Clothing For suits and evening suits for both sale and rental, **Hans Allde** (Birger Jarlsgatan 58, tel. 08/200835), provides good, old-fashioned service. **Kostymex** (Hunlegårdsgatan 10, tel. 08/663-3667; Odengatan 30, tel. 08/347888; and Renstiernasgatan 27, tel. 08/422030) is a chain store. For shirts, there is **La Chemise** (Smålandsgatan 11, tel. 08/101494).

Women's Clothing There are many boutiques in **Biblioteksgatan** and **Västerlånggatan** in Gamla Stan, in addition to stores such as **Twilfit** (Nybrogatan 11, tel. 08/662–3817; Gallerian, tel. 08/216221; and Gamla Brogatan 36–38, tel. 08/201954).

Hennes & Mauritz (Hamngatan 14 and 22; Drottninggatan 53 and 56; Hötorget 1–3; Sergelgatan 1, 11, 22; and Sergels Torg 12; all tel. 08/796–5500) is one of the few Swedish-owned clothing stores to have achieved international success.

Sports and Fitness

Bicycling Stockholm is well supplied with bicycle routes and, except during peak traveling times, bikes may be taken aboard commuter trains for excursions to the suburbs. **Cyckelfrämjandet** (tel. 08/321680), a local bicyclists' association, publishes an English-language guide to cycling trips. Bicycles may be rented from **Cykel & Mopeduthyrning** (Strandvägen at Kajplats 24, tel. 660–7959) or from **Skepp & Hoj** (Gälarvärvsvägen 10, tel. 08/660–5757). Rental costs average around SKr80 per day.

Golf There are numerous golf courses around Stockholm, among them **Lidingö Golf Club** (Sticklinge on Lidingö, tel. 08/765–7911) and **Nacka Golfbana** (Nacka, tel. 08/773–0431).

Health and Fitness Centers Keeping fit is an obsession with Swedes. **Friskis & Svettis** (Eriksgatan 63, 100 28 Stockholm, tel. 08/520470) is a legendary local gym specializing in aerobics. Farther along the same road is the **Atalanta Girls Gym** (Eriksgatan 34, tel. 08/506625). For relatively inexpensive massage, try **Axelsons Friskvård** (Gästrikegatan 12, tel. 08/338988). Otherwise, consult the yellow pages under "Frisk-, hälsovård."

Jogging Numerous parks and footpaths dot the central city area, among them **Haga Park,** which also has canoe rentals, **Djurgården,** and **Liljans Skogen.** An interesting track runs alongside the Karlbergssjö; it can be reached from an alleyway and steps at the side of Eriksbron (the Eric bridge). The nearest subway station is s:t Eriksplan.

Swimming In the center of town, **Centralbadet** (Drottninggatan 88, tel. 08/242402), newly renovated, boasts an extra-large pool and numerous other facilities, including something called a "meditation pool." **Sturebadet** (Sturegalleriet, tel. 08/206700) also has excellent facilities.

Tennis There are many excellent tennis courts in and around Stockholm. **Kungliga Tennishallen** (the Royal Tennis Hall, Lidingövägen 75, tel. 08/667–0350) is where former champion Björn Borg plays. Another fine venue is **Tennisstadion** (Fiskartorpsvägen 20, tel. 08/215454).

Spectator Sports

There are two main sports stadiums in Stockholm, featuring soccer in summer and ice hockey in winter. The **Globe** (Box 10055, S-12127, tel. 08/725–1000), at 281 feet claimed to be the world's tallest spherical building, has its own subway station just across the water from Söder. The Stockholm Open Tennis Tournament is held here each November. To the north there is **Råsundastadion** (Solnavägen 51, Solna, tel. 08/735–0900).

Beaches

The best bathing places in central Stockholm are on the island of **Långholmen** and at **Rålambshov** at the end of Norr Mälarstrand. Neither is really a beach but more grassy or rocky lakeside hideaways. Topless sunbathing is virtually de rigueur.

Dining

Stockholmers traditionally treat restaurants as places where one goes on special occasions, to celebrate, rather than to dine regularly. The restaurant simply is not part of the normal social fabric as it would be elsewhere in Europe. Restaurants tend to cater almost exclusively to the upscale sector; cheap, out-of-the-way spots with exquisite home cooking do not exist. Nonetheless, culinary standards are high. Among Swedish dishes, the best bets are fish, particularly salmon, and the smörgåsbord buffet, which usually is a good value. Many restaurants close for either July or August, and most close at Christmas and New Year. It is advisable to telephone first to check that the restaurant is open. Unless otherwise stated, casual dress is acceptable.

Highly recommended restaurants are indicated by a star ★.

Very Expensive

Grands Franska. This classic French restaurant in the Grand Hotel has an inspiring view of the Old Town and the Palace across the inner harbor waters. The food is equally inspiring, and the recent acquisition of Sweden's Chef of the Year for 1989, Roland Persson, can only improve matters further. The duckling in coriander with honey-and-cinnamon sauce, and the medallions of deer with shiitake mushrooms in wild-berry cream sauce are highly recommended. The restaurant imports its own wines, which is unusual in Sweden. The thick carpets and elegant decor should be matched by your thick wallet. *Grand Hotel, Blasieholmshamnen 8, tel. 08/221020. Reservations required. Jacket and tie required. AE, CB, DC, MC, V.*

L'Escargot. Australian chef Neil Ponsonby has located his excellent French restaurant somewhat askew from the city center, on the island of Kungsholmen. It boasts the best selection of cheeses in town and an almost baffling array of desserts. Downstairs is a bistro with a cheaper menu and simpler food. *Scheelegatan 8, tel. 08/530577. Reservations advised. Jacket and tie required. AE, DC, MC, V.*

Operakällaren. Stockholm's best-known restaurant has a magnificent location in the Opera House at the end of Kungsträdgården. Operakällaren started business in 1787, so the tone is predictably snobbish, but not intrusively so. The decor is lavish Old World–Style, with deep Oriental carpeting, shiny polished brass, and handsome carved wood chairs and tables. The crystal chandeliers are said to be Sweden's most magnificent, and the high windows on the south side give fine views of the Royal Palace. Werner Vögeli, Sweden's best-known chef, oversees a grand smörgåsbord table; top selections include pickled herring, rollmops (rolled herring), reindeer and elk in season, and ice cream with cloudberry (a yellow blackberry native to Scandinavia) sauce. Operakällaren chefs are tradition-bound to prepare any fish caught in the waters between the restaurant and the Royal Palace, no more than casting distance away. A beautiful wine cellar offers an extensive collection of vintages. Resting on its laurels, Operakällaren tends to be more a Swedish institution than a great gastronomic experience. *Operahuset, tel. 08/111125. Reservations required. Jacket and tie required. AE, DC, MC, V.*

★ **Ulriksdalsvärdshus.** This beautifully situated country inn, built in 1868, offers both Swedish and international cuisine, but is particularly noted for its lunchtime smörgåsbord. It provides a specifically Swedish experience in the park of an 18th-century palace, overlooking orchards and a peaceful lake. The interior is traditional, and guests even stand and sing the Swedish national anthem, *Du Gamla, Du Fria* (Thou Ancient, Thou Free), as the flag is lowered. *Ulriksdals Slottspark, Solna, tel. 08/850815. Reservations advised. Jacket required. AE, DC, MC, V. Closed Christmas. No dinner Sun.*

Wedholms Fisk. This restaurant, tucked away in a renovated period building, is disarmingly informal, with tall, straight-back chairs and cheerful tablecloths. Lots of mirrors and good lighting impart an open feel. The traditional Swedish cuisine is simple, straightforward, generous, and delicious, and consists almost exclusively of seafood. Try the poached sole in lobster-and-champagne sauce or the Pilgrim mussels Provençal. Owner Bengt Wedholm (also the head chef) takes particular care with the cooking, allowing no room for compromise. *Nybrokajen 17, tel. 08/104874. Reservations advised. AE, DC, MC, V. Closed Sun.*

Expensive

Aurora. Extremely elegant, if a little staid, this Old-Town cellar restaurant is set in a beautiful 300-year-old house. A largely foreign clientele enjoys top-quality Swedish and international cuisine served in intimate small rooms. The adjacent Old City Club, under the same management, is open for moderate-price lunch Monday through Friday. *Munkbron 11, tel. 08/219359. Reservations required. Jacket and tie required. AE, DC, MC, V. Closed Sun.*

Blå Gåsen. This is a classic Östermalm restaurant: very classy, cozy, and costly. The Swedish/French food is excellent, the service usually impeccable. *Karlavägen 28, tel. 08/100269. Reservations advised. Jacket and tie required. AE, DC, MC, V.*

★ **Clas på Hörnet.** In the small, intimate ground floor of a restored inn built in 1739 on what was once the edge of the city, this restaurant is today only a little off the beaten track but well worth seeking out for its extremely pleasant, relaxed, and old-fashioned atmosphere. It offers a choice of Swedish or international cuisine, including outstanding *stromming* (Baltic herring). *Surbrunnsgatan 20, tel. 08/165136. Reservations required. Jacket and tie required. AE, DC, MC, V. Closed Christmas.*

Den Gyldene Freden. Sweden's most famous old tavern, "Freden" has recently been restored after being closed many years. The building dates from 1721 and the restaurant from the following year. The stone street and the hand-drawn angles of the building itself make getting there a good part of the pleasure. The haunt of bards and barristers, artists and ad people, Freden could probably serve sawdust and still be popular, but the new staff is worthy of the restaurant's hallowed reputation. The cuisine is classic Swedish, with a few new dishes thrown in. "SOS" (the Swedish initials for Butter [smör],

Stockholm Dining and Lodging

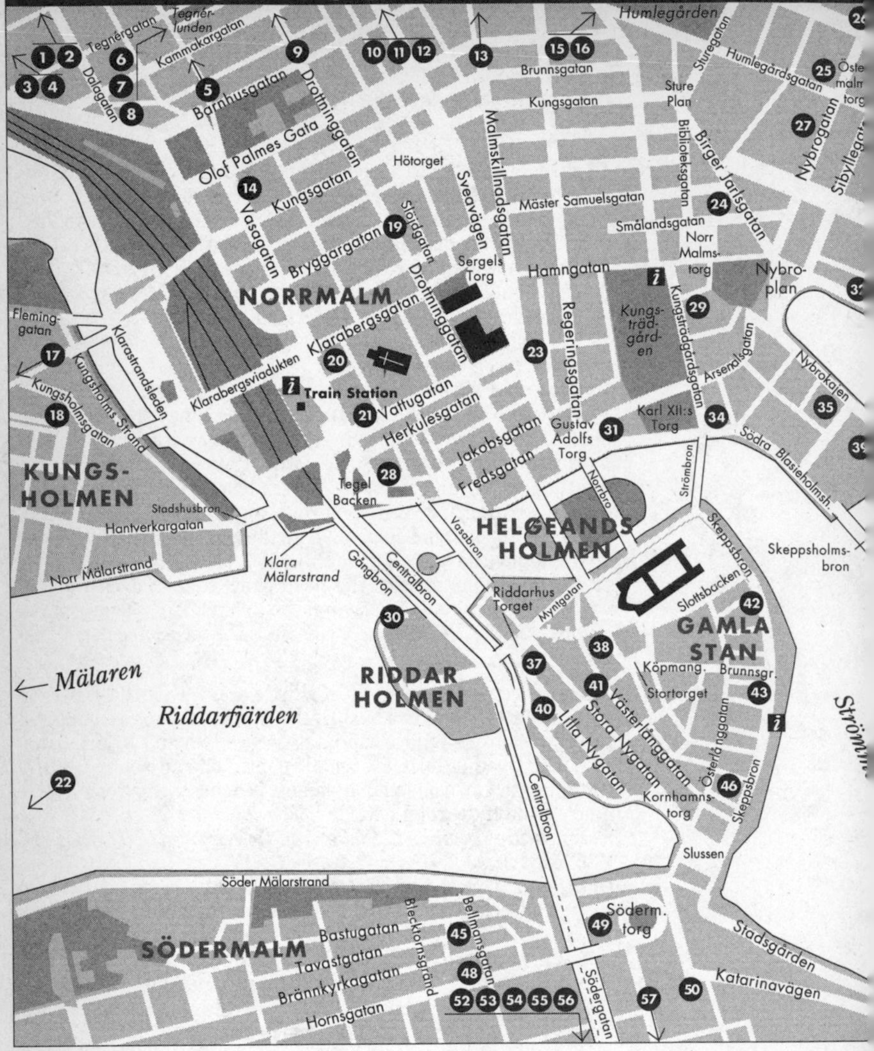

Dining

Aurora, **37**
Bakfickan, **31**
Blå Gåsen, **15**
Bröderna Olsson, **57**
Butler's, **4**
Cassi, **36**
Clas på Hörnet, **12**
Edsbacka Krog, **11**
L'Escargot, **17**
De Fyras Krog, **45**
Glada Enkan, **10**
Gourmet, **7**
Grands Franska, **34**
Greitz, **14**
Den Gyldene Freden, **46**
Les Halles, **25**
Hannas Krog, **56**
Invito, **16**
Källaren Diana, **43**
KB, **24**
Nils Emil, **55**
Oden Gate, **52**
Operakällaren, **31**
Örtagården, **27**
Rolfs Kök, **8**
Söders Hjärta, **48**
Stallmästaregården, **9**
Tranan, **1**
Ulriksdalsvärdshus, **3**
Wasahof, **2**
Wedholms Fisk, **39**

Lodging

af Chapman, **44**
Alexandra, **54**
Alfa, **53**
Amaranten, **18**
Anno 1647, **50**
Bema, **5**
Berns, **29**
Birger Jarl, **13**
Bosön, **33**
City, **19**

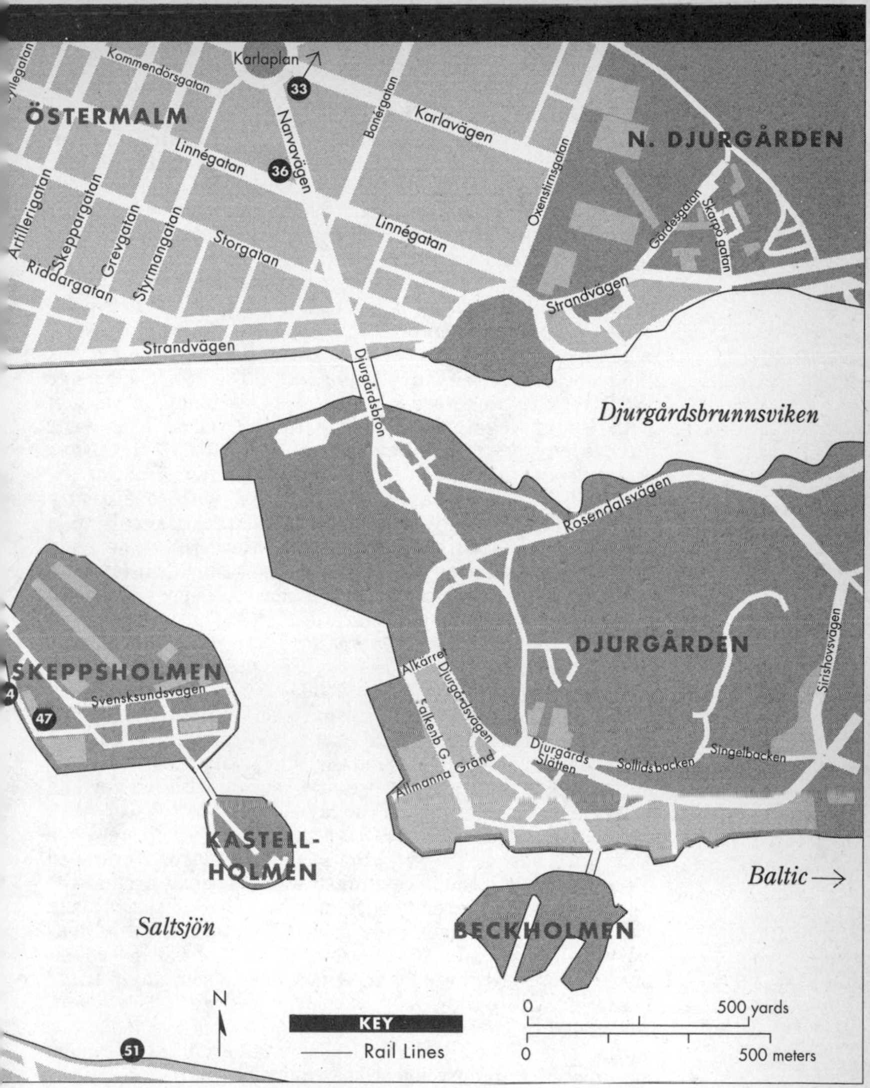

Clas på Hörnet, **12**
Continental, **20**
Diplomat, **32**
Grand, **34**
Gustav af Klint, **51**
Lady Hamilton, **38**
Långholmen, **22**
Lord Nelson, **41**
Mälardrottningen, **30**
Mornington, **26**
Reisen, **42**
Royal Viking, **21**
Scandic Crown, **49**
Sergel Plaza, **23**
Skeppsholmen, **47**
Stockholm, **28**
Strand, **35**
Tegnérlunden, **6**
Victory, **40**

Cheese [ost], and Herring [strömming]) is as Swedish a starter as you can get. It consists of three variations of raw, pickled herring served on hard bread with slices of cheese on the side. For a main dish, try oven-baked fillets of turbot, served with cantarelles and cepes. The gray hen fried with spruce twigs and dried fruit is another good selection. The building is owned by the Swedish Academy, whose members presumably discuss next year's Nobel laureates over the traditional Thursday yellow-pea soup in a dining room above the main restaurant. *Österlånggatan 51, tel. 08/109046. Reservations advised. AE, DC, MC, V. Closed Sun. No lunch.*

Edsbacka Krog. In 1626, Edsbacka became Stockholm's first licensed inn. These days, it is a classic Swedish restaurant located 20 minutes from downtown by taxi. With its exposed, rough-hewn beams, plaster walls, and open fireplaces, it has the feel of a country inn for the gentry. The owner, Christer Lindström, is an award-winning chef; his tarragon chicken with winter vegetables is worth the occasional long wait. *Sollentunavägen 220, Sollentuna, tel. 08/963300. Reservations recommended. AE, DC, MC, V. Closed Sun. No lunch Sat.*

Gourmet. Expensive, quiet, and secluded, with consistently high standards, Gourmet is a fail-safe choice. The cuisine is classical French without being too conservative. The fried monkfish in a spicy sweet sauce, and the grilled spit (smoked calf liver, beef, and veal) in a green- and red-pepper sauce are especially good. The atmospheric decor leans on dark paneling and thick, red curtains. *Tegnérgatan 10, tel. 08/314398. Reservations required. Jacket and tie advised. AE, DC, MC, V. Closed Sun. and July. No lunch Sat.*

Greitz. Home-style Swedish cuisine is served in this classy and comfortable restaurant, with owner Bo Greitz in attendance, often assisting longtime friend Christer Lindgren in the kitchen. Try their *Sotare* (grilled Baltic herring with parsley and butter); Bo's home-flavored aquavit and a beer chaser work well with it. Also good is the *burbot* (local white fish) stewed in wine with burbot roe and croutons. The decor is Revamped Cafe Style, with the once-stained wood paneling around the room now painted a trendy burgundy red. The wine list is bland but, for Sweden, moderately priced. The restaurant adjoins the plain-but-friendly International Press Club bar. Do not sit near or opposite the door in winter unless you enjoy frigid blasts. *50 Vasagatan, tel. 08/234820. Reservations advised. Jacket and tie advised. AE, DC, MC, V. Closed weekends.*

Invito. This elegant and airy Italian restaurant in Östermalm has a pleasant dining room on the ground floor and atmospheric cellar rooms below. *Engelbrektsgatan 37, tel. 08/203817. Reservations required. Jacket and tie required. AE, DC, MC, V.*

Källaren Diana. This is one of the best cellar restaurants in Gamla Stan, with a menu that includes such Swedish specialties as cuts of elk and reindeer meat and cloudberry desserts. Nowadays in the summer the customers may be predominantly foreign or businesspeople from the provinces. *Brunnsgränd 2, tel. 08/107310. Reservations advised. Jacket required. AE, DC, MC, V.*

KB. The most urbane of Stockholm's quality restaurants serves Swedish country fare, painstakingly prepared. The middle-age waitresses are familiar in the best sense, and the patrons are among the city's most relaxed. There are soft, fitted benches around the smallish dining room, and another room one floor up. Chef Örjan Klein pushes low-cal, low-fat dishes in the best modern tradition (i.e., with visible homage to France). Try the pot-au-feu with chicken and almond potatoes, or the Swedish freshwater crayfish in season. Don't be put off by having to enter the restaurant by the cloak room. The initials stand for *Konstnärsbaren*, the artists' bar just across the corridor from the restaurant. *Smålandsgatan 7, tel. 08/110232. Reservations advised. AE, DC, MC, V. Closed Sun. No lunch Sat.*

Stallmästaregården. A historic old inn with an attractive courtyard and garden, Stallmästaregården is located in the Haga Park, half an hour from the city center. The fine summer meals are served in the courtyard overlooking the waters of Brunnsviken. A lower, fixed-price menu is available. *Norrtull, near Haga, tel. 08/243910. Reservations advised. AE, DC, MC, V.*

Moderate

★ **Bakfickan.** The name means "hip pocket" and is appropriate because this restaurant is tucked round the back of the Opera House complex. It's a budget-price alternative to the nearby Operakällaren and is particularly popular at lunchtime, offering Swedish home cooking and a range of daily dishes. Counter and table service are available. *Operahuset, tel. 08/242700. No reservations. AE, DC, MC, V. Closed Sun.*

Bröderna Olsson. Two brothers from the province of Småland have made a stunning success in the capital with this small restaurant and their formula of culinary ability, good humor—and garlic with almost everything. *Folkungagatan 84, tel. 08/408446. Reservations required. No credit cards.*

Butler's. The menu is short but dependable, featuring Mediterranean cuisine. Try the saddle of lamb with mixed vegetables Provençal, or the steak tournedos in creamy mustard sauce with garlic and mushrooms. The checkered tablecloths and the French bistro chairs give Butler's an indefinable Continental atmosphere, while an eclectic mix of artists, writers, computer hackers, and local residents make up the clientele. Butler's is noisy but very trendy for lunch. *Rörstrandsgatan 11, tel. 08/323823. Reservations advised. AE, DC, MC, V. No lunch on weekends.*

De Fyras Krog. The Inn of the Four Estates boasts a good traditional Swedish menu and an intimate, cozy atmosphere. *Tavastgatan 22, tel. 08/586405. Reservations required. AE, DC, MC, V.*

Hannas Krog. Newly opened, this restaurant features a modern menu and a staff whose good humor makes up for the occasional lapses in service. *Skånegatan 80, tel. 08/438225. Reservations required. AE, DC, MC, V.*

Les Halles. Appropriately, you'll find Les Halles over Stockholm's mini version of that Parisian landmark, the Östermalmstorg food hall, supplying French cuisine at reasonable prices. It has a cheerful Continental atmosphere. *Humlegårdsgatan 3, tel. 08/662–8424. Reservations required. AE, DC, MC, V.*

Nils Emil. This restaurant is known for good food and generous helpings at reasonable prices. It attracts members of the royal family on occasion. *Folkungagatan 122, tel. 08/407209. Reservations required. Jacket and tie required. AE, DC, MC, V.*

Rolfs Kök. Small and modern, this restaurant combines an informal atmosphere with excellent Swedish/French cuisine at reasonable prices. The lamb usually is a good bet. *Tegnergatan 41, tel. 08/101696. No reservations. AE, DC, MC, V.*

Söders Hjärta. Conveniently located on Söder just across from a floodlit church, this bistro is not far from the Slussen subway station. The cuisine is Stockholm standard, but the adjacent large bar is cheerful and friendly. *Bellmansgatan 22, tel. 08/401462. Reservations required. AE, DC, MC, V.*

Tranan. A young, yuppie crowd uses Tranan for its bar, which often features live music, and for its unpretentious restaurant that offers basic Swedish fare. The stark walls and checkered floor are from Tranan's days as a workingman's beer parlor. Chef Rolf Durr improvises the menu almost daily. Traditional Swedish dishes like boiled pork sausage and mashed turnip with lashings of sweet mustard are more delicious than they sound. *Karlbergsvagen 14, tel. 08/300765. Reservations advised. AE, DC, MC, V.*

★ **Wasahof.** This is the closest you will come in Stockholm to the friendly ambience of an English pub or a Continental cafe. The bar and restaurant are combined, the cuisine is variable, but who cares when you can actually meet people? *Dalagatan 46, tel. 08/323440. Reservations advised. AE, DC, MC, V.*

Inexpensive

Cassi. This centrally located restaurant specializes in French cuisine at reasonable prices. *Narvavägen 30, tel. 08/661–7461. Reservations advised. MC. Closed Sat.*

Glada Enkan. This so-called artists' restaurant, housed in a former widow's home in Vasastan, serves excellent food and wine at (for Sweden) reasonable prices. It's a short walk from the Odenplan subway station. *Norrtullsgatan 42, tel. 08/339575. No reservations. No credit cards.*

Oden Gate. Located near the Slussen locks, on the south side of Stockholm harbor, this is a popular, trendy Art Deco Italian-style trattoria. Pasta dishes are the house specialty. *Högbergsgatan 40, tel. 08/439776. No reservations. AE, DC, MC, V.*

★ **Örtagården.** This is a truly delightful vegetarian, no-smoking restaurant over the Östermalmstorg food market. The excellent-value buffet includes soups, salads, and hot dishes and is served in a turn-of-the-century atmosphere. *Nybrogatan 31, tel. 08/662–1728. No reservations. DC, MC, V.*

Lodging

The price of staying in Stockholm nowadays can horrify even those undertaking the exercise on expense accounts. Check out special offers and consult carefully with your travel agent or the Swedish Tourist Board before committing yourself. The plus side of the coin is that hotels usually are scrupulously clean and well run and staffs are honest and courteous. All rooms in the hotels reviewed are equipped with showers/bath unless otherwise noted.

Highly recommended hotels are indicated by a star ★.

Very Expensive

Amaranten. A little out of the way, on the island of Kungsholmen, this large, modern hotel is, however, just a few minutes' walk from Stockholm's central train station. Built in 1969, it was refurbished in 1988. A roof garden is featured atop the "executive tower," which contains 52 rooms. The brasserie-style restaurant features cuisine with a French touch. *Kungsholmsgatan 31, Box 8054, 104 20, tel. 80/654–1060, fax 08/652–6248. 410 rooms. Facilities: restaurants, piano bar, pool, sauna, solarium. AE, DC, MC, V.*

Berns. In a successful attempt to distinguish itself from the rest of the crowd, the 130-year-old Berns opted for a Spartan look in its 1989 renovation. Indirect lighting, modern Italian furniture, and expensive marble, granite, and wood inlays now dominate the decor of the public areas and guest rooms. The best rooms are on the top floor; while views are nowhere spectacular, the interiors are pleasant enough to compensate. Berns has been a meeting place for literati and bon vivants for generations. It was one of August Strindberg's haunts; guests can breakfast in the Red Room, immortalized by his novel of the same name. *Nackstrimsgatan 8, S–111 47, tel. 08/614–0700 or 800/448–8355, fax 08/611–5175. 59 rooms, 3 suites. Facilities: restaurant, bar. AE, DC, MC, V.*

Continental. Located in the city center across from the train station, the Continental is popular with American guests. It was first opened about 25 years ago and is now undergoing renovation that's scheduled for completion in 1992. It offers four restaurants in different price brackets, all of which have recently been renovated. *Klara Vattugränd 4, S–101 21, tel. 08/244020, fax 08/113695. 250 rooms with bath. Facilities: 4 restaurants. AE, DC, MC, V.*

★ **Diplomat.** Located within easy walking distance of Djurgården, this elegant hotel is less flashy than most. Rooms facing the water have magnificent views over Stockholm's harbor. Originally a turn-of-the-century house, it was converted to its present use in 1966. The atmosphere is calm and dignified, and the hotel has a very popular tea room. *Strandvägen 7C, S–104 40, tel. 08/663–5800, fax 08/783–6634. 133 rooms. Facilities: restaurant, bar, sauna, office, conference room. AE, DC, MC, V. Closed Christmas and New Year's Day.*

Grand. The city's showpiece hotel is an 1874 landmark on the quayside at Blasieholmen, just across the harbor from the Royal Palace. Visiting political dignitaries and Nobel prizewinners are accommodated here. The gracious Old-World atmosphere extends to the comfortable and well-furnished rooms. One of the hotel's best features is a glassed-in veranda overlooking the harbor, where an excellent smörgåsbord buffet is served. *Södra Blasieholmshamnen 8, Box 164 24, S–103 27, tel. 08/221020, fax 08/218–6880. 299 rooms, 20 suites. Facilities: restaurant, piano bar, shop, conference and banquet rooms. AE, DC, MC, V.*

★ **Lady Hamilton.** This small but highly desirable hotel is in a house dating from 1470 near the Royal Palace in the Old Town. Converted to its present use in 1980, it boasts an extensive collection of antiques, including one of George Romney's portraits of Lady Hamilton, the English beauty who was mistress of Lord Nelson at the beginning of the 19th century. *Storkyrkobrinken 5, S–111 28, tel. 08/234680, fax 08/111148. 34 rooms. Facilities: cafeteria, sauna, pool. AE, DC, MC, V. Closed Christmas.*

Reisen. This hotel, dating from 1819, successfully manages to combine elegance with modernity, class with liveliness. It has a magnificent central location on the Old Town waterfront. The rooms have all been modernized and are well furnished, while the swimming pool is built under medieval arches. The Quarter Deck restaurant serves high-quality Swedish-French food and the piano bar attracts a lively crowd at night. *Skeppsbron 12–14, S–111 30, tel. 08/223260, fax 08/201559. 114 rooms. Facilities: 2 restaurants, 2 bars, indoor pool, sauna, conference rooms. AE, DC, MC, V. Closed Christmas and New Year's Day.*

Royal Viking. Only yards from the central station and from the airport bus terminal, the SAS-owned Royal Viking, built in 1984, could not be more centrally located. The large atrium lobby is spacious, and the split-level lounge is elegant—but one looks in vain for anything on a Swedish or Viking theme. Last renovated in early 1990, the guest rooms lack nothing except space; they have attractive natural textiles and art work, sturdy writing desks, minibars, separate seating areas, and plush robes in the large bathrooms. Triple-glazed windows and plenty of insulation keep traffic noise to a minimum, but check whether the current bar pianist is the exuberant type before taking a room on the atrium. The atrium breakfast is one of Stockholm's best. The ninth-floor Sky Jazz bar and nightclub offers panoramic views of the city. The staff is young and inexperienced, and service is at best formal. *Vasagatan 1, S–101 24, tel. 08/141000 or 800/448–8355, fax 08/108180. 319 rooms. Facilities: 3 restaurants, 2 bars, nightclub, indoor pool, sauna, solarium, massage, conference rooms, SAS ticket counter and check-in, rooms for disabled guests. AE, MC, V.*

Sergel Plaza. This stainless-steel-paneled high-rise was originally built in the late '70s to provide offices and beds for parliamentarians attending the Riksdag, which was then located next door. It became a hotel after Parliament returned to its original quarters in 1984. The lobby is welcoming, with cane chairs in a pleasantly skylighted seating area. Well-lighted rooms are practical, but lack the luxury feel the price tag might lead you to expect; the decor is almost disappointing, with run-of-the-mill furnishings and too many grays in the uninspired color scheme. The location is central, right on the main pedestrian mall and adjoining the City Theater, but most windows view only office buildings. The best rooms are high up, with a view of the inner city rooftops and beyond. *Brunkebergstorg 9, S–103 27, tel. 08/226600 or 800/843–6664, fax 08/215070. 406 rooms. Facilities: restaurant, 2 bars, rooms for nonsmokers and the disabled, conference rooms. AE, DC, MC, V.*

Strand. This Old-World yellow-brick hotel, built in 1912 for the Stockholm Olympics, has been completely and tastefully modernized since its purchase by SAS in 1986. The waterside location is right across from the Royal Dramatic Theater. No two of its rooms are the same; many are furnished with antiques and have rustic touches such as flower painting on woodwork and furniture. The Piazza Italiano restaurant offers pleasant ambience in the glassed-in yard. *Nybrokajen 9, Box 163, S–103 27, tel. 08/678–7800, fax 08/611–2436. 138 rooms. Facilities: sauna, kiosk, conference rooms. AE, DC, MC, V.*

Victory. Slightly larger than its brother and sister hotels, the Lord Nelson and Lady Hamilton, this is an extremely atmospheric lodging place in a building that dates from 1640 in the Old Town. *Lilla Nygatan 5, S–111 28, tel. 08/143090, fax 08/202177. 48 rooms. AE, DC, MC, V.*

Expensive

Birger Jarl. This is one for nondrinkers: a hotel with no liquor license that is connected to a neighboring church, with weekly services in English. The modern, characteristically Scandinavian hotel opened in 1974. It is a quiet, unpretentious place, only a short walk from Stureplan and the city center. *Tulegatan 8, S–104 32, tel. 08/151020, fax 08/317366. 248 rooms. Facilities: cafeteria, fitness center, sauna, pool. AE, DC, MC, V.*

Clas på Hörnet. This may be the most exclusive—and smallest—hotel in town: 10 rooms (eight doubles) in an 18th-century inn converted into a small hotel in 1982. The rooms, comfortably furnished with antiques of the period, go quickly. The restaurant (*see* Dining, *above*) is worth a visit in its own right; a bar opened in 1991 in the adjacent glassed-in pavilion. *Surbrunnsgatan 20, S–113 48, tel. 08/165130, fax 08/612–5315. Facilities: restaurant, bar. AE, DC, MC, V.*

Lord Nelson. A small hotel with nautical atmosphere right in the middle of the Old Town, this is in the same hotel family as the Lady Hamilton and the Victory. Space is at a premium, and the rooms are little more than cabins, though service is excellent. Noise from merry-makers in the pedestrian street outside can be a problem in the summer months. *Västerlånggatan 22, S–111 29, tel. 08/232390, fax 08/101089. 31 rooms. Facilities: sauna, conference room. AE, DC, MC, V.*

Mälardrottningen. One of the more unusual places to stay in Stockholm, *Mälardrottningen* (Queen of Lake Mälar) was at one time Barbara Hutton's yacht, given to her on her 18th birthday by a father who ought to have known better. Since 1982, it has been a quaint and pleasant hotel, with a crew as service-conscious as any in Stockholm. The ship is tied up on the freshwater side of Gamla Stan, minutes from everything. Beds take up most of the room in the small suites, which are suitably decorated in a navy-blue and maroon nautical theme. Some of the below-deck cabins are a bit stuffy. Mälardrottningen is recommendable chiefly because of its novelty and absence of traffic noise. There is a tennis court on the quay. *Riddarholmen 11, S–111 28, tel. 08/243600 or 800/448–8355, fax 08/243676. 59 rooms. Facilities: restaurant, grill, bar, conference rooms. AE, DC, MC, V.*

Mornington. A quiet, modern hotel that prides itself on a friendly atmosphere, the Mornington is within easy walking distance of Stureplan and downtown shopping areas and particularly handy to Östermalmstorg, with its food hall. *Nybrogatan 53, S–102 44, tel. 08/663–1240, fax 08/662–2179. 141 rooms. Facilities: restaurant, bar, rooms for the disabled and nonsmokers, 4 conference rooms, sauna, steam baths. AE, DC, MC, V.*

Scandic Crown. Working with what appears to be a dubious location (perched on a tunnel over a six-lane highway), the Scandic Crown has pulled a rabbit out of a hat. The hotel was built in 1988 on special cushions; you know the highway is there but it intrudes only minimally, mainly in view. The Scandic Crown is a charming labyrinth of levels, separate buildings, and corridors, filled with such details as a rounded stairway lighted from between the steps. The guest rooms are exquisitely designed and decorated in modern style, with plenty of stainless steel and polished wood inlay to accent the maroon color scheme. Desks are sturdy and well lighted, beds are firm and large, and bathrooms are spacious and generously stocked. The staff is friendly but appears inexperienced. The hotel is located on the cliffs of Söder overlooking Riddarfjärden and the Old Town and is easily accessible from downtown. *Guldgränd 8, S–104 65, tel. 08/702–2500, fax 08/428358. 264 rooms. Facilities: 2 restaurants, bar, shops. AE, DC, MC, V.*

Moderate

Alfa. About 20 minutes from the city center, Alfa is a medium-size, medium-class hotel. Opened in 1972, it has recently been refurbished. *Marknadsvägen 6, S–121 09, tel. 08/810600. 104 rooms with bath. Facilities: restaurant. AE, DC, MC, V.*

★ **Anno 1647.** The name is the date the building was erected. A small, pleasant, friendly hotel on Söder, the south island, it is three stops on the subway from the city center. *Mariagränd 3, S–116 21, tel. 08/440480, fax 08/433700. 42 rooms, 30 with baths. Facilities: restaurant serving light foods only. AE, DC, MC, V.*

Bema. This small hotel has a reasonably central location, on the ground floor of an apartment block near Tegnérlunden. *Upplandsgatan 13, S–111 23, tel. 08/232625, fax 08/205338. 12 rooms with showers. Facilities: breakfast. AE, DC, MC, V.*

City. A large, modern-style hotel built in the 1940s but modernized in 1982–83, City is located near the city center and Hötorget market. Breakfast is served in the atrium Winter Garden. *Slöjdgatan 7, S–111 81, tel. 08/222240, fax 08/208224. 300 rooms with bath. Facilities: restaurant, café, sauna, rooms for the disabled. AE, DC, MC, V.*

Stockholm. Occupying the upper floors of a downtown office building, this hotel has mainly modern decor offset by traditional Swedish furnishings that help create its friendly atmosphere. *Norrmalmstorg 1, S–111 46, tel. 08/221320, fax 08/611–2103. 92 rooms. Facilities: breakfast. AE, DC, MC, V.*

Tegnérlunden. An extremely good bet for the budget tourist, this moderate-size hotel is situated only a short walk from the city center opposite a small park, close to the Strindberg Museum. *Tegnérlunden 8, S–113 59, tel. 08/349780. 104 rooms. Facilities: rooms for nonsmokers. AE, DC, MC, V.*

Inexpensive

Alexandra. Although it is in the Södermalm area, to the south of the Old Town, the Alexandra is only five minutes by subway from the city center. It is a small, modern hotel, opened in the early 1970s and renovated in 1988. Only breakfast is served. *Magnus Ladulåsgatan 42, S–118 27, tel. 08/840320. 79 rooms with bath. Facilities: sauna, solarium. AE, DC, MC, V. Closed Christmas and New Year's Day.*

Gustav af Klint. A "hotel ship" moored at Stadsgården quay, near Slussen subway station, the Gustav af Klint is divided into two sections—a hotel and a hostel. It was refurbished in 1989. There is a cafeteria and restaurant, and you can dine on deck in summer. *Stadsgårdskajen 153, S–116 45, tel. 08/404077. 28 cabins, none with bath. AE, DC, MC, V. Closed Christmas and New Year's Day.*

Youth Hostels

Don't be put off by the "youth" bit: There's actually no age limit. The standards of cleanliness, comfort, and facilities offered usually are extremely high.

Af Chapman. This is a sailing ship built in 1888, which is permanently moored in Stockholm harbor, just across from the Royal Palace. It is a landmark in its own right and in the summer has a decktop cafeteria. *Västra Brobänken, Skeppsholmen S–111 49, tel. 28/103715. 136 beds; 2- to 6-bed cabins. Facilities: breakfast.*

Bosön. This hostel is out of the way on the island of Lidingö but is pleasantly situated close to the water. *Bosön, S–181 47 Lidingö, tel. 08/767–9300. 26 beds; 2- to 3-bed rooms. Facilities: breakfast, cafeteria, washing machine, sauna, canoes for rent. V.*

Långholmen. This former prison, built in 1724, was converted into a combined hotel and hostel in 1989. It is located on the island of Långholmen, which has popular bathing beaches. The Inn, next door, serves Swedish home cooking, and the wine cellar offers light snacks. *Långholmen, Box 9116, S–102 72,tel. 08/668–0510. Summer weekends: 254 beds (101 2- to 4-bed rooms, all but 10 with showers and WC). Sept.–May, weekdays: 26 beds with shared bath. 32 beds adapted for the disabled. Facilities: cafeteria, restaurant, laundry room, sauna, beach. AE, DC, MC, V.*

Skeppsholmen. A former craftsman's workshop in a pleasant and quiet part of the island after which it is named, it was converted into a hostel for the overflow from the af Chapman, which is nearby. *Västra Brobänken, Skeppsholmen, S–111 49, tel. 08/202506. 152 beds. 2- to 4-bed rooms. Facilities: special rooms for disabled guests, breakfast. No credit cards.*

Camping There are camping sites at Enskede (tel. 08/773–0100), Haninge (tel. 08/745–8259), Slagsta (tel. 0753/77788), Bredäng (tel. 08/977071), and Sollentuna (tel. 08/353475). Camping in the Stockholm area costs SKr50–SKr100 per night.

The Arts and Nightlife

The Arts

Theater **Kungliga Dramatiska Teatern** (or Dramaten: the Royal Dramatic Theater) (Nybroplan, tel. 08/667–0680) sometimes stages productions of international interest, even though they are in Swedish. These include works directed by Ingmar Bergman, who has retired from films.

The **Regina Theater** (Drottninggatan 71a, tel. 08/207000) stages English-language productions.

Music Free concerts are held in **Kungsträdgården** every summer. For details contact the tourist office. International orchestras often visit **Konserthuset** (Hötorget 8, tel. 08/221800), the main concert hall.

Opera **Operan** (the Royal Opera House) (Jakobs Torg 2, tel. 08/791–4300), dating from 1898, continues a tradition going back to 1755, when Queen Lovisa Ulrika introduced opera to her subjects. Sweden has continued to produce such names as Jenny Lind, Jussi Björling, and Birgit Nilsson.

Folkoperan (Hornsgatan 72, tel. 08/585300), a lively, modern company with its headquarters in Söder, features "opera in the round." It rides roughshod over traditional methods of presentation and interpretation of the classics, generally to scintillating effect, and has established an international reputation for itself.

Dance There are demonstrations of Swedish folk dancing in **Kungsträdgården** and at **Mosebacken** in Söder during the summer months. Consult the tourist office for details.

Film Foreign movies are not dubbed. The best quality cinema in town is the **Grand** (Sveavägen, tel.08/112400). The cinema at **Filmhuset** (Borgvägen 1–5, tel. 08/665–1100), headquarters of the Swedish Film Institute, usually features an interesting program.

A curiosity is **Folkets Bio** (The People's Cinema) (Vegagatan 17, tel. 08/736–0035), a leftover from more idealistic times, which shows films that don't get general release, in a cellar just off Odenplan. It has an adjoining coffee bar.

Nightlife

Bars
Piano bars are also an important part of the Stockholm scene. Try the **Anglais Bar** at the Hotel Anglais (tel. 08/249900) or the **Clipper Club** at the Hotel Reisen, Skeppsbron (tel. 08/223260).

Cabaret
Stockholm's biggest nightclub, **Börsen** (Jakobsgatan 6, tel. 08/249210), offers high-quality international cabaret shows. Another popular spot is the **Cabaret Club**, Barnhusgatan 12 (tel. 08/110608). Although it can accommodate 450 guests, reservations are advised.

Casinos
These simply do not exist as such. Most hotels and bars have a roulette table and sometimes blackjack, operating according to Swedish rules aimed at restricting the amount you can lose.

Discos
Café Opera (tel. 08/110026) enjoys a magnificent locale in the Opera Building at the end of Kungsträdgården. A popular meeting place for young and old alike, it features a restaurant, roulette tables, and the longest bar in town with a disco that starts at midnight, closing at 3 AM. **Daily News** (tel. 08/215655), a glitzy disco located at the other end of Kungsträdgården near the Sweden House, has a restaurant and is open until 3 AM. **King Creole** (Kungsgatan 18, tel. 08/244700) offers big-band dance music alternating with rock.

Jazz Clubs
The best venue is **Fasching** (Kungsgatan 63, tel. 08/216267), close to the city center and featuring international and local bands. **Stampen** (Stora Nygatan 5, tel. 08/205793), an overpriced but atmospheric club in the Old Town, features traditional jazz nightly.

Rock Clubs
The best local and international groups can be seen at the following venues: **Melody** (Kungsträdgården, tel. 08/215665); **Galaxy** (on Strömsburg, an islet in the middle of Strömmen, tel. 08/215400); **Ritz** (Götgatan 51, on Söder, subway: Medborgarplatsen; tel. 08/424737); and **Lido** (on Söder, at Hornsgatan 92, subway: Zinkensdamm; tel. 08/668233).

Gay Bars
Pride (Sveavägen 57, tel. 08/315533) has a restaurant, café, bookshop, and disco, run by homosexuals for homosexuals. It's all totally respectable by local standards and backed by grants from the authorities.

Excursions from Stockholm

Uppsala

Sweden's principal university town vies for that position with Lund in the south of the country. August Strindberg, the nation's leading dramatist, studied here—and by all accounts hated the place. Ingmar Bergman, his modern heir, was born here. It is a historic site where pagan (and extremely gory) Viking ceremonies persisted into the 11th century. Uppsala University, one of the oldest and most highly respected institutions in Europe, was established here in 1477 by Archbishop Jakob Ulusson. As late as the 16th century, nationwide *ting*s, early parliaments, were convened here. Today it is a quiet home for around 155,000 people, built along the banks of Furu River, a pleasant jumble of old buildings dominated by its cathedral, which dates from the early 13th century.

Tourist Information The main **tourist office** (tel. 018/117500 or 018/161825) is at Fyris Torg in the center of town. In summer a small tourist-information office is also open at Uppsala Castle.

Getting There
By Car Uppsala is an easy drive 40 kilometers (25 miles) north from Stockholm along the E4 motorway.

By Train There is regular train service from the central station. The journey takes 45 minutes.

By Bus Buses leave the city terminal at Klarabergsviadukten on Friday and Sunday. For information, tel. 08/237190. There is direct bus service to Uppsala from Arlanda Airport.

Guided Tours You can explore Uppsala easily by yourself on foot, but guided tours in English for groups can be arranged through the tourist office. Usually a bus tour, with a recorded commentary in English, leaves from the railway station during July and August at 11 AM and 1 PM.

Numbers in the margin correspond with points of interest on the Excursions from Stockholm map.

Exploring Uppsala Ideally, you should start your visit with a trip to **Gamla Uppsa-
5 la** (Old Uppsala), 5 kilometers (3 miles) north of the town. This is a 15-minute ride on Bus No. 14, which you pick up at Dragarbrunnsgatan, a short walk from the station toward the town center.

Here under three huge **mounds** lie the graves of the first Swedish kings, Aun, Egil, and Adils, of the 6th-century Ynglinga dynasty. Close by in pagan times was a sacred grove containing a legendary oak from whose branches were hung animal and human sacrifices. By the 10th century, Christianity had eliminated such practices. A small church, which was the seat of Sweden's first archbishop, was built on the site of a former pagan temple. Today, the archbishopric is in Uppsala itself, and the church, **Gamla Uppsala Kyrka,** is largely for the benefit of tourists. A small open-air museum nearby, **Disagården,** features old farm buildings, most of them from the 19th century. *Admission free. Open May–Sept., daily 9–5.*

Time Out You can drink mead brewed from a 14th-century recipe at the nearby **Odinsborg Restaurant.**

---

6 Back in **Uppsala,** your first visit should be to Uppsala **Domkyrka** (cathedral), whose twin towers (362 feet high) dominate the city. They are the same height as the length of the nave. Work on the cathedral was begun in the early 13th century; it was consecrated in 1435 and restored between 1885 and 1893. The cathedral remains the seat of Sweden's archbishop. It is important in the nation's history as the site of the tomb of Gustav Vasa, the king who established Sweden's independence in the 16th century. It also houses a silver casket containing the bones of St. Erik, Sweden's patron saint.

Work on **Uppsala slott** (Uppsala Castle) was started in the 1540s by Gustav Vasa, who intended it to symbolize the dominance of the monarchy over the church. It was completed under Queen Christina nearly a century later. Students gather here every April 30 to celebrate the Feast of Valborg and optimistically greet the arrival of spring.

Time Out

Fyrishall (Gamla Uppsalagatan, tel. 018/274950) is Sweden's largest sports complex, with a 50-meter pool, a special heated pool for the handicapped, and three different sauna baths. There are a café, a restaurant, and terraces for sunbathing.

One of Uppsala's most famous sons, Carl von Linné, also known as Linnaeus, was a professor of botany at the university during the 1740s and created the Latin nomenclature system for plants and animals. The **Linné Museum** in his old botanical garden, **Linnaeusgården,** which has been restored to its former glory, is dedicated to his life and works. The orangery houses a pleasant cafeteria and is used for concerts and cultural events. *Svartbäcksgatan 27, tel. 018/136540. Admission to garden free. Open May–Aug., daily 9–9; Sept.–Apr., daily 9–7. Admission to museum: SKr10. Open May–Sept., daily 1–4.*

Uppsala Universitetet (the Uppsala University), founded in 1477, features the **Carolina Rediviva** (the university library), which contains a copy of every book published in Sweden, in addition to a large collection of foreign literature. One of its most interesting exhibits is the *Codex Argentus*, a silver Bible written in the 6th century.

The university's collection of art and historical items is housed behind the cathedral in the **Gustavianum,** completed in 1625 by Casper Panten, the Dutch master builder. *Akademigatan 3, tel. 018/182500. Admission: SKr15. Open daily noon–3.*

Dining

Domtrappkällaren. Located in a 14th-century cellar near the cathedral, Domtrappkällaren features excellent French and Swedish cuisine. *Eriksgränd 15, tel. 018/130955. Reservations required. Dress: casual but neat. AE, DC, MC, V.*

Gotland

Gotland is Sweden's main holiday island, a place of wide, sandy beaches and wild cliff formations called *raukar*. Inland, there is verdant sheep-farming country and glades in which 35 different varieties of wild orchids thrive, attracting botanists from all over the world. Lying in the Baltic just 85 kilometers (53 miles) from the mainland, the island is 125 kilometers (78 miles) in length and 52 kilometers (32 miles) across at its widest point.

Gotland was first inhabited around 5000 BC, and by the time of the Roman Iron Age had become a leading Baltic trading center. Germans arrived later and built most of its churches in the 13th century. They established close trading links with the Hanseatic League in Lübeck. The Danes followed, and it was not until 1645 that Gotland finally became part of Sweden.

Tourist Information

The main tourist office is at Donnersplan, Visby (tel. 0498/47060 or 0498/47065).

Getting There

By Plane

Fifteen flights a day arrive in Gotland's airport from Stockholm. For information, call SAS, tel. 08/240000.

By Boat

There are car-ferry sailings from Nynäshamn, a small port on the Baltic an hour by car or rail from Stockholm. (Commuter trains leave regularly from Stockholm's central station for Nynäshamn.) Boats leave daily at 12:30 PM year-round, with an extra sailing at midnight in summer. The voyage takes about five hours. *Gotlandslinjen, Kungsgatan 48, Gotland City, tel. 08/236170 or 08/233180; Nynäshamn, tel. 0752/64000.*

Guided Tours

Guided tours of Visby, the capital, are available in English by arrangement with the tourist office.

Exploring Gotland

7

If you have a limited time schedule, you may be content to visit **Gotland**'s capital, **Visby,** a delightful, hilly town of about 20,000 people, in which medieval houses, ruined fortifications, and churches blend with cobbled lanes of fairy-tale cottages, their facades covered with roses reputed to bloom even in November because the climate is so gentle.

In its heyday, Visby was protected by a wall, of which three kilometers survive today, along with 44 towers and numerous gateways. It is considered the best-preserved medieval city wall in Europe after that of Carcassonne in southern France. The north gate provides the best vantage point for an overall view of the wall.

The cathedral, **Maria Kyrka,** is the only one of the town's 17 medieval churches still intact and in use. The ruins of 11 others can be visited, however, and in those of St. Nicolai, a Dominican monastery dating from 1230, an operatic pageant is performed from mid-July to mid-August. Tickets are available from the tourist office.

Near the harbor is **Det Gamla Apoteket** (the Old Apothecary), a late-medieval four-story merchant's house, where a silversmith now works and demonstrates his trade to visitors. *Strandgatan 28, tel. 0498/12889. Admission free. Open daily 9–5.*

In the same street, you'll find **Burmeisterska huset,** the home of the Burmeister or principal German merchant, which today houses the tourist office. *Strandgatan 9, tel. 0498/10982. Admission: SKr10. Open weekdays 8–8, Sat., Sun. 10–7.*

Fornsalen (the Fornsal Museum) contains examples of medieval artwork, hordes of silver from Viking times, and impressive picture stones that predate the Viking rune stones. *Strandgatan 14, S–62102, tel. 0498/47010. Admission: SKr20 adults, children under 16 free. Open mid-May–Sept., daily 11–6; Sept–mid-May, Tues.–Sun. noon–4.*

The rest of the island is best explored by bicycle. Bicycles, tents, and camping equipment can be rented from **Gotlands Cykeluthyrning** (Skeppsbron 8, tel. 0498/14133). Details of Gotlandsleden, a 200-kilometer (120-mile) route around the island, which avoids military installations, off-limits to foreigners, are available from the tourist office.

The stalactite caves at **Lummelunda,** about 10 kilometers (6 miles) from Visby, are unique in this part of the world and are worth visiting, as is the **Krusmyntagården** (herb garden), 12 kilometers (7 miles) north of Visby, close to the sea.

There are approximately 100 old churches on the island that are still in use today, dating from Gotland's great commercial era. Outstanding among them are: **Barlingbro,** dating from the 13th century, with vault paintings, stained-glass windows, and a remarkable 12th-century font; the exquisite **Dalhem,** constructed about 1200; **Gothem,** built during the 13th century, with a notable series of paintings of that period; **Grötlingbo,** a 14th-century church with stone sculpture and stained glass (note the 12th-century reliefs on the facade); **Tingstäde,** a mix of six building periods from 1169 to 1300; **Roma Kloster Kyrka**

(Roma Cloister Church), the massive ruins of a Cistercian monastery founded in 1164; and **Öja,** decorated with paintings and housing a famous holy rood from the late-13th century.

There are a number of other sights well worth your time. Among them are curious rock formations along the coasts and two bird refuges, **Stora** and **Lilla Karlsö,** off the coast south of Visby. The bird population consists mainly of guillemots, which look like penguins. Visits to these refuges are permitted only in the company of a recognized guide. (Stora Karlsö, tel. 0498/40500; Lilla Karlsö, tel. 0498/41111 or 0498/41139).

Dining
Visby

Lindgården. This atmospheric restaurant specializes in both local dishes and French cuisine. *Strandgatan 26, tel. 0498/18700. Reservations required. AE, DC, MC, V. Expensive.*

Gutakällaren. Despite the name, this is not a cellar restaurant. Located aboveground in a building that dates back to the 12th century, it features local specialties, many involving lamb. *Stora Torget 3, tel. 0498/10043. Reservations required. AE, DC, MC, V. Expensive.*

Göteborg

Introduction

If you arrive in Goteborg by car, don't drive straight through the city in your haste to reach your coastal vacation spot; it is well worth spending a day to two exploring this attractive port. A quayside jungle of cranes and warehouses attests to the city's industrial might, yet within 10 minutes' walk of the waterfront is an elegant, modern city of broad avenues, green parks, and gardens. It is an easy city to explore: Most of the major attractions are within walking distance of each other, and there is an excellent streetcar network. In summer you can take a sightseeing trip on an open-air streetcar.

Sprawling, mostly modern Göteborg (Gothenburg), with a population of 700,000, is Sweden's second-largest city. Its heart is Avenyn (the Avenue; actually Kungsportsavenyn, but over the years shortened to simply Avenyn), a 60-foot-wide, tree-lined boulevard that bisects the center of the city in a south–north direction, linking its cultural heart, Götaplatsen, at the southern end, with the main commercial area, now dominated by the huge, modern Nordstan shopping center. Also toward the northern end of Avenyn is the pleasant park of Trädgårdsföreningen (the Horticultural Society—called Trägårn), the best-known of the city's 20 parks.

Beyond Nordstan is the harbor, 22 kilometers (14 miles) of quays with warehouses and sheds covering more than 1.5 million square feet and spread along both banks of the Göta Älv (river), making Göteborg Scandinavia's largest port. It is also the home of Scandinavia's largest corporation, the automobile manufacturer Volvo (which means "I roll" in Latin), as well as of the roller-bearing manufacturer SKF and the world-renowned Hasselblad camera company.

Historically, Göteborg owes its existence to the sea. Tenth-century Vikings sailed from its shores, and a settlement was founded here in the 11th century. Not until 1621, however, did King Gustav II Adolf grant Göteborg a charter in order to establish a free-trade port on the model of others already thriving on the Continent. The west-coast harbor would also allow Swedish shipping to avoid Danish tolls exacted for passing through Öresund, the stretch of water separating the two countries. Foreigners were recruited to make these visions real: The Dutch were its builders—hence the canals that thread the city—and many Scotsmen worked and settled here, though they have left little trace.

Today, Göteborg resists its second-city status by being a leader in terms of attractions and civic structures: The Skandinavium was until recently Europe's largest indoor arena; the Ullevi Stadium stages some of the Nordic area's most important concerts and sporting events; Nordstan is Europe's largest indoor shopping mall; and Liseberg is Scandinavia's largest amusement park in area, attracts some 2.5 million visitors a year. Over the Göta River is Älvsborgsbron, at 3,000 feet the longest suspension bridge in Sweden, and under it is the Gnistäng Tunnel, at 62 feet the world's widest cut through rock for motor vehicles.

Göteborg is a pleasantly relaxed place from which to explore the west coast of Sweden, where wide, unspoiled beaches alternate with timbered fishing villages. From here, too, you can set out on the Göta Canal, Sweden's "blue ribbon," down which barges once sailed laden with exports and imports, but which today provides a picturesque water journey through the Swedish countryside.

Important Addresses and Numbers

Tourist Information The main tourist office is Göteborg's Turistbyrå Kungsportsplatsen 2, S–411 10 Göteborg, tel. 031/100740. There is also an office at the Nordstan shopping center (Nordstadstorget, 411 05 Göteborg).

Consulates **U.S. Consulate:** Södra Hamngatan 2, tel. 031/100590; **U.K. Consulate:** Norra Hamngatan 32, tel. 031/800778.

Emergencies Dial 90000 (*see* Stockholm, *above*).

Doctors Dial 031/415500 for information on medical services. Emergencies are handled by the **Sahlgrenska Hospital** (tel. 031/601000), **Östrasjukhuset** (tel. 031/374000), and **Mölndalssjukhuset** (tel. 031/861000). There is a private medical service at **City Akuten** (Drottninggatan, tel. 031/101010).

Dentists The national health service emergency number is 031/803140, the private dental service emergency number is 031/117017.

English-language Bookstores Nearly all bookshops stock English-language books. The broadest selection is at **Esselte's Eckersteins** store (Grönsakstorget, tel. 031/171100).

Pharmacy **Vasen** (Götgatan 12, tel. 031/804410), in the Nordstar shopping mall, is open 24 hours.

Travel Agencies **American Express** is at Kyrkogatan 56 (tel. 031/178230). **SJ,** the state railway company, has a bureau at Östra Hamngatan 35 (tel. 031/176100). For other travel agencies see the yellow pages under "Resor-Resebyråer."

Arriving and Departing by Plane

Airports and Airlines The airport, **Landvetter,** is approximately 26 kilometers (16 miles) from the city center. Among the airlines operating from it are **SAS** (tel. 031/942000), **British Airways** (tel. 031/941315), **Air France** (tel. 031/801110), and **Lufthansa** (tel. 031/805640).

Between the Airport and City Center
By Bus Landvetter is linked to Göteborg by freeway. Buses leave Landvetter every 15 minutes, traveling to the air terminal near the central railway station and stopping at the SAS Park Avenue Hotel. The price of the trip is SKr50. For more information, tel. 031/941000.

By Taxi A taxi to the city center will cost between SKr250 and SKr300. For SAS limousine service, tel. 031/942424.

Arriving and Departing by Car, Train, and Bus

By Car You arrive on the E3 highway from Stockholm (495 kilometers/307 miles) and the east or on the E6 coastal highway from the south (Malmö is 290 kilometers/180 miles away.) Markings are excellent, and roads are well sanded and plowed in winter.

By Train There is a regular service from Stockholm, taking a little over four hours. All trains arrive at the central railway station in Drottningtorget, downtown Göteborg (tel. 031/175000). Streetcars and buses leave from here for the suburbs.

By Bus Buses all arrive in the downtown area. The principal companies are **SJ** (tel. 031/103100) and **GDG Continentbus** (tel. 031/800390).

Getting Around

By Car **Avis** has offices at the airport (tel. 031/946030) and the central railway station (tel. 031/170410). **Hertz** is at Engelbrektsgatan 73 (tel. 031/810790).

By Bus and Tram Göteborg has an excellent transit service. Books of 24 tickets, costing SKr100, are available at the Pressbyrån shops and kiosks. However, the best bet for the tourist is the **Göteborg Card,** which costs SKr95 and gives free use of public transport, various sightseeing trips, and admission to Liseberg and local museums.

By Taxi To order a taxi, telephone 031/200400; for advance bookings, call 031/200570.

Guided Tours

Orientation A 90-minute bus tour of the chief points of interest leaves from outside the main tourist office (Kungsportsplatsen 2) at 10:30, 11:30, and 12:30 each day in summer.

Highlights for First-time Visitors

Götaplatsen (*see* Tour 1)
Avenyn (*see* Tour 1)
Elfsborg Fortress (*see* Tour 3)
Harbor (*see* Tour 2)
Liseberg Amusement Park (*see* What to See and Do with Children)

Exploring Göteborg

Numbers in the margin correspond with points of interest on the Göteborg map.

Tour 1: The City Center

Start in **Götaplatsen,** a fine, light, modern square dominated by Carl Milles' statue of **Poseidon,** whose shy, downturned gaze and gentle demeanor lend him a distinctly Swedish aura.
1 Grouped around the square, you will find **Konserthuset** (the Concert Hall), the art museum and the municipal theater, three quite imposing contemporary buildings in which the city celebrates its important contribution to Swedish cultural life. Konserthuset is the home of the highly acclaimed Göteborg Symphony Orchestra (Konserthuset, Götaplatsen, tel. 031/200130).

2 **Konstmuseet** (the Art Museum), opened in 1925, contains an impressive collection of the works of leading Scandinavian painters and sculptors; it encapsulates some of the moody introspection of the artistic community in this part of the world. Among the artists represented are Swedes such as Carl Milles, Sergel, the impressionist Anders Zorn, the Victorian idealist Carl Larsson, and Prince Eugen. There is a small collection of old masters, including Rubens, Rembrandt, and van Dyke, and the best collection in Sweden of 19th- and 20th-century French art. This includes works by Monet, Pissaro, Sisley, Renoir, Cézanne, Gauguin, van Gogh, Rousseau, Matisse, and Picasso. *Götaplatsen, tel. 031/139010. Admission: SKr20. Open weekdays 10–4 (Wed. until 9), Sun. 11–5.*

3 **Stadsteatern** (the Municipal Theater) (Götaplatsen, tel. 031/019900), while it has a good reputation in Sweden, remains very much a local phenomenon because the vast majority of its pro-
4 ductions are in Swedish. Also in Götaplatsen, **Stadsbiblioteket** (the Municipal Library) (Götaplatsen, tel. 031/810480), boasts a collection of more than 550,000 books, many of them in English.

From Götaplatsen, stroll northward past the cafés and restaurants along the **Avenyn** to the intersection with Vasagatan. A short way to the left down Vasagatan, at the junction with
5 Teatergatan, you can visit the **Röhsska Konstslöjdsmuseet** (Museum of Arts and Crafts), with its fine collections of furniture, books and manuscripts, tapestries, and pottery. *Vasagatan, tel. 031/200605. Admission: SKr20. Open Tues. noon–9, Wed.–Sun. noon–4.*

6 Continue left along Vasagatan to **Folkhögskolan,** Göteborg's university, and, if the weather's good, to relax in neighboring **Vasa Park.** Walk northward along Viktoriagatan, crossing the canal and then making an immediate left to visit one of the
7 city's most peculiar attractions, **Feske Körkan,** an archaic spelling of *Fisk Kyrkan,* the Fish Church. It resembles a place of worship but is actually an indoor fish market.

Following this you may feel inspired to visit the city's principal
8 place of worship, **Domkyrkan** (Göteborg Cathedral). To get here from Feske Körkan, follow the canal eastward until you come to Västra Hamngatan, then head north to Kyrkogatan. The Cathedral, in neoclassic yellow brick, dates from 1802;

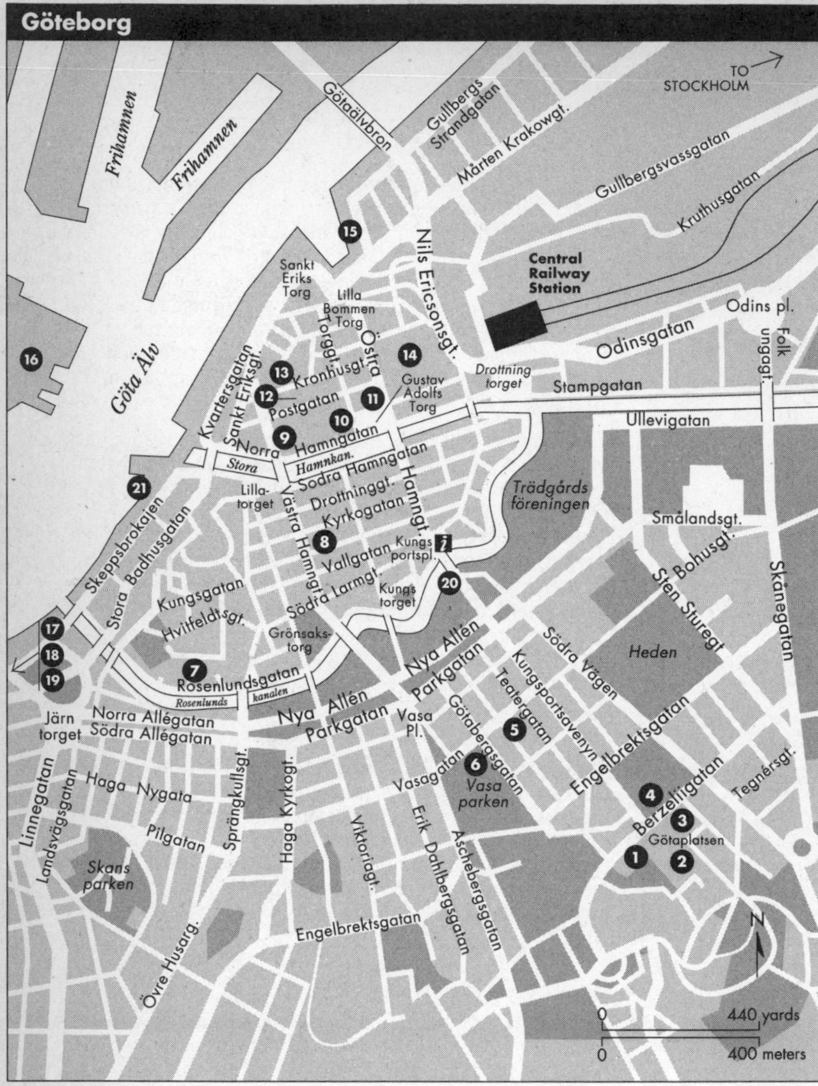

Älvsborgsbron, **18**
Börshuset, **11**
Domkyrkan, **8**
Elfsborgs fästning boat, **21**
Feske Körkan, **7**
Fiskhamnen, **17**
Folkhögskolan, **6**
Götaverkan, **16**
Konserthuset, **1**
Konstmuseet, **2**
Kronhusbodarna, **13**
Kronhuset, **12**
Kulturhistoriska Museet, **9**
Maritima Centret, **15**
Nordstan, **14**
Paddan boats, **20**
Rådhuset, **10**
Röhsska Konstslöjdsmuseet, **5**
Skarvikshamnen, **19**
Stadsbiblioteket, **4**
Stadsteatern, **3**

while it's not particularly attractive from the outside, the interior is impressive. *Kungsgatan 20. Open weekdays 8–5, Sat. 8–3, Sun. 10–3.*

9 Continue northward on Västra Hamngatan to the **Kulturhistoriska Museet** (the Museum of Cultural History) at the junction with Norra Hamngatan. This was founded in 1861, and its Department of Ethnography has interesting collections of Sami artifacts. (It also has one of the best collections of South American Indian artifacts anywhere in the world. The pre-Columbian textiles from Peru are its pièce de résistance.) The Department of History is mainly concerned with Göteborg itself and the Swedish west coast, with the emphasis on crafts and industries of times past. The Department of Archaeology has a similar local focus, some of its exhibits dating from the Stone Age. *Norra Hamngatan, tel. 031/139010. Admission: SKr20. Open weekdays 10–4 (Wed. until 9), Sun. 11–5.*

Follow Norra Hamngatan eastward to **Gustav Adolfs Torg,** the
10 city's official center, which is dominated by **Rådhuset** (the City Hall) (Gustav Adolfs Torg, tel. 031/611000), built in 1699, with a modern extension by Swedish architect Gunnar Asplund that caused great controversy when it was completed in 1937. Tours must be prearranged.

11 On the north side of the square is **Börshuset** (the Stock Exchange) (Gustav Adolfs Torg, tel. 031/835900), built in 1849.

Head northwest from the square along Östra Hamngatan,
12 turning into Kronhusgatan, to visit **Kronhuset,** the city's oldest secular building, which dates from 1643. It was once the armory, and in 1660 Sweden's Parliament met here to arrange the succession for King Karl X Gustav, who died suddenly while visiting the city. *Postgatan 628, tel. 031/112238. Admission: SKr20. Open weekdays 10–4, Sun. 11–5.*

13 Close by are the attractive **Kronhusbodarna,** carefully restored turn-of-the-century shops and handicraft boutiques. *Kronhusgatan. Open daily 10–4, some shops open later in summer.*

The quaintness of Kronhusbodarna as a shopping experience contrasts sharply with the coldly modern functionalism of
14 **Nordstan,** the vast indoor shopping mall a short distance away off Östra Hamngatan.

Tour 2: The Harbor

Walk across the Götaälvbron (Göta River bridge) to **Hisingen,** now the mainly industrial area of the city, on the far bank, which was the site of earlier settlements before Göteborg was built. When the city was founded, boats at first anchored in its canals, but larger vessels had to put in farther west, and as a consequence, the harbor developed on both banks of the river.

A good starting point for a tour of the docks is **Gasverkskajen** (Gas Works Quay), just off Gullbergsstrandgatan. Today this is the headquarters of a local boating association, its brightly colored pleasure craft contrasting with the old-fashioned working barges either anchored or being repaired at Ringön, just across the river. Walk back under the Göta River Bridge and head for
15 **Maritima Centret** (the Maritime Center) at Lilla Bommen. This modern development is aimed at revitalizing the inner harbor. Its **Ship Museum** contains historic vessels, including a destroy-

er, a lightship, a cargo vessel, and various tugboats, that can be visited. *Lilla Bommenshamnen, tel. 031/101290. Admisssion: SKr20 adults, children under 16 free. Open Mon.–Sat. 9–4, Sun. 9–5.*

Continue along the river, down Skeppsbrokajen, for views
16 across the river of the **Götaverkan** and **Cityvarvet** shipyards, which were once the pride of the city but now look distinctly forlorn. Farther along the river bank, past Masthuggskajen, you come to **Stigbergskajen,** where the transatlantic liners once docked. In the city's heyday, mighty vessels like the *Gripsholm*, the *Drottningholm*, and the *Kungsholm* landed American visitors. Today, most international visitors arrive by air in Stockholm.

17 Just past Stigbergskajen is **Fiskhamnen,** the fishing harbor, where the day's catch is auctioned each morning at 7. Continue walking and you will see signs of changing times all around. From the London Pier, where boats once left for England,
18 there is today an excellent view of **Älvsborgsbron,** (the Älvsborg bridge), the longest suspension bridge in Sweden. Built in 1967, it stretches 3,000 feet over the river and is built so high that ocean liners can pass beneath. Plans now are before the government to turn this part of the harbor into a scenic walkway with parks and cafés. Return to the city side of the river over the mighty bridge and from it look toward the sea to
19 the large container harbors, **Skarvikshamnen, Skandiahamnen,** and **Torshamnen,** which bring most of the cargo and passengers to the city today.

Tour 3: Göteborg from the Water

For a view of the city from the water and an expert commentary in English and German on its sights and history, take one of the
20 **Paddan** sightseeing boats. Paddan means "toad" in Swedish, an apt commentary on the vessels' squat appearance. The boats pass under 16 bridges and take in both the canals and part of the Göta River. *Kungsportbro, tel. 031/133000. Fare: SKr35. Open May 1–Sept. 13, daily 10–5 (until 6 in July and 1st week in Aug.).*

There also are regular **boat** trips from the quayside close to the
21 city center to the **Elfsborgs Fästning** (Elfsborg Fortress), built in 1670 on a harbor island to protect the city from attack. *Elfsborg båtar, Stenpiren, tel. 031/752565. Boats leave 5 times daily, Apr. 11–Sept. 8. Cost: SKr55 adults, SKr7 children round-trip.*

What to See and Do with Children

Here Göteborg comes into its own with **Lisebergs Nöjes Park,** Scandinavia's largest amusement park, one of the best-run, most efficient in the world. It not only features a wide selection of carnival rides but also has numerous restaurants and theaters, all set amid beautifully tended gardens. It's only a short walk from the city's center. *Södra Vägen, tel. 031/400100. Admission: SKr25; SKr35 June 21–Aug. 4. Open Apr. 13–Sept. 29.*

Shopping

Department Stores The local branch of **NK,** Sweden's leading department store, is at Östra Hamngatan 42 (tel. 031/173300), while that of **Åhléns** is in the Nordstan mall (tel. 031/800200).

Specialty Stores
Antiques **Antikhallarna** (the Antiques Hall) (Västra Hamngatan 6, tel. 031/137799) claim to be the largest of their kind in Scandinavia. You'll find Sweden's leading auction houses, **Bukowskis,** on Avenyn (Kungsportsavenyn 1, tel. 031/116783).

Handicrafts The most atmospheric settings for the purchase of Swedish handicrafts and glassware are in the various shops in **Kronhusbodarna** (*see* Tour 1, *above*), but excellent examples of local handicrafts can also be bought at **Bohusslöjden** (Kungsportsavenyn 25, tel. 031/160072).

Men's Clothing **Gillblads** (Kungsgatan 42–44, tel. 031/108846) and **Ströms** (Kungsgatan 27–29, tel. 031/177100) have good selections.

Women's Clothing For furs, try **Amoress** (Kungsgatan 31, tel. 031/118780); for other fashions, **Gillblads, Ströms** (*see* Men's Clothes, *above*), and **Hennes & Mauritz** (Kungsgatan 55–57, tel. 031/110011) all have standard choices.

Sports and Outdoor Activities

Fishing Fishing for mackerel is a popular sport. Among the boats that take expeditions into the archipelago is M/S *Daisy*, which leaves from Hjövik on the Hisingen side of the Göta River (tel. 031/963018).

Water Sports Boating, sailing, and windsurfing are all well provided for. Check with the tourist office for details.

Beaches

There are several excellent local beaches. The two most popular (though visitors are unlikely to find them crowded) are **Näset,** reached by taking streetcar No. 2 or 3 to Frölundatorg, then changing to bus No. 92, and **Askim,** reached by taking streetcar No. 1 or 2 to Linnéplatsen and then changing to bus No. 82 or 83.

Dining

You can eat well in Göteborg, but you must expect to pay dearly for the privilege. If anything, there is a more casual approach here than in Stockholm, so, unless otherwise indicated, you won't need to dress up. Fish dishes are the best bet here. Check that restaurants are open first, as many close for a month in summer.

Highly recommended restaurants are indicated by a star ★.

Very Expensive **La Scala.** This long-established restaurant located in a corner close to the Konstmuseet currently is hitting new highs with marvelous French cuisine from Leif Mannerström and Crister Svantesson, who have achieved almost legendary status in the city as a result. It is especially known for its excellent fish dishes and desserts, including cardamom pie. *Götaplatsen, tel. 031/182212. Reservations advised. Jacket and tie required. AE, DC, MC, V.*

★ **The Place.** This restaurant has an intimate atmosphere in a dining room with large, arched windows and prides itself on both its elegant, contemporary cuisine and the quality of the ingredients used. *Arkivgatan 7, tel. 031/160333. Reservations required. Jacket and tie required. AE, DC, MC, V.*

Expensive

Chablis. Long popular in Göteborg, this excellent fish restaurant has two locations: *Aschebergsgatan 22, tel. 031/203545; and Linnégatan 52, tel. 031/242444. Reservations advised. AE, DC, MC, V.*

Johanna. Once the city's most exclusive gourmet restaurant, this is today a shadow of its former self. The interior suggests a London club and the cuisine is nouvelle, with an accent on seafood. *Södra Hamngatan 47, tel. 031/112250. Reservations required. Jacket and tie required. AE, DC, MC, V. Closed Sun.*

Sjömagasinet. The specialty of this seafood restaurant with its 18th-century atmosphere and pleasant view of the sea is filet of sole Walewska. *Klippans Kulturreservat, tel. 031/246510. Reservations required. AE, DC, MC, V.*

Stallgården. This is a high-quality fish restaurant, one of whose specialties is curry-stuffed lobster. *Kyrkogården 33, tel. 031/130316. Reservations required. AE, DC, MC, V.*

Moderate

Bräutigams. Near the tourist office, Bräutigams is an elegant café, ideal for a snack or light meal in a turn-of-the-century atmosphere. The restaurant specializes in homemade cakes and coffee, but light lunches—open-faced sandwiches and salads—are also available. *Östra Hamngatan 50B, tel. 031/136046. Reservations not necessary. AE, DC, MC, V. Closed Christmas Eve.*

Fiskekrogen. Its name means "Fish Inn," and it has more than 30 fish and seafood dishes to choose from. Lunches are particularly good here. *Lilla Torget 1, tel. 031/112184. Reservations advised. AE, DC, MC, V.*

Weise. A centrally located restaurant with a German beer-cellar atmosphere. Owned by the same family since 1907, it was once a haunt of local painters and intellectuals and still retains something of that ambience. The tables and chairs date from 1892. It specializes in traditional Swedish home cooking, serving dishes such as pork and brown beans, pea soup, and homemade apple cake. *Drottninggatan 23, tel. 031/131402. Reservations advised. AE, DC, MC, V.*

Inexpensive

Amanda Boman. This little restaurant is in one corner of the market hall and keeps early opening hours, so unless you eat an afternoon dinner, it is primarily a lunch place. It serves Swedish specialties—fish soup, gravlax, and daily hot dishes. *Saluhallen, tel. 031/137676. AE, DC, MC, V. Closed Sun.*

Gabriel. Fresh shellfish and the fish dish of the day draw crowds to this restaurant on a balcony over the fish hall. You can eat lunch and watch all the trading. *Feskekorka, tel. 031/139051. MC, V. Closed dinner and weekends.*

Minus. This restaurant proves that health food doesn't have to be boring. All food is marked with calorie count, but, fortunately, that dosen't affect the taste. *Andra Långgatan 4B, tel. 031/144199. No credit cards. Closed weekends.*

Lodging

In Göteborg, many hotels offer special summer discounts.

Highly recommended hotels are indicated by a star ★.

Very Expensive

Sheraton Hotel and Towers. Opened in 1986, the Sheraton Hotel and Towers is Göteborg's most modern and spectacular international-style hotel. It features an atrium lobby. There are several restaurants with varying prices, including a popular Italian café, open at lunchtime, and a more formal restaurant serving international cuisine. *Södra Hamngatan 59–65, S–401 24, tel. 031/806000, fax 031/159888. 340 rooms with bath. Facilities: restaurants, nightclub, health club, 16 rooms for the disabled, swimming pool. AE, DC, MC, V. Closed Christmas.*

Expensive

★ **Eggers.** Dating back to 1859, Eggers has more Old World character than any other hotel in the city. It is located near the train station and was probably the last port of call in Sweden for many emigrants to the United States. The rooms feature antique furnishings, and there is a popular brasserie. *Drottningtorget, S–401 25, tel. 031/806070, fax 031/154243. 77 rooms with bath. AE, DC, MC, V. Closed Christmas.*

Gothia. In a good central location, this quality hotel specializes in conference visitors. *Mässans gata 24, S–402 26, tel. 031/409300, fax 031/189804. 300 rooms. Facilities: 2 restaurants, coffee shop, bar, swimming pool, 2 saunas, Jacuzzi, parking. AE, DC, MC, V.*

SAS Park Avenue. The lobby of this modern luxury hotel was renovated in 1991, but it still lacks ambience. The well-equipped rooms are decorated in earth tones. Its excellent location on Avenyn and the bright, airy cocktail bar on the top floor are its chief attractions. *Kungsportsavenyn 36–38, S–400 16, tel. 031/176520, fax 031/169568. 318 rooms. Facilities: restaurant, bar, nightclub, sauna, swimming pool, conference room, SAS airline check-in counter. AE, DC, MC, V.*

Moderate

★ **Europa.** Large and comfortable, this hotel is situated close to the Central Railway Station and the Nordstan mall. *Köpmansgatan 38, S–401 24, tel. 031/801280, fax 031/154755. 475 rooms, 5 suites. Facilities: restaurant, bar, piano bar, nightclub, gift shop, garage, rooms for the disabled. AE, DC, MC, V.*

Opalen. If you are attending an event at the Scandinavium stadium or if you have children and are heading for the Liseberg amusement park, this hotel is ideally located. Completely renovated in 1990, the rooms are bright and modern with large windows. *Engelbrektsgatan 73, S–402 23, tel. 031/810300, fax 031/187622. 241 rooms. Facilities: restaurant, bar, swimming pool, sauna, tennis courts, 2 nonsmoking floors. AE, DC, MC, V.*

Panorama. Within reach of all downtown attractions, this hotel nevertheless manages to provide a quiet, relaxing atmosphere. *Eklandagatan 51–53, S–400 22, tel. 031/810880, fax 031/814237. 340 rooms. Facilities: restaurant, nightclub, swimming pool, sauna, Jacuzzi, garage. AE, DC, MC, V.*

Ramada. A little off the beaten path, but still only five minutes from the city center by car the Ramada has large, pastel rooms equipped with desks and sofas in addition to the standard amenities. *Gamla Tingstadsgatan 1, S–402 76, tel. 031/222420, fax 031/512100. 121 rooms. Facilities: restaurant, bar, sauna, squash courts, conference rooms. AE, DC, MC, V.*

Riverton. Convenient for people arriving in the city by ferry, this hotel is close to the European terminals and overlooks the harbor. Built in 1985 and regularly renovated, it has a glossy marble floor and reflective ceiling in the lobby and rooms decorated with abstract-pattern textiles and whimsical prints.

Stora Badhusgatan 26, S–411 21, tel. 031/101200, fax 031/130866. 190 rooms. Facilities: restaurant, bar, swimming pool, sauna, Jacuzzi, garage, conference rooms. AE, DC, MC, V.

Rubinen. Here's an excellent central location on Avenyn, but it can be noisy during the summer months. *Kungsportsavenyn 24, S–400 14, tel. 031/810800, fax 031/167586. 190 rooms. Facilities: restaurant, bar, conference rooms, garage. AE, DC, MC, V.*

Scandinavia. This large modern redbrick hotel has harbor views and comfortably furnished, if smallish, rooms decorated in muted greens and neutrals. The restaurant specializes in fish and seafood. *Kustgatan 10, S–402 42, tel. 031/427000, fax 031/122965. 323 rooms. Facilities: restaurant, bar, piano bar, sauna, indoor pool, rooms for the disabled and for nonsmokers, conference room. AE, DC, MC, V.*

Inexpensive ★

Royal. Located in the city center near the train station, Göteborg's oldest hotel is small, family-owned, and traditional. It was built in 1852 and refurbished in 1991. The rooms are individually decorated with reproductions of elegant Swedish traditional furniture. *Drottninggatan 67, S–411 21, tel. 031/80610. 86 rooms with bath. Facilities: breakfast room. AE, DC, MC, V. Closed Christmas and New Year's Day.*

Youth Hostels

Oskupan. Situated in a modern apartment block this hotel is 5 kilometers (3 miles) from the railway station. *Merjerigatam 2, S–412 76, tel. 031/401050. 220 beds; 6-bed apartments. Facilities: breakfast.*

Pastille. This hotel is in a pleasant old house 15 kilometers (9 miles) outside the city. *Box 201, Landvettersvägen, S–433 24, tel. 031/446163 or 031/446501. 120 beds; 2- to 4-bed rooms. Facilities: meals to order.*

Camping

There are camping sites at **Delsjö** (tel. 031/252909) and **Karralund** (tel. 031/252761).

The Arts and Nightlife

Two free publications in English, available in hotels and at the tourist office, list events, shows, and restaurants: *What's On in Gothenburg* is published monthly, *Gothenburg This Week* weekly in the summer, fortnightly in winter. The principal morning newspaper, *Göteborgs Posten*, publishes a weekly listings supplement titled "Aveny," which, while it is in Swedish, is reasonably easy to decipher. "Miss Tourist" (tel. 031/117450), a taped telephone service, lists events in English.

Excursions from Göteborg

Bohuslän

This coastal region north of Göteborg, with its indented, rocky coastline, provides a foretaste of Norway's fjords farther north. It was from these rugged shores that the 9th- and 10th-century Vikings sailed southward on their epic voyages. Today, small towns and attractive fishing villages nestle among the distinctively rounded granite rocks and the thousands of skerries and islands that form Sweden's western archipelago, best described by Prince Vilhelm, brother of the late King

Gustav V, as "an archipelago formed of gneiss and granite and water which eternally stretches foamy arms after life."

Tourist Information The principal tourist office for the region is **Västkustens Turistråd** (Kungsportsplatsen 2, 411 10 Göteborg, tel. 031/100750). There are local offices in **Kungälv** (Fästningsholmen, tel. 0303/12035), **Kungshamn** (Torget, tel. 0523/37150), **Ockerö** (Hamnplan, tel. 031/965080), **Strömstad** (Tutlhuset, Norra Hamnen, tel. 0526/14364), **Tanum** (Affärsvägen 16, 457 00 Tanumshede, tel. 0525/20400), and **Uddevalla** (Södra Hamnen 2, tel. 0522/11787).

Getting There

By Car The best way to explore Bohuslän is by car. The E6 highway runs the length of the coast from Göteborg north to Strömstad, close to the Norwegian border, and for campers there are numerous extremely well-equipped and uncluttered camping places along the coast's entire length.

By Train There is regular service along the coast between all the major towns of Bohuslän. The trip from Göteborg to Strömstad takes around two hours, and there are several trains each day. **SJ,** *Göteborg, tel. 031/103000 or 031/804980.*

By Bus Buses leave from behind the central railway station in Göteborg (bus lines are: Göteborg bus, tel. 031/801235, and Bohustrafiken, tel. 0522/14030). The trip to Strömstad takes two to three hours.

Exploring Bohuslän *Numbers in the margin correspond with points of interest on the Excursions from Göteborg map.*

Ideally you should drift slowly north, taking full advantage of the uncluttered beaches and small, picturesque fishing villages. Painters and sailors haunt the region in summer.

❶ The first stop north of Göteborg is **Kungälv,** strategically placed at the confluence of the two arms of the Göta River and site of **Bohus Festning,** a ruined fortress built by the Norwegians in 1308 where many battles between Swedish, Norwegian, and Danish armies took place. Today Kungälv has become something of a bedroom suburb for Göteborg, but it has a white wood church dating back to 1679, with an unusual Baroque interior. (*See also* Exploring the Göta Canal, *below*).

There is excellent deep-sea mackerel fishing from **Skärhamn** on the island of Tjörn, which can be reached by road bridge from Stenungsund.

❷ **Uddevalla,** a former shipbuilding town at the head of a picturesque fjord, is best known for a battle in which heavy rains doused musketeers' matches, effectively ending hostilities.

Lysekil, off the E6 highway on a promontory at the head of the Gullmarn fjord, has been one of Sweden's most popular summer resorts since the 19th century. It specializes in boat excursions to neighboring islands and deep-sea fishing trips. The best bathing is at Pinnevik Cove.

A little to the north lies the **Sötenäs** peninsula and the attract-
❸ ive island of **Smögen,** which can be reached by road bridge. It locally is renowned for its shrimps.

Stop at **Tanumshede** to see Europe's largest single collection of Bronze-Age rock carvings at **Vitöycke.** They cover 673 square feet of rock and depict battles, hunting, and fishing. The carvings are close to the main road and well marked.

Excursions from Göteborg

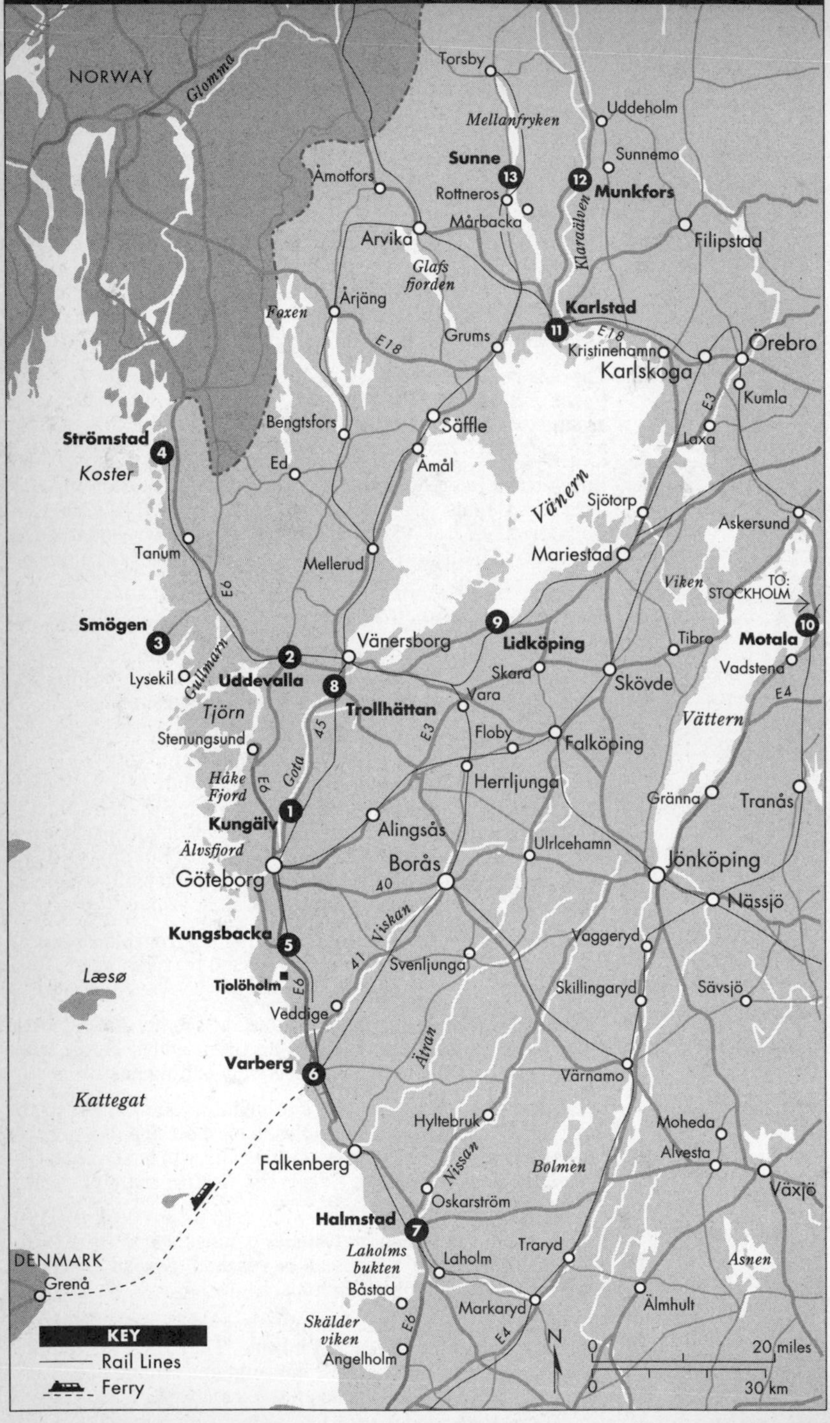

4 **Strömstad,** a popular Swedish resort, boasts it has more summer sunshine than any other town north of the Alps. Formerly Norwegian, it has been the site of many battles between warring Danes, Norwegians, and Swedes. A short trip over the Norwegian border takes you to Halden, where Sweden's warrior king, Karl XII, died in 1718.

There are regular ferry boats from Strömstad to the **Koster Islands,** another favorite holiday spot, with uncluttered beaches and trips to catch prawn and lobster.

The Swedish Riviera

The coastal region south of Göteborg is the closest that mainland Sweden comes to having a resort area (locally dubbed the "Swedish Riviera"). Fine beaches abound, and there are plenty of opportunities for many sporting activities. The region stretches down to Båstad in the country's southernmost province, Skåne.

Tourist Information The regional tourist office is **Västkustens Turistråd** (Kungsportsplatsen 2, 411 10 Göteborg, tel. 031/100750). Local offices are in **Båstad** (Stortorget 1, tel. 0431/75045), **Falkenberg** (Holgergatan 22B, tel. 0346/17410), **Halmstad** (Lilla Torg, tel. 035/109345), **Kungsbacka** (Storgatan 41, tel. 0300/34619), **Laholm** (Rådhuset, Stortorget, tel. 0430/15216 or 0430/15450), and **Varberg** (Brunnsparken, tel. 0340/88780 and 0340/88770).

Getting There

By Car To reach the Swedish Riviera, simply follow the E6 highway south from Göteborg. It parallels the coast.

By Train Regular service connects the Göteborg central station with all major towns. Contact **SJ** (Göteborg, tel. 031/103000 or 031/804980).

By Bus Buses leave from behind Göteborg's central railway station.

Exploring the Swedish Riviera

5 The first stop heading south from Göteborg is **Kungsbacka,** today fast becoming one of its bedroom suburbs; it holds a market on the first Thursday of every month. From the top of an Ice-Age sand ridge at the nearby village of Fjärås, there is a fine view of the coast, and on the slopes of the ridge are Iron-Age and Viking graves.

At **Tjolöholm,** 12 kilometers (7 miles) down the road, you encounter Tjolöholms Slott (Tjolöholm Castle), a manor house built by a Scotsman at the beginning of this century in mock English Tudor style. *S–43033 Fjärås, tel. 0300/44200. Admission: SKr25 adults, SKr5 children 4–14. Open June–Aug., daily; Apr.–May, Sept., weekends; Oct., Sun.*

Nearby is the tiny 18th-century village of **Asthult,** the site of Byarum, open-air museum. *S–56700 Vaggeryd, tel. 0393/22112. Admission free. Open June–Aug.*

6 The next town along the coast is **Varberg,** a busy port with connections to Grenå in Denmark and some good beaches. It is best known for a suit of medieval clothing preserved in the museum in the 13th-century **Varberg Fästninger** (Varberg Fortress). The suit belonged to a man who was murdered and thrown into a peat bog. The peat preserved his body, and his clothes are the only suit of ordinary medieval clothing in existence. The museum also contains a silver bullet said to be the one that killed

Sweden's warrior king, Karl XII. *Tel. 0340/18520. Admission: SKr10. Open daily 10–7.*

Falkenberg, 29 kilometers (18 miles) farther south, is one of Sweden's most attractive resorts, with fine beaches and salmon fishing in the Ätran River. Its 12th-century church is decorated with ceiling paintings dating from the 17th century. The town has an excellent golf course and international-class tennis courts.

7 **Halmstad,** 148 kilometers (92 miles) south of Göteborg, is the largest seaside resort on the west coast, with a population of 50,000. The **Norreport** town gate, all that remains of the town's original fortifications, dates from 1605. The modern Town Hall has interior decorations by the so-called Halmstad Group of painters formed here in 1929. A 14th-century church in the main square contains fragments of medieval murals and a 17th-century pulpit.

By the time you reach **Båstad,** 188 kilometers (117 miles) from Göteborg, you are in Skåne, Sweden's southernmost province. Båstad is the most fashionable resort in Sweden, where ambassadors and local captains of industry have their summer houses. Aside from this, it is best known for its tennis. In addition to the **Båstad Open,** a Grand Prix tournament in late summer, there is the annual **Donald Duck Cup** in July for children ages 11 to 15; it was the very first trophy won by Björn Borg, who later took the Wimbledon men's singles title an unprecedented five times in a row. Spurred on by Borg and other Swedish champions such as Stefan Edberg and Mats Wilander, thousands of youngsters take part in the Donald Duck Cup each year. For details, contact **Svenska Tennisförbundet** (the Swedish Tennis Association), Lidingövägen 75, Stockholm, tel. 08/6679770).

Time Out **Norrviken Gardens** (tel. 0431/71070), 3 kilometers (2 miles) northwest of Båstad, are beautifully laid out in different styles, with a restaurant, a shop, and a pottery studio.

The Göta Canal

The **Göta Canal** is actually 565 kilometers (350 miles) of interconnected canals, rivers, lakes . . . and even a stretch of sea. It links Stockholm with Göteborg and was a Swedish dream ever since it was first suggested by Bishop Hans Brask of Linköping in the 16th century. In 1718 the Swedish inventor Christopher Polhem and his compatriot, the scientist and engineer Emmanuel Swedenborg, actually made a start on the canal, acting under the instruction of King Karl XII, who saw in the project considerable military advantage. However, work was abandoned when the king was killed in battle the same year. It was not until 1810 that the idea was once again taken up in earnest. The driving force was a Swedish nobleman, Count Baltzar Bogislaus von Platen (1766–1829), and his motive was commercial. Von Platen saw in the canal a way of beating Danish tolls on shipping passing through the Öresund and of enhancing the importance of Göteborg by linking the port with Stockholm on the east coast. At a time when Swedish fortunes were at a low ebb, the canal also was envisaged as a means of reestablishing faith in the future and boosting national morale.

The building of the canal took 22 years and involved a total of 58,000 men. The linking of the various stretches of water required 97 kilometers (60 miles) of man-made cuts through soil and rock, the building of 58 locks, 35 bridges, 27 culverts, and three dry docks. Unfortunately, the canal never achieved the financial success hoped for by von Platen. By 1857 the Danes had removed shipping tolls and in the following decade the linking of Göteborg with Stockholm by rail effectively ended the canal's chances of achieving great commercial success. The canal has come into its own as a 20th-century tourist attraction, however.

Tourist Information

Regional tourist offices are **Båhusturist** (Uddevalla, tel. 0522/ 14055), **Västergötlands Turistråd** (Skövde, tel. 0500/18050), and **Östergötlands Länsturistnämnd** (Linjäping, tel. 013/227600). Local tourist offices along the route include **Linköping** (Agatan 39, tel. 013/206835) and **Vadstena** (Rådhustorget, tel. 0143/ 15125).

Exploring the Göta Canal

Drifting lazily down this lovely series of waterways, across the enormous lakes, Vänern and Vättern, through a microcosm of all that is best about Sweden—abundant fresh air, clear, clean water, pristine nature, well-tended farmland—it is difficult to conceive of the canal's industrial origins.

Traveling the entire length of the canal to Stockholm takes three full days. If you have a limited time schedule, there are both one-day trips to Trollhattan and two-day outings to Vadstena, a lovely, well-preserved historic town by the shores of Vättern, dating back to the 14th century. For details contact the **Göta Canal Steamship Company** (Box 272, S–401 24, Göteborg, tel. 031/806315).

The trip from Göteborg takes you first along the Göta Älv (river), a wide waterway that 10,000 years ago, when the ice cap melted, was a great fjord. Some 30 minutes into the voyage the boat passes below a rocky escarpment, topped by the remains of **Bohus Festning** (Bohus Castle), distinguished by two round towers known as Father's Hat and Mother's Bonnet. It dates from the 14th century and was once the mightiest fortress in western Scandinavia, commanding the confluence of the Göta and Nordre rivers. It was strengthened and enlarged in the 16th century and successfully survived 14 sieges. From 1678 onward, the castle began to lose its strategic and military importance, fell into decay, and its stones were removed for other buildings until 1838 when King Karl XIV passed by on a river journey, admired the old fortress, and ordered its preservation.

The boat passes **Kungälv** (*see also* Exploring Bohuslän, *above*), a pleasant riverside town, then **Lödöse,** once a major trading settlement and a predecessor of Göteborg that is today a quiet village. The countryside becomes wilder, with pines and oaks clustered thickly on either bank between cliffs of lichen-clad granite.

Some five hours after leaving Göteborg the boat arrives in
8 **Trollhättan,** 89 kilometers (55 miles) up river. This is a pleasant industrial town of around 50,000 inhabitants, where a spectacular waterfall was in 1906 rechanneled to become Sweden's first hydro electric plant. Most years, on specific days the waters are allowed to follow their natural course, a fall of 106 feet in six torrents. This is a sight that is well worth seeing.

Trollhättan is still worth a visit for other sights. The main point of interest is the area between what were the falls and the series of locks that allowed the canal to bypass them. Here are disused locks from 1800 and 1844 and a strange Ice-Age grotto where members of the Swedish royal family have carved their names since the 18th century. Trollhättan also has a fine, wide market place and pleasant waterside parks.

Soon after leaving Trollhättan, the boat passes **Hunneberg** and **Halleberg,** two strange, flat-top hills, both over 500 feet high. The woods surrounding them are extraordinarily rich in elk, legend, and Viking burial mounds. The boat proceeds through **Karls Grav,** the oldest part of the canal. This was begun early in the 17th century, its purpose to bypass the Rännum Falls on the Göta River, which have been harnessed to a hydro-electric project. Finally the boat reaches **Vänern,** Sweden's largest and Europe's third-largest lake: 3,424 square kilometers (2,123 square miles) of water, 145 kilometers (90 miles) long and 81 kilometers (50 miles) wide at one point. The canal enters the lake at **Vänersborg,** a town of around 30,000 inhabitants that was founded in the mid-17th century. The church and the governor's residence date from the 18th century, but the rest of the town was destroyed by fire in 1834. Vänersborg is distinguished by its fine lakeside park, the trees of which act as a windbreak for the gusts that sweep in from Vänern.

It takes around eight hours to cross Vänern. On an inlet at the southernmost point of its eastern arm lies the town of
9 **Lidköping,** which received its charter in 1446 and is said to have the largest town square in Sweden. Lying 24 kilometers (15 miles) to the north of it, on an island off the point dividing the eastern arm of Vänern from the western, is **Läckö Slött** (Läckö Castle), one of Sweden's finest 17th-century Renaissance palaces. Its 250 rooms were once the home of Magnus Gabriel de la Gardie, a great favorite of Queen Christina. Only the Royal Palace in Stockholm is larger. In 1681 Karl XI, to curtail the power of the nobility, confiscated it, and in 1830 all its furnishings were auctioned. Many of them have since been restored to the palace.

On a peninsula to the east, the landscape is dominated by the great hill of **Kinnekulle,** towering 900 feet over the lake. The hill is rich in colorful vegetation and wildlife and was a favorite hike for the botanist Linnaeus.

Then, at the lakeside port of **Sjötorp,** the **Göta Canal** proper begins: a cut through earth and granite with a series of locks raising the steamer to Lanthöjden, the highest point on the canal at 304 feet above sea level. The boat next enters the narrow, twisting lakes Viken and Botten and continues to Forsvik though the canal's oldest lock, built in 1813. It then sails out into **Vättern,** Sweden's second-largest lake, nearly 129 kilometers (80 miles) from north to south and 31 kilometers (19 miles) across at its widest point. Its waters are so clear that in some parts, the bottom is visible at a depth of 50 feet. The lake is subject to sudden storms that whip its normally placid waters into a choppy maelstrom.

Some 259 kilometers (161 miles) from Göteborg, the boat finally anchors at **Vadstena,** a little-known historic gem of a town. Vadstena grew up around the monastery founded by St. Birgitta, or Bridget (1303–1373), who wrote in her *Revela-*

tiones that she had a vision of Christ in which He revealed the rules of the religious order she went on to establish. These rules seem a precursor for the Swedish ideal of sexual equality, with both nuns and monks sharing a common church. Her order spread rapidly after her death, and at one time there were 80 Bridgetine monasteries in Europe. Little remains of the Vadstena monastery, however; in 1545 King Gustav Vasa ordered its demolition, and its stones were used to build **Vadstena Slott** (Vadstena Castle), the huge fortress dominating the lake. Swedish royalty held court here until 1715. It then fell into decay and was used as a granary. Today it houses part of the National Archives and is also the site of an annual summer music festival. *Tel. 0143/15123. Admission: SKr20. Open daily 10–5.*

Vadstena Kyrka is also worth visiting. The triptych altarpiece on the south wall features St. Birgitta presenting her book of revelations to a group of kneeling cardinals. There is also a fine wooden carving of the Madonna and Child from 1500.

If you continue down the canal to Stockholm, you sail through
10 **Motala,** where Gustav von Platen is buried close to the canal. He had envisaged the establishment of four new towns along the waterway, but only Motala fulfilled his dream. He designed the town himself, and there is a statue of him in the main square.

At Borenshult a series of locks takes the boat down to Boren, a lake in the province of Östergötland. On the southern shore of the next lake, Roxen, lies the city of **Linköping,** capital of the province and home of Saab, the aircraft and automotive company. Once out of the lake, you follow a new stretch of canal past the sleepy town of **Söderköping.** A few miles east, at the hamlet of Mem, the canal's last lock lowers the boat into Slätbaken, a Baltic fjord presided over by the ruins of the ancient **Stegeborg** fortress. The boat then steams north along the coastline until it enters Mälaren through the Södertälje Canal and finally anchors in the capital at Riddarholmen.

Lodging
Vadstena

Kungs-Starby Wärdshus. This manor house is surrounded by a park on the outskirts of town, reached on Route 50. *S–59200, tel. 0143/11420. 59 rooms, 45 with shower. Facilities: restaurant, sauna, swimming pool, solarium. AE, DC, MC, V. Inexpensive.*

Munkklostret. This hotel is housed in what is Sweden's oldest secular building, parts of which date from the 13th century. *Klosterområdet, Vadstena, tel. 0143/11530. 28 rooms with bath. Facilities: restaurant, satellite TV, rooms for allergy sufferers. AE, DC, MC, V. Inexpensive.*

Värmland

This province, close to the Norwegian border on the north shores of Vänern, is rich in folklore. It was also the home of Alfred Nobel and the birthplace of other famous Swedes, among them the Nobel-prize–winning novelist Selma Lagerlöf, the poet Gustaf Fröding, former Prime Minister Tage Erlander, and present-day opera star Håkan Hagegård. It is a part of the country favored by artists, with a timeless quality to it, a place where Swedes often take their own holidays. Värmland's forested, lake-dotted landscape, along with that of Dalarna, farther north, embodies Sweden as a whole.

Tourist Information The regional tourist office is **Värmlands Turistråd** (Karlstad, tel. 054/102160). There are local tourist offices in **Karlstad** (Södra Kyrkogatan 10, tel. 054/195901) and **Sunne** (Sunne Turistcentrum, tel. 0565/13530).

Getting There
By Car Follow E3 and then E18 west from Stockholm or Route 45 north to E18 from Göteborg.

By Train There is regular service to Karlstad from Stockholm and Göteborg on SJ.

Exploring Värmland Värmland's principal city, **Karlstad** (population 74,000), 255 kilometers (158 miles) from Göteborg, is situated on Klaraälven
11 (the Klara River) at the point where it empties into Vänern. Karlstad was founded in 1684, when it was known as Tingvalla. It later changed its name to honor King Karl IX, Karlstad meaning "Karl's Town." It was totally rebuilt after a fire in 1865. In **Stortorget,** the main square, there is a statue of Karl IX by the local sculptor Christian Eriksson. The **Värmlands Museum** has rooms dedicated to both Eriksson and the poet Fröding. *Sandgrun, Box 323, S-65108, tel. 054/102160. Admission free. Open daily noon–4.*

The **Marieberg Skogspark** (Marieberg Forest Park) is also worth visiting. It has a small animal park and, in the summer, an outdoor theater. Karlstad is also the site of an **Emigrant Registret** (Emigrant Center, tel. 054/111419) that maintains detailed records of the Swedish emigration to America. Visitors of Swedish extraction can trace their ancestors at the center's research facility.

Värmland is, above all, a rural experience. You can drive along the Klaraälven, through the beautiful Fryken Valley, to Ransater, where author Erik Gustaf Geijer was born in 1783 and where Erlander, the former prime minister, also grew up.
12 The rural idyll ends in **Munkfors,** where some of the best quality steel in Europe is manufactured, but just past it, you'll find the little village of **Sunnemo,** with its beautiful wood church. A little farther north, the town of **Uddeholm** on Lake Råda is home of the Uddeholm Corporation, which produces iron and steel, forestry products and chemicals. Continuing north around the lake, you can return to Munkfors and then make a
13 diversion west to **Sunne** from where it is only 55 kilometers (34 miles) to **Mårbacka,** the estate where nobelist Selma Lagerlöf was born in 1858. It is preserved as it was when she died in 1940. *Östra Ämtervik, S-68600 Sunne, 0565/31027. Admission: SKr10. Open daily 10–7.*

Turning south and heading back toward Karlstad, you can stop off at **Rottneros Herrgårds Park** (Rottneros Maron), the Ekeby of Lagerlöf's *Gösta Berlings Saga* (The Tale of Gösta Berling). The house is privately owned, but its park can be visited and features a fine collection of Scandinavian sculpture, including works by Carl Milles, Norwegian artist Gustav Vigeland, and Wäinö Aaltonen of Finland. *S-68602 Rottneros, tel. 0565/60295. Admission: SKr45 adults, SKr20 children under 15. Open daily 10–6.*

Dining
Karlstad **Inn Alstern.** Overlooking Lake Alstern, this restaurant serves Swedish and Continental cuisine in an elegant atmosphere. *Morgonvägen 4, tel. 054/134-900. Reservations advised. Dress: casual but neat. AE, MC, V. Expensive.*

Dining and Lodging
Karlstad

Stadshotellet. On the banks of Klaraälven (the Klara River), this hotel built in 1870 is steeped in tradition. Completely renovoted in 1991, all the rooms are decorated differently: some in modern Swedish style, others evoking their original look. *Kungsgatan 22, S-651 04, tel. 054/115220, fax 054/188211. 143 rooms. Facilities: 2 restaurants, bar, nightclub, sauna. AE, DC, MC, V. Expensive.*

Gösta Berling. Located in the center of town, this small hotel, named after the hero of the Selma Lagerlöf novel, surrounds guests in genuine Värmland ambience. *Drottninggatan 1, S-652 24, tel. 054/150190, fax 054/154826. 66 rooms. Facilities: restaurant, bar, sauna. AE, DC, MC, V. Moderate.*

The South and the Kingdom of Crystal

Introduction

The southernmost provinces of Sweden—Halland, Skåne, and Blekinge—are different in character from the rest of the country, both in appearance and in the temperament of their inhabitants. This is an extension of the fertile plain of northern Europe, rich farming country, and its inhabitants generally are more easygoing than their compatriots farther north. The south is a place of windswept, flat meadows and gently rolling hills, of timber-framed farmhouses in whose yards strut geese being fattened to supply local restaurants with the region's specialty dish. Danish for hundreds of years before being incorporated into Sweden in 1658, the region even today seeks its inspiration from mainland Europe, viewing the rest of Sweden—especially Stockholm—with some disdain. Skåne even has its own independence movement, and the dialect here is so akin to Danish that many Swedes from other parts of the country have trouble understanding it.

While not strictly part of the south, the so-called Kingdom of Crystal, in Småland, is easily reachable from here. This is an area of small glassblowing firms, such as Kosta Boda and Orrefors, that are world-renowned for the quality of their products. In addition to visiting these works (and perhaps finding some bargains), the traveler forms an insight into a poorer, harsher way of life that led thousands of peasants to emigrate from Småland to the United States in search of a better life. Those who stayed behind developed a reputation for their inventiveness in setting up small industries to circumvent the region's traditional poverty and are also notorious for being extremely careful—if not downright mean—with money.

Important Addresses and Numbers

Tourist Information

Skånes Turistråd, the Skåne Tourist Council, is at Stora Södergatan 8c, Lund (tel. 046/124350). There are tourist offices in the following towns: **Helsingborg** (Rådhuset, tel. 042/120310), **Kalmar** (Ölandshamnen 6, tel. 0480/15350), **Karlskrona** (Södra Smedjegatan 6, tel. 0455/83490), **Lund** (Kattesund 6, tel. 046/155040), **Malmö** (Hamngatan 1, tel. 040/341270), **Ronneby** (Snäckebacksplan, tel. 0457/17650), and **Ystad** (S:t Knuts Torg, tel. 0411/77279 or 0411/77288). For visitors to the

Kingdom of Crystal, the **Småland Tourist Office** is at Jönköping (tel. 036/199570) and Växjö (tel. 0470/47575).

Arriving and Departing by Plane

Airport and Airlines **Malmö**'s airport, **Sturup,** was opened in 1972. Sturup is approximately 30 kilometers (19 miles) from Malmö and 25 kilometers (16 miles) from Lund. It has six international destinations: London, Amsterdam, Hamburg, Cologne, Helsinki, and Århus (in Denmark). Oslo joins this list in 1992. The airlines represented include: **SAS** (tel. 040/357200), **KLM** (tel. 040/76655), and **Lufthansa** (tel. 040/71710).

SAS/Linjeflyg offers day trips to The Kingdom of Crystal from Stockholm in conjunction with the Avis car rental firm for $177 per person, if one person; $149 each for a minimum of two. A two-day trip, with overnight accommodations in either Växjö or Kalmar costs $223 (summer) and $252 (winter). For more details, contact **SAS** (161 87 Stockholm, tel. 08/797–0000).

Between the Airport and City Center
By Bus Buses leave hourly for Malmö and Lund from the Sturup airport. The price of the trip is SKr35 to either destination. For further information on bus schedules, routes, and fares, telephone 040/501100.

By Taxi A taxi from the airport to Malmö costs around SKr250 and to Lund approximately SKr200. For SAS limousine service, tel. 040/501834 or 040/357140.

Arriving and Departing by Car, Train, and Boat

By Car Malmö is 620 kilometers (384 miles) from Stockholm. You take the E4 freeway to Helsingborg, then the E6 to Malmö and Lund. From Göteborg, take the E6.

By Train There is regular service from Stockholm to Helsingborg, Lund, and Malmö. The journey takes around 6½ hours. All three railway stations are centrally situated.

By Boat The most common form of arrival in southern Sweden is by boat. Several regular services run from Copenhagen to Malmö, including a hydrofoil that makes the trip in less than an hour, and a bus/ferry service from Copenhagen Station, which also goes to Lund. There also are regular ferry connections to Denmark, Germany, and Poland from ports such as Malmö, Helsingborg, Trelleborg, and Ystad. Each year an estimated 25 million people cross back and forth. **Stena Line** is one of the major Swedish carriers, with offices at Kungsgatan 12–14, Stockholm, tel. 08/141475, and Danmarksterminalen, Göteborg, tel. 031/858000.

Getting Around

By Car Roads are uncluttered and extremely well marked and maintained. Traveling around the coast counterclockwise from Helsingborg, you take the E6 to Landskrona and then on to Malmö, then the E66 to Lund, Kristianstad, Solvesborg, Karlshamn, Ronneby, Karlskrona, and up the east coast to Kalmar.

By Train The major towns of the south are all connected by rail. A special *Öresund Runt* (Around Öresund) ticket for trains and ferries to

Denmark is available from the Malmö tourist office (Hamngatan 1, tel. 040/343447; price: SKr95).

Exploring the South and the Kingdom of Crystal

Numbers in the margin correspond with points of interest on the South and the Kingdom of Crystal map.

Southern Sweden is a world of its own, clearly distinguished from the rest of the country by its geography, culture, and history. Skåne (pronounced *Skoh*-neh), the southernmost province, is known as the granary of Sweden. It is a comparatively small province of beautifully fertile plains, sand beaches, scores of castles and chateaus, thriving farms, medieval churches, and summer resorts. The two other southern provinces, Blekinge and Halland, are also fertile and rolling and edged by seashores. Historically, these three provinces are distinct from the rest of Sweden: they were the last to be incorporated into the country, having been ruled by Denmark until 1658. They retain the influences of the Continental culture in their architecture, language, and cuisine. Småland, to the north, is larger than the other provinces, with harsh countryside of stone and woods. It is noted for its glass industries, as well as furniture and other wood products, and for the historic region around Kalmar.

Tour 1: The South

1 The first town of any importance is **Helsingborg** (still sometimes spelled the old way, Hälsingborg). With a population of 108,000, the town seems little more than a nondescript ferry terminal (it has connections to both Denmark and Germany). Actually, it has a rich history, having first been mentioned in 10th-century sagas and since been the site of many battles between the Danes and the Swedes. Together with its twin town, Helsingör, across the Öresund (Elsinore in William Shakespeare's *Hamlet*), it controlled shipping traffic in and out of the Baltic for centuries. Helsingborg was officially incorporated into Sweden in 1658 and totally destroyed in a battle with the Danes in 1710. It was then rebuilt, and Jean-Baptiste Bernadotte, founder of the present Swedish royal dynasty, landed here in 1810. The **Stadshuset** (Town Hall) has a small museum featuring exhibits on the history of the town. *Södrastorgatan, tel. 042/120310. Admission free. Open May–Aug., daily 11–6, Sun. noon–6.*

All that remains of Helsingborg's castle is **Kärnan** (the Keep). The surviving center tower, built to provide living quarters and defend the medieval castle, is the most remarkable relic of its kind in the north. The interior is divided into several floors, where there are a chapel, a kitchen, and other medieval fittings. It stands in a park and offers fine views over the Öresund from the top. *Kärngränden. Admission: SKr5. Open June–Aug., daily 10–8.*

Solfiero Slott (Solfiero Palace), 5 kilometers (3 miles) outside the town, was once a royal summer residence. Built in 1865 in Dutch Renaissance style, it has a fine park designed by Crown Princess Margareta. *Solfierovägen (on road to Lärod), tel. 042/145259. Admission: SKr10. Open May–Sept., daily 10–6.*

The South and the Kingdom of Crystal

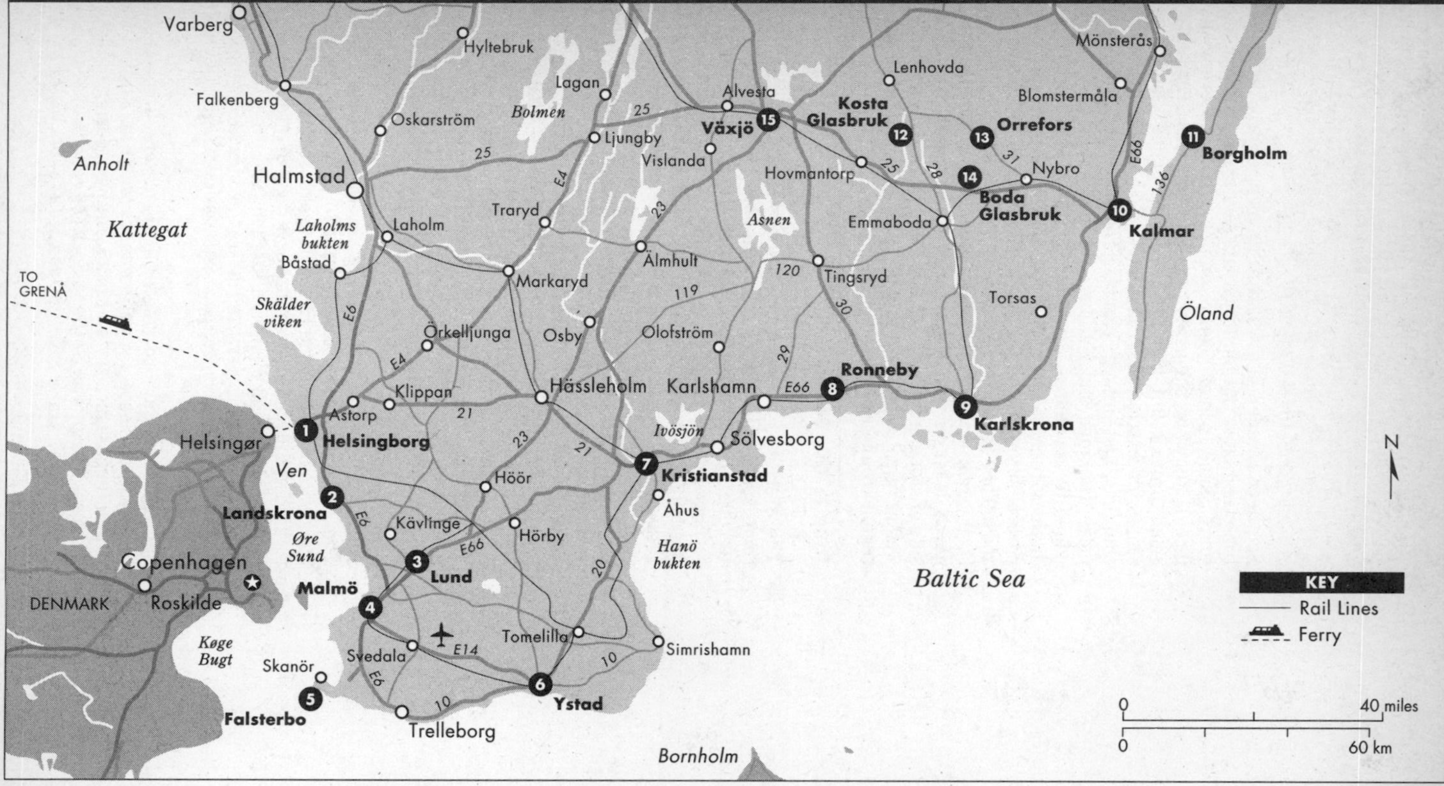

2 The 17th-century Dutch-style fortifications of **Landskrona,** 40 kilometers (25 miles) down the coast, are among the best preserved of their type in Europe. Though it appears to be just another modern town, Landskrona actually dates from 1413, when it received its charter. Author Selma Lagerlöf worked here at the town's elementary school in 1888 and began her novel *Gösta Berlings Saga.*

Landskrona's **Citadell** (castle) was built under orders of the Danish King Christian III in 1549 and is all that remains of the original town, which was razed in 1747 on orders of the Swedish Parliament to make way for extended fortifications. The new town was then built on land reclaimed from the sea. Local handicraft workshops in the castle grounds sell their products in the summer. *Slottsgatan, tel. 0418/16980. Admission: SKr10. Open June–Aug., daily 11–4.*

Three kilometers (2 miles) north of the town lies the **Borstahusen** recreation area, with long stretches of beach, a marina, and a holiday village with 74 summer chalets. The village is surrounded by a 36-hole golf course and overlooks the sound.

From Landskrona harbor there are regular 25-minute boat trips to the island of **Ven** where the Danish astronomer Tycho Brahe lived from 1576 to 1597 and conducted his pioneering research. The foundations of his Renaissance castle, **Uranienborg,** can be visited, as can **Stjärneborg,** his reconstructed observatory. The small **Tycho Brahe Museet** is dedicated to Brahe and his work. *Landsvägen, Ven, tel. 0418/72058. Admission: SKr3. Open May–Sept., daily 10:30–12:30 and 1:30–4:30.*

Ven also is ideal for camping (check with the local tourist office in Landsvägen, tel. 0418/79493), and there are special paths across the island for bicycles (rentals are available at Bäckviken, the small harbor).

3 Head inland now to **Lund,** one of the oldest towns in Europe, founded in 1020 by the legendary King Knud (Canute), monarch of Scandinavia and Britain, who reputedly thought he could turn the tide but wound up getting his feet wet. From 1103 Lund became the religious capital of Scandinavia and at one time had 27 churches and eight monasteries, before King Christian III of Denmark ordered most of them razed to use their stones for the construction of Malmöhus Castle in Malmö. Lund lost its importance until 1666 when its **university** was established. It is now one of Sweden's two chief university towns and one of the nicest of Swedish towns, having managed to preserve its historic character.

Its Romanesque **cathedral,** a monumental gray stone edifice, is the oldest in Scandinavia, consecrated in 1145. Its crypt features 23 finely carved pillars, but its main attraction is an astrological clock, *Horologum Mirabile Lundense* (the miraculous Lund clock), dating from 1380, which was restored in 1923. It features an amazing pageant of knights jousting on horseback, trumpets blowing a medieval fanfare, and the Magi walking in procession past Virgin and Child as the organ plays *In Dulci Jubilo.* It plays at noon and 3 PM on weekdays and 1 PM and 3 PM on Sunday.

Esaias Tegnér, the Swedish poet, lived from 1813 to 1826 in a little house immediately behind the cathedral. Today it is the

Tegnér Museet in his honor. *Gråbödersgatan, Admission: SKr10. Open first Sun. each month noon–3.*

Kulturen (the Museum of Cultural History), is both outdoor and indoor museum, featuring 20 old cottages, farms, and manor houses from southern Sweden plus an excellent collection of ceramics, textiles, weapons, and furniture. *Adelgatan, tel. 046/150480. Admission: SKr20. Open daily 11–5.*

Botaniska Trädgården (the **Botanical Gardens**), contain specimens of thousands of plants from all over the world and are east of the cathedral, very pleasant on a summer's day.

4 **Malmö,** just 31 kilometers (19 miles) to the southwest, is very different from Lund. Capital of the province of Skåne, with a population of about 250,000, this is Sweden's third largest city. The city's castle, **Malmöhus,** completed in 1542, was for many years used as a prison (James Bothwell, husband of Mary, Queen of Scots, was one of its notable inmates). Today it houses four museums, including one with a comprehensive collection of local art. *Malmöhusvägen, tel. 040/341000. Admission: SKr20. Open Mon.–Wed. and Fri. noon–4, Thurs. noon–9, Sun. noon–4:30.*

Nearby is the old town, where the **St. Petri** Church, from the 14th century, is an impressive example of the Baltic Gothic style, with its distinctive stepped gables. Inside there is a fine Renaissance altar.

Rådhuset (the City Hall), dating from 1546, dominates Stortorget, a huge, cobbled market square, and makes an impressive spectacle when illuminated at night. In the center of the square stands an equestrian statue of Karl X, the king who united this part of the country with Sweden in 1658. Off the southeast corner of Stortorget is Lilla Torg, an attractive small cobblestone square surrounded by restored buildings from the 17th and 18th centuries. A sports museum in **Baltiska Hallen** features equipment that has contributed to sports and athletics history. *John Ericssons Väg, tel. 040/342688. Admission free. Open Mon.–Fri. 8–4.*

On a tiny peninsula, 32 kilometers (20 miles) from Mälmö, at the country's southwesternmost corner, are the idyllic towns of
5 **Falsterbo** and **Skanör,** both popular summer resorts. Ornithologists gather at Falsterbo every fall to watch the spectacular migration of hundreds of raptors.

Continuing on from Malmö, you can make your way through
6 **Trelleborg,** Sweden's southernmost town, to **Ystad,** a medieval city on the coast, and a smuggling center during the Napoleonic Wars. If you are driving, go by way of **Torup Slott** (Castle), a good example of the square fortified stronghold, built about 1550. Ystad has preserved its medieval character with winding, narrow streets and hundreds of half-timbered houses from four or five different centuries. The principal ancient monument is **St. Maria Kyrka,** begun shortly after 1220 as a basilica in Romanesque style, but with later additions.

The plains, gentle rolling hills, and fields of Skåne are broken every few miles by lovely castles, chronologically and architecturally diverse, which have given this part of Sweden the name "Chateau Country." Often they are surrounded by beautiful grounds and moats. A significant number of the estates have remained in the hands of the original families and are still inhabited. **Bosjökloster** at Ringsjön, **Christinehof** in eastern Skåne and **Svaneholm** in the south, **Bäckaskog** near Kristianstad, **Snogeholm** near Sjöbo, and **Bjärsjölagård** near Hörby regularly are open to the public (contact local tourist offices for hours).

7 **Kristianstad** was founded by Danish King Christian IV in 1614 as a fortified town to keep the Swedes at bay. Its former ramparts and moats are today wide, tree-lined boulevards. **Holy Trinity Church,** consecrated in 1628, is an excellent example of so-called Christian IV-style architecture.

8 **Ronneby,** a spa town 85 kilometers (53 miles) east of Kristianstad on Route 66, has a picturesque waterfall and rapids called **Djupadal,** where a river runs through a cleft in the rock just five feet wide but 50 feet deep. There are boat trips on the river each summer.

9 A little farther along the coast is **Karlskrona,** a small city built on the mainland and five nearby islands. It achieved great notoriety in 1981 when a Soviet submarine ran aground a short distance from its naval base. The town was laid out in Baroque style on the orders of Karl XI in 1679. In 1790 it was severely damaged by fire. Its **Admiralitetskyrkan** (Admiralty Church) is Sweden's oldest wooden church, and two other churches, **Holy Trinity** and **Frederiks,** were designed by the 17th-century architect Nicodemus Tessin. **Arsenal Museet** (the Arsenal Museum), dating from 1732, is the oldest museum in Sweden, detailing the history of the country's navy. *Admiralitetsslatten, tel. 0455/83490. Admission: SKr10. Open daily 9–8.*

If you follow E66 north for 82 kilometers (51 miles), you'll reach
10 the attractive coastal town of **Kalmar.** Opposite the Baltic island of Öland, the town is dominated by the imposing **Kalmar Slott,** Sweden's best preserved Rennaissance castle, part of which dates from the 12th-century. Here in 1397 Sweden, Norway, and Denmark signed the Kalmar Union, which lasted until 1521, when King Gustav Vase rebuilt the castle. The living rooms, chapel, and dungeon can be visited. The castle now houses **Kalmar Läns Museum** (Kalmar District Museum), which has a good archaeological and ethnographic collection. *Skeppsbrogatan, tel. 0480/15350. Admission: SKr25. Open daily 10–4.*

The **Kronan Museet** in the harbor area features the remains of the royal ship *Kronan,* which sank in 1676. Primarily consisting of cannon, wooden sculptures, and old coins, they were raised from the seabed in 1980. *Skeppsbrogatan, tel. 0480/15350. Admission: SKr25. Open daily 10–4.*

The limestone plateau of **Öland,** 139 kilometers (86 miles) long and 37 kilometers (23 miles) at its widest point, was first settled some 4,000 years ago. It is linked to the mainland by one of the longest bridges in Europe (6 kilometers/4 miles). Öland is fringed with fine sandy beaches and is dotted with old windmills and such archaeological remains as the massive stone walls of the 6th-century Gråborg Fortress, the 5th-century fortified village of Eketorp, and the medieval Borgholm castle. The royal family has a summer home at Solliden, on the out-
11 skirts of **Borgholm,** the principal town. In spring and fall, Öland is a way station for hundreds of species of migrating birds.

Tour 2: The Kingdom of Crystal

An hour or so west of Kalmar off Route 25, scattered among the rocky woodlands of Småland province, are isolated villages whose names are bywords for quality when it comes to fine crystal glassware. In the streets of Kosta, Orrefors, Boda, and Strombergshyttan, red-painted cottages surround the actual factories, which resemble large barns. The region is the home of 16 major glassworks, and visitors may see glass being blown and crystal being etched by skilled craftspeople. *Hyttsil* evenings are also arranged, a revival of an old tradition in which Baltic herring (*sil*) are cooked in the glass furnaces of the *hytt* (literally "cabin" but meaning the works). Most glassworks also have shops selling seconds at a discount.

Fifteen kilometers (9 miles) north of Route 25 on Route 28 is
12 **Kosta Glasbruk,** the oldest works, dating from 1742 and named after its founders, Anders *Ko*skull and Georg Bogislaus *Sta*el von Holstein, two former generals. Faced with a dearth of talent locally, they initially imported glassblowers from Bohemia. The Kosta works pioneered the production of crystal (to qualify for that label, glass must contain at least 24% lead oxide). *Tel. 0478/50705 or 0478/50705. Open daily 8–3.*

On Route 31, 17 kilometers (11 miles) north of Route 25 is
13 **Orrefors,** onc of the best known of the glass companies. It came on the scene late—in 1898—but set particularly high artistic standards. The skilled workers in Orrefors dance a slow, delicate minuet as they carry the pieces of red-hot glass back and forth, passing them from hand to hand, blowing and shaping them. The basic procedures and tools are ancient, and the finished product is the result of unusual teamwork, from designer to craftsman to finisher. One of Orrefors's special attractions is a magnificent display of pieces made during the past century. *Tel. 0481/30159. Open 8–3.*

14 **Boda Glasbruk,** part of the Kosta Boda company, is just off Route 25, 42 kilometers (26 miles) west of Kalmar. *Tel. 0481/24138. Open 8–3.*

15 Farther west on Route 25 is **Växjo,** where the **Småland Museum** has the largest glass collection in northern Europe. *Södra Jarnvägsgatan 2, S-35104, tel. 0470/45145. Admission: SKr10. Open weekdays 9–4, Sat. 11–3, Sun. 1–5. Closed holidays.*

Växjö is also an important sightseeing destination for some 10,000 American visitors each year, for it was from this area that their Swedish ancestors set sail in the 19th century. The Emigrants' House, located in the town center, tells the story of the migration, during which close to a million Swedes—one quarter of the population—departed for the promised land. The museum exhibits provide a vivid sense of the rigorous journey, and an archive room and research center allow American visitors to trace their ancestry. On the second Sunday in August, Vaxjo celebrates Minnesota Day. Swedes and Swedish-Americans come together to commemorate their common heritage with fun and festivities.

Dining and Lodging

Highly recommemded establishments are indicated by a star ★.

Helsingborg
Dining and Lodging
★

Grand Hotel. In one of Sweden's oldest hotels, the dining room has a long reputation for excellence, with a good selection of wines at reasonable prices. There are special rose-colored rooms for women guests. The hotel is near the railway station and ferry terminals. *Stortorget 8–12, S–251 11, tel. 042/120170. 130 rooms. Facilities: restaurant, piano bar. AE, DC, MC, V. Expensive.*

Villa Thalassa. This youth hostel has fine views over Öresund. *Dag Hammarskjölds väg, tel. 042/110384. 145 beds, 4- to 6-bed rooms (in winter 2-bed rooms are also available). Facilities: conference rooms. No credit cards. Inexpensive.*

Kalmar
Lodging

Stadshotellet. Located in the city center, Stadshotellet is a fairly large, Old World hotel. The main building dates from the 19th century. It features a fine restaurant. *Storgatan 14, tel. 0480/15180. 150 rooms with bath or shower. Facilities: restaurant, Jacuzzi, disco. AE, DC, MC, V. Closed Christmas. Expensive.*

Slottshotellet. Situated in a gracious old town house on a quiet street, Slottshotellet bears no resemblance to a hotel from the outside. But inside, it offers a host of modern facilities. Only breakfast is served. *Slottsvägen 7, tel. 0480/88260. 36 rooms with shower. AE, DC, MC, V. Expensive.*

Continental. Located about 93 meters (100 yards) from the train station, the Continental is a fairly basic but comfortable family hotel. Only breakfast is served. *Larmgatan 10, tel. 0480/15140. 40 rooms, most with bath or shower. AE, DC, MC, V. Closed Christmas. Inexpensive.*

Lund
Dining

Fiskaregatan. Owner Lars Fogelklous believes in getting to know his guests and in taking an unconventional approach to do so. One example is his "gourmet evening" with nine courses—interrupted by a stroll around the town at the halfway stage. A specialty is stuffed breast of pheasant. *Lilla Fiskaregatan 14, tel. 046/151620. Reservations advised. Dress: casual. AE, DC, MC, V. Moderate.*

Lodging

Grand. This elegant red-stone hotel is located close to the railway station in a pleasant square. *Bantorget 1, S–221 04, tel. 046/117010. 87 rooms. Facilities: restaurant with vegetarian menu by arrangement, conference rooms, sauna. AE, DC, MC, V. Very Expensive.*

Concordia. Located in a 100-year-old building in the city center, this hotel was completely renovated recently. *Stålbrogatan 1, S–222 24, tel. 046/135050. 50 rooms. Facilities: rooms for nonsmokers and the disabled. AE, DC, MC, V. Moderate.*

Djingis Khan. This English-style hotel has a pleasing aspect and is situated in a quiet part of town. *Margarethevägen 7, S–222 40, tel. 046/140060. 55 rooms. Facilities: rooms for allergy sufferers and the disabled, conference rooms, sauna, solarium, gymnasium, bicycles for rent (SKr25). AE, DC, MC, V. Moderate.*

Sparta. This hotel is about 1 kilometer (½ mile) from the center of town. Buses to the center stop outside four times an hour, and the airport bus stops at the hotel. *Tunavägen 39, S–223 63, tel. 046/131885. 75 rooms. Facilities: restaurant, rooms for* *nonsmokers and the disabled, conference rooms, sauna. AE, DC, MC, V. Moderate.*

STF Youth Hostel. Situated 5 kilometers (3 miles) from the railway station, this grim-looking building provides high standards inside. *Backavägen 18, S–214 32, tel. 040/82220. 174 beds. 2-, 4-, and 6-bed rooms. Facilities: laundry room. No credit cards. Inexpensive.*

Malmö
Dining

★ **Anno 1900.** Here is a curiosity: a charming little restaurant smack in the middle of an industrial area. It is a popular local luncheon place with a cheerful outdoor garden terrace for summer eating. Try the *dagens rätt*, which may be meat or fish. *Norra Bulltoftavägen 7, tel. 040/184747. Reservations required. Dress: casual. AE, MC, V. Expensive.*

Årstiderna. Marie and Wilhelm Pieplow's restaurant (the name means "The Seasons" in Swedish) has a pleasant, intimate atmosphere. It is known for large portions and a good medium-priced wine list. *Grynsbodsgatan 9, tel. 040/230910. Reservations advised. Jacket and tie required. AE, DC, MC, V. Expensive.*

Hamnpaviliongen. The accent is on fish in this restaurant, which has fine views over the harbor. *Grimsbygatan, Nyhamnen, tel. 040/113717. Reservations advised. Dress: casual. AE, DC, MC, V. Expensive.*

Winecellar. Centrally located in the St. Jörgen hotel, this white-walled cellar restaurant sparsely decorated with ironwork may have the best wine list in southern Sweden. The cuisine is Swedish with a French accent, and there's an emphasis on grilled meats and fish. *Stora Nygatan 35, tel. 040/77300. Reservations advised. Dress: casual. AE, DC, MC, V. Expensive.*

B & B. It stands for *Butik och Bar* (Bar shop) because of its location in a covered market. There's always good home cooking, and sometimes even entertainment at the piano. Saturday afternoons are best for atmosphere. *Saluhallen, Lilla Torg, tel. 040/127120. Reservations advised. Dress: casual. AE, DC, MC, V. Moderate.*

La Mélisse. This friendly little restaurant usually gives extremely good value. The special menu, *Kvartersmenyn*, is an excellent bet, with four courses for SKr175. *Foreningsgatan 37, tel. 040/116816. Reservations advised. Dress: casual. AE, DC, MC, V. Moderate.*

Dining and Lodging

SAS Royal. This modern luxury hotel has rooms in four styles: Scandinavian, Oriental, Italian, and Grand. *Östergatan 10, S–211 25, tel. 040/239200, fax 040/112840. 221 rooms. Facilities: restaurant. AE, DC, MC, V. Expensive.*

★ **Savoy.** This was the atmospheric setting for the Sjöwall and Wahlöö detective story *Murder at the Savoy. Norra Vallgatan 62, S–201 80, tel. 040/70230. 100 rooms. Facilities: restaurant, nightclub. AE, DC, MC, V. Expensive.*

Sheraton. Ultramodern, in steel and glass, the Sheraton opened in 1989. *Triangeln 2, S–200 10, tel. 040/74000, fax 040/232020. 214 rooms. Facilities: restaurant, bar, fitness center, sauna. AE, DC, MC, V. Expensive.*

Anglais. Opened in 1912, this hotel has a central location with views over the main square. *Stortorget 15, S–211 22, tel. 040/71450, fax 040/71450. 86 rooms. Facilities: restaurant, cafeteria, bar. AE, DC, MC, V. Moderate.*

★ **Baltzar.** A turn-of-the-century house in central Malmö has been converted into a small, comfortable hotel. *Södergatan 20, tel. 040/72005. 41 rooms. AE, DC, MC, V. Moderate.*

Öland
Dining and Lodging

Halltorps Gästgiveri. This manor house from the 17th century has modernized duplex rooms decorated in Swedish landscape tones and an excellent restaurant. *S-38792 Borgholm, tel. 0485/85000, fax 0485/85001. 25 rooms. Facilities: restaurant. AE, DC, MC, V. Expensive.*

Växjö
Lodging

Sara Statt. A conveniently located, traditional hotel, Sara Statt is popular with tour groups. The building dates from the early 19th century, but the rooms themselves are modern, and the hotel has a resident piano bar and à la carte restaurant. *Kungsgatan 6, tel. 0470/13400. 130 rooms with bath or shower. AE, DC, MC, V. Closed Christmas Eve. Expensive.*

Esplanad. Centrally located, Esplanad is a small, family hotel offering basic amenities; it has been recently renovated. Only breakfast is served. *Norra Esplanaden 21A, tel. 0470/22580. 27 rooms, most with shower. MC, V. Closed Christmas and New Year's. Inexpensive.*

Dalarna: The Folklore District

Introduction

Dalarna is considered to be the most typically Swedish of all the country's 24 provinces, a place of forests, mountains, and red-painted wood farmhouses and cottages by the shores of pristine, sun-dappled lakes. It is the favorite site for Midsummer celebrations, in which Swedes don folk costumes and dance to fiddle and accordion music around maypoles garlanded with wildflowers.

Dalarna played a key role in the history of the nation. It was from here that Gustav Vasa recruited the army that freed the country from Danish domination in the 16th century.

The city is also important artistically, both for its tradition of naïve religious decoration and for producing two of the nation's best-loved painters, Anders Zorn (1860–1920) and Carl Larsson (1853–1915), and one of its favorite poets, the melancholy, mystical Dan Andersson, who sought his inspiration in the remote camps of the old charcoal burners deep in the forest.

Important Addresses and Numbers

Tourist Information

There are tourist offices in the following towns and villages: **Falun** (Stora Torget, tel. 023/83637), **Leksand** (Norsgatan, tel. 0247/80300), **Mora** (Ångbåtskajen, tel. 0250/26550), **Rättvik** (Torget, tel. 0248/10910), **Siljansnäs** (tel. 0247/22224), and **Sälen** (Sälen Centrum, tel. 0280/20150).

Emergencies

For **emergencies,** dial 90000, **Falu Hospital** (tel. 023/82900) or **Mora Hospital** (tel. 0250/25000).

Pharmacies

There are no late-night pharmacies in the area, but doctors called to emergencies can supply medicines. **Vasen** pharmacy (Åsagatan, tel. 023/20000) is open until 7 PM.

Arriving and Departing by Plane

Airports and Airlines Dalarna is served by two airports: **Dala Airport** at **Borlänge** and **Mora Airport.** There are regular daily **Linjeflyg** (tel. 0243/39090) flights from Stockholm to Dala Airport (nine each weekday, four on Saturday, five on Sunday). Mora Airport is served by the private company **Salair** (tel. 0250/30175), with six flights daily from Stockholm.

Between the Airport and Town Dala Airport is 7 kilometers (4 miles) from Borlänge, where there are half-hourly bus connections to Falun, 17 kilometers (11 miles) away. Mora Airport is 6 kilometers (4 miles) from town.

By Bus There are buses every half hour from Dala Airport to Borlänge. The price of the trip is SKr10. From Mora Airport there are buses four times daily into town. The fare is SKr7.

By Taxi A taxi from Dala Airport to Borlänge costs around SKr100, to Falun approximately SKr200. A taxi to town from Mora Airport costs SKr70–SKr80.

Arriving and Departing by Car, Train, and Bus

By Car From Stockholm it is 275 kilometers (170 miles) on Highway 70 leads to Borlänge. From Göteborg the drive is 438 kilometers (272 miles): E3 to Örebro and Route 60 north from there to Borlänge.

By Train There is regular daily train service from Stockholm to both Mora (tel. 0250/11619) and Falun (tel. 023/10058).

By Bus Buses run only on weekends: for information, call **Swebuss** (tel. 08/237190).

Getting Around

By Car **Avis** has offices in **Borlänge** (tel. 0243/87080) and Mora (tel. 0250/16711). **Hertz** has an office at **Dala** Airport (tel. 0243/39807) and agents in **Falun** (tel. 023/18440) and **Mora** (tel. 0250/11760). **InterRent** and **Europcar** have offices in **Borlänge** (tel. 0243/19050) and **Falun** (tel. 023/18850).

Guided Tours

The tourist office in **Falun** can arrange one-day guided coach tours in English of Falun and the region around Lake Siljan. The guide costs around SKr850, the coach, with driver, SKr4,200 (coaches can seat around 50 persons). Other tourist offices can arrange tours or advise on public transport.

Exploring Dalarna

Numbers in the margin correspond with points of interest on the Dalarna map.

1 **Falun** is the traditional capital of Dalarna, though in recent years the nondescript railway town of Borlänge has been growing in importance. Falun's history has always been very much bound to its copper mine. This has been worked since 1230 by Stora Kopparbergs Bergslags AB (today just *Stora),* which claims to be the oldest limited company in the world. Its great-

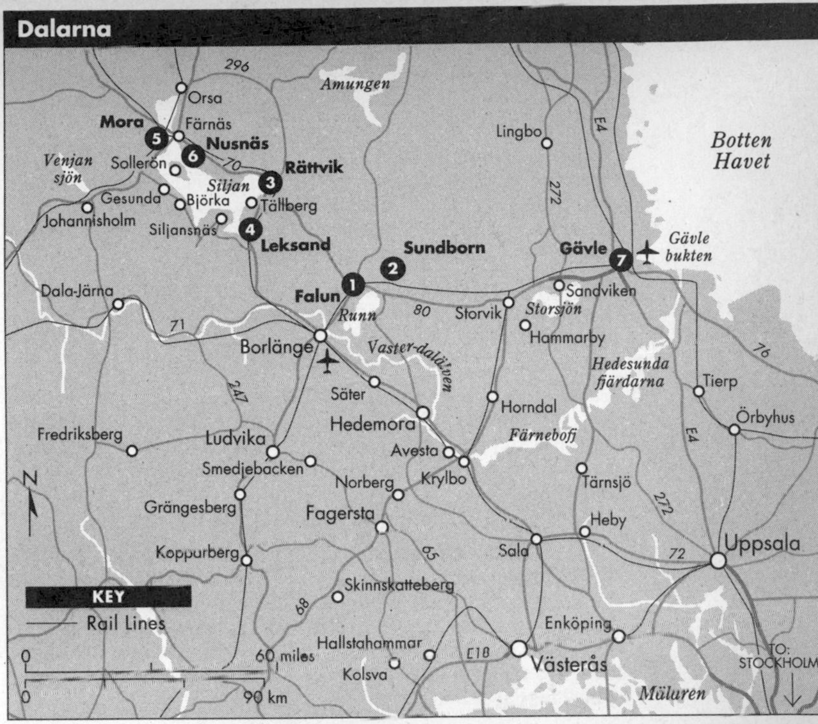

est period of prosperity was the 17th century, when it financed Sweden's "Age of Greatness," and the country became the dominant Baltic power. In 1650, Stora produced a record 3,067 tons of copper; probably as a result of such rapid extraction, 37 years later its mine shafts caved in. Fortunately the accident was on Midsummer's Day when most of the miners were off duty, and as a result no one was killed. Today the major part of the mine is an enormous hole in the ground that has become Falun's principal tourist attraction, with its own museum, **Stora Museum.** It actually does continue to function, however, producing small quantities of pyrites, zinc, and lead. *Tel. 023/114750. Admission: SKr50, including entry to mining museum; admission to museum alone, SKr5. Open May–Aug., daily 10–4:30. Sept.–Apr., daily 12:30–4:30.*

❷ At **Sundborn,** a small village east of Falun off Route 80, you can visit **Carl Larsson Gorden,** the lakeside home of the Swedish artist Carl Larsson, its turn-of-the-century fittings and furnishings carefully preserved. Larsson was an excellent draftsman who painted idyllic scenes from his own family's apparently unceasingly happy and well-adjusted life. His grandchildren and great-grandchildren are on hand to show you the house and a selection of his paintings, which owe much to local folk-art traditions. *Tel. in summer, 023/60053; in winter, 023/60069. Admission: SKr45. Open May 1–Sept. 30, Mon.–Sat. 10–5, Sun. 1–5.*

The real center of Darlana folklore is the area around **Lake Siljan,** the largest of the 6,000 lakes in the province. From

3 Falun take Route 80 north to **Rättvik,** a pleasant town of timbered houses on the eastern tip of Lake Siljan surrounded by wooded slopes. Rättvik is a center for local folklore, and several shops sell handmade articles and produce from the surrounding region.

Every year hundreds of people wearing traditional costumes arrive in longboats to attend Midsummer services at the town's 14th-century church, **Rättvik Kyrka,** which stands on a promontory stretching into the lake. Its interior contains some fine examples of local naïve religious artwork.

Only a short distance away, the open-air museum **Rättvik Gammalgård** gives the visitor an idea of the peasant lifestyles of bygone days. *Admission: free; guided tour: SKr10. Open June 16–Aug. 18, 11–6, Sun. 12–6.*

4 South of Rättrik on Route 70 is **Leksand,** on which thousands of tourists converge each year for the Midsummer celebrations and, in July, for *Himlaspelet* (The Play of the Way that Leads to Heaven), a traditional musical with an all-local cast, staged in the open near the town's church. It is easy to get seats for this; the local tourist office will have details.

Leksand is also an excellent vantage point from which to watch the "church boat" races on Siljan. These vessels are claimed to be successors to the Viking longboats and traditionally were used to take peasants from outlying regions to church on Sunday. Today, crewed by people in folk costumes, they are one of the region's great tourist attractions. Consult the local tourist office for dates and times.

In the hills around Leksand and elsewhere near Siljan you will find the *fäbodar,* small settlements in the forest where cattle were taken to graze during the summer. Less idyllic memories of bygone days are conjured up by **Käringberget,** a 720-foot-high mountain north of town where alleged witches were burned to death in the 17th century.

After Leksand, take the small road toward Mora along the southern shores of Siljan, passing through the small communities of Siljansnäs and Björka, before stopping at **Gesunda,** a pleasant little village at the foot of a mountain (with a chair lift) from which there are unbeatable views over the lake.

It is also worth paying a quick visit to **Sollerön,** a large island connected to the mainland by bridge, from where there are fine views of the mountains surrounding Siljan and several excellent bathing places. The church here dates from 1775.

5 **Mora,** a pleasant, relaxed lakeside town of 20,000, was the home of Anders Zorn (1860–1920), Sweden's leading Impressionist painter, who lived in Stockholm and Paris before returning to his roots here, painting the local scenes for which he is now famous. His former home is now **Zorn Museet,** which contains many of his best works; the lovingly tended garden is also open to the public. *Vasagatan, tel. 0250/16560. Admission: SKr15. Open Mon.–Sat. 9–5, Sun. 11–5.*

South of town, near the lake, you'll find **Zorns Gammalgård,** a fine collection of old wood houses from local farms, brought here and donated to the town by the artist.

Mora is also renowned locally as the finishing point for the *Vasalopp,* the world's longest ski race, 86 kilometers (53 miles), running from Sälen, a ski resort close to the Norwegian border. Variously described as "the last great adventure of our time," and "the way of the suffering thousands," the race actually commemorates a fundamental piece of Swedish history: the successful attempt by Gustav Vasa in 1521 to rally local peasants to the cause of ridding Sweden of Danish occupation. Vasa, aged only 21, arrived in Mora and described to the locals in graphic detail a bloodbath of Swedish noblemen ordered by the Danish King Christian in Stortorget in Stockholm. Unfortunately, no one believed him and the dispirited Vasa was forced to abandon his attempts at insurrection and take off on either skis or snow shoes for Norway, where he hoped to evade Christian and go into exile. After he had left, confirmation reached Mora of the Stockholm bloodbath, and the peasants, already discontented with Danish rule, relented, sending two skiers after Vasa to tell him they would join his cause. The two men caught up with the young nobleman at Sälen. They returned with him to Mora where an army was recruited. Vasa marched south, defeating the Danes to become king and the founder of modern Sweden. The race, held on the first Sunday in March, attracts thousands of competitors from all over the world. There is a spectacular mass start at Sälen before the field thins out. The finish is eagerly awaited in Mora, though in recent years the number of spectators has fallen, thanks to the often frigid temperatures and the fact that nowadays the race is usually televised live. The winner is presented with a garland by a local girl, chosen each year for her beauty.

From Mora, take Route 70 back along the eastern shore of Siljan to Rättvik and Falun, leaving it at Färnäs to make an excursion to **Nusnäs,** the small lakeside village where the small, brightly red-painted wood Dala horses are made. These were originally carved by the peasants of Dalarna as toys for their children, but their popularity rapidly spread with the advent of tourism in the 20th century. "Mass production" of the little horses started at Nusnäs in 1928. In 1939 they achieved international popularity after being shown at the New York World's Fair. Since then they have become a Swedish symbol. Today some of the smaller versions available in Stockholm's tourist shops are even made in East Asia. However, at Nusnäs you can watch the genuine article being made, now with the aid of modern machinery but still painted by hand. Naturally, you'll be able to buy some to take home.

Directly east of Falun, on the coast of the Gulf of Bothnia, is the town of **Gävle,** which achieved dubious renown at the time of the Chernobyl nuclear accident in 1986 by briefly becoming the most radioactive place in Europe. A freak storm dumped extra large amounts of fallout from the Soviet Union on the town. For a while farmers had to burn newly harvested hay and keep their cattle inside. However, the scare soon passed and today one can visit the town in perfect safety. Gävle is worth visiting for two relatively new museums.

Joe Hill Museet (the Joe Hill Museum), dedicated to the Swedish emigrant who went on to become America's first well-known protest singer and union organizer, is located in Hill's former home in the oldest section of Gävle. Once a poor, working-class area, ironically this is now the most picturesque and highly sought-after residential part of town, and nearby are some art studios and handicraft workshops. The museum is furnished in the same style as when Hill lived here. Though it contains very few of his possessions, it does display Hill's prison letters. The house itself bears witness to the poor conditions that forced so many Swedes to emigrate to the United States (an estimated 850,000 between 1840 and 1900). When his mother died in 1902, Joe and his brother sold the house and used the money to emigrate to the United States. He became a founder of the International Workers of the World and was executed for the murder of a Salt Lake City grocer in 1914 but right up to the end protested his innocence. *Nedre Bergsgatan 28, tel. 026/112022. Admission: SKr10. Open 10–5.*

Also in Gävle you will find the **Skogsmuseet Silvanum** (Silvanum Forestry Museum). Its name means "The Forest" in Latin, and when it was inaugurated in 1961, it was the first such museum in the world; it remains the largest. The museum provides an in-depth picture of the forestry industry in Sweden, still the backbone of Sweden's industrial wealth. As a traveler in the country soon discovers, there are trees everywhere, covering over 50% of the country's surface area. Forest products account for 20% of Swedish exports. Silvanum includes a forest botanical park and an arboretum that contains examples of every tree and bush growing in Sweden. The museum itself is built from slag from old iron furnaces, once a local industry. *Kungsbäcksvägen 32, tel. 026/614100 or 026/615570. Admission: SKr20. Open Tues.–Sun. 10–4.*

What to See and Do with Children

Near Gesunda, **Tomteland** (Santaland) somewhat unconvincingly claims to be the home of Santa Claus or Father Christmas. It features Santa's workshop and kiosks where you can buy toys. There are rides in horse-drawn carriages in summer and sleighs in winter. *Gesundaberget Sollerön, S–79200 Sollerön-Gesunda, tel. 0250/29000. Admission: SKr60. Open mid-June–mid-Aug., Dec.*

Shopping

Apart from its little red wooden horses (*see* Nusnäs, above), Dalarna offers knitwear and handicrafts, available in *hemslöjd* shops throughout the region.

Sports

All the region's tourist offices can supply details of **skiing** vacations. The principal ski resort is Sälen, starting point for the Vasalopp. **Canoes** and **kayaks** can also be rented at most of the lakeside campgrounds.

Dining and Lodging

Do not expect too much in Dalarna. Traditionally, visitors to the area—many from elsewhere in Scandinavia or from Germany—make use either of the region's many well-equipped camping sites or of *stugbyar* (small villages of log cabins, with cooking facilities), usually set idyllically by lakesides or in forest clearings.

Highly recommended establishments are indicated by a star★.

Falun
Dining and Lodging

Grand. Part of the SARA chain, this conventional, modern hotel has fine light rooms and is close to the town center. *Trotzgatan 9–11, S–791 71, tel. 023/18700, fax 023/14143. 183 rooms. Facilities: restaurant, bar, rooms for allergy sufferers and the disabled, conference center, gymnasium, sauna, pool, solarium. AE, DC, MC, V. Expensive.*

Birgittagården. This small hotel, 8 kilometers (5 miles) out of town, run by the religious order Stiftelsen Dalarnas Birgitta Systrar (The Dalarna Sisters of Birgitta), is alcohol-free and set in a fine park. It is open year-round. *Uddnäs Hosjös S–79146, tel. 023/32147 fax 023/32471. 25 rooms. Facilities: restaurant, rooms for the disabled, conference rooms. No credit cards. Inexpensive.*

Samelsdals Herrgårdspensionat. This small hotel is set in a former manor house 3 kilometers (2 miles) southwest of Falun but with regular bus connections to the town. There is a beach nearby. *10 rooms. Facilities: restaurant, sauna, pool, jogging tracks. AE, DC, MC, V. Inexpensive.*

Lodging

★ **Bergmästaren.** This is one of Dalarna's best hotels. Situated in the middle of town, it is decorated according to local custom and was completely refurbished in 1985. It is open year-round. *Bergskolegrand 7, S–791 26, tel. 023/63600, fax 023/22524. 90 rooms. Facilities: breakfast, gymnasium, sauna, solarium, conference center, parking with engine warmers. AE, DC, MC, V. Expensive.*

Scandic. This modern hotel is 2 kilometers (1 mile) from the center of town on Route 80 and is well equipped. *Kopparvagen 21, Norslund, S–791 05, tel. 023/22160, fax 023/12845. 107 rooms. Facilities: rooms for the disabled, conference center, gymnasium, sauna, pool, solarium. AE, DC, MC, V. Moderate.*

Falun. Ulf Henriksson and Bernt Brick run this small, friendly hotel just 1,300 feet from the railway station and open year-round. *Centrumhuset, Trotzgatan 16 S–791 71, tel. 023/29180. 25 rooms, 15 with bath/shower. Facilities: breakfast. AE, DC, MC, V. Inexpensive.*

Mora
Dining and Lodging

King's Inn. This modern, reasonably sized hotel is 2 kilometers (1 mile) from the center of town. *Kristeneberg, S–792 01, tel. 0250/15070, fax 0250/17078. 47 rooms. Facilities: restaurant, rooms for the disabled, conference rooms, gymnasium, sauna, pool, solarium. AE, DC, MC, V. Moderate.*

Mora. A pleasant little hotel, situated in the center of town, 5 kilometers (3 miles) from the airport, the Mora is part of the Great Western Hotels chain. *Strandgatan 12, S–792 01, tel. 0250/18981, fax 0250/18981. 145 rooms. Facilities: restaurant, bar, rooms for nonsmokers, conference rooms, sauna, pool, game room. AE, DC, MC, V. Moderate.*

Moraparken. This modern hotel sits in a park by the banks of the Dala River, not far from the center of town. *Parkgarten 1, S–79201, tel. 0250/17800. 75 rooms. Facilities: restaurant; rooms for the disabled, nonsmokers, and allergy sufferers; conference rooms; sauna; indoor pool; tennis courts; jogging tracks; beach; fishing. AE, DC, MC, V. Inexpensive.*

Siljan. Part of the Sweden Hotel group, this small, modern hotel affords views over the lake. *Moragatan 6, S–79200, tel. 0250/13000, fax 0250/13098. 46 rooms. Facilities: restaurant, rooms for nonsmokers and the disabled, sauna, conference rooms. AE, DC, MC, V. Closed Sept. 1–May 31. Inexpensive.*

Norrland

Introduction

The north of Sweden, Norrland, is a place of wide-open spaces, where you can "listen to the silence." Golden eagles soar above snowcapped crags, huge salmon fight their way up wild, tumbling rivers, rare orchids bloom in Arctic heathland, and wild rhododendrons splash the land with color.

In the summer the sun shines at midnight. In the winter it hardly shines at all. The weather changes with bewildering rapidity. A June day can dawn sunny and bright; then the skies may darken and the temperature drop to around zero as a snow squall blows in. Just as suddenly, the sun comes out again and the temperature starts to rise.

Here live the once-nomadic Lapps, or Sami, as they prefer to be known, generally smaller and darker than Swedes, with high cheekbones and slightly slanting eyes. They jealously guard what remains of their culture. Many of them still earn their living, and often grow rich, herding reindeer. There are 17,000 Sami in Sweden. Often the Sami exhibit a sad resignation to the gradual disappearance of their way of life as the modern world makes incursions. This is best expressed in one of their folk poems: "Our memory, the memory of us vanishes/We forget and we are forgotten."

Yet there is a growing struggle, especially among younger Sami, to maintain their identity and, thanks to their traditional closeness to nature, they are now finding allies in Sweden's "Green" movement. They refer to the north of Scandinavia as *Sapmi*, their spiritual and physical home, making no allowance for the different countries that now rule it.

Nearly all Swedish Sami now live in ordinary houses, having abandoned the *kåta* (Lapp wigwam), and some even herd their reindeer with helicopters. Efforts are now being made to protect and preserve their language, which is totally unlike Swedish, bearing much more resemblance to Finnish. The language reflects their closeness to nature. The word *goadnil*, for example, means "a quiet part of the river, free of current, near the bank or beside a rock."

Nowadays many Sami depend on the tourist industry for their living, selling their artifacts, such as expertly carved bone-handled knives, wood cups and bowls, bark bags, silver jewelry, and leather straps embroidered with pewter thread.

The trouble with Norrland, from the traveler's point of view, is its size. It stretches for 1,000 kilometers (620 miles) from south to north, makes up more than half of Sweden, and is about the size of Britain. On the west there are mountain ranges, to the east a wild and rocky coastline, and in between boundless forests and moorland. Its towns are usually little more than one street, built around a local industry such as mining. However, thanks to Sweden's excellent transportation infrastructure, Norrland is no longer so inaccessible and even a traveler with a limited time schedule should be able to get at least a taste of it. Its wild spaces are ideal for open-air holidays. Hiking, climbing, canoeing, river rafting, and fishing are all popular in summer; skiing, skating, and dogsledding in winter.

A word of warning: In summer mosquitoes are a constant nuisance, worse even than in other parts of Sweden, so be sure to bring plenty of repellent. The fall is perhaps the best season to visit Norrland. Roads are well maintained, but you should watch out for *guppar* (holes) following the thaw. Highways are generally traffic free, but keep an eye out for the occasional reindeer or two.

Important Addresses and Numbers

Tourist Information **Norrbottens Turistråd** covers the whole area (Sandviksgatan 53, Luleå, tel. 0920/94070). There are tourist offices at **Kiruna** (Hjalmar Lundbohmsvägen 42, tel. 0980/18880) and **Jokkmokk** (Porjusvägen 4, tel. 0971/12140).

Emergencies For **emergencies** dial 90,000. You can also call **Kiruna Health Center** (Thulegatan 29, tel. 0980/16677), **Luleå district nurse** (emergency tel. 0920/71400), and **Jokkmokk Health Center** (Lappstavägen 9, tel. 0971/11350).

Pharmacies There are no late-night pharmacies in the area, but doctors called to emergencies can supply medicines. The pharmacy at Kiruna Hospital (Thulegatan 29, tel. 0980/12220) is open until 5 PM.

Arriving and Departing by Plane

There are two SAS flights a day from Stockholm to **Kiruna Airport** (tel. 0980/17777).

Between the Airport and Town It is 9 kilometers (6 miles) from the airport to the center of Kiruna. **Buses** connect with the flights from Stockholm. The fare is SKr20. A **taxi** from the airport to the center of Kiruna costs SKr70–SKr80.

Arriving and Departing by Train

The best and cheapest way to get to Kiruna is to take the 5:43 PM sleeper from Stockholm on a Tuesday or Wednesday when the fare is reduced to SKr482 single. The regular single price is SKr804, double for return. You arrive at 12:03 PM the following day.

Getting Around

By Car In Kiruna **Avis** has a branch at Industrivägen 10 (tel. 0980/16060). **Hertz** is at Industrivägen 5 (tel. 0980/19000), and **InterRent** and **Europcar** are at Växlaregatan 20 (tel. 0980/14365).

Guided Tours

The Kiruna Tourist Office organizes numerous guided tours. There is a two-hour tour of the local iron mine costing SKr65, a day-trip to a Same holy place for SKr150, and a trip by bus and boat to a Same camp for SKr170. Most exotic is a 45-minute flight in a seaplane, taking off from a nearby lake at 11 PM to see the midnight sun. Tickets are SKr465.

Exploring Norrland

Norrland is best discovered from a base in Kiruna, the largest city in the region. You can tour south and west to the mountains and national parks, east and south to Sami (Lapp) villages, and farther south still to Baltic coastal settlements.

Numbers in the margin correspond with points of interest on the Norrland map.

Tour 1: Kiruna

1 **Kiruna** is the most northerly city in Sweden, spread over a large area between two mountains mostly composed of iron ore, which are its raison d'être. They are called Luossavaara and Kirunavaara. The city, named after the latter, was established in 1890 as a mining town, but true prosperity came only with the building of the railway to the Baltic port of Luleå and the northern Norwegian port of Narvik in 1903. Kiruna has the world's largest underground iron mine, with reserves estimated at 500 million tons. There is also much open-pit mining, quite dramatic to witness, with tons of dynamite ripping the ore out of the ground.

Kiruna lies at the southern end of Lake Luossajärvi and with its 30,000 inhabitants is Norrland's largest center of population. It is, at 1,670 feet above sea level, the highest city in Sweden, with an estimated fifth of its population Finnish immigrants who came to work in the mine.

Because the municipality is spread over such a large area, Kiruna is often called "the world's biggest city" yet it remains a vastly ordinary place, with few facilities or cultural events. In recent years the city has diversified its economy and now houses the Esrange Space Range, which sends rockets and balloons to probe the upper reaches of the earth's atmosphere, and the Kiruna Geophysical Institute, which has pioneered the investigation of the phenomenon of the northern lights. The city received a boost in 1984 with the opening of *Nordkalottvägen*, a 170-kilometer-long (105-mile) road to Narvik.

One of Kiruna's few buildings of interest is **Kiruna Kyrka** (Kiruna church), on Gruvvägen, near the center of the city. It was built in 1921, its inspiration a blending of a Same *kåta* with a Swedish stave church. The altarpiece is by Prince Eugen, Sweden's painter prince (1863–1947).

Tour 2: Kebnekaise

At 7,000 feet above sea level, **Kebnekaise** is Sweden's highest mountain, but you'll need to be in good physical shape just to get to it. From Kiruna you travel about 60 kilometers (37 miles)
2 south, then west to the Sami village of **Nikkaluotka.** There are two buses a day from Kiruna in the summer. From Nikkaluotka it is a hike of 21 kilometers (13 miles) to the Fjällstationen
3 (mountain station) at the foot of **Kebnekaise,** though you can take a boat for 7 kilometers (4 miles) across **Lake Ladtjojokk.** Kebnekaise itself is easy to climb in good weather, with no need for mountaineering equipment. If you feel up to more walking, the track continues past the Mountain Station to become part of what is known as **Kungsleden** (The King's Way), a trail through the mountains and Abisko National Park to Riksgränsen on the Norwegian border.

Tour 3: Jukkasjärvi and Jokkmokk

Jukkasjärvi is just 16 kilometers (10 miles) east of Kiruna and can be reached by bus. The history of this Sami village by the
4 shores of the fast-flowing **Torneälven** (Torne River) dates back

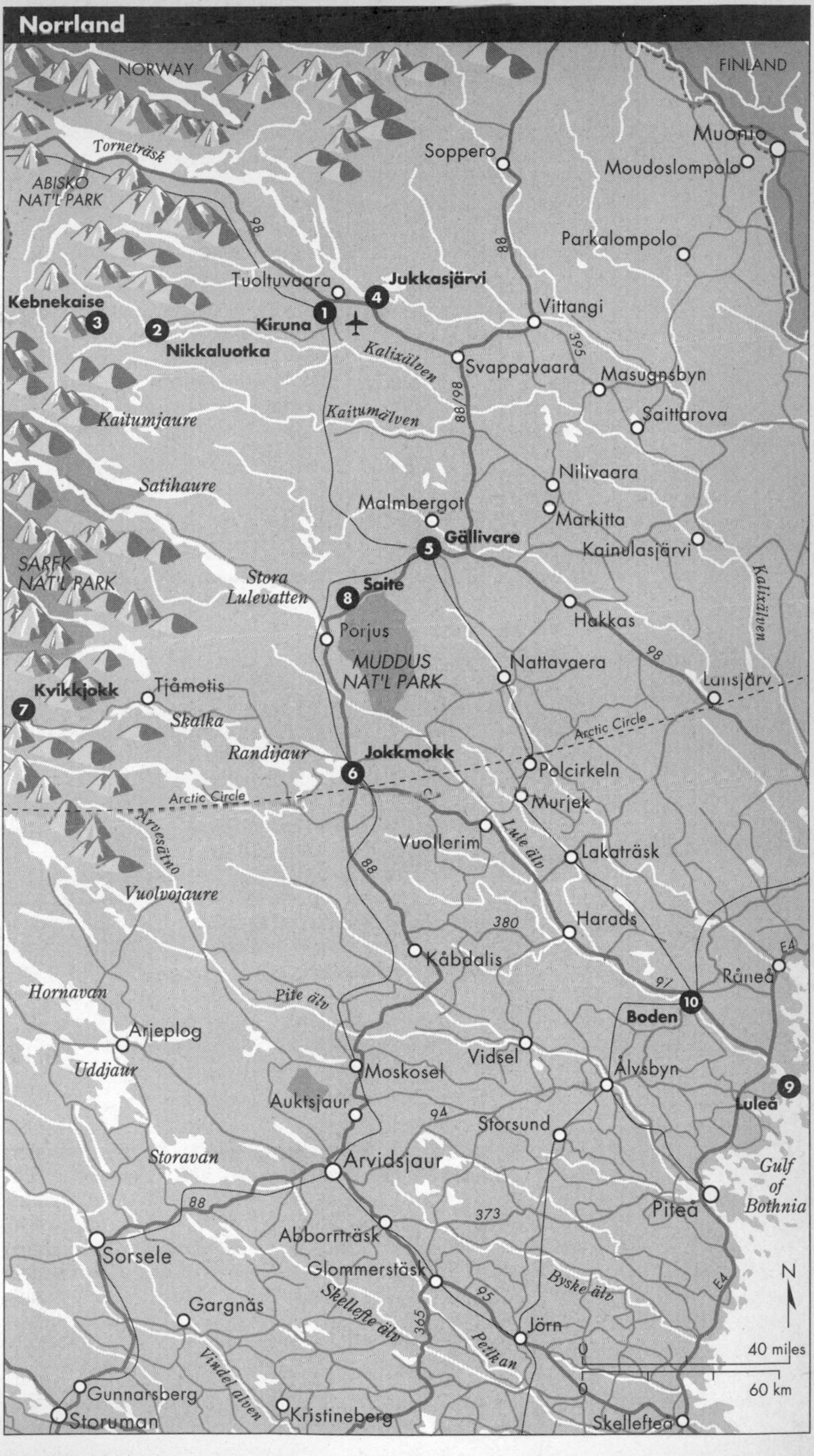
Norrland
NORWAY
FINLAND
Torneträsk
ABISKO NAT'L PARK
Muonio
Soppero
Moudoslompolo
Parkalompolo
Tuoltuvaara
Jukkasjärvi
Kebnekaise
Kiruna
Nikkaluotka
Vittangi
Kalixälven
Svappavaara
Masugnsbyn
Saittarova
Kaitumjaure
Kaitumälven
Satihaure
Nilivaara
Malmbergot
Markitta
Gällivare
Kainulasjärvi
SAREK NAT'L PARK
Stora Lulevatten
Saite
Hakkas
Porjus
MUDDUS NAT'L PARK
Nattavaera
Kvikkjokk
Tjåmotis
Skalka
Lansjärv
Arctic Circle
Randijaur
Jokkmokk
Polcirkeln
Murjek
Vuollerim
Lule älv
Lakaträsk
Arvesätno
Vuolvojaure
Harads
Kåbdalis
Råneå
E4
Hornavan
Pite älv
Boden
Arjeplog
Vidsel
Uddjaur
Moskosel
Älvsbyn
Auktsjaur
Luleå
Storsund
Storavan
Arvidsjaur
Gulf of Bothnia
Piteå
Abborrträsk
Sorsele
Glommerstäsk
Byske älv
Skellefte älv
Gargnäs
Jörn
Petikan
Vindel alven
Gunnarsberg
Storuman
Kristineberg
Skellefteå
40 miles
60 km
N

to 1543, when a market was recorded here. There is a wood **church** from the 17th century and a small **open-air museum** that gives a feeling of Sami life in times gone by.

Here, if you are gastronomically adventurous, you may sample one of the most unusual of Sami delicacies: a cup of thick black coffee and small lumps of goat cheese. These you marinate in the coffee, fish out with spoons, and consume. Then you drink the coffee. The taste sensation is intriguing, to say the least. Afterward, try riding the rapids of the Torne River in an inflatable boat. In winter Jukkasjärvi also offers dogsled rides.

5 Follow Route 98 104 kilometers (65 miles) south to **Gällivare,** a mining town with a population of 22,000, then Route 88 106 ki-
6 lometers (66 miles) farther to **Jokkmokk,** an important center of Sami culture. It is the scene each February of the region's largest market, nowadays an odd event featuring everything from stalls selling frozen reindeer meat to computerized fortune-telling.

Jokkmokk makes perhaps the best base in Norrland for the outdoor vacationer. The village has three campsites and is surrounded by wilderness.

The local tourist office sells fishing permits, which cost SKr25 to SKr40 for 24 hours, with special weekly and monthly rates. The office can also supply lists of camping and housekeeping cabins.

Tour 4: Sarek National Park

Sarek is Sweden's largest high mountain area and was moulded by the last Ice Age. It totals 197,000 hectares (487,000 acres), a small portion of which is forest, bogland, and waterways. The remainder is bare mountain. The park contains 200 peaks more than 6,000 feet above sea level, and six of the country's 13 mountain peaks more than 6,600 feet high. The mountains are some of the most beautiful in Sweden, having been sculpted by glaciers, of which there are around 100 in the park. The Rapaätno River, which drains the park, runs through the lovely, desolate **Rapadalen** (Rapa Valley). There is a surprising variety of landscape, luxuriant green meadows contrasting with the snowy peaks of the mountains. Animals to be found here include elk, bear, wolverine, lynx, ermine, hare, Arctic fox, red fox, and mountain lemmings. Birdlife includes ptarmigan, willow grouse, teal, wigeon, tufted duck, common scoter, bluethroat, brambling, and warbler, with the meadow pipit and the Lappland bunting common on the bare mountainsides. Golden eagles, rough-legged buzzards and merlins also have been spotted here.

Visiting Sarek demands a good knowledge of mountains and a familiarity with the outdoors. Sarek can be dangerous in winter because of avalanches and snowstorms. However, in the summer, despite its unpredictable, often inhospitable climate, it attracts large numbers of hikers. The best entry point is at
7 **Kvikkjokk,** a village reached by a small road to the east of Jokkmokk (*see* Tour 3, *above*). Hikers can then choose between a trail through the Tarradalen (Tarra Valley), which passes through the western part of Sarek, or part of the Kungsleden trail (*see* Tour 2, Kebnekaise, *above*), which crosses the southern end for a distance of about 16 kilometers (10 miles).

Tour 5: Muddus National Park

Established in 1942, this park is less mountainous and spectacular than Sarek, its 49,300 hectares (121,770 acres) comprising

mainly virgin coniferous forest, some of whose trees may be up to 600 years old. The park's 1,490 hectares (3,680 acres) of water is composed primarily of two huge lakes at the center of the park and the Muddusjokk River, which tumbles spectacularly through a gorge with 330-foot-high sheer rock walls and includes a 140-foot-high waterfall. Muddus is reached by taking
8 the road southwest of Gällivare to **Saite** en route to the Porjus power station and is well signposted. The highest point of Muddus is **Sör-Stuobba** Mountain, 658 meters above sea level. Well-marked trails lead through the park, where you can pick cloudberries in the autumn. There are four well-equipped overnight communal rest huts and two tourist cabins. The park contains bears, lynx, wolverines, moose, ermines, weasels, otters, and many bird species, but all but the mosquitoes tend to be shy.

Tour 6: Luleå and the East Coast

Driving south from Kiruna, continuing along Route 98 at Gällivare, you pass several small former mining villages before coming into the **Kalixälv** (Kalix River Valley), where the countryside becomes more settled, with small farms and fertile meadows replacing the wilder northern landscape. Some 347
9 kilometers (215 miles) from Kiruna, you reach **Luleå,** a port at the top of the Gulf of Bothnia, at the mouth of the Luleäl (Lule River). The most northerly major town in Sweden, Luleå was situated some 10 kilometers (6 miles) farther inland when it was first granted its charter in 1621, but by 1649 trade had grown so much that the town was moved closer to the sea. The development of Kiruna and the iron trade is linked, by means of a railway, with the fortunes of Luleå, where a steelworks was set up in the 1940s. Luleå has never really achieved all that was intended for it, but nonetheless, along with Piteå, Skellefteå, Umeå, and Sundsvall, farther south down the coast road, it remains an important northern port. Luleå, like most of its fellow ports on the east coast, is a very modern and nondescript city, but it has some reasonable hotels. There is also, at **Norrbottens Museet** (the Norbotten Museum), one of the best collections of Same ethnography in the world. *Hermelinsparken, tel. 0920/93829. Admission: SKr10. Open daily 10–5.*

10 From Luleå you can take Route 97 to **Boden,** the nation's largest garrison town, dating from 1809 when Sweden lost Finland to Russia and feared an invasion of its own territory. **Garnisonsmuseet** (the Garrison Museum), contains exhibits from Swedish military history, with an extensive collection of weapons and uniforms. *Garnisonsmuseet, Boden, tel. 0921/62000. Admission: SKr10. Open daily 10–5.*

You can then return through ever wilder and more desolate countryside to Jokkmokk and Kiruna.

Sports and Outdoor Activities

All the regional tourist offices can supply details of skiing holidays, but never forget the extreme temperatures and weather conditions. For the really adventurous, Kebnekaise Mountain Station (*see* Tour 2, *above*) offers combined skiing and climbing weeks at SKr3,475. It also offers week-long combined dogsledding, skiing, and climbing holidays on the mountains, which vary in price from SKr3,995 to SKr4,995. Because of the extreme cold and the danger involved, be sure to have proper equipment. Consult the Mountain Station well in advance for advice (tel. 0980/55042).

Dining and Lodging

The two are often synonymous at these latitudes. Standards of cuisine and service are, unlike prices, not high, but hotels usually are exceptionally clean and staffs scrupulously honest.

Highly recommended establishments are indicated by a star★

Dining Norrland specialties include *surströmming* (fermented herring), *pält* (a stuffed dumpling), and *tunnbröd* (thin bread made from barley flour) with either butter, buttermilk, or sour cream. Trout and salmon are common, as are various cuts of elk and reindeer. But the most acceptable of Norrland's culinary specialties to the foreign palate is undoubtedly *löjröm*, pinkish caviar from a species of Baltic herring, which is eaten with chopped onions and sour cream, and the various desserts made from the cloudberries that thrive here.

Lodging This is limited, but the various local tourist offices can supply details of bed-and-breakfasts and of holiday villages equipped with housekeeping cabins. The area is also rich in camping sites, though, with the highly unpredictable climate, this may appeal only to the very hardy.

Jokkmokk
Dining and Lodging
★

Jokkmokk. In the middle of a remote, empty region this modern luxury hotel seems incongruous, but welcome nevertheless. The hotel can arrange helicopter trips to the Sarek and Muddus national parks, and there is excellent fishing nearby. *Solgatan 45, S–96040, tel. 0971/11320. 82 rooms. Facilities: restaurant, pool, solarium, sauna, gymnasium, conference rooms. AE, DC, MC, V. Expensive.*

Gästis. This small hotel in central Jokkmokk was opened in 1915. *Herrevägen 1, S–96040, tel. 0971/10012. 30 rooms. Facilities: restaurant, dancing, sauna. AE, DC, MC, V. Moderate.*

Jokkmokks Turistcenter. This complex is prettily situated in a forest area, near a lake, 3 kilometers (2 miles) from the railway station. *Box 75, S–96040, tel. 0971/12370. 26 rooms, 84 cabins. Facilities: conference rooms, sauna, solarium, 4 outdoor swimming pools, canoe and bicycle rentals. No credit cards. Inexpensive.*

Jukkasjärvi
Dining and Lodging
★

Jukkasjärvi Wärdshus och Hembygdsgård. The restaurant specializes in Norrland cuisine and is the lifework of its manager, Yngve Bergqvist. The hotel has four rooms, and there are 45 cabins around it. *Box 24, S–98021, tel. 0980/21190, fax 0980/21406. 4 rooms, 45 cabins, 30 with bath and kitchen. Facilities: restaurant, rooms for the disabled, conference rooms. AE, DC, MC, V. Inexpensive.*

Kebnekaise
Lodging

Kebnekaise Fjällstation has been recently renovated. Conditions are remarkably good considering its isolation. *S–98129, tel. 0980/55042. 160 beds. Facilities: restaurant. AE, V. Moderate.*

Kiruna
Dining and Lodging

Ferrum. Part of the Reso Hotels chain, this late-1960s-vintage hotel, renovated in 1991, is situated near the railway station. *Lars Janssonsgatan, S–981 31, tel. 0980/18600, fax 0980/14505. 170 rooms with shower. Facilities: 2 restaurants, bar, sauna, solarium. AE, DC, MC, V. Moderate.*

Fyra Vindar. This small hotel, dating from 1903, also has the advantage of being close to the railway station. *Bangårdsvägen 9, S–98134, tel. 0980/12050. 18 rooms, not all with bath. Facilities: breakfast. DC, MC, V. Moderate.*

Kebne och Kaisa. These twin modern hotels are close to the railway station and the airport bus stop. *Konduktörsgatan 7, S–98134, tel. 0980/12380. 54 rooms with shower. Facilities: restaurant (closed Fri.–Sun.), sauna, solarium. AE, DC, MC, V. Moderate.*

STF Vandrarhem. This youth hostel, nicely situated just 800 meters from the railway station, is surrounded by forest and park. *7 4-room cabins, 90 beds with bath in separate cabin. Facilities: pool. No credit cards. Inexpensive.*

Luleå
Dining and Lodging

Luleå Stads Hotell. This large, centrally located hotel has nightly, sometimes rowdy dancing. *Storgatan 15, S–951 31, tel. 0920/10410, fax 0920/67092. 135 rooms, 3 suites. Facilities: restaurant, rooms for the disabled and allergy sufferers, conference rooms, sauna, solarium. AE, DC, MC, V. Expensive.*

SAS Luleå. As you might expect of an SAS hotel, this one is large, modern, and centrally situated. *Storgatan 17, S–951 24, tel. 0920/94000, fax 0920/88222. 212 rooms. Facilities: restaurant, rooms for the disabled and allergy sufferers, conference rooms, sauna, swimming pool, solarium. AE, DC, MC, V. Expensive.*

Amber. A particularly fine old building houses this centrally situated hotel close to the railway station. *Stationsgatan 67, S–95132, tel. 0920/10200. 16 rooms. Facilities: restaurant, nightclub, 2 bars, rooms for allergy sufferers and nonsmokers. AE, DC, MC, V. Moderate.*

Arctic. Right in the center of town, it's renowned locally for its restaurant. *Sandviksgatan 80, S–95132, tel. 0920/10980. 95 rooms. Facilities: restaurant, rooms for the disabled, conference rooms, sauna. AE, DC, MC, V. Moderate.*

Aveny. This small hotel is close to the railway station. *Hermelinsgatan 10, tel. 0920/21820 or 0920/21821. 24 rooms. Facilities: rooms for nonsmokers and allergy sufferers, solarium. AE, DC, MC, V. Moderate.*

Scandic. This hotel, alongside Luleälven (the Lule River), has an extremely pleasant location but is 8 kilometers (5 miles) from the railway station. *Mjölkudden, S–951 56, tel. 0920/28360, fax 0920/69472. 158 rooms. Facilities: restaurant, rooms for the disabled and allergy sufferers, conference rooms, gymnasium, sauna, indoor pool, solarium. AE, DC, MC, V. Moderate.*

Conversion Tables

Distance

Kilometers/Miles To change kilometers to miles, multiply kilometers by .621.
To change miles to kilometers, multiply miles by 1.61.

Km to Mi	Mi to Km
1 = .62	1 = 1.6
2 = 1.2	2 = 3.2
3 = 1.9	3 = 4.8
4 = 2.5	4 = 6.4
5 = 3.1	5 = 8.1
6 = 3.7	6 = 9.7
7 = 4.3	7 = 11.3
8 = 5.0	8 = 12.9
9 = 5.6	9 = 14.5

Meters/Feet To change meters to feet, multiply meters by 3.28.
To change feet to meters, multiply feet by .305.

Meters to Feet	Feet to Meters
1 = 3.3	1 = .31
2 = 6.6	2 = .61
3 = 9.8	3 = .92
4 = 13.1	4 = 1.2
5 = 16.4	5 = 1.5
6 = 19.7	6 = 1.8
7 = 23.0	7 = 2.1
8 = 26.2	8 = 2.4
9 = 29.5	9 = 2.7

Weight

Kilograms/Pounds To change kilograms to pounds, multiply by 2.20.
To change pounds to kilograms, multiply by .453.

Kilo to Pound	Pound to Kilo
1 = 2.2	1 = .45
2 = 4.4	2 = .91
3 = 6.6	3 = 1.4
4 = 8.8	4 = 1.8
5 = 11.0	5 = 2.3

6 = 13.2	6 = 2.7
7 = 15.4	7 = 3.2
8 = 17.6	8 = 3.6
9 = 19.8	9 = 4.1

Grams/Ounces To change grams to ounces, multiply grams by .035.
To change ounces to grams, multiply ounces by 28.4.

Grams to Ounces	**Ounces to Grams**
1 = .04	1 = 28
2 = .07	2 = 57
3 = .11	3 = 85
4 = .14	4 = 114
5 = .18	5 = 142
6 = .21	6 = 170
7 = .25	7 = 199
8 = .28	8 = 227
9 = .32	9 = 256

Liquid Volume

Liters/U.S. Gallons To change liters to U.S. gallons, multiply liters by .264.
To change U.S. gallons to liters, multiply gallons by 3.79.

Liters to U.S. Gallons	**U.S. Gallons to Liters**
1 = .26	1 = 3.8
2 = .53	2 = 7.6
3 = .79	3 = 11.4
4 = 1.1	4 = 15.2
5 = 1.3	5 = 19.0
6 = 1.6	6 = 22.7
7 = 1.8	7 = 26.5
8 = 2.1	8 = 30.3
9 = 2.4	9 = 34.1

Vocabulary

Danish Vocabulary

	English	*Danish*	*Pronunciation*
Basics	Yes/no	Ja/nej	yah/nie
	Please	Vær så god	**ver** soh god
	Thank you very much	Tak	tak
	You're welcome	Velbekomme	**vel**-be-ko-me
	Excuse me (to apologize)	Undskyld	**unsk**-ul
	Hello	Goodag	gu-**day**
	Goodbye	Farvel	fa-**vel**
	Today	I dag	ee **day**
	Tomorrow	I morgen	ee **morn**
	Yesterday	I går	ee **gore**
	Morning	Morgen	**more**-n
	Afternoon	Eftermiddag	**ef-tah**-mid-day
	Night	Nat	nat
Numbers	One	een/eet	**een**/eet
	Two	to	toe
	Three	tre	tre
	Four	fire	fear
	Five	fem	fem
	Six	seks	sex
	Seven	syv	syoo
	Eight	otte	**oh**-te
	Nine	ni	nee
	Ten	ti	tee
Days of the Week	Monday	mandag	**man**-day
	Tuesday	tirsdag	**tears**-day
	Wednesday	onsdag	**ons**-day
	Thursday	torsdag	**trs**-day
	Friday	fredag	**free**-day
	Saturday	lørdag	**lore**-day
	Sunday	søndag	**soo**(n)-day

Useful Phrases	Do you speak English?	Taler du engelsk	te-ler **doo** in-galsk
	I don't speak . . .	Jeg taler ikke Dansk	yi tal-ler **ick** Dansk
	I don't understand.	Jeg forstår ikke	yi fahr-store **ick**
	I don't know.	Det ved jeg ikke	deh **ved** yi ick
	I am American/ British.	Jeg er amerikansk/ britisk	yi ehr a-mehr-i-**kansk**/ bri-**tisk**
	I am sick.	Jeg er syg	yi ehr **syoo**
	Please call a doctor.	Kan du ringe til en læge?	can **doo** rin-geh til en lay-eh
	Do you have a vacant room?	Har du et værelse?	har **doo** eet va(l)r-sa
	How much does it cost?	Hvad koster det?	va cos-ta **deh**
	It's too expensive.	Det er fahr duurt	deh ehr **fohr** dyrt
	Beautiful	Smukt	smukt
	Help!	Hjælp	yelp
	Stop!	Stop	stop
	How do I get to . . .	Hvordan kommer jeg til?	vore-**dan** kom-mer yi til
	. . . the train station?	banegarden	**ban**-eh-gore-en
	. . . the post office?	postkonoret	**post**-kon-toh-raht
	. . . the tourist office?	turistkonoret	too-**reest**-kon-tor-et
	. . . the hospital?	hospitalet	hos-peet-**tal**-et
	Does this bus go to . . . ?	Går denne bus til?	**goh** den-na boos til
	Where is the W.C.?	Hvor er toilettet	vor **ehr** toi-le(tt)-et
	On the left	Til venstre	til **ven**-strah
	On the right	Till højre	til **hoy**-ah
	Straight ahead	Lige ud	**lee** u(l)
Dining Out	Please bring me . . .	Mø jeg få	mo yi **foh**
	menu	menu	me-**nu**
	fork	gaffel	gaf-**fel**
	knife	kniv	kan-**ew**
	spoon	ske	skee

	napkin	serviet	serv-**eet**
	bread	brød	brood
	butter	smør	smoor
	milk	mælk	malk
	pepper	peber	**pee**-wer
	salt	salt	selt
	sugar	sukker	**su**-kar
	water/bottled water	vand	van
	The check, please.	Regning	**ri**-ning

Finnish Vocabulary

	English	*Finnish*	*Pronunciation*
Basics	Yes/no	Kyllä/Ei	kue-la/**ee**
	Please	Olkaa hyvä	**ol**-kah **hue**-va
	Thank you very much.	Kiitoksia paljon	**kee**-tohk-syah **pahl**-yon
	You're welcome.	Olkaa hyvä	**ol**-kah **hue**-va
	Excuse me. (to get by someone)	Anteeksi	**ahn**-teek-see
	(to apologize)	Suokaa anteeksi	**soo**-oh-kah **ahn**-teek-see
	Hello	Hyvää päivää terve	**hue**-va **paee**-va **tehr**-veh
	Goodbye	Näkemiin	**na**-keh-meen
	Today	Tänään	**ta**-naan
	Tomorrow	Huomenna	**hoo**-oh-men-nah
	Yesterday	Eilen	**ee**-len
	Morning	Aamu	**ah**-moo
	Afternoon	Iltapäivä	**eel**-tah-**pay**-va
	Night	Yö	**eu**-euh
Numbers	One	Yksi	**uek**-see
	Two	Kaksi	**kahk**-see
	Three	Kolme	**kohl**-meh
	Four	Nelja	**nel**-yah
	Five	Viisi	**vee**-see
	Six	Kuusi	**koo**-see
	Seven	Seitseman	**sate**-seh-man
	Eight	Kahdeksan	**kah**-dek-sahn

	Nine	Yhdaksän	**uef**-dek-san
	Ten	Kymmenen	**kue**-meh-nen
Days of the Week	Monday	maanantai	**mah**-nahn-tie
	Tuesday	tiistai	**tees**-tie
	Wednesday	keskiviikko	**kes**-kee-veek-koh
	Thursday	torstai	**tohrs**-tie
	Friday	perjantai	**pehr**-yahn-tie
	Saturday	lauantai	**loo**-ahn-tie
	Sunday	sunnuntai	**soon**-noon-tie
Useful Phrases	Do you speak English?	Puhutteko englantia?	**poo**-hoot-teh-koh **ehng**-lahn-tee-ah
	I don't speak . . .	En puhu suomea . . .	ehn **poo**-hoo **soo**-oh-mee-ah
	I don't understand.	En ymmärrä.	ehn **eum**-mar-ra
	I don't know.	En tiedä.	ehn **tee**-eh-da
	I am American/ British.	Mina olen amerikkalainen/ englantilainen.	**mee**-na **oh**-len **ah**-mehr-ee-kah-lie-nehn/**ehn**-glahn-tee-lie-nehn
	I am sick.	Olen sairas.	**oh**-len **sigh**-rahs
	Please call a doctor.	Haluan kutsua lääkärin.	**hah**-loo-ahn **koot**-soo-ah **lay**-ka-reen
	Do you have a vacant room?	Onko teillä vapaata huonetta?	**ohn**-koh **teel** la **vah**-pah-tah **hoo**-oh-neht-tah?
	How much does it cost?	Paljonko tämä maksaa?	**pahl**-yohn-koh **ta**-ma **mahk**-sah
	It's too expensive.	Se on liian kallis.	**say** ohn **lee**-ahn **kah**-lees
	Beautiful	Kaunis	**kow**-nees
	Help!	Auttakaa!	**ow**-tah-kah
	Stop!	Seis!/ Pysähtykka!	say(s) **peu**-sa-teu-kay
	How do I get to . . .	Voitteko sanoa miten pääsen-n . . .	**voy**-tay-koh **sah**-noh-ah **mee**-ten **pay**-sen
	. . . the train station?	asema (. . . pääsen asemalle?)	**ah**-say-mah (**pay**-sen **ah**-say-mah-lay)
	. . . the post office?	posti (. . . paasen postiin?)	**pohs**-tee (**pay**-sen **pohs**-teen)

	. . . the tourist office?	matkatoimisto (. . . pääsen matkatoimistoon?)	**maht**-kah-**toy**-mees-toh (**pay**-sen **maht**-kah-**toy**-mees-tohn)
	. . . the hospital?	sairaala (. . . pääsen sairaalaan?)	**sigh**-rah-lah (**pay**-sen **sigh**-rah-lahn)
	Does this bus go to . . . ?	Kulkeeko kämä bussi-n?	**kool**-kay-koh **ta**-ma **boo**-see -n?
	Where is the W.C.?	Missä on W.C.?	**mee**-sa ohn **ves**-sah
	On the left	Vasemmalle	**vah**-say-mahl-lay
	On the right	Oikealle	**ohy**-kay-ah-lay
	Straight ahead	Souraan eteenpäin	**swoh**-rahn **eh**-tayn-pa-een
Dining Out	Please bring me . . .	Tuokaa minulle . . .	**too**-oh-kah **mee**-new
	menu	ruokalista	**roo**-oh-kah-lees-tah
	fork	haarukka	**hahr**-oo-kah
	knife	veitsi	**vayt**-see
	spoon	lusikka	**loo**-see-kah
	napkin	lautasliina	**low**-tahs-lee-nah
	bread	leipä	**lay**-pa
	butter	voi	**voh**(ee)
	milk	maito	**my**-toh
	pepper	pippuri	**pee**-poor-ee
	salt	suola	**soo**-oh-lah
	sugar	sokeri	**soh**-ker-ee
	water/bottled water	vesi/ kivennäisvesi	**veh**-see/**kee**-ven-eyes-veh-see
	The check, please.	Lasku, olkaa hyvä/Saanko maksaa	**lahs**-kew, **ohl**-kah **heu**-va/ **sahn**-koh **mahk**-sah

Icelandic Vocabulary

	English	*Icelandic*	*Pronunciation*
Basics	Yes/no	já/nei	yow/nay
	Thank you very much.	kærar þakkir	**kie**-rahr **thah**-kihr
	You're welcome.	Þù ert veikumin (nn)	thoo ehrt **vehl**-kohm-in
	Excuse me. (to get by someone)	Afsakið	**ahf**-sah-kith(e)
	(to apologize)	Fyrirgefið	**feer**-ee-geh-vith(e)

	Hello	Hallo	**hah**-loh
	Goodbye	bless	bless
	Today	í dag	**ee dahgh**
	Tomorrow	á morgun	ow **mohr**-gun
	Yesterday	í gær	ee **gah-eer**
	Morning	morgun	**mohr**-gun
	Afternoon	eftirmiðdagur	**ehf**-teer-mihth-dahg-ur
	Night	nótt	noht
Numbers	One	einn	**ehnn**
	Two	tveir	**tveh**-eer
	Three	Þrír	threer
	Four	fjórir	**fyohr**-eer
	Five	fimm	fehm
	Six	sex	sex
	Seven	sjö	sy-uh
	Eight	átta	**owt**-tah
	Nine	níu	**nee**-uh
	Ten	tíu	**tee**-uh
Days of the Week	Monday	mánudagur	**mown**-ah-dah-gur
	Tuesday	Þriðjudagur	**thrithe**-yoo-dah-gur
	Wednesday	miðvikudagur	**meethe**-veek-uh dah-gur
	Thursday	fimtudagur	**feem**-too-dah-gur
	Friday	fóstudagur	**fuhs**-too-dah-gur
	Saturday	laugardagur	**loy**-gahr-dah-gur
	Sunday	sunnudagur	**soon**-noo-dah-gur
Useful Phrases	Do you speak English?	Talar Þú ensku?	**tah**-lahr thoo **ehn**-skoo
	I don't speak . . .	Ég tala ekki islensku . . .	**yeh** tah-lah **ehk**-keh ehn-skoo
	I don't understand.	Ég skil ekki	yeh **skeel ehk**-keh
	I don't know.	Ég veit ekki	yeh **vayt ehk**-keh
	I am American/ British.	Ég er ameriskur/ breskur	yeh ehr **ah**-mehr eeskur/brehs-koor brehsk
	I am sick.	Ég er veik(ur)	yeh ehr vehk(oor)
	Please call a doctor.	Viltu hringja í lækni	veel-too **hreeng**-yah ee **lahk**-nee

Do you have a vacant room?	Átt þú laust herbergi	owt thoo laysht **hehr**-behr-ghee
How much does it cost?	Hvað kostar það	kvathe kohs-tahr thathe
It's too expensive.	Það er of dýrt	thahthe ehr ohf deert
Beautiful	Falleglur/t	**fahl**-lehg-loor
Help!	Hjálp	hyalp
Stop!	Stopp	stohp
How do I get to . . .	Hvernig kemst ég	**kvehr**-neeg kehmst **yehg**
. . . the post office?	á pósthúsið	ow pohst-hoos-ihthe
. . . the tourist office?	á ferðamálaráð	ow **fehr**-tha-mow-lahr-owthe
. . . the hospital?	á spitalan	ow **spee**-tah-lahn
Does this bus go to . . . ?	Fer þessi vagn	fehr **thehs**-see **vakn**
Where is the W.C.?	hvar er salernið	kvahr ehr sahl-ehr-nihthe
On the left	til vinstri	teel **veen**-stree
On the right	til hægri	teel **hie**-ree
Straight ahead	beint áfram	baynt **ow**-frahm

Dining Out

Please bring me . . .	get ég fengið	geht yehg **fehn**-gihthe
menu	matseðil	**maht**-seh-theel
fork	gaffal	**gah**-fahl(t)
knife	hnif	hneef
spoon	skeið	skaythe
napkin	servetta	sehr-**veht**-tah
bread	brauð	braythe
butter	smjör	smyoor
milk	mjólk	myoolk
pepper	pipar	**pay**-pahr
salt	salt	sahlt
sugar	sykur	**say**-koor
water/bottled water	vatn	vahtn
The check, please.	reikninginn	takk **rehk**-nihn-ghihn

Norwegian Vocabulary

	English	*Norwegian*	*Pronunciation*
Basics	Yes/no	Ja/nei	yah/nigh
	Please	Vær så snill	**vehr** soh snihl
	Thank you very much.	Tusen takk	**tews**-sehn tahk
	You're welcome.	Vær så god	**vehr** soh goo
	Excuse me.	Unnskyld	**ewn**-shewl
	Hello	God dag	goo **dahg**
	Goodbye	Adjø	ah-**dyur**
	Today	i dag	ee **dahg**
	Tomorrow	i morgen	ee **moh**-ern
	Yesterday	i går	ee **gohr**
	Morning	morgen	**moh**-ern
	Afternoon	ettermiddag	**eh-terr**-mid-dahg
	Night	natt	naht
Numbers	One	en	ehn
	Two	to	too
	Three	tre	tray
	Four	fire	**feer**-eh
	Five	fem	fehm
	Six	seks	sehks
	Seven	syv, sju	shew
	Eight	åtte	**oh**-teh
	Nine	ni	nee
	Ten	ti	tee
Days of the Week	Monday	måndag	**mahn**-dahg
	Tuesday	tirsdag	**teesh**-dahg
	Wednesday	onsdag	**oonss**-dahg
	Thursday	torsdag	**tohsh**-dahg
	Friday	fredag	**fray**-dahg
	Saturday	lørdag	**loor**-dahg
	Sunday	sondag	**suhn**-dahg
Useful Phrases	Do you speak English?	Snakker De engelsk?	**snahk**-kerr dee **ehng**-ehlsk
	I don't speak Norwegian.	Jeg snakker ikke norsk.	yay **snahk**-kerr **ik**-keh nohrshk
	I don't understand.	Jeg forstår ikke	yay fosh-**tawr** **ik**-keh
	I don't know.	Jeg vet ikke.	yay veht **ik**-keh

	I am American/ British.	Jeg er amerikansk/ engelsk	yay ehr ah-mehr-ee-**kahnsk/ehng**-ehlsk
	I am sick.	Jeg er darlig	yay ehr **dahr**-lee
	Please call a doctor.	Vær så snill og ring etter en lege	vehr soh snihl oh ring **eht**-ehr ehn **lay**-geh
	Do you have a vacant room?	Jeg vil gjerne ha et rom	yay vil **yehr**-neh hah eht room
	How much does it cost?	Hva koster det?	vah **koss**-terr deh
	It's too expensive.	Det er for dyrt	deh ehr for **deert**
	Beautiful	vakker	**vah**-kehr
	Help!	Hjelp!	yehlp
	Stop!	Stopp	stop
	How do I get to . . .	Hvor er	voor **ehr**
	. . . the train station?	jernbanestasjonen	yehrn-bahn-eh sta-**shoon**-ern
	. . . the post office?	posthuset	**pohsst**-hewss
	. . . the tourist office?	turistkontoret	tew-**reest**-koon-toor-er
	. . . the hospital?	sykehuset	**see**-keh-hoo-seh
	Does this bus go to . . . ?	Går denne bussen tel ?	gohr **den**-nah boos teel
	Where is the W.C.?	Hvor er toalettene?	voor ehr too-ah-**leht**-ter-ner
	On the left	Til venstre	teel **vehn**-streh
	On the right	Til høyre	teel **hooy**-reh
	Straight ahead	Rett fram	reht **frahm**
Dining Out	menu	meny	meh-**new**
	fork	gaffel	**gahff**-erl
	knife	kniv	kneev
	spoon	skje	shay
	napkin	serviett	ssehr-**vyeht**
	bread	brød	brur
	butter	smør	smurr
	milk	melk	mehlk
	pepper	pepper	**pehp**-per
	salt	salt	sahlt
	sugar	sukker	**sook**-kerr

water/bottled water	vand	vahn
The check, please.	Jeg vil gjerne betale	yay vil **yehr**-neh beh-**tah**-leh

Swedish Vocabulary

	English	*Swedish*	*Pronunciation*
Basics	Yes/no	Ja/nej	yah/nay
	Please	Var snäll; Var vänlig	vahr snehll vahr **vehn**-leeg
	Thank you very much.	Tack så mycket.	tahk soh **mee**-keh
	You're welcome.	Var så god.	vahr shoh **goo**
	Excuse me. (to get by someone)	Ursäkta.	oor-**shehk**-tah
	(to apologize)	Førlåt.	fur-**loht**
	Hello	God dag	goo **dahg**
	Goodbye	Adjø	ah-**yoo**
	Today	I dag	ee **dahg**
	Tomorrow	I Morgon	ee **mohr**-ron
	Yesterday	I går	ee **gohr**
	Morning	Morgon	**mohr**-ron
	Afternoon	Eftermiddag	**ehf**-ter-meed-dahg
	Night	natt	naht
Numbers	One	en	ehn
	Two	tva	tvoh
	Three	tre	tree
	Four	fyra	**fee**-rah
	Five	fem	fem
	Six	sex	sex
	Seven	sju	shoo
	Eight	åtta	**ot**-tah
	Nine	nio	nee
	Ten	tio	tee
Days of the Week	Monday	Måndag	**mohn**-dahg
	Tuesday	Tisdag	**tees**-dahg
	Wednesday	Onsdag	**ohns**-dahg
	Thursday	Torsdag	**tohrs**-dahg
	Friday	Fredag	**freh**-dahg
	Saturday	Lørdag	**luhr**-dahg
	Sunday	Sondag	**sohn**-dahg

Useful Phrases

Do you speak English?	Talar ni engelska?	**tah**-lahr nee **ehng**-ehl-skah
I don't speak . . .	Jag talar inte svenska . . .	yah **tah**-lahr **een**-teh **sven**-skah
I don't understand.	Jag förstår inte.	yah fuhr-**stohr** **een**-teh
I don't know.	Jag vet inte.	yah **veht** **een**-teh
I am American/ British.	Jag är amerikan/ engelsman.	yah ay ah-mehr-ee-**kahn**/ **ehng**-ehls-mahn
I am sick.	Jag är sjuk.	yah ay **shyook**
Please call a doctor.	Jag vill skicka efter en läkare.	yah veel **shee**-kah **ehf**-tehr ehn **lay**-kah-reh
Do you have a vacant room?	Har Ni något rum ledigt?	hahr nee noh-goht **room** **leh**-deekt
How much does it cost?	Vad kostar det?/ Hur mycket kostar det?	vah **kohs**-tahr deh/hoor **mee**-keh **kohs**-tahr deh
It's too expensive.	Den är for dyr.	dehn ay foor **deer**
Beautiful	Vacker	**vah**-kehr
Help!	Hjälp	yehlp
Stop!	Stopp, stanna	stop, **stahn**-nah
How do I get to . . .	Kan Ni visa mig vägen till	kahn nee **vee**-sah may **vay**-gehn teel
. . . the train station?	stationen	stah-**shoh**-nehn
. . . the post office?	posten	**pohs**-tehn
. . . the tourist office?	en resebyrå	ehn-**reh**-seh-**bee**-roh
. . . the hospital?	sjukhuset	**shyook**-hoo-seht
Does this bus go to . . . ?	Går den här bussen till ?	gohr dehn hehr **boo**-sehn teel
Where is the W.C.?	Var är toilett/ toaletten	vahr ay twah-**leht**
On the left	Till vänster	teel **vehn**-stur
On the right	Till höger	teel **huh**-gur
Straight ahead	Rakt fram	rahkt **frahm**

Dining Out

Please bring me . . .	Var snäll och hamta åt mig	vahr snehl oh **hehm**-tah oht may
menu	matsedeln	**maht**-seh-dehln
fork	en gaffel	ehn **gahf**-fehl
knife	en kniv	ehn **kneev**
spoon	en sked	ehn **shehd**
napkin	en servett	ehn sehr-**veht**
bread	brød	bruh(d)
butter	smør	smuhr
milk	mjølk	myoolk
pepper	peppar	**pehp**-pahr
salt	salt	sahlt
sugar	socker	**soh**-kehr
water	vatten	**vaht**-n
The check, please.	Far jag be om notan?	fohr yah beh ohm **noh**-tahn

Index

In this index the Scandinavian letters å, æ, ä, ø, ö, and þ have been alphabetized as though they were the English letters a, o, and p. In Scandanavia these letters are found at the *end* of the alphabet in telephone directories and other alphabetized lists.

Personal Itinerary

Departure *Date*

Time

Transportation

Arrival *Date* *Time*

Departure *Date* *Time*

Transportation

Accommodations

Arrival *Date* *Time*

Departure *Date* *Time*

Transportation

Accommodations

Arrival *Date* *Time*

Departure *Date* *Time*

Transportation

Accommodations

Personal Itinerary

Arrival *Date* *Time*

Departure *Date* *Time*

Transportation

Accommodations

Arrival *Date* *Time*

Departure *Date* *Time*

Transportation

Accommodations

Arrival *Date* *Time*

Departure *Date* *Time*

Transportation

Accommodations

Arrival *Date* *Time*

Departure *Date* *Time*

Transportation

Accommodations

Personal Itinerary

Arrival *Date* *Time*

Departure *Date* *Time*

Transportation

Accommodations

Arrival *Date* *Time*

Departure *Date* *Time*

Transportation

Accommodations

Arrival *Date* *Time*

Departure *Date* *Time*

Transportation

Accommodations

Arrival *Date* *Time*

Departure *Date* *Time*

Transportation

Accommodations

Personal Itinerary

Arrival *Date* *Time*

Departure *Date* *Time*

Transportation

Accommodations

Arrival *Date* *Time*

Departure *Date* *Time*

Transportation

Accommodations

Arrival *Date* *Time*

Departure *Date* *Time*

Transportation

Accommodations

Arrival *Date* *Time*

Departure *Date* *Time*

Transportation

Accommodations

Personal Itinerary

Arrival *Date* *Time*

Departure *Date* *Time*

Transportation

Accommodations

Arrival *Date* *Time*

Departure *Date* *Time*

Transportation

Accommodations

Arrival *Date* *Time*

Departure *Date* *Time*

Transportation

Accommodations

Arrival *Date* *Time*

Departure *Date* *Time*

Transportation

Accommodations

Personal Itinerary

Arrival *Date* *Time*

Departure *Date* *Time*

Transportation

Accommodations

Arrival *Date* *Time*

Departure *Date* *Time*

Transportation

Accommodations

Arrival *Date* *Time*

Departure *Date* *Time*

Transportation

Accommodations

Arrival *Date* *Time*

Departure *Date* *Time*

Transportation

Accommodations

Arrival *Date* *Time*

Departure *Date* *Time*

Transportation

Accommodations

Arrival *Date* *Time*

Departure *Date* *Time*

Transportation

Accommodations

Arrival *Date* *Time*

Departure *Date* *Time*

Transportation

Accommodations

Arrival *Date* *Time*

Departure *Date* *Time*

Transportation

Accommodations

Addresses

Name

Address

Telephone

Name

Address

Telephone

Name

Address

Telephone

Name

Address

Telephone

Name

Address

Telephone

Name

Address

Telephone

Name

Address

Telephone

Name

Address

Telephone

Name

Address

Telephone

Name

Address

Telephone

Name

Address

Telephone

Name

Address

Telephone

Name

Address

Telephone

Name

Address

Telephone

Name

Address

Telephone

Name

Address

Telephone

Addresses

Name

Address

Telephone

Name

Address

Telephone

Name

Address

Telephone

Name

Address

Telephone

Name

Address

Telephone

Name

Address

Telephone

Name

Address

Telephone

Name

Address

Telephone

Name

Address

Telephone

Name

Address

Telephone

Name

Address

Telephone

Name

Address

Telephone

Name

Address

Telephone

Name

Address

Telephone

Name

Address

Telephone

Name

Address

Telephone

Addresses

Name

Address

Telephone

Name

Address

Telephone

Name

Address

Telephone

Name

Address

Telephone

Name

Address

Telephone

Name

Address

Telephone

Name

Address

Telephone

Name

Address

Telephone

Name

Address

Telephone

Name

Address

Telephone

Name

Address

Telephone

Name

Address

Telephone

Name

Address

Telephone

Name

Address

Telephone

Name

Address

Telephone

Name

Address

Telephone

Addresses

Name

Address

Telephone

Name

Address

Telephone

Name

Address

Telephone

Name

Address

Telephone

Name

Address

Telephone

Name

Address

Telephone

Name

Address

Telephone

Name

Address

Telephone

Name

Address

Telephone

Name

Address

Telephone

Name

Address

Telephone

Name

Address

Telephone

Name

Address

Telephone

Name

Address

Telephone

Name

Address

Telephone

Name

Address

Telephone

Fodor's Travel Guides

U.S. Guides

Alaska
Arizona
Boston
California
Cape Cod, Martha's Vineyard, Nantucket
The Carolinas & the Georgia Coast
The Chesapeake Region
Chicago
Colorado
Disney World & the Orlando Area
Florida
Hawaii
Las Vegas, Reno, Tahoe
Los Angeles
Maine, Vermont, New Hampshire
Maui
Miami & the Keys
National Parks of the West
New England
New Mexico
New Orleans
New York City
New York City (Pocket Guide)
Pacific North Coast
Philadelphia & the Pennsylvania Dutch Country
Puerto Rico (Pocket Guide)
The Rockies
San Diego
San Francisco
San Francisco (Pocket Guide)
The South
Santa Fe, Taos, Albuquerque
Seattle & Vancouver
Texas
USA
The U. S. & British Virgin Islands
The Upper Great Lakes Region
Vacations in New York State
Vacations on the Jersey Shore
Virginia & Maryland
Waikiki
Washington, D.C.
Washington, D.C. (Pocket Guide)

Foreign Guides

Acapulco
Amsterdam
Australia
Austria
The Bahamas
The Bahamas (Pocket Guide)
Baja & Mexico's Pacific Coast Resorts
Barbados
Barcelona, Madrid, Seville
Belgium & Luxembourg
Berlin
Bermuda
Brazil
Budapest
Budget Europe
Canada
Canada's Atlantic Provinces
Cancun, Cozumel, Yucatan Peninsula
Caribbean
Central America
China
Czechoslovakia
Eastern Europe
Egypt
Europe
Europe's Great Cities
France
Germany
Great Britain
Greece
The Himalayan Countries
Holland
Hong Kong
India
Ireland
Israel
Italy
Italy 's Great Cities
Jamaica
Japan
Kenya, Tanzania, Seychelles
Korea
London
London (Pocket Guide)
London Companion
Mexico
Mexico City
Montreal & Quebec City
Morocco
New Zealand
Norway
Nova Scotia, New Brunswick, Prince Edward Island
Paris
Paris (Pocket Guide)
Portugal
Rome
Scandinavia
Scandinavian Cities
Scotland
Singapore
South America
South Pacific
Southeast Asia
Soviet Union
Spain
Sweden
Switzerland
Sydney
Thailand
Tokyo
Toronto
Turkey
Vienna & the Danube Valley
Yugoslavia

Wall Street Journal Guides to Business Travel

Europe
International Cities
Pacific Rim
USA & Canada

Special-Interest Guides

Bed & Breakfast and Country Inn Guides:
Mid-Atlantic Region
New England
The South
The West
Cruises and Ports of Call
Healthy Escapes
Fodor's Flashmaps New York
Fodor's Flashmaps Washington, D.C.
Shopping in Europe
Skiing in the USA & Canada
Smart Shopper's Guide to London
Sunday in New York
Touring Europe
Touring USA